Essentials for Working with Young Children

THIRD EDITION

The Council for Professional Recognition
2460 16th Street, NW, Washington, DC 20009-3547
(202) 265-9090

Visit the Council's website at ***www.cdacouncil.org***.

Essentials for Working with Young Children - Third Edition

First Printing, Printed and bound in the United States of America

February 2023

ISBN: 978-0-9889650-8-9

Acknowledgements

The Council for Professional Recognition would like to acknowledge the following people who contributed to the creation of this textbook:

Calvin E. Moore, Jr., Ph.D., CEO, The Council for Professional Recognition

Edited by Lisa Yarkony, Ph.D., The Council for Professional Recognition and Annie Cassidy, The Creative Technique, LLC

Design and layout by Otero Cunha and Tevin Johnson, The Council for Professional Recognition and Stacy Kleber Jensen, Stacy Kleber Design, LLC

Vilma M. Williams, Manager, Multilingual and Special Programs, The Council for Professional Recognition

Carol Day, Ph.D., Fellow, The Council for Professional Recognition

Rosemarie Allen, Ph.D. Associate Professor, Early Childhood Education and President and CEO Institute for Racial Equity & Excellence

Shantel Meek, Ph.D., Professor of Practice and Founding Director, Children's Equity Projects

Ellen Senisi Education Photographs for providing images throughout

The children, families and staff of School for Friends, St. Columba's Nursery School and the Thurgood Marshall Child Development Center for appearing in the many images throughout

Table of Contents

What's New in This Edition

Dr. Calvin E. Moore, Jr.

Equity has always been the heartbeat of the *Essentials for Working with Young Children*. The first edition came out in 1991 as the Council for Professional Recognition worked to provide more skilled, qualified teachers to meet the needs of low-income children. This mission has stirred early childhood teachers and advocates since the birth of the Child Development Associate® (CDA) Credential™ 46 years ago at the behest of Head Start. The challenge was to conceive an inclusive, structured way for colleges and training groups to give teachers the competence and confidence they need to bring out all children's best.

The Council paved the way ahead in the first edition of the *Essentials*. Our goal in the new textbook was to lay out an approach that would guide teachers in helping young children "master skills, develop friendships, grow in independence, and move to new levels of thinking and understanding about the world," as we explained to readers. The result was a model curriculum to help build a model world based on tolerance and inclusion.

But we didn't just tout these high ideals. We gave our values teeth by showing teachers how to impart them in the early childhood classroom. And we made this clear by presenting the second edition of the *Essentials* as a "practical manual" that conveyed the latest research and advice on helping young learners advance. Still, the step-by-step tools we gave CDA students all added up to promote our longtime social mission.

Recent events have led the Council to be even more committed to the advancement of equity in the early childhood classroom. In the past few years, there's been a rise in racial and ethnic tensions, pointing to the need to teach tolerance when young minds are most open. Equally pressing is the shortage of early childhood teachers, a persistent issue that took the spotlight during the pandemic. The gap between supply and demand is especially glaring in low-income communities and those of color—precisely the ones that suffered the greatest losses from the pandemic.

All this fueled public support for a fairer, more balanced system. So, we seized the moment to work with the Children's Equity Project and embed equity throughout our new edition of the *Essentials*, from the type of books we recommend to techniques for settling conflicts and talking to families. We've honed our focus on how teachers can use the microcosm of the classroom to make a macro impact by giving children a sense of social justice when they are still small.

That's also a prime time for children to learn to value differences among their peers in our increasingly diverse classrooms. So, *Essentials* includes a new section on cultural capital. We urge teachers to view young children through a strengths-based lens and recognize the cultural richness they contribute. In today's multicultural classrooms, children also have a wide range of attitudes toward eating, sleeping, playing, and more. So, *Essentials* now offers new tips on how to help young learners rejoice in what joins them and respect what sets them apart.

Our children have changed, so we have broadened our discussion on the best ways to help them succeed. Still, we have stayed true to our roots as we support our early childhood teachers in earning their CDA. A key step in the credentialing process is careful study of *Essentials*, and it, too, has paved the way for change while preserving the past. Now—as 46 years ago—we're determined to give all children the head start that they deserve in school and life. Building equity is still the essence of *Essentials*.

Introduction

An Interview With "the Father of the CDA®," Edward Zigler, Ph.D. (1930-2019)

Edward F. Zigler, Ph.D., eminent psychologist, rigorous scholar, advisor to presidents, and senior political officials, and one of the key architects of Head Start and the CDA, passed away on February 7, 2019. Zigler's contributions to the field of early care and education, along with his influence on other social action programs, have been and will continue to be felt and recognized for years to come.

In May 2012, Richard Cohen, former Associate Chief Officer of the Council for Professional Recognition, conducted an interview with Dr. Zigler. Excerpts from that interview follow:

Why do you think the field of child care and early education is important?

Preschool education, in the years since we invented Head Start in 1965, has just grown by leaps and bounds.

The research has now made very clear to us that the single most important determinant of a child's educational performance, whether it be in preschool or fifth grade, or high school for that matter, is how good the teacher is. So, it's absolutely imperative that we make sure that our children are taught by teachers who have demonstrated their competency. It's really at the heart of our whole educational issue in the United States.

There are four systems that determine children's healthy growth and development where we should be concentrating. The first is the family, particularly the parents. The second, which we still have work to do on, is health. Children are not going to develop properly, and they are not going to learn properly, if they are ill. The third is education and the fourth is child care where so many children spend those first five formative years of life before they ever go to school. These systems are not independent, they're synergistic – each one affects the other. If you're not healthy you're not going to do well anywhere. If you have five lousy years of child care before you go to school, you're not optimally ready for school.

What were the origins of the Child Development Associate® (CDA) Credential™?

I don't think it's too much hubris for me to say that I am the father of the CDA®. There was no such thing; there wasn't anything like that in anyone's mind until I invented the concept.

In 1971, I revamped Head Start: we started home-based services, resource centers, and a number of programs that were new. I was also deeply immersed in the drafting the Child Development Act of 1971. That bill was going to put into place a huge national child care system in America that any parent could access. But, the primary question was "Who's going to staff all these child care centers?" That was my primary motivation for inventing the Child Development Associate® Credential.

What was revolutionary about it was the performance-based or competency idea behind the CDA® Credential. I didn't care if you knew who Piaget was but I did want to know if you could effectively interact with children and teach them. The fact is, a paper and pencil test alone is really not valid to the degree that an observation of a person actually functioning is in determining that person's qualifications.

But we needed a template for how to evaluate them. I mean, you go in and look at a teacher and anybody that knows early childhood education can tell you in fifteen minutes whether the teacher is competent or not, but it had to be more than that.

But what exactly should we look at that? The emotional warmth between the teacher and the child, the independence that the teacher gives the child to lead, to discover what "Teachable Moments" are – these are the things you look at. But I handed that specific task to my colleagues at the National Association for the Education of Young Children and they really did the "heavy lifting". I can't thank NAEYC enough. They really made it whole. Bank Street College then led the group to develop what became the thirteen Functional Areas that they now look at. So it evolved from a kind of look-see into a much more formal, evaluation process.

What do you think about the way the CDA® Credentialing process is evolving?

The CDA® is a good, solid certificate for new caregivers. The changes to the credentialing process sound like a very good move. Everything should evolve. Nobody should ever stand pat on anything, I don't care who invented it. We need to be always trying to upgrade and improve what we're doing.

I also think the reflection aspect of the new CDA® process is very solid and very worthwhile. People should become conscious and reflect on what it is that they're doing and putting that into the credentialing process is a very good step.

Any final thoughts about the CDA®?

The Council overshot my goal by 50%. When I started this, my goal was 200,000 credentialed caregivers and, given the needs in child care at that time, that wasn't too many. Now there are over 300,000 – I think that's great!

Dr. Edward F. Zigler is the Sterling Professor Emeritus of Psychology; Emeritus Faculty; Director, Emeritus, The Edward Zigler Center in Child Development & Social Policy, Yale University. Dr. Zigler was interviewed by Richard Cohen, former Associate Chief Officer of the Council for Professional Recognition, on May 23, 2012.

Purpose of This Book

Welcome to *Essentials*!

This textbook is a practical manual for parents, teachers, and providers who work with children from birth to age five, either in homes, centers or school settings. It is also an essential companion and study guide for candidates working towards the Child Development Associate® (CDA) Credential™. It has been designed to provide the comprehensive breadth of information needed to effectively care for and educate young children, for those who are either new to the field, or are new to formally studying child development and early childhood best practices. *Essentials* is a practical guide, yet deeply rooted in current childhood development research and theory.

The Child Development Associate® (CDA) Credential™ is the most widely recognized credential in early childhood education (ECE) and is a key stepping stone on the path of career advancement in ECE. The CDA® Credential is based on a core set of Competency Standards, which guide early care and learning professionals as they work toward becoming qualified teachers of young children. These professionals have the knowledge of how to put the CDA Competency Standards into practice and the understanding of how the Standards help children move with success from one developmental stage to another.

The Child Development Associate® (CDA) Credential™ is the "best first step" because: The CDA® National Credentialing Program is based on the knowledge of the nation's leading scholars in early care and learning. Utilizing multiple sources of evidence, the Program is the only comprehensive system of its kind that recognizes the essential competencies needed by entry-level and all early childhood professionals. The CDA® credentialing process is now a powerful cohesive professional development experience, infused with meaningful activities that facilitate the reflective practice of working professionals.

For more information about obtaining a CDA®, please visit *www.cdacouncil.org*

In particular, this *Essentials* textbook is the perfect companion for anyone preparing to earn a Child Development Associate® (CDA) Credential™ because:

- The ideas and examples contained throughout were specifically written to correlate with many of the questions asked in the required CDA® Exam taken by every CDA® Candidate as part of the credentialing process.
- Each Competency Standards section of this book is followed by the specific reflective activities required of CDA® Candidates as they create their Professional Portfolios.

By reading the thirteen *Essentials* chapters in order and then following the "Reflections" section after each Competency Standard, you will be well prepared to both take the CDA® Exam and create a valuable Professional Portfolio that meets the credentialing requirements.

Structure

Essentials has been structured around the CDA® Competency Standards and Functional Areas (please see Figure 1. for the full Competency Standards chart).

Candidates seeking to earn the CDA® Credential are assessed based upon the CDA® Competency Standards. These national standards are the criteria used to evaluate an early care and learning professional's performance with children, families, colleagues, and their community.

There are six *Competency Standards*—statements that set the standard of competency for professional behavior. The first four Standards relate directly to the experiences of young children and are therefore presented within a *Developmental Context.* Each Developmental Context presents a brief overview of relevant child development principles related to the Functional Areas within that Standard. The last two standards relate to program management and professionalism.

The six Standards are then defined in more detail in 13 *Functional Areas,* which describe the major tasks or functions that an early care and learning professional must complete in order to meet each Competency Standard.

Figure 1. CDA® Competency Standards At-A-Glance

Competency Standard	Functional Area	Definitions
I. To establish and maintain a safe, healthy learning environment	1. Safe	Candidate provides a safe environment and teaches children safe practices to prevent and reduce injuries.
	2. Healthy	Candidate provides an environment that promotes health and prevents illness, and teaches children about good nutrition and practices that promote wellness.
	3. Learning Environment	Candidate organizes and uses relationships, the physical space, materials, daily schedule, and routines to create a secure, interesting, and enjoyable environment that promotes engagement, play, exploration, and learning of all children, including children with disabilities.
II. To advance physical and intellectual competence	4. Physical	Candidate uses a variety of developmentally appropriate equipment, learning experiences and teaching strategies to promote the physical development (fine motor and gross motor) of all children.
	5. Cognitive	Candidate uses a variety of developmentally appropriate learning experiences and teaching strategies to promote curiosity, reasoning, and problem solving and to lay the foundation for all later learning. Candidate implements curriculum that promotes children's learning of important mathematics, science, technology, social studies, and other content goals.
	6. Communication	Candidate uses a variety of developmentally appropriate learning experiences and teaching strategies to promote children's language and early literacy learning, and help them communicate their thoughts and feelings verbally and nonverbally. Candidate helps dual-language learners make progress in understanding and speaking both English and their home language.
	7. Creative	Candidate uses a variety of developmentally appropriate learning experiences and teaching strategies for children to explore music, movement, and the visual arts, and to develop and express their individual creative abilities.
III. To support social and emotional development and to provide positive guidance	8. Self	Candidate develops a warm, positive, supportive, and responsive relationship with each child, and helps each child learn about and take pride in their individual and cultural identity.
	9. Social	Candidate helps each child function effectively in the group, learn to express feelings, acquire social skills, and make friends, and promotes mutual respect among children and adults.
	10. Guidance	Candidate provides a supportive environment and uses effective strategies to promote children's self-regulation and support acceptable behaviors, and effectively intervenes for children with persistent challenging behaviors.
IV. To establish positive and productive relationships with families	11. Families	Candidate establishes a positive, responsive, and cooperative relationship with each child's family, engages in two-way communication with families, encourages their involvement in the program, and supports the child's relationship with their family.
V. To ensure a well-run, purposeful program that is responsive to participant needs	12. Program Management	Candidate is a manager who uses observation, documentation, and planning to support children's development and learning and to ensure effective operation of the classroom or group. The Candidate is a competent organizer, planner, record keeper, communicator, and a cooperative co-worker.
VI. To maintain a commitment to professionalism	13. Professionalism	Candidate makes decisions based on knowledge of research-based early childhood practices, promotes high-quality in child care services, and takes advantage of opportunities to improve knowledge and competence, both for personal and professional growth and for the benefit of children and families.

Competency Standard I:

To establish and maintain a safe, healthy learning environment

Developmental Contexts

Functional Area 1: Safe

Young and mobile infants *(birth–17 months)* need affectionate and competent physical care geared to their individual needs and rhythms. Adults support infants by establishing routines that regulate their eating, sleeping, and other activities gradually, while continuing to balance the infant's and the group's needs.

Toddlers *(18–36 months)* imitate and learn from the activities of those around them. Safety awareness can be established through modeling, encouraging, and discussions about safe behaviors. Toddlers are increasingly curious about their world. They stretch boundaries and test everything in their surroundings. Adults must be attentive to their activities and ensure their safety while giving them simple explanations for safety precautions.

Preschoolers *(3–5 years old)* are gradually able to understand the relative danger or safety of situations. In a safe setting, children will gradually learn to protect themselves and look out for others.

Functional Area 2: Healthy

Young and mobile infants *(birth–17 months)* need affectionate and competent physical care geared to their individual health, physical growth, and nutrition. Adults *individualize* infants' eating, sleeping, and other daily routines, while continuing to balance the infant's and the group's needs.

Toddlers *(18–36 months)* imitate and learn from those around them. Good health habits can be established through modeling and encouraging handwashing, nutritious eating, etc.

Preschoolers *(3–5 years old)* are ready to learn the reasons and take responsibility for good health practices including, hygiene, handwashing, and good nutrition. They are fascinated by their own bodily functions and can gradually learn about them.

Competency Standard I (continued)

Functional Area 3: Learning Environment

Young infants *(birth–8 months)* are learning from their immediate surroundings and daily experiences with a few important people. The sense of well-being and emotional security conveyed by a loving and skilled provider create a readiness for other experiences. Before infants can creep and crawl, adults should provide a variety of sensory experiences and encourage movement and playfulness.

Mobile infants *(9–17 months)* are active, independent, and curious. They are increasingly persistent and purposeful in doing things. They need many opportunities to practice new skills and explore the setting within safe boundaries. Adults can share children's delight in themselves, their skills, and discoveries and gradually add variety to the learning setting that will continue to foster relationships and exploration.

Toddlers *(18–36 months)* are developing new language skills, physical control, and awareness of themselves and others each day. They enjoy participating in planned and group activities, but they are not yet ready to sit still or work in a group for a very long time. Adults can support their learning in all areas by maintaining a setting that is dependable but flexible enough to provide opportunities for them to extend their skills, understanding, and judgment in individualized ways.

Preschoolers *(3–5 years old)* continue to develop new language skills, physical control, and awareness of themselves and others each day. They enjoy participation in planned and group activities. They learn by doing. Adults can support their learning in all areas by maintaining a setting that has a wide range of exploratory and adaptive materials; provides opportunities for them to extend their vocabulary, mathematical, and scientific skills; and promotes social and emotional growth. Adults can observe children's play; give them time and space to repeat familiar activities; and expand the learning setting in response to their developing skills, interests, and concerns about themselves and their world.

CHAPTER 1: Safe

CDA® Functional Area 1: Candidate provides a safe environment and teaches children safe practices to prevent and reduce injuries.

Safe

Introduction

The National Association for the Education of Young Children's Code of Ethical Conduct states that early educators "shall place the welfare and safety of children above other obligations" (NAEYC 2011). Children's safety is your first priority. When children feel secure in a safe, stable, and trusting setting, they are better prepared to develop well and learn. Although other dimensions of safety, such as emotional, intellectual, and spiritual safety of children contribute to children's sense of security as well, these dimensions will be discussed throughout this book and not specifically in this section.

In this chapter, we examine five strategies for ensuring children's physical safety while in your care:

- **Keeping Children Physically Safe**
- **Teaching Children about Safety**
- **Modeling Safe Practices**
- **Responding to Injuries and Emergencies**
- **Engaging Families in Safe Practices**

Keeping Children Physically Safe

Quality early childhood education begins with a safe environment. Safety has been identified as one of the top priorities used by families in selecting a child care option (ACF 2015). Your first and most important responsibility to families is to keep their children free from harm. Between 2009 and 2011, over half of the States upgraded their licensing requirements for child development centers and Family Child Care homes by making safety regulations more stringent. (ACF 2015). Familiarize yourself with your local, state, and federal safety requirements. For example, if you work in an Early Head Start or Head Start program, you must know and follow national safety regulations that apply to all settings. Safety regulations cover such topics as early childhood educator to child ratios and which plants and pets are allowed and which are prohibited in your program. Your setting needs to comply with all requirements to maintain licensure and funding. Ideally, you will help your program exceed those minimum requirements to reflect even higher standards.

In addition to state, local safety, and applicable federal standards, such as those that govern Head Start programs, these are two excellent references to have on hand. They describe the latest safety recommendations for the early childhood education field:

1. *Caring for Our Children: National Health and Safety Performance Standards; Guidelines for Early Care and Education Programs.* Fourth Edition. American Academy of Pediatrics, American Public Health Association, National Resource Center for Health and Safety in Child Care and Early Education. Itasca, IL: American Academy of Pediatrics, 2019.

2. *Caring for Our Children Basics: Health and Safety Foundations for Early Care and Education.* Administration for Children and Families. U.S. Department of Health and Human Services, June 25, 2015. *www.acf.hhs.gov/sites/default/files/ecd/caring_for_our_children_basics.pdf*

The first publication sets forth health and safety standards for infants, toddlers, and preschoolers in both centers and family child care homes. The second publication builds on this foundation, providing the latest health and safety information that will help programs improve the quality of their centers and FCC homes serving infants and toddlers.

Maintaining a Safe Physical Setting

There are many things to think about in a broad topic like safety. You need to consider your every action and interaction with children to prevent accidents and injuries. Above all, you have to ensure that your indoor and outdoor environments are safe havens for children. The last thing you ever want to have to tell a family member is that their child was harmed while under your protection. Reflect on the following topics and think about how you can best keep children safe.

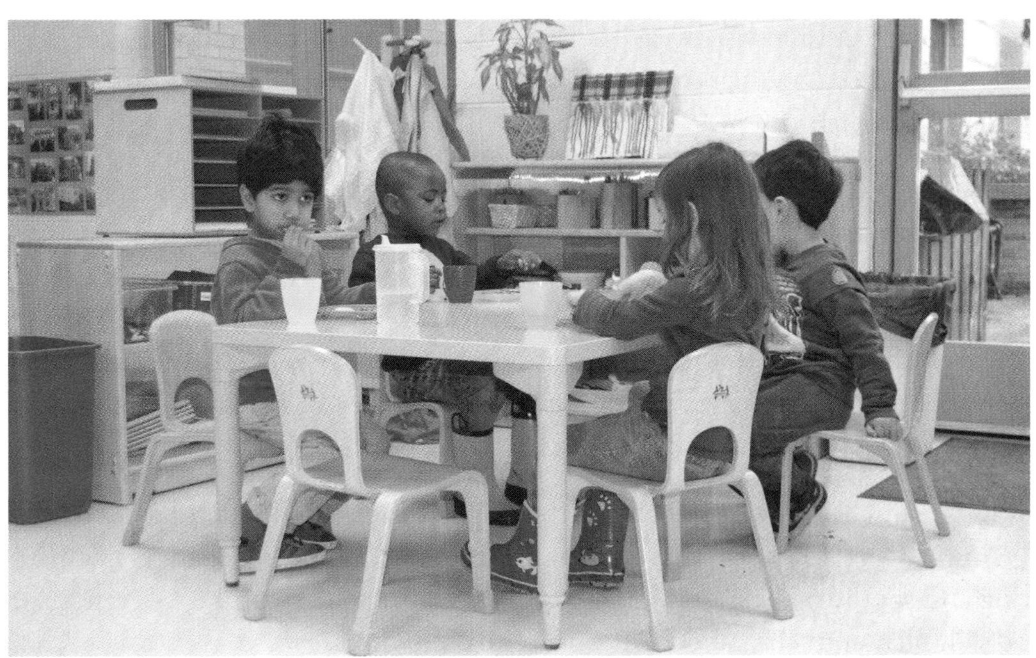

All equipment and furniture should be appropriate for the children's sizes and developmental levels.

Following Adult-Child Ratios for Supervision

Find out the governing regulation concerning adult–child ratios in your setting and adhere to this requirement at all times. Additional staff may be required to appropriately serve children with disabilities. The Administration for Children and Families (2015) sets forth these standards for children in center-based programs (p. 8):

Child's Age	Maximum Child: Teacher Ratio
12 months or less	4:1
13-23 months	4:1
24-35 months	4:1 to 6:1
3 years old	9:1
4 to 5 years old	10:1

For family child care homes (FCC), the following adjustments to these ratios should be made:

- The provider's own children under six are included in the ratio.
- If mixed ages are present, a maximum ratio of 6:1 is maintained, which includes no more than two children 24 months of age or younger.
- If all children in care are under three years of age, a ratio of 4:1 is maintained, with no more than two children 18 months of age or younger.
- If all children are three years old, a maximum ratio of 7:1 is maintained.
- If all children are four or five years old, a ratio of 8:1 is maintained.

In a center-based setting, early childhood educators must be able to see and hear all of the children at all times. The classroom team works together to provide this level of supervision. In FCC homes, you can supervise by sight or sound. During nap time, supervision by sound should be supplemented by visual check-ins. This means that you will need to periodically look in on children, even when you hear nothing out of the ordinary.

When caring for infants, it is critical to be aware of their growing skills, particularly their abilities to accomplish new physical feats. For example, you need to carefully monitor infants, as they learn to roll on their sides. Be aware and attentive. There may be times when you need to step away to take a phone call from a family member or respond to an emergency. If you work in a classroom, alert a colleague so they can supervise the children. If you are changing a diaper, place the infant on the floor and make sure a colleague can take over, or take the child with you. In an FCC home, you will have to take the children with you.

When enrolling families and when updating the original paperwork, ask for a written statement naming the individuals who are authorized to pick up their child. Any changes to this list must be in writing and should be kept on file. This includes family, such as when a grandparent is visiting and will pick up their grandchild. Ensure that children leave your setting at the end of the day with only those whom the family has authorized to pick up their child.

Protecting Children from Exposure to Lead

Lead is an extremely dangerous poison. Lead poisoning occurs when lead builds up in the body, often over a period of months or years. Even small amounts of lead can cause serious mental and physical health problems that can lead to life-long impairments. Children under the age of six are especially vulnerable to lead poisoning. Because they are undergoing rapid neurological and physical development, they are at great risk.

The Centers for Disease Control (CDC) reports that 6 percent of all children one to two years old have blood lead levels in the toxic range (American Academy of Child & Adolescent Psychiatry [AACAP] 2012). This figure jumps to 11 percent in African-American (non-Hispanic) children one to five years old (AACAP 2012). Lead poisoning is the leading environmentally-induced illness in children. When exposed to only small amounts of lead, children may appear inattentive, hyperactive, and irritable. Children exposed to higher levels of lead may also experience problems reading and learning, delayed growth, and hearing loss. At its highest levels, lead can cause permanent brain damage and even death (AACAP 2012). Early identification and treatment of lead poisoning reduces the risk that children will suffer permanent damage.

Common sources of additional lead exposure and contamination include storage of acidic foods in open cans or ceramic containers/pottery with a lead glaze, certain types of art supplies, some imported toys and inexpensive play jewelry, and vinyl products, such as beach balls, soft PVC-containing dolls, rubber ducks, chew toys, and nap mats (AAP, APHA, and NRC 2019). It is also advisable to promote children's blood testing for lead exposure and then promptly remove any items that may be contributing to increases in the body's lead levels.

Dust and chips from deteriorating lead paint on interior surfaces of buildings are the source of most lead poisoning detected in children today. Contaminated soil and water may, however, also contain lead. Most buildings built before 1978 are known to have used lead-based paint (CDC 2012). Children who live or spend a lot of time in buildings built before 1978 are at the highest risk for lead poisoning. If your center or FCC home was built before 1978, it must be tested for lead hazards by an EPA-certified firm. Your local health department can provide a list of these firms.

Even for settings built after 1978, the soil should be tested for lead and other contaminants.

Figure 2a. Protecting Children from Lead Poisoning

Whether the program owns or rents the facility and whether the FCC provider owns or rents their home, it is necessary to protect children from lead poisoning. This may be a shared responsibility between program operators and building owners. The State of New York Department of Health (SNYDOH July 2009, 1-2) offers the following tips on lead safety.

Remove lead paint and repair the building

A qualified firm should:

- Fix lead paint and make building repairs safely.
- Remove all peeling paint and paint chips.

Figure 2b. Protecting Children from Lead Poisoning

- Repair peeling or damaged paint or plaster promptly.
- Insist that children be kept away while old paint is sanded or scraped.
- Clean area using wet cleaning methods and a HEPA vacuum (not dry sweeping).

(Note: Before making repairs to a building built before 1978, program administrators or an FCC provider should contact the local health department to learn how to keep dust levels down during the repair. Administrators should share this information with early childhood educators.)

Ensure child safety during lead removal

- Wash children's hands and faces after play, before meals, and before bed.
- Wash toys, stuffed animals, pacifiers, and bottles with soap and water often.
- Mop floors often, and use damp paper towels to clean window wells and sills.

Prevent child contact with lead from other sources

- Remove from your setting any toys recalled due to lead content.
- Test your soil for lead and other toxins. Cover bare soil that might be contaminated with grass or woodchips. Never allow children to play in bare soil as lead might be present. This is especially possible in urban settings and on sites that previously housed factories.
- Examine old painted toys, high chairs, and furniture because they can contain lead paint and varnish. Regulations ban the use of toxic paints or finishes on anything in an early childhood setting that children use or is within their reach.
- Prevent children from chewing on metal, brass, lead, or pewter objects, such as keys or figurines, fishing weights, blinds, old furniture, or window sills.

Keep lead out of food and water

- Let tap water run for one minute before using it, if it has not run for a few hours. Both town and well water could contain lead from old plumbing.
- Use cold tap water only for drinking, cooking, and making baby formula. Boiling water does not get rid of lead.
- Cook, serve, and store food using lead-free dishes. Do not use cracked china, pewter, crystal, or pottery from Central America or the Middle East.
- Use bottled water if local water supply is known to include lead.

Protecting Children from Exposure to Carbon Monoxide

Carbon monoxide—labeled "The Silent Killer"—is an odorless, colorless gas that can be extremely dangerous and even deadly if inhaled. It is produced whenever fuel is burned. It only becomes a problem, though, when it builds up in the air. This happens when small gasoline stoves, grills, generators, lanterns, and gas ranges are not properly installed or ventilated. Blocked flues/chimneys and leakage from faulty appliances like clothes dryers can also cause carbon monoxide to accumulate.

When carbon monoxide is inhaled, the carbon monoxide replaces the oxygen in blood. Low oxygen levels kill cells and can lead to organ failure and death. Babies and young children are among the most susceptible. Over 450 people in the U.S. die every year from carbon monoxide poisoning and some 20,000 people seek emergency help in hospitals. (CDC 2014). Of those hospitalized from carbon monoxide poisoning, children under five are most likely to be affected. Carbon monoxide is the most common cause of accidental poisoning-related deaths.

Carbon monoxide poisoning is more likely to occur in an FCC home than a center, because of the type of heating and cooling systems used in a residence and the absence of chimneys and fireplaces in centers. However, centers can experience carbon monoxide leakage and are especially susceptible following power outages, if back-up generators are used. Also, some centers are housed in current or former residences such as in a housing complex.

If you observe that a child in your program shows symptoms such as headache, dizziness, vomiting, shortness of breath, disorientation, and seizures, carbon monoxide poisoning could be the cause. Stay calm, but act quickly:

- Take the child outdoors immediately.
- Turn off the source of the carbon monoxide, if safe to do so.
- Call 911.
- Start Cardiopulmonary Resuscitation (CPR) if the child has stopped breathing and do not stop until the child starts breathing or someone can take over for you.

Figure 3. Preventing Carbon Monoxide Poisonings

- Install carbon monoxide detectors and have them checked annually at the same time as your fire detectors.
- Clean and inspect furnaces, fireplaces, and wood stoves yearly.
- Use space heaters and lanterns in well-ventilated areas.
- Run generators only where the exhaust cannot enter an enclosed area.
- Avoid using gas ovens, stove tops, or dryers for heat.
- Avoid using grills and hibachis indoors.

While Head Start, Early Head Start, and a growing number of states require centers and FCC homes to have carbon monoxide detectors, not all programs are mandated to have detectors installed and regularly inspected. If your program does not require detectors, discuss the situation with your supervisor and advocate for installing them. If your FCC home does not have a detector, install one in your home as an added safety precaution.

Preventing Choking, Suffocation, and Strangulation

A main consideration when creating a safe early childhood setting is to make sure that children won't accidentally choke, suffocate, or strangle themselves. What could be worse than having a child in your care choke on the hot dog you served for lunch or get caught on a climber when his scarf is tangled in the equipment?

Accidental choking, suffocation, and strangulation lead to asphyxia, a lack of oxygen supply to the brain. This can cause serious injury or death. Choking is the interruption of respiration by an internal obstruction of the airway, usually a food item or small object. Suffocation is obstruction of the airway by an external object that blocks the nose and mouth, such as a plastic bag, bedding, or mattress. Strangulation is external constriction of the neck that interferes with respiration, often caused by a window blind cord or a drawstring on clothing.

While some accidents are impossible to predict and prevent, choking, suffocation, and strangulation can be prevented in almost every case. What it takes is vigilance on your part and a willingness to ban items that would cause these accidents. If you remove the problem, you eliminate a potential tragedy.

Choking is the fourth leading cause of accidental deaths in children under five. Children under three are particularly prone to choking on food because they don't have a full set of teeth to chew and grind food before swallowing. Children between three and four years of age have molars, but are still learning how to chew. Even five-year-olds are in danger, because they may "inhale" their food rather than taking the time to slowly chew it well. To keep children from choking:

- DO NOT offer toys and materials that are smaller than 1¼ inches in diameter.
- DO NOT provide toys and materials with detachable parts that are smaller than 1¼ inches in diameter.
- DO NOT use balls smaller than 1¾ inches in diameter.
- DO NOT allow safety pins, coins, button-type batteries, Styrofoam objects, marbles, bottle caps, magnets, foam blocks, erasers, or jewelry, such as rings or earrings.
- DO NOT feed hot dogs to children under age four. While cutting them into coin-sized pieces would seem like good practice, it is actually most dangerous. Pieces this size become the perfect choking hazard. According to Johns Hopkins pediatrician Nisha Kapadia, M.D., "Every food poses a choking risk in young kids but the hot dog has just the right size and consistency to perfectly block the airway; it's the perfect plug that doesn't allow any air to get through" (Johns Hopkins Children's Center 2010). Hot dogs are the number one cause of choking in children under three years old.
- DO NOT serve children under four foods with pits (olives or cherries), hard candies, whole grapes, gum, popcorn, peanuts, raisins and other dried fruit, uncooked peas,

peanut butter that is not on a cracker, ice cubes, cheese cubes, marshmallows, or jelly beans. For older children, make sure food is cut into small pieces and that children sit up straight while eating and have plenty of water to drink.

- DO supervise children at all times.
- DO put adult purses, totes, and all plastic bags out of children's reach.
- DO make sure children are seated when eating.
- DO supervise children while they are eating to monitor the amount of food they consume.
- DO provide menus of food that reflect the age and developmental needs of individual children.
- DO create, distribute and post lists of high-risk foods.

Suffocation and strangulation were responsible for 1,176 children's deaths in 2010. Seventy-seven percent of these children were less than one year old (CDC 2013). Most infant suffocation injuries and deaths are due to unsafe sleeping environments. Older children tend to be injured or die from strangulation incidents on playground equipment. To keep children safe from suffocation and strangulation:

- ALWAYS Put infants to bed on their backs on firm, flat mattresses, with less than two fingers' width between the mattress and the crib on all sides.
- ALWAYS Check to be sure crib slats are no more than 2 ⅜ inches apart (the width of a soda can); if they cannot meet this standard, stop using the crib.
- ALWAYS Use fitted sheets to cover the mattress.
- ALWAYS Remove, or ask families to remove, cords and drawstrings from all clothing, including hooded items.
- NEVER Place pillows, comforters, toys, stuffed animals, or rattles in cribs.
- NEVER Install mobiles, crib mirrors, or crib gyms in or near cribs as a child could pull them down.
- NEVER Hang pacifiers, rattles, or teething rings around a child's neck.
- NEVER Allow uninflated balloons or plastic bags in the setting.
- NEVER Use window blinds or shades with cords attached.
- NEVER Put head bands or ribbons on babies.
- NEVER Offer toys with cords over 12 inches long.

Food Safety for Children

As noted above, food can be a possible cause of choking in young children. It can also pose dangers to children if they have food allergies or it is not stored and handled properly. In Chapter 2, we will focus on food allergies and other health-related matters. For now, consider the strategies for safe food handling presented below. If you work in a center, it is important to be aware of these concerns, especially if you are supervising activities involving food experiences. If you work in a family child care home, it is vital that you familiarize yourself with all aspects of food safety, since you are, in essence, the food manager and cook.

- Serve food that is fresh, nutritious, and properly stored. If you have any questions about how long food can be safely stored in the refrigerator or freezer, check online or contact your local U.S. Department of Agriculture Cooperative Extension Service.

Figure 4. Food Storage Tips from the U.S.D.A.*

- Always refrigerate perishable food within 2 hours—1 hour when the temperature is above 90°F (32.2°C).
- Cook or freeze fresh poultry, fish, ground meats, and variety meats within 2 days; beef, veal, lamb, or pork, within 3 to 5 days.
- Wrap perishable food, such as meat and poultry, securely to maintain quality and to prevent meat juices from getting onto other food.
- Maintain quality by freezing meat and poultry in its original package, after wrapping the package again with foil or freezer-grade plastic wrap.
- Serve canned foods indefinitely as long as they are not exposed to freezing temperatures, or temperatures above 90°F. If the cans look okay, they are safe to use. Discard cans that are dented, rusted, or swollen. High-acid canned food (tomatoes, fruits) will keep their best quality for 12 to 18 months; low-acid canned food (meats, vegetables) for 2 to 5 years.
- Separate the food preparation areas from eating, playing, laundry, diapering, and toileting areas.
- Keep all pets and their food out of the children's food preparation area.
- Keep the refrigerator and freezer clean.
- Check the temperature of your refrigerator and freezer with an appliance thermometer. The refrigerator should be at 40°F (4.4°C) or below and the freezer at 0°F (-17.7°C) or below.
- Store canned goods and other shelf-stable items in a cool dry place; rotate foods so you use older supplies first. Store your dry foods including flour, cereal, corn meal, and dry beans on shelves in tightly covered containers to protect from rodents.
- Ensure that everyone washes their hands before and after preparing and cooking foods, and that an adult is always present while children are preparing, cooking, and eating food.

(U.S. Department of Agriculture March 2015)

Ensuring Sleep Safety and Protecting Infants from SIDS

The Centers for Disease Control estimate that each year in the United States 3,500 infants one year old and younger die suddenly of no immediately obvious cause. Known as Sudden Unexpected Infant Death (SUID), about 45% of these infant deaths are due to SIDS (Sudden Infant Death Syndrome). Although most common among infants from two to four months of age, SIDS is the leading cause of death among infants ages one to twelve months. The CDC defines SIDS as "the sudden death of an infant less than one year of age that cannot be explained after a thorough investigation is conducted, including a complete autopsy, examination of the death scene, and review of the clinical history" (CDC 2013).

Twenty percent of SIDS cases occur when a child is being cared for by someone other than a family member (AAP 2012). Being aware of the conditions that are linked with SIDS, however, helps early childhood educators guard against SIDS and SUIDS. Thanks to the availability of information about SIDS, the SIDS rates, in fact, have gone down dramatically. In 1990, the SIDS rate was 130.3 deaths per 100,000 live births; in 2013, there were 39.7 deaths per 100,000 live births (CDC 2013).

To fight against SIDS and ensure that all children in your care sleep safely, implement these strategies at your center or FCC home:

- Ensure that cribs, beds, and cots are set up and secured properly.
- Allow babies to sleep only in cribs. It is unsafe for infants to fall asleep on chairs, sofas, cushions, or adult beds. (Indoor baby swings should not be present in the setting.)
- Have children share rooms when sleeping, but never have them share cribs, cots, mats, or beds.
- Place all infants ages up to 12 months on their backs when sleeping. Cover crib mattresses with fitted sheets. Do not place any other soft materials—including pillows or soft toys—inside cribs. Keep soft or loose bedding away from sleeping infants and out of safe sleep environments.
- Place all sleeping equipment—including cribs, cots, and mats—away from windows, electrical sockets, and hanging decorations. Do not string toys across cribs for infants or toddlers to use.
- Maintain a smoke-free environment.
- Set the room thermostat at a temperature that would be comfortable for a lightly-clothed adult. Overheating has been linked to SIDS.
- Dress babies lightly for napping.

Ensuring Safe Field Trips

Field trips are both enriching learning experiences for young children and a lot of fun. They also raise a number of safety concerns that need to be prepared for and resolved. For instance:

- How can I keep track of all the children?
- How do I make sure that our transportation is safe?
- What if a child wanders off?
- What if the museum is not childproofed?
- What if an animal at the farm we visit bites a child?
- What if the firemen are called out on an emergency while we're visiting the firehouse?
- What if a child gets burned touching hot machinery at the bakery?

Field trip preparation can be hampered when educators are consumed by all of the "what ifs." Rather than bury yourself in worry, the best approach is to prepare for the event and figure out ahead of time how you will address any safety concerns that arise. Koralek, Dodge, and Pizzolongo (2004) offer these suggestions:

- Collect signed permission slips from families for the trip.
- Recruit family members as volunteers, so there will be more adult supervision on the trip. Familiarize them with all trip and safety procedures.
- Collect emergency phone numbers.
- Collect signed family emergency forms (should children need to go to a hospital or see a doctor).
- Visit and scout out the site in advance. Find out where you would go in an emergency and whom you would talk to. Locate bathrooms and facilities for bad weather.
- Decide on the best means of transportation for getting there and back—on foot, public transportation, car, or bus. Check on the safety of vehicles, if they will be used.
- Familiarize yourself with the route ahead of time. Make sure that you have clear directions and have allowed sufficient travel time.
- Inspect the first-aid kit to be sure it is complete before collecting it for the trip. Replace items that are out of date.
- Make name tags, including the program's name, address, and telephone number (or your cell phone number), but do not display the child's name on the tag as a safety measure. Children tend to trust adults who know their name; not displaying this information helps guard against abductions.

- Plan for the children's unique needs, including children with disabilities. If a child uses a wheelchair, is blind, or deaf, make sure that the site is accessible. If a child needs medication that you typically administer at the time of day you'll be on the field trip, be sure to bring it along. You need to know how to respond to children's medical emergencies if they were to occur on a field trip, so be sure to collect all needed information, supplies, and written medical plans.
- Prepare the children for the trip ahead of time. Go over all safety rules for walking near traffic and standing in line. Make sure children know what to do if they are separated from the group. Try role-playing scenarios of getting lost or getting hurt.
- Bring along water and food, if needed.

Once the group is safely at the site, count all of the children to make sure everyone is accounted for and then closely supervise the group. Before leaving, count the children again and review safety procedures for returning home to the program. If possible, assign a number of children to one adult for closer supervision. Count children periodically throughout the field trip. By paying attention to these safety details, you can ensure that everyone enjoys the visit.

Monitoring the Program for Safety

Take a proactive approach to safeguarding your indoor and outdoor settings for children. The only way that you can ensure that your program is truly safe for children is to regularly inspect it. Get down on the floor—at the children's level—and look around the room. From a child's perspective, you can pinpoint where dangers may lie. Ask yourself questions like the following:

- Does this space protect young infants' play from toddlers' play?
- Are all the toys and materials nontoxic and nonflammable?
- Is the equipment and furniture appropriate for the children's sizes and developmental levels?
- Are all of the furnishings secured to the ground or wall to prevent them from falling on a child?
- Are materials stored so that children can safely use them on their own?
- Are computer cords secured to prevent tripping accidents?
- Is my setting free of lead paint and exposed asbestos?
- Are all choking hazards removed?
- Are all electrical sockets covered?

Outside, check to see that play areas are free of debris, structural hazards, matches, chipping paint, toxic plants, and objects that could be choking hazards, such as uninflated balloons and plastic bags.

Use Figures 5 to 9 to conduct safety checks of your indoor/outdoor settings. Figure 5 is a checklist for early childhood educators who teach infants and toddlers to assess the indoor environment. Figure 6 is for early childhood educators who teach preschoolers to assess their indoor environment. Figure 7 is for teachers of infants and toddlers in center-based programs to assess their outdoor environment. Figure 8 is for teachers of center-based preschool programs to assess their outdoor environments. And finally, Figure 9 is for family child care educators to assess their outdoor environments.

Secure all heavy furniture and structures to the wall.

Consider these checklists as master safety inventories. Some items like "Crib slats are no more than a soda can's width apart (2 ⅜ inches) to prevent head entrapment" don't have to be continually checked once you determine that the cribs in your program comply with this standard. Other items such as "the setting has functioning smoke alarms and carbon monoxide detectors (if required)" have to be checked only monthly, in accordance with stated codes or regulations. Other items, however, like the outdoor area is "free of debris including glass, standing water, ice, and animal wastes" need to be checked daily. For your convenience, we have grouped items according to whether they need to be done yearly, monthly, or daily.

In addition, because these are master lists, not every item on these lists is your responsibility if you work in a center-based program. For example, you are not likely to be the one to ensure that heating and cooling systems are inspected. Before attempting to use the checklists, discuss them with your supervisor and together decide which items you are responsible for monitoring and which items will be someone else's domain.

If you operate a FCC home, then you are responsible for monitoring every item on the checklist for FCC homes.

Figure 5a. Indoor Safety Checklist for Center-Based Infant/Toddler and Family Child Care Environments

Initially (to determine compliance), then Yearly or as Noted

- ☐ Radiators, fans, and space heaters are covered and located out of children's reach.
- ☐ Fireplace/heater/furnace (if present in FCC home) is either off-limits and behind locked doors or enclosed by barricades and separated by at least 3 feet from area used by children.
- ☐ Smoke and carbon monoxide detector batteries work and are in place and changed or recharged every 6 months.
- ☐ A-B-C type fire extinguishers are visible, easy-to-reach, and charged for use.
- ☐ Closet and bathroom doors have release/rescue hardware.
- ☐ Cribs have latches and locks on drop-sides.
- ☐ Crib slats are no more than a soda can's width apart (2 ⅜ inches).
- ☐ Crib mattresses are firm and fit tightly (less than two fingers' width on all sides).
- ☐ Chairs with attachable trays that are used by infants are sturdy and stable.
- ☐ Tables and chairs used by toddlers are child-size, sturdy, and stable.
- ☐ All furnishings in children's environment are sturdy and stable.
- ☐ All shelves and furniture have protective corners or edge bumpers.
- ☐ The height of classroom furniture and changing tables does not impair visual access to children.
- ☐ Small stepladders or stools, no higher than the children's knees and with rubber slats, are available so children can reach sinks that are not child-size (as in FCC homes).
- ☐ Steps, inclines, and platforms are padded and have nonslip treads and protective railings.
- ☐ Decals or other signs on glass doors (if present) are placed at children's eye levels.

Monthly

- ☐ The environment is smoke-free, lead-free, and toxin-free.
- ☐ The setting has no flammable furnishings.
- ☐ Heating and cooling systems, as well as air quality, are inspected for safety.
- ☐ Water temperature is tested to ensure that it is at 120°F or below, or faucets have scald-guards.
- ☐ The setting has functioning smoke alarms and carbon monoxide detectors (if required).
- ☐ Instructions for operating fire extinguishers are posted in English and in home languages of staff and families. Pictured directions should be available for those who are not able to read the directions, especially during an emergency.

Figure 5b. Indoor Safety Checklist for Center-Based Infant/Toddler and Family Child Care Environments

Monthly (continued)

- ☐ Poison control, fire, police, EMS, and other emergency services phone numbers are visibly posted and updated.
- ☐ A well-stocked first aid kit (see Figure 10) is stored in a locked cabinet out of children's reach.
- ☐ Emergency lighting (including flashlights) is available and batteries are in working order.
- ☐ Emergency exits are marked, lit, and unlocked from the inside.
- ☐ Evacuation procedures for fires and other natural disasters are visibly posted and clearly diagrammed with instructions in English and the home languages of staff and family members.
- ☐ Evacuation procedures are practiced according to regulations. Documentation of drills is available for review.
- ☐ Safety gates with latching devices are used to block access to stairs and other areas that are off-limits to children. Gates are at least ¾ of the children's height. Spacing is either too small to entrap children's heads or covered with rigid mesh screen. Accordion and/or pressure gates are not used.
- ☐ Cribs have no gyms, toys, mirrors, mobiles, or hanging toys.
- ☐ Cribs are positioned near exits in case of emergency.
- ☐ Space is organized so that babies will not be knocked down by older children.
- ☐ Play areas are located away from doorways.
- ☐ Room arrangement allows mobile infants and toddlers to easily move to activity areas.
- ☐ All toys and equipment are developmentally appropriate and in good repair.
- ☐ Toys and materials are displayed on shelving with heavier items at the bottom.
- ☐ Toys, furnishings, equipment, and space are adapted as necessary to provide for safe use by children with disabilities.

Daily

- ☐ Children are supervised in center-based programs by sight and sound at all times.
- ☐ Children are supervised by sight or sound in family child care homes. Sleeping children are supervised by sound with frequent visual checks.
- ☐ Children are released only to those with written permission to pick-up them up.
- ☐ Children do not wear around their necks rattles, pacifiers, or teething toys on strings or laces.
- ☐ Toys and equipment have no sharp edges, chipped paint, lead paint, or loose nuts and bolts.
- ☐ Toy pieces and removable parts are larger than 1¼ inches in diameter.

Figure 5c. Indoor Safety Checklist for Center-Based Infant/Toddler and Family Child Care Environments

Daily (continued)

- ☐ All plants are nontoxic (see Figure 11).
- ☐ Only animals that pose no danger to children are in the setting (see Figure 12). This includes children with allergies and extreme fear of an animal that interferes with the child's ability to fully engage in activities.
- ☐ A working telephone is accessible; cordless or cellular phones are fully charged.
- ☐ Child-resistant caps cover unused electrical outlets.
- ☐ Electrical cords are not frayed or damaged.
- ☐ Electrical cords and wires are tied together, on top of carpeting, and located in low-traffic areas, away from water.
- ☐ Small appliances are unplugged when not in use and stored out of children's reach.
- ☐ Window blinds and/or shades have plastic rods to open and close. There are no cords long enough to encircle a child's neck.
- ☐ Adult purses, tote bags, and personal items are stored out of children's reach.
- ☐ Sharp objects (scissors, knives, safety pins) and potential choking hazards (buttons, coins, uninflated balloons, marbles, magnets, foam blocks, plastic bags, and Styrofoam objects) are banned from the setting or stored in locked cabinets.
- ☐ Chemicals and potentially dangerous products, such as cleaning supplies, bleach, and medications are stored in original, labeled containers in a locked cabinet that is not accessible to children.
- ☐ Bleach solution is kept in a marked spray bottle in a locked cabinet. It is used only when children cannot inhale fumes. Alternatives to bleach solutions are used for children and adults at risk of having asthma triggered by droplets from bleach solutions.
- ☐ Empty cleaning product bottles are rinsed prior to disposal and placed in trash containers out of children's reach.
- ☐ Cribs and mats/cots for toddlers are spaced at least three feet apart.
- ☐ Cribs have no pillows, comforters, toys, stuffed animals, or rattles.
- ☐ All infants under the age of 12 months are placed on their backs to sleep; they do not wear hats.
- ☐ Early childhood educators use safety straps to secure children during diapering on changing tables.
- ☐ Pot handles on the stove (in FCC homes) are turned towards the back of the stove out of children's reach.
- ☐ Carpeting and area rugs are secured and lay flat, with no frayed edges.
- ☐ Flooring is clean, dry, and has no-skid surfaces.

Figure 6a. Indoor Safety Checklist for Center-Based Preschool and Family Child Care Environments

Initially (to determine compliance), then Yearly or as Noted

- ☐ Radiators, fans, and space heaters are insulated/covered and located out of children's reach.
- ☐ Fireplace/heater/furnace (if present in FCC home) is either off-limits and behind locked doors or enclosed by barricades and separated by at least 3 feet from area used by children.
- ☐ Smoke and carbon monoxide detector batteries work and are in place and changed or recharged every 6 months.
- ☐ Closet and bathroom doors have release/rescue hardware.
- ☐ Room dividers and storage units are stable and secured.
- ☐ Furniture is child-size, in good condition, and with protective corners, if needed.
- ☐ Furniture placed flush against a wall does not exceed 30 inches in height.
- ☐ Small stepladders or stools, no higher than the children's knees and with rubber slats, are available so children can reach sinks that are not child-size (as in FCC homes).
- ☐ Steps, inclines, and platforms are padded and have nonslip treads and protective railings.
- ☐ A-B-C type fire extinguishers are visible, easy-to-reach, and charged for use; one is located near the cooking learning center.
- ☐ Decals or other signs on glass doors (if present) are placed at children's eye level.

Monthly

- ☐ The environment is smoke-free, lead-free, and toxin-free.
- ☐ The setting has no flammable furnishings.
- ☐ Heating and cooling systems, as well as air quality, are inspected for safety.
- ☐ Water temperature is tested to ensure that it is at 120°F or less, or faucets have scald-guards.
- ☐ The setting has functioning smoke alarms and carbon monoxide detectors (if required).
- ☐ Instructions for operating fire extinguishers are posted in English and in home languages of staff and families. Pictured directions should be available for those who are not able to read the directions, especially during an emergency.
- ☐ Poison control, fire, police, EMS, and another emergency services phone numbers are visibly posted and updated.
- ☐ A well-stocked first aid kit (see Figure 10) is stored in a locked cabinet out of children's reach.
- ☐ Emergency lighting (including flashlights) is available and batteries are in working order.
- ☐ There are no long pathways between learning centers; space is arranged so children cannot run into and around learning centers.

Figure 6b. Indoor Safety Checklist for Center-Based Preschool and Family Child Care Environments

Monthly (continued)

- ☐ Play areas are located away from doorways.
- ☐ Open stairwells are blocked off.
- ☐ Emergency exits are marked, lit, and unlocked from the inside.
- ☐ Evacuation procedures for fires and other natural disasters are visibly posted and clearly diagrammed with instructions in English and the home languages of staff and family members.
- ☐ Evacuation procedures are practiced according to regulations. Documentation of drills is available for review.
- ☐ All toys and equipment are developmentally appropriate and in good repair.
- ☐ Toys and materials are displayed on shelving with heavier items at the bottom.
- ☐ Toys, furnishings, equipment, and space are adapted as necessary to provide for safe use by children with disabilities.

Daily

- ☐ Children are supervised in center-based programs by sight and sound at all times.
- ☐ Children are supervised by sight or sound in family child care homes. Sleeping children are supervised by sound with frequent visual checks.
- ☐ Children are released only to those with written permission to pick-up them up.
- ☐ Toys and equipment have no sharp edges, chipped paint, lead paint, or loose nuts and bolts.
- ☐ Toy pieces and removable parts are larger than 1¼ inches in diameter.
- ☐ All plants are nontoxic (see Figure 11).
- ☐ Only animals that pose no danger to children are in the setting (see Figure 12). This includes children with allergies and extreme fear of an animal that interferes with the child's ability to fully engage in activities.
- ☐ A working telephone is accessible; cordless or cellular phones are full charged.
- ☐ Child-resistant caps cover unused electrical outlets.
- ☐ Electrical cords are not frayed or damaged.
- ☐ Electrical cords and wires are tied together, on top of carpeting, and located in low-traffic areas, away from water.
- ☐ Carpeting and area rugs are secured and lay flat, with no frayed edges.
- ☐ Flooring is clean, dry, and has no-skid surfaces.

Figure 6c. Indoor Safety Checklist for Center-Based Preschool and Family Child Care Environments

Daily (continued)

- ☐ Small appliances are unplugged when not in use and stored out of children's reach.
- ☐ Window blinds and/or shades have plastic rods to open and close. There are no cords long enough to encircle a child's neck.
- ☐ Adult purses, tote bags, and personal items are stored out of children's reach.
- ☐ Sharp objects (scissors, knives, safety pins) are stored in locked cabinets.
- ☐ Chemicals and potentially dangerous products, such as cleaning supplies, bleach, and medications are stored in original, labeled containers in a locked cabinet that is not accessible to children.
- ☐ Bleach solution is kept in a marked spray bottle in a locked cabinet. It is used only when children cannot inhale fumes. Alternatives to bleach solutions are used for children and adults at risk of having asthma triggered by droplets from bleach solutions.
- ☐ Empty cleaning product bottles are rinsed prior to disposal and placed in trash containers out of children's reach.
- ☐ Mats/cots are spaced at least three feet apart.
- ☐ Mats/cots are stored out of the way when not in use. Early childhood educators place cots in racks from bottom to top, so they will not topple over.
- ☐ Water tables are filled to a height of no more than 4 inches of water and emptied daily.
- ☐ Water tables are located on washable flooring or placed atop a piece of vinyl, a drop cloth, toweling, or a shower curtain.
- ☐ Pot handles on the stove (in FCC homes) are turned towards the back of the stove out of children's reach.
- ☐ Early childhood educators supervise all woodworking activities; participating children must wear safety goggles.

Figure 7a. Outdoor Safety Checklist for Center-Based Infant/Toddler Environments

Initially (to determine compliance) then Yearly

- ☐ The area where infants play is adjacent to, but physically separated from, space for mobile infants and toddlers; in center-based programs both areas are separate from the area used by preschoolers.
- ☐ At least 33 square feet of play space is available for each infant and 50 square feet of space for each toddler.
- ☐ The play area is enclosed by a natural barrier or a fence at least 4 feet in height.
- ☐ The fence has no openings larger than 3½ inches.
- ☐ Exit gates have self-closing, child-proof latches.
- ☐ All play equipment including sandbox, climbers, slides, and swings are developmentally appropriate, securely anchored to the ground, and free of sharp edges.
- ☐ Play structures that are 30 inches or lower in height are placed at least 6 feet apart; taller play structures are placed at least 9 feet apart.
- ☐ The area has no trampolines, teeter-totters, belt swings, single-chain tire swings, or enclosed tunnel slides.
- ☐ Elevated surfaces, such as platforms have guardrails.
- ☐ Swings for infants are fully enclosed and have seat belts.
- ☐ Swings for toddlers are "bucket shaped."
- ☐ A use zone of 48 inches is established around swings and other equipment.
- ☐ Cushioning material, such as wood chips, mulch, or sand are located under and around play equipment, according to the depth specified for each type of equipment by the U.S. Consumer Product Safety Commission.
- ☐ The ground and sandbox allow for drainage.
- ☐ Sprinklers, hoses, and plastic tubs are available for water play in warm weather, but wading pools are not present.
- ☐ A track for riding toys is located on the perimeter of the play area.
- ☐ Riding toys are age-appropriate and have a low center of gravity.
- ☐ Play equipment and play surfaces are designed to accommodate children with disabilities, including those who use walkers and wheelchairs.

Daily

- ☐ Area is free of debris including glass, standing water, ice, and animal wastes.
- ☐ There are no toxic plants (See Figure 11).

Figure 7b. Outdoor Safety Checklist for Center-Based Infant/Toddler Environments

Daily (continued)

- ☐ There are no animals that pose danger to children (See Figure 12).
- ☐ Fence is free of splinters and sharp edges.
- ☐ Play area is free of holes and tripping hazards.
- ☐ All play equipment is free of rust, rot, cracks, peeling paint, and protruding nails and bolts.
- ☐ The sandbox is raked before use and covered when not in use.
- ☐ Water play takes place in plastic tubs filled with no more than two inches of water.
- ☐ Children do not wear neck scarves and clothing with drawstrings.
- ☐ At least six feet of shade from trees, a canopy, or umbrellas is available.
- ☐ All children must wear helmets while using riding toys. Plastic liners are used if helmets are shared.
- ☐ Children in strollers are fastened with safety straps.
- ☐ Storage sheds are locked.
- ☐ Early childhood educators have a first aid kit (see Figure 10) and cell phone.

Figure 8a. Outdoor Safety Checklist for Center-Based Preschool Environments

Initially (to determine compliance) then Yearly

- ☐ The play space for preschoolers is separated from the play space for infants and toddlers.
- ☐ At least 75 square feet of play space is available for each child.
- ☐ The play area is enclosed by a natural barrier or a fence of at least 4 feet in height.
- ☐ Fence has no openings larger than 3½ inches.
- ☐ Exit gates have self-closing, child-proof latches.
- ☐ All play equipment including sandbox, climbers, slides, and swings are developmentally appropriate, securely anchored to the ground, and free of sharp edges.
- ☐ Elevated surfaces, such as platforms, have guardrails.
- ☐ Single axis swings that rest a minimum of 12 inches off the ground are used. S-hooks are closed completely.

Figure 8b. Outdoor Safety Checklist for Center-Based Preschool Environments

Initially (to determine compliance) then Yearly (continued)

- ☐ Six feet fall zones are established around swings and other play equipment.
- ☐ Cushioning material, such as wood chips, mulch, or sand are located under and around play equipment, according to the depth specified for each type of equipment by the U.S. Consumer Product Safety Commission (an average of 10 to 12 inches).
- ☐ Climbers are no more than 60 inches in height.
- ☐ The ground and sandbox allow for drainage.
- ☐ A track for tricycles and wagons is located away from play areas.
- ☐ Tricycles have a low center of gravity, no spokes, and are sized for the age group.
- ☐ The area has no trampolines, glider swings, free-swinging ropes, swinging exercise rings, or trapeze bars.
- ☐ Play equipment and play surfaces are designed to accommodate children with disabilities, including those who use walkers and wheelchairs.

Daily

- ☐ Area is free of debris including glass, standing water, ice, and animal waste.
- ☐ There are no toxic plants (See Figure 11).
- ☐ There are no animals that pose danger to children (See Figure 12).
- ☐ Fence is free of splinters or sharp edges.
- ☐ Play area is free of holes or tripping hazards.
- ☐ All play equipment is free of rust, rot, cracks, peeling paint, and protruding nails and bolts.
- ☐ Children do not wear neck scarves and clothing with drawstrings.
- ☐ The sandbox is raked before use and covered when not in use.
- ☐ At least six feet of shade is available.
- ☐ All children must wear helmets while riding tricycles and other riding toys. Plastic liners are used if helmets are shared.
- ☐ Storage sheds are locked.
- ☐ Early childhood educators have a first aid kit (see Figure 10) and cell phone.

Figure 9a. Outdoor Safety Checklist for Family Child Care Environments

Determine that these items are in place:

- ☐ The play space is located no more than ⅛ mile from the FCC home.
- ☐ Play area is enclosed by natural barriers or securely fenced.
- ☐ Fence has no openings larger than 3½ inches.
- ☐ Exit gates have self-closing, child-proof latches.
- ☐ Any swimming pools, creeks, or ponds on the property are fenced and out-of-bounds for children.
- ☐ Any exposed air conditioning units or other electrical appliances are behind fences and out-of-bounds for children.
- ☐ Outdoor grills are not present in the play space.
- ☐ All play equipment, including sandbox, climbers, slides, and swings are developmentally appropriate, securely anchored to the ground, and free of sharp edges.
- ☐ Elevated surfaces, such as platforms, have guardrails.
- ☐ Fully enclosed swings with straps are used for infants. Bucket-type swings are used for toddlers. Single axis swings that rest a minimum of 12 inches off the ground are used for preschoolers and school-age children. S-hooks are closed completely.
- ☐ Six feet fall zones are established around swings and other play equipment.
- ☐ Cushioning material, such as wood chips, mulch, or sand are located under and around play equipment, according to the depth specified for each type of equipment by the U.S. Consumer Product Safety Commission (an average of 10 to 12 inches).
- ☐ Climbers are no more than 60 inches in height.
- ☐ The ground and sandbox support drainage.
- ☐ A track or paved surface for riding toys and wagons is located away from play areas.
- ☐ Riding toys are age-appropriate, have a low center of gravity, and no spokes.
- ☐ There are no trampolines, glider swings, free-swinging ropes, swinging exercise rings, or trapeze bars.
- ☐ Play equipment and play surfaces are designed to accommodate children with disabilities, including those who use walkers and wheelchairs.

Figure 9b. Outdoor Safety Checklist for Family Child Care Environments

Check these items daily:

- ☐ Area is free of debris, including glass, standing water, ice, and animal waste.
- ☐ There are no toxic plants (See Figure 11).
- ☐ There are no animals harmful to children (See Figure 12).
- ☐ Fence is free of splinters or sharp edges.
- ☐ Play area is free of holes or tripping hazards.
- ☐ All play equipment is free of rust, rot, cracks, peeling paint, and protruding nails and bolts.
- ☐ Children do not wear neck scarves and clothing with drawstrings.
- ☐ The sandbox is raked before use and covered when not in use.
- ☐ At least six feet of shade is available.
- ☐ All children must wear helmets while riding tricycles and other riding toys. Plastic liners are used if helmets are shared.
- ☐ Storage sheds, barns, and garages are locked.
- ☐ Trash cans are placed outside the yard or behind barriers.
- ☐ Educator has a first aid kit (see Figure 10) and cell phone.

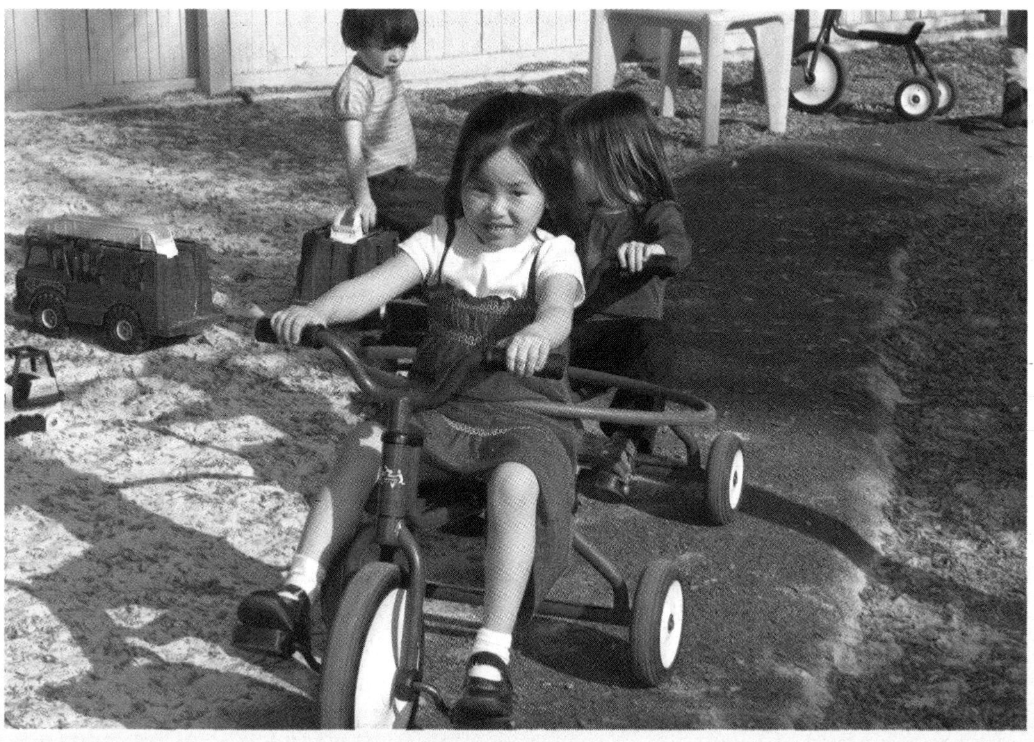

Riding toys should be developmentally-appropriate and in good or excellent condition. These toys should also have a low center of gravity.

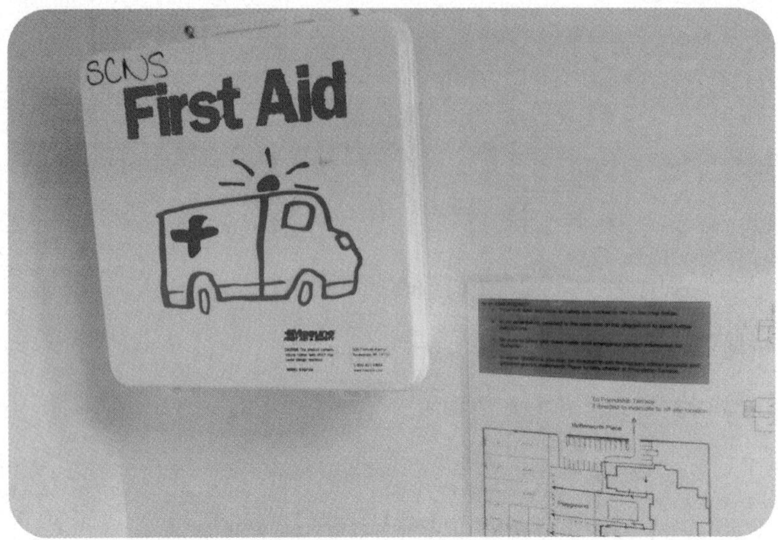

First aid kits should be easily available to staff and out of children's reach.

Figure 10. Suggested First-Aid Kit Contents and Uses

- **Disposable nonporous, latex-free or non-powdered latex gloves** (latex-free recommended)
- **Scissors**
- **Tweezers**
- **Non-glass, non-mercury thermometer** to take a child's temperature
- **Bandage tape**
- **Sterile gauze pads**
- **Flexible roller gauze**
- **Triangular bandages**
- **Safety pins**
- **Eye patch or dressing**
- **Pen/pencil and note pad**
- **Cold pack**
- **Current American Academy of Pediatrics (AAP) standard first-aid chart or equivalent first-aid guide,** such as the AAP Pediatric First Aid for Caregivers and Teachers (PedFACTS) Manual
- **Phone (cell or other)**
- **Water** (two liters of sterile water for cleaning wounds or eyes)
- **Liquid soap** to wash an injury and hand sanitizer, to be used under supervision, if hands are not visibly soiled or if no water is present
- **Tissues**
- **Wipes**
- **Individually wrapped sanitary pads** to contain bleeding of injuries
- **Adhesive strip bandages, plastic bags for clothes, gauze and other materials** used in handling blood
- **Flashlight**
- **Whistle**
- **Battery-powered radio**
- **List of children and their emergency contact information** (i.e., home, work and cell phone numbers for parents, guardians and emergency contacts)
- **Special care plans for children who have medical conditions**
- **Emergency medications or supplies** as specified in the special care plans
- **List of emergency contacts** (i.e., address and phone numbers for nearby poison control center, hospitals, or emergency care clinics and other community resource agencies)

(List is from AAP, APHA, and NRC 2019)

Sample pictures of poinsettia, split leaf philodendron, and hydrangea.

Figure 11a. Indoor and Outdoor Plants that May Be Harmful to Children

- Amaryllis
- Arrowhead Plant
- Asparagus Fern
- Avocado
- Azalea
- Bird-of-Paradise
- Bittersweet
- Boston Ivy
- Caladium
- Chenille Plant
- Christmas Rose
- Chrysanthemum
- Creeping Charlie, Ground Ivy
- Creeping Fig
- Croton
- Crown of Thorns
- Cyclamen
- Dieffenbachia
- English Ivy
- Gold Toothed Aloe
- Heartleaf Philodendron
- Hydrangea
- Jerusalem Cherry
- Lantana
- Lily-of-the-Valley
- Marble Queen
- Majesty
- Narcissus
- Needlepoint Ivy
- Oleander
- Poinsettia
- Pothos
- Primula (Primrose)
- Red Princess
- Rhubarb
- Ripple Ivy
- Saddle Leaf
- Split Leaf Philodendron
- Umbrella Plant
- Weeping Fig

(University of Nebraska Cooperative Extension [UNCE] n.d.)

Figure 11b. Indoor and Outdoor Plants that May Be Harmful to Children

Nonpoisonous plants:

- African violet
- Begonia
- Christmas cactus
- Coleus
- Dandelion
- Dracaena
- Forsythia
- Impatiens
- Jade
- Marigold Calendula
- Petunia
- Rose
- Spider plant
- Swedish ivy
- Wandering Jew
- Wild strawberry

(List is from AAP, APHA, and NRC 2019)

Figure 12. Animals Prohibited from Early Childhood Programs

- Bats
- Hermit crabs
- Spiders, venomous insects
- Wolf-dog hybrids
- Stray animals
- Chickens and ducks
- Aggressive animals
- Reptiles and amphibians
- Psittacine birds (parrots, parakeets, budgies, and cockatiels) unless tested for psittacosis
- Ferrets
- Animals in heat
- Animals less than one year of age.

(AAP, APHA, and NRC 2011, 121)

Teaching Children about Safety

Early childhood educators are responsible for keeping children physically safe. One important way of doing this is by teaching toddlers and preschoolers how to help keep themselves safe. They will be learning a skill they can use now and in the future.

Creating and Reinforcing Safety Rules

Think about the rules in your setting. They are probably ones like these:

- We need to walk indoors. If we want to run, it must be outdoors.
- We need to be kind to one another. Biting, pushing, and hitting are not allowed.
- We need adults to help us use sharp tools like knives or paper cutters, they will show us how to use them safely.

Are you surprised at how many of these rules target children's physical safety? In Chapter 10, we will examine more closely how a few simple rules can guide young children's behavior. In this section, however, we will focus on rules to keep young children safe.

At what age can you begin involving children in safety rules? Start when they are toddlers. Even young toddlers can begin to understand the need for safety rules—that rules are needed to keep both themselves and others safe. Older toddlers can understand simple safety guidelines, like take turns at the slide, so that children don't bump into one another, use words when you are upset, and use blocks for building not throwing. When crossing a street, teach toddlers how to look and listen for approaching vehicles. Toddlers can also learn that matches are tools used only by adults, not toys for children's play. By the time children are preschoolers, they can cognitively understand that their actions lead to consequences and that there are specific steps they can follow to stay safe.

People of all ages—but especially children—are more invested in and willing to follow rules that they helped set. If your family thinks it's important, for example, for everyone to have dinner together, then this is likely to be a rule everyone wants to follow. If you give young children a voice in rulemaking, they will want to remember those rules. Preschoolers can take an active role in rulemaking, while toddlers can have a beginning role. Here are some thoughts on making rules:

- Begin with just a few short, clear rules that children can repeat easily. With all there is to know about staying safe, children can become overwhelmed quickly and easily. Do not bombard them with too much information at once. Add more rules, if needed, once the children master these short, clear rules.
- Relate rules to ideas children already know.
- Help children to understand the "why" behind a rule.
- State rules positively. Tell them what they can do rather than what they cannot (e.g., instead of "Do not run inside," try "Be safe, walk inside").
- Illustrate rules with pictures for children who are not yet readers or are learning English as a second language.
- Repeat the rules in all the children's home languages.
- Let children practice using the rules.
- Apply rules consistently over time.
- Give gentle reminders when children forget the rules.
- Use puppets and stories—in books or written by the children in the group—to introduce and reinforce safety rules.
- Help children notice when they are following a rule and acknowledge their efforts.

The most effective way to reinforce safety rules is to make them a natural part of the daily program. Weave safety discussions gradually and naturally into your conversations with all of the children about new and existing toys, equipment, and materials. Describe what you are doing and explain the safety reasons behind those actions. For example, when introducing a waterwheel at the water table, say, "Here are towels and a mop for wiping up spills. It's easy to splash water on the floor when we're having fun. It's also easy to slip and fall on wet floors. That's why we need to have towels and a mop handy."

Here are other examples of safety conversations you might have with the children in your setting:

- "Antonio, thank you for telling me that the wheel on the ride-on car is broken. We'll put it in the cupboard until one of the maintenance staff can fix it. We wouldn't want anyone to get hurt driving a broken car."
- "I know that everyone's excited about baking bread today. Before we begin, let's go over the safety rules for using the oven."
- "Aarika, I'm sorry that Eduardo bumped into you when you went down the slide. I think we need to review our safety rules for playing on the slide so that this doesn't happen again."
- "Sammi, thank you for rinsing your plate after lunch. Let's double-check to see that no water splashed on the floor. Whoops, the floor is wet. Could you please get a paper towel to dry the floor? Thank you. Now nobody will slip and fall on the wet floor."

When introducing children to new safety messages, give them lots of opportunities to test and practice them with you. Be realistic about the children's ability to grasp and retain these messages successfully. You will most likely have to offer numerous reminders until they remember what to do to stay safe.

Teaching Safety Content

In addition to teaching children safety rules, it is important that they learn safety content. Children cannot depend on you alone to keep them safe. Even though you are there to supervise them, they need to know what they should do if there is a fire or how they can walk safely in traffic. Taking some personal responsibility for safety will not only keep them safer, it will better equip children to make their way in the world.

Pedestrian Safety

When children accidentally kick a ball and it rolls into the street or a beloved pet runs at a passing car, safe pedestrian practices are not the first things to come to mind. Help guard children against pedestrian accidents by teaching them a few necessary safety behaviors:

Selecting Teaching Safety Aids

Various commercial materials and curricula exist that are designed to help you teach children about safety—particularly fire and water safety or how to deal with strangers. Some of these materials are designed by educators who understand how young children learn and may include excellent activities to try in your setting. Others are not developmentally appropriate and often rely on coloring activities and stickers. Before using any of these materials, read them carefully. Select only those that are developmentally appropriate for the children in your setting.

- Hold on to an adult's hand when crossing the street.
- Walk on sidewalks. If there is no sidewalk, walk on the left, facing traffic, while holding an adult's hand.
- When crossing a street, look for the pedestrian crosswalk. Before crossing a street, look left, right, and left again.

Many accidents result from children surrendering all of the responsibility for their safety to adults. Be sure that children are active participants in the pedestrian safety process. As you walk with children, point out the safe walking behaviors you are both performing. Narrate your actions: "Before we cross the street we need to make sure no cars are coming. Let's stand on the curb and look to the left. Now let's look to the right. Now let's check to the left again. I don't see any cars coming. Do you? I don't hear any car motors either. Do you? It looks like it's safe to walk across the street now. Let's keep checking both sides as we cross to make sure no cars are coming."

There will be times when it is not possible for each child to have an adult's hand to hold while walking near traffic. In these cases you and children can use a knotted travel rope for neighborhood or nature walks. Each child holds onto a knot while adults lead and follow the rope "train." Multi-seat strollers will similarly work for younger children who are not yet stable walkers or do not have the stamina needed to walk as far as you plan to go.

Get into the habit of following these safety precautions while walking with a group:

- Make sure that each child wears a tag with the name of your setting and phone number on it. (Do not include the child's first or last name.)
- Carry a list of the names of all the children you are supervising and their emergency contacts.
- Maintain required adult–child ratios.
- Bring a cell phone and a first-aid kit.
- Practice traffic safety rules with children ahead of time. Games such as "red light, green light" help young children become aware of traffic lights and safety measures.

Safe Use of Riding Toys

Riding toys include vehicles with and without pedals. Toddlers use the ones without pedals by moving their feet on the ground. Trikes with pedals come in different sizes, appropriate for children of different heights, usually from age three on. Before they take their first ride, teach children these rules:

Safe

- Children's feet should reach the ground for riding toys without pedals. A trike is the right size for a child if they can reach the foot pedals.
- Children should use only riding toys in good repair with seats, handlebars, and wheels firmly attached.
- Children may ride only on flat, hard surfaces, such as designated tracks or blacktops, and need to obey any traffic safety signs.
- Children must put on helmets before riding.
- Children must ride alone.
- Bumping other drivers is not permitted.

Children should use only riding toys that are in good repair.

Car Passenger Safety

Whether you work in a center or an FCC home, car passenger safety is a topic you need to be up to date on. You may use the following information yourself and/or pass it along to families.

> All states and territories require child safety seats for infants and children fitting specific criteria, but requirements vary based on age, weight and height. Often, this happens in three stages: infants use rear-facing infant seats; toddlers use forward-facing child safety seats; and older children use booster seats. To learn more about state requirements governing the use of car seats, go to the website: *www.ghsa.org/html/stateinfo/laws/childsafety_laws.html*

The use of car seats and booster seats reduces the rate of injury and death for infants under one year of age by 71%, for toddlers by 54%, and for preschoolers by 45% (CDC 2015). Infants, toddlers, and preschoolers should sit in the backseat of vehicles. Airbags in the front dash, if released during an accident, could crush children's bodies. Allowing a child to sit in an adult's lap is illegal and dangerous. If the car stops suddenly, the child will fly out of the adult's arms and into a window, windshield, or another passenger.

The American Academy of Pediatrics recommends that all infants and toddlers be secured in a rear-facing car seat until they reach the highest weight or height allowed by the car seat manufacturer. Some car seats are just for rear-facing use; others, convertible seats, can be used in different ways as the child gets taller and heavier. When a toddler has outgrown the requirements for safe use of a rear-facing seat, the child will move to a new seat designed for forward facing, a seat that allows for forward-facing use now and as a booster later, or continue in a convertible seat, now adjusted for forward-facing use. It is best for children to ride in a seat with a harness for as long as possible, at least until age four. Depending on the four-year-old's height and weight, the child will move to a booster seat that is secured with the car's lap and shoulder belts. With a little assistance, toddlers and preschoolers can learn to fasten their own seat belts. It is best to always check so there is no more than an inch of "give" in the straps.

Make Teaching Traffic Safety Fun

Children can practice both pedestrian and vehicle safety using road signs when they play with blocks or when they use ride-on toys. Use children's books like the following to teach traffic safety messages:

- *The ABC's of Traffic Safety* by Whitney M. Hemstock.
- *Safety on the School Bus* by Sarah Florence
- *Road Safety* by Sue Barraclough

Toddlers and preschoolers can be taught where to sit and why. You can emphasize concepts as:

- "Buckling up" is a necessary habit for everyone for every ride.
- The driver will not move the car until everyone is buckled. If someone undoes a buckle or gets out of the car seat, the driver will stop the car. This could mean missing out on something fun like a field trip.
- If something falls on the floor, it stays on the floor.
- Talking and singing are permitted, but yelling and fighting are not.

School Bus Passenger Safety

The children who attend your center or FCC home may or may not ride on a school bus. Nevertheless, the following is important information for anyone who works with children and families.

School buses come in a variety of shapes and sizes. Some are vans, some are small buses, and some are large school buses, weighing 10,000 pounds or more. Most often, if children are bused to your center, they will be riding on a van or small school bus. These vehicles are equipped with child restraints, and if carrying infants or toddlers, they will have the appropriate-sized car seats installed. Monitors are assigned to buses to ensure safe boarding, riding, and exiting procedures.

Occasionally, children are transported on large school buses. In a few states, these large school buses use seat belts and restraints, similarly to the way vans and small buses do. More often though, large buses do not have seat belts. They depend on compartmentalization to keep children safe. Compartmentalization provides a protective envelope consisting of strong, closely spaced seats that have energy absorbing seat backs (NHTSA 2006).

Since more young children are killed getting on and off school buses than riding on them, you want to focus your attention on teaching children how to enter and exit school buses. (Savage, Kawanabe, Mejeur, Goehring, and Reed 2002). For example, teach children to look at the driver and make eye contact before stepping onto the bus or crossing in front of it. Children should wait for the driver to wave them on before crossing.

Among other content points you should teach children are these:

- Check that your shoes are fastened before walking to the school bus.
- Stand at least three giant steps back from the curb as the bus approaches.
- Board the bus one-at-a-time.
- Hold on to the handle bar to safely climb up and down steps.
- Wait for the person ahead to move on before stepping onto or off the bus.
- Sit facing forward on the bus.
- Hold your backpack on your lap.
- Fasten your seat belt or ask the bus monitor to help you, if you are riding on a bus equipped with seat restraints.
- When exiting, wait to stand up until children in the row ahead are exiting.
- Take everything with you when you leave the bus.
- Always walk in front of the bus, taking five giant steps.
- Wait for the driver to signal you to cross.
- Signal the driver through the window if you drop something in front of the bus. Never bend over in front of the bus to pick something up.
- When crossing the street, look left-right-and left again, as you always do when walking in traffic.

If you are transporting children in a van, bus, or passenger car, have an index card for each child that includes the child's name, birthday, emergency contact, and the child's picture. This will be an invaluable resource in case of an accident or other emergency.

At the end of the trip, make sure the driver checks all the seats in the bus to ensure no child has fallen asleep and to avoid leaving any child behind on the bus.

Fire Safety

Children under age five are more than twice as likely to die in a fire than older children and adults (U.S. Fire Administration [USFA] 2003).

Playing with matches is the leading cause of home fires (USFA 2003). Children are naturally curious about fire and attracted to flames. Toddlers as young as two years old have started home fires. Teach children that matches and lighters are tools for adults only. Children should learn to never pick up matches or lighters and to tell an adult if they find these items.

There are four important things you can do to prevent fires and to respond if there is a fire.

1. Ensure that smoke alarms and fire extinguishers are accessible and in working condition.
2. Devise and practice fire emergency plans (see the last section in this chapter). Fire experts recommend having both primary and back-up plans. If the proposed fire exit is blocked or engulfed in flames, take your back-up route out of the building.
3. Designate a meeting place outdoors where everyone can reunite should the group separate during evacuation.
4. Hold fire drills monthly so that escape procedures become second nature for everyone in your setting.

In addition to preparing yourself, early childhood educators also need to prepare children for what to do in case of an actual fire emergency:

Make Learning Fire Safety Engaging

Your local fire station can help you teach the children in your setting about fire safety. For children, a trip to the fire station is not only an opportunity to learn about what to do in a fire emergency, but a chance to see where the firefighters eat and sleep—and to try on a firefighter's helmet. In many communities firefighters are willing to visit the program in their truck and show the children how their equipment works and how their clothing keeps them safe.

Also, read aloud fiction and non-fiction books about fire safety to the children. Relate the stories and information to what children already know about fire safety. Here are a few titles to consider:

- *Firehouse Fun!* by Abby Klein.
- *Sparkles the Fire Safety Dog* by Dayna Hilton.
- *Fire Drill* by Paul DuBois Jacobs and Jennifer Swender.
- *Stop Drop and Roll (A Book about Fire Safety)* by Margery Cuyler.

- Have children leave the building with a responsible adult. This is the best way to stay safe.
- Make sure children understand that they cannot hide from a fire. Taking shelter in a closet or waiting under furniture until the worst is over places children at high risk. Evacuation is the only plan that works.
- Teach children that inhaling smoke is dangerous. If children encounter smoke while trying to leave the building, have them get down on their knees and crawl low to the ground. Practice this skill. Set up a ceiling of bed sheets and have children crawl below the sheets to safety.
- Tell children to stay out of the building after evacuating. No one—child or adult—should ever go back into a burning building for any reason.

- Prepare children for fire emergencies. For example, teach them what to do if their clothing catches fire. Children should "stop, drop, and roll" immediately —meaning that they stop whatever they are doing, fall to the ground, and roll their bodies. As they roll, they should cover their eyes with their arms until the fire is smothered. Again, practice this skill often. Let children know that you will be practicing fire safety that day. When children are indoors or outdoors, yell, "Stop, drop, and roll!" Have everyone—including you—act it out.

Water Safety

Accidents can occur any time children use or play near water. In the art center, at the water table, or even in the bathroom, water can spill on the floor and cause children to slip and fall. Wipe or mop any floor spills immediately—with children's assistance, if possible.

Young children can drown in as little as one inch of water. Within 4 to 6 minutes underwater, children can suffer irreversible brain damage (National Safe Kids Campaign [NSKC] 2004). While residential swimming pools and open water sites pose the greatest danger to young children, many places in your setting can be deadly, like wading pools, sinks, baby bathtubs, water tables, buckets of water, or even toilets. A toddler falling head first can drown in a toilet in two minutes.

Supervise children during water play and while they are using the toilet. Guard against leaving standing water anywhere other than inside the toilet. If you are in an FCC home, consider installing a safety latch that will keep the lid on the seat. Empty your setting's water table every day, both to guard against bacteria growth and to prevent accidental drowning.

You can also teach children the following water safety content:

- Stay dry by wearing smocks when playing with water.
- Play with only a few props at a time in a water table, tub, or wading pool.
- Avoid splashing indoors.
- Tell an adult immediately if water gets on the floor during indoor water play or when using the bathroom. Help mop up spills.
- Put away all water toys and props when finished using them.

Poison Safety

Every day three hundred children in the U.S. are treated for accidental poisonings. Two of these children will die (CDC 2012). Your primary defense against accidental poisoning is to make sure that no poisonous substances are available in your center or FCC home. This means that you should:

- Lock hazardous items like drain cleaners, toilet bowl cleaners, insecticides, and the bleach solution you use in disinfecting toys in a locked cabinet, out of children's reach.
- Store batteries in a locked cabinet, out of children's reach.
- Use medicines safely and store them in a locked cabinet, out of children's reach.
- Post the Poison Control number prominently: 1-800-222-1222.

Helping Children Hear and Listen to Their Inner Voices

As adults we work hard to keep children safe. We prepare and monitor the indoor and outdoor environments. We teach children the rules for walking safely in traffic and what to do in case of a fire. We also offer guidance on what they should do if they find a potentially poisonous plant outdoors.

All of this practice, knowledge, and guidance goes a long way in helping children to be safe. Still, it's not the whole answer. We don't want children to become 100% dependent on us for their safety. Part of our role as early childhood educators is to help children start to develop their own instincts—to know if something is not right. Hearing one's inner voice evolves from learning and knowing what is right and then practicing the rules (Greer 2011). By internalizing the rules and practicing them over and over, children will start developing an instinct about safety.

They will sense when something is not right and act as you have taught them.

How can we actually help children learn to listen to that voice inside? Some children will naturally be able to process and follow specific rules and expectations just by hearing what is being taught and provided. Others will benefit from books and additional resources to help them learn how to respond to difficult situations. Role-playing and dramatic demonstrations of proper responses to negative situations will also aid certain children. Games, activities, or specific routines that are practiced regularly can be quite effective. Children will NOT internalize information with limited or singular methods of practice. The younger the child, the more important rehearsal and practice become. Multiple methods of information delivery are also critical. Each child will respond to a technique or practice that appeals to their learning style. Books, games, routines, role-playing, and other activities may seem like fun and perhaps not reflect the gravity of a situation as adults perceive it. Yet the upbeat and positive nature of playful activities will allow young children to make the necessary cognitive connections. Meanwhile, fear and constant negative instruction will only stymie learning and responses.

In addition to these preventive measures, educate children about poisons. Make these content points when talking with toddlers and preschoolers about poisons:

- A poison is something that if you eat, smell, taste, or touch, can make you sick or even kill you.
- Poisons are found both inside and outside.

- Some poisons are things that we use to clean like sink or toilet cleaner; some poisons are used in the garden, like sprays to get rid of bugs.
- Medicines—that usually make us well—can be poisonous if we take too much or accidentally take someone else's medicine. That's why they are kept in a locked cabinet.
- All inside poisons should be locked away. If you see any sitting out, tell an adult.
- Sometimes plants growing outside can be poisonous, like holly berries or certain mushrooms.

It's hard to know if a plant or food growing outside is bad for us by looking at it. You need to ask an adult before touching or eating it.

Modeling Safe Practices

Children will understand the importance of safety when they see you respecting safety rules and doing everything you can to keep everyone around you safe. There are many things you do to model safe practices:

- Have a background check that validates that it is safe for you to work with children.
- Complete training in pediatric first aid and CPR so that you can treat injuries and respond to emergencies.
- Supervise children carefully and always maintain required adult–child ratios.
- Work safety topics into your daily conversations with children. For example, telling Marcus, "Be careful not to make your block construction taller than your shoulders. We don't want it to hurt anyone if it falls over."
- Practice and enforce safety rules. For example, every time you drive or ride in a car, you use a seatbelt.
- Teach and practice emergency routines with the children, such as fire drills.
- Talk calmly and with authority in an emergency. You offer reassurance and address children's fears, whether real or imagined. "I saw you fall off the slide and I know your leg hurts. I've called your mom and she's going to have the doctor check you out. I'm quite certain that you won't need a new leg. The doctor will get this one working right again."
- Stay abreast of current safety practices and the latest safety regulations for children's toys, equipment, and furnishings.
- Know the signs of abuse and provide a setting that encourages children to share their feelings.

Always be on the lookout for ways to make early childhood education settings safer for children and explain to children how you do it. Let them see and understand how you solve safety issues. Not only will you model safety practices, but you will illustrate the vital skill of problem solving.

Teaching Safety and Problem-Solving

Darnell (age 5): *"Teacher, I hurt my hand on the tray."*

Mr. Frank: *"I've noticed lately that a lot of us have been burning our hands when we take something out of the oven. Let's figure out what's happening and see if we can do something to prevent it."*

Sharmaine (age 4): *"Maybe Darnell had the oven on too hot."*

Mr. Frank: *"That's a good thought, Sharmaine. But I remember helping Darnell adjust the oven temperature. We had it at 350 degrees, which is the same temperature we usually use for baking. So I don't think the oven was hotter than usual."*

Louis (age 4): *"You showed us how to use potholders when we want to take things out of the oven. You even showed us how to hold them to protect our fingers. Maybe Darnell didn't use any potholders."*

Darnell: *"I did not forget! You can ask Miss Washington. She was helping me take the tray out. I told her our teacher said that we need to use potholders."*

Sharmaine: *"I saw him. He used potholders."*

Mr. Frank: *"Well, let's take a look at these potholders. Darnell, would you please bring me the potholders you used?"*

Darnell: *"Here you go."*

Mr. Frank: *"Oh, these are the beautiful ones you made for us in the art center, Suzanna. They're very pretty, but they're also very thin. See? When we hold them up to the window, light goes through them. That means heat can go through them, too. I think these are a little too thin for using in our kitchen. However, they'd be great in the dramatic play center. Suzanna, would you please move these potholders to the play kitchen area?"*

Darnell: *"Well, what do we use in the real kitchen?"*

Mr. Frank: *"That's an excellent question, Darnell. For safety reasons, we won't be able to use the oven until I get us some new oven mitts. As soon as I can, I'm going to get us some made out of silicone. Silicone allows you to touch things as hot as 500 degrees."*

Sharmaine: *"Wow! That's hot!"*

Mr. Frank: *"It sure is. Silicone mitts should protect everyone's hands when we take something out of the oven. I think our problem is solved."*

Safe

Responding to Injuries and Emergencies

Teaching children about safety and modeling safe practices are critical components of CDA Functional Area 1. So too, is knowing what to do if children are injured while in your care. Whether you work in a center or in an FCC home, you have to know how to respond if a child falls off a swing, is bitten by a bee, or chokes on a peanut butter sandwich. Your best preparation for this all-important challenge is the pediatric first aid and CPR training that you receive as part of the CDA process. Through this course, you will learn to treat the following:

- Choking
- Insect, animal, or human bites
- Falls
- Cuts or scrapes
- Injuries that result in heavy bleeding
- Accidental poisonings
- Allergic reactions
- Head injuries
- Dental emergencies
- Eye injuries
- Sprains and fractures
- Accidental drowning

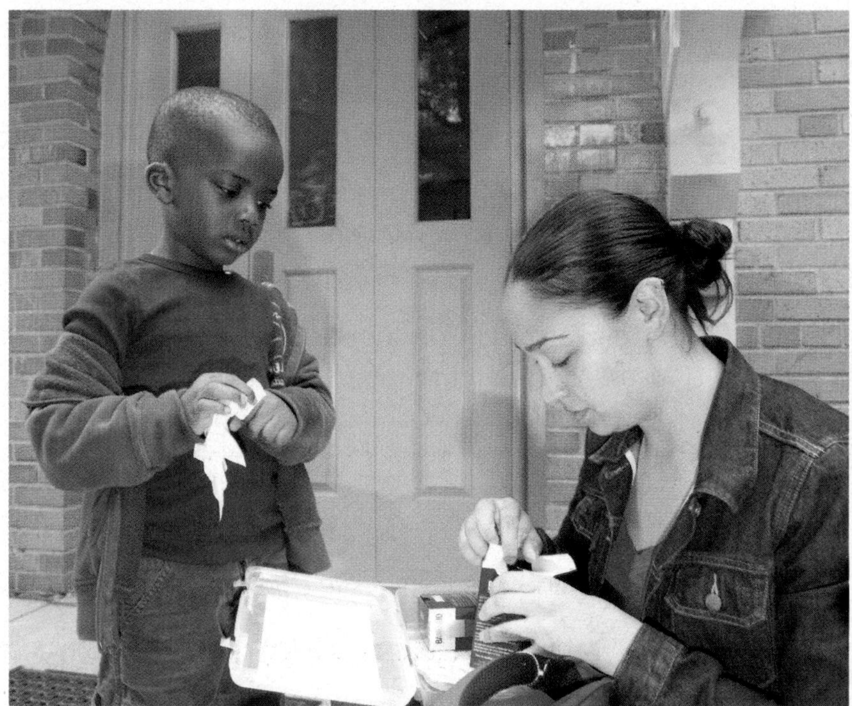

Keep two, well-stocked first-aid kits in your setting.

Knowing how to handle these emergencies will help prevent additional injury and even death. Every time a child is injured and you respond, you'll need to fill out an incident report and report the injury to the child's family the day it occurs. In Figure 13a-b, you will find examples of how you might apply your first-aid knowledge to injuries that might occur in your program.

Figure 13a. Administering First-Aid Treatment

Incident	First-Aid Response
Keisha (age 3) burns herself when touching a hot pot on the stove.	• Since this is a minor burn, hold Keisha's affected hand under cold, running tap water. • Dry and bandage the affected area. • Fill out an incident report and notify Keisha's family. • (Later, review stove-top safety rules with all of the children.)
Timothy (age 4) breaks a glass when trying to pour juice, and cuts his hand. It is bleeding.	• Because there is only light bleeding involved, hold Timothy's cut thumb under cold, running tap water. • Clean the wound with soap and paper towels. • Dress the wound with clean gauze. • Fill out an incident report and notify Timothy's family. • (Later, replace the glass cups with plastic ones.)
Tonio (age 5) trips and falls on a rock while playing outdoors. His knee is scraped and bleeding lightly.	• Treat the wound as above in Timothy's example. • Clean the scrape thoroughly to prevent infection. • Fill out an incident report and notify Tonio's family. • (Later, check the area for more rocks like the one Tonio tripped on. Remove or rake them, as needed.)
Emilia (age 14 months) begins choking while eating lunch.	• Stand behind Emelia and wrap your arms around her waist. • Place a fist just above the child's belly button. • Try to dislodge the food by holding the fist with your other hand and quickly pushing in and up. • When the food comes out of her mouth, comfort her and explain what has happened. There is no need to call 911 if she is conscious and breathing. • Fill out an incident report and notify Emilia's family. • (Later, figure out what Emilia was eating and why she choked on it.)

Figure 13b. Administering First-Aid Treatment

Incident	First-Aid Response
Mary Lou (age 6 months) is stung by a bee while sitting outside on a blanket.	• Remove the stinger from Mary Lou's arm. • Check to see that the child is not having a reaction to the bee venom (e.g., shortness of breath or hives). • Apply ice if there is redness and swelling at the site of the sting. Check Mary Lou's file to see if there are any allergens listed, if not, due to her age, call her family to pick her up and watch for certain allergic symptoms, which, if apparent, mean bringing Mary Lou to the hospital to make sure swelling of her trachea does not occur which would obstruct her breathing. Very often, families are unaware of this kind of allergy because their child has not been stung yet by a bee or wasp, so asking family members to monitor their child at home is not an overreaction to the situation. (Later, check the garden to see if there is a bee's nest or certain flowers that are attracting bees. Spraying or removal of the nest may be necessary.)
Anna (age 2) bites Pedro (age 2) in a fight over a coveted toy; she does not break Pedro's skin.	• Comfort Pedro. Involve Anna in comforting him. • Get an ice pack for Pedro. • State the rule about being kind to our friends calmly and firmly. Tell Anna that if she still has an urge to bite, she can bite an apple. • Fill out an incident report and notify Pedro's family. • Notify and discuss the situation with Anna's family. Together, discuss strategies to discourage biting that can be used at school and at home. Keep in mind, biting is a typical behavior for this age. • (Later, discuss the incident with Anna and remind her to use her words to explain her feelings.

Treat children's injuries calmly, but be direct. Children will take comfort in knowing that you are in charge and know what to do in this situation. They receive the message that their safety is important to you and that you will ensure it. Likewise, when you immediately tell families what has happened, they realize that their child's safety is a high priority for you.

Sometimes your intervention is not enough and the child will need to see a doctor or be taken to the hospital. You need to know when you should reach out for assistance in an escalated emergency situation.

Call 911 and get children to the hospital if they experience any of the following symptoms (AAP, APHA, and NRC 2011):

- Loss of consciousness
- Breathing difficulties
- Severe bleeding
- Unequal pupils
- Seizure or convulsions
- Neck, back, or head injuries
- Continuous clear drainage from nose/ears after a blow to the head
- Severe headache
- Stiff neck or neck pain when head is moved
- Hives that appear quickly
- Repeated forceful vomiting or vomiting blood
- Severe abdominal pain that causes a child to double-over
- Possible broken bones
- Shock

Treat children's injuries calmly but straightforwardly.

In these instances, notify the child's family of the emergency and ask them to meet either you or the person assigned to accompany their child at the hospital. If you are the one accompanying a child to the hospital, bring all medical records and emergency authorization forms that your program has on file for the child.

Developing Emergency Plans

Beyond administering first aid and responding to individual emergencies, every early childhood educator needs to know how to respond to emergencies that threaten the entire group of children and adults in your setting.

The most effective way of doing this is for the program to devise emergency plans (sometimes called emergency preparedness plans) to properly respond to potential emergencies and disasters. Depending on where you are located, the program will need plans for the following types of emergencies:

- Fire
- Weather-related disasters, such as tornadoes, flash floods, landslides, earthquakes, tsunamis, and hurricanes/typhoons
- Interruptions in water or electricity service
- Hazardous material/chemical spill
- Criminal incidents, such as kidnappings, intruder or hostage situation, bomb threats, or acts of terrorism
- Mandated evacuations in response to military actions (for example, if your setting is located in or near a war zone)

For programs in centers, emergency plans are usually developed under the direction of the Administrator, with input from teachers. Your supervisor will share with you what your responsibility is. Even if your role in writing the plan is minimal, it is important that you become familiar with the plans and fully able to implement them.

In FCC homes, educators will need to develop plans for their program. Your licensing agency should be able to give you assistance in doing this, including sharing sample plans that you can use as models in formulating your own plans.

In developing emergency plans the Federal Emergency Management Agency (FEMA 2011) recommends compiling the following:

- Basic information: program name, address, phone number and email address
- A list of emergency phone numbers: police, fire, rescue, hospital, poison control, insurance, and out-of-area contact. (Long-distance phone calls may go through even if local lines and cell networks are down or jammed. Be sure to make wallet cards of this number for the children's families, as they may be able to get information from this contact if they cannot get through to your program.)
- Child/Family Information: names, phone numbers, parent or guardian's place of work and contact information, unique needs or accommodations for children with disabilities, including medications and comfort items, two emergency contacts, child's pediatrician/ health service.
- Scenarios for three types of evacuations:
    - o In-place evacuation—children and staff stay at the center or FCC home in a secured location, as for tornadoes
    - o On-site evacuation—children and staff move out of the affected area but relocate to another area on the premises, as for a localized fire
    - o Off-site evacuation—some or all of the children and staff move to a designated area off-site, as for a chemical spill

These scenarios need to include:

- The specifics of the evacuation route, including maps and written instructions in all languages spoken by staff and the children's families.
- Detailed information on how infants and toddlers will be evacuated as well as children with mobility problems.
- How pets will be cared for.
- The back-up routes to be used in case you are unable to evacuate via your first chosen route.
- Where the designated outdoor meeting place is in case your group separates during the evacuation.
- Steps the program has taken to reduce risk (e.g., testing smoke and carbon monoxide detectors monthly and changing batteries yearly; drills).
- Role playing exercises used to prepare children (e.g., Stop, Drop, and Roll.)
- The emergency supplies that will go with you (e.g., medications/medical supplies; charged cell phone; first aid kit; flashlights with extra batteries; battery operated radio with extra batteries; wipes and tissues; disposable cups; water and nonperishable food; nonelectric can opener; diapers and formula for infants; blankets; keys for vehicles, if driving; hard hats, masks, and gloves; fluorescent tape for roping off dangerous areas).
- Information needed in an emergency (e.g., the contact list for staff and families; children's emergency information; attendance sheet of all children and staff present that day; insurance information; contact information for utilities; contact information for landlord or property manager, if applicable, vehicle identification number, if applicable; financial information).
- Who will do what (e.g., call 911; call children's families; check bathrooms and other locales to make sure everyone has evacuated, take attendance, carry first aid kits and provide needed first aid; transport the children's medical files; transport cash/checks; accompany children to a doctor or hospital; turn off gas, electricity, and water if needed; post relocation information; and of course, supervise the children).
- Specific procedures for reunification with families.

The program should share all emergency plans with the children's families in their home languages. Diagrams, sketches, or photos can be added to these plans if it seems they will help reinforce the messages. Children's families should be familiar with these plans so they can discuss them with their children and participate in drills when they are visiting your setting. In addition, program staff should provide families with specific information about creating a family emergency plan. This makes a good topic for a family workshop (see the next section).

Creating a Fire Emergency Plan

Of all the emergency plans developed by an early childhood program, fire emergencies are considered a top priority. Have on hand plans for both on-site evacuations and off-site evacuations as described in the section above.

In implementing the plans, follow these procedures (South Carolina Child Care Services 2013):

- Evacuate the building/house
- Call 911 to confirm that the fire department has been alerted and is on its way
- Activate your written plan
- Check weather conditions on a cell phone app or battery-operated radio; move children and staff upwind of any smoke
- Make sure all children, staff, and visitors and pets are accounted for
- Assess weather again and decide if an off-site evacuation is needed
- Release children to families, checking appropriate forms.

The fire emergency plan should have explicit instructions for determining whether staff should attempt to put out a fire with an extinguisher or call 911.

If your instructions say that staff should use a fire extinguisher, evacuate the children before attempting to use it to put out the fire. Ensure that they are outside of the building with a colleague or other responsible adult to supervise. It is appropriate to use an extinguisher if it seems that the fire is small and contained, such as a kitchen or wastebasket fire. Standing approximately eight feet from the fire, aim the extinguisher at the fire's base—not the flames. Do not underestimate the power of a fire. If it appears out of control, it is. If you have any doubts, do not use the extinguisher; instead get out of the building and join the children and your colleagues.

The emergency plan also describes the program's risk-reduction measures. Practice implementation of the fire emergency plans monthly to make sure that children and adults know what to do. Regular fire drills ensure that children will be able to leave the building quickly without thinking about it. Have children practice crawling on the floor to get outside in the event that smoke fills the play area. Practice checking the door to see if it is hot. And as noted earlier, make stop, drop, and roll a regular part of your curriculum.

Test smoke alarms monthly and replace batteries every six months. Check extinguishers monthly to ensure the following:

- They arc charged and in their designated places.
- There are no obstructions to accessing them.
- Safety seals are intact.
- Operating instructions are clearly legible (and in all staff members' home languages).

Engaging Families in Safe Practices

Children's safety is a top priority for their families as well as for you. Ease family members' minds by sharing with them the many ways you work to keep your setting safe:

- Releasing their children only to authorized persons who must sign children in and out of the setting.
- Supervising children at all times.
- Developing emergency plans in the families' home languages and posting them.
- Regularly practicing emergency procedures with children. (Pay special attention to children with sensory issues who might have a strong response to loud noises, smells, and unplanned transitions.)
- Being certified in pediatric first-aid and CPR.
- Performing safety checks on indoor and outdoor settings daily.
- Developing and enforcing safety rules with children.
- Teaching children how to prevent accidents and injuries from fire, water, riding toys, and poisons.

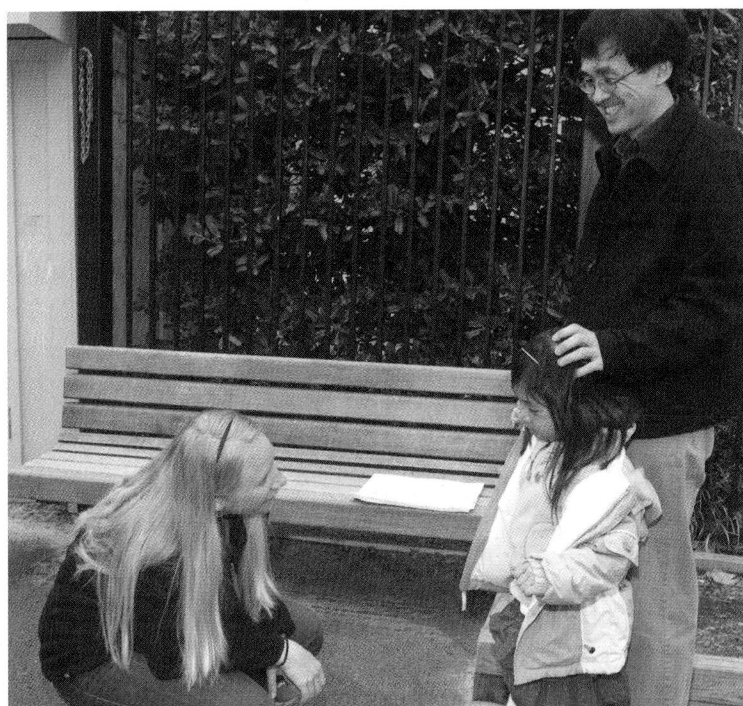

Reassure families that their children will be safe at your setting.

- Helping children learn how to walk safely in traffic and ride safely in cars and buses.
- Involving children in developing safety rules.

- Filling out an incident report and informing families every time their child is injured or involved in an accident.
- Modeling appropriate safety practices.

Like all aspects of your curriculum, children benefit most when their families are engaged in their education. To engage families in your setting's safety program, obtain the following information from them:

- Emergency addresses and phone contacts (both cell and landline) for them, their emergency contacts, and their child's doctor.
- A list of persons to whom children are permitted to be released and the names of any individuals to whom their children are specifically not allowed to be released.
- Permission to photograph their child (or instructions not to).
- Disabilities that their child may have that could impact safety and evacuation procedures.
- Languages that their child understands.
- Best ways to comfort their child, should there be an emergency or injury.
- Specific circumstances that could affect their child's safety and ability to follow evacuation procedures.

Make sure that families are aware of how you deal with injuries and accidents. Provide copies of your emergency procedures and encourage families to read them.

Family members should understand that you will inform them if there is an accident or injury involving their child. When you use incident reports and share them with families, you ensure that they are aware of every safety concern that has involved their child during the day. Reassure family members that you will call 911 and have their child transported to the hospital during an emergency and that you will notify them. Staff will consult them before making any decisions regarding their child's treatment.

Keep families informed of any changes in your safety program. If you encounter a new safety challenge, involve families in solving the problem. For example, if Doug is hurting other children—either by biting or throwing things—confer with his family. Ask: Have these behaviors happened before? Are they occurring at home? Are there any new circumstances in Doug's life that might be causing him stress? Has he had any physical or medical changes? Involve the family in developing a plan of action to address the cause of the behavior and to help the child learn to use an acceptable behavior instead.

The same safety measures children are learning at your program will help keep them safe at home. Invite families into your classroom to be a part of your safety program. If families speak a home language other than English, make sure safety information is available in their home languages. Hold workshops during the year to share safety information with families. Here are some sample newsletter or workshop topics:

- **Keeping smoke and carbon monoxide detectors in working order.** Two thirds of home fires in which children die occur in homes without working smoke detectors (USFA 2003). Invite a firefighter to speak to families on this topic. At the same time, inform families about the dangers of exposure to carbon monoxide and explain how these detectors work. In some communities, local government provides new detectors to those who do not have them in their homes.

- **Calling 911.** Family members with preschoolers can teach their children to dial 911 if there is a home fire or other emergency. You can walk families through the process of teaching this skill, offering advice on teaching children what's a real emergency (Mommy fainted) and what isn't (I can't find my stuffed bear).

- **Protecting children from accidental poisoning.** Describe how you store household cleaning products, medicines, and other potentially harmful substances in their original containers, in locked cabinets, out of reach. Invite a pediatrician to offer advice on what to do if a child does get poisoned.

- **Pretty or poisonous?** Inform families about which plants are potentially toxic and how to recognize them. As part of the session, alert families that in case of an emergency, they should contact the National Capital Poison Center from anywhere in the United States at 1-800-222-1222. Families can get immediate information in their own language when they call.

- **"Stranger Danger."** Many families worry about a stranger's intent on doing children harm. By the time they are in preschool, children can learn what they should do if approached by a stranger. Focus this workshop on strategies for keeping children safe without instilling fear. The goal is for children to use caution, not to be afraid of everyone they don't know.

- **Partner with families to create a family emergency plan.** Share with families, in their home languages, the emergency plans for fire and other disaster programs. Provide templates and work with the families to create their own emergency plans, including evacuation routes. Having plans in place at your setting and in the children's homes not only keeps children safer, it confirms that safety is a vital concern to everyone important in the child's life.

Work with families to review safety procedures thoroughly so they are active partners in ensuring their children's safety. By working together, you give children a clear, consistent message on the importance of safety in your program, at home and in our communities.

Additional sources for children's books related to health and safety issues can be found at the following:

Capstone
1710 Roe Crest Drive
North Mankato, MN 56003
800.747.4992
www.capstonepub.com

The Book Vine for Children
3980 W. Albany Street, Suite 7
McHenry, IL 60050
800.772.4220
www.bookvine.com

Free Spirit Publishing
6325 Sandburg Road, Suite 100
Minneapolis, MN 55427
612.338.2068
www.freespirit.com

CHAPTER 2:

Healthy

CDA® Functional Area 2: Candidate provides an environment that promotes health and prevents illness, and teaches children about good nutrition and practices that promote wellness.

Healthy

Introduction

Among the fundamental responsibilities of early childhood educators is to maintain a healthy environment that fosters wellness and to teach children what they can do to ensure their own health--now and later in life. When you work daily to keep children safe, nourished, and healthy, you enhance their learning significantly and promote lifelong healthy habits.

Keeping children healthy, like keeping children safe, requires educators to follow a number of specific procedures. In this chapter, we will spell out this guidance while exploring a number of important aspects involved in keeping children healthy:

- **Promoting Wellness**
- **Supporting Wellness During Routines**
- **Responding to Illness**
- **Helping Children Develop Good Health Practices**
- **Partnering With Families**

Promoting Wellness

Wellness can be defined as the active process of making choices that result in a healthy life. To promote a healthy lifestyle for young children, it is important to be proactive. This means that early childhood educators must work closely with families to take steps to prevent illness and health problems instead of reacting to them once a child is sick. Wellness also includes being physically active and fit. Fitness and strategies for encouraging young children's fitness is discussed in Chapter 4.

In Chapter 1, we discussed how you could prevent choking, suffocation, and strangulation by removing objects and food that were likely to cause these accidents. In this section, we will discuss what you can do to prevent illnesses and the spread of communicable diseases.

There are four basic strategies for making wellness an ongoing part of your program. First, develop trusting, respectful relationships with families as they provide the foundation for wellness and health. Second, monitor your setting to be sure that the indoor and outdoor environments support health and wellness by being sanitary and germ-free. Third, perform daily health checks on children to determine if they are healthy enough to participate in the program. Fourth, maintain complete and thorough health records on each child. Through these records you can follow each child's progress towards wellness. An important part of the health record is a log of each child's immunizations, created with information provided by a child's family. Positive actions like these go a long way toward creating settings that keep children healthy and ready to learn.

Maintaining a Germ-Free, Sanitary Setting

To ensure that indoor and outdoor settings are as sanitary and germ-free as possible, familiarize yourself with the health requirements mandated by your local and state licensing agencies. Early Head Start, Head Start, and military child development programs also have specific health standards that must be addressed. These regulations serve as a baseline for quality. Your setting requirements should match or exceed them. The more rigorous your requirements, the healthier the setting will be for children. Contact your child care licensing agency to obtain a copy of licensing rules and regulations. Ask your supervisor for help if you have trouble locating the documents that list and explain the requirements.

Cleaning, sanitizing, or disinfecting surfaces is critical for reducing the spread of disease in child care settings. Routine cleaning is often the most common method for removing some germs (bacteria and viruses) from surfaces. However, sanitizing or disinfecting AFTER cleaning to further reduce the number of germs on a surface is frequently needed as well (AAP, APHA, and NRC 2019).

Is there a difference between sanitizers and disinfectants? Absolutely. A sanitizer reduces but does not eliminate germs. A disinfectant destroys or inactivates germs. It is always important to note which surfaces, objects or materials may require sanitizing or disinfecting.

Use Figure 14 to review your setting's compliance with health requirements. Be sure to learn and keep current with any new guidelines, such as the guidance on preparing bleach solution or alternative (see Figure 16). As you read this checklist, you'll note that if you work in a center, not all of these items are your responsibility. Requirements like mopping floors and vacuuming carpets will likely be done by cleaning staff, however, teachers and aides are responsible if meals or snacks are provided in the classroom. Meet with your supervisor and decide which of these items you are responsible for. Family child care educators, however, must address all items in order to maintain a healthy environment.

Figure 14a. Indoor Health Checklist for Infant/Toddler, Preschool, and Family Child Care Environments

- ☐ Ensure rooms are ventilated. Clean air conditioners regularly (if used) to remove dust and prevent mold. Do not use chemical air fresheners and scented products. (These products can trigger children's asthma attacks or nausea.)
- ☐ Keep room temperature 70°F or slightly lower. If the climate in your setting is dry during the winter months, use a cool mist humidifier. Clean and disinfect this humidifier daily.
- ☐ Maintain well-lit, glare-free rooms.

Figure 14b. Indoor Health Checklist for Infant/Toddler, Preschool, and Family Child Care Environments

- ☐ Mop floors daily. Sweep floors throughout the day, especially after meals or snacks. (Broom sweeping is the best method for removing food scraps on the floor/carpet area when children are present.)
- ☐ Vacuum carpets and large area rugs when children are not present. Spot clean as needed. Fully clean twice per year.
- ☐ Shake small rugs outside or vacuum daily. Launder at least weekly.
- ☐ Prepare fresh bleach solution, or alternative, daily to sanitize surfaces and disinfect toys and all washable learning materials. (See Figure 16 for guidelines on preparing bleach solution.)
- ☐ Wash dress-up clothes and accessories weekly.
- ☐ Wash, rinse, and sanitize tables at the start of each day, in between activities, and before any food is served. Use bleach solution only when children will not be near enough to inhale fumes. Allow bleach solution to air dry (at least 2 minutes) before a child sits at the table.
- ☐ Wash, rinse, and sanitize food preparation surfaces, counters, chairs with trays (if used for infants), eating utensils, and dishes before and after each use.
- ☐ Line trash cans with plastic bags and empty daily. If children eat in the room, empty trash after lunch and at the end of the day. If you care for infants and toddlers, discard disposable diapers in a covered trash can with a foot pedal. Change the liner at least once daily.
- ☐ Store children's toothbrushes so that they can air dry without touching one another.
- ☐ Keep tissues, liquid soap, and paper towels accessible to children throughout the setting and always in bathrooms.
- ☐ Use a plastic cover for the diaper table and sanitize after each diaper change or use a paper cover that you discard after every diaper change. (See section on Diapering and Toileting later in this chapter for more detailed information.)
- ☐ Wear nonporous disposable gloves to clean bodily fluids (e.g., blood, urine, vomit, feces, mucus, and saliva).
- ☐ Use bleach solution to immediately clean any surfaces exposed to bodily fluids. Rinse any mops, sponges, or dishrags used to clean body fluids immediately afterwards with bleach solution.
- ☐ Wash, rinse, and sanitize bathrooms including sinks, faucets, countertops, toilets, diaper pails, and potty chairs (if used) daily using bleach solution prepared that day.
- ☐ Remove bathroom odors through exhaust system ventilation.
- ☐ Wash, rinse, and sanitize doors and cabinet handles daily.
- ☐ Clean and sanitize computer and tablet keyboards daily.
- ☐ Empty and sanitize water tables with bleach solution daily.

Figure 14c. Indoor Health Checklist for Infant/Toddler, Preschool, and Family Child Care Environments

- ☐ Spray sand in tables with bleach solution weekly. Replace sand as often as necessary to keep the sand visibly clean. Clean and sanitize cribs after each child. If used by one child only, clean and sanitize weekly. Disinfect daily any crib parts (such as railings) that children mouth.
- ☐ Set up individual toddler and preschooler cots/mats at least 3 feet apart at naptime. Use mats that are at least 2 inches thick, waterproof, washable, and appropriate for the size and weight of the children. Position children head to toe on mats for nap time. Clean and sanitize cots and mats after each child.
- ☐ Use bedding, including crib bedding, for one child only. Wash bedding weekly or when soiled. Store bedding between use in a labeled bag or in the child's cubby. Do not allow one child's bedding to touch the bedding of another child.
- ☐ Store children's clean personal care items (e.g., combs or change of clothing) in individually labeled containers or cubbies. Do not allow children to share these items. Older children can access their own personal care items without assistance.
- ☐ Keep children clean and dry. Change their clothing as needed after outdoor play, food spills, or toileting accidents.
- ☐ Have drinking water available at all times. (Provide child-size water fountains, ask families to bring individual refillable water bottles labeled with the child's name daily, or offer pitchers of water so older children can pour their own drinks.)
- ☐ Discard single-serve disposable drinking cups after use. Sanitize reusable sippy cups/drinking cups by hand or in a dishwasher. Clean and disinfect drinking fountains (if used) daily.
- ☐ Choose classroom pets according to setting and other applicable regulations.
- ☐ Maintain pets' health certificates documenting immunizations. Ensure that pets do not pose a health threat to children or staff. (See Figure 12 in Chapter 1 for a list of prohibited animals.)

Allow only animals that do not pose a health or safety risk to children.

- ☐ Keep animals away from food preparation and eating areas.
- ☐ Clean animal habitats and sanitize all areas affected by animal droppings immediately. Children should not clean animal habitats or animal droppings, even if supervised.
- ☐ Keep pet food and litter boxes out of children's reach.
- ☐ Teach children how to feed pets, with adult supervision.

Figure 15. Outdoor Health Checklist for Infant/Toddler, Preschool, and Family Child Care Environments

Check all of the following items daily:

- ☐ Take children outside daily if the wind chill factor is at or above -15°F. and the heat index is at or below 90°F., as determined by the National Weather Service (AAP, AHA, and NRC 2011).
- ☐ Touch young children's hands and feet at least every 15 minutes when they are outdoors in cold weather to be sure they are warm and retain their usual color.
- ☐ Dress children in hats, scarves, or knit masks to cover the face and mouth in cold weather; sleeves should be snug at the wrist. Have children wear mittens/gloves, and a water and wind-resistant jacket or coat and shoes or boots. Ensure clothing is dry to prevent frostbite.
- ☐ Encourage children to play in snow, but not to eat it.
- ☐ Dress children in lightweight cotton clothing and sun hats in warm weather.
- ☐ Keep children under six months of age out of the sun.
- ☐ Apply sunblock with an SPF of 15 or higher to all children above six months in age, 30 minutes before going out in the sun. Spray sunblock directly on the child's skin, except for the facial area. Spray sunblock into adults' hands before applying to a child's face.
- ☐ Check for air quality daily at *www.airnow.gov* and use that information to determine if it is healthy for children to be playing outdoors. Children with asthma are particularly sensitive to pollution in the air. An AQI (air quality index) of 101-150 is considered "unhealthy for sensitive groups," which include young children.
- ☐ Have drinking water available at all times. (Provide child-size water fountains, ask families to bring individual refillable water bottles labeled with the child's name daily, or offer pitchers of water so older children can pour their own drinks.)

Figure 16. Preparing and Using Bleach Solution for Disinfecting Surfaces

The use of bleach solution remains the most common method of sanitizing and disinfecting in child care settings. According to the American Academy of Pediatrics (2019), only a sanitizer or disinfectant product with an EPA registration number on the label can make public health claims to be effective in reducing or inactivating germs. Many bleach (and hydrogen peroxide) products are EPA-registered and can be used to sanitize or disinfect.

Wash surfaces with soap before applying bleach solution.

It is important to always follow the manufacturers' instructions when using EPA-registered products described as sanitizers or disinfectants. EPA-registered bleach products are described as sanitizers and disinfectants. Yet when purchasing bleach, make sure it is for household use and not for industrial applications. Household chlorine bleach is typically sold in retail stores as an 8.25% sodium hypochlorite solution.

Pay attention to the mixing recipe and required contact time for each use. The recipe and contact time are most likely different for sanitizing and disinfecting.

To safely prepare bleach solutions:

- Dilute bleach with cool water, and do not use more than the recommended amount of bleach.
- Select a bottle made of opaque material.
- Make a fresh bleach dilution daily; label the bottle with the contents and date mixed.
- Wear gloves and eye protection when diluting bleach.
- Use a funnel.
- Add bleach to the water rather than water to the bleach to reduce fumes.
- Make sure the room is well ventilated.
- Never mix or store ammonia with bleach or products that contain bleach.

To safely use bleach solutions:

- Apply the bleach dilution after cleaning the surface with soap or detergent and rinsing with water if visible soil is present.
- If using a spray bottle, adjust the setting to produce a heavy spray instead of a fine mist.
- Allow for the contact time specified on the label of the bleach product.
- Apply when children are not present in the area.
- Ventilate the area by allowing fresh air to circulate and let the surfaces air dry completely or wipe dry after the required contact time before allowing children back into the area.
- Store all chemicals securely, out of reach of children and in a way that prevents them from tipping or spilling.

(AAP, APHA, and NRC 2019)

Performing Daily Health Checks

Daily health checks are an important part of an early childhood wellness routine. They determine who is healthy enough to attend the program and who is ill and needs attention. They also stop the spread of germs that could put other children and staff at risk for communicable diseases. Most important, daily health checks send children and families the message that health is something to pay attention to every single day.

As each child enters the setting the early childhood educator greets the new arrival and conducts a daily health check. Fortunately for busy educators, this check usually takes less than a minute. Observe children as they arrive. Ask the children and whoever brings the child that day a few questions. If children usually arrive via bus, set up a system for communicating with their families about their children's health each morning. This could be via e-mail or text, notes the child brings to the setting, or a daily checklist completed by parents and sent with their child. Remember, the daily health check is not a physical exam. Respect the children, their feelings, and their cultures.

Figure 17. Sample Daily Health Check

- Ask older children questions like "How are you today?" and "How are you feeling?"
- Ask family members questions like: "How is LeShawn today?" "Did he sleep well," "When were the last times Emily ate, drank, had her diaper changed? "Has Isabella been around anyone who is sick?" "Are there any changes in Mikey's behavior?" and "Is there anything new that I should know about?"
- Hold children or kneel down to their height to observe them.
  - Do they seem different somehow? Listless or clingy? Unusually irritable?
  - Check their breathing.
  - Listen for coughs.
  - Are there any rashes or swelling on their skin?
  - Are they scratching their scalps?
  - Does their skin look yellowish or pale?
  - Are their eyes watering, swollen, or crusty?
  - Are they pulling at their ears?
  - Does their breath smell fruity or different than usual?
  - Do you smell any odors?
  - Gently touch children's foreheads or cheeks with the back of your hand. Do they feel feverish or clammy?

If you do see signs of illness, refer to the information in the section on Responding to Illness later in this chapter.

Even if children appear fine physically when you greet them in the morning, continue to observe them throughout the day for such things as frequent visits to the bathroom, loss of appetite, scratching, listlessness, or irritability. Should a child show signs of illness, refer to the section on Responding to Illness on page 89.

Another reason to conduct health checks is to add to your observational data about each child. Use your daily records to chart children's behavior and physical symptoms over time. Health experts recommend that you keep a record of these daily health checks for a month at a time. You can use a checklist or record notes on paper or electronically. Check your setting requirements to ensure that you are performing and recording daily health checks properly. If you identify changes or patterns, talk with the child's family about your observations. They can then determine if their child needs further assessment by a health professional and potentially treatment for a specific condition.

Maintaining Children's Health Records

Early childhood programs are required by licensing and most funders to monitor children's health, growth, and development by using health records. Children's health records serve multiple purposes. Early childhood educators use them to:

- Identify preventive health needs, such as immunizations or dental care.
- Prepare a special care plan (in collaboration with specialists and the child's family) for children with chronic health conditions or special health needs such as asthma.
- Determine whether to continue a child's enrollment or ask the family to temporarily remove the child from care because it is not possible to ensure the child's healthy participation in the program.

Content of Health Records

At a minimum, health records should include:

- Telephone numbers where parents or guardians and at least two emergency contacts can be reached at all times
- Name of the child's regular source of health care and any other usual sources of health care, including the name of a specific contact person, address, and telephone number
- Child's pre-admission medical examination/health assessment and subsequent update at each checkup, including immunization status
- Developmental health history (physical and developmental milestones and significant events)

- Results of all screenings and assessments
- Notations about allergies, special diet, chronic illness, or other special health concerns
- Emergency permission for medical care
- All permission slips authorizing non-emergency health care and giving of medications
- Reports of all injuries or illnesses that occur while the child is in the program
- Medication logs
- Reports of referrals and follow-up action
- Notes about any health communication with family or health providers
- Written correspondence about the child's health
- Health observations from staff members

Health experts recommend maintaining a file for each child in a central location within the facility or FCC home. Maintaining accurate records is essential to providing quality care and protecting the health of children in child development settings. Updating records can be tedious when done by hand. Computer software is available to make this job more accurate and efficient. If your program is still doing manual updates, ask your supervisor whether the program has access to this kind of software or is willing to purchase it (AAP, APHA, and NRC 2011).

Immunizations

The most important preventive health measure is to be sure that all children are immunized against preventable diseases, such as measles, mumps, rubella, polio, pertussis (whooping cough), diphtheria, tetanus, deep tissue infections such as meningitis, cellulitis, and abscess caused by Hib bacteria, chickenpox, pneumococcus, influenza, and rotavirus-caused infant/toddler diarrhea. The Centers for Disease Control and Prevention (CDC), the American Academy of Pediatrics (AAP), and the American Academy of Family Physicians (AAFP) jointly publish a schedule each year of what immunizations children under age six should receive and when. Visit the CDC website to access the most recent schedule.

In addition to checking immunization records, check annually that each child has received the health care mandated by local, state, and federal entities, including Early Head Start and Head Start and military child development programs. Typically, these requirements include annual dental and physical exams (with identification of any allergies or other health concerns); entry vision and hearing exams; and developmental screening for signs indicating possible developmental delays.

Like all confidential records, keep health records in a locked file cabinet and available to program staff only as needed.

Immunizations and Autism

Autism Spectrum Disorder (ASD). ASD is a developmental disability that is caused by differences in how the brain functions. People with ASD may communicate, interact, behave, and learn in different ways.

For many years, concerned family members and other individuals have questioned whether there is a link between childhood vaccinations and ASD. Fearing that vaccinating their child will cause autism, a significant number of parents refused to have their children vaccinated, despite regulations mandating that vaccinations are required for enrollment in public schools.

Extensive research has shown that the fears about vaccinations are groundless. Yet, even in the face of this research, many families have held onto the belief that immunizations are dangerous. Trying to put this myth to rest once and for all, in the summer of 2015, the CDC issued a definitive judgment: Vaccines do not cause autism. The CDC writes (2015):

> Some people have had concerns that ASD might be linked to the vaccines children receive, but studies have shown that there is no link between receiving vaccines and developing ASD. In 2011, an Institute of Medicine (IOM) report on eight vaccines given to children and adults found that with rare exceptions, these vaccines are very safe.

A 2013 CDC study added to the research showing that vaccines do not cause ASD. The study looked at the number of antigens (substances in vaccines that cause the body's immune system to produce disease-fighting antibodies) from vaccines during the first two years of life. The results showed that the total amount of antigen from vaccines received was the same between children with ASD and those that did not have ASD.

In 2019, an extensive study published in the Annals of Internal Medicine examined the specific interactions of the MMR vaccine and autism identification over the course of several years and multiple variables. The factors related to autism diagnosis indicated that issues other than the vaccine were often possible contributors and that the vaccine did not cause or have any connection to these factors when an autism diagnosis was determined. The other factors that feature in the literature on autism diagnosis include maternal age, paternal age, smoking during pregnancy, method of baby delivery, preterm birth, low birthweight, head circumference and sibling history.

There is no question that vaccines are both safe and needed. All children must be immunized to protect their health, the health of the other children, and adults in the setting.

(CDC 2015, Annals 2019)

Supporting Wellness During Routines

Routines—handwashing, diapering and toileting, nap time, toothbrushing, and eating meals and snacks—take up a lot of the day in early childhood settings. The younger the child, the more time is spent carrying out routines. They are important opportunities to build relationships and support learning. At the same time, they require early childhood educators to carry them out with health and hygiene in mind.

In this section we focus on what early childhood educators do to keep children well. Later on in this chapter we will take a look at how you can use these same routines to teach children good health practices.

Handwashing

There is no other health practice more important to maintaining a healthy setting than handwashing. Expect that you and the children will wash your hands numerous times every day. Consider these facts:

- Handwashing can reduce the risk of respiratory infections by 16%.
- Washing hands with soap and water could reduce diarrhea-associated deaths by up to 50%.
- Researchers estimate that if all individuals routinely washed their hands 1,000,000 deaths could be prevented each year (CDC 2011b).

Caring for Our Children (AAP, APHA, and HRA 2011) recommends that children and staff wash their hands at these times during the day:

- Upon arrival for the day or when moving from one group setting to another.
- Whenever hands look dirty.
- Before and after
    - o handling food
    - o feeding a child
    - o eating
    - o providing medication or first aid
    - o diapering an infant or toddler
    - o playing in water used by more than one child

- After
  - o helping a child use the toilet or a potty seat
  - o using the toilet
  - o wiping children's noses or mouths
  - o handling bodily fluids (e.g., mucus, blood, urine, vomit, feces, saliva) or clothes soiled by bodily fluids
  - o assisting a sick child
  - o sneezing
  - o coughing
  - o blowing your nose or assisting a child in doing so
  - o handling pets, pet wastes, pet toys, and cages
  - o playing in the sandbox
  - o cleaning and sanitizing surfaces
  - o handling garbage and changing the trash can liner
  - o playing outdoors

Give children lots of practice handwashing.

Figure 18. The Steps of Proper Handwashing

Review the steps with children. You could take photos of children performing each step and make a poster to hang near the sink.

1. First, check to make sure a clean, disposable paper towel or single-use cloth towel is available.
2. Turn on faucet and adjust temperature of water to be warm and not hot.
3. Moisten hands with water.
4. Apply one squirt of liquid soap from a dispenser onto hands (make sure soap is NOT antibacterial).
5. Rub hands together until a lather forms out of the stream of water.
6. Continue to rub hands for at least 20 seconds (think "Happy Birthday" mentally sung twice or "The ABCs" songs). Make sure to wash the backs of hands, between fingers, and around and under nails.
7. Rinse hands under clean, running water until they are free of soap and dirt.
8. Keep water running while drying hands.
9. Use a clean, disposable paper towel or single-use cloth towel to dry hands.
10. If water does not turn off automatically, turn taps off with the disposable paper towel or single-use cloth towel.
11. Throw the disposable paper towel away in a lined trash container. If a single-use cloth towel was used, place the towel in a laundry hamper.

(AAP, APHA, and NRC 2019)

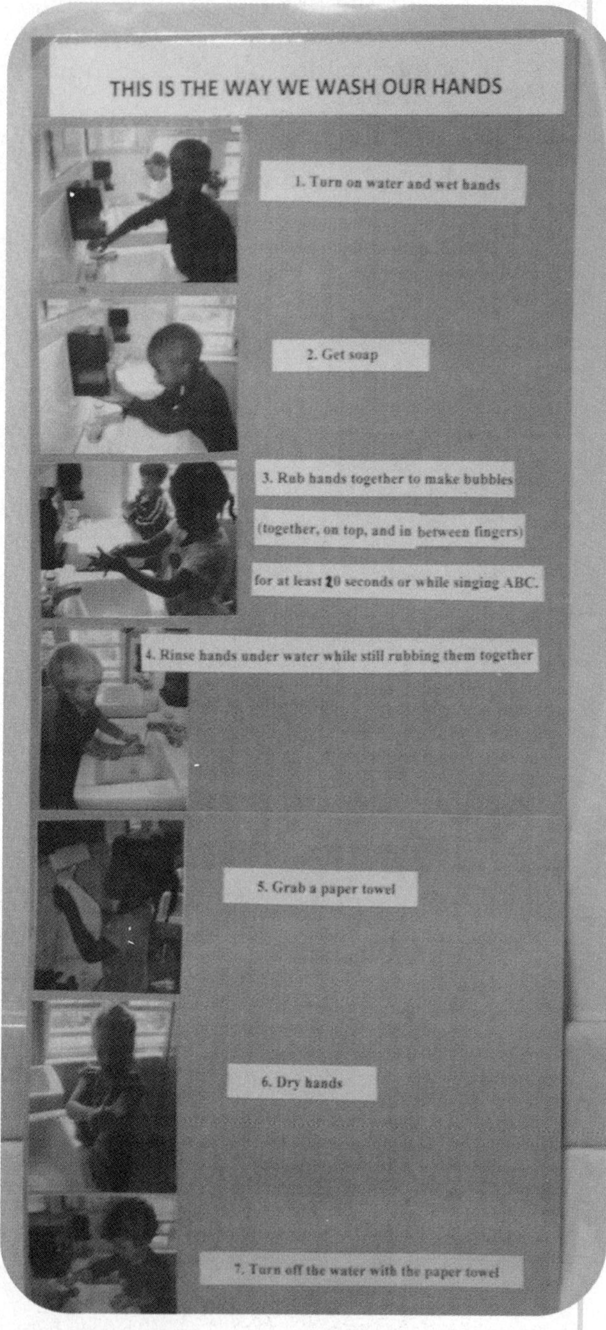

THIS IS THE WAY WE WASH OUR HANDS
1. Turn on water and wet hands
2. Get soap
3. Rub hands together to make bubbles
(together, on top, and in between fingers)
for at least 20 seconds or while singing ABC.
4. Rinse hands under water while still rubbing them together
5. Grab a paper towel
6. Dry hands
7. Turn off the water with the paper towel

Diapering and Toileting

Diapering and toileting are important and frequent routines in an early childhood setting. They can be times for relaxed, one-on-one time with a child and contribute to strong relationships. Although they carry distinct health challenges for children and adults, well-planned diapering and toileting times can reduce the spread of infectious diseases. Diligence in frequent, proper handwashing; sanitizing the changing area; and good personal hygiene habits are the first line of defense.

Changing Diapers

To prevent diaper dermatitis (diaper rash), change children's diapers soon after they are wet or soiled. In addition to keeping an infant clean and sanitary, diaper changes are opportunities to talk about what you are doing and what you will do next. Set a gentle, calm, and unhurried tone. When you are gentle, nurturing, and relaxed, children will learn that you respect them and their bodies and that body waste is a natural part of life. During this one-on-one time, you can forge a bond of attachment with each child.

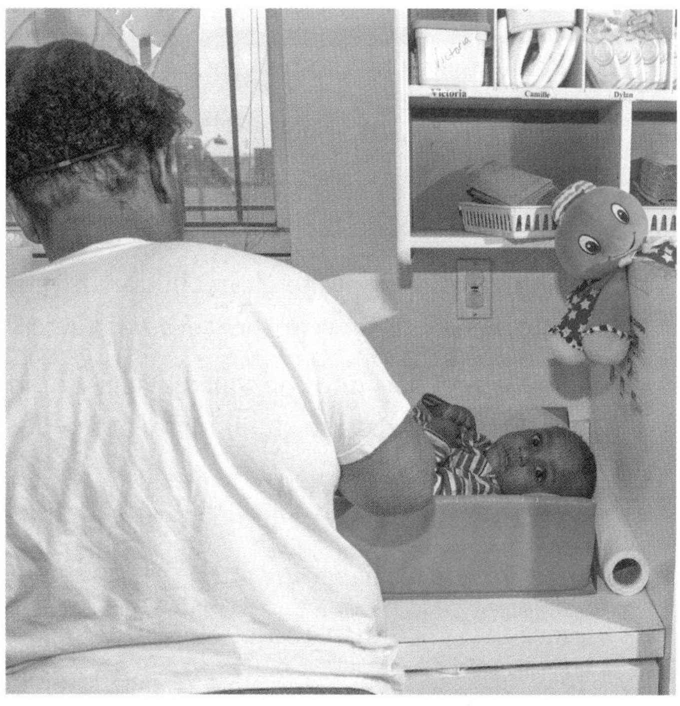

Change infants' diapers soon after they are wet to prevent diaper rash.

Follow these steps when changing children's diapers:

1. Get organized.
   - Before you bring a child to the diaper-changing area, wash your hands.
   - Make sure everything you need is within reach:
     - o nonabsorbent paper liner (large enough to cover the sanitized changing surface from the child's shoulders to below the child's feet)
     - o fresh diaper
     - o clean clothes (if needed)
     - o wipes (removed from the container)
     - o plastic bag (for soiled clothes)
     - o disposable gloves

- o diaper cream (if the program allows and if the family has asked that you use it)
- Place a dab of diaper cream, if used, on a corner of the disposable paper.
- Put on the disposable gloves.

2. Carry an infant to the changing table, keeping soiled clothing away from your clothing; walk a toddler to the stable stairs attached to the table.
   - If children's feet and clothing cannot be kept out of diapers during the changing process, completely remove their shoes, socks, and other clothing items to prevent contamination.
   - Place any soiled clothes in the plastic bag, and tie it securely so that parents can take it home safely.

3. Clean child's genitals and bottom.
   - Place child on the diaper table, and unfasten the diaper. Leave soiled diaper under the child for now.
   - Keep one hand on the child at all times when on the changing table.
   - Use disposable wipes to clean child's bottom. Remove stool and urine by wiping from front to back to prevent the spread of bacteria. Repeat using as many wipes as needed.
   - Place used wipes into the soiled diaper or directly into a plastic-lined, hands-free, covered can. (This covered can should have a step pedal.)

4. Remove the soiled diaper without contaminating other surfaces.
   - Fold the soiled diaper inward.
   - Place the soiled diaper into the plastic-lined step can.
   - If children wear reusable cloth diapers, place soiled cloth diapers and their covers in plastic bags to give to children's parents or a laundry service. Do not rinse or wash the contents. Emptying and rinsing soiled diapers poses the greatest health risk for early educators and children.
   - Check under the child to see if the paper liner is wet or soiled. If so, fold over the paper under the child's feet so that a fresh unsoiled paper surface is now under their clean bottoms.
   - Remove disposable gloves and place them into the plastic-lined step can. Do not perform other tasks while wearing these gloves, as it poses a health and safety risk to you and the child.
   - Use separate disposable wipes to clean your hands and the child's hands. Place the wipes in the plastic-lined step can.

5. Put clean diapers and clothing on the child.
    - Apply any necessary ointments or creams (for example, a diaper rash treatment provided by the family).
    - Note and record on the daily log any skin problems, such as redness.
    - Slide a fresh diaper under the child and adjust and fasten it. For cloth diapers, place your hand between the children and the diapers when inserting the pin.

6. Wash child's hands and return them to a supervised area.
    - Use soap and water at a sink to wash the child's hands, if possible. If not, use the following method:
        - o Wipe the child's hands with a damp paper towel or a clean disposable wipe.
        - o Discard the towel or the wipe into the plastic-lined step can.
    - Return the child to a supervised area.

7. Clean and sanitize the diaper changing surface.
    - Place the paper liner you used on the diaper changing surface in the plastic-lined step can.
    - Clean any visible soil from the changing surface with water and soap or detergent.
    - Spray a bleach solution to wet the entire changing surface. (See Figure 16 for guidance on preparing bleach solution.)
    - Store the bleach solution in a locked cupboard.
    - Leave the bleach sanitizer on the diaper changing surface for at least 2 minutes. Wipe the surface dry or air dry.

8. Wash your hands. Record diaper change in child's daily log.
    - Wash your hands using soap and warm water.
    - Use a paper towel to turn off the faucet.
    - Use hand lotion to keep your hands moisturized.
    - Describe the contents of diapers and any problems, such as diarrhea, an unusual odor, blood in the stool, or any skin irritations in children's daily logs.

Toilet Learning

Toilet learning is one of children's major developmental milestones that will test and enhance their cognitive, social, emotional, and physical skills. Typically, this takes place between age two and three. It is not unusual, though, for a three-year-old child to still wear diapers.

It is essential to collaborate with the child's family to determine the best timing and method for their child to learn to use the toilet. Discuss what words you will use (see the next page) and what you will do at the program and at home. Put these plans in writing in all of the families' home languages so all are clear about the approach you plan to use.

NEVER rush, shame, tease, or punish children during toilet learning. Instead, encourage toilet learning when children have the skills needed to use the toilet on their own and demonstrate signs they are ready to learn.

Cultural Differences in Toilet Learning

There are cultures from countries, such as Nigeria, India, and China that began toilet "training" in infancy. This is called assisted infant toilet training. Adults pick up cues from the baby and assist them with toileting or they place infants on a schedule, helping them toilet throughout the day. You may have a parent who insists on using assisted toilet training in your program. It is important to respect the culture of the family. Avoid touting Western methods of toilet learning as better or more desirable. Instead stress that it is merely different. You will also need to discuss licensing regulations related to toilet learning and other demands of group care that will make it difficult to engage in assisted infant toilet training in your program.

Toilet Learning for Children With Disabilities

Children with disabilities may learn to use the toilet earlier or later than other children. They may also have specific or unique needs to be met in order to be successful in toilet learning. It is important to avoid shaming or pressuring children in general when learning to use the toilet, and this is particularly important for children with disabilities who may be learning these skills on a different timetable. Work closely with the child's family and with other relevant service providers who work with the child, such as early interventionists, special educators, or medical professionals, to ensure the child is supported and has the appropriate accommodations needed to be successful and included.

Encourage children to make up toileting scenarios with their dolls and puppets. Perhaps their doll has an accident or two puppets talk about stopping their play to go to the bathroom. Read books like *Who's in the Bathroom?* by Jeanne Willis and *Everyone Poops* by Taro Gomi that will make children feel more confident about expressing that they need to use the toilet.

What words will you use when you talk about toileting? Some experts suggest you use only formal terms such as urinate and bowel movement. On the other hand, some families and children are more comfortable with terms like pee-pee, tinkle, go potty, or poop. Respect a family's wishes for what they want to call these bodily functions. Try to be flexible and accept any terms that are not offensive. Children in a group will generally all start using the same word—especially one that is fun to say.

Figure 19. Signs that a Child is Ready for Toilet Learning

A child is ready to learn to use the toilet when they:

- Stay dry for at least 2 hours at a time, or after naps.
- Recognize that she is urinating or having a bowel movement. For example, a child goes in a corner when having a bowel movement.
- Are developing physical skills that are critical to toilet learning—the ability to walk, to pull pants up and down, and to get onto/off the potty (with some help).
- Copy an adult or older sibling's toileting behavior.
- Can follow simple instructions.
- Most importantly, the child wants to use the toilet. He may say "I want to wear 'big boy' pants, or learn to use the toilet "like Daddy does." He may feel uncomfortable in a soiled diaper and ask to be changed, or ask to use the toilet himself.

(Adapted from Zero to Three 2010)

When children use toileting terms that some people find offensive, speak with them privately and calmly. For example, explain, "We don't use words like that here. We say 'poop' and 'pee.' Usually, children will use offensive language less often if you ignore it.

Toddlers should feel good about themselves, their bodies, and their accomplishments—particularly during toilet learning. The encouragement and patience of important adults are crucial for toddlers to develop successful skills and attitudes concerning toileting.

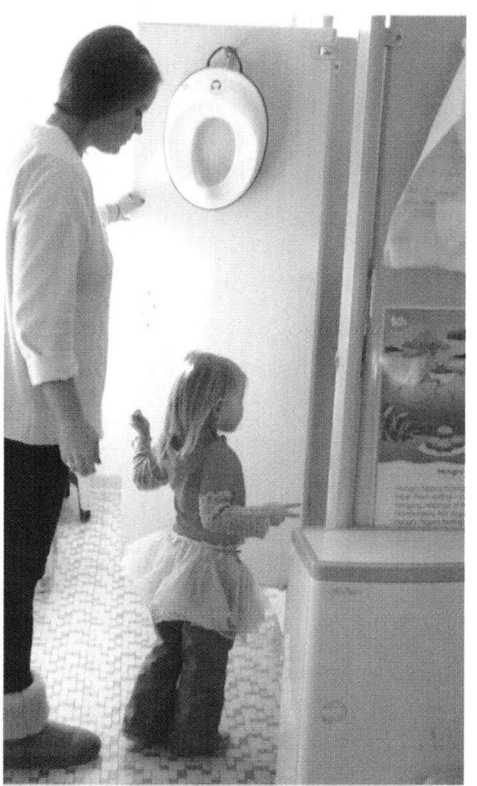

Bathroom stalls provide children privacy.

Using the Toilet

Many of the preschoolers in your care may use or be fully ready to use the bathroom independently. For those who are not, watch their behavior to learn when they might be ready to learn this major skill. The information above about toilet learning for toddlers applies to preschoolers too.

Make sure children feel comfortable about going to the bathroom whenever they need to. Girls and boys this age can share the facilities; closed stalls provide privacy.

As with toddlers, accidents happen. However, you can help children recover from these accidents calmly and respectfully. Explain to children that these accidents are common, but they will happen less and less frequently as the children grow. Help them retrieve their emergency clothing from their cubby, remove the wet or soiled items, wash their hands, and change into a clean outfit.

Nap Time

Nap time is a key component of a child's day in your setting. Sleep directly impacts children's cognitive and physical development. Well-rested children are more likely to get maximum benefit from your program and enjoy playing and learning with others.

Infants

Infants nap according to their own individual schedules for sleeping. Very young infants sleep most of the day. By the time they arrive in your care, however, most infants will take 2 to 4 naps a day. Ask the infant's family to describe the napping routine and schedule at home. Try to follow it as much as possible at the program to help the infant adjust to and feel secure in the new setting.

You can look for signs that an infant is getting tired. Again, families can help by sharing what they have observed at home. "Portia pulls her ear when she is tired." "Danny makes little squeaking sounds when he is getting tired." It's best to put infants in their cribs before they fall asleep. That way they can learn to soothe themselves and put themselves to sleep.

At nap times, infants should be placed in cribs, on their backs, even after they have learned to roll over. This practice should continue until the child is 12 months of age.

Family members often carry sleeping infants into the setting in their car seats. In these instances, gently loosen the buckles and lift the infant into their crib to continue sleeping. Sometimes the child will continue to sleep, but not always. In the latter case, look for signs of sleepiness and try again later.

Sleepy infants might fall asleep somewhere other than their cribs. For example, an infant might fall asleep in your lap or in a bouncy chair. As in the car seat example above, gently move the baby to the crib and place them on their back to sleep.

An early childhood educator should supervise sleeping infants at all times. Check regularly to make sure the infant's head is not covered and that clothing is in place.

The cribs used by infants should be set up at least three feet apart and have no Plexiglas® partitions. They should be placed away from open windows and window coverings with cords. When infants sleep in an assigned crib—recommended, but not always possible--each crib should be cleaned and disinfected weekly. Change the sheets whenever wet or soiled. Refer back to the health checklists for further guidance in this area.

If more than one child sleeps in a specific crib, clean it every time a different child uses it. Be sure to change the sheet and clean and sanitize the mattress and any crib parts, such as railings, that children can mouth.

Toddlers and Preschoolers

By the time children are toddlers, their nap times are predictable and can be scheduled, most of the time. Typically, toddlers take one, two-hour nap after lunch. Preschoolers too settle into a daily afternoon nap of about an hour to two hours, but older preschoolers may nap for a shorter time or not at all.

Plan how to handle naps and rest times just as you would plan any other part of the daily program. The plan should include helping children fall asleep and offering a snack and quiet activities when they wake up.

Children must each rest on their own mat or cot, placed at least 3 feet apart. Mats should be at least two inches thick, waterproof, washable, and appropriate for the size and weight of the children. Position children head to toe on these mats during nap time. If different children use the same cot or mat, clean and sanitize each of them after each use.

Children should not share bedding, nor should one child's bedding touch that of another child. Wash bedding weekly or whenever soiled. Between uses, store bedding in a labeled bag or in the child's cubby.

Some children can be fearful at nap time or have difficulty relaxing and falling asleep. Early childhood educators can rub backs, sing songs softly, or just be available at a child's side to offer comfort. See Chapter 10, Guidance, for more information on helping children relax and cope with stress.

Some preschool children do not take naps. These children should be encouraged to rest quietly, but never forced to sleep. If after 20 minutes, the child does not fall asleep, an alternative, quiet activity should be offered. Children with disabilities may have more specific routines or needs for nap time. You should work closely with the family to provide optimal support during nap or quiet time.

Toothbrushing

Dental decay is the number one chronic disease of children. This disease is painful, can lead to other illnesses, and can even affect learning. In one state, the statistics caused legislators to respond. Almost half (48%) of four-year-olds in Massachusetts suffer from tooth decay. As a result, the state passed a law in 2010 requiring that children who eat meals at state-licensed child care centers have their teeth brushed (Santos 2010).

Children learn about toothbrushing even before they have teeth. When you wash your hands then wipe infants' gums with a soft cloth, you are not only maintaining infants' oral health, but you are teaching them that it is important to keep their mouths clean. When their first teeth appear and you brush them with a soft toothbrush and a thin smear of toothpaste, these children see this process two or three times daily. By the time these children are toddlers, you can narrate the process, describing how you use a small dab of toothpaste and brush both sides of their teeth to make sure they are clean. Explain to them the relationship between food and dental health and that sweets and sticky foods like raisins and dried fruits can cause tooth decay.

Preschoolers can learn to brush their own teeth with supervision. Show them how, step by step:

1. Moisten the child-size toothbrush.
2. Apply a pea-size dab (these are steps for preschoolers) of fluoride toothpaste to the bristles.
3. Start with the upper left back teeth. Clean all of the front teeth in a circular motion, moving clockwise.
4. Repeat the same procedure with the bottom teeth, starting with the lower left teeth.
5. Brush the backside of all teeth.
6. Brush the tongue.
7. Have children rinse their teeth with water and spit.

The entire process should last two to three minutes. Bring in a timer to let them see that this is probably a longer process than they realize. After watching you go through the steps, gradually transfer responsibility for the task to them. Let children narrate the steps for you, explaining how they position the toothbrush to clean their teeth and gums.

In time, children will know to retrieve their labeled toothbrushes and brush their teeth after snacks and meals. Instead of using the sink, give each child a paper cup of water. They can use it to wet their toothbrushes, rinse their teeth, and spit before discarding. When children consume meals or snacks outside the setting, give them cups of water to rinse and spit with before discarding the empty cups.

Providing Nutritious Meals and Snacks

As an early childhood educator you plan, or contribute to the planning, of age-appropriate, nutritious meals and snacks for the children in your group. Collaborate with families and frequently share with them information concerning nutrition, including appropriate ages for weaning and introducing solid foods. Ask for recipes related to the family's culture that might be incorporated into the menu. Respect each family's practices and values. Be aware of any foods the child or family does not eat, for religious, cultural, or other reasons. (See Figure 20 for information on planning to meet the needs of a child with a food allergy.) Also, teach children healthy attitudes about food and eating. Let them know that it is important to eat a variety of nutritious foods in moderation. Explain that food helps our bodies grow strong and healthy. It is never appropriate to use food as a reward or to deny food as a punishment.

Figure 20a. Planning for Food Allergies

Early childhood education programs have legal and ethical reasons to be ready to ensure the health and safety of children with food allergies. Many programs have written plans and offer staff training on how to make sure the child does not have contact with the allergen and how to respond if the child does accidently eat the food. At minimum, early childhood programs should take the following steps:

- **Provide training:** Make sure everyone who comes in contact with the child—educators, bus drivers, assistants, cooks, supervisors, and so on—take part in food allergy training. They need to know which children have allergies, how to recognize reactions, and how to respond. Training can also cover how to read food labels. For more information see the Food Allergy and Research Education (FARE) website, *www.foodallergy.org*.
- **Involve the child's family:** Work with families to prepare an allergy procedure for the child. This should include information about the allergen and what foods might contain the allergen, the child's symptoms should they ingest the allergen, and the recommended emergency response. Post the information in food preparation areas and in the setting. Also, in center settings, have parents provide two emergency kits—labeled with the child's name, classroom, and photo. Keep one kit in the classroom (and take it outdoors and on trips) and one in the nurse's office. One kit is sufficient for an FCC home. Each kit should contain a copy of the child's medical file and injectable epinephrine (EpiPens). The EpiPens should be checked regularly to ensure they are not expired. They should be stored out of children's reach, but easily accessible to adults, preferably in an unlocked cabinet that is not within children's reach.
- **Make the setting allergen-free:** Notify all parents that there is a child in the setting who is allergic to a specific food—for example, peanuts. Explain that you are asking them to help keep the classroom free of this allergen, so the child will be safe. Include a list of substitute foods that are safe for the child and appropriate for celebrations and snacks. You can find a list on the FARE website, *www.foodallergy.org*.
- **Teach all of the children:** Help the child with the food allergy and the other children in the group understand and accept that certain foods make the child sick. Read and discuss books about characters who have food allergies, such as *Can I Have Some Cake Too?* A Story about Food Allergies and Friendship by Melanie Nazareth or Nutley, the *Nut-Free Squirrel*, by Stephanie Sorkin. Use puppets or persona dolls to tell a story about how a child with a food allergy might feel and how the other children were and perhaps, were not, supportive.

Figure 20b. Planning for Food Allergies

When an Allergic Emergency Takes Place

After eating or coming in contact with the allergen, a child's symptoms of an anaphylactic reaction may occur within seconds or be delayed for 15 to 30 minutes or longer. The child might say, "I don't feel good," but not know why. Or the child might have symptoms such as swelling of the tongue and throat, hoarseness, difficulty swallowing, and difficulty breathing. Take action immediately if the child has any of these symptoms.

1. Stay calm.
2. Get out the emergency kit and check for the appropriate dose of epinephrine.
3. Inject the child using the EpiPen.
4. Call 911.
5. Call the family.
6. Call the physician.

(Thelan, P. and E. A. Cameron 2012, 106-112)

Feeding Infants

The American Academy of Pediatrics (AAP) and the American Medical Association (AMA) recommend breast milk for infants from birth to 12 months. Although breast milk defends young infants against allergies, infections, and numerous chronic illnesses, breastfeeding may not be possible for all mothers. Some women are unable physically to breastfeed or choose not to because of medical considerations or lifestyle. These mothers feed their infants formula.

Before their first days in your setting, discuss infants' feeding patterns and routines with their family. Following an infant's individual schedule and routines helps to ease the child's transition into your setting and strengthens your relationship with the child and the family. Be attentive and follow the infants' cues. For example, infants may make sucking sounds to indicate that they are hungry 20 minutes before their usual feeding times. Meet infants' needs on demand. Record daily the amount of breast milk, formula, or solids infants consume and the time of each feeding. Share this information with infants' families.

Storing Breast Milk

Ask parents to label each breast milk container with their child's name and the date the milk was expressed. Store the containers in the refrigerator or freezer. See chart below for guidelines. Do not mix recently expressed breast milk with frozen breast milk. Never save milk from a used bottle for another feeding.

To thaw frozen breast milk, the Centers for Disease Control recommend placing the frozen milk container in the refrigerator or submerging it in warm water. Do not use a microwave oven to thaw or heat containers or bottles of breast milk. These ovens heat the milk unevenly, destroy the milk's nutrients, and may cause the container to explode. The hot liquid could scald an infant. Do not refreeze breast milk once it has thawed (CDC 2010).

Location	Temperature	Duration	Comments
Countertop, table	Room temperature (up to 77°F or 25°C)	6–8 hours	Keep containers covered and cool. Covering the container with a cool towel may keep milk cooler.
Insulated cooler bag	5-39°F or -15-4°C	24 hours	Keep ice packs in contact with milk containers at all times. Limit opening cooler bag.
Refrigerator	39°F or 4°C	5 days	Store milk in the back of the refrigerator.
Freezer			
Freezer compartment of a refrigerator	5°F or -15°C	2 weeks	Store milk toward the back of the freezer, where temperature is most constant. Though milk stored for longer durations in the ranges listed is safe, some of the milk lipids will degrade, resulting in lower quality.
Freezer compartment of a refrigerator with separate doors	0°F or -18°C	3–6 months	
Chest or upright deep freezer	-4°F or -20°C	6–12 months	

(CDC 2010)

Preparing and Storing Infant Formula

Follow the directions on the infant formula container to prepare infants' bottles. It is safe to use room-temperature tap water to mix the formula, as long as local/state health departments have deemed the tap water in your area safe to drink.

Formula is ready for an infant's feeding immediately after you prepare it, without additional refrigeration or warming. Within one hour of preparation, the infant should consume the prepared formula—or you should store the prepared, unused formula in the refrigerator. Discard any prepared formula that has been at room temperature for more than 1 hour. If an infant does not consume all the formula in the bottle, discard the unused portion. Never save used, prepared formula.

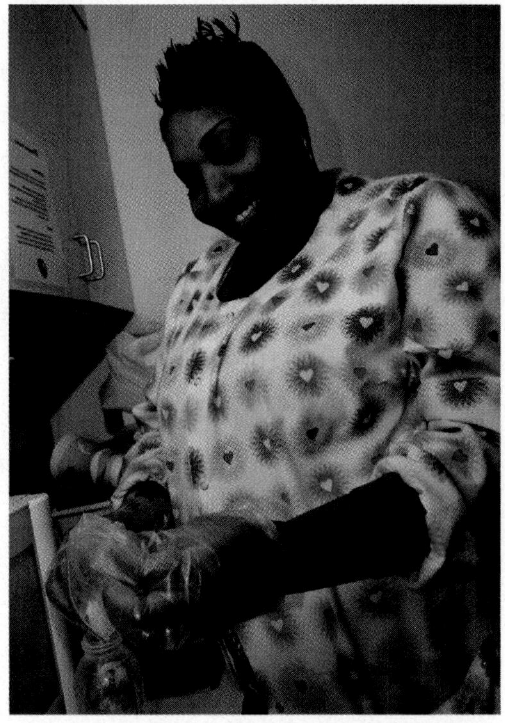

When preparing infant formula, follow the directions written on the formula packaging.

You can prepare formula up to 24 hours in advance, as long as you store it in the refrigerator, preventing the formation of bacteria. Open containers of ready-made formula, concentrated formula, and formula prepared from concentrate can be stored safely in the refrigerator for up to 48 hours (Nemours Foundation 2013).

Bottle Feeding

Bottle feeding times strengthen your bond with each infant in your care and promote attachment. Wash your hands properly and wear a clean pair of disposable gloves before and after handling breast milk and feeding each infant.

Infants should consume only the breast milk or formula their families have provided. If an infant drinks from another infant's bottle, notify both sets of parents immediately. Consult and follow your local health department's guidelines concerning HIV exposure in the event that an infant consumes breast milk from a source other than their mother.

To learn infants' unique feeding cues, it's best for early childhood educators to feed the same infants each day. This is part of a primary caregiving approach. Make sure infants are comfortable and snug in your lap during feedings. Even after infants have the fine motor skills needed to hold a bottle independently, it's best to continue feeding them in your lap. They thrive on the one-on-one attention you provide during these times.

Introducing and Feeding Solid Foods

Experts recommend introducing solid foods to infants who are between 4 and 6 months old, with a preference for waiting to 6 months. Solid foods are added to complement, not replace, the breast milk or formula the infant is already getting. Family members will typically decide when to introduce solid foods based on their pediatrician's recommendations.

Some families and pediatricians may wait longer to introduce solid foods and wean infants from their bottles. Other times families are excited to start solid foods and seem to see it as a sign of their infants' healthy development. Families and early childhood educators must communicate clearly to ensure that everyone understands the goals and expectations for feeding the infant while in the caregiving setting.

Among the signs of readiness to try solid foods, are when infants can:

- hold their head steady without it wobbling.
- sit with support (as in a feeding chair).
- put hands, toys, and other items in the mouth.
- pay attention to others when they are eating—reaches for food on their plates.
- communicate yes and no—for example, through nonverbal actions and turning their heads away (to say no) or towards someone (to say yes).

Introducing solid foods to infants too early can be associated with digestive issues and some food allergies. Also starting solid foods too soon can cause the child to take in less formula or breast milk, which in turn interferes with the iron and nutrients needed at this age.

When it is time to introduce solid foods, you and the family should discuss the approach to be used at home and at the program, and put a plan in writing in the family's home language. The pediatrician may have shared useful information with the family to help with this process. Communicate in great detail during this introductory period—it may turn out that the infant rejects the food—in which case you can stop and look for signs of readiness in a month or so.

You might feed the infant food brought from home or prepared on site. Regardless, transfer the food from its container into a dish and offer a small spoonful to the infant. Offer another small spoonful if the first one goes well. Discard any food left in the dish. Always use a clean spoon and dish for each child.

Experts believe that it is not appropriate to mix food with liquids in a bottle for the baby to eat nor is it helpful to use infant feeders—syringe-like devices that are filled with food that is squirted in the infant's mouth.

Infants' first solid food is often a semisolid, iron-fortified infant cereal, but some infants start with mashed bananas. If these foods are accepted, between 6 and 8 months, vegetables and fruits—such as pears, applesauce, carrots, sweet potatoes, and avocados—come next. Many of these foods can be cooked and prepared by families—often using leftovers from adult meals—so it is not always necessary to use prepared food in jars or containers. Keep in mind that at this point the primary goal is not nutritional—instead, the goal is for the infant to get used to the different tastes and textures of foods and learn to swallow them.

By eight or nine months, most infants are ready to try eating food in one-quarter inch cubes or lumps that they can easily mash, chew, or swallow whole. By 12 months, infants are ready to eat most table foods—as long as hard foods are cut into bite-size pieces.

On occasion, when an infant tries a new food for the first time, they experience food intolerance. Symptoms might be indigestion or a rash. To avoid these symptoms while the infant is with you, only feed them foods that have already been introduced successfully at home. Ask the family about newly introduced foods and encourage them to wait several days to make sure the food agreed with the infant before introducing a new food. Then it is okay to introduce another food and go through the waiting period again. If an infant eats more than one new food at a time, and experiences food intolerance, you and the family will not know the cause. Babies get most of their nutritional needs met through formula or breast milk so there is no hurry to fill them up with solid foods.

Weaning

Infants can start to drink from a cup at about six to nine months. Work with the family to determine the right time. Pour two to three ounces of water in the cup and hold it up to the infant's mouth. If the infant is ready to try using a cup they will lean forward to drink it. There will be spills at first, but practice does make perfect.

A sippy cup is fine for now. Use ones with handles, lids, and a hard spout. It's best to not allow children to walk around with the sippy cup to avoid tooth decay, oral injury, and the child becoming overly attached to the cup. Breast milk or formula can also be provided in a sippy cup. This helps children learn to associate drinking from a cup with something that tastes familiar.

The American Academy of Pediatrics (AAP) recommends teaching children to drink from regular cups once they are from 12 to 15 months old. The AAP also suggests that at this age infants may also be ready to be start being weaned from a bottle to a cup and drink whole (often recommended) milk (usually cow's milk if the baby is not allergic to dairy products). Again, all of these decisions are made by families with their pediatrician's input.

Some families and pediatricians believe it is okay to offer diluted juice to mobile infants. Others think it best to avoid sweet drinks because they can cause tooth decay or prevent children from drinking enough water. While infants do not really need the water now, once they are toddlers they should be drinking several cups of water a day. Drinking water is an excellent habit to acquire now and for the future.

Serving Meals and Snacks to Older Children

With growing small motor skills and a desire for independence, one-year-olds, toddlers, and preschoolers are eager and able to feed themselves. Ask the family about feeding and eating practices at home. Some cultures use their hands to eat, some feed their children through preschool age. Discuss these practices with families and decide together what can happen in group care and licensing/health regulations related to eating practices. To reinforce children's growing independence, provide healthy, nutritious meals and snacks and encourage children to adopt positive attitudes toward foods and eating. It works well to establish and follow regular meal and snack times, while being flexible enough to offer food to a child who is hungry before or after the scheduled times.

Display dated meal and snack menus (in families' home languages) in the classroom. Identify specific food items—for example, specify "orange juice" rather than "fruit juice." Any substitutions should be indicated on the menus.

Cut food into small pieces before serving it to young children. The younger the child, the smaller the pieces should be to prevent choking. For example, slice hot dogs lengthwise and then into smaller pieces. (As noted in Chapter 1, children under age four should not even be served hot dogs, due to their potential to be a choking hazard.) Cut sandwiches into fourths and present on a serving platter so that children may help themselves to manageable portions. Finely cube fruit, such as pears and apples.

Meal Planning

- Offer children different foods daily.
- Encourage children to choose from a variety of fresh fruits and vegetables.
- Serve low- or no-sugar foods and foods rich in vitamin C, like berries, oranges, cantaloupe, broccoli, and spinach. These foods promote dental health.
- Avoid all processed foods and foods containing artificial additives, coloring, and flavorings.
- Serve foods in small portions. Allow children to have seconds.
- Do not insist that children finish all the food on their plates.
- Reward children with your attention, not food. Using food as a reward (or punishment) forms unhealthy attitudes toward food.
- Involve children in preparing the food they eat.
- Make mealtimes a social affair. Sit with children. Ask questions, lead conversations, and set a pleasant tone.
- Set a good example by trying new foods and making healthy choices children can model.
- Experts say that babies do not need to drink water until they are about 6 months, about the same time as they begin eating solid foods. Toddlers, ages 1 through 3, should consume a total of 5 ½ cups, including water from foods and beverages. For preschoolers, the amount increases to a total of 7 cups. It's best to offer small amounts of water throughout the day than to expect a child will drink a full glass at a time.

Offer small amounts of food so children are not overwhelmed. Offer second servings when they finish or if they request more food. Set up a safe, pleasant, and relaxed eating environment to further reinforce positive attitudes toward eating. As small motor skills become more refined, children can serve themselves from bowls and platters. Remind them to take as much as they think they can eat. They can always have more if they are still hungry.

Use food to nourish children's bodies, not to reward or punish them.

One-year-olds, toddlers, and preschoolers probably receive one or more daily meals or snacks in your setting. A trained nutritionist may plan these meals and snacks in a center, but all early educators need to know that healthy meals and snacks include foods that are low in salt, fats, and sugar and high in nutrients. Ensure that the meals and snacks you serve contribute to children's nutritional needs. Dietary Guidelines for Americans (USDA and HHS, 2010), published by the U.S. Department of Agriculture (USDA) and Health and Human Services (HHS), can help you plan these meals. If your program participates in the federal Child and Adult Care Food Program (CACFP), you will need to follow those guidelines. The guidelines emphasize three major goals:

1. Balance calories with physical activity to manage weight.
2. Consume more of certain foods and nutrients, such as fruits, vegetables, whole grains, seafood, and fat-free and low-fat dairy products.
3. Eat fewer foods with sodium (salt), saturated fats, trans fats, cholesterol, added sugars, and refined grains.

Visit *www.choosemyplate.gov* to explore USDA dietary information and food plans for young children. Use this interactive website as a tool for planning menu items and portion size for children. Figure 21 provides a checklist for ensuring healthy snacks and meals are provided in your setting.

Children with disabilities often have the same nutritional needs as children without disabilities. It may be necessary to modify the texture and consistency of certain foods for children who have difficulty chewing, swallowing, or feeding themselves (always check with parents or a nurse for clear instructions). Also, be aware of children's food allergies and make sure the problematic foods are not on the menu. Check children's health records and be aware of conditions, such as metabolic problems, when planning meals. The program's nutritionist or nurse can help you plan how to meet these needs.

Figure 21. Checklist for Ensuring Healthy Nutrition

- ☐ Meet all state, local, and setting guidelines for food selection and preparation.
- ☐ Post a list of children's food allergies—in all staff and children's home languages—in both the food preparation area and in the setting.
- ☐ Maintain excellent communication with families.
- ☐ Be aware of the general health of children in your care and be attentive to their needs.
- ☐ Plan menus in advance and share them with children's families in their home languages.
- ☐ Serve foods that represent a variety of cultural preferences, especially family favorites.
- ☐ Respect dietary restrictions and family preferences.
- ☐ Provide plates, cups, utensils, and serving pieces that are an appropriate size for the children to use on their own.
- ☐ Provide adaptive plates, cups, and utensils for children with physical disabilities so they can eat independently.
- ☐ Establish relaxed feeding and/or snack and mealtime routines that are pleasant experiences for each child.
- ☐ Encourage families to pack healthy snacks and meals if the program does not serve food. These foods should be low in sugar and salt and should not contain unnecessary chemical additives, or artificial coloring and flavoring. For celebrations or cooking experiences, ask parents to bring similar high nutrition foods.

Dining Family Style

Although families choose different styles of dining at mealtime, programs often use a group style called "family style" because mealtimes are opportunities to promote toddlers' and preschoolers' physical, social, emotional, cognitive, and language development. During meals, children make decisions and share. They also learn good manners, responsibility, how to communicate with others, and how food nourishes their bodies. Their participation during mealtimes—whether they are eating or setting the table—helps develop their eye–hand coordination, muscle control, and overall independence. In addition, conversations at meal and snack times build language skills and teach children about the give and take of sharing ideas and information with others. Family-style dining reinforces these skills in children.

When children dine family style, they eat in their setting, enjoy all the same foods, and discuss topics of interest. Children serve themselves (if able) and decide their portions, which makes them more likely to try new foods. Early childhood educators sit and eat at tables with the children, and family members who are present are invited to join the group.

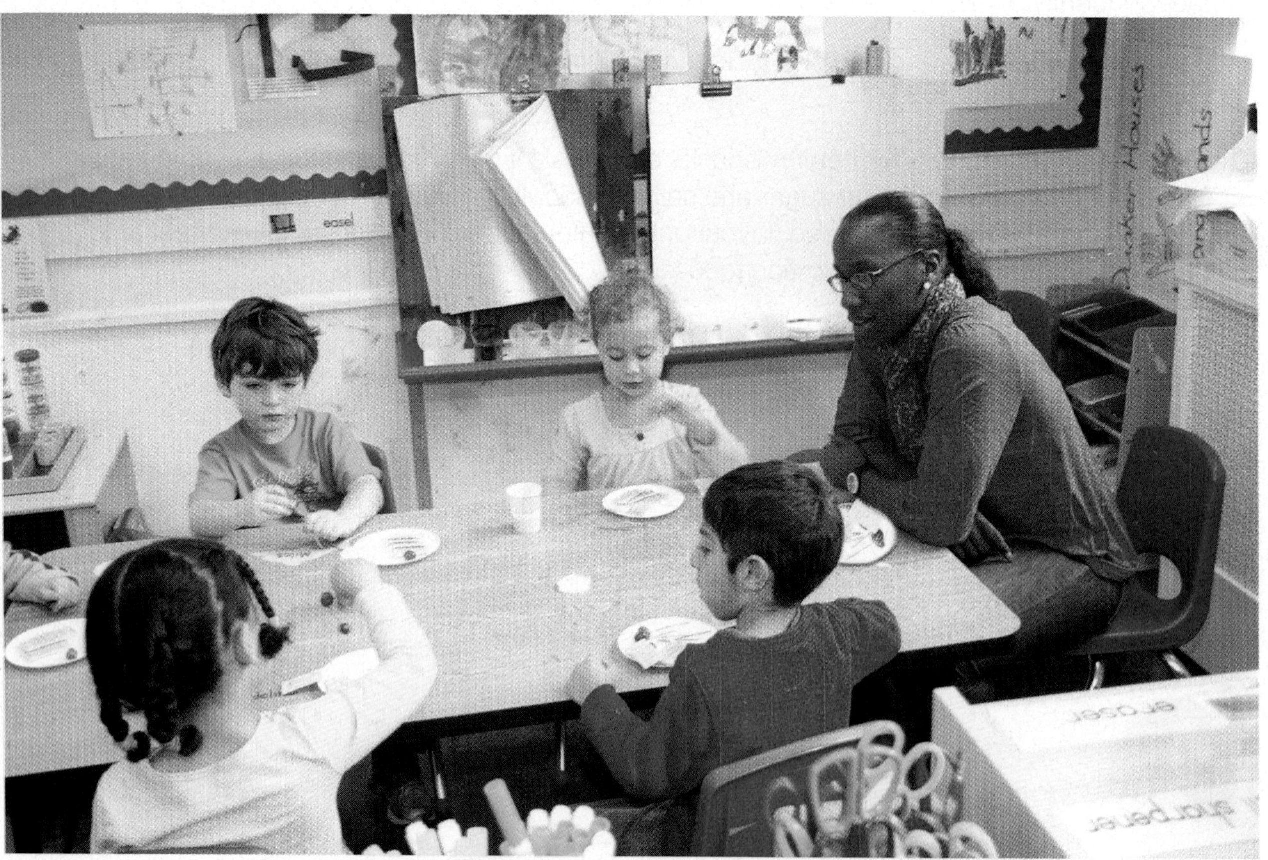

While dining family style, encourage conversation on topics that will interest the children.

In FCC homes and many center-based programs, it is possible to have true family-style meals. In some programs, though, educators will have to adapt the family style dining model to accommodate the situation. For example, if a program is in a primary school, the preschoolers probably eat in the cafeteria. They may purchase lunch or bring lunch from home. In some programs, all of the children bring their lunch and snacks from home. In still others, single-serve meals are delivered to the program from a catering company. In situations such as these, educators can determine which elements of family style dining can be implemented, and which ones are just not feasible. For example, even in a cafeteria, the preschoolers and their teachers can sit together and enjoy mealtime conversations. Or, perhaps the characteristics of family style dining can be incorporated at snack time, with children serving themselves.

Figure 22. Tips for Family-Style Dining in a Center Setting

- Plan to seat four to six children and one adult at each table.
- Leave tables in the learning centers instead of moving them to a central location.
- Wash, rinse, and sanitize all tables before and after eating.
- Assign children to set the table, place platters and bowls on the table, and wipe the table clean.
- Serve food in child-size bowls and platters with child-size serving utensils.
- Serve drinks, including milk, from small pitchers (not cartons) so children can serve themselves.
- Leave salt and sugar off the tables.
- Wait for all of the children and adults to be seated at their table before anyone begins to eat.
- Invite children to begin passing the food clockwise.
- Encourage children to serve themselves only as much as they think they can eat. However, if they find they took too much food, don't force them to finish.
- Ask children who do not want to eat a certain food to take one bite to try. Do not push them to eat more.
- Encourage all adults who join a table group—whether staff, parents, or volunteers—to eat, model appropriate manners, promote self-help skills, and engage children in conversation.
- Maintain a leisurely dining pace so children do not feel hurried.
- Encourage conversation about the foods served, the day's events, or other topics of interest to the children.
- Have sponges and paper towels handy so children can clean up their own spills.
- Allow children to leave the table when finished. They can clear their dishes, wash their hands, brush their teeth, and after lunch get ready for nap time. Allow slower eaters enough time to finish eating.
- Ask the children to help clean up and wipe down the tables using a wet cloth and soapy water.
- Spray wiped tables with bleach solution. Children should not use the bleach solution nor be around the tables when the bleach solution is being sprayed.

Serving Snacks

Have nutritious snacks available to children throughout the day. These snacks should contribute to the children's total daily nutritional needs according to USDA guidelines. Choose snack foods that contribute not only to the children's nutrient needs but also to good dental health. Serve high-fat snacks (under a nutritionist's recommendation) to children struggling to maintain weight. Serve low-cholesterol snacks to children with documented high cholesterol levels. Avoid sweet, salty, and fried foods.

Responding to Illness

Although you and children's families partner to promote health and wellness, young children do get sick. When this happens while a child is in your care, the first response is to make sure the child is safe and comfortable. Then determine whether the child can remain at the program or should go home. Just because children show symptoms of illness does not mean you should automatically send them home. For example, a low-grade fever in a child over six months is not necessarily a sign of illness. Sometimes a child is just overheated or overdressed. Children with thrush, chronic hepatitis B, HIV, or any of the following symptoms do not have to be sent home (AAP, APHA, and NRC 2011):

- Common colds and runny noses (if the child feels well enough to participate in the program).
- A cough not associated with an infectious disease.
- Fever below 101°F (when taken orally).
- Eye discharge.
- Pink eye (unless experienced by multiple children in the program).
- Rash (without fever and behavioral changes).

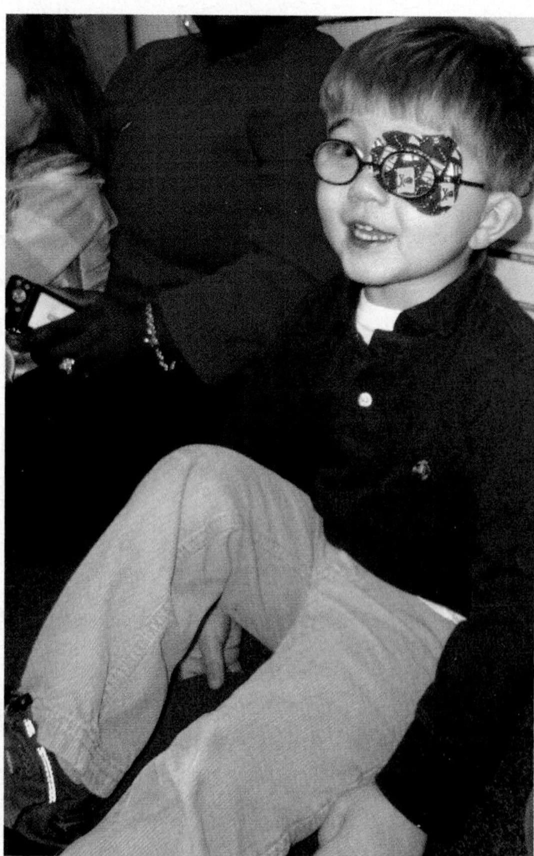

Some sick children can remain in the setting and participate in activities.

According to *Caring for Our Children* (AAP, APHA, and NRC 2011, 132), there are in fact only three reasons to exclude a sick child from your setting:

1. The illness prevents the child from participating comfortably in activities.
2. The illness results in a need for care that is greater than the staff can provide without compromising the health and safety of other children.
3. The illness poses a risk of spreading harmful diseases to others.

The following symptoms are deemed serious enough for a child to go home (AAP, APHA, and NRC 2011):

- Fever at or above 101°F (when taken orally).
- Diarrhea.
- Blood or mucus in stools.
- Vomiting.
- Abdominal pain.
- Mouth sores with drooling.
- Rash with fever or behavioral change.
- Signs of untreated contagious conditions such as impetigo (red sores that crust over), strep throat (sore throat), head lice (itchy scalp; nits), and chickenpox (rash of raised pink bumps) which are easily spread in close and crowded conditions.

Sick children may be upset, in pain, feeling awful, or frightened by their symptoms. They need your compassion. Establish a quiet place away from others where sick children can rest until a family member can pick them up. Offer them water to drink. If you think the illness may be contagious, keep the number of staff exposed to the child to a minimum.

If a child does need to go home, you or the supervisor should contact the child's family or emergency contact. This is one reason why it is important to have current emergency phone numbers for each child's family members and medical providers. Please review state/federal standards concerning sick children in your setting. Just as your setting will have specific policies in place concerning when to send sick children home, your setting has also developed policies concerning when these children are allowed to return. The following guidelines are typical (AAP, APHA, and HRA 2011; Colker, 2009):

Children may return to the program as follows:

- Fever at or above 101°F (when taken orally): after they have been free of fever for 24 hours without taking fever-reducing medications.
- Uncontrollable diarrhea: when they have been free of diarrhea symptoms for 24 hours.
- Strep throat: must have been on antibiotics for 24 hours.
- Pertussis (whooping cough): five days after beginning antibiotics.
- Chickenpox: when lesions are dry, crusted, fading, and/or disappearing. This is usually 6 days after the onset of the rash.
- Impetigo: 24 hours after beginning medical treatment.

- Head lice: after a first treatment with lice medicine, called pediculicide.
- Scabies: after medical treatment is completed.
- Rubella: six days after the rash appears.
- Measles: four days after the rash appears.
- Mumps: five days after glandular swelling begins.

Meeting the Needs of Children with Chronic Illnesses

There may be children at your setting who have a chronic illness, defined as a health problem that lasts more than 3 months, affects a child's normal activities, and requires extensive medical care (University of Michigan Health System [UMHS] 2012). Based on this definition, UMHS (2012) estimates that 15 to 18% of children living in the US have chronic illnesses. The following chronic illnesses are most common:

- Asthma and allergies
- Diabetes
- Cerebral palsy
- Sickle cell anemia
- Cystic fibrosis
- Cancer
- HIV/AIDS
- Epilepsy
- Spina bifida
- Congenital heart problems

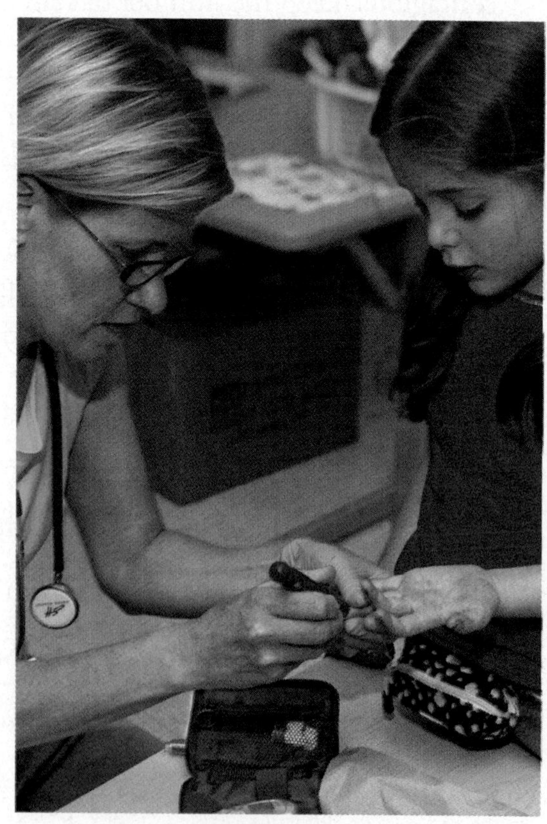

Teacher conducting blood sugar check for child with diabetes.

Chronic conditions vary widely from child to child and from illness to illness. To illustrate, a child with allergies may need only seasonal treatment while a child with diabetes needs daily medication and monitoring of diet and exercise. Conditions may change over time and in severity. Some forms of cancer, for example, may go into remission. As an early childhood educator for a child with a chronic health problem, it is imperative that you learn what this child's specific needs are. It's not enough to know the name of the chronic condition. You have to know how to respond to the needs of this particular child. You can learn about the condition from the child's family and from specialists and other resources suggested by the family.

If you've never cared for a chronically ill child before you probably have a lot of questions. What if the child faints or has a seizure? What if I call her father to take her to the doctor and he can't come? What if I forget to give him his medicine on time? It can feel overwhelming and fearful. Still, it's important to ensure that children with chronic illnesses, disabilities or other special healthcare needs are welcomed and that you partner with the family and other service providers to ensure they are appropriately supported and have the accommodations they need to stay healthy, safe, and engaged in learning alongside their peers.

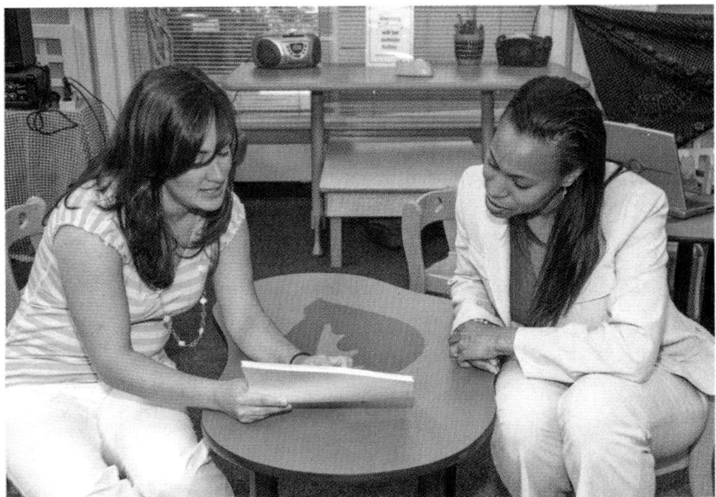

Develop an Individualized Health Plan to help answer questions and support you in caring for children with chronic illnesses.

To answer all of your questions and support you in supporting children with chronic illnesses, most programs (like Head Start) recommend that you develop an Individualized Health Plan in conjunction with the child's family and health provider. This plan should give you all of the specifics you need so there are no unanswered "what ifs?" Head Start (2015) recommends that your plan provide detailed answers to the following questions:

- What accommodations in daily programming are needed, including meals and snacks, playing, sleeping, and toileting?
- When and how should the child receive medication, and who may give it?
- When and how should any required medical procedures be performed, and who may perform them?
- What procedures should be followed in the event of a medical emergency?

Depending on the child's condition and how it affects the child's participation in program routines and activities, some children may qualify to receive special services through an Individualized Family Service Plan (IFSP) if they are under three years old or an Individualized Education Program (IEP) if they are over three. They may also be eligible for case management services under IDEA or Section 504 of the Rehabilitation Act.

Work closely with the child's family, health providers and any early intervention or special education staff who are involved. The more you work as a team, the better you will serve the child and the easier the child's life will be.

Supporting a Child with Chronic Illness: Samantha

Four-year-old Samantha has epilepsy, a seizure disorder. It is choice time, and Samantha is in the dramatic play area, washing a baby doll. Suddenly her body stiffens and she falls to the floor. Her teeth clench and her arms and legs jerk rapidly and rhythmically.

Eduardo rushes toward you. "Samantha needs help," he shouts. Remaining calm, you reassure Eduardo and the other children that Samantha will be okay. You ease Samantha to the floor, ensuring that the area around her is clear. You place a folded blanket from the doll's crib under Samantha's head. Then you turn Samantha gently onto her side to keep her airway clear. Samantha's parents have instructed you not to force her mouth open, hold her tongue, put anything in her mouth, or restrain Samantha's movements.

After a minute, the seizure stops, and Samantha returns to consciousness. You tell her calmly what has happened and that she is okay. You encourage her to rest for a few minutes before she returns to play with the dolls. You fill out an incident report to be shared with Samantha's parents detailing the seizure's time, severity, length, and type.

Whether children have epilepsy, asthma, or other chronic illnesses, always keep in mind that they are children first. Because of their illnesses, they may feel that they do not fit in with other children. The ongoing need for medical attention can be unsettling and make children feel different from their peers. The unpredictable nature of chronic illness can be frightening to children who yearn for predictability. If a child receives special education services, this too can add to the feeling of being different.

Though their conditions are part of their daily lives, chronically ill infants and toddlers understand very little about their illnesses. These children are just beginning to develop a sense of trust and security. Be accessible to them at all times and work to make their days as safe and predictable as possible. Preschoolers, who are learning to be independent, may find that being sick and having to visit doctors interferes with their desire to be in control. As a result, some children with chronic illnesses may act out and test limits. Try some of the following approaches to help children deal with their frustration, stress, and anger:

- Offer choices to give children some sense of control: "Emily, which medicine would you prefer to take first—the blue pills or the syrup?"
- Suggest play opportunities to calm children's emotions (e.g., water or sand play) or act out their fears (e.g., puppets or dramatic play). Dramatic play can be especially helpful for helping children deal with negative emotions. Giving sick children an opportunity to play a doctor or nurse puts them in control. For once, they can administer shots and care for a sick patient.

- Teach stress-reducing techniques, such as deep breathing exercises, yoga, meditation, or visualization. (These are good techniques for the whole group.)
- Read aloud and discuss children's books about dealing with chronic illnesses. The following titles can get you started:
    - o *Little Tree: A Story for Children With Serious Medical Problems* by Joyce C. Mills.
    - o *Lara Takes Charge (For Kids With Diabetes, their Friends, and Siblings)* by Rocky Lang.
    - o *I Have Asthma* by Jennifer Moore-Mallinos.
    - o *Just Ask* by Justice Sonia Sotomayor.
- Help children understand that their illnesses are not caused by anything they have done.

Administering Medication

Many local, state, and federal early childhood programs allow early childhood educators to administer medicine to young children. As noted above, the Americans with Disabilities Act (ADA) may even require educators to administer medication to children with chronic health conditions. Before doing so, however, every educator must take a course in medication administration—taught by a licensed health professional. During this course, you will learn your state and local regulations concerning dispensing medication. Even after you have finished training, it is recommended (Aronson 2012) that you have a health professional observe you until you feel competent—and are competent—in this all-important task.

Explain to family members that their child's medications must be in the original labeled bottle/packaging so that there are no misunderstandings about dosage. This bottle/packaging should be childproof. Confirm that the label includes the following:

- Child's first and last names.
- Name and phone number of the health professional who prescribed the medication.
- Date the prescription was filled.
- Date the prescription will expire.
- Specific instructions for administering, storing, and disposing of the medication.

Also, families should ask the pharmacist, when picking up and refilling the medication, to place some of the prescription in an extra labeled bottle to bring to the program. Families can keep and use the rest at home.

Health experts recommend that you check and double-check to ensure you are giving the child the correct medication and dosage before proceeding. Document the time and amount of medicine you give and any side effects you have witnessed in the child. Fill out a daily medication form and give a copy to the child's family. Store the medicine in a locked cabinet, out of children's reach, away from food (especially if stored in the refrigerator), and at the appropriate temperature.

For over-the-counter medications, do not accept parents' vague instructions, like "Give Sam some medicine if he starts coughing" as sufficient instruction. Make sure that the child's health provider has written the dosage and frequency to administer it.

Always bring emergency medications along when you and the children leave the setting for field trips or other outings. For example, if you care for a child who is highly allergic to bee stings, be sure to have the child's auto-injector on your person if you both will be outdoors or on a field trip.

In summary, Aronson (2012, 164-165) states that there are five RIGHTS when it comes to administering medication: Give the RIGHT medication to the RIGHT child. Give the RIGHT dose by the RIGHT method at the RIGHT time. Please check to ensure that you are following all local child care licensing regulations.

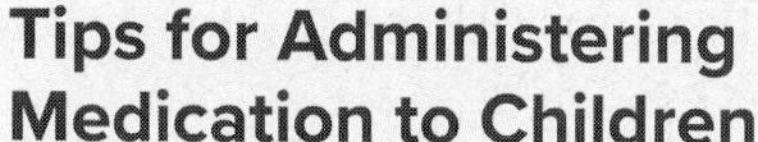

Tips for Administering Medication to Children

Some children resist taking their medicine. Here are some tips to make administering medications easier for them (and you):

- Have children suck on ice to numb their taste buds.
- Administer liquid medicine along the side of their mouths. Medicine poured down the center of children's palates triggers their gag reflexes.
- Place tablets and capsules on the backs of children's tongues to prevent the child from spitting out the medication.
- Combine liquid medicine with strongly flavored food, like pudding, or dilute the medicine in strong-tasting liquid, like cranberry juice—with the pediatrician's permission.
- Never refer to medicine as "candy." Children should never confuse medication with M&M's® or other treats.
- Be warm and supportive, but do not bargain with children. The bottom line is that children must take their medicine.

(Dixon and Rosas n.d.)

Assisting Children with Coughing, Sneezing, and Nose Blowing

Coughing, sneezing, and runny noses can be symptoms of a common cold, the flu, or seasonal allergies. Children can also show these symptoms with no other signs of illness or infection. When these symptoms are accompanied by a fever of 101°F. or higher, the child should be cared for at home. Keep plenty of tissues on hand—for older children, place them within reach—and dispose of used tissues in a covered, foot-operated trash container. Always wash your hands after wiping your nose or the child's.

Caring for Infants When They Cough or Sneeze

Place infants with stuffy noses upright in a seat so that mucus will drain away from their ears. Because infants cannot blow their own noses, use an aspirator—soft, rubber bulb with a soft, narrow tip—to suck out (aspirate) mucus for them. Ask families to bring in an individual aspirator for their infant, labeled with the child's name, and use it only for that child. Wash your hands before and after using the aspirator. To clean inside the aspirator, submerge the tip in warm, soapy water and squeeze the bulb. Shake the soapy water inside the bulb before squeezing. Rinse well by repeating the process several times with clear, warm water. Suspend the syringe, tip side down, in a glass to dry. Do not allow multiple aspirators to touch. Store the child's aspirator in his cubby with his other belongings from home.

Assisting Older Children When They Cough, Sneeze, and Blow Their Own Noses

By about two years old, many children can blow their noses successfully and can learn to cough or sneeze into either a tissue or their elbow. Remind them when they forget and acknowledge their healthy behaviors when they remember. However, some preschoolers still may have trouble blowing their noses. Teach them how by holding one nostril shut and having the child breathe through the other. Hold the tissue for children who just learned to blow their own noses. Most children delight in copying adults. When they see you doing this for them, they will learn to do it on their own. Again, wash your hands and remind children to wash their hands after coughing, sneezing, or nose-blowing.

Helping Children Develop Good Health Practices

Infants need adults to feed them, put them down for naps, and attend to their personal hygiene in order to keep them well. As children grow older, gain new skills, and become eager to do things on their own, adults can transfer some of these self-help responsibilities to children. Empowering children to learn about and do things on their own helps them become independent and teaches them problem-solving and decision-making skills. It also builds children's competence and confidence. Work with the child's family as these new skills are being promoted.

As an early educator, you model and teach children healthy habits that will last a lifetime. There are a number of skills you can work on with children, such as handwashing, sneezing, coughing, and nose-blowing, diapering, toileting, napping, toothbrushing, and making nutritious choices at meal and snack times.

For the very youngest children, like 9 month old Michael for example, start talking about these routines as you perform them. Explain to him, "I'm going to put you in your crib now, Michael, since you're starting to fall asleep. Getting rest is very important for both your body and your mind." As he grows, begin involving him in helping you with the task. "Michael, can you hold the other end of the blanket and help me put it on your mat, please? It's time to get Mr. Bear out of your cubby and get ready for nap time." By the time he is a toddler, Michael will recall your step-by-step directions and get his mat out on his own to ready himself for nap time.

Another excellent way to help children master self-help skills and learn about health and nutrition is through dramatic play. Children can feed their baby doll, put her to bed, brush her teeth, and comb her hair—doing for the doll all the tasks they are learning to do for themselves. They also learn by mimicking you and your colleagues as you model washing your hands and sneezing into your elbow. In just a few short years, children will move from being totally dependent on adults to feeding themselves when they are hungry, putting themselves down to nap when they are tired, and using the bathroom on their own.

Research shows that children who participate in preparing their own foods are more motivated to eat them than are children who do not help with preparation. To help older toddlers and preschoolers prepare their own snacks, provide recipe cards with pictorial instructions. Children can also consult a posted picture menu and sign a snack sheet to record that they ate a snack.

Below are some additional examples of how young children can learn about health and nutrition during routines.

Handwashing

Modeling the procedure is the best way to teach children how to wash their hands. Have them copy your actions while you narrate the steps. Use soap with a hand pump so they can learn to pump once to get enough soap on their hands. Have children sing the "Happy Birthday" song twice to time their handwashing. (See Figure 18 for guidance on teaching handwashing.) Supervise children when they wash their hands by themselves. Ensure that the water temperature is warm—not cold—so children will rinse their hands thoroughly. (Some children like handwashing a lot and it can be difficult to convince them that their hands are completely clean and rinsed!)

Tell children you notice their competence when they can do the task on their own. "I saw you get one pump of soap and sing the Happy Birthday song before rinsing and drying your hands. They look very clean." Give them lots of practice, reminding them that it's time to wash their hands after they come in from outside or before they eat a snack. Offer children opportunities to wash their dolls' hands in water play or pretend to wash a stuffed animal's hands during a make-believe picnic. Read aloud and discuss, such books as *Why Do I Wash My Hands?* by Angela Royston.

Using Tissues

Place boxes of tissues around the room where children can reach them. Ask children to let you know if a box is empty so you can replace it.

Have children practice what to do when they have to sneeze, cough, or blow their noses—before the need arises. Explain that the following practice will help prevent their germs from spreading to someone else. You can also explain in simple terms that germs cause coughs, colds, and other illnesses.

- Cover your nose and mouth with a tissue.
- Throw away the used tissue in a trash receptacle.
- Wash your hands.

OR, if there's no time to get a tissue

- Cough or sneeze into your inner elbow.
- Wash your hands.

Model this process and gently remind children of the steps. You take photos of children using this procedure and use them to make a poster to hang in the setting. With practice, this procedure will become part of your routine and theirs.

Diapering and Toileting

Always tell children what you will do before carrying them to the diapering table. "Hannah, it's time for a clean diaper. I'm going to pick you up now and carry you to the diapering table." Continue your step-by-step description throughout the process. As children get older, invite them to help. "Leon, thank you for holding the clean diaper. You can give it to me now." Toddlers are likely to help in another way, by telling you when they need a clean diaper. This may seem like a small thing, but being aware of their bodily functions is a necessary stage on the way to toilet learning.

Toilet learning is likely to be most successful when children have the small motor skills needed to remove and replace their clothes. Ask parents to dress their children in pants with an elastic waist so they are easier to pull down and back up. Toddlers and preschoolers also help care for themselves by changing into clean clothes when theirs get wet or soiled and by washing their hands every time they use the toilet.

Diapering and bathroom times are opportunities for young children to see how their bodies work and learn the names of body parts. Children are naturally curious, so use a matter-of-fact tone as you respond to their questions and comments. Provide factual information that fits their stage of development. When children begin noticing how the bodies of boys and girls differ, stay calm. Focus on the facts, at the child's level, and without getting emotional.

Discovering Gender Differences

Ms. Duncan is in the bathroom with 3-year-old Keisha. "Larry's a boy," Keisha tells Ms. Duncan after 3-year-old Larry walks out of a stall, washes his hands, and leaves the bathroom.

"Yes, Larry's a boy," Ms. Duncan says, wary of the conversation's direction.

"Do you know how I know Larry's a boy?" Keisha asks.

"No, Keisha, how do you know Larry's a boy?" Ms. Duncan asks cautiously.

"Because Larry's a boy's name!" Keisha says proudly.

Toothbrushing

The American Academy of Pediatric Dentistry (AAPD) recommends that a child's first visit to the dentist take place by age one or within six months after the child gets a first tooth. Some families think that because the child's first teeth are not permanent, it is not necessary to take care of them. This is an incorrect assumption. Permanent teeth are developing under the "baby" teeth and a dentist can make sure that there are not problems with the first or permanent teeth.

Having a dentist or a dental hygienist as a guest at the program can help make dental visits a lot less frightening. Talk to families about their dental care routines. You can also incorporate the family's dental care into your activities. Provide a model tooth so children can practice their brushing technique. Help them use puppets to brush other puppets' teeth or set up a dental office in the dramatic play area. Read aloud and discuss books like *Brush, Brush, Brush!* by Alicia Padron.

Napping

Infants follow individual schedules for napping, often two or more times during the day. Older children however, nap at a set time—usually after lunch. Typically, the early childhood educator creates a calming transition, by singing a particular song or reciting a rhyme that cues children that it is now time to prepare for naps.

Although they cannot lift cots or mats down from where they are stacked, older toddlers and preschoolers can help early childhood educators carry cots or mats to spots around the room. They can help get ready for nap time by cleaning their lunch dishes, brushing teeth and washing hands, and retrieving bedding from cubbies or storage units. And, they can help place their

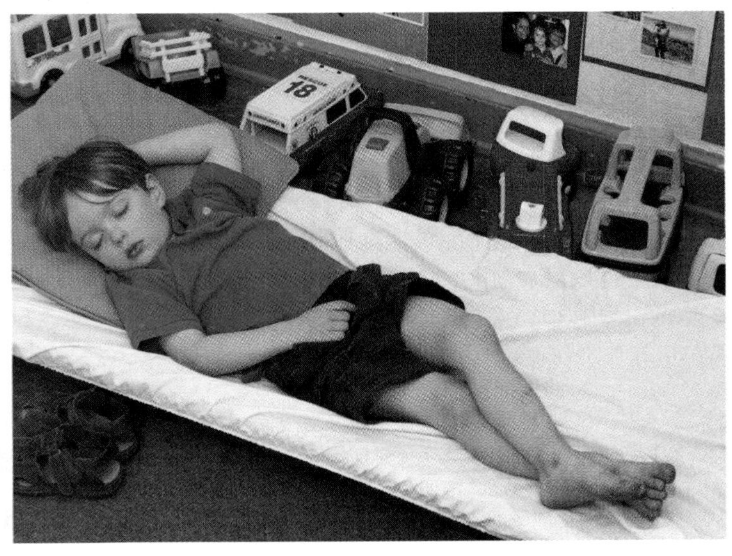

bedding on their cot or mat and snuggle up with a stuffed animal from home.

Older children who do not nap, can rest and look at books or play quietly, for example with puzzles. You might designate specific items that are available only for quiet play while the others sleep. Some programs ask families to pack a shoe box filled with small items to use while the other children nap. It is never appropriate to make children feel uncomfortable or embarrassed because they do not nap. This is one of the times when it is important to remember that every child follows their own schedule for development.

Making Nutritious Choices at Snack and Meal Times

Eating a diet that includes foods high in nutrients and low in sugar, fats, and salt, is an important part of a healthy life style. Young children learn about healthy nutrition from the way you plan and serve meals and snacks and from specific activities. For example, the following food-related activities support learning about language and literacy, color, texture, math, science, social skills, and hygiene. You and the children could:

- Make place mats to use at meal times
- Take a field trip to a restaurant or grocery store
- Have a tasting party (e.g., seasonal fruits and vegetables)
- Grow a garden
- Plant, grow, and harvest a garden
- Make a favorite family recipes cookbook
- Read aloud books about foods and food preparation (e.g., *Everybody Cooks Rice* by Norah Dooley and *Sophie's Squash*, by Pat Zietlow Miller
- Shop for food and cook it together (See Figure 23 for specific tips for cooking with young children.)

Figure 23a. Teaching Healthy Behaviors through Cooking

The best way to teach children healthy behaviors is naturally through the activities they do every day. Instead of setting aside time to teach children healthy practices, you can introduce health information and safe practices in the context of what the children are doing while they are playing in learning centers or outside on a nature walk. Perhaps no other activity lends itself better to this than cooking. Think about the many opportunities you have to educate children about health (Colker 2005):

- **Hand washing:** Every food activity begins and ends with hand washing. Make handwashing a part of the cooking curriculum, so that children will automatically begin and finish their cooking experiences with germ-free hands.
- **Safe food handling:** When preparing recipes, teach children these rules:
    - Just like hands, fruits and vegetables (especially raw sprouts) need to be washed before handling and eating.
    - Wash tops of cans before opening them with an adult's help.
    - If you taste a dish while cooking it with a spoon, do not reuse the spoon.
    - Cook foods thoroughly and to the appropriate temperature.
    - Keep hot foods hot and cold foods cold to prevent bacteria from growing.
    - Return foods that need refrigeration to the refrigerator within 2 hours of taking them out to prevent spoilage.
- **Good nutrition:** While children are tasting foods and making recipes, make them aware of the nutritional value of the foods they cook. You can use tools like *ChooseMyPlate.gov* to let children take a lead in what they are going to prepare for snacks and choose for cooking experiences. For example, you can encourage children to eat fruits and vegetables by introducing ones that may be new and enticing. Offer spaghetti squash and star fruit as tasting experiences and baked sweet potato fries as a small group cooking activity. Talk about how spaghetti squash is healthier than regular pasta (and gluten-free) and how baked sweet potato fries provide more nutrition than regular fries.

  Challenge children to come up with healthier alternatives to standard fare and then make the suggested dishes. If the suggestions get too wild, temper them with your own alternatives. For example:
    - Instead of a gingerbread house covered with icing and candy, children could make a graham cracker house with a celery stick roof and decorations of dried fruits and nuts attached with nut butter (if children have no nut allergies).
    - Instead of chips and dip, children can cut carrots into coins and make a Greek-yogurt based dip.
    - Instead of ice cream, children could, under your supervision, blend frozen bananas in a blender. It will look like ice cream, and taste like it, too.

Figure 23b. Teaching Healthy Behaviors through Cooking

- o Instead of nachos made with chips, children can use pepper slices to scoop the melted cheese.
- o Instead of sloppy joes made with ground beef, children can use lentils just as sloppily.

Cooking activities like these allow you to integrate health education into your ongoing curriculum in a natural way. And while they are learning—and eating—children have fun and take pride in their creations.

Partnering With Families

Collaborate with families so they can share what they are doing at home to ensure that their children receive similar, consistent health messages in your setting and at home. For example, if families model and encourage proper handwashing at home, then children will see the value of taking personal responsibility for this habit. It's vital, therefore, that you and the children's family agree on an approach to keeping their children healthy.

Provide Information on Healthy Young Children

Help to forge a bond with families by including a section on health practices in the program's handbook of policies and practices. This handbook should be provided in English and the home languages of families. The handbook might address the following:

- Expectations for health visits and immunizations
- Daily health checks
- Sick child policy (when children are sent home/when they can return)
- Incident reports
- Caring for children who are chronically ill
- Medication policy
- Food and nutrition practices
- Handwashing—when it is required during the day
- Personal hygiene practices (sneezing, coughing, blowing nose, toothbrushing, toileting)
- Child abuse reporting policies
- Maintenance of health records and safeguards for privacy

Some families may need help locating appropriate health resources, such as a community health clinic or a pediatrician who speaks their home language. Check to see if the program has this information available for parents and families. If not, consult the health staff in your setting or ask your supervisor for assistance in finding appropriate referrals, if you work in a center.

For each child, keep names and phone numbers on file for the following people and places:

- Medical providers, including specialists.
- Dentist.
- The preferred hospital to go to in an emergency.
- Authorization to seek medical care in case of an emergency.
- Family members authorized to pick up each child, in the order staff should contact them in an emergency. Keep both landline and cell numbers for these individuals.

Families need to know that they will be called as soon as staff determines that their child is too sick or contagious to remain in your setting. Explain that in a medical emergency you will call 911 and have their child transported to the hospital by ambulance, with a staff member if you cannot reach them in time. Reassure them that staff will never make any decisions regarding their child's treatment without first consulting them. Although you are the families' partners in caring for their children, they are the ones who are ultimately responsible for their children's well-being.

Figure 24. Troubleshooting as a Team

Mackenzie, a 3-year-old, has been using the toilet since she was 2 ½ years old. However, she is suddenly having frequent toileting accidents. She does not know why this is happening. Mackenzie's behavior offers no clues. However, when you speak to her parents, you learn that they are adopting a baby and Mackenzie is not excited. She may worry that her parents will spend too much time with the new baby and not enough time with Mackenzie.

Could her toileting accidents be her way of expressing her fears? Share your theory with her parents and work together to rectify the situation.

Work with families to plan workshops during the year to address relevant, health-related issues. Families might want to learn more information on how to choose healthy meals and snacks. During this workshop, share recommended nutritional goals for young children and how you plan menus. Ask families about the foods they serve at home. Together, identify what foods are healthy to serve at school and to send for their child to eat.

Here are some additional topics families might identify for workshops:

- **Family-style dining.** How it teaches toddlers and preschoolers self-help skills and good eating habits.

- **Involving children in food preparation.** Help families understand that when children make snacks and meals it motivates them to eat the food. Show them how to make picture-based recipe cards to use when cooking with their children. Offer examples to show how cooking teaches literacy, math, fine-motor, and science skills.
- **Creating a classroom or family cookbook.** Invite families to submit family favorites. Plan a hands-on workshop to create copies of a classroom cookbook featuring family favorites.
- **Coping with head lice.** Discuss head lice outbreaks—especially after they occur. Ask a nurse or other health care worker to be present. Make sure everyone gets the message that head lice, hygiene, and socio-economic status are unrelated. Discuss the program's policy for when children who have had head lice can return to the program. Let families know what you are doing in the setting to eliminate head lice and what they should do at home. Organize a group clean-up day to launder linens and vacuum stuffed animals.
- **Preventing the flu and other contagious viruses and illnesses.** Describe the hygiene and sanitation practices that are known to prevent or curb their spread in the setting. If families are interested, you could arrange for a pediatrician or nurse to attend the session to administer flu or other shots to adults and children, with parents' written permission.

Teaming with families ensures your joint efforts make a difference. Working together keeps their children healthy.

Identifying/Reporting Child Maltreatment

According to the Children's Defense Fund, 750,000 children are abused or neglected each year in the United States. That is one child every 42 seconds. Children who suffer abuse and neglect suffer side effects beyond the maltreatment, during childhood and throughout their lives. They might have behavioral problems, learning difficulties, and low self-esteem, and may repeat the pattern by maltreating others (Karageorge and Kendall 2008).

Identifying and reporting child abuse is never easy, but your actions can save a child's life. Prepare for this challenge by doing the following:

- Learn the signs of abuse and neglect and be alert to them.
- Make sure children feel comfortable talking to adults and expressing their feelings in your setting.
- Share with children's families the program's clear policies on responding to the signs of child abuse and neglect. Write them in the families' home languages. Have families initial this section of the handbook to ensure they understand your legal responsibility to report any suspicion of child abuse.
- Know how to report any suspicions in accordance with your setting's policies and applicable laws.
- Be an advocate for children. Support children without overreacting or blaming the perpetrator. Reassure the child they are safe.

Identifying Abuse and Neglect

Karageorge and Kendall (2008) describe four types of maltreatment:

- Physical abuse includes any non-accidental physical injury, including burning, beating, biting, kicking, hitting, or punching a child. Children under five years old are at the greatest risk of injury or death from physical abuse.
- Sexual abuse includes any sexual behavior with a child. It also includes commercial exploitation of a child through pornographic photos and videos.
- Psychological maltreatment, sometimes called emotional abuse, involves belittling, rejecting, isolating, and terrorizing children. It also includes passive-aggressive behaviors toward a child, in which the adult expresses their anger at the child indirectly.
- Neglect involves omissions of care that result in harm to the child. There are at least seven types of neglect:
    - **Physical neglect:** abandonment or failure to meet children's basic nutritional, clothing, or hygiene needs;
    - **Medical neglect:** failure to meet children's medical and dental needs when resources are available;
    - **Inadequate supervision:** exposing children to hazards or leaving children in the care of someone who does not or cannot appropriately care for them;
    - **Environmental neglect:** exposing children to unsanitary or hazardous living conditions;
    - **Emotional neglect:** failure to meet children's needs for affection and attention;
    - **Educational neglect:** failure to meet children's needs for education and schooling; and
    - **Newborns' addiction/exposure to drugs:** exposing unborn children to drugs, causing them to be born with addiction or the side effects of drugs.

There is no clear profile of perpetrators of abuse and neglect. They might be known to the child or strangers, family members or unrelated to the child. They can be of any gender and young or old. Child abuse and neglect can be found at all economic levels and in all cultures and family structures. The child's immediate family may not be aware of the maltreatment.

Abuse and neglect may involve one incident or a pattern of ongoing behavior. Some signs of abuse and neglect are obvious, such as unexplained bruises, burns, or broken bones. Look for these physical signs that might indicate a child is being abused:

- **Physical abuse:** extensive and frequent bruises, especially in areas of the body that wouldn't be hurt in an accidental fall, such as the abdomen, head, neck, backs of legs, and genitals. Other signs can include burns, bite marks, bald spots on the scalp, or dental injuries.
- **Sexual abuse:** pain when walking, running, or sitting; problems with urination; pain/itching or discharge in the genital area.
- **Psychological maltreatment:** eating problems, sleeping problems, bed-wetting, self-abusive behaviors, such as head banging and hair pulling.
- **Neglect:** height and weight significantly below normal expectations, poor hygiene, wearing inappropriate clothing for the weather, fatigue, and sleepiness.

Other kinds of abuse, such as psychological maltreatment and neglect, may have no outward physical signs. Behavioral changes may be your only clue. Children may seem overly afraid of upsetting their parents or have sudden crying jags. Perhaps a lively girl may suddenly withdraw from everyone around her. A boy who is always happy to greet his mother at the end of the day may freeze and cry suddenly when his aunt arrives at the setting. Children may act out their feelings during play. A child may involve two dolls in sexual gestures. Or during a puppet show, the "father" puppet may start vigorously beating the "little boy" puppet.

Observing Possible Signs of Abuse

Tomas, a 5-year-old, is a quiet, shy child. He seldom spends much time in the art center, but today he paints a picture entirely in black and brown.

Ms. Turner: *"Tomas, can you tell me about your painting, please?"*

Tomas: *"The daddy had to spank the little boy with his belt."*

Ms. Turner: *"I don't understand why he had to do that."*

Tomas: *"Because the little boy wouldn't listen."*

Ms. Turner: *"I hope the little boy wasn't hurt."*

Tomas: *"He has to learn to be good."*

Ms. Turner: *"Does the little boy know that he can talk to his mother or his teacher about this problem? No one should be hurting him this way."*

Tomas does not answer Ms. Turner's question and walks toward the block area.

Ms. Turner knows to monitor Tomas's behavior carefully for other signs that Tomas may be a victim of abuse. She will speak with her supervisor about the situation and follow state legal requirements.

Reporting Abuse and Neglect

Early childhood educators residing and practicing in the United States and all U.S. territories and U.S. military bases worldwide, are legally required to report signs that a child might be abused or neglected. Proof of abuse is not required; suspicion is all you need to file a report. Waiting for proof leaves a child at risk for further abuse or neglect.

However, because not all suspicions will be confirmed as actual abuse, the law protects people who report abuse in good faith. Legally, mandatory reporters cannot be sued or prosecuted. You cannot let fear stop you from reporting abuse.

You also have an ethical responsibility to report your suspicions. The National Association for the Education of Young Children (NAEYC 2011) states the following in Principle 1.8 of its Code of Ethical Conduct and Statement of Commitment:

> We shall be familiar with the risk factors for and symptoms of child abuse and neglect, including physical, sexual, verbal, and emotional abuse and physical, emotional, educational, and medical neglect. We shall know and follow state laws and community procedures that protect children against abuse and neglect.

Check the state law regarding how and to whom you should report abuse. This information should be shared with families in their home languages at the start of the year.

Identifying and reporting abuse is only the beginning. No matter what the situation's outcome may be, you are obligated to inform the family that you and your colleagues are there to support, not condemn, them. Your objective is to keep the children in your setting safe and healthy. Be patient and support these families once treatment plans are established. Reassure parents and guardians that everything regarding their child and their family will remain confidential. ■

CHAPTER 3: Learning Environment

CDA® Functional Area 3: Candidate organizes and uses relationships, the physical space, materials, daily schedule, and routines to create a secure, interesting, and enjoyable environment that promotes engagement, play, exploration, and learning of all children, including children with disabilities. This space is culturally responsive and culturally sustaining. It promotes the positive racial identity and home language development of all children.

Learning Environment

Introduction

The learning environment you create within your setting is the foundation for children's growth and development. This environment comprises the setting itself (indoors, outdoors, and all materials and equipment); the people within the setting (early childhood educators, children, parents, volunteers, administrators, and visitors); and any learning experiences, routines, and schedules you establish within the setting. How this environment is configured directly impacts children's progress in building social, emotional, cognitive, language and literacy, and physical skills.

In this chapter, you will learn how the following critical elements work together to create an effective learning environment:

- **10 Fundamental Principles that Support Learning and Development**
- **Designing an Environment to Promote Development and Learning**
- **Selecting Appropriate Materials**
- **Planning Curricula for Children**
- **Developing the Daily Schedule**
- **Implementing the Daily Schedule**

10 Fundamental Principles That Support Learning and Development

An effective and meaningful learning environment is crucial to optimize learning potential in all children. In order to establish and promote the learning environment, it is important to keep in mind several principles that impact all other aspects of the learning environment's design and implementation. These principles, which are supported by extensive research and review of practice, should influence decisions on curriculum, room design, selection of materials, and programs in general.

Principle 1: Discovery and Divergent Learning

The brain responds well to opportunities for discovery and divergent learning. Discovery relates to new experiences, different ways of approaching a situation or activity, and exposure to unique, delightful options that are not necessarily typical or previously part of a child's worldview. Divergent learning refers to the use of materials or participation in activities or events in nontraditional or unconventional ways. The use of what are often referred to as open-ended materials provides wonderful examples of how to combine principles of discovery and divergent learning, then put them into practice. Blocks, dough, paint, balls, crayons, pencils, markers, blank paper, water, sand, natural objects like acorns, rocks/stones, twigs, leaves, pine cones, bark, seeds, and miscellaneous or random items that may be considered "waste" or "garbage" are examples of open-ended types of materials that lead to different kinds of interactions and experiences.

Principle 2: High Challenge and Low Threat

The brain—and by extension the learning process—responds well to situations that involve high challenge and low threat. What is meant by high challenge and low threat? High challenge refers to opportunities and experiences that go beyond routines or activities that are always easily and readily completed. Low threat involves a sense of comfort and trust, a lack of feelings such as fear, anger, frustration, stress, hopelessness or helplessness. All learners thrive when they are in situations where they feel comfortable, have experiences they can deal with and engage in activities they can accomplish with limited anxiety.

Principle 3: Novelty

Like options for discovery and divergent learning, novelty provides opportunities to work in environments or with materials that encourage creativity, imagination, wonder and joy. Novelty builds renewed interest in actions, activities, materials or spaces that have been used or completed too often and lost appeal. While routines, schedules, and anticipation of what may happen next are important, a lack of novelty may lead to indifference or limited focus. Individuals of all ages will pay closer attention to an environment or situation when a bit of novelty is part of the experience. More attention drives deeper learning.

Principle 4: Manipulatives

There are many neural connections from the fingertips and skin to the brain. Touch and engagement with objects create unique opportunities to know about the characteristics and defining properties of what is being manipulated. Hands-on experiences are "minds-on" experiences. Manipulatives promote the development of concepts. Along with the joy of interacting directly with materials, manipulatives help in the formation of brain connections that are responsible for understanding dimensionality and the existence of objects in space. All of this neural formation also promotes a variety of conceptual designations responsible for later cognitive processes that help children understand letters, numbers, and shapes. Therefore, manipulatives strengthen literacy, numeracy, and the foundation for other learning.

Principle 5: Play and Exploration

The Russian psychologist Lev Vygotsky stated that when a child is engaged in play the child is functioning a "head taller." By using the term "head taller," Vygotsky helps us understand the central role of play in encouraging creative thought, imagination, problem-solving, meaning-making, risk-taking—and prompting cognitive and physical growth, along with well-being. One aspect of play is further exploration of an idea, action, or material. Exploration, like discovery and other productive learning experiences, increases awareness of what is available in an environment. Awareness leads to engagement, which in turn leads to more understanding and interest. Learning is always enhanced when more attention and engagement are part of an experience.

Principle 6: Social Situation

Humans have varying degrees of social interaction and preferences for social engagement. However, learning is generally enhanced when people connect with each other through conversation, physical engagement and interactions, proximity, relationships, team work, observation, modelling, and other means of social activity. Setting up learning environments where social engagement can readily occur promotes dramatic and subtle opportunities for learning to happen.

Principle 7: Inquiry

Children have questions. Infants gaze intently at objects and faces or point to what has sparked their interest. Toddlers naturally investigate every possible facet and nuance of their environment. Preschoolers constantly experiment with language, objects, ideas, materials, and behaviors. All of these activities and experiences are parts of the inquiry process involved in learning about the world. While children may not always voice their questions, inquiry and wonder are part of an ideal environment for them to learn. Children should be provided with a wide range of experiences, materials, and spaces in order to stimulate their exploration of many questions: what, how, when, where, why, what if, is it possible, can I do it, what will happen, how many, what is it, is there enough, and where did it go? By setting up environments where inquiry is expected and encouraged, we will help children come naturally to understand and appreciate more of their world.

Principle 8: Environments that Are Appealing and Stimulating

Children learn about what they are exposed to in their world experience. When something is fascinating, enjoyable, exciting, playful, engaging, pleasurable, meaningful, and intriguing to children, it offers them limitless possibilities for learning. Setting up learning spaces or providing opportunities to explore the broader world can be challenging and requires understanding and knowledge of children in a program and its facility. Depending on the needs and preferences of the children, the design, setup, and opportunities available to any group require lots of thought and action. What works for one particular group or individual children may not be effective and desirable for another set of children. Learning spaces—whether inside or outside—should be constantly monitored and modified as needs and preferences change. While it is important to provide an appealing and stimulating learning environment, one that is too hectic, inappropriate, or just not a good match with the décor, furniture, and materials can create a less than optimal experience for children. Knowing the children and families is critical to making good choices on what to provide for children.

Principle 9: Support Resiliency

Resiliency is the ability to deal with less than optimal circumstances and be able to go on with life. In many ways, children are naturally resilient. Consider how often adults miss children's cues and clues and yet children somehow are able to make sense of their world and thrive. When setting up learning environments, it is important to think about how to help children succeed in progressing through their day and what is necessary to help them do so. Whether it is room/space design, labels, schedules, routines, materials, adult attitudes, language/vocabulary, expectations, color scheme, lighting, seating arrangements, access to necessary objects, or simply the daily experience—all this and more will benefit children or hinder them from being resilient and capable individuals.

Principle 10: Cultural Relevancy

The concept of culture is broad. Culture is not just about artifacts and simple representations of traditional or generic pieces of a child's background. When establishing a learning environment, it is imperative to consider the various and unique persons and families that will be involved in the space. Getting to know families, along with their expectations and understanding of learning and education, is also important. Expressing dominant or misguided cultural beliefs in the learning environment will create alienation and frustration. As much as possible, provide experiences, materials, and classroom setups that resonate with the many cultural and family groups represented in your site or facility.

These ten principles represent a foundation on which to build and create learning environments. Each of the learning environment elements addressed in the rest of this chapter have incorporated these general principles that are vital to help children reach their potential.

Designing an Environment to Promote Development and Learning

The layout of your setting—both indoors and outdoors—influences what and how children learn and offers them rich and meaningful early learning experiences. When you begin thinking about how to arrange your space, ask yourself: How do I arrange the setting to promote relationships, exploration, and experimentation? How can the setting support children in reaching learning and developmental goals? How can I ensure that the setting respects children's individual characteristics—abilities, needs, interests, home language, and culture? How can I welcome both children and families? Questions like these will help you translate what you know about the children you serve into a design that truly allows everyone to develop and learn.

Creating a High-Quality Setting for Infants and Toddlers

Both the indoor and outdoor play areas for infants and toddlers need to be designed to focus on developmental, individual, and cultural needs. Think about what the children in your program can do. What developmental challenges are they working on? What are their special interests, home languages, and cultural influences? How can your environment support their growth and development?

Designing Infant and Toddler Environments to Meet Developmental Needs

Because children think and behave like this:	Arrange the space to do this:
Young infants (birth–8 months) are attached to their family members	• Welcome family engagement. • Include a space for nursing mothers. • Display family photos at infants' eye levels. • Provide greeting areas and furniture that invites adults to comfortably sit while interacting with children. • Allow plenty of time at drop off and pick up to make the transition smoother for both children and families.
Young infants learn through moving their bodies and using all of their senses	• Offer soft, protected spaces where babies can move safely. • Provide safe, appropriate toys that infants can reach and explore. • Lift and carry babies so they can see, smell, touch, and feel items in the indoor and outdoor settings. • Provide a variety of textures, scents, and vibrant materials to enhance sensory experiences.
Mobile infants (8–17 months) move from place to place	• Provide protected spaces where children can creep, crawl, and walk out of the way of infants who are not yet mobile. • Have sturdy furniture and railings that infants can use to pull themselves up.
Mobile infants find comfort in familiar adults	• Incorporate photos, tape recordings, and verbal reminders of family members. • Use low room dividers so children can see adults whenever they need reassurance, and so adults can supervise all children at all times.
Young toddlers (18–24 months) often eat and sleep at scheduled times	• Have tables and chairs where small groups can eat together. • Set up cots or mats at nap time and remove them when children are awake.
Young toddlers like to play close to another friend	• Provide play spaces where two or three children can work together on activities of their choosing.
Older toddlers (24–36 months) can climb, run, jump, and hop.	• Offer open spaces and equipment where children can move freely and safely.
Like younger toddlers, older toddlers have a difficult time sharing	• Provide duplicates of favorite toys and materials. It would be helpful if duplicates are exactly the same color, size, and shape to avoid conflicts over materials.

Designing the Indoor Setting for Infants and Toddlers

A well-planned indoor setting for infants and toddlers uses design techniques to effectively create a calm, playful, and home-like space that welcomes children and their families. The ideal indoor setting is stimulating (not overwhelming) and designates areas for both play experiences and routines like diapering and toileting, feeding and eating, napping, dressing, and for storing individual belongings. Space for the early childhood educators and other visiting adults to sit and play with the children and store belongings are also incorporated into the design.

An effective indoor space also reflects children's home cultures and languages through music, writing, books, foods, and more.

When teaching children with disabilities, offer accommodations based on their physical, intellectual, or emotional differences so all children can take full advantage of the program and reach their potential. Rely on early interventionists and special education staff (including an occupational therapist if the program has access to one) to make recommendations and train you in how to use adaptive equipment. Here are some thoughts on what you might do to include everyone:

- **For children with physical (orthopedic) disabilities:** Include soft mats, foam climbing shapes, and pools of balls to provide children with motor delays a safe environment for developing their large muscle skills. Children who need support to sit or stand may need therapeutic chairs, prone standers, or grab bars. If children use walkers or wheelchairs, arrange the indoor and outdoor spaces so children can use their equipment to move freely through the environment.

Including Home Languages and Culture in Infant and Toddler Settings

Experts (Nemeth and Erdosi 2012)* recommend the following practices to help infants and toddlers feel valued, strengthen their identities, and build language and literacy skills:

- Post photos of families at the children's eye level.
- Purchase or check out board books from the public library written in children's home languages.
- Create and display posters using photos of the children's homes, neighborhoods, stores, and parks.
- Stock dolls, block people, and books featuring people with diverse facial features and skin colors.
- Provide snacks and tasting/cooking experiences using ethnic foods familiar to the children.
- Label key areas of the room in English and the children's home languages.
- Post phonetic spellings of key words in the children's languages throughout the settings to remind adults how to introduce these words during conversations with children.
- Learn songs, key words, and phrases in home languages, such as diaper, lunch, hello, goodbye, and read. Play music in children's home languages.

- **For children with visual impairments:** Well-defined spaces with bright lighting will help children recognize where they are. Use textural clues to mark spaces, such as a change in flooring from carpeting to linoleum. This tells children that they have moved into the eating area. Adorn the child's cubby with fake fur or netting to set it apart from others. Provide large print books and signage to help children distinguish print. Use music to alert everyone to transitions.

- **For children with hearing impairments:** Provide visual clues, such as photos of classroom toys and materials to communicate with children. Make sure that you talk directly to the child when conversing so that they can read your face.

- **For children with tactile sensitivities:** Children with sensory disorders who are hypersensitive typically have low tolerance for noise, light, or messy materials like paint or mud. You can work with an occupational therapist to learn how to control the environment so as not to trigger sensitivity. Making homemade playdough and offering crunchy foods to eat seem to benefit many children. Some children can be desensitized by slowly increasing their exposure to materials like shaving cream (for finger painting), glue, and sand. Some children wear gloves or Lycra garments under their clothing. The pressure seems to help control sensitivities. Children who are hypo-sensitive, may need to touch different textures, enjoy messy play and need vibrating toys. They may have difficulty with zipping, buttoning, and understanding where their body is in space. These children like to be in constant motion. Spinning, crashing, jumping, and hopping helps with sensory input.

The following tips will help you design an indoor setting that promotes the growth and development of infants and toddlers:

- Set up carpeted areas for children to sit, crawl, and walk to soften falls.
- Designate areas with linoleum floors for eating, or messy experiences like art.
- Paint the walls a neutral color such as off-white. Environmental designers Louis Torelli and Charles Durrett (n.d.) caution that bold colors on walls can be overstimulating. Bring color into the room through decorations, flooring, and toys.
- Use natural and halogen incandescent light sources. Avoid fluorescent lighting as it tends to create an institutional feel. Use dimmer switches to control the intensity of the lighting.
- Use separate sinks for diapering, handwashing, and food preparation.
- Designate a place for each routine, play and learning experience, and activity.
- Create a variety of defined spaces for infants and toddlers at every stage of development to move their bodies and explore toys and other materials.

- Include carpeted risers and low room dividers or platforms to protect children, add variety, and help define space.
- Use corners, nooks, and tunnels to create private spaces where children can get away from the action, calm themselves, and cope with emotions.
- Plan an arrangement that allows children to be seen and supervised from any vantage point in the room.
- Strategize on where to place noisy and quiet activities. For example, choose the quietest areas to arrange cribs or cots/mats for nap time.
- Include comfortable spaces such as rocking chairs or gliders for adults to use when feeding, comforting, or interacting with children.
- Include space for adults to safely store their belongings.
- Provide locked cabinets in activity areas where adults can store and return potentially hazardous materials.

For young infants the Early Head Start National Resource Center (2010) suggests creating a "YES" indoor setting. In other words, ensure that everything infants can reach is safe and acceptable for them to use. These infants require soft, comfortable areas throughout the setting and a variety of views. Design areas for infants to explore, be creative, engage in parallel play, or have quiet time. Make sure that there are spaces designated for napping, diapering, food preparation and eating, carpeted spaces for sitting and playing with toys or looking in a mirror, and places for nestling together with an adult.

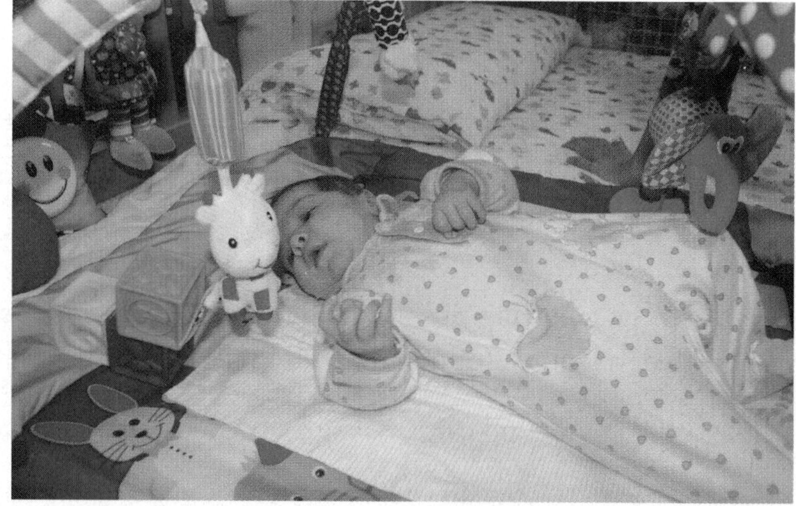

Ensure that everything infants can reach is safe and acceptable for them to use.

Mobile infants also need "YES"-protected areas where they can crawl, climb, pull themselves up, and walk. Their areas should include sturdy furniture with rounded edges; low, secure railings for them to pull up on as they attempt to stand; and low dividers or risers so that adults and infants can see each other as the infants move around and explore freely. Mobile infants' areas should also include seating and spaces for eating, diapering, and other routines. They also need areas designed for exploration, parallel play, creativity, language and literacy, and quiet time.

Figure 25, offers a sample layout for an infant program. Depending on the ages and needs of the children in your program, you can tailor this design to meet your requirements.

Figure 25. Sample Infant Setting

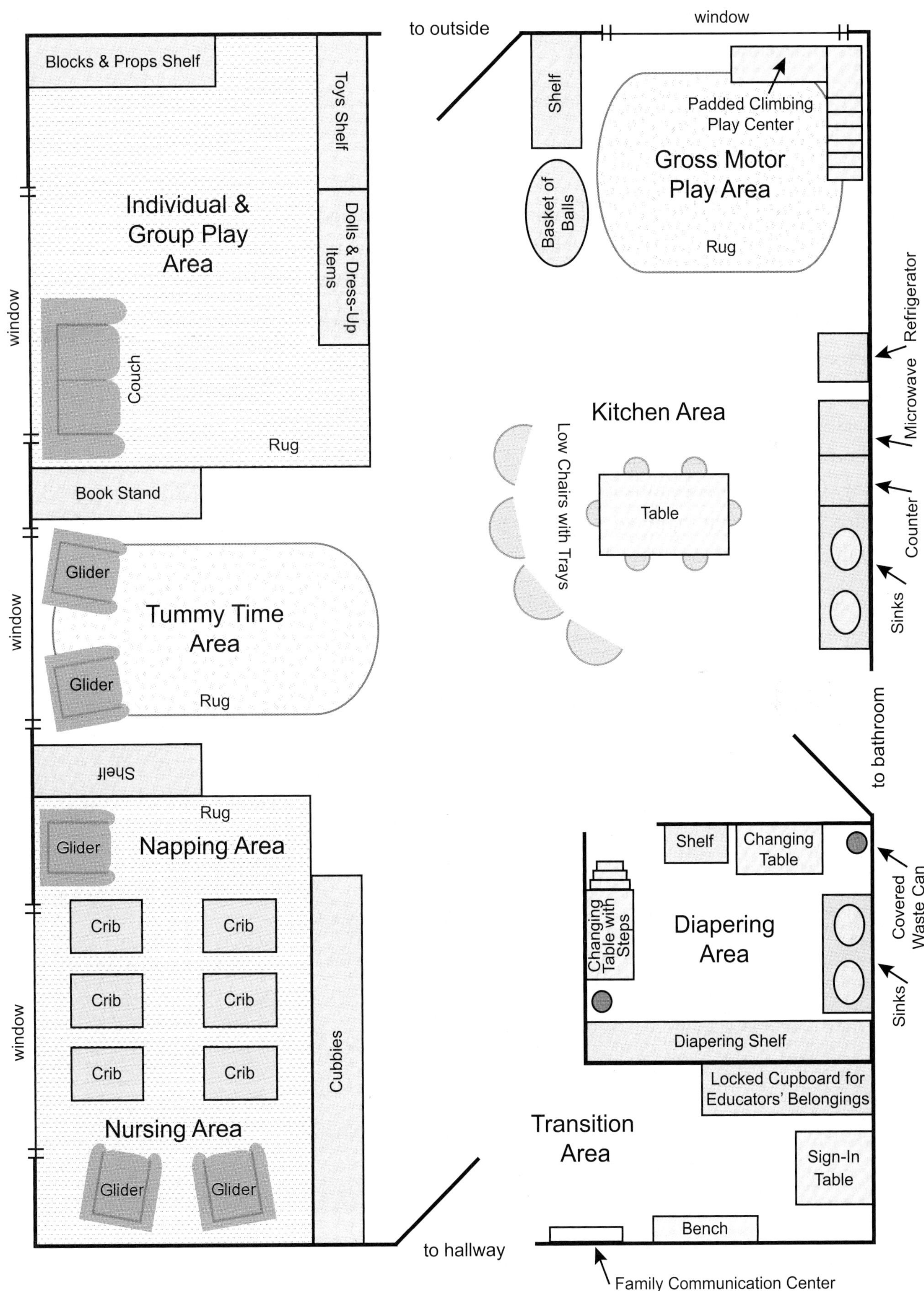

Toddlers need many of the same features in the indoor setting as do mobile infants. However, because of their rapidly growing skills, you will need to adjust the design to challenge and engage toddlers in development and learning.

Young toddlers can come together in small groups for eating and doing activities. Small tables with toddler-size chairs work best.

Toddlers are struggling with learning to be independent, so they need spaces where they can work by themselves, be alone or with other children as the mood strikes them. Depending on their skill levels, you can introduce activity areas for creating art, pretending—solo or parallel play, singing songs and making music, looking at books and listening to stories, doing puzzles, building with blocks, manipulating toys, and exploring natural items.

Older toddlers, who have more refined skills than they did as younger toddlers, are in constant motion and move quickly. They need well defined spaces that control traffic patterns to keep these active youngsters focused. Provide defined play areas for art, sand and water play, pretend play, books and storytelling, toys and puzzles, music and movement, and food tasting and cooking. Children this age can also be introduced to tablets (such as the iPad), if your program can afford them. In addition, older toddlers will enjoy coming together as a group for a quick group meeting or music activity, so set up spaces to accommodate these activities.

Figure 26 offers a sample layout for a toddler setting. Again, you will need to customize this design plan to address your program's individual needs.

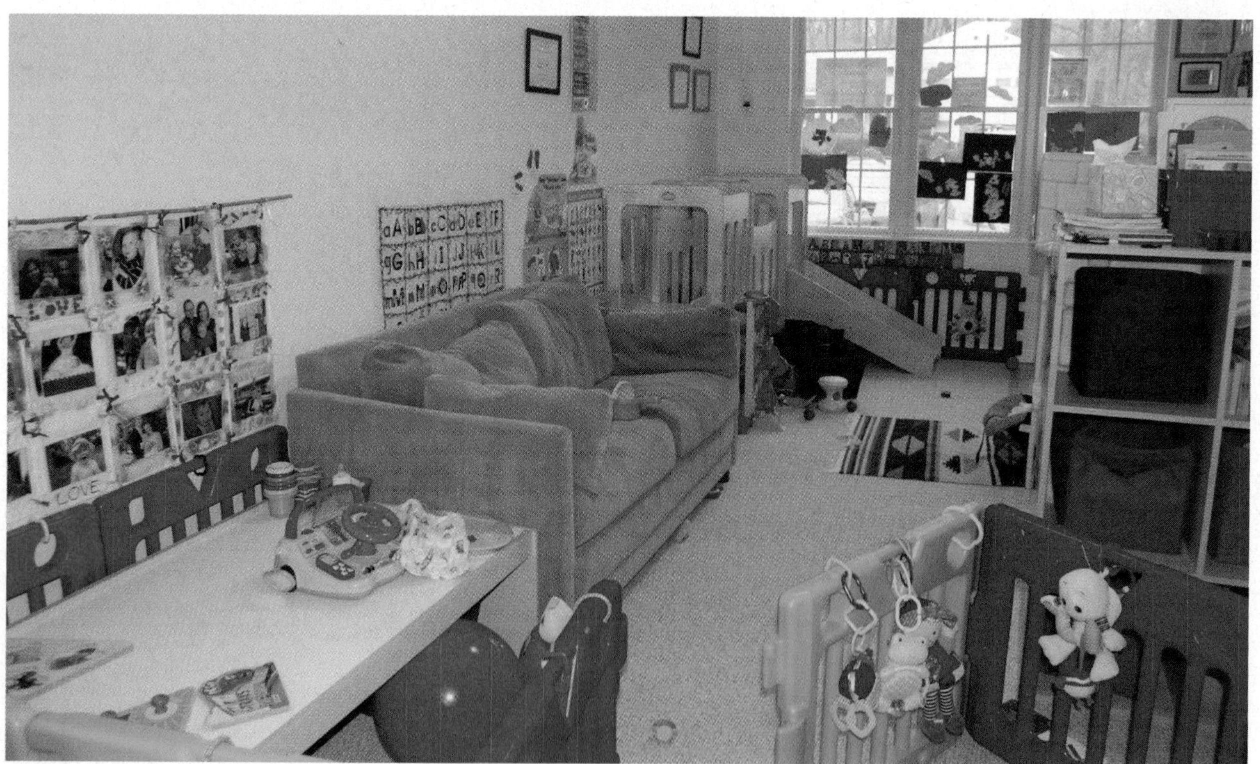

Your setting should be large enough to accommodate the wider range of activities in which children will engage.

Figure 26. Sample Toddler Setting*

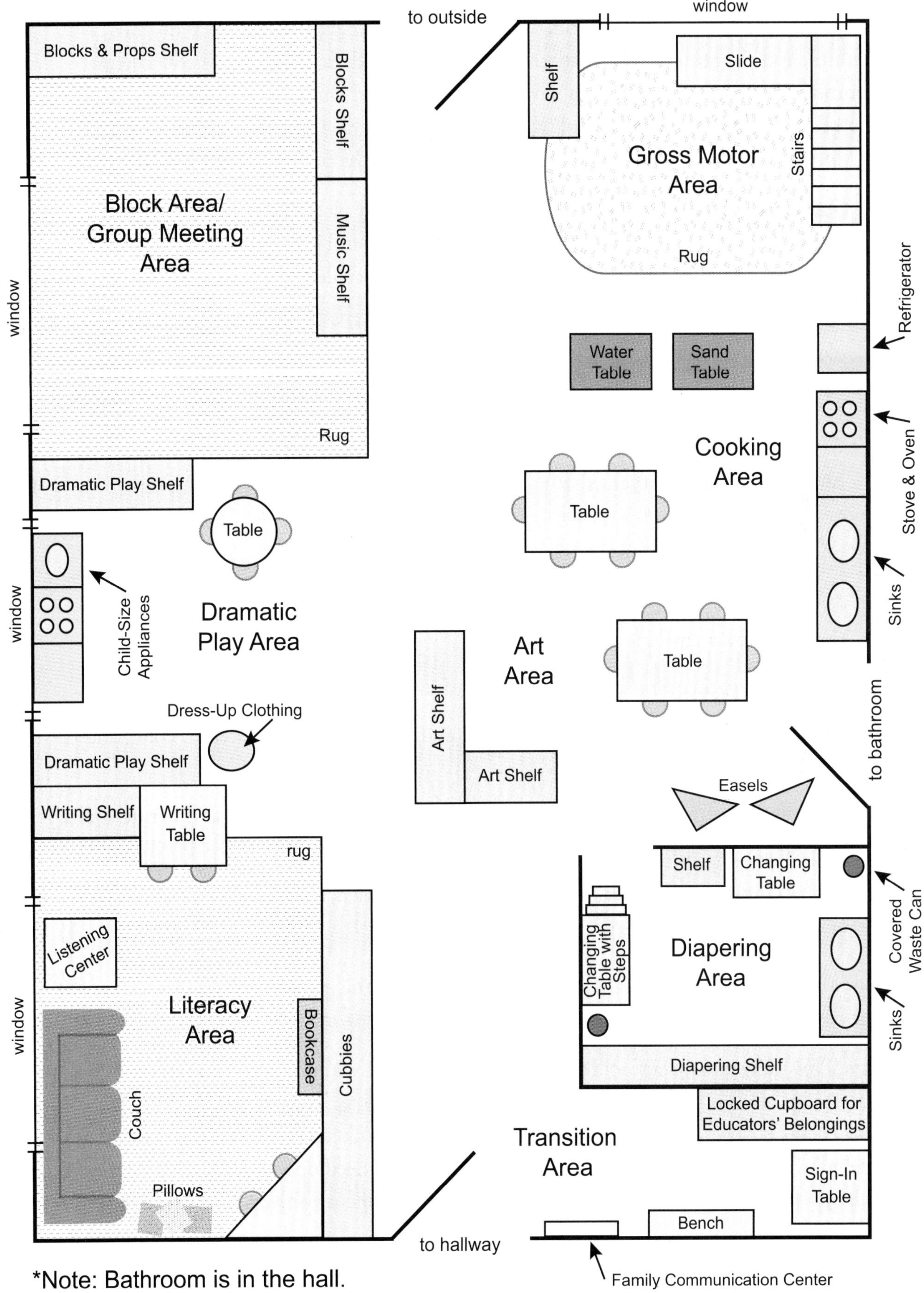

*Note: Bathroom is in the hall.

Designing the Outdoor Setting for Infants and Toddlers

Bringing infants and toddlers outdoors promotes children's development, extends the curriculum, and connects young children with nature. Outdoor time affords children an opportunity to move freely, explore a new environment, and enjoy the feel and smell of sun and wind on their cheeks. The Early Head Start National Resource Center (Technical Assistance Paper No. 14, 2013) offers these strategies for configuring the outdoor space:

- Separate the infant space from the toddler space, but place them adjacent to one another. The goal is to have children play where they can see and hear each other, but not be in physical contact so that boisterous toddlers do not accidentally injure infants.
- Separate noisy and quiet activities. Locate swings or trike paths towards the edges of the play space.
- Make sure that there is a 48-inch use zone in every direction around swings and other playground equipment.
- Ensure that there is proper drainage throughout the play space. Standing water becomes a breeding ground for mosquitoes.
- Provide a shaded area of at least six feet, if no natural shading exists.
- Offer safe, developmentally appropriate materials and equipment that engage and challenge children.
- Plant small gardens both in the ground and in planters.
- Hang bird feeders, wind chimes, banners, and streamers to add interest, color, and to bring nature into the play space.
- Use wagons, carriages, or strollers to take children on short outings and nature walks.
- Make sure play spaces are accessible and that appropriate accommodations are made to ensure children with disabilities can enjoy and experience outdoor space and activities alongside their peers.

Because the outdoor environment supports children's learning goals in the same way that the indoor environment does, it's important to plan for the following.

Infants. Physically, infants are rolling over, sitting with and without assistance, pulling themselves up, waddling and walking, climbing, and swinging. The outdoor area needs to support these activities. There should be grassy areas for blankets or carpet squares where non-mobile infants can interact with an adult or nature. Babies need opportunities for "tummy time" and sitting (with or without support), reaching for and throwing objects, and splashing water.

Mobile infants. Now that they can move from place to place, pull-up bars, walking paths, tunnels, and room for push and pull toys are required. Toy baby carriages, shopping carts, and wagons with handles, provide the extra support beginning walkers need. Mobile infants need large enclosed spaces where they can climb and roll around. They also need space for throwing beach balls and dropping bean bags into baskets. Fully enclosed swings with safety belts allow infants to see what is taking place in the world around them from a higher, moving perspective.

Educators can read with infants, do music activities, and introduce them to plants and naturally found objects in a refreshing environment. Mobile infants also enjoy digging in a sandbox, splashing water in a tub, and crawling through a tunnel.

Toddlers. Being outside offers exciting new learning experiences. Toddlers are physically active, so they need an outdoor play area where they can freely run, hop, jump, march, tiptoe, leap, and gallop. There needs to be room to push and pull toys, wagons, and wheelbarrows. They need an environment that allows them to enjoy riding in bucket swings, climbing up platforms and climbers (no higher than 18 inches), and going down slides. The outdoor space also needs areas where toddlers can balance on a beam, swing on a rope, throw balls of various sizes, and balance on a wheeled toy or pedal a tricycle.

Toddlers will also enjoy an outdoor space where they can play in a sandbox, wash a rubber doll in a tub of water, engage in pretend play, and draw with thick crayons on chart paper at a picnic table. Early childhood educators can read to toddlers at a table or under a tree (while being aware of all children). Children can sing a song or shake a tambourine. They can build with blocks and hide in a large cardboard box. The outdoors is an exciting place for toddlers—and adults.

Both infants and toddlers. Children in these age groups benefit from having access to what is known as "loose parts" for outdoor play. The term loose parts refer to toys and materials that are safe and not fixed in place. Children can manipulate loose parts in a number of ways. They can collect, stack, sort, dump, pick up, and line up loose parts such as stones, twigs, leaves, seed pods, and other naturally found objects. (Early Head Start National Resource Center, Technical Assistance Paper No. 14, 2013). Loose parts stimulate children's senses and help young children learn. That's what being outdoors is all about.

Creating a High-Quality Setting for Preschoolers

A high-quality learning environment for preschoolers promotes learning, creativity, and fun. How you arrange your indoor and outdoor spaces has a deep impact on what children learn and the messages they receive about being there. You want every child to feel safe, valued, and eager to learn.

Your first consideration in creating this type of environment is to incorporate what you know about preschoolers' culture, and how they develop and learn into a design plan. The chart that follows will give you some ideas on how to go about doing this:

Designing Preschool Environments to Meet Developmental Needs

Because preschoolers (3–5 years) think and behave like this:	Arrange the space to do this:
Preschool children like playing cooperatively with other children	• Offer activity areas that are large enough to play together and give children enough time to be fully engaged in projects. Promote inclusive play. Pay attention to how children naturally group themselves, being aware of bias and other hurtful interactions.
Children enjoy using their large muscles to climb, run, jump, throw, and kick balls	• Provide indoor and outdoor spaces that are large enough for children to safely practice and perfect these skills.
They are working on refining their small muscle skills and eye and hand coordination	• Offer many opportunities to develop these skills by setting up learning centers where children can turn pages in a book, build with Legos, complete a puzzle, weave streamers through a fence, and play a musical triangle.
They have expanding interests	• Divide the space into learning areas that will appeal to most children—art, music, blocks, sand and water play, and the like.
They enjoy being independent and doing things for themselves	• Display materials so that children can get them themselves and provide play spaces where they can work on their own.

Designing the Indoor Setting for Preschoolers

The most effective way to incorporate the principles of child development noted above, is to divide the indoor space into learning centers (defined areas where specific learning activities occur). This design feature ensures that children are motivated to explore, experiment, and master learning goals and objectives. Learning centers are able to support learning through play and help children progress as they attempt and accomplish challenging tasks. These centers allow children to choose interesting activities and concentrate on them for extended periods of time. Learning centers provide room for children to play in pairs, small groups, or alone.

While creating these centers, consider the children's interests. Make a list of possible learning centers and think about the learning opportunities these centers will provide. How will these centers—and the stimulating, varied materials that they are stocked with—help to develop the children's social, emotional, cognitive, and physical development? Will the centers support the children's content learning in language and literacy, mathematics, science, technology, social studies, and the arts?

To help you begin thinking about the best learning centers for your indoor setting, here is a suggested list of learning centers from the National Association for the Education of Young Children (NAEYC) used in its publication for preschool educators, *Teaching Young Children*:

- Blocks
- Art
- Literacy
- Dramatic Play
- Music & Movement
- Science
- Math & Manipulatives
- Sand Play/Water Play
- Cooking

Create learning centers in your indoor-setting design where children can play in pairs, small groups, or alone.

When you have finalized the list of learning centers your indoor setting will include, draw a plan for your room on chart paper. This blueprint will help you visualize where you will place each learning center and its furnishings and equipment. Though you may realize during planning that your indoor space does not accommodate all of your plans, you can discover how to make the most of the space you do have. For example, you could place bean bag chairs or large pillows in an odd-shaped corner to create a nook where one or two children can sit and read together or by themselves.

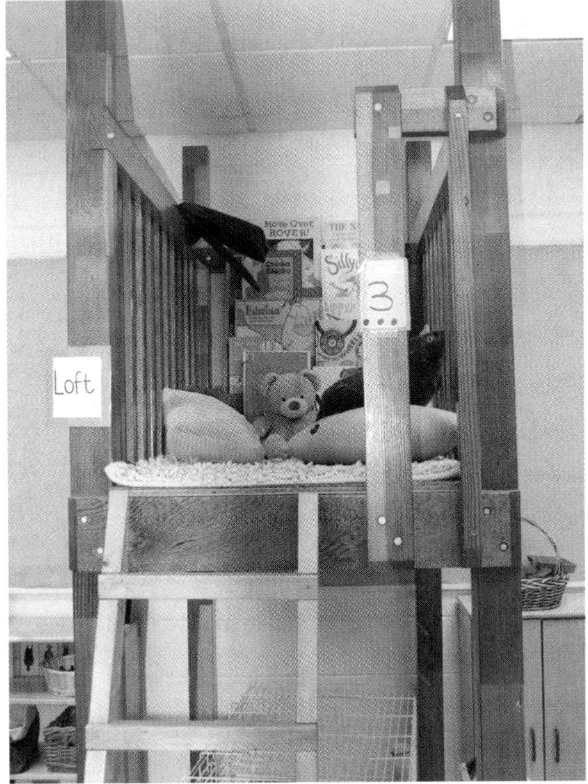

Include cozy places in your indoor-setting design where children can play or relax alone or in small groups.

Or you can turn a loft into a library with two levels. Alternatively, a loft can become an extra dramatic play area that doubles as a pretend townhouse or department store. Is there a chalkboard affixed to one wall, as is common in preschool classrooms housed in elementary schools? Use this wall for the writing area of your literacy center. Or use the area as your art center. The children can create chalk drawings or draw on butcher paper attached to the board.

Do any of the children in your setting have disabilities? Meet with your program's special education staff or consultants as you consider their needs in your blueprint.

Finally, think about how you can incorporate the children's families, cultures, and home languages into your program. Some strategies you may wish to use are:

- Write labels and signage in all of the children's home languages as well as in English. Develop color codes for each language so, for example, Spanish signage is always green, and French is red. See Chapter 6 for more information on this topic.
- Stock the library with books that reflect each child's family, culture, and home language.
- Provide dress up clothes and dramatic play accessories that reflect the children's heritage.
- Offer foods and cooking experiences that include family favorites.
- Feature music and dance reflective of the children's cultures.
- Post photos of family members in the children's cubbies and the greeting area of the room.
- Learn and use a few important words and phrases in the children's home languages. For example, learn to say good morning, welcome, clean up time, lunch, let's go outdoors, and so on.

Consider these factors when drawing the blueprint for an indoor setting that fosters engaging play and learning:

Accommodating Children's Disabilities

For children with **physical (orthopedic) impairments:** Passageways should be wide enough (usually 3½ feet) to accommodate wheelchairs and walkers. Ramps, stepstools, and raised toilets can make bathroom fixtures accessible. Add adaptive tools, paint brushes, drawing implements, and utensils for children with manual dexterity issues. Review your state/federal requirements for additional information about ensuring the setting is accessible for all.

For children with **developmental delays:** Use room dividers and bookcases to block out distractions and offer adapted tools and utensils to encourage independence.

For children diagnosed with **autism spectrum disorder:** Use picture icons to clarify directions and provide tables children can work at while standing. This is often a preferred stance for children with this disorder.

For children with **visual impairments:** Use hardware and software configurations on computers, provide large text books, and offer textured toys and learning materials that children can identify through touch.

For all children, including those with **social and emotional concerns**: Provide quiet spaces like a "be by myself" space or a comfy corner that children can go to when they need a break. Reduce the noise level through carpeting and acoustic paneling. Help children to self-regulate their nervous systems through heavy block play or by wearing a weighted vest. Ensure all of these strategies are done in consultation and partnership with children's families and other relevant service providers, including early interventionists and special educators.

Size. If the children who use your setting vary in age and development (for example, the program includes three to five-year-olds), then the setting should be large enough to offer a wide range of materials and equipment that will meet the needs of the entire age group. Also, define a spacious meeting area where children can sit without distracting each other, If you do not have enough room to have a dedicated meeting space, set up a learning center (such as the block center) with a large space for meetings. This avoids staff having to move furniture before and after each meeting. Also, consider the size of each learning center, so there will be space for all nine. This presents a challenge in small spaces. However, you have options, like conducting music activities indoors and movement activities outdoors. Or if your program is in a school, movement activities can be moved to a gym or all-purpose room, if one is available. Some learning centers, like the block center, need as much space as possible so that children can carry out their creative plans.

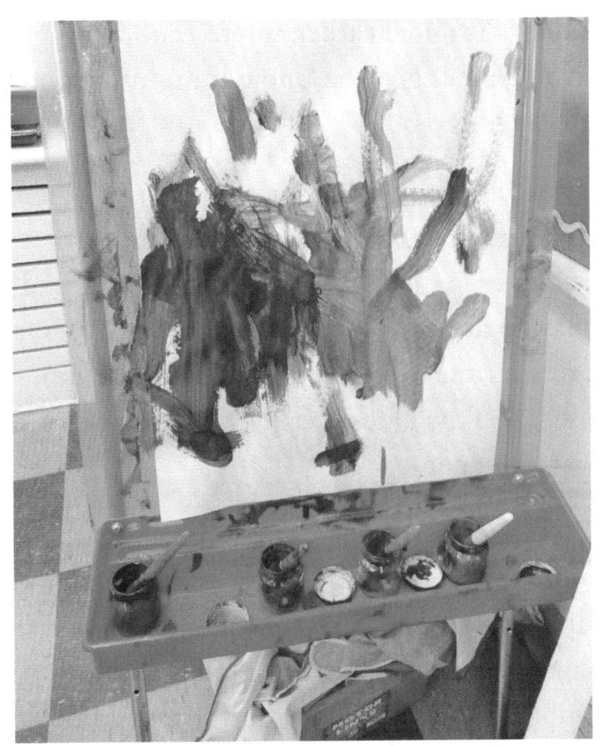

Assign messy activities, like art, to areas with washable flooring.

Power sources. Place learning centers near the resources they require. For example, electrical outlet locations determine where you will place computers, chargers for tablets, CD/DVD players, light tables, kitchen appliances, or other equipment.

Water. Determine where the water sources are and which learning centers—including art, sand and water play, and cooking—should be located near them.

Lighting. The art, science, and literacy centers will be enhanced if they can be located near natural light. If this is not possible, lamps with halogen incandescent bulbs can create pools of light that warm the room and define areas

Lamps create incandescent pools of light that warm the room and define areas subtly.

subtly. As noted earlier, fluorescent lighting should be avoided as it gives an unpleasant, institutional look to the setting.

Flooring. Ideally, indoor settings have both carpeted and washable flooring, like linoleum. Assign messy activities, such as cooking, art, and sand and water play, to areas with washable flooring. Reserve carpeted areas for the other learning centers, including noisier areas like the block area, to provide a welcoming, safe environment.

Placements. Are there any centers that should be adjoined? Perhaps the block center should be near the dramatic play center to encourage children to wear construction helmets while building block towers, bridges, or cities. The centers that yield the most noise should be close to each other. Group the quietest centers together so children can play undisturbed.

Determine how to best incorporate cubbies into your room design.

Cubbies. Determine how to best incorporate cubbies into your room design. Each child should have a private space to display photos of their families, store special possessions, hang their coats and book bags, and place items to take home. In essence, a cubby is a preschooler's locker. Cubbies don't have to be built in or purchased. Milk crates and other storage containers placed on their sides will serve the purpose well. Cubbies can be the anchor for a welcoming transition area at the entrance of the room where children and families can sign-in and say good-bye.

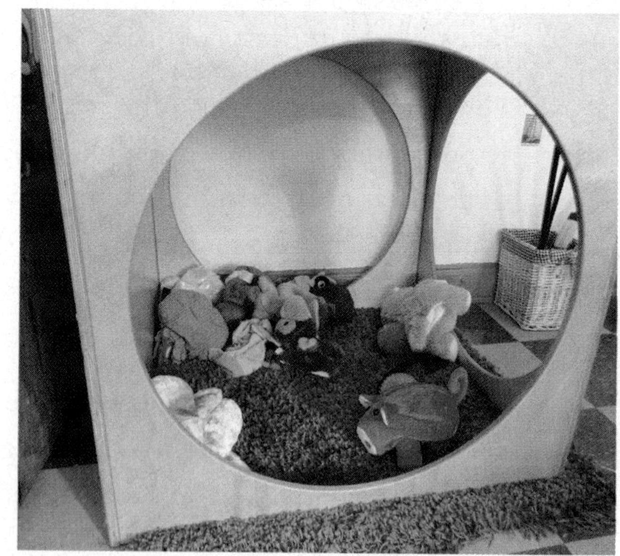

Nooks provide children opportunities to be alone or engage in very small groups.

Nooks. Children need cozy places where they can play or relax alone or in small groups. Sometimes children just need to get away from the commotion of the classroom and take a break. Place a rocking chair in a corner or fill an area under a loft with pillows to offer children this respite.

Putting the Blueprint into Action

After drawing your working blueprint for the indoor setting, ask yourself: What will greet the children when they first enter the setting? Is it clear where they go to place their belongings and play? Have I placed all the centers so that children can easily access them, out of the way of foot traffic? Have I placed quieter learning centers close together? Have I positioned noisier centers next to each other? Now stand and ask: Am I, as the early childhood educator, able to see everywhere, so that I can supervise all the children effectively? Correct long corridors or large open areas in your design that invite children to run. Create clear pathways around every learning center.

Consider what families will think of your design. Will they see this as a space where their child will be safe and healthy? Do they feel welcome to participate in their child's care and education? Will their child's individual needs be met here? Is their family's home language and culture embraced in this space?

Low room dividers or shelves (no more than 36 in. high) that are anchored securely will help you enclose and separate learning centers and allow you to supervise the children. The dividers also give children easy access to materials in each learning center. Also, use furniture, equipment, or room accents—including couches, easels, or rugs—to define learning centers.

Tips on setting up each of the learning centers are provided in the chart below.

Figure 27a. Preschool Learning Center Setup Tips

Learning Center	How Children Use This Center	Setup Tips
Blocks	Children learn math skills, such as proportion, shape and size, seriation, numbers, patterns, and measurement. As children recreate the world around them by building constructions, block play becomes a stepping-stone to abstract thinking. Children also learn skills, such as collaboration, planning, cooperation, perseverance, and social studies as they build neighborhoods and cities out of blocks.	Use walls and divider shelves to enclose the block center on three sides; locate it near the dramatic play center, to promote pretend play and keep it near another noisy center. Cover the floor with smooth, flat carpeting.
Art	Children use open-ended materials creatively—perform activities that are safe and that fulfill their desire to express themselves and create beauty. They also develop fine motor skills, solve problems, and learn about cause and effect when they paint, draw, mold clay, create collages and mobiles, and weave potholders.	Locate the art center near a water source, on washable flooring (or use oilcloth, a small tarp, or newspapers to protect carpet). Use double-sided easels to enclose the center. Include a table that seats 4 to 6 children for drawing, molding clay, weaving, or making collages. Include a drying rack for paintings.

Figure 27b. Preschool Learning Center Setup Tips

Learning Center	How Children Use This Center	Setup Tips
Literacy	Children learn the fundamental skills needed to read, write, and operate a computer or tablet. They learn to recognize and write letters, recreate stories, and create their own books using photographs they take or drawings they make. Most importantly, they learn to love books and reading.	Provide ample space for using computers or tablets, writing, and reading books. Computer and listening activities (using devices, like CD or DVD players) require electrical outlets. Include a table that seats 2 to 4 children for writing and a computer table with two chairs. Use a couch, rocker, or large pillows for a quiet reading area.
Dramatic Play	Children recreate familiar experiences and confront anxiety-producing situations. They make up new scenarios, negotiate roles, and learn how to regulate their own emotions and behavior. Pretending and imagining sets the stage for abstract thinking.	Use toy appliances—including stoves, refrigerators, and sinks and communication, devices including play phones, small pads, pencils, and tape—and child-size furnishings to define the area. Locate next to the block center so that pretend play can influence block construction.
Music & Movement	They express themselves and find comfort through music, dance, and movement. They learn about tone and rhythm in language. And, they learn about patterning and create a foundation for math when they chant and keep time with music.	Designate a large carpeted area for floor exercises, like yoga and meditation, and for marching and dancing. Locate near electrical outlets for playing recorded music. Use a rack or shelf to hold musical instruments and to section off the center.
Science	Children observe natural collections, insects and worms, small animals, observe weather and other natural phenomena. They predict, experiment, document, and graph results.	Set up near a window so that children can view natural objects and conduct experiments that require sunlight. House aquariums and pet cages in this center. The table in this area should seat 4 to 6 children.
Math & Manipulatives	Children learn counting, patterning, seriation, and geometry by playing with puzzles and games. They also learn to follow directions for games and practice fine motor skills.	Provide an area for children to work on puzzles, parquetry blocks, string beads, construct with preschool Legos and other table blocks and construction toys and play games while seated on the floor, at a table, or while standing.
Sand/Water	Children express feelings and calm themselves through sand and water play. They experiment with math skills, such as patterning, volume, and shape as they make sand constructions or pour water.	Locate near a water source and on washable flooring. Define the area with tables. Keep mops, sponges, brooms, a mini-vac, and cleaning supplies nearby.
Cooking	Children express creativity through cooking projects. They learn math (measuring), science (watching bread dough rise), and literacy skills (using recipe cards). Children also develop fine motor skills through cutting, kneading, pouring, and mixing.	Locate near electrical outlets for kitchen appliances and a water source. Use the back of a shelf or a wall to hang large versions of recipes for children to see. Use a table that seats 4 to 6 children where self-service snacks can be served or children can conduct cooking activities. Children can also use this table for meals.

As you set up your indoor setting according to your working blueprint, ensure that you are creating an inviting and organized space that accommodates the needs of every child. You want each child to feel acknowledged, respected, and excited about learning. Have you addressed all of the children's interests in your choices of centers and materials? Have you accommodated every child's unique needs and abilities? Have you brought each child's home language and culture into the program? Are the children's family members reflected in the design? Do children see themselves in the design of your room?

Learning centers should be well-equipped but not overcrowded. They should incorporate a variety of textures and finishes. Ensure that all furnishings are sturdy, safe, and appropriately sized for the children in your setting. Furnish the setting with tables and chairs that vary in size so that all children can sit comfortably. Include tables in centers where it makes sense for children to be using them, such as the art center, the math and manipulatives center, and the cooking center. Also include just enough tables and chairs for each child. Additional tables and chairs may clutter the room. Other furnishings to include are area rugs; open-shelf room dividers to enclose learning centers and hold materials; and pegboards for displaying props, utensils, and tools.

Again, your indoor-setting blueprint is a working document. There is no one correct way to configure a setting. What works well for your setting today may not work as well next year or with a different group of children. Each group of children you teach is unique and the setting should reflect their individual characteristics. Monitor how children move and operate within your setting's design and tweak it to adjust to the children's changing developmental needs.

Figure 28 offers a sample layout for a preschool setting. Use this design to spark your own ideas as you arrange your classroom for preschoolers.

Low shelves that are anchored securely will help you enclose and separate learning centers.

Figure 28. Sample Preschool Setting*

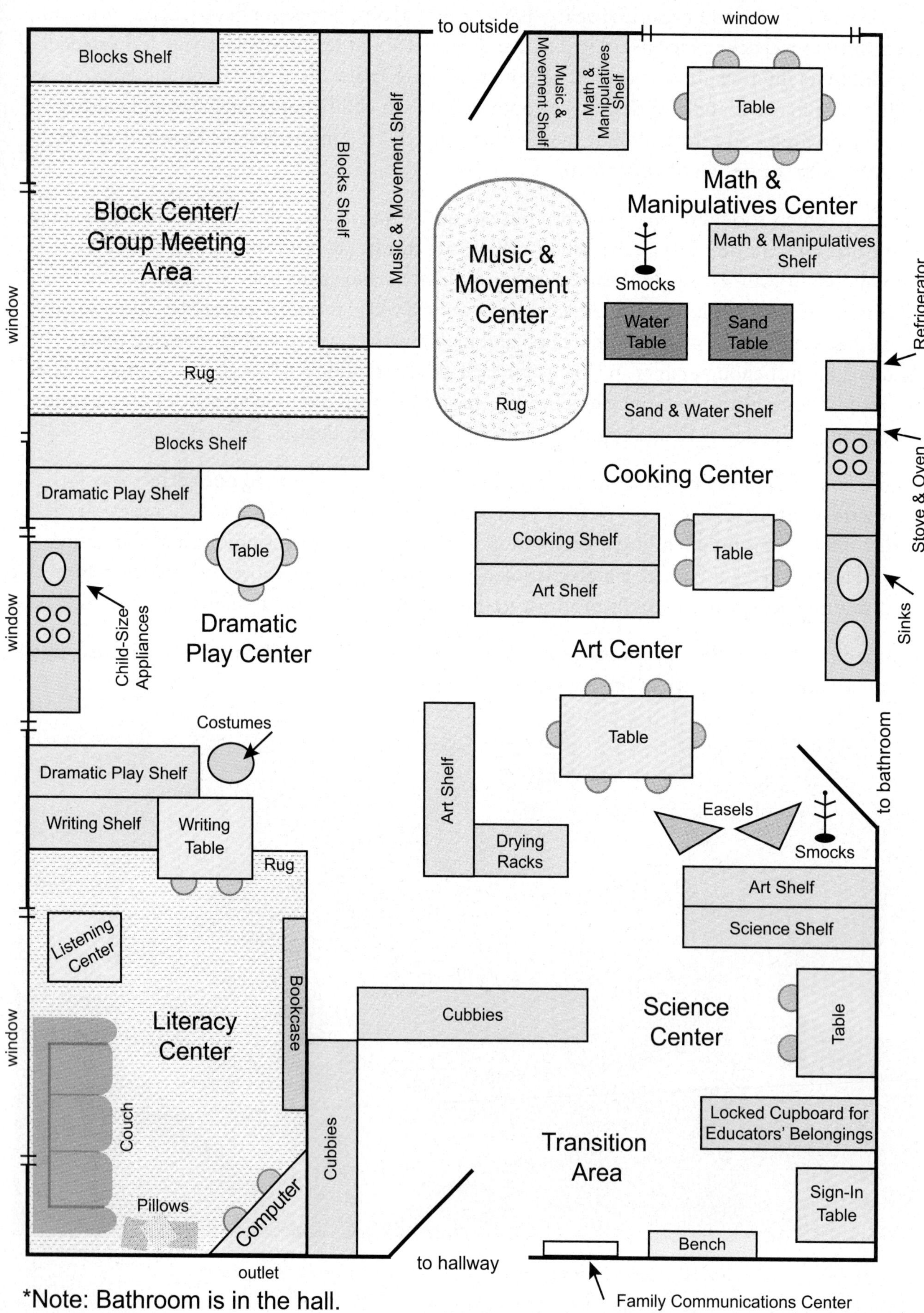

*Note: Bathroom is in the hall.

Designing the Outdoor Setting for Preschool Programs

Your outdoor setting should support the same types of learning activities that occur indoors and engage children in all areas of development and learning. The goal is for children to experience learning from a different perspective. Doing artwork outside allows children to create in the glow of sunlight. Children can collect leaves and pinecones to examine and study right in their natural habitats. Sand, water, and mud play can get as messy as they want it to be when children are allowed to play with abandon. Children don't have to use their "indoor voices" outside.

Setting up an outdoor space can be challenging, though, because programs vary greatly in the type and amount of space available. If you are lucky, you have a grassy, fenced-in playground with age-appropriate equipment designed specifically for preschoolers. For those not as fortunate, setting up an appropriate play space may take both creativity and perseverance.

Working with your administrator, designate an area where all preschoolers can be outdoors at once. This translates into 80-100 square feet of space per child. Make sure that the space is protected by a locked fence or landscaping, and safely away from traffic, electrical wires, and other potential hazards. In addition, make sure that your space meets these conditions:

- It is easily accessible from the indoor area (including bathrooms).
- Anchored equipment (swings, slides, etc.) are installed on soft, shock-absorbing material that will reduce injuries if children fall.
- A lockable storage shed is handy so that materials/equipment do not have to be brought in and out every day.
- A covered area is available for rainy days.
- A shaded area is available for hot weather.
- Children have access to a drinking fountain or hose with a spigot attachment.

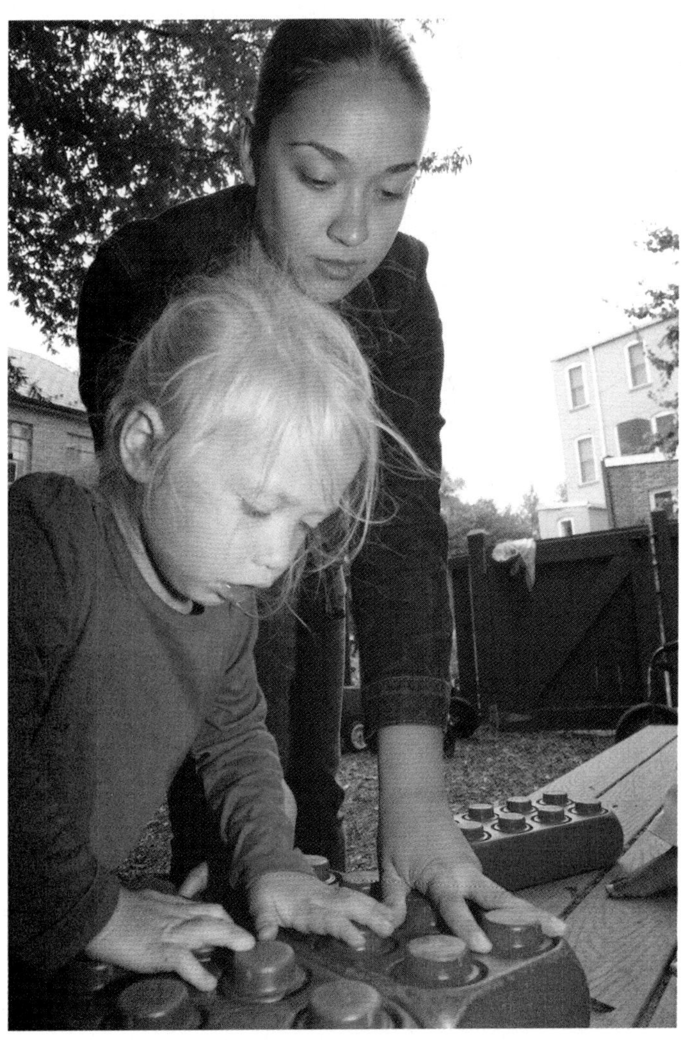

Provide weather-resistant large blocks in your outdoor setting.

- If there is an outdoor sandbox, make sure it has a cover, to prevent contamination from animals.

Just as you divided your indoor space into learning centers, think about how you can divide the outdoor space into distinct learning areas. What activities would you like children to engage in outdoors? Here are some ideas.

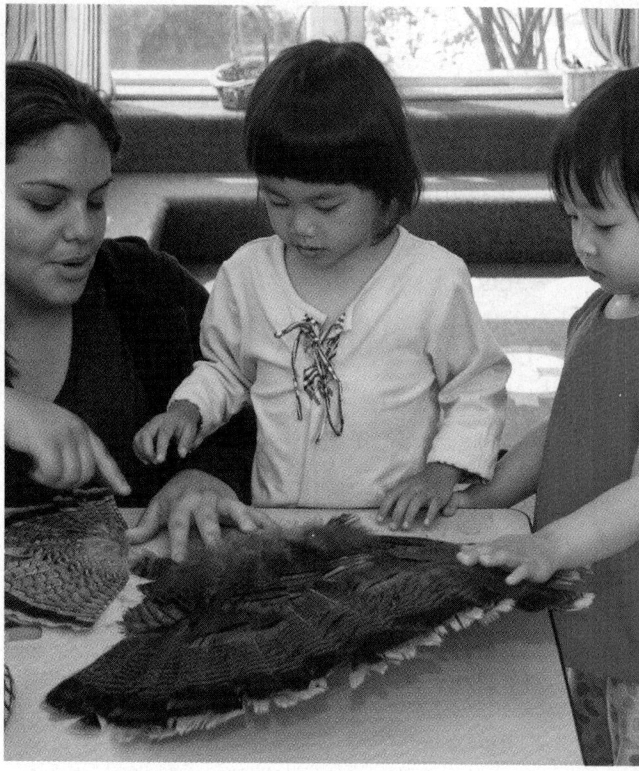

Be sure to use materials that are safe and engaging.

- **Gross motor play.** Children need room to run, jump, climb, crawl, roll, hop, throw, catch, and chase. Anchored play equipment is the most common way of providing many of these opportunities. Swings, climbing structures, slides, and riders enable children to develop and refine large muscles in a way that most every child enjoys. Children also need space to run and throw balls to each other and through hoops. Tunnels, balance beams, and obstacle courses continue the fun. A hard surface track that children can safely use (while wearing helmets) for riding tricycles, big wheels, scooters, and wagons both develops skills and creates excitement. Children can also use the gross motor space to play games like "Tag," "Simon Says," or "Duck, Duck, Goose." Children can also march with instruments and streamers or unfold a giant parachute. The opportunities for gross motor play and games are seemingly endless.
- **Sand, water, and mud play.** Children can dig in the ground, play in a sandbox, frolic with water from a hose or sprinkler on a warm day, use a wading pool to sail boats, or play with sand and water in plastic tubs. Combine sand and soil (in a proportion of one-third sand to two-thirds soil) with water to form mud, which makes a wonderful sculpting medium for pies, muffins, and other pretend baked goods.
- **Science.** Outdoors children can watch science in action. They can grow plants and record the effects of sunlight and water. They can plant vegetables such as carrots or bok choy and eat their home-grown veggies for snacks. If space is limited, grow plants in planters or a wheelbarrow filled with soil. Children can conduct science experiments like collecting and comparing leaves, looking at a ladybug through a magnifying glass, washing stones, or tracing shadows. They can blow bubbles using homemade frames, like a plastic six-pack holder, a mesh net, or plastic hangers.

- **Art.** Children can draw, paint, use finger paints, or mold playdough and clay at a picnic table. Butcher paper taped to a fence or wall creates an easel for children to paint on. Sidewalk chalk can be used to decorate concrete surfaces. And all it takes is water and a paintbrush to paint the side of a building. On a sunny day, children can watch the "paint" evaporate.
- **Dramatic play.** A playhouse, tent, or old wooden boat offer structures for children to use in pretend play. Different props can turn the playhouse into a school, fire station, or a bakery. Based on the children's interests, use props and signage to stretch children's imaginations as they take on different roles.
- **Literacy area.** Locate in a shaded area where children can look at books alone, read with another child, or have a book read to them. Early childhood educators can sit with children under a shade tree and enjoy reading a story together. Afterwards, children can re-enact the story. A picnic table can readily become a writing table.
- **Construction.** Offer large weather-resistant blocks for building cities, space stations, and airports. Carry hollow blocks outside for this purpose. Bring out large appliance boxes and challenge children to make a train or a garage for a pretend racing car. Provide safety goggles, hammers, nails, wood scraps, and glue to do woodworking on a tree stump or a carpenter's bench.

Although outdoor learning centers do not require boundaries the way that indoor ones do, consider using landscaping to designate play areas. For example, use stones or a planter box to frame a garden, or designate a paved track for riding toys. Also consider filling your outdoor setting with natural decor like flowers, plants, herbs, boulders, and a willow tunnel or shaded walkway. Hang sun catchers and wind chimes.

Creating a High-Quality Setting in Family Child Care Programs

The indoor and outdoor environments play the same role in family child care homes that they do in center-based programs serving infants and toddlers or preschoolers. In both centers and FCC homes, the environment provides the foundation for learning. It sets the stage for implementing the curriculum and determines what and how effectively children will learn. In setting up the FCC environment, the same considerations apply. Both the indoor and outdoor environments need to be safe and welcoming. This means that every child—including those with disabilities—is able to participate fully in the program.

Ensuring Appropriate Accommodations for Children With Disabilities

The same types of accommodations noted earlier for teachers of infants and toddlers and teachers of preschoolers apply to family child care providers. If you care for a child with a physical (orthopedic) disability who uses a walker or wheelchair, and there are steps leading up to the front or back door of your home, you may need to install a ramp (or provide a portable one that can be set up at the entrance when needed). This will allow the child to get in and out of your home with ease. Rearrange furniture as needed to allow unobstructed passageways for the walker or wheelchair. Install grab bars in the bathroom, as well as a raised toilet seat. If the child needs seating or positioning assistance or to use adaptive utensils, toys, and materials, the child's family may be able to provide this equipment.

For children with other types of disabilities, the same types of adaptations noted earlier apply. The use of textures can help guide children with vision impairments. Use soft, foam dividers and area rugs to define space. Music and dimmer light switches can soothe children who experience sensory overloads.

In most instances, an infant or toddler with disabilities will have an IFSP (Individualized Family Service Plan) and a preschool or school-age child with disabilities will have an IEP (Individualized Education Program). These plans are developed by a team of special educators and administrators in collaboration with a child's family. Both documents specify the types of accommodations needed and take the guesswork out of trying to figure out what is the best way to ensure children with disabilities reach their potential. Most importantly, following the plans allows you to fully include children in their program.

Including All Children's Families, Cultures, and Home Languages in the Family Child Care Program

As with infant and toddler and preschool settings, your indoor and outdoor environments need to reflect the families, home languages, and cultures of each child enrolled in the program. This is relatively easy to do in family child care homes. With a small group size, providers can readily focus on each child and get to know them at a deep level. Moreover, as the name implies, the children's families are an integral part of the program. You are in a unique position to intimately know each child and family, including the home language and culture that defines those families. As such, bringing home languages and culture into the daily curriculum is a natural extension of the way the program operates. Work hand-in-hand with family members to ensure that there are books, signage, music, musical instruments, dance, dramatic play clothing and accessories, toys, manipulatives, and food experiences reflective of each child's background.

There are two big differences in setting up an FCC program that distinguish it from center-based programs. First, you are likely to serve a multi-age group of children. While some FCC providers only care for infants and toddlers or all preschoolers, it is most common for FCC homes to serve children in both groupings together, often with school-age children as well. This type of grouping brings additional challenges to your planning, as you have to meet the developmental needs of children of varying ages and skill levels.

The second big difference, of course, is that educators care for children in their homes. By homes, we mean any type of housing that a family child care educator lives in—be it a detached house, a townhouse, an apartment, a farmhouse, or military base housing. It may be a home that the family owns or rents.

What separates it from center-based care is that space is either shared or given over to the FCC program by family members who live in the residence full time. The size of the home and the educator's philosophy about family child care will determine how this space is allocated. And of course, the chosen space must be approved by the governing licensing agency, be it local, state, Head Start, or military.

Designing the Indoor Setting for Family Child Care

There are a number of approaches to setting up your home for family child care. As mentioned, you may use shared space, create a devoted space for FCC in your home, or use a combination approach. Whatever design plan you choose must stay in place once your licensing agency certifies your home.

Shared Space

Historically, the thought behind family child care was that care is most effective when it brings in the elements of a home. Children feel welcomed, valued, and safe when they are in a real home atmosphere. Accordingly, the setup of the indoor environment is based on the way the home itself is laid out. Reading books and playing with puzzles and other manipulatives takes place in the living room, making use of couches, comfy chairs, and rugs or carpeting. Likewise, block play is set up on the living room or family room floor. Writing and art as well as meals and snacks make use of the dining room table. School-age children can also use the kitchen or dining room table for doing homework. Cooking activities naturally occur in the family kitchen and snacks and meals at either the kitchen or dining room table. Naps take place in the bedrooms, making use of the family's beds. Cribs are set up in the bedrooms, as needed. Dramatic play might also takes place in a bedroom with clothing and dress-up props stored in a closet. Children enjoy water play at a kitchen or bathroom sink, standing on a secure step stool so they can reach the water. The family computer or tablet is used by the children where it is currently set up in the home, though a dedicated tablet for children in the program is preferred. Music is portable and movement and sand play are typically moved outdoors.

In a shared space setting, the children's activities are fully incorporated into the FCC home as it currently exists. However, because the provider's family lives in this same space when FCC is not in session, careful consideration needs to be given to how the FCC program can be balanced with the family's home life. To do this effectively, adjustments and creativity are needed. Consider the following as part of your layout and licensing plan:

- What rooms do you want to devote to your family child care program? Are there some rooms like your master bedroom that for privacy reasons you'd rather not open up to the children? Do you have a room that would be difficult to childproof, such as one with a fireplace that mobile infants or toddlers might be able to crawl into? Decide what rooms you want to keep off limits and plan to keep them locked or blocked off. Make sure that rooms that are open to FCC use are thoroughly childproofed.
- Where will you keep your family's personal items so that they feel that this is still their home? Your children may have toys or special keepsakes that they don't want to share with the FCC children. Your spouse likely has strong feelings as well that certain household items should be off-limits. Store these items on high shelves or in locked closets. Identifying these items ahead of time and finding an agreeable way to keep them private, will go a long way in keeping your family happy and supportive of having other children using their personal spaces.
- How will you arrange the rooms that you'll be using for Family Child Care? You will need to consider how to involve children in activities so they do not run around from place to place. Moving furniture and using rugs can be a solution to this issue.
- Where will children work on specific activities and participate in routines? While you do not need to establish actual learning centers, you can designate certain places in your home for learning center-type activities, such as drawing and writing at the dining room table and making a cozy reading area at the living room couch. If you care for babies, be sure to provide a protected floor space where they can safely move and explore.
- How will you display and store materials so children can use them independently, including children with disabilities? You might clear or set up some low shelves so children can choose what they need and return items at clean up time. A children's book rack would make a nice addition for your reading area and a child-size clothes tree could be used to hang smocks needed for painting or water play.
- How will you set up an entry area that is accessible to children and families with disabilities and encourage exchanges of information between yourself and family members at drop off and pick-up times? You might install hooks for children to hang coats and backpacks and a space for cubbies perhaps fashioned out of crates.
- Where can children be alone when they want to retreat from the action? You could create a private space in a corner or a space under the stairs where you can place soft cushions and books and balls to squeeze.
- Where might mildly ill children sit or lie down comfortably while waiting for a family member to pick them up? Consider setting up an inflatable or small mattress, blanket, or pillows in the corner of a room so you can keep an eye on the child, while still interacting with the other children.

The answers to these questions will enable you to create a design plan that meets the needs of your FCC goals, while respecting the fact that this is your own family's home. A sample floor plan that you can use for inspiration in drawing up your own indoor design appears as Figures 29 and 30.

Figure 29. Sample Family Child Care Setting: Shared Space

(Note: Children take naps in family bedrooms and use the family bathroom.)

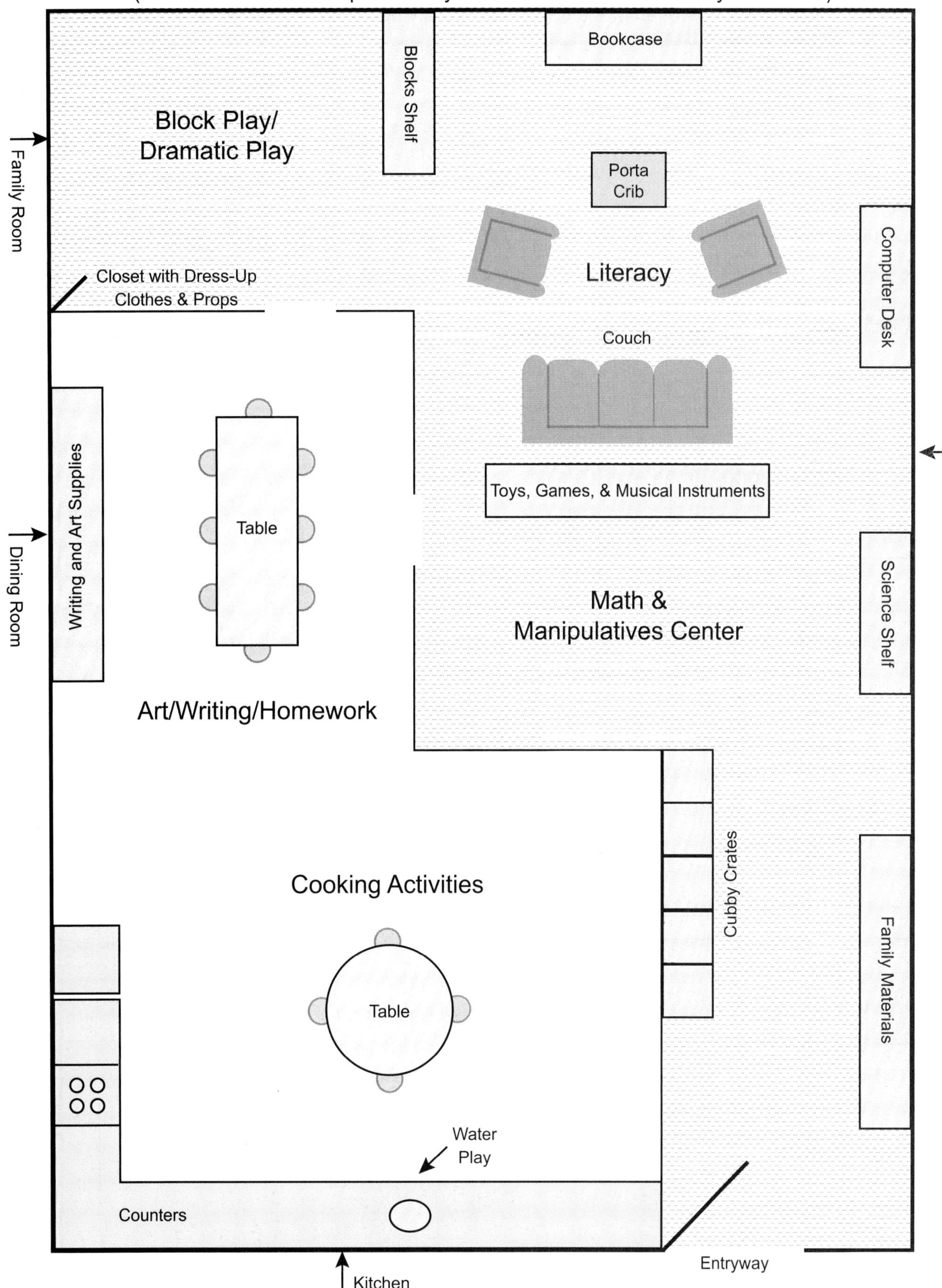

Figure 30. Sample Family Child Care Setting: Dedicated Space

(Note: Children cook in the family kitchen, nap in family bedrooms, and use family bathroom.)

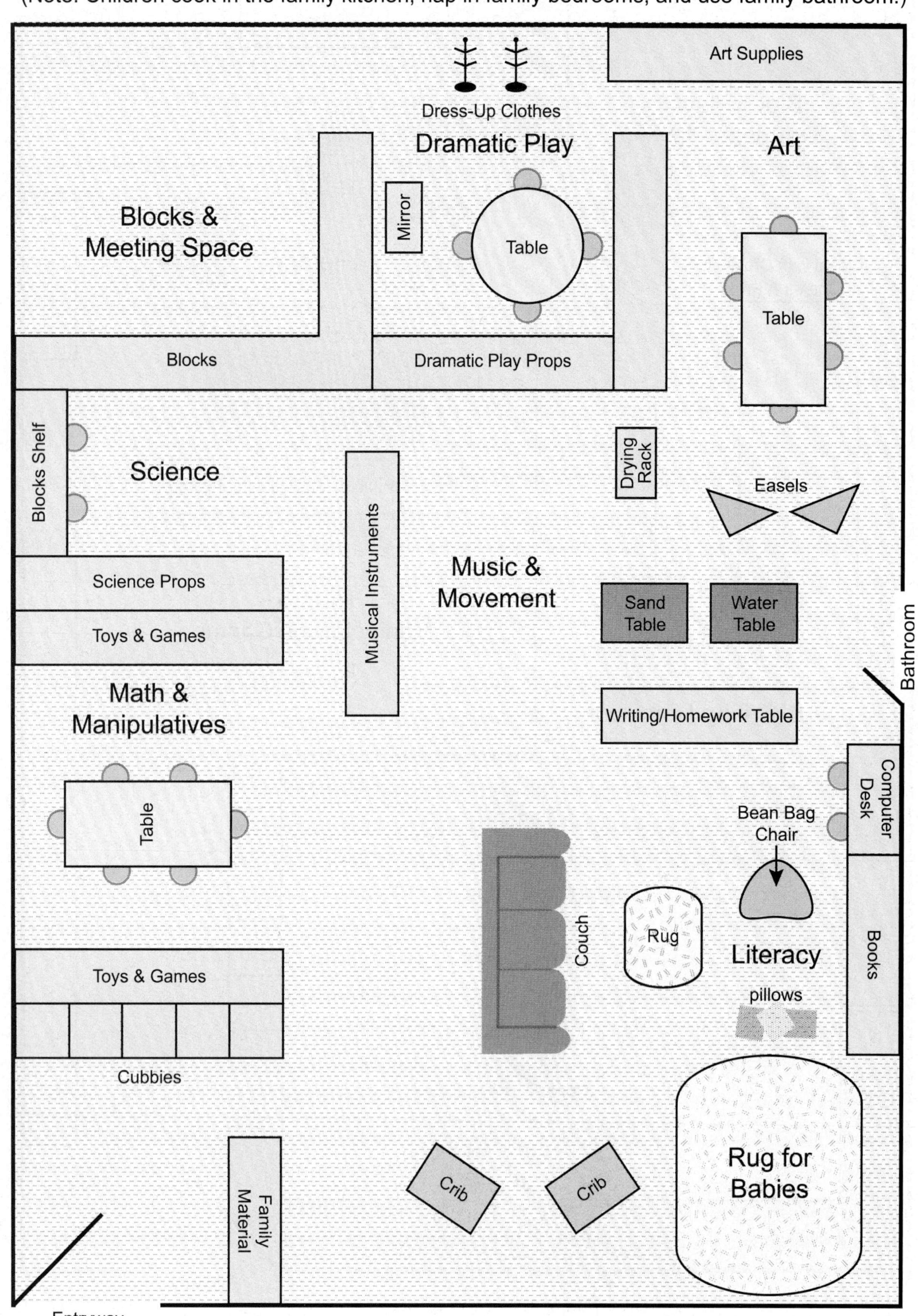

Making the Outdoors Fully Accessible

- Use ramps and inclines to enable children to maneuver the ground in a wheelchair
- Add grab bars to climbing structures
- Use bucket style swings with seat belts
- Provide pedal straps on wheeled riding toys
- Have picnic tables that a wheelchair can fit under for art, science, writing, and cooking/eating activities.

Dedicated Space

Some family child care providers prefer to dedicate an area of their home for their FCC program. Rather than incorporate the program into their own family's living space, they designate a specific room or rooms to the FCC program. Often a basement, recreation room, or large family room serves this purpose. While still bringing home-like touches into their arrangement, this set-up closely resembles that of a center-based program. The main difference is that if children of varying ages of development are in the program, the design must contain elements of center design for all ages served.

Because of the blending of ages, learning centers are usually more loosely defined than in a center setting. Rugs, furniture, and even tape can be used to define space and ensure that areas that need protection, such as a floor area for babies to sit and move or a construction area for preschoolers, are in fact blocked off. In setting up this area, keep these design principles in mind:

- Locate art, water, and cooking activities near a water source.
- House computers, tablet chargers, light tables, and kitchen appliances near power sources.
- Separate noisy areas and quiet areas.
- Divide space so that infants are protected and older children can engage in activities of their choosing.
- Include private spaces in the design.
- Designate spaces for school-age children to quietly do homework.
- Include child-size furnishings along with adult seating.

In some programs using this arrangement, all of the indoor program takes place in the dedicated room or rooms—including eating and napping. Other FCC homes follow a combination approach—that is, all of the activities take place in the designated area but routines such as eating and napping take place in the family's kitchen and bedroom respectively.

While there will be great variation among FCC homes, Figures 29 and 30 present sample designs. You can modify the designs to address the make-up of your home and the ages of the children in your care. Work closely with your licensing agent to determine which areas of your home are used for children and those that are not included in your license and off limits to children.

Designing the Outdoor Setting for Family Child Care

The outdoor play space for FCC homes will be as unique as the indoor design. It can range from the ideal—a large fenced-in backyard with naturally shaded areas—to none at all. The greatest challenge is to turn whatever currently exists into an outdoor play space where children can stretch their muscles and learn and develop. If you live in an apartment building or have no usable yard, you may need to depend on a nearby park or safe rooftop play area for your outdoor play space and augment the children's outdoor time with daily nature and neighborhood walks.

In selecting and setting up your outdoor space, the children's health and safety has to come first. Consider the following before determining how to refine the space to meet children's individual needs. An appropriate space must be:

- Fenced in with a lockable gate.
- Free of debris and potential dangers like wires or nails.
- Free of any potentially toxic plants, such as poison ivy or oak, mushrooms, and lily of the valley.
- Able to be shaded if natural shade does not exist.
- Large enough so that infants can be away from older children who might bump or accidentally hurt them.
- Large enough for mobile children to be able to creep, crawl, walk, run, jump, hop, skip, and gallop with abandon.
- Adjacent to a paved surface where children can ride tricycles and pull wagons.
- Equipped with safe and developmentally appropriate swings, slides, or climbers. There must be 6-foot fall zones around the equipment with shock-absorbent material underneath.
- Accessible to children with disabilities.

Once you have identified a suitable and safe outdoor space, the next step is to design it to foster learning for the ages and stages of the children in your program. The goal is for children to be able to experience the same types of learning activities they have indoors in an outdoor arena. Again, your design plan will be unique to the ages of the children in your program and the layout of the outdoor space you have available. Depending on the makeup of your group, consider the following options:

- A protected place for babies to have tummy time, sit, watch, and interact with you, other children, and nature.

- A grassy area where children can stretch their big muscles; push and pull toys; throw, catch, and kick balls; and play group games like Ring Around A Rosie or Hide and Seek.
- A protected driveway or asphalt surface where children can ride tricycles, big wheels, bicycles (for older children), or scooters, while wearing protective helmets.
- A place for gardening and growing fruits and vegetables that children can ultimately eat in snacks and cooking projects.
- A sandbox for digging.
- A wading pool filled with water for water play, for preschoolers and older children.
- A playhouse, tent, or old canoe for dramatic play.
- A picnic table for doing art, writing, and making and eating snacks.
- A space for making constructions out of hollow blocks or large cardboard boxes.

In many instances, the FCC program's outdoor play space is also a family's back yard. For this reason, it is not appropriate to carve it into formal learning centers. However, you can use plants and other landscaping techniques to alert children to particular play areas. What you want to avoid is having children run wild through the yard—especially if younger children could be accidentally bumped by vigorous play. Set up different areas in the yard where children can become involved in play activities. As always, try to group quiet activities apart from louder, more boisterous ones. The child who wants to read a book alone under a tree needs to be able to do so uninterrupted while her friends are laughing loudly on the swings.

Selecting Appropriate Materials

The materials in your setting should be age, individually, and culturally appropriate for the children in the group (Copple and Bredekamp 2009). They also need to be safe and engage children in play, exploration, and learning. Select toys and materials that invite children to participate. This kind of active learning supports children's social, emotional, cognitive, physical, and language development.

In addition to having materials that match the children's ages and stages of development, include items that support a range of abilities. This means you will offer materials appropriate for children six months younger than the youngest child in the group through six months older than the oldest child in your setting. For example, if the youngest child is 18 months old and the oldest child is four years old, make sure there are materials considered appropriate for children from 12 months to four-and-a-half years old. This range affords children opportunities to play comfortably with familiar items as well as be challenged by new ones.

The children in any early childhood setting are likely to have a variety of interests and skills. For example, one preschool classroom includes Tameka, who can count more than 20 objects accurately and struggles to write her name. Malcolm is interested in postal workers and the process of sending and receiving mail. Rochelle loves cars and can identify makes and models effortlessly. Think about how you can select toys and materials that will engage all of the children like Tameka, Malcolm, and Rochelle in your program.

There may be children in your group who have disabilities or delays. Talk with the children's families and their special education or early intervention teams to determine what adaptations would help to ensure the child's full participation. You may need to research the types of adaptive materials and resources that are available so all children can learn and play independently. For example, for a child with manual dexterity problems, include larger materials and toys that he can grasp more easily. Some with visual impairments are more able to read books with larger print. Likewise, enlarging the windows on computer screens will make the illustrations and print more visible.

Educators can also modify materials so that they are easier for children to use. For example, attach padding to the handles of flatware so that children with manual dexterity problems can eat independently. Or add different fragrances to paints so that children with vision problems can distinguish colors by smelling them. Always meet with children's parents and intervention teams to determine what adaptations would be helpful to address children's particular needs.

It's also important to include materials and print that introduce and expose dual language learners to both their home languages and the other language(s) they are learning—usually English. Look for children's books published in both English and the children's home languages. Display these books in your program's reading area or literacy center. Include books in the child's home language and/or bilingual books in construction areas where children play with blocks. In the art area, bring in bilingual books and/or books in the child's home language about artists and painting techniques. Likewise, for the music area, include books on composers and musical instruments. So too, when selecting music, choose music and audio recordings that are sung or spoken in the children's home languages, as well as in English. Invite family members to visit the program where they can talk with children, record songs and books, and help hang signage and labels in the language spoken in the classroom and in children's home languages.

Early childhood materials should not only address children's language backgrounds, but should also reflect their individual cultures and heritages. Culture and heritage refer to the way we eat, sleep, talk, pray, play, and value things and concepts. You help children identify with race, ethnicity, and customs daily through the music, books, dolls, games, toys, and other materials you provide as well as the foods you prepare and serve. This sends children the vital message that their cultures are an important part of your learning community every day—not just during holidays and special occasions. For additional ideas about introducing young children to the reality of our world's diversity see books like, *What If All the Kids Are White?: Anti-Bias*

Multicultural Education with Young Children and Families 2nd. Ed. by Louise Derman-Sparks and Patricia G. Ramsey, with Julie Olsen Edwards and *Anti-Bias Education for Young Children and Ourselves*, by Louise Derman-Sparks and Julie Olsen Edwards.

Display materials for children so that they can retrieve and return these items independently.

Though usually well-intentioned, the text, characters, and illustrations in children's books sometimes reinforce stereotypes. A stereotype is a generalization about a particular group, race, or gender. These stereotypes can be subtle. Does the mother in a storybook stay home while the dad works? Do heroes tend to be only white men? Do grandparents do anything other than dote on children?

When searching for books and other materials for your program think about the messages they convey. Choose materials that defy stereotypes. For example, does the story feature a female construction worker, an overweight child who is popular, or a child of color who stands up to a bully. Look for illustrations of characters who have distinct, not exaggerated facial features and who wear clothing that represents their everyday appearances instead of costumes worn only for celebrations.

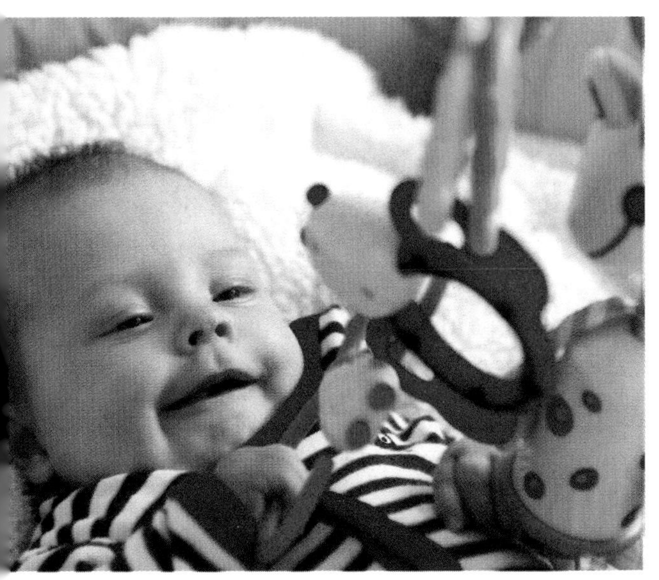

Provide infants materials with bright or contrasting colors and interesting shapes and designs.

Of course, you want to expose children to classic books and stories that are not always sensitive to bias. However, when children are old enough to understand, make sure they are aware of the bias when you read these stories with them. Discuss how this story does not reflect what we think about racial, age, or gender roles today, nor the way we view people with disabilities.

See Figure 31 for a checklist that will help you check for biases in children's books and materials.

Figure 31. Eight Quick Ways to Analyze Children's Books (and Other Materials) for Biases

Preview books and other materials before including them in your setting. Some children's books or materials may unintentionally promote biases—including racism, sexism, ageism, ableism, and homophobia. In your review, consider the following:

- ☐ **Check the illustrations and text for stereotypes of various ethnic/racial groups.** Do characters of a particular ethnic or racial group have overly exaggerated features? Also, be wary of "token" illustrations in which all African Americans and Hispanics appear as dark-skinned people with Caucasian facial features.
- ☐ **Check the plot.** Examine the roles of the women and men in the story. Are men active and women passive? Do the White characters help resolve the non-White characters' problems? Do seniors need to be cared for? Do people with disabilities appear helpless? Was the book written to promote a particular religion or belief system? (This would be appropriate, however, in faith-based programs.)
- ☐ **Look at the characters' lifestyles.** Do people of color only live in ghettos, barrios, or migrant camps? Are some people always wearing traditional clothing? Are elderly people only in nursing homes? Are families only headed by both a mother and a father?
- ☐ **Consider the relationships among the characters.** Do only the White characters possess power and show leadership? Do only men take charge and solve family problems?
- ☐ **Note the heroes and heroines.** Do non-White heroes exhibit the same positive qualities as White heroes? Are they admired for the same attributes? Do only boys perform brave and important deeds? Are heroes all young, handsome, and strong men? Are there powerful female heroes?
- ☐ **Consider the effects on a child's self-image.** Are there positive characters children can identify with, including people of color, girls, children with diverse family makeups, and people with disabilities?
- ☐ **Watch for loaded words.** These are words or phrases with insulting or historically negative overtones, like *savage, primitive, conniving, superstitious, treacherous, wily, crafty, lazy, Indian giver, sit Indian-style,* and *oriental* (when used to describe a human being). In addition, a word may assume a different meaning when used with a different audience. *Ambitious*, for example, is a complimentary term to describe a man, but is often less than complimentary when used to describe a woman.
- ☐ **Check the copyright date.** Recent books, maps, or posters are more likely to mirror our diverse world and the lives of the children and families in your setting. Do not disregard classic books and fairy tales, but know that some materials with earlier copyright dates may not reflect today's diversity *(Derman-Sparks and Edwards 2010).*

Materials should positively reflect the lives of the children in the program. Children's racial identities and home languages should be promoted in books, stories, songs, block area prompts, dramatic play materials, art, and music.

Stocking Your Setting with Materials for Each Age Group

Intentional early childhood educators look for materials that will promote children's development and learning and encourage further progress. The goal is not to amass all the materials you can. Rather, thoughtfully choose items that will contribute to children's social, emotional, cognitive, language, and physical progress, including children with disabilities.

Consider the children in your setting and apply what you know about the developmental and individual characteristics of the children and how they think, learn, and behave. The sections that follow provide guidelines for each age group to help you select appropriate toys and materials for your center or FCC home. However, it's important to consider that children with disabilities may develop on a different timetable than other children, with some abilities developing sooner and some later.

Young infants (birth–8 months). The youngest babies are not yet mobile, so they look, listen, and rely on you to change their scenery and their access to play materials. Toys and materials for this age group should stimulate their senses, appeal to their developing self-awareness, and produce effects when manipulated. Look for these attributes when selecting toys and materials for young infants:

Provide materials that help children balance, rock, and climb.

- Bright or contrasting colors (e.g., grasping toys, hand puppets [held by adults], and wall hangings).
- Interesting shapes and designs (e.g., mobiles and floor play gyms).
- Movable parts (e.g., jack-in-the-box, plastic discs on a ring, interlocking rings, and pop beads).
- Shiny, reflective surfaces (e.g., unbreakable mirrors hung in a crib or on the wall next to the changing table).
- Noisy parts (e.g., rattles, wrist and ankle bells, pots and pans, music boxes, and squeaky toys).
- Tactile surfaces (e.g., texture balls, and washable rag dolls).
- Large "chewable" materials that children cannot swallow (e.g., washable soft animals and cloth books).

Mobile infants (8–17 months). Besides creeping, crawling, and walking, mobile infants' receptive and productive language skills are growing and they can increasingly use their hands to make things happen. Materials for this age group should invite exploration and experimentation and be self-rewarding. Look for items the help children master age-appropriate developmental tasks such as the following:

- Crawling over, under, and through (e.g., low, softly padded climbing platforms, tunnels, and empty boxes).
- Walking with assistance (e.g., push and pull toys like shopping carts, strollers, and lawn mowers).
- Throwing (e.g., clutch and texture balls, flutter balls, and chime balls).
- Developing fine motor skills (e.g., jumbo markers, maracas, puzzles with two to four knobbed pieces, puppets, stacking toys, and drop objects on string,)
- Scribbling and noticing print (e.g., large crayons or watercolor markers and large pieces of paper, small books [cloth, plastic, board]).
- Trying out familiar roles (e.g., phones, dolls with ethnic features and skin colors, cradles, dishes and pitchers, purses and tote bags, and steering wheels).
- Solving problems (e.g., nesting baskets, activity baskets, texture pads, stacking ring cones).

Younger toddlers (18–24 months). Toddlers are active in every way. In addition to walking, kicking, and throwing, they like to push and pull. They also like to dump, pull, pile, and knock down most anything. They are becoming increasingly independent and like to play alone or with adults. Toys and materials for this age group should promote development of the following skills:

- Dumping and refilling (e.g., buckets of spools or beads, different size containers, and pieces that can be placed inside; toy dump trucks).
- Pushing, pulling, riding (e.g., push/pull toys with multiple objects, doll carriages, wagons, shopping carts, large trucks and steerable ride-on vehicles).
- Constructing (e.g., large blocks made of cloth, rubber, or plastic, wooden unit blocks, large plastic interlocking bricks).
- Honing fine motor skills (e.g., spools or beads to string, blunt-end scissors, wide brushes for use at easels, watercolor markers, sturdy crayons, puppets, transportation toys, grasping toys, simple 3-5 piece puzzles with knobs, activity boxes, matching board games, board books, and musical instruments).
- Pretending (e.g., dress-up clothing and accessories, medical props, baby care items, play food and appliances, dolls, small realistic vehicles, and rubber animals).

Older toddlers (24–36 months). Two-year-olds are energy in action and can do many large muscle activities. At this age children typically play alone or with one or two other children and are just beginning to learn how to share and take turns. They are curious, learning more about language and numbers and want to be independent—most of the time. Materials for older toddlers allow them to develop these skills:

- Practicing and gaining new fine motor skills (e.g., pegboards with large pegs, matching and sorting toys, chalk and chalkboard, watercolor markers, tempera paint and brushes and large sheets of paper, blunt-end scissors, playdough and tools, finger paints, paste, and glue).
- Using numbers and letters in real situations (e.g., picture books, fit in puzzles, lotto games, giant dominoes, matching and sorting games, watercolor markers and paper, magnetic letters and numbers).
- Running, jumping, pushing, pulling, galloping, and riding (e.g., balls, tricycles, large cardboard blocks, ride-on vehicles, foot-propelled trucks, obstacle courses, and climbers).
- Playing make-believe (e.g., dress-up clothing and accessories, full length unbreakable mirror, dolls, child-size housekeeping furniture, housekeeping equipment like toy vacuum cleaner, wood/plastic/rubber people and animal figures, puppets, and other items like those found in the children's homes or related to a theme or study topic).
- Exploring cause and effect (e.g., sand and water props such as scoops, funnels, and cups; toys that come apart, latch, open, and/or close; rhythm sticks, drums, tambourines; and construction sets with large pieces).

Preschoolers (3–5 years old). Preschoolers' play is more sophisticated, complex, and social. Materials for preschoolers should support the following developmental tasks:

- Becoming independent (e.g., materials and games that they can use and play with alone, such as puzzles, balance scales, lock boxes, magnifying glass and collections).
- Devising and implementing plans (e.g., blocks with blueprints for building towers, bridges, airports and cities; using recipes, kitchen utensils, and gadgets to prepare snacks and meals; puppets for creating puppet shows; and books that they can reenact).

Provide opportunities for children to cooperate with others.

- Engaging in cooperative play (e.g., board games, lotto, plastic interlocking building bricks; wooden unit blocks and props, musical instruments; balls and large bats; toy food items; toy utensils and dishware).
- Learning literacy and math content (e.g., books and magazines, flannel boards with letters and numbers, magnetic letters and numbers and boards, writing implements and paper, reading and writing software, recipe cards, parquetry boards, counting puzzles, dominoes, and magnetic tiles).
- Experimenting with science (e.g., materials for making volcanoes and tornadoes in a bottle; magnifying glasses, prisms, and collections of natural objects; graph-making materials; and an ant farm or fish aquarium to observe).
- Learning about themselves and others (e.g. dress-up clothes representing genders, occupations, and cultures, books like *Bread, Bread, Bread* [Around the World Series] by Ann Morris; music like *Multicultural Children's Songs* by Ella Jenkins; instruments from around the world, like a Russian balalaika or a djembe drum from Africa; and ingredients and appliances for cooking Jewish latkes or Greek tzatziki).
- Engaging in complex dramatic play roles and scenarios (e.g., prop boxes to create additional dramatic play scenes, such as a doctor/vet office, beach, school, or store).
- Refining gross motor skills (e.g., balls, tricycles, swings, slides, climbers, parachutes, and tunnels).
- Refining fine motor skills (e.g., beads for stringing, writing tools, safety scissors and collage materials, drawing tools, painting tools, musical instruments to play, and puzzles).

In addition to creating an inventory of toys and materials for each age group that you serve, review the collection to be sure that you have offered a balanced array of items. Your inventory should allow children to engage in the following:

- small and large muscle activities
- quiet and exuberant learning experiences
- messy and neat kinds of play
- close-ended (forced choices, such as puzzles) and open-ended (unlimited possibilities, such as crayons) play opportunities

Organizing Materials

No matter the age group served by your program or the age make-up of each group, there are standard principles for effective display and storage of toys and materials. Keep these recommendations in mind when organizing the toys and materials.

Locate materials in the area where they will be most frequently used. For example, in an infant room, place a basket of books next to the rocking chair where you read with one or two older babies. Think about using baskets from other countries that reflect the culture of the children. In a preschool room, learning centers offer natural groupings. Art materials go in the art center and books go in the literacy area. In an FCC home, art projects might take place in the kitchen, so you would keep art supplies on an open shelf in the pantry and books could go in shared space, such as a bookshelf or book basket near the living room couch.

Decide how many materials to make available at one time. Seldom would you offer every toy and game at any one time. For one thing, it is important to display materials in a neat and inviting way. In addition, young children can be easily overwhelmed by too many choices. It makes good sense to start out the year with fewer choices and add to or rotate your inventory to meet children's growing skills and changing interests.

Provide duplicates of favorite toys and materials for children of all ages. This will prevent the problems that arise when children are not developmentally ready to share and take turns and it can encourage cooperative play, as when two firefighters are needed to save the kitty that climbed up the tree.

Display materials so children can retrieve and return these items independently. Typically, this is accomplished by using low shelving so children can easily reach what they need.

Group materials by function. For example, store all plastic and rubber figures in a clear, plastic container on a shelf in the block center. Store larger items, like puppets and stuffed animals, in baskets placed on the floor or on a shelf. Store toys with small parts in plastic containers labeled with pictures and words.

Group wooden unit blocks by size and shape and store on low, open shelves. Label the block shelves by using solid-colored adhesive paper to create the block shapes. Place the shape on the shelf where the block pieces are stored so children can retrieve and return blocks independently.

Label all storage containers and items stored on shelving. Use a written label and a photo (or picture from a toy catalog) of the items inside. (Laminate all labels.) This helps children begin to associate words with pictures. Print the written labels as words appear in books with an initial capital letter and the remaining letters in lower case. (It is difficult for pre-readers to recognize words written in all capital letters.)

Write labels in the language spoken in your setting and the home languages of each child. Assign each language a different color to help children differentiate them (Nemeth 2012). For example, designate the color blue for Spanish or the color green for French. Place a blue sticker on Spanish CDs, books, puzzles, games, and menus/food containers in the dramatic play area and green stickers on the French materials.

Planning Curricula for Young Children

In this chapter, you have discovered that children learn best through play. Your setting is a learning environment that lays the foundation for children's development and learning. A more structured approach to laying that foundation—beyond your indoor and outdoor settings, the people in them, and the materials—involves planning and delivering a curriculum. Copple and Bredekamp (2009, 20) say that "the curriculum consists of the knowledge, skills, abilities, and understandings children are to acquire and the plans for the learning experiences through which those gains will occur."

Your program may choose to deliver one of the well-known established early childhood curricula. These include Montessori, HighScope (versions for infants and toddlers and for preschoolers), Tools of the Mind (preschoolers), and The Creative Curriculum (versions for infants and toddlers, preschoolers, and family child care). Many of these approaches are founded upon the work of theorists like Jean Piaget, Lev Vygotsky, and Maria Montessori—whom you will learn more about in Chapter 5—and the concept of engaging children in hands-on play and learning. The curriculum implemented in your setting should match the program's overall early childhood education philosophy and mission.

To implement a curriculum effectively, it is essential to be completely familiar with it. The curriculum is the framework for your teaching, and allows you to make intentional decisions about the environment, activities, experiences, interactions, and more. If you have not received training to deliver this curriculum, ask your supervisor to help you learn to implement it successfully. An appropriate early childhood curriculum clearly aligns with domains of learning and your state's early learning standards. In determining how to implement the methods, approaches, and/or strategies to help young children learn, consider the following:

- Familiarize yourself with the curriculum's goals for children's learning and development, as well as the materials, experiences, and teaching strategies that you can use to help children to achieve these goals.
- Use the curriculum to support all children, their families, their cultures, and their home languages. Appreciate and plan for individual differences. Use the curriculum as a springboard for building relationships.
- Choose learning experiences and teaching strategies that help children reach curriculum goals.
- Observe and listen to children when they express their interests and share their ideas. Keep track of their progress—both efforts and accomplishments.
- Ask: What are children learning through these experiences and activities? How can we build on their learning? What additional materials and experiences will enhance their learning? How can I extend children's learning to a higher level?
- Encourage children to ask questions, experiment, and research information independently. Pose questions that will spark children's inquiries.

- Ask lots of open-ended questions that stretch children's minds (What would happen if…? or Why did this…?) rather than questions that have one correct answer and stifle thought.
- Encourage children's creativity and provide many open-ended opportunities. Avoid models, coloring books, worksheets, and patterns. Invite children to create original artwork, stories, and ideas.
- Provide real, hands-on experiences. For example, provide a basket of buttons to sort, categorize, and count rather than pencil and paper worksheets.
- Ensure that children are spending more time doing and learning versus watching and copying an adult's actions. Ensure that children spend most of the day doing child-directed activities so they learn to make choices and solve problems.
- Help children learn to appreciate beauty and diversity in the world around them (art, nature, music, and literature) through daily, culturally authentic activities.
- Support something more interesting when it diverts children's attention from a current activity. Offer new materials, interactions, and encouragement.
- Present activities with enthusiasm to build children's interest and curiosity. Exhibit a playful, cheerful attitude. Model being a learner.
- Treat children and their work with respect and interest. Instead of asking, "What is it?" engage children in conversation about their work and play. "Tell me about your . . . "
- View every minute of the day as a learning opportunity. Seize the teachable moment.

Developing the Daily Schedule

A daily schedule tells the adults and the children in a program what they will be doing at various times of the day. The schedule shows when routines and transitions are likely to take place, when there will be individual, large, and small group activities, and approximately when each event will begin and end. The schedule lists events in order. This is very important for young children who thrive on predictability. They feel more secure and gain a sense of control as they learn how a typical day will proceed. The schedule is the framework for your planning and children's development and learning.

Observing and learning each child's interests, skills, knowledge, and attitudes is paramount to creating daily schedules that meet their specific needs. Also, it is important to regularly review and reflect on your documentation of the children's experiences—including the time they spend in routines and transitions, playing indoors and outdoors, and engaging in small and large group activities. Ask: How did these experiences promote development and learning? How long did the children choose to remain engaged? What did the children learn? Were they interested? Then ask, what did I learn from these experiences? What will I do next based on these experiences? The answers to these specific questions will help you increase the effectiveness of planned routines, transitions, and activities—all parts of a schedule for young children.

Routines

In early childhood settings, routines—including arrival and departure, dressing and undressing, mealtimes, handwashing, toileting, and napping—are opportunities for children to learn. There is no need to hurry through these events as they are important opportunities to build relationships with individual children—particularly infants and toddlers—and times when older children build self-help and academic skills. Educators can show children how to put on their coats, pull off their socks, hold a diaper, button their sweaters, or fasten the Velcro straps on their shoes. Allow them to practice pumping soap to wash their hands and setting the table for meals. When four-year-old Delia places one placemat on the table in front of each chair, she is learning one-to-one correspondence. Or when you lead a discussion during the meal about how eating carrots protects our eyesight, toddlers learn life science. Remember that routines are chances for children to learn life skills, increase content knowledge, and build self-esteem.

Transitions

Transitions are the times between events and activities. It is important that children are not forced to wait idly during transitions. Early childhood educators can plan ways to keep children engaged while they shift from one activity or setting to the next. To achieve this goal, incorporate transitions into your routines and activities. Sing songs, play games, and keep children engaged while you help toddlers put their shoes on after naptime or walk like different animals on the way to the playground. If the preschoolers still have a few minutes of inside choice time and need to use the bathroom before outside choice time, take a few children at a time to the bathroom while the rest continue to play (make sure you are maintaining licensing ratios). This strategy keeps children engaged while they wait for their turn in the bathroom. Or appoint a few children to work with a staff member or family volunteer to prepare for lunch while you read a board book aloud to the rest of the children. Another staff member can take a few children at a time to wash their hands. Again, these strategies keep the children engaged until they sit down for lunch.

Here are tips for incorporating smooth transitions into your daily routines:

- **Give children a 5-minute warning before a transition occurs.** For example, hearing the familiar sound of a soft chime lets children know when it is time to return their toys and materials to the shelves and prepare for another activity. Give additional, whispered time-warnings to children who have difficulty with transitions.
- **Turn the transition into a learning activity.** For example, announce, "All children whose names begin with an S sound may go put on their coats to go outside," or "Everyone who has a birthday in the summer may go wash their hands now."
- **Convert the transition into a game.** For example, announce, "Let's all go outside hopping like kangaroos," or "Let's do the chicken dance to our cubbies to put away our jackets." Other ideas include singing cleanup songs or having children count the steps it takes to put on their coats.

- **Allow children to leave out their work for future play.** If Hector is in the middle of building an elaborate block construction or creating an art project, let him leave out the work so that he can finish it at a later time. Help him make a *Building in Progress* or *Please Do Not Touch* sign to protect the work from others
- **Avoid completing transitions as a full group.** Small group transitions ensure that children remain occupied while they wait.

Choice Time

During indoor and outdoor choice times, toddlers and preschoolers can select which activities are of most interest to them and with whom they want to play. Early childhood educators observe children's play, discuss with them what they see and hear (when appropriate), and ask open-ended questions that will expand their thinking and take it in new directions. Interact with all children individually so you can get better acquainted with them. Be nurturing, enthusiastic, playful, and respectful. Children should be able to express themselves to you openly while viewing you as an authority and a role model.

Supporting Learning During Choice Time

Ms. Bennett is observing Yan in the block center. Yan has built his tower several times, but it keeps collapsing. After several tries, he says, "I don't like these blocks."

Ms. Bennett: *"What is it that you don't like about the blocks, Yan?"*

Yan: *"They don't work. They keep falling."*

Ms. Bennett: *"Let's take a look at the blocks and see if we can understand why they fall. Will you make another tower, so we can watch what happens together?"*

Yan and Ms. Bennett count blocks as Yan stacks four of them. When he adds the fifth block, the tower falls.

Yan: *"I can only make a tower of four blocks."*

Ms. Bennett: *"True. We know that four blocks make a sturdy tower. But what if you wanted a higher tower?"*

Yan: *"I can't do that, Ms. Bennett. It'll fall. The blocks are too skinny to stand."*

Ms. Bennett: *"I think you're on to something, Yan. What could you do to make a fatter base? A fatter base might just hold a fifth block."*

Yan: *"Um…I could put two blocks at the bottom."*

Ms. Bennett: *"That's an interesting idea. Let's try that now!"*

Group Meetings and Small Group Times

These sessions—also referred to as "circle time"—assemble the entire group to start the day, recap the day's learning, or participate in an activity, such as a finger play or an introduction to new equipment. However, in center-based programs, not every child can or will participate in a group meeting. Offer an alternative activity, supervised by one teacher, for children who are upset, ill, unable, or do not want to sit to remain with the group. Ensure this alternative activity is not perceived as punitive. If children wander regularly during this particular session, evaluate whether the activity or information you are presenting is engaging and developmentally appropriate.

On the other hand, small group times allow you and other educators to engage more deeply with a few children at a time, working on specific skills or knowledge. This may occur during choice time. For example, a group of children in your setting may have difficulty using scissors. Invite these children to work with you in the art area. Guide them in using scissors as a group or individually.

The following sections present sample daily schedules for infants, toddlers, and preschoolers and for children in a family child care home. Use these sample schedules as a starting point. Compare them to the schedule you currently follow. You may need to plan for special activities (such as visits from specialists) or your setting may operate for different hours than presented here. Adjust your schedules accordingly. For example, in a half-day program, the schedule would omit lunch, nap, and afternoon activities, and end with the closing meeting and departure.

An Infant Room Schedule (2 to 18 months)

For young infants, much of the day is taken up with routines—sleeping, eating, and diapering, and by arrival and departure times when families and staff exchange important information about the child. Therefore, an infant room schedule should be flexible so as to accommodate each baby's personal rhythms for eating, sleeping, and diapering and to allow early childhood educators to respond to needs with prompt and consistent care. Flexibility also allows educators to give infants their full attention during routines and use them as opportunities to build relationships with individual babies, support development and learning, and, as the infants gets older, involve the child in the routine. Throughout the day, educators are talking with infants, describing what they and the child are doing, pointing out interesting things indoors and outdoors, and encouraging the infant to respond with coos and gurgles.

Older infants spend less time engaged in routines, and therefore have more time for play—usually with an early childhood educator and sometimes alongside another baby. They too need a flexible schedule that allows for planned activities and responding spontaneously to interests and needs. They are also likely to begin self-feeding. This means that they may need additional time for snacks and meals.

Figure 32. Sample Daily Schedule for Infants*

Time	Activity
8:00–9:00 AM	Arrival
8:00–9:15	Play/lap book reading
8:00–10:00	Diapering/bottles
8:30–11:00	Naps/individual play/diapering
10:30–12:00	Outdoor walk/play
11:30–1:00	Diapering/lunch/mid-day bottles
12:30–2:30 PM	Naps/individual play/diapering
2:00–4:00	Bottles/outdoor play/diapering
3:00–5:00	Naps/songs/lap book reading/play/diapering
4:30–6:00	Play/bottles/leave

*Notice the extended time from 8:00 a.m.–11:00 a.m. allotted for infants' diapering, feeding, napping, and individual play. Infants have unique needs, so follow their individual schedules. Also infants should spend most of their day at play. They want to move, vary their scenery, and get involved with what is happening around them. Push younger infants in their strollers outside. Allow mobile infants plenty of time and space to crawl and walk.

A Toddler Room Schedule (18 to 36 months)

Rigid time restrictions may frustrate toddlers. Plan how you can help them transition from one activity to another in your schedule. For example, it is helpful to give a child a signal (like singing a particular song) that it is nap time.

Structure your daily schedule for toddlers so that they are engaged and moving during the day. Give these children your individual attention. Have lots of conversations with all children, and include their home languages. Greet each child personally, talk throughout the day about what you and the child are doing, thinking, and feeling, and say goodbye at the end of the day. Small group times provide opportunities for interactions that address developmental skills at the child's individual level.

Figure 33. Sample Daily Schedule for Toddlers*

Time	Activity
7:30–8:30 AM	Arrival
8:30–9:15	Diapering and toileting
7:30–10:15	Individual and group activities
10:15–11:00	Outdoor play
10:45–11:00	Diapering and toileting
11:00–11:30	Lunch
11:30–12:00	Diapering, washing up, tooth brushing, singing
12:00–2:30 PM	Nap time
1:30–2:30	Individual and group activities
2:30–3:00	Self-initiated snack
2:00–3:00	Diapering and toileting
3:00–4:00	Outdoor play
4:00–4:30	Diapering and toileting
4:00–5:30	Individual activities, story reading, departure

*Group activities hold a toddler's attention for no more than 5 min. They need to be active, so expect them to spend little time in one place or on one activity—unless it is extremely engaging. Rather, offer a variety of activities. For example, some children might blow bubbles while others play in the sandbox.

A Preschool Room Schedule (3 to 5-year-olds)

As for other age groups, a well-planned daily schedule for preschoolers reflects the children's individual and developmental characteristics. Consider the children's needs, interests, and skills when allocating time to each activity. For example, most preschoolers require 40–45 minutes to become fully involved in an activity, so plan for at least one-hour for self-selected activities in learning centers. Include outdoor activities (lasting 45 minutes to 1 hour) in the daily schedule during both morning and afternoon, following periods where children have engaged in less active indoor activity. Keep large group activities (such as the morning meeting) to 15–20 minutes. Begin the year with shorter meetings (10 minutes), and then lengthen the meeting gradually during the year.

Work to achieve a balance in your daily schedule. Plan for both child-initiated and teacher-directed learning; alternate quiet times with active times; sequence outdoor play to follow indoor play or naps; and plan for individual, small group, and full group activities.

Because preschool children are aware of the daily sequence, post a picture version of the schedule at their eye level. Use photographs or illustrations to represent different daily events. Also, post a written schedule for all adults—including staff, visitors, parents, and volunteers. Note periods of the day, from the setting's opening in the morning to the children's departure in the evening, on this schedule.

Figure 34a. Sample Daily Schedule for Preschoolers*

Time	Event	How Educators** Support the Children
8:00–8:30 AM (30 min)	**Planning Time**	• Meet with colleagues to review day's plans before the children arrive. • Conduct daily health and safety checks. (See Chapters 1 and 2 of your Essentials textbook for more information.) • Ensure breakfast foods and all necessary materials are ready for children.
8:30–9:00 (30 min)	**Arrival.** Families and children enter the setting. Children can serve themselves healthy breakfast foods. Quiet centers, such as the math & manipulatives and literacy centers, are open.	• Greet families and children individually. • Exchange information with families. • Help children store belongings and select an activity, such as "writing" in their journals or reading books.
9:00–9:15 (15 min)	**Group Meeting.** Discuss what the children and educators did the night before or over the weekend. Take attendance (ask children to count who is present and absent). Assign helper jobs for the day. Read a story aloud or introduce songs and finger plays. Review the daily schedule and ask children to predict what activity comes next. Complete a shared reading, choral reading, song, or group writing activity related to current concepts and studies.	• Introduce group meeting and encourage children's participation. • Lead activities, for example counting and word-sound. Note: Assigned staff do activities with individual children who are not yet ready for large group activities.
9:15–10:15 (1 hour)	**Indoor Choice Time.** Children select a center and/or a small group activity. Children may explore materials or concepts introduced at the group meeting. At end of choice time, all children clean up and put on jackets, if needed, for going outdoors.	• Observe and interact with individual children in ways that extend play and learning. • Lead a small-group activity to build on children's skills and interests and/or is related to the current project study. • Encourage children to clean up; help them as needed. • Help children who are not quite finished to save a project or give them extra time to complete their play.
10:15–10:30 (15 min)	**Small group time.** Children work in small groups with educators on specific literacy, science, or math activities, that are engaging and interesting to children and will support development of skills and learning.	• Select developmentally appropriate activities that you and other early educators in your setting can work on with small groups, like cooking experiences or math games. • Document children's progress as related to relevant early learning standards.

Figure 34b. Sample Daily Schedule for Preschoolers*

Time	Event	How Educators** Support the Children
10:15–11:00 (45 min)	**Outdoor Choice Time.** Children select an activity, like playing on swings, climbers, and slides; riding tricycles; or playing ball games. Some children do quiet activities such as reading a book, drawing with sidewalk chalk, or tending a garden.	• Supervise play on equipment. Interact individually with children, engaging in conversations and asking open-ended questions. • Lead small group activities such as weeding the garden, woodworking, or blowing bubbles.
11:15–11:30 (15 min)	**Story/Lunch Preparation.** Children store their jackets. Children use toilet and wash hands in small groups. Educator reads aloud to the children, while selected helpers work with staff and family volunteers to set tables for lunch.	• Read a story using props. • Help children setting the table with placemats, dishes, glasses, flatware, and napkins. • Fill serving dishes and bowls with food and place on tables with serving utensils. • Supervise children as they use the bathroom.
11:30–12:15 (45 min)	**Lunch.** Children and adults enjoy a family-style meal together. After eating, children clear their dishes, wash hands, brush teeth, and get cots/mats for nap time. Every child has enough time to finish eating at their own pace.	• Help children settle in for lunch. • Sit with children and encourage conversations about nutrition and topics of interest to the children. • Guide children in eating, cleaning up, washing hands, brushing teeth, and preparing for nap time. • Help children set out cots/mats.
12:15–1:45 PM (1½ hour)	**Nap Time.** Children sleep or rest quietly on cots/mats. Nonsleepers have books, puzzles, or other small items to play with quietly.	• Help children relax, if needed, by rubbing backs, singing softly, and playing soft music to help children fall asleep. • Use this time for breaks and planning (once children are settled).
1:45–2:45 (1 hour)	**Indoor Child Choice.** Children wake up, put away mats or cots, use the bathroom, and wash their hands. Children choose a learning activity or conduct small-group investigations as part of project work. After clean up children dress for going outdoors.	• Interact with children one-on-one and in groups. Help take their play to the next level. • Make comments, ask open-ended questions, suggest research materials, and otherwise help children with investigations.

Figure 34c. Sample Daily Schedule for Preschoolers*

Time	Event	How Educators** Support the Children
2:45–3:45 (1 hour)	**Outdoor Choice Time.** Children choose their outdoor activity, like playing on swings, climbers, and slides; riding tricycles; or playing ball games. They may take part in a special project such as playing drums or taking a nature walk.	• Plan and lead special projects. • Interact with children one on one or as part of a group. • Make comments, ask open-ended questions, suggest research materials, and otherwise help children during activities.
3:45–4:00 (15 min)	**Afternoon Meeting.** Children come in from outdoor play, store jackets, wash hands, and sit in the meeting area. Educators and children review the day and discuss how what they learned applies to the children's lives.	• Lead the group meeting and encourage children's participation. • Discuss plans for next day.
4:00–4:30 (30 min)	**Departure.** Children clean up and prepare to leave. Families pick up children.	• Help children clean up and prepare to leave the setting. • Greet families and exchange information about the children. • Say goodbye to individual children and their families, making sure that children take home artwork, projects, and family information from their cubbies.
4:30–5:00 (30 min)	**Planning Period**	• Review and discuss the day's events—what worked, what needs improvement. Note the participation and progress of individual children—skills, needs, interests. • Plan for the next day, week, and month and prep learning centers for the next day. • Complete paperwork and messages to families, specialists, supervisors, and so on.

* Build morning and afternoon snacks into choice times. When snack time is a separately scheduled component, valuable learning time is lost. Give children control over eating when they are hungry, which helps them develop healthy eating habits. Build activities like cleanup, going to the bathroom, brushing teeth, and putting on coats into choice time activities. Incorporate these activities into play (Colker 2009).

** Educators includes all adult staff and volunteers on duty.

A Daily Schedule for Family Child Care

There is probably no greater challenge than trying to figure out how best to schedule learning in a program that serves children of multiple ages, who arrive and leave at various times. Babies need to be fed, changed, and put down to nap on-demand—at the same time that older children need to be engaged in play and learning. If your program also includes school-age children, the challenges multiply as you need to meet their needs before and after school through the daily program as well.

To help you put a plan together, try some of these ideas:

- As children arrive, offer breakfast. (Some programs invite family members to have a cup of coffee or join in the meal.)
- Have quiet activities available for children who arrive at differing times.
- Plan for routines to be unhurried; incorporate them into the schedule.
- Offer the most challenging activities in the morning when everyone is fresh.
- Include outdoor time in both the morning and the afternoon.
- Schedule nap time directly after lunch.
- Provide quiet activities for children to do as they wake up from nap.
- Schedule both a short morning and an afternoon meeting when the whole group is together.
- Invite family members to participate in the daily schedule as fully as they are comfortable with and have time for.

Every FCC program will ultimately have a unique schedule since every program has unique characteristics. Do not fret if your program operates somewhat differently from another FCC home or from the sample in this book. The goal is to create a schedule that works for you and the children and families you serve. Use the sample schedule in Figure 35a-b as a guidepost. Then refine your own schedule to conform to your own needs.

Figure 35a. Sample Daily Schedule for Family Child Care

Time	What Children and Providers Do
6:30-8:30 AM (2 hours) Families drop off children at program	As provider readies own children for school, FCC children arrive on a staggered basis. Children eat breakfast upon arrival. Provider changes babies and puts them down for naps, as needed. Older children clean up after themselves, use toilet, wash hands, and play quietly. School age children leave for school.

Figure 35b. Sample Daily Schedule for Family Child Care

Time	What Children and Providers Do
8:30-8:45 (15 min) Morning meeting	Everyone shares what is new in their lives. They sing or hear a story. Provider discusses the day's plans with the group and refers individual children to toys and materials of probable interest to them.
8:45-9:45 (1 hour) Indoor choice time	Older children select an activity on their own; provider helps younger children make choices. Children of different ages play alone or together with peers or children who are younger or older. Provider engages children and supports their development and learning through small group activities, interactions, and other appropriate teaching strategies.
9:45-10:45 (1 hour) Outdoor play	Everyone goes outdoors to enjoy being in nature, move their bodies, explore materials, ride bikes, pull wagons, and do whatever other outdoor activities are available and of interest to them.
10:45-11:15 (30 min) Story time; preparation for lunch	Everyone comes inside, stows their outdoor gear, and washes hands. A few children help the provider prepare for lunch while the others play with table toys.
11:15 am-12:00 PM (1 hour) Lunch	Everyone eats together sharing a family-style meal and talking about the morning's events and other topics of interest to the group.
12:00-2:00 (2 hours) Naps (including wake-up snack)	Children wash hands, brush teeth, and get ready for naptime. Each child has an assigned place for napping. Babies are in cribs; older children in cots or sleeping bags or on beds with safety rails. As children wake up on their own schedule they have a snack and play quietly.
2:00-3:00 (1 hour) Outdoor play	Same as above. Group may take a walk in the neighborhood.
3:00-4:00 (1 hour) Indoor choice time	Same as above. This time activities are less challenging and tend to be quieter. School-age children may arrive home during this period. Provider may work with children on special projects such as publishing their own books or baking bread.
4:00-4:15 (15 min) Afternoon meeting	Everyone discusses the day's events. They might learn a new song or share what they learned about a study topic. Provider reminds the group of upcoming events such as a field trip or visit from a guest or a special activity.
4:15 -6:00 (1 hour, 45 min) Quiet play, journaling: pick-up	Family members arrive to pick up their children. They exchange information with the provider and share any news that affects their child's participation. Provider tells everyone something special she remembers from the day and wishes everyone a great evening.

Implementing the Daily Schedule

The schedule exists on paper, but until it is implemented by thoughtful early childhood educators, it is not very useful. Putting the schedule to work facilitates children's learning and engages them in activities that foster their growth and development. Your relationships with each child are fortified as you continue to observe their actions, document their learning, discuss what you see happening, ask probing questions, and engage families in their children's development and learning.

An effective early childhood daily schedule should be flexible enough to adjust for field trips, guest presenters, and other occasional activities. This flexibility allows early childhood educators to extend children's learning and interests. For example, if the toddlers are particularly interested in the roly poly bugs on the playground, it should be okay to stay outdoors a bit longer so they can thoroughly investigate these interesting creatures.

A flexible schedule also helps you to accommodate teachable moments that may interrupt your plans for the day. Owocki (1999) describes *teachable moments* as "knowledgeably observing children and seeking out relevant opportunities to help them extend their understandings." For example, snowstorms and rainbows are examples of times you will forgo the scheduled activity and take advantage of these opportunities to teach and learn. Bring a shovelful of snow to the water table so the children can touch and experience it. Read a book aloud—or research rainbows on the Internet—so children can learn about the colors of the rainbow. Ask the children to look for these colors in the rainbow outside the window. Other teachable moments stem from children's home lives, like the arrival of a new sibling, or questions like, "How did the worms get under the swing set?"

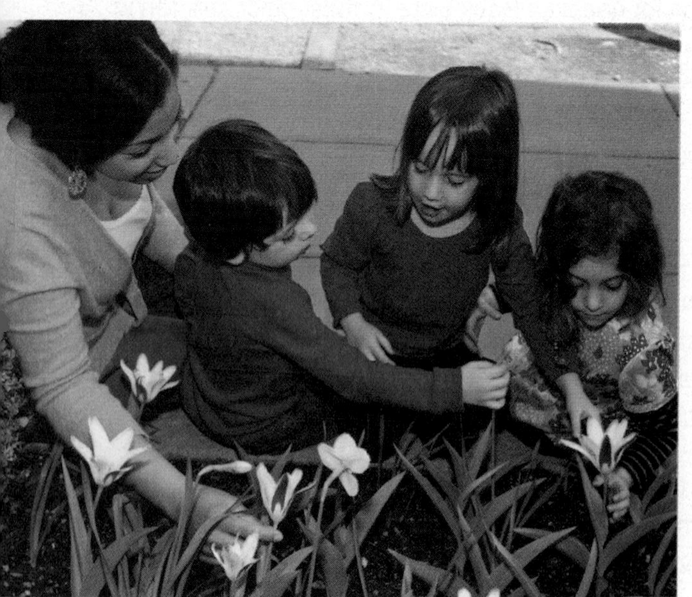

Teachable moment with children asking questions about flowers they discovered during neighborhood walk.

As always, be aware of the children's interests, feelings, and questions. They may be worth taking an unplanned turn in your day to follow the children's lead.

Infants and Toddlers

We recommend the primary caregiving model for educators of infants and toddlers. To implement this model teachers are assigned primary responsibility for the same small group of infants or toddlers from the moment these children arrive until the moment they leave the setting each day. The primary caregiving model ensures that infants and toddlers create secure attachments with the same early educators daily and maintains continuity in the children's care. Families like this approach too because they know one person is truly getting to know and meet the needs of their child.

It is critical, however, for educators to communicate with each other clearly and frequently throughout the day regardless of what caregiving model is implemented in your setting.

The goal is for all children to develop secure attachments and close, reciprocal relationships with their primary early childhood educator. Strong attachments enable children to gain a sense of trust and the secure feelings needed to explore the world.

To ensure continuity in children's care, we also recommend that the same individuals work with the same small group of children from birth until three years old. Though it is not possible to do this in some settings, it is important that educators pass along information about the individual characteristics of a child and family whenever the child transitions to a new classroom. It is also critical to plan for the transition and help children gradually get used to their new teacher, environment, and classmates.

Early childhood educators who work with infants and toddlers, are most effective when they pay attention to children as much as possible. This flexibility promotes the children's interest in and engagement with different materials and helps them build a sense of self, positive self-concept, and strong bonds with adults and other children.

Toddlers will enjoy small group activities that they choose to participate in. An activity for toddlers can be quite simple and does not need to involve a lot of materials and planning. Suggestions include cooking experiences, such as making fruit smoothies, working with specific open-ended art materials such as finger painting on trays, and making, listening, and moving their bodies to music.

Again, reflecting on specific experiences in your setting and your role as an early childhood educator will help you grow professionally, develop deeper relationships with the children, and refine your teaching strategies. Ask questions like: Why did that child react that way to the situation? What could I have done differently? What will I do next time with the specific child or with other children in a similar situation?

Preschoolers

A major component in planning for effective early childhood programs is a consistent daily schedule. Dodge and Colker (2002) note the importance of consistency in the daily routine:

> Young children feel more secure when they can predict the sequence of events and have some control over their environment. They delight in reminding a teacher that 'snack time comes next' or telling a visitor that 'now we go outside.' In addition, predictability provides children with a rudimentary sense of time, as they begin to learn what comes first in the day, second, next, and last. A consistent schedule also helps build trust in the environment (p. 37).

Children should have ongoing opportunities to learn important skills, knowledge, and dispositions. Early childhood educators implement the daily schedule in a setting that is busy with conversations, projects, experiments, reading, and building activities. These materials and activities are individualized and challenge children's intellectual development.

Use these opportunities to reflect on specific learning experiences to improve your teaching practices and support children's learning and development. Evaluate and improve your schedule often.

Family Child Care

Implementing a family child care schedule requires plenty of patience and flexibility. When caring for a group of children who may range in age from infancy through school-age, it is critical to remain calm and respond to needs as they arise. It's also important to be an excellent planner. For example, before going outside with the group, make sure the babies have had recent diaper changes and everyone has used the toilet. Bring water bottles outdoors with you so thirsty children do not have to go back in for a drink.

It's also important to consider and take advantage of the multiple ages of the children. Older children can minimize wait times for the younger ones by pitching in to help at mealtimes or when getting ready for naps. They will feel proud of their abilities and will be practicing their own self-help skills. Similarly, an older child might demonstrate how to clean up, find a puzzle piece under the sofa, or look at a picture book with a toddler.

Having reasonable expectations is also critical. Be sure to anticipate what might happen and plan for it accordingly. If you plan to offer clay to the older children, you might decide to put out playdough for the younger ones because they are still exploring the properties of this substance. Or, to meet the needs of experienced and new painters, you could put out five colors on one side of the easel and two on the other.

While the daily events may not always happen according to the schedule, be assured that the children will still be developing and learning. Your individual attention and interactions will be contributing to the reciprocal caring relationships that are the hallmark of family child care.

Weekly Lesson Planning

Weekly planning allows you to view the activities you have scheduled each day over the course of one week. Use a grid, like Figure 36 to record the time and duration of daily and weekly routines and activities. This grid may also detail staff responsibilities, necessary preparations, target objectives, and learning standards, ideas for involving families and the community, planned field trips, and the arrival of special invited guests. Post the completed grid to keep early educators and children's family informed of setting activities. Your setting may also require early educators to develop daily lesson plans, using forms like Figure 37a-b that detail specific activities and the materials you will use. The purpose of these plans is to explain how an activity will be performed and match the activity to specific learning outcomes or objectives. ■

Figure 36. Sample Weekly Planning Grid

	Monday	Tuesday	Wednesday	Thursday	Friday
Group Meeting					
Learning Centers (changes to centers including materials added or removed)					
Small Group					
Outdoor Time					
Transitions					

Figure 37a. Lesson Plan Form

Lesson plan title: ____________________ **Date of lesson:** ____________________

Concept / topic to teach: ____________________

☐ Small group ☐ Full group ☐ Individual activity

Early Learning Standards addressed: ____________________

Specific learning outcomes/objectives/learning domains: ____________________

Required materials and preparation needed: ____________________

How I will introduce the activity: ____________________

Figure 37b. Lesson Plan Form (continued)

Step-by-step procedures: ______________________________

____

____

____

____

____

____

____

____

____

____

Follow-up (for example, related materials I may put in a learning center after this lesson): ______

____

____

How I will evaluate the activity: ______________________________

____

____

Adaptations (for children with disabilities) **if needed:** ______________________________

____

____

Adaptations (for dual language learners) **if needed:** ______________________________

____

____

Possible connections to other topics: ______________________________

____

____

Competency Standard II:

To advance physical and intellectual development

Developmental Contexts

Functional Area 4: Physical

Young infants *(birth–8 months)* use physical movement, taste, touch, smell, sight, and sound to explore and learn about their world. By moving their arms, hands, legs, and other body parts, by touching and being touched, infants develop an awareness of their bodies and their ability to move and interact with the environment. By using their mouths to explore, hands to reach and grasp, whole bodies to roll over and sit up, they master the necessary strength and skills needed for the developmental stages that follow.

Mobile infants *(9–17 months)* delight in practicing and achieving new physical skills—crawling, standing, sitting down, and walking. They interact with their environment in a practical way, using all senses to examine and manipulate objects and begin to understand cause and effect, space, and distance in this way.

Toddlers *(18–36 months)* continue to master physical skills at their own individual rates. Their learning and interaction with the environment continues to be active. Although they are gaining greater control and satisfaction through use of their small muscles (for example, painting, drawing, or working with puzzles), they need opportunities to exercise their large muscles often each day.

Preschoolers *(3–5 years old)* are gradually refining new skills: skipping, drawing, threading, throwing, and catching. They are interested in learning subtle differences through their senses: sweet and sour, rough and smooth, high and low, loud and soft. They can attend and persist for longer periods of time when they are absorbed in using their small muscles on a puzzle or an art project. They also need daily opportunities to exercise their large muscles in free play and organized activities. Daily physical activities can promote children's cognitive, creative, and language growth as well as their physical development.

Competency Standard II (continued)

Functional Area 5: Cognitive

Young infants *(birth–8 months)* learn best within the context of their relationships with caring adults in a secure environment. Some of their early cognitive (intellectual) development includes becoming familiar with distance and space, sounds, similarity and differences among things, and visual perspectives from various positions—front, back, under, and over.

Mobile infants *(9–17 months)* actively learn through trying things out; using objects as tools; comparing, imitating, looking for lost objects; and naming familiar objects, places, and people. By giving them opportunities to explore their environment, objects, and people and by sharing children's pleasure in discovery, adults can build children's confidence in their ability to learn and understand.

Toddlers *(18–36 months)* enter into a new and expansive phase of mental activity. They are beginning to think in words and symbols, remember, and imagine. Their curiosity leads them to try out materials in many ways and adults can encourage this natural interest by providing a variety of new materials for experimentation. Adults need to create a supportive social environment that contributes to learning by showing enthusiasm for children's individual discoveries and by helping children use words to describe and understand their experiences. Children's cognitive and social development are deeply connected.

Preschoolers *(3–5 years old)* continue their cognitive development by actively exploring their world and manipulating objects, thinking and solving problems, talking and engaging with adults and other children in a variety of roles, and repeating and practicing their learning. Their increasing ability to describe objects and experiences with words reinforces their understanding of abstract concepts. Adults can expand learning through play, introduce a variety of new opportunities for learning, and ensure that preschoolers experience a balance of challenge and success.

Functional Area 6: Communication

Young infants *(birth–8 months)* need adults who are attentive to their nonverbal and preverbal communication. Adults can provide better care when they respond sensitively to the individual signals of each infant. Infants' early cries, babblings, and coos are early forms of communication. An infants' speech development is facilitated by an encouraging partner who responds to their beginning communications and who sings and talks with them about themselves and their world.

Mobile infants *(9–17 months)* begin to babble expressively, name familiar objects and people, and understand many words and phrases. Adults can build on this communication by showing an active interest in children's expressions, interpreting their first attempts at words, repeating and expanding on what they say, talking to them clearly, singing songs, and telling stories.

Competency Standard II (continued)

Toddlers *(18–36 months)* increase their vocabularies and use of sentences daily. Although there is a wide range of typical language development during this time, it can also be an opportunity for early intervention if there are language delays or difficulties. Adults should communicate actively with all toddlers—model good speech, listen carefully, and provide a wide range of vocabulary. Language should be used in a variety of pleasurable ways each day, including songs, stories, instructions, comfort, conversations, information, and play. This is an especially busy time for dual language learners who are developing their home language alongside English. It is critical to provide a strong base of first language development. Therefore, to the extent possible, dual language learners should have plentiful exposure to their home language through songs, stories, instruction, and play. Family partnerships to encourage strong language development, especially for dual language learners who may not share the same language as their teacher, are critical.

Preschoolers *(3–5 years old)* develop a wide range of abilities to communicate both verbally and nonverbally. Adults should communicate actively with each child—modeling good speech, listening carefully, responding actively to their expressions, engaging in conversations with them, and building on their verbal and nonverbal understanding and vocabulary. During the preschool years, early literacy experiences provide the foundation for later success in learning to read and write. Dual language learners continue to need exposure to their home language in the learning setting, alongside increased exposure to English.

Functional Area 7: Creative

Young and mobile infants *(birth–17 months)* are creative in their individual styles of interacting with the world. Adults can support their creativity by respecting and enjoying the variety of ways very young children express themselves and act on their environment.

Toddlers *(18–36 months)* are interested in using materials to create their own product—sometimes to destroy and create it again or to move on. For example, they become absorbed in dipping a brush in paint and watching their stroke of color on paper. They use their voices and bodies creatively—swaying, chanting, and singing. They enjoy making up their own words and rhythms, as well as learning traditional songs and rhymes. Adults can provide water, sand, blocks, and other open-ended and raw materials and opportunities for toddlers' creativity and can show respect for what they do. Make-believe and pretend play appear gradually and are signs of emerging cognitive capacity to understand symbols. Adults can join in imaginative play, while helping toddlers distinguish between what is real and what is not.

Preschoolers *(3–5 years old)* can express their creativity in increasingly symbolic ways through the use of their bodies, words, and materials (building blocks, music, dance, art) and through make-believe. Adults can promote creativity by providing space, time, and materials for children to create and recreate their individual works, their own dramas, and their unique solutions to problems and by respecting the process of creativity as much as the product.

CHAPTER 4:

Physical

CDA® Functional Area 4: Candidate uses a variety of developmentally appropriate equipment, learning experiences, and teaching strategies to promote the physical development (fine motor and gross motor) of all children.

Physical

Introduction

Some adults—including parents and early childhood educators—think of physical development as something that just happens. While educators play a dear role in children's cognitive, social, emotional, and language development, how do educators promote children's physical development? Doesn't it just enfold? With maturation, won't children develop physical skills on their own? To the contrary, children's physical development is not just a matter of biology. It is a process fueled by experience and opportunity (Bredekamp 2013).

Physical development has important implications for children's learning. Among these are:

- Mastering physical skills strengthens children's self-esteem.
- Peer and adult perceptions of children are enhanced by observing their physical skills.
- Physical activity helps children build and maintain healthy bones and muscles.
- Physical activity reduces the risk of developing obesity and chronic diseases, such as diabetes, cardiovascular disease, and colon cancer.
- Physical activity reduces stress.
- Physical activity leads to increased attention spans and improved academic learning.
- Physical activity is a gateway to fitness and enjoyment of creative movement activities like dancing.

As an early childhood educator, you promote physical development by giving children chances to use their large and small muscles, build their coordination, stay fit, and enjoy active play with peers.

In this chapter, we will discuss the following ways you can support children's physical development:

- **Understanding the Physical Development of Infants, Toddlers, and Preschoolers**
- **Promoting Gross Motor Development**
- **Promoting Physical Fitness**
- **Promoting Fine Motor Development**
- **Connecting Physical Development to the Development of the Whole Child**

Understanding the Physical Development of Infants, Toddlers, and Preschoolers

During the early childhood years, children acquire physical skills at a rapid pace. Indeed, more physical development occurs between birth and 35 months of age than at any other time in life. The physical development of young children typically follows predictable patterns, according to these two principles of physical development:

1. **Development goes from the top down.** As newborns start off their lifelong course of physical development, movement begins with their heads and extends down through their bodies to their lower limbs and toes. This is known as cephalocaudal development, from the Latin words for head and tail. Babies first learn to control head movements, as the muscles in their necks develop. As they notice light and sounds, during the first month of life curious infants turn their heads from side to side, developing strength and coordination in their necks and upper back muscles. At about the age of two months, infants can hold their heads up to see the world around them. Before this age, neck muscles are usually too weak to support their heads. At four to five months of age, infants will often roll over for the first time while trying to reach for a favorite toy. Around six months of age, when placed in a sitting position, infants will prop themselves up with both arms to stay balanced.

   Within another month or two, at around seven to eight months, infants can get into and out of a sitting position without help and use both hands to explore a toy. They can scoot across the floor on their tummies and use their hands and knees to crawl. Generally, infants begin to stand at around 10–12 months, walk at around 12–16 months, and walk up stairs at around 18–20 months.

2. **Development goes from the center of the body to the extremities.** Development moves from the central portions of the body (i.e., the spinal cord) out through the extremities to the fingers and toes. This type of development is known as proximodistal development, from the Latin words for close in and far away. Infants can move their shoulders before they develop the fine motor skills in their hands to tear paper. Typically, children can hold objects with the whole hand at around five to six months; pick up objects using the thumb and forefinger (what is known as the pincer grasp) at around 12 months; hold a spoon at around 16 months; scribble with a fat crayon at around 18 months; and eat with a fork at around 24 months. The skeletal system also grows rapidly in infancy, slows, and then returns to rapid growth during adolescence.

The order in which children are able to perform new movements—known as motor sequence—depends on the development of the brain and nervous system. This is why movements begin in the head with the brain (cephalocaudal trend) and the spinal cord (proximodistal trend).

Midlines, Motor Tools, and Mind

While the development of gross and fine motor skills is considered the primary area of physical development, other aspects of motor development must also be addressed. The body has midlines—critical points of reference that divide it in half, whether left and right, top and bottom or front and back. These lines and divisions are what actually help to align our bodies and promote various types of development. The midlines serve as pivot points for all movement patterns.

Midline development is a slow, natural process that eventually leads to independence of movement as well as coordination of movements for multiple parts of the body (Connell and McCarthy, 2014). The body works at linking and communicating what is going on within its physical structure and also how movements and information impact understanding and ultimately brain function.

Connell and McCarthy refer to the aspects of movement that lead to physical, cognitive, emotional, and social development as motor tools that allow children to make sense of the world. In other words, it is through the use of these tools that children begin to make sense of the world and the available learning environment. It is through engagement of that learning environment with different types of motor movements that children achieve understanding.

What is generally considered to be gross and fine motor development requires strength, stamina, flexibility, and agility. It is through this strength, stamina, flexibility, and agility that all motor movement and development progresses.

How is strength developed? Through experience. When a child tries to do something, they build strength. It is not so much a specific action or repeated action like exercise that matters but just the simple act of doing it. As Connell and McCarthy point out, strength is related to effort. A child's efforts become an internal understanding of what that child can do and accomplish.

Stamina refers to the ability to maintain or sustain effort. We often think of stamina as being able to continue on when doing something. However, for young children, stamina is related to how they feel about something and how they remain engaged. If a child is attempting to do something and is yet unable to accomplish that task or action, that is not a sign of lack of stamina. The persistence and dedication the child exhibits reflect the stamina the child possesses.

Flexibility is how the body can be manipulated and used in a relatively easy manner to pursue an action. Young children are born extremely flexible simply because the body has yet to create a more rigid skeletal structure. As children attempt new and different actions, flexibility allows them to experience a broad range of sensations and body configurations.

Agility takes time. Children achieve agility when they are confident and able to successfully make coordinated movements. The body and brain work in tandem to promote agility. As children use their muscles and perform body movements, their confidence is reinforced, and they achieve ease, quickness and fluidity of movement.

Gross and fine motor development also requires control (Connell and McCarthy, 2014). It is not enough to just be able to move and engage with the environment. Moving in precise and dedicated ways aids in the acquisition of information and understanding of one's world.

Control promotes additional skills and learning. Self-organization, the ability to adapt, understanding position, pacing, and the use of pressure or force are some of the skills related to control that become evident as a child progresses and develops gross and fine motor movements.

It is the combination and promotion of both gross and fine motor skills that will benefit a child. Because the body works as a whole, it should not be limited by emphasizing one component or part while neglecting another. So, a program that encourages and incorporates a variety of strategies and engagements is critical.

Children who have extensive and diverse motor experiences improve not only their physical selves but also their cognitive abilities. By undertaking a broad range of actions, children are able to determine movements that are possible, enjoyable, repeatable and informative about their world of learning. These experiences, in turn, inspire new and varied interests.

Daniel Siegel, noted psychiatrist, researcher, and proponent of a neurobiological perspective of development and learning (2015), discusses how what we experience and enjoy leads us to seek out more opportunities to work with similar materials and have similar experiences. In other words, what we positively experience influences our future choices and decisions. Siegel refers to this as the creation of mind—not to be confused with the brain, which is the gray matter and mechanism for recording and influencing information.

How is the mind related to physical development and particularly gross motor and fine motor skills? As children participate in gross motor and fine motor activities, they are increasing their strength, stamina, flexibility, and agility, motor tools and control. The choices and decisions children make regarding their learning environment will subsequently influence their lives. If children feel confident, comfortable and capable, their minds will drive them to pursue new learning opportunities with excitement and joy.

Reflexes—The Inborn Part of Physical Development

Reflexes are automatic physical responses to stimuli. While most of physical development involves voluntary movements, reflexes are involuntary. We have no control over them. They occur without us even thinking about them. We are born with these movements. In fact, most begin in the womb. Reflexes help protect us. For example, if an object comes close to our face we blink, protecting our eyes.

Most of the reflexes that appear at birth disappear within months. They serve a specific purpose for infants, and then they go away forever. Consider the following newborn reflexes:

Reflex	What it is and its Purpose	Age of Disappearance
Stepping	When an infant is held with the feet flat on a surface, the child lifts one foot and then the other in stepping fashion. Like the Palmar grasp, this later becomes a learned voluntary behavior as a precursor to walking.	2 to 3 months
Rooting	This reflex causes infants to turn their heads towards anything that brushes their face. When it's a nipple, the child is able to find its food source.	3 months
Palmar grasp	When a finger or rattle is placed in the palm of a baby's hand, the child grasps the object tightly enough to support his weight. It is thought that this aids in later development of voluntary grasping. The grasping reflex also appears in the feet, with the toes curling inward.	3 to 4 months
Moro	Known as the startle reflex, babies extend and then retract their arms and legs and cry in response to a loud noise or sudden movement. It is the body's attempt to protect the child from possible harm.	5 to 8 months
Babinski	When the sole of the baby's foot is stroked from the heel to the toe, the toes fan out and the heel twists in. This aids in belly crawling as babies push off from their big toes and propel themselves forward.	8 to 12 months

Physical Development milestones are divided into two major components: gross motor and fine motor development. *Gross motor development* refers to the large muscles of the legs, arms, and torso. *Fine motor development* refers to the smaller muscles of the body including the muscles of the hands, feet, and eyes. Because of the principles of cephalocaudal and proximodistal development described above, gross motor development starts before fine motor development.

Promoting Gross Motor Development

Gross motor development involves large muscle movements of the torso and limbs—including rolling, crawling, running, jumping, twisting, dancing, and skipping, to name a few skills. These skills can be grouped into three areas (Gallahue and Ozmun 2011):

1. **Moving from one place to another (or "locomotion"):** crawling, running, leaping, jumping, galloping, and hopping.
2. **Giving or receiving objects with force:** throwing, catching, and kicking. This type of movement is sometimes called "gross motor manipulative movement" because in addition to body movements, it involves handling objects, like balls.
3. **Stability movements:** balancing, stopping and starting, and using a riding toy or tricycle.

In general, gross motor skills develop in an orderly fashion and develop predictably based on experience and practice. These skills move from simple to complex. For example, before children can run, they must first be able to walk independently. Before they can gallop, they must be able to run. Typically, each skill is sequential and dependent on the one before it. Factors such as heredity, gender, nutrition, and health, including access to health care, may impact how children's large muscles develop.

Children's bodies crave movement.

Developmental milestone charts offer general information about children's development at particular ages. Each child is unique; we cannot rely on these charts as an exact standard. For example, some infants may begin walking at eight months whereas other infants may not begin walking until 15 months. Joshua, a three-year-old in your setting, might be able to balance himself well enough to carry a beanbag on his head while walking a wavy line while Xavier, a five-year-old, might not be able to keep the beanbag on his head. Both Joshua and Xavier are developing typically—according to their own biological clocks.

In addition, while children follow the same sequence in development, they may not go through every step. For example, some children do not crawl; they go directly to pulling themselves up and walking. For children with orthopedic impairments such as cerebral palsy, development may be at a slower pace and—some children—depending on the severity of their disability—may never reach certain milestones.

What if an Infant Doesn't Crawl?

We know that not every baby does. Since 1994, pediatricians have counseled family members to put babies to sleep on their backs as a SIDS-prevention measure. One byproduct of this life-saving practice is that more and more babies are skipping the crawling milestone, apparently because they have less upper body strength due to spending less time on their stomachs where they have an opportunity to practice pushing themselves up with their arms and legs.

So what does this mean? Is this bad for development or does it even matter? Some pediatricians worry that babies who don't crawl will have weaker upper body strength, reduced coordination skills, and less developed fine motor skills including poorer writing, since crawling stretches the ligaments in the wrist.

Others claim that crawling is in no way vital to children's physical development, noting that the Denver Development Screening Test, a tool used by pediatricians to measure children's development, doesn't even list crawling as a milestone because it is a variable skill. As pediatrician Pamela High puts it, "It's a prominent misconception that it is important for kids to include crawling in their development" (Port 2015).

So whether or not being a crawler is important is still up for debate. If you care for children who became walkers without ever crawling, you might want to focus on activities that will promote their upper body strength—just to make sure there are no lasting effects. Try activities that will have them crawling through tunnels or moving to music like four-legged animals. It's never too late to gain the benefits of crawling.

If you care for very young infants, offer them lots of tummy time on the floor. This can counteract the effects of being on their backs so much while in their cribs. Tummy time seems to increase the likelihood that a child will crawl.

But don't overly concern yourself. Just be aware that this is a topic under study. The important thing is that a baby is able to explore their surroundings and strengthen their body in preparation for walking. If you or a family members feels a child is not moving normally, this should be discussed with the child's pediatrician.

As mentioned earlier, individual gross motor development can be affected by heredity and environmental factors, such as nutrition and health. It is also influenced by cultural expectations. When it comes to culture, for example, there is considerable variation in the amount of freedom of movement children receive. For example, at the Pikler Institute, started by Dr. Emmi Pikler in Budapest, Hungary, to serve children who lost families in World War II, freedom of movement is a hallmark. Adults do not move children in any way. Babies stay on their backs until they can roll themselves over. Once in motion, they propel themselves to crawl and walk. Babies are never put in high chairs, infant seats, or jumpers. As a result, Pikler-raised babies have great body awareness, balance, and coordination.

In contrast, babies in the Au tribe of Papua, New Guinea, are carried for much of the day by their mothers. When put down for rest, they are placed in a sitting position. Children tend to hitch (drag their bottoms) across floors rather than crawl. Most Au children learn to walk without ever having learned to crawl, although they generally reach this milestone a few months later than Western babies (Bredekamp 2013).

Throwing and catching are gross motor manipulative movements.

These two examples of cultural extremes differ with common infant care practices in the U.S. where babies are routinely placed on the floor for tummy time and infant seats and high chairs are nearly universally used. However, it is important to consider the cultural diversity within the United States and respect families' diverse cultural child rearing practices.

Figure 38 describes some of the gross motor skills that children are typically developing during the early childhood years. Use this chart as a guidepost to physical development, always remembering the uniqueness of individual development and the potential influence of factors, such as culture, nutrition, and health.

Figure 38. Gross Motor Skills for Young Children

Age	Developing Gross Motor Skills
Young Infant (birth–8 months)	• Turns head from side to side. • Rolls from back to stomach. • Holds up head and chest when lying on stomach. • Uses arms and legs to move forward when on stomach and back. • Sits with assistance. • Begins to sit without assistance.
Mobile Infant (9–17 months)	• Sits without assistance and maintains balance while playing with a toy. • Scoots on stomach. • Crawls after a toy. • Pulls self up from sitting to standing positions or lowers self from standing to sitting positions. • Walks while holding onto furniture or people and later walks without assistance.
Toddler (18–36 months)	• Throws large ball. • Carries large objects. • Walks easily or runs from place to place without assistance. • Propels riding toys with feet. • Walks up stairs alternating feet. • Runs. • Builds with large blocks. • Jumps on two feet. • Balances on one foot.
Young Preschooler (3–4 years old)	• Stands on tiptoes with hands overhead for more than 3 seconds. • Hops on one foot forward 1–3 times. • Walks down stairs by placing one foot on each step (alternating gait). • Able to walk on 2 inch line for 10 feet without stepping off once. • Throws tennis ball underhand 10 feet using upper trunk rotation, arms, and legs moving in opposition. Initiates throw by moving arm down and back. • Pedals tricycle for long distances, turns corners, and makes U-turns. • Gallops 5 feet.
Older Preschooler (4–5 years old)	• Completes somersaults with chin tucked and without turning to side. • Gallops 10 feet with weight transferred smoothly and evenly; arms move freely in opposition to legs. • Jumps and turns so feet land in opposite direction from starting position (180-degree turn in the air). • Hops eight consecutive times on one foot followed by eight hops on other foot. • Skips eight steps using opposing arm and leg movements and using alternating feet while maintaining balance. • Hits a target 12 feet away with tennis ball using overhead throw. • Catches tennis ball from 5 feet away with hands outstretched. • Runs while pumping arms.

While there is wide variation in children's mastery of physical milestones, there is also an outer limit of expectations. If children have not reached the following milestones by the ages noted below, you need to confer with the children's families about having them tested for a possible delay (Shelov 2014):

- By 3-4 months, child is not able to lift his head.
- By 4 months, child does not push down on her legs when placed on a firm surface.
- By 5 months, does not roll over in either direction.
- By 9 months, cannot sit without assistance.
- By 1 year, cannot stand with support.
- By 18 months, cannot walk.
- By 2 years, cannot push a wheeled toy.
- By 3 years, cannot walk down steps.
- By 4 years, cannot throw a ball overhand.
- By 4 years, cannot ride a tricycle.

Supporting Gross Motor Development

Early childhood educators need to be intentional in planning for and fostering children's physical development. While nearly every child will develop the gross motor skills listed in Figure 38, in the absence of a disability, children's mastery of these skills is dependent on support from educators and family members. The indoor and outdoor setting should be arranged and stocked with materials and equipment that support gross motor development. In addition, your interactions can encourage children to build and practice skills.

Young Infants (Birth–8 Months)

During this stage, infants are growing and developing rapidly. Yet, for the first few months of life, infants are developing the muscle strength that will enable movement. They enjoy being rocked, held, and seated in an infant seat (for short periods of time) while an adult talks, sings, or reads to them. By four to six months, they are beginning to roll over, sit up independently, and grab and hold objects. Configure your setting so that infants can safely experience open spaces while lying on a blanket on the floor. Place materials including mobiles, squeaky toys, rattles, bells, balls, hand puppets, plastic measuring spoons, teething rings, and hollow building blocks where children can grab, shake, and mouth them. When infants are ready to roll over onto their stomachs, leave them in this position to help them develop the use of their legs, neck, arms, and hands. Place toys or safe items within infants' reach to encourage them to roll over when they are able to do so. When infants begin crawling, place toys nearby that they can choose to investigate.

Seven-month-old Marie is starting "hitching" movements, that is, while sitting upright without support, she moves her arms and legs and scooches her bottom along the floor. To encourage her movements, her family child care educator Ms. Downing holds out Marie's favorite penguin puppet just out of reach. Cooing and smiling, Marie scoots towards Ms. Downing, with her arms reaching out towards the puppet.

Mobile Infants (9–17 Months)

As their name says, mobile infants are movers. Provide safe and interesting places where they can move around and safely explore, and ensure that there is ample interesting and stimulating space for crawling and walking around the setting. Place materials around the room that mobile infants can access—including books, large hollow blocks, balls, and manipulatives. Provide push toys, such as toy strollers and shopping carts. Provide materials and equipment that are safe for infants to use to pull themselves up to a standing position, such as a low bookshelf containing age-appropriate toys that is anchored to the wall or floor. If infants pull themselves up then fall to a sitting position, observe their reactions and encourage them to stand again. Take time to observe mobile infants, so you will know when you need to step in to offer your support and when they can maneuver independently.

Children can practice gross motor skills while playing alone or with peers.

Ten-month-old Ruby likes to pull herself up to a standing position, but keeps falling down. When she does this with the room divider in the tasting area, she cries as she hits the tile floor. Her teacher leads her to a carpeted area where she can use the bookshelf to pull herself up.

Toddlers (18–36 Months)

Create safe spaces and opportunities—both indoors and outdoors—for toddlers to walk, run, jump, and climb. Allow them to explore your setting and to practice and use their recently-acquired motor skills. Observe their developing skills, along with their newfound balance and coordination, and provide toddlers with interesting materials and equipment that will test these skills. Riding toys and climbing structures with steps, swings, and slides are ideal for this age group. These toys promote toddlers' developing pedaling, balancing, climbing, jumping, running, and hopping skills. Provide balls, beanbags, and rings that children can roll, toss, and catch. When children are excited by rolling a new toy across the floor, think of other materials you have in your setting that the child can roll safely.

Two-year-old Eddie loves listening to music and singing along. To get him up and moving, his teacher Dr. Cromwell suggests that he listen to the music with cordless headphones and dance along to the songs. She also plays movies like Born to Move, which ensure that he will want to move his body along with the music.

Preschoolers (3–5 Years Old)

Engage preschoolers daily in enjoyable gross motor activities that require them to use their entire bodies and promote fitness. Stock your program with equipment and toys that will support the use of children's large muscles. Outdoor equipment should include swings, slides, climbing structures, tricycles, wagons, and hollow blocks. Smaller equipment, like roller boards and scooters, will provide exciting experiences for older preschoolers who are adept at balancing themselves. Indoor equipment for promoting gross motor development include balance boards, large blocks, large foam wedges, ramps, and crawl-through tunnels. Other materials that will encourage large muscle movement include jump ropes (7-foot ropes are recommended), balls, beanbags, hula hoops, balance beams, tumbling mats, large blocks, foam or plastic bats, paddles, parachutes, and streamers. While choosing equipment and materials, ask family members to suggest games, activities, music, and dances to incorporate into your gross motor program. Make children feel more at home by incorporating these experiences into your setting.

Four-year-old Julian's mom tells his FCC educator that Julian's older sister taught him a freeze dance, that she thinks the children at Mrs. Hendricks' FCC program would enjoy. After rest time, Mrs. Hendricks puts on some Latin music, telling the children that when the music stops, they have to freeze in the position they are in. She has Julian demonstrate how this works. The children enjoy freezing their actions and do so with great fanfare. The next day, she introduces a new feature: after freezing their motions, they have to hop backwards until the music resumes.

Play games that allow children to get their bodies moving.

No matter what age children you care for, you can promote their gross motor development and physical fitness by providing age appropriate toys and materials that can be used safely during uninterrupted play times. By understanding children's development, Ms. Downing is able to help seven-month-old Marie reach for a puppet while hitching across the floor in much the same way Mrs. Hendricks uses what she knows about how children learn to help four-year-old Julian hop backwards in a freeze dance. Both educators are supporting gross motor development in ways appropriate for the children they care for.

To further support children's gross motor development, try some of the following strategies with older infants, toddlers and preschoolers, as appropriate.

Schedule time for extended periods of unstructured play. According to the National Association for Sport and Physical Education (NASPE 2004), children from birth through age five should not be at rest or sitting for more than 60 minutes at a time unless they are sleeping. Children crave movement. Early educators can support this need by ensuring that there is plenty of time for children to move and explore. For example, if you see children climbing on a book shelf or other structure in your setting, work with your colleagues to figure out how to promote the development of the children's climbing skills in a safe manner on the playground or on an indoor climber.

Schedule outdoor play for 45 min to an hour both in the morning and afternoon.

Plan opportunities for children to explore and develop gross motor skills every day. Use space indoors on days when you are unable to go outdoors. Do you have a space inside where children can climb, skip, and crawl? If there is no gym or "gross motor room" available to you, then find or create a space in your setting that children can use for movement activities. If your music area has ample space, children can march, dance, or exercise. Or use the space in the block area for movement activities. Provide equipment like balance boards, tunnels, hula hoops, and tumbling mats if they are available.

Plan daily movement experiences. In addition to unscheduled gross motor activities, you want to plan scheduled activities. Include opportunities for movement such as forming a marching band, performing tumbling routines, dancing to music, running an obstacle course, doing yoga poses, or making an outdoor parachute billow into a temporary "tent"—during both indoor and outdoor choice times.

Introduce games that require children to use their large muscles. Games like "Duck, Duck, Goose" get children moving and stopping on demand. Other games, like "Simon Says," "Follow the Leader," "Tag," and "Hide and Seek," enable children to practice advanced motor skills. While you regard these games as gross motor and fitness opportunities, children will play them to have fun. In addition, include short (1–2 minute) activities during group meetings or during routines, such as after nap time, that will get children's blood flowing. For example, stretching after an activity clears children's minds and exercises their muscles.

Incorporate gross motor activities into transitions. Suggest that children gallop like gazelles when coming indoors. Or, everyone can try putting on their coats while hopping on one foot. Not only does this give children a chance to work on their gross motor skills, it is sure to bring laughs to an otherwise routine gross activity.

Make gross motor activities exciting and interesting. Consider ways to challenge and motivate children to move, like running obstacle courses, wandering through simple mazes, and crawling through pretend tunnels. Try changing the rules to a familiar game. For example, instead of playing Simon Says, have children play Reverse Simon Says. In this version of the game, if you say, "Simon says touch your head," children should touch their toes.

Encourage children to enjoy the process of learning gross motor skills. Help children focus more on the activity itself rather than the final result or product. For example, when Ms. King demonstrates how to saw wood safely her goal is for the four-year-old children to enjoy the process of sawing the wood as they develop their large muscle skills, not to produce a heaping pile of wood.

Plan movement experiences that allow children to participate according to their skills and interests. These activities, like dancing, moving like wheat blowing in the wind, or pretending to be snakes crawling through the rainforest, should be open-ended rather than competitive. The goal is for everyone to participate, not to see who performs the activity best.

Challenge children to expand their skills. Provide individual children with new personal challenges. For example, if Marta has learned to kick a ball but gives no thought to where it goes, give her some targets to practice her aim. Likewise, if Louis can walk a straight line on the ground, challenge him to walk along the edge of the sandbox. Give children group challenges, such as "Jump in the air as many times as I clap." Or, as you slowly lift a jump rope off the ground, ask the children to "One at a time, jump forward, backward, and sideways over the rope." Children will enjoy using and mastering these skills.

Adapting Gross Motor Play to Meet Children's Disabilities

Let children show you what they can do, rather than setting your expectations prematurely. Follow their lead, and you will learn how best to adapt your program to meet their individual needs.

The children in Ms. Prince's class are scheduled to run relay races this afternoon. Juwan, a 4-year-old with physical disabilities, can walk, but not run. Ms. Prince wants Juwan to join in the children's gross motor play, but worries that he will fall and become frustrated. She does not want Juwan to "fail" in front of his peers. She considers appointing him scorekeeper so that he can still be involved in the activity and avoid failure. However, this would deprive him of the chance to really experience gross motor activity. Ms. Prince decides to forego the relay races and instead schedules a scavenger hunt, during which the children will work in teams and walk around the playground in search of items found in clues. This activity successfully meets Juwan's skills where they are and allows him to fully participate with his peers.

Children with disabilities like Juwan may have difficulty participating in certain gross motor activities. For example, a child diagnosed with cerebral palsy or dyspraxia (a motor-skills disorder that affects how well the brain sends signals to muscles), may have delays in their motor development. Children with visual impairments are also likely to have delayed physical fitness because of their anxiety about moving where they cannot see (Gould and Sullivan, 2004).

As an early educator, identify gross motor activities in which all the children in your setting can participate. See what children can do and tailor activities to build on these strengths. Children who use wheelchairs, for example, can steer around obstacles and objects. They can also practice throwing and catching beanbags. If you have access to equipment specially designed for children who use wheelchairs, such as scooter boards, platform swings, or prone standers, help children out of their wheelchairs and let them experience these gross motor activities. You can work with the children's therapists and family members to help plan a gross motor program that will address children's needs more specifically and ensure that they are included with appropriate accommodations, across all learning activities.

All children in your setting need and deserve your support in promoting their gross motor development. Observe them all to see if children who are not receiving special education services might be in need of such assistance. Are there any children who are not walking, running, jumping, hopping, or balancing themselves? If you have concerns about children's development, discuss them with the children's families. They may want to consult the child's pediatrician or have you bring in a special education consultant to conduct further observation.

Expanding Gross Motor Skills

Work with children to refine their skills to a higher level. If a child can run, encourage him to gallop. If she can throw underhand, help her to try overhead ball throwing, if you think they're developmentally ready. Here's how one educator helped a child hone his balancing skills over time.

Five-year-old Eduardo can balance in place. He can even stand on one foot for 10 seconds, with his arms extended. His teacher, Mr. Kennedy, thinks that Eduardo has the muscle development to increase his balancing skills. First, he gives Eduardo objects to hold, like beanbags, while balancing.

Mr. Kennedy then challenges Eduardo to stand on stationary objects that are higher than the ground, like a sturdy bench or a tire in the outdoor obstacle course. As Eduardo's skills catch up to the challenges, Mr. Kennedy asks Eduardo to stand on various beams, even rounded ones—first alone and then holding objects.

Once he's competent in balancing, Mr. Kennedy encourages Eduardo to balance while moving. He first asks Eduardo to walk back and forth along a line on the floor, using alternate foot stepping. Next, Eduardo tries walking along an uneven surface, such as a rope on the ground. After accomplishing this, Eduardo walks along a beam. Each time he completes a walk across the beam, Mr. Kennedy raises it a bit higher.

At this point, Eduardo can balance himself both standing and moving. Because Eduardo is so adept at balance skills, Mr. Kennedy decides to make Eduardo a pair of stilts by attaching a Velcro™ foot fastener atop two upside-down metal pails. Eduardo thrills himself and the other children with his newfound stilt-walking skill.

Fostering Mastery of Gross Motor Skills

As you try out the strategies listed above, observe children carefully to see how they are progressing and think about how you might further facilitate their development. For instance, to help children learn to throw, catch, and kick, consider using visual aids. Because children's optic nerves are still developing tracking objects is somewhat difficult. These ideas will help children keep track of the ball (Binelli and Yongue 2004):

- Use bright, colorful balls.
- Use soft balls that are easy to catch, such as beach balls, balloons, balls of yarn, Koosh® balls, or Nerf® balls.
- Throw balls at a consistent speed and height.

In addition, it helps to give children specific cues—that is verbal instructions or demonstrations of the most effective way of accomplishing gross motor feats. In this example, it would be helpful to instruct children on how to position their hands and feet:

- To catch above the waist, point thumb tips toward each other.
- To catch below the waist, point pinkie tips toward each other.
- To throw overhand, place the throwing hand behind the head while stepping forward with the opposite foot.

Cues like these prevent children from becoming frustrated with their early attempts. Brooklyn's first tries at galloping ended with her tripping over her own feet. But when her teacher cued her in with the advice that she keep the same foot forward as she moved rather than reversing her feet, she galloped like a colt. Some other helpful cues are:

- Running: "Keep your head up, bend your elbows, and swing your arms."
- Hopping: "Bend one knee and lift that leg; keep your arms out for balance."
- Balance: "Tighten your muscles while you stand very still; keep your arms out wide."
- Skipping: "Hop and land on one foot; then, hop and land on the other foot."

Again, observe children as they work to master these skills, and keep a record of their progress. For example, watch Justin as he walks, runs, skips, hops, throws, kicks, rides a tricycle, and performs all of the other gross motor activities discussed in this section. In which skills is he at a beginning level, mastery level, or somewhere in between? Do his skill levels increase when he plays with one or two friends? How about with the whole group? Is he having fun while also making progress?

After you have learned this information, think about how you can help children develop their skills further. For example, Tiffany, age four, can throw a ball underhand, and seems ready and interested in learning to throw overhand. What could you do to help her learn this new skill? Here are a few options:

- Demonstrate how to throw a ball overhand so it lands where she wants it to.
- Watch her throw overhand; give her tips, if needed, to help her be more successful.
- Walk her through the process and give her pointers, like: "Point your shoulder of the arm that you don't throw with, toward the target. Now keep your throwing arm way behind your head and move your opposite foot toward the target. Let your throwing arm move across your body."
- Place markers, like pieces of tape or footprints and arrows, on the ground to illustrate where Tiffany should move her feet as she throws.

- Have her practice throwing the ball against a wall.
- Encourage her to practice with a friend who has mastered this skill. Have them practice an underhand throw first, and then move on to the overhand throw. Start the children off at a relatively close and comfortable distance from one another. Then, as Tiffany gains skill, move the children farther apart.
- Have a circle of children toss balls to one another overhead, in turn. They can start with beach balls and move on to beanbags and then balls of varying sizes and softness.

Because you know Tiffany and have insight into how she learns best, you can decide which of these strategies is most appropriate for her. Practice is paramount to mastering gross motor skills. Build time into your schedule for Tiffany to practice throwing—alone, with your assistance, with a friend, or with a small group. Keep a variety of balls in various sizes, weights, and textures available for the children to use on their own. The goal is to individualize your curriculum so that all of the children in your program—including Tiffany—have an opportunity to develop, refine, and master gross motor skills.

Learning and mastering gross motor skills helps children feel good about their bodies and gives them confidence in their abilities. Most children are eager to get outdoors and move. However, occasionally children do not want to participate in these activities for a variety of reasons. Perhaps they are having trouble mastering certain skills and are frustrated or embarrassed. Or they may be reluctant to participate because of illness, abuse, or overprotection at home. Maybe they just do not like these kinds of activities. Gently encourage these children to join in movement activities. Try to find out why they are reluctant, and see if you can address the problem. Build on what interests the children.

For example, Kareem, age two-and-a-half, is passionate about cars. He loves to talk about different makes and models, look at picture books about cars, and use the cars in his pretend play. Think about creating a space for cars outdoors to promote Kareem's engagement in gross motor skill activity. Create roads with intersections in your outdoor space. Kareem can pretend he is a car and walk, run, or push a ride-on car with his feet through make-believe traffic.

If children do not want to be around others because they are embarrassed, find a private area to work with these children one-on-one. If they find an activity too difficult, find a way to make it less frustrating. For example, if three-and-a-half year old Elizabeth cries at the thought of riding a tricycle, offer her a four-wheel pedal toy to use until she is more confident in her ability. If she will try this toy, Elizabeth will still get the benefits of gross motor exercise in a way that meets her skill and comfort level. If children remain resistant to an activity, however, do not force their participation.

Figure 39a-b examines some of the basic gross motor skills that children will work on and master as they grow.

Figure 39a. Mastering Basic Gross Motor Skills

Gross Motor Skill	Physical Prerequisites for this Skill	What Constitutes Mastery
LOCOMOTOR MOVEMENT		
Rolling over	Lifting head, using arms to raise upper body.	Turns from back to stomach and stomach to back.
Hitching	Sitting without support.	From a sitting position, moves arms and legs, sliding buttocks across the ground.
Creeping	Supporting weight on hands and arms.	From a tummy-down position, uses arms and legs to drag body across the ground.
Crawling, scooting, or slithering	Supporting weight on arms and legs, with body raised off ground, moves forward on hands and knees. Or scooting on bottoms to move forward; or slithering on their stomachs to move forward.	With body raised off ground, moves forward on hands and knees.
Walking	Standing in an upright position without support.	Walking with balance and without assistance, with legs in narrow base of support and arms at side.
Running	Walking without assistance.	Running backward and forward.
Jumping	Jumping off a step with an adult holding their hand.	Jumping forward from a standing position; jumping 12–16 in. on either foot and 36 in. using both feet.
Leaping	Moving through the air with an adult holding their hands.	Putting their hands on the back of a squatting child and vaulting over the child ("Leap Frog").
Standing on one foot	Standing on one foot, holding on to an adult for balance.	Standing on one foot unassisted for 10 seconds.
Hopping	Hopping on one foot in place, holding on to an adult for balance.	Hopping on either foot to a targeted landing point; hopping eight times consecutively.
Galloping	Running.	Moving by leading one foot and having the other follow; changing the lead foot.
Skipping	Running and galloping, but without changing the lead foot.	A combined leg movement of stepping and hopping; skipping 8 to 10 times.
Climbing stairs	Climbing upstairs with both feet on each step, no hand support; climbing downstairs with both feet on each step while holding on to a wall or railing.	Climbing up and down stairs using alternating feet and no hand support.
Rolling (somersault)	Tucking head into body while an adult pushes the child forward and turns the child over, with feet going over the child's head.	Rolling 360 degrees.

Figure 39b. Mastering Basic Gross Motor Skills

Gross Motor Skill	Physical Prerequisites for this Skill	What Constitutes Mastery
MANIPULATIVE MOVEMENT		
Throwing	Throwing a beanbag or ball underhand a short distance.	Throwing objects with controlled, smooth overhand motions; throwing a tennis ball 12 feet at target.
Catching	Trapping a thrown object with their whole body.	Catching an object in their hands with control, elbows bent.
Kicking	Kicking an object with adult holding the child's hand to maintain balance.	Kicking an object unassisted with a smooth, fluid motion of the leg.
STABILITY MOVEMENT		
Balancing	Walking along a line, sometimes on toes, occasionally stepping off of the line.	Walking forward or backward along an edge or beam for four or more steps without falling off; standing on elevated or unstable objects.
Stopping and starting	Stopping or starting with adult prompting and assistance.	Stopping and starting upon command, avoiding obstacles and changing directions.
Riding a trike	Sitting on tricycle and using feet to push forward or backward.	Using feet to pedal tricycle and handle bars to control direction and avoid obstacles.
Using a ride-on toy	Sitting atop toy and using feet to push forward or backward	Using feet to propel toy forward or backward and using handle bars to control path.
Swinging	Sitting on swing, pushed and caught by adult positioned behind swing.	Using feet to push up on swing; moving forward and backward seamlessly.

(Goodway, Ozmun, Gallahue 2012) (Herr, 2012)

Promoting Physical Fitness

When children are young, there is a natural compulsion to use their large muscles and to constantly be in motion. Unfortunately, this love of movement tends to fade away. According to the Center for Disease Control, 80% of adults in the U.S. over 18-years-old do not get the recommended amount of exercise needed to stay physically fit and healthy (Jaslow, 2013).

As an early childhood educator, you are in a unique position to emphasize the benefits of fitness. By promoting regular exercise and teaching children to value these efforts, you can help children make gross motor activity a habit that will carry on into adulthood. Children don't need to go to a gym to become physically fit. All they have to do is make movement a regular part of their daily routine.

Take A Look at Your Own Attitudes about Physical Activity

Along with the children's families, you can have a major influence on children's behavior. Your attitudes and actions about exercise and movement send children powerful messages. Consider your own beliefs and practices.
Do you:

- View physical development skills as important as cognitive, social, and emotional ones?
- Believe that early childhood educators should support all kinds of development and learning, including physical development?
- Believe that taking children outdoors at least twice a day helps to promote their health and fitness?
- Take children outside to play in all kinds of weather?
- Think that children and adults can have fun and benefit from staying physically fit?

If you answered "yes" to these questions, you are probably conveying to children a belief that physical activity is a priority in your program. These beliefs affect your teaching. If you want children to develop a lifelong desire to be physically fit, then you need to send messages that are consistent with this belief.

Age	Minimum Daily Activity Needed	Type of Activity
Infant	No specific requirement	Physical activity should encourage motor development.
Toddler	1½ hours	30 minutes planned physical activity and 60 minutes unstructured free play.
Preschooler	2 hours	60 minutes planned physical activity and 60 minutes unstructured free play.

In the chart above, you can see how much exercise the children you care for need, according to the National Association for Sport & Physical Education (NASPE) (Gavin, 2015).

As shown in the chart and mentioned earlier in this section, children need both unstructured and planned physical activity. In addition to providing these times for gross motor activity, it is also important that children be exposed to a balance of types of activity. To become fit, children need to participate in three types of activities:

1. Endurance
2. Strength
3. Flexibility

Endurance develops through aerobic activity. By moving vigorously, the heart strengthens and delivers more oxygen to the body. Activities that involve running, pedaling, and jumping all build endurance. To promote endurance, children can play games like tag, run relay races, or push a riding toy or ride a trike around a track.

Strength-building activities by definition make children stronger. When children do activities where they have to push, pull, and bend, they tone their muscles. To promote strength, children can climb a slide or swing on the monkey bars.

Flexibility comes from stretching the muscles. This enables children to bend more easily and use the full range of motion in their joints. Gross motor activities that enhance flexibility include such things as reaching out for a toy that is out of reach, attempting to do a cartwheel, and dancing enthusiastically to music.

By promoting fitness you help guard against what has become an epidemic of obesity. Children who engage in active play are not eating chips in front of a video game. If you make physical activity a regular and routine part of the day, children will value the role of fitness in their lives. The more this routine becomes a habit, the more likely it is that children will make fitness a part of their lives as they grow up. Hopefully the children you teach now will grow up to reverse the current trend and make fitness a way of life, their whole lives.

Supporting Fine Motor Development

Fine motor skills involve coordinating the small muscles of the hand, wrist, and fingers. These skills can be difficult to master, because they require muscular control, patience, judgment, and brain coordination. Children need to have a foundation in large muscle skills before they can develop fine motor skills. The hands and fingers need stable torso and shoulder muscles to function properly.

Like gross motor development, fine motor development is sequential and predictable. Children go through four stages in the development of fine motor skills, all during the first year of life. They spend the next four years of early childhood refining these movements (Huffman and Fortenberry 2011).

Fine motor skills can be difficult to master, because they require muscular control, patience, judgment, and brain coordination

1. Whole arm movements
2. Whole hand movements
3. Pincher movements, in which the thumb and index finger are pressed together and released
4. Pincer movements, in which the thumb and index finger coordinate to grasp an object

Here are some examples of how the progression works. First, babies need to develop the muscles in their arms with large movements of the whole arm before their hand muscles can be developed. We've all seen this when babies fling their arms to bat at a mobile. Older children continue refining their arm muscles by using large, circular motions to paint with water on the side of a building or to stir a bowl of fruit salad. As the arm muscles develop, the baby is able to use hand muscles to grasp a ring toy or rattle and squeeze a stuffed animal. Older children refine their hand muscles by squeezing a sponge or a baster in the water table. With practice, the baby learns to pinch a rag doll or a piece of edible playdough. Older children refine their pinching skills by using clothespins to hang laundry in the dramatic play area or squeeze an eyedropper with colored water in the science center. Ultimately, the hand movements become refined enough that pinching turns into grasping and the baby can grasp a piece of food or pick up beads using his thumb and index finger. From this point on, children can refine their small muscle skills to the point where they can feed and eventually dress themselves as toddlers. By the age of five years old, most children have the coordination to eat peas with a fork, use scissors to cut out collage materials, hold and turn the pages of a book, and play a kazoo. This is a long way from the newborn infant who could only grasp and hold an object by reflex.

Figure 40a. Fine Motor Skills for Young Children

Age	Developing Fine Motor Skills
Young Infants (birth–8 months)	• Hold and shake rattle. • Follow moving objects with eyes and head. • Grasp objects. • Look at an object in hand while bringing it to mouth. • Drop and put small blocks into a container.
Mobile Infants (9–17 months)	• Transfer a block or another toy from hand to hand. • Use pincher grasp with thumb and forefinger together to pick up small objects. • Push or pull toys while standing or walking. • Use spoon.
Toddlers (18–36 months)	• Hold cup or glass in one hand. • Unbutton large buttons. • Turn doorknobs. • Make lines, circles, or scribbles with fat crayons. • Stack small blocks. • Push and pat puzzle pieces into place. • Tear tissue paper into small pieces to glue onto paper. • Turn pages of books, though not always one at a time.

Figure 40b. Fine Motor Skills for Young Children

Age	Developing Fine Motor Skills
Young Preschooler (3–4 years old)	• Place large pegs into pegboards; string large beads; pour liquids with some spills. • Build block towers; easily do puzzles with whole objects represented as a piece. • Draw shapes, such as the circle; begin to design objects, such as a house or figure; draw objects in some relation to each other. • Hold crayons or markers with fingers instead of the fist. • Undress without assistance but needs help getting dressed; unbutton skillfully but button slowly. • Begin to cut with scissors.
Older Preschooler 4–5 years old	• Use small pegs and board; string small beads and may do so in a pattern. • Pour sand or liquid into small containers. • Build complex block structures that extend vertically; show limited spatial judgment and tend to knock things over. • Enjoy manipulating play objects that have fine parts; like to use scissors; practice an activity many times to gain mastery. • Draw combinations of simple shapes; draw persons with at least four parts and objects that are recognizable to adults. • Dress and undress without assistance; brush teeth and comb hair; spill rarely with cup or spoon; lace shoes or clothing, and learning to tie laces.

(American Academy of Pediatrics [AAP], 2013)

As with gross motor skills, children develop these skills at somewhat different rates. Each child is an individual, with his own unique timetable for development. Figure 40a-b presents an overview of fine motor skill development from birth to five years old. The timetable for children with disabilities may look different, depending on their specific disability. Talk with the family and other service providers about the child's development to ensure you are supporting the child's development, wherever they are on the timetable.

Even though there is a wide range of what is considered typical development during the early childhood years, it may be cause for concern if a four-month-old is not bringing an object to her mouth, a two-year-old is not drinking from a cup, or a preschooler is still having trouble using drawing and writing tools. Should you observe delays in development, discuss your concern with the child's family. As with gross motor difficulties, the parents may wish to consult the child's pediatrician or call in an early interventionist or special educator if the child is not yet on an Individual Education Plan or Individual Family Service Plan to conduct a more in-depth observation.

Supporting Fine Motor Development

While nearly every child will develop the fine motor skills listed earlier, children's mastery of these skills is greatly dependent on the support they receive. You need to create an environment where children have both the materials, opportunities, and the interactions they need to hone these skills.

Provide lots of open-ended experiences. Materials, like modeling clay, Lego® building bricks, and crayons, help children continue to develop their skills and abilities. Use these materials to create open-ended activities that promote children's fine motor skills as well as their cognitive skills and creativity.

Let children choose activities and tools that match their skills. For example, if a group of children are making a collage for the bulletin board, invite them either to tear paper or use scissors, depending on their preference and skill levels. Likewise, they can use glue sticks or paste—depending on their interest and skills. This allows children with varying skills to participate in the same activity and enjoy being part of the group experience.

Offer materials to explore and manipulate. As children explore and experiment, they become familiar with the materials, refine small motor skills, and take pleasure in the activities. However, forcing children to perform tasks or participate in activities before they are ready developmentally will thwart their progress. For example, children who are not yet ready to write letters or numbers will quickly become frustrated if they are required to do this task. But if they are free to experiment, children will start writing letters and numbers spontaneously when they are ready.

Adapting Fine Motor Play to Include and Support Children with Delays or Disabilities

There may be children in your setting who have difficulty moving the small muscles in their hands or who have developmental delays. Children with cerebral palsy or those who use a wheelchair are most likely to need extra help. Make sure children are positioned correctly by supporting their trunks so that their heads and hands are at the midpoint on their bodies.

Continue to observe children who have disabilities. Look for ways to adapt your materials and setting to include, stimulate, engage, and challenge all children as they develop their fine motor skills.

Some things you might try include the following (Gould and Sullivan 2004):

- Offer larger beads to string on pipe cleaners.
- Attach knobs to puzzle pieces to make them easier to grasp.
- Make use of vertical planes. Place books and puzzles on easels and tape pegboards against the wall.
- Replace buttons and zippers on dress-up clothes with Velcro® closures.
- Use shower curtain rings as zipper pulls on jackets.
- Glue magnets to the backs of small blocks and toys and place them on cookie sheets.

Provide vertical surfaces for scribbling, drawing, and writing. Vertical surfaces help children develop the small muscles in their hands and wrists, as well as the larger muscles in their arms and backs. Tape pieces of paper to the wall or use easels and encourage children to scribble, draw, and color on the paper.

Include natural opportunities to develop fine motor skills. You do not need to teach children specific fine motor skills like holding objects between their fingers and thumbs or making a circle with their thumbs and index fingers. Rather, when you encourage children to perform activities using materials that require these skills—including holding a paintbrush, fastening Velcro closures on shoes, or placing a puzzle piece in a frame—they will develop these skills naturally.

Stock the setting with materials that require fine motor skills. Children will not only have lots of opportunities to practice and refine their fine motor skills, but they can pick the type of activity that will interest them and motivate them to practice. For example, Santiago may choose to play with a puzzle while Ava may opt to play with blocks. Both children will be developing fine motor skills while doing what they enjoy.

Model and/or demonstrate how to use materials correctly, when appropriate. For example, you might model how to use musical instruments or tools like hammers. Materials that are new to children, like digital cameras or board games, may also require modeling or direct instruction before you introduce them into play.

Offer activities that give children opportunities to practice their fine motor skills over and over. The only way that children will master fine motor skills is to practice. Experts (Huffman and Fortenberry 2011) suggest activities such as the following to target fine motor development:

Targeted Muscle	Activity
Whole Arm	• Tape paper to the underside of a table and have children draw, lying on their backs. • Place pebbles in a pot and in the dramatic play area have children stir up some stone soup.
Whole Hand	• Using a divided food dish or bowl, have children use a sponge to transfer water from one side of the dish to the other and back again. • Have children pour one cup of cornmeal through a crank-handled sifter.
Pincher	• Have children sort buttons and then place them through slits into color-coded containers. • Have children use tongs to sort buttons into egg cartons. • Have children use tweezers to capture corks floating in water. • Give children closed locks with keys and let them determine which keys open which locks.

Below we offer age-specific guidance on materials that promote children's fine motor development.

Young Infants (Birth–8 Months)

Provide space and opportunity for infants to move their legs, feet, arms, and hands and to kick, hit, and grasp objects. Place interesting objects and toys within infants' reach to look or swipe at, hit, or kick. Be careful not to place objects into infants' hands until they are ready to grasp and release objects independently, starting at about three months of age. In addition to grasping, babies like to shake, mouth and suck most everything. Offer them rattles, squeeze toys, large rings, teething toys, soft dolls and balls, and vinyl and cloth books.

Six-month-old Donovan loves when his FCC educator Ms. Garcia sits in a rocking chair and reads to him. Today she is holding a board book of Goodnight, Moon. Donovan smiles and rocks his body against Ms. Garcia's as she starts reading. When she turns to the second page, Donovan reaches for the book. Ms. Garcia decides to let Donovan pick up the book and mouth it, rather than to try continuing to read. She is pleased that he is grasping so many objects and feels that Donovan is learning about books just as much by using his senses as when he hears the story read. She smiles at him and says, "It's a very tasty story, don't you think, Donovan?"

Mobile Infants (9–17 Months)

Provide toys and materials that encourage fine motor skills including shape sorters, nesting toys, large beads, containers for inserting and removing objects, and toys with pieces that separate, fit together, fit inside, and stack. Play games with infants that require physical actions. Include a variety of board books in your setting that infants can look through independently. Allow plenty of time for infants to explore and manipulate a variety of items. Support infants in learning how to feed themselves independently. For example, most one-year-old children are ready to drink from a cup. Providing appropriate cups for infants to drink from will help them develop fine motor skills as they grasp the cups and move them toward their mouths.

Twelve-month-old Tasha delights in feeding herself. However, her preferred method of doing this is to grasp a spoon in her right hand and lift up the food with her left. Since she's having applesauce, there's a trail of sauce from the bowl to her face. After washing Tasha's face and dirty hand, her teacher Mr. Manillo announces to Tasha that now that she is able to hold a spoon so well, he wants to show her how a spoon works.

Toddlers (18–36 Months)

Provide opportunities for toddlers to play and interact with other children. Provide toys and materials that help them practice fine motor skills and eye–hand coordination, such as puzzles, pegs and pegboards, blocks, construction toys, beads to string, and lacing cards, and musical instruments. Provide sensory experiences too, using sand or water with toys, such as shovels and buckets, cups, spoons, squirt bottles, and other containers. Art materials like jumbo crayons, markers, large paintbrushes, blunt-tipped scissors, jumbo chalk, clay and fingerpaint allow children to create while refining fine motor skills. Introduce pretend play props that require children to develop the small muscles in their hands: foods, kitchen equipment, table settings, and dress-up clothes.

Two-year-old Sophie loves doing puzzles. She adeptly lifts the puzzle pieces up by their knobs and moves them around until the puzzle is complete. She then claps for herself. Seeing that Sophie is starting to get bored doing four-piece puzzles, her FCC educator Mrs. Brown makes a mental note to get some 8- and 12-piece puzzles to better challenge Sophie's cognitive and fine motor skills.

Preschoolers (3–5 Years Old)

Preschoolers enjoy a wide variety of toys and materials that help them refine the fine motor skills they have been working on since infancy. The best way for children to practice using these skills is to manipulate materials as part of their normal play experiences. Think of how you might help a child work on fine motor skills while doing art or pretending to cook a meal in the dramatic play center. The goal for educators of preschoolers is to provide a rich environment that will facilitate children's acquisition and mastery of fine motor skills in every learning center in the setting. Children are motivated to use these materials because they are encouraged to play in centers that are of most interest to them.

Three-year-old Miguel has been trying to use scissors to cut tissue paper for a collage. His attempts have all led to frustration and his teacher Ms. Nguyen sees that he is on the verge of tears. Because she doesn't think that Miguel's fine motor skills are at a point where he can successfully use scissors and because she wants Miguel to experience success, she suggests that Miguel tear the tissue papers with his hands rather than the scissors. She starts to tear down the top of one of the tissue papers to demonstrate how it's done, and then hands it over to Miguel to finish.

In Figure 41 you'll find a list of materials you can add to the learning centers in your setting to promote fine motor development. Regard these ideas as suggestions to spark your thinking. Materials should represent diversity in various categories, including race, culture, language, gender, and ability.

Figure 41. Materials for Promoting Fine Motor Development in Preschoolers (3–5 Years Old)

Learning Center	Materials
Blocks	Foam blocks, hardwood blocks, animal figures, people figures, small cars, buses, trains, traffic signs, books, markers and chart paper, ramps, and pulleys
Art	Paints, brushes, chalk, crayons, markers, scissors, stapler, puncher, stencils, clays, wires, pipe cleaners, potholder loops and looms, feathers, paste, glue, rubber bands, and wires
Literacy	Books, felt letters and numbers, magnetic letters and numbers, puppets, letter stamps, markers, paper clips, pencil sharpener, stencils, computer or tablet keyboard, mouse, and printer
Dramatic Play	Dress-up clothing, hats, purses, jewelry, plastic foods, telephones, writing pads, cookbooks, and dolls
Music & Movement	Musical instruments (drums, kazoos, rhythm sticks, bells, triangles, maracas, etc.), headphones, and CD/DVD/tape/MP3 players
Science	Seeds, prisms, magnifying glasses, eyedroppers, tweezers, tongs, magnets, pet food, markers and chart paper, books, and egg cartons for sorting
Math & Manipulatives	Lego® building bricks, people figures, props, beads, sewing cards, pegs and pegboards, geoboards, Cuisenaire® rods, parquetry blocks, interlocking links and cubes, lotto games, dominoes, card games, board games, puzzles, self-help frames, nesting boxes and cups, shape sorters, attribute blocks, and Unifix® cubes
Sand/Water	(Sand Center) Measuring cups, measuring spoons, pails and shovels, cookie cutters, muffin tins, ladles, magnifying glasses, shakers, toothbrushes, combs, scoops, funnels, tongs, tweezers, colander, and rakes (Water Center) Basters, squirt bottles, whisks, eggbeaters, sponges, dolls, straws, eyedroppers, fishnets, gutters, tubing, waterwheels, toy boats, and bubble wands
Cooking	Measuring spoons, measuring cups, pastry brushes, pitchers, rolling pins, can openers, mixers, mortars and pestles, graters, timers, colanders, eggbeaters, funnels, ladles, spatulas, tongs, sifters, and pastry bags and tips
Outdoors	Gardening shovels, rakes, hoes, sand and water shovels and pails, miniature animal figures, people figures, cars and trucks, books, writing paper and markers, and board games

Connecting Physical Development to the Development of the Whole Child

In the early years of life, the varied domains of development and learning are interconnected. Think about the following. Is building a structure out of hollow blocks an example of a physical development task? Cognitive development? Social and emotional development? Language development? All of these answers are correct.

How about toilet learning? Obviously, the successful potty chair user must possess a number of physical skills like walking, being able to pull down one's pants, and sit on a chair. They also have to be able to control the sphincter muscles around the anus. Beyond this, they need to have acquired the cognitive skill of following directions and the language skill of using potty-related vocabulary. Perhaps most importantly, the child needs to have the social and emotional desire to want to use the chair and act like a grown-up. The pride the child feels in mastering the task will be second only to their parents' joy. Keep in mind that toilet learning is also cultural. Talk to families about their preferences.

The point is that it is almost impossible to separate physical development from the rest of children's development. With young children, social, emotional, cognitive, and language development are interrelated. Every time a child learns a physical skill, it has an impact on the other domains of development. For example, a toddler may pull a friend in a wagon—a physical task. At the same time, the two friends are working on social skills and as they converse, they refine their language skills.

The Interconnectedness of Development During Play

Jessica and Cheyenne decide to build a fort out of hollow blocks together (social development). They discuss the need to take the blocks outdoors (language development). They carry the blocks outdoors and set them on a level area of ground (physical development). They devise a plan (language development; cognitive development) to make a square out of the blocks first (cognitive development) and then stack them (physical development). When they finish, they admire their fort and high-five each other to celebrate their success (social-emotional development).

Not only is physical development interrelated to the development of the whole child, it is linked to academic gains. Contemporary brain research has shown that both gross and fine motor skill development are related to brain development. More specifically, research has also shown that the ability to skip improves reading skills (Teacher Support Force [TSF] 2011). According to the CDC's review of research literature (Carollo 2012) physical activity has a positive impact on cognitive skills and academic behavior, including enhanced concentration and attention. In addition, every time children move the small muscles in their hands, brain connections are strengthened (Bredekamp 2013).

There is no denying that when children master physical skills and use them daily, they are fostering their whole development and predisposing themselves for academic success.

Promoting Perceptual-Motor Skills

In addition to the interrelatedness of physical development with the other domains of learning (cognitive, language, social, and emotional development), we also know that sensory input affects physical development. The information provided through our senses (touching, seeing, hearing, smelling, and tasting) impacts our physical movements. For young children who are dependent on sensory learning, this means that their physical development is influenced by how they use the information they receive from their senses. The process known as "perceptual motor development" focuses precisely on this relationship.

To understand how this works, think about an infant crawling from room to room in an FCC home. As the texture and slant of the crawling surface changes, the child uses this visual and tactile input to change the speed and direction of his crawling. The sensory input that the child received and processed made the child adjust his physical movements. In a similar fashion, a toddler learning to string beads orients the beads towards the needle according to where she sees and feels the holes in the beads. Sensory input influences both gross motor and fine motor skills. It is an "in-out" process. Information comes "in" to the mind and is processed; it comes "out" in a response of bodily movement.

You are probably already familiar with the term "eye-hand coordination." When people talk about eye-hand coordination they are actually talking about sensory awareness, which is a part of perceptual-motor development. If Elyse wants to put a ball into a pail, she visualizes where she has to move the ball and then lifts her arm and grasps the ball, moving it to where her vision showed her the ball should go. Although vision is the dominant sense used by young children, children learn through all of their senses. From infancy, children are able to combine sensory awareness with movement. When a baby grasps a book and puts it in her mouth, she is learning what books are like, including how they taste.

Perceptual-motor skill development is based on the works of Montessori and Piaget, whom you'll read about in Chapter 5. It is a process that allows children to use their mind and bodies together as a unified whole. You can promote perceptual-motor development by offering children activities that tie sensory learning to physical movement. For example, during group time, have children sing and chant finger plays, like "Open, Shut Them" which involves physical movements:

Open, shut them, *(open and shut fists)*,

Open, shut them,

Give a little clap, clap, clap *(clap)*.

Open, shut them *(open and shut fists)*,

Open, shut them,

Fold them in your lap, lap, lap *(place hands in lap)*.

Creep them, creep them *(walk hands up body to chin)*,

Slowly creep them,

Right up to your chin, chin, chin.

Open wide your little mouth,

But do not put them in, in, in.

Other songs, like "Head, Shoulders, Knees, and Toes;" "Where Is Thumbkin?;" and "The Hokey Pokey" also incorporate physical movements and help children develop body awareness—a sense of their body parts and how they are connected. More active games like "Duck, Duck, Goose" and "Hide and Seek" teach spatial awareness—where children are in relation to their environments. Ask families to suggest songs and games from their cultures and home languages. Whenever you encourage children to use their senses, you are facilitating perceptual-motor development. ■

CHAPTER 5:

Cognitive

CDA® Functional Area 5: Candidate uses a variety of developmentally appropriate learning experiences and teaching strategies to promote curiosity, reasoning, and problem-solving and to lay the foundation for all later learning. Candidate implements curriculum that promotes children's learning of important mathematics, science, technology, social studies, and other content goals.

Cognitive

Introduction

Cognitive development refers to children's increasing ability to think, reason, and understand. Children's brains develop rapidly during early childhood. They are learning to expand their memories, increase their powers of attention, solve problems, think symbolically, employ logic, predict situation outcomes, understand others' perspectives, and understand cause and effect.

Your role in supporting children's cognitive growth is vital, and in this chapter, you will learn the following:

- **Understanding the Cognitive Development of Infants, Toddlers, and Preschoolers**
- **Major and Related Theories of Cognition**
- **Learning Through Play**
- **Learning Throughout the Day**
- **Supporting Children's Content Learning**

Understanding the Cognitive Development of Infants, Toddlers, and Preschoolers

In the early childhood years, cognitive development is the process of growth and change in intellectual abilities. During this time, from birth through age five, children make rapid advances in how they process, store, and use the information gained from observing and interacting with the world around them. They use the information they take in to expand and develop their abilities to pay attention, to remember, and to think and reason. As experts have put it, "Complex human reasoning is … rooted in early childhood" (Shonkoff and Phillips 2000). The question of when cognitive development begins has long been debated by educators and researchers. Up until about 35 or 40 years ago, researchers believed that even though cognitive development started early, it didn't really begin until children were verbal. The philosopher John Locke said that we are born with minds that are blank slates and the psychologist William James described the baby's world as one of "blooming, buzzing confusion" (Gopnik 2009). Experts thought that infants entered this world with very few cognitive powers. The idea that babies had memories, could grasp mathematical concepts, and had beginning understandings of cause and effect would have been regarded as absurd. Yet, recent research has shown that infants can do all of these complex processes and more. In fact, we now know that children learn more in the first 12 months of life than they will at any other time in their lives (Royal Children's Education Institute 2011).

Beginning in the 1970s, researchers began looking at what children did rather than what they said. The result of this research confirms that "Even the youngest children know, experience, and learn far more than scientists ever thought possible" (Gopnik 2010). They approach learning in much the same way that an actual scientist does—by observing, conducting experiments, and analyzing data. In her groundbreaking work, *The Scientist in the Crib*, Gopnik and her co-authors present studies showing babies can understand the principles of everyday physics and throughout the early childhood years have an extraordinary ability to learn from statistical patterns and use this information to draw conclusions about the world. From as early as the first two days of life, newborns have an approximate sense of numbers. Researchers can tell this by measuring the amount of time babies stare at certain grids of dots. Those babies who showed a high sense of number at six months of age, statistically outperformed their age-mates in math skills at three-and-a-half years of age (Pappas 2013).

Our current understanding of cognitive development is that children enter this world "wired" to learn. It is not necessary to motivate infants to learn—they are born wanting to learn. The job of families and early childhood educators is to encourage a child's drive to learn. In 2000, the National Research Council and the Institute of Medicine of the National Academies published the landmark book *From Neurons to Neighborhoods: The Science of Early Childhood Development.* In this book, the authors explain that infants are born with millions of brain cells (neurons) that connect (synapses) as a result of experiences during the early years of life. Their research emphasizes the importance of four essential aspects of learning for young children (Shonkoff and Phillips 2000):

- Loving and caring relationships with adults.
- Many opportunities to explore the world through seeing, touching, hearing, tasting, and smelling.
- Conversation and language richness in the environment.
- Play.

In addition to the debate over when learning begins, another long-time debate in the field of early childhood education concerns the roles of nature and nurture in cognitive development. Does heredity predetermine cognitive ability or do the child's experiences and environment determine what a child will become? Nativists take the position that all or most behaviors and characteristics are the result of inheritance. Genetic traits, in their view determine our intellectual abilities: smart parents have smart children. Empiricists like John Locke (and his blank slate) and behaviorists like James B. Watson, take the position that all or most behaviors and characteristics result from learning. Watson believed he could train anyone of any background to do anything. Over the years, both sides have prevailed in the argument, and the pendulum swung back and forth accordingly.

Today, we understand that both heredity and environment work in tandem to support cognitive development. It is often referred to metaphorically as a delicate dance that goes on throughout life. Rather than continue the debate, it has become a non-issue. Jack Shonkoff (2005) has declared that "Nature vs. nurture is simplistic and scientifically obsolete. No gene exists without the influence of environment."

Gaining Cognitive Skills

Young children are active learners who use all of their senses to interact with the people and objects in their world. Through active explorations in the context of loving relationships, young children begin to learn what their world is like and how to make associations, compare and contrast, and categorize. Preschoolers need adults to support their learning and guide them to higher levels of thinking and reasoning through modeling, questioning, exploration and experimentation. What and how children learn during the first five years of their lives lays the foundation for successful lifelong learning. Children become confident learners when adults encourage their discoveries and explorations. The degree of cognitive learning in the early childhood years is dramatic. For the most part, these skills fall into nine categories (Gordon and Browne 2016):

1. **Skills of inquiry.** Children listen to others, look for patterns, organize what they hear, make hypotheses, test them out, and evaluate the results. They are scientists and investigators.

   At the water table, Lanny, age three, is upset that water is only coming out of a few holes in his straining ladle. "Ms. Lance," he says, "The water is stuck." Ms. Lance suggests that they hold the ladle up to the light to examine it. "The holes are dirty," declares Lanny. "I see what you mean," says Ms. Lance. "Do you think that is the problem?" "I think that's it. Can we clean them out?" suggests Lanny. Ms. Lance hands Lanny a pipe cleaner, retrieved from the art center. Lanny hurries to the trash can where he punches through the holes. He races back to the water table to test the newly cleaned ladle. "It works!" exclaims Lanny.

2. **Knowledge of the physical world.** Children use all of their senses to learn about the people and objects in the world around them. A baby picks up and examines a doll using his senses. He looks, touches, and tastes the doll. A toddler picks up and releases everything he sees to watch and learn about what happens when things are dropped. A preschooler rings a series of bells to see which has the loudest tone. All are learning about the properties of objects and how they work. Explorations of their environment turn children into scientists and provide the foundation for learning about cause-and-effect and problem solving.

   Eighteen month old Maurice lifts and drops several different stuffed animals. After noticing that the rabbit squeaks when dropped, he singles in on dropping the rabbit only. He greets each squeak with his own squeal. His FCC educator Mrs. Campbell is thrilled that Maurice is learning about cause and effect.

3. **Knowledge of the social world.** At the same time that children are using all of their senses to learn about the objects in their world, they are learning about the people who inhabit it. A newborn learns to distinguish between people familiar to her and those who are strangers. A toddler can tell you with confidence that anything you pick up is his. Many four-year-olds can feel empathy for a child who is hurt and share a favorite toy without first fighting over it. Children learn how they are alike and different from others and what it means to negotiate with others.

   Two-year-old Tomas and his age-mate Marnie both want to crawl through the tunnel. When Marnie says, "Me first," Tomas bites her arm. Now both children are crying. Their teacher Ms. James first tends to Marnie and makes sure she is okay. Then she beckons Tomas to her side and says, "Tomas, it is not okay to bite other people. Use your words to tell people what you want." Tomas hugs Ms. James and she puts her arms around both children, letting Tomas know that while she doesn't like his behavior, she still cares about him. Tomas hugs Marnie, then both children go back to crawl through the tunnel.

4. **Classification.** Through their interaction with the physical world, children begin to notice that people and objects have specific attributes. A plum is round, a rug is rectangular, bananas are yellow, and beards are prickly. Classification is the ability to group, sort, categorize, and connect objects and people by these various characteristics. While toddlers may sort objects according to their own criteria ("foods I like") over time and with language they use consistent criteria like shape, color, and size. Preschoolers are learning to sort using two or more criteria, noting that an apple is both green and round.

   Three-year old Ava is examining the natural items collected on a morning nature walk. Her teacher, Mr. Spinelli, lifts up a leaf, a twig, and an acorn and asks her where the children found these things. Ava replies, "On the ground, near the big tree." Mr. Spinelli then holds up a carrot, a beet, and a cabbage leaf and again asks Ava where she found these things. She replies, "In our garden." Mr. Spinelli offers Ava two boxes and a pair of tongs and suggests that she sort the materials into the two boxes. Ava agrees, saying, "I'll put the tree stuff in one box and the garden vegetables in the other one."

5. **Seriation.** Seriation may be defined as the ability to put objects in order based on a particular property of those objects. Size is the most common form of seriation in which objects are arranged by increasing size. But seriation can pertain to any attribute such as shades of a color, weights of objects, or even their number.

Four-year old Julie has brought in wooden babushka (nesting) dolls that her grandmother brought back from the Ukraine to share with everyone during morning group time. When her FCC educator Ms. Domingo asks her if she knows why they are called babushka dolls, she points to the red painted scarf that the doll is wearing and proudly says, "Because she's wearing a babushka." She then starts to pull the doll apart and says "Here's the best thing. There's lots of dolls inside." Everyone watches in amazement as Julie pulls apart a second doll, a third doll, and a fourth doll, lining up the five dolls in order of size. Julie says, "The little one doesn't come apart." "Wow," says Ms. Domingo, "Let's count them now from biggest to smallest." Touching each babushka doll in turn, Julie counts out loud, 1-2-3-4-5.

6. **Numbers.** The concept of number involves learning about quantity—its amount, its degree, and its position. Typically, between 8 and 12 months of age, babies have learned that objects still exist even if they cannot be seen (object permanence). This understanding comes after numerous interactions with the environment and countless games of peek-a-boo. Building on this understanding, preschoolers start to learn about quantity. This is when they can start counting items and learning that objects are counted in a specific order and are only counted once.

   There are four children at the art table this morning wanting to finger paint. Their teacher Ms. Butler tells them that she will get the paints for them. While she is doing that, she asks three-year-old Andre if he will hand out the finger painting paper, telling him that each child should get a piece of paper and that he should remember to put a paper in front of his chair so that he will have one, too. Andre counts out four pieces of paper and hands them out. Ms. Butler makes a quick note on an index card to record this example of how Andre is learning one-to one correspondence.

7. **Symbols.** Symbols stand for something else. When we talk about symbols in early childhood cognition, we are referring to the ability to picture, remember, understand, and replicate objects that are not immediately in front of us. It involves creating mental images of objects and storing them in our minds for later use. Like numeracy, this is a process that cannot occur prior to the development of object permanence, and usually does not develop before 18 months. You see lots of symbolic thought in toddlers and preschoolers during dramatic play. In addition, older children might represent a figure in their paintings or choose an avatar on the computer.

   Today, the dramatic play area is set up like an office. Four-year-old Kaylee is playing there with Kevin, who is pretending to be her assistant. Kevin comes rushing in and tells Kaylee she has an important phone call. Kaylee lifts her right hand to her ear and says to her hand. "This is Kaylee. How can I help you?"

8. **Spatial relationships.** Spatial relationships involve mentally determining the position of objects and people in space and how they relate to each other in movement. Infants start developing this skill as they reach for an object and place it in their mouths. As babies start moving they begin to learn what is nearby and what is far away, what is above and what is below, and what is in front and what is behind. By three years of age, children can use this vocabulary to describe what they observe.

   Ms. Rubenstein, a toddler educator, gives two-year-old Lee a four piece puzzle to play with. Lee has no problem getting the first two pieces in, but is getting frustrated trying to orient the third piece correctly. After watching Lee continuing to have trouble and sensing he is about to start crying, Ms. Rubenstein kneels down and puts her hand over Lee's, which is holding the puzzle piece by its knob, and gently suggests, "Let's try turning the piece this way." She then releases Lee's hand and lets Lee triumphantly put the piece in the puzzle board.

9. **Time.** Advanced cognitive concept involves understanding several interrelated dimensions: present time, past time, future time, and time as a continuum. Mobile infants gain a beginning concept of time when their educators flip a light switch to indicate that an activity has ended. Toddlers and preschoolers learn to understand the sequence of time when they follow a picture-based daily schedule. They begin to get a sense of clocks and calendars and recall what happened yesterday and how long it will be until their birthdays.

   Ms. Harris teaches preschool on an Army base. Five-year-old Jonah arrives seeming very sad and withdrawn. His mother tells Ms. Harris that Jonah's father was deployed and won't be back for two months. Ms. Harris sits down with Jonah and talks with him about how he feels with his dad away. Feeling a bit better after their talk, Jonah says, "I can't wait to see him. How much longer will it be?" Ms. Harris then brings over a calendar and hands it to Jonah. She flips over two months and tells Jonah, "This is when your dad will be back. Let's put a picture of him here on December 5th. Today is October 6th, right here. Every day, I want you to make a painting or a sculpture or a story that you can dictate to me for your dad. We'll take a photo of it, and put it on the day that you did it. When we fill up all of the days between now and dad's picture, he will be home. Let's keep the calendar in your cubby and we'll take it out every day when you've made something for your dad. How does that sound?"

Cognitive Development Milestones

As noted above, children are acquiring a dazzling number of cognitive skills from birth through age five. From a baby sticking out her tongue to indicate she is hungry to a five-year-old experimenting to see how much water yields the ideal growth of mung beans, children are developing cognitive powers in all of the nine skill categories noted above. Figure 42a-c (Berk 2012; Learning Disabilities Association of America 1999; Administration for Children & Families 2015) presents some of major milestones of cognitive development during the early childhood years. Because there are so many things happening in the area of cognitive development during the early years, these are just a sampling of some of the major milestones. As with the discussion of milestone charts in Chapters 4, 6, and 9, it's important to remember that milestones are norms and children develop according to an their own individual timetable. In addition, nutrition, health care, temperament, culture (including linguistic background), and the presence or absence of disabilities can all affect development.

Stages of Racial Awareness

Many early childhood professionals and families wonder how to talk to young children about race. Some believe children are too young, while others fear that talking about race might promote racism. The failure to talk about race contributes to racial inequities (Plaut, et al., Romano, 2018). Adults may be uncomfortable talking about race because they were taught to be "colorblind" and do not have experience having such discussions. Children develop an awareness of race in infancy, and by the time they are two-years-old, children show a strong preference for those in the same racial group (Baron & Banaji, 2006). Stages of racial awareness:

Infants (Birth–17 Months)

Shortly after birth, babies are able to distinguish the features of caregivers of all races. By the time a child is 3-months-old, they show a strong preference for same race caregivers (Kelly, et al., 2005). At this age, they demonstrate a significant preference for faces from their own-ethnic group. By the time they are 9-months-old, they are only able to distinguish the facial features of same race caregivers. This is called perceptual narrowing or Other Race Effect (ORE). As infants grow older, they have difficulty distinguishing faces of ethnic groups (Maurer & Werker, 2013). Perceptual narrowing does not occur in infants who are exposed to caregivers of different races (Anzures, 2012). Exposure to caregivers of different races not only prevents perceptual narrowing, it can also reverse the effects of perceptual narrowing.

Toddlers (18–36 Months)

By the time children are two years old, they show a strong preference for those in the same racial group (Baron & Banaji, 2006). Toddlers are very aware of differences and at this age, they begin to sort and classify people based on skin color. They are also beginning to pick up on stereotypes and social attitudes about race. Young children are naturally curious and may ask questions like, "Why is her skin brown?" It is important to talk to children openly and candidly about skin color and differences. When they are hushed or reprimanded, they may develop negative associations related to race and begin to draw their own conclusions based on very limited knowledge.

Preschoolers (3–5 Years Old)

Three- to five-year-olds categorize people by race and express bias based on race (Aboud, 2008; Hirschfeld, 2008). They use racial categories to identify themselves and to categorize others. Preschoolers use race as a determinant to include or exclude children from activities, and to wield power "in their own social/play networks" (Winkler, 2009). It is important to talk about race and promote racial identity in a positive way so children are less likely to internalize racial discrimination. Silence can reinforce racism or discomfort with talking about race. The adult should actively help children feel positive about their racial identity, have accurate words to describe and understand other's racial identities, and the skills to challenge racist behaviors. Talk about how we want to treat other people the way we would want to be treated. "We treat everyone fairly. We try to make sure everyone in the class gets what they need." Be careful to promote empathy and not sympathy. It is important that White children not feel sorry for children of color so that superior attitudes are not developed. You can say, "We all have different skin color, but we are all the same. We have families, we eat food, and we like to play. It isn't right to treat someone differently based on the color of their skin."

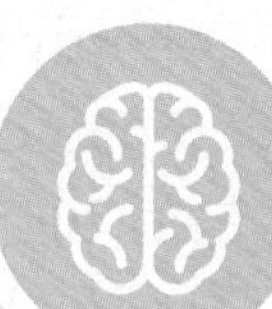

The Impact of Culture on Cognition

Until a couple of decades ago, the idea that culture could influence cognition was outright dismissed (Wiseman 2006). It was widely assumed that basic cognitive processes are universal. However, recent research contrasting cultures has uncovered subtle differences in cognitive development that are influenced by culture. For example, in tests of categorization, American children form categories according to type: a cow and a pig go together because they are both animals. In contrast, Asian children form categories according to relationships. Asian children group a cow with grass, because the cow eats the grass. In general Asian cultures are more intuitive and less linear in thinking and reasoning than are Americans and Europeans.

The Impact of Culture on Cognition (continued)

Culture affects all aspects of cognition. It affects the way we think and the way we interact with others. Tone of voice, choice of words, facial expressions and eye contact are a byproduct of the culture we live in. And since so much of cognitive learning is dependent on children asking questions and learning from adults who guide them, differences in cultures will impact the acquisition of skills. A child who is taught that it's rude to look an adult in the eye or that one must reflect before answering will not do well with an early childhood educator who regards these practices as signs of inattention and slowness.

As an early childhood educator, it is important to get to know, respect, and value all cultures. Think also about your own cultural values and practices so you are truly supporting children's cognitive development in your interactions.

As an early educator, it is important to understand the cultural lens through which you view the world. Your culture influences your perception of others, expectations, values, and sense of right and wrong. Make an effort to identify areas where your cultural values and beliefs may be misaligned with the culture of the families and children you serve. "Misunderstandings about the role of culture in behavior, communication, and learning often lead to assumptions about the abilities of children to be successful in school. An awareness and understanding of the role of culture in the classroom, and the different values and behaviors that may accompany culture can remove unintentional barriers to a child's success" (Zion & Kozleski, 2005).

Further, these unintentional barriers are sometimes precipitated not by your individual cultural lens, but by the cultural values embedded in the program practices that you implement. So it is also important to begin what will become a career long quest to identify those that may impede the development of the children in the program, or cause conflict with family cultural values, and determine ways to become an effective advocate for change on behalf of those children and families. We will discuss more about strategies for this in the Competency Area of Professionalism.

Figure 42a. Cognitive Skills for Young Children

Age	Developing Cognitive Skills
Young Infants (birth–8 months)	• Imitates facial expressions and gestures of others, like smiling. • Explores using motor skills, such as turning head, sucking, kicking, grasping. • Recognizes familiar faces and voices; smiles back at people. • Detects differences in senses of hearing and taste: pitch and volume; salty, bitter, and sour tastes. • Awareness of shape and size constancy. • Repeats actions to make things happen or to get adults to repeat an action. • Begins to understand object permanence. • Remembers earlier toys played with; show excitement at their return. • Begins to categorize objects by function and behavior. • Uses gestures like waving to communicate.

Figure 42b. Cognitive Skills for Young Children

Age	Developing Cognitive Skills
Mobile Infants (9–17 months)	• Imitate everyday actions of others. • Point to objects and pictures. • Put small objects in and out of container with intention. • Understand object permanence. • Categorize many objects by function and behavior. • Make things happen intentionally, like pulling a string to retrieve attached toy. • Understand and respond to words or commands appropriately. • Name familiar objects. • Use quantity-related words like "more" or "all gone". • Actively sort objects into one category. • Are beginning to match objects through toys such as shape sorters. • Can match two similar objects. • Recognize own image in mirror. • Initiate play activities. • Understand and follow simple directions. • Anticipate routines.
Toddlers (18–36 months)	• Can point out and name familiar objects in books. • Explore how objects such as balls move through space. • Can find object moved out of sight. • Sort objects into sub-groups of categories. • Sequence objects from smallest to largest. • Represent ideas symbolically in pretend play. • Act out routines, stories, and social roles. • Recognize difference between self and others. • Aware of own gender. • Know own name and age and will show age by raising fingers. • Enjoy watching and playing with other children. • Begin to understand whole/part concepts. • Understand two-step directions. • Relate memories to others. • Can build on past experiences. • Use problem solving and experimentation to determine solutions to everyday problems. • Use quantity-related vocabulary. • Understand how objects fit together. • Solve the same problem in different ways. • Plan ways to solve problems. • Begin counting small number of objects.

Figure 42c. Cognitive Skills for Young Children

Age	Developing Cognitive Skills
Preschoolers (3–5 years)	• Understand and follow multi-step directions. • Make up own games. • Anticipate cause-and-effect of own actions. • Engage in elaborate pretend play scenarios. • Demonstrate awareness of past and present. • Identify and use senses in observations. • Ask what, why, and how questions for information. • Observe, gather and record data to answer questions and solve problems. • Draw conclusions from investigations. • Verbalize cause-and-effect relationships. • Distinguish animate from inanimate objects. • Sort objects into hierarchically organized categories. • Grasp conservation (See section on Piaget). • Begin to understand differences between fantasy and reality. • Rhyme. • Name, identify, and match six or more colors. • Count to 20 and higher by ones. • Pair objects with numbers up to 10 and higher. • Represent addition and subtraction with fingers, objects, and drawings. • Fill in missing elements in patterns. • Measure using nonstandard tools such as blocks and standard tools. • Compare and measure objects according to size and weight. • Know basic shapes in any orientation. • Understand directionality and positioning. • Tell where they live (street and town). • Write their own name. • Increased understanding of time: can talk about yesterday or last week, today, and tomorrow.

Possible Developmental Concerns

As always in development, while it's important to realize that not all development takes place according to standards in milestone charts, there are times when you should be concerned about lags in development. Developmental delays—which include thinking skills—are in fact the most common form of disability in young children. If you do not observe the following by the ages noted, meet with the children's family and together decide if you should consult with a special educator who can do further testing. Cultural differences in practices, values, and child rearing can influence the timing when milestones are reached. Therefore, it is important to ask questions about family priorities and philosophies.

By 12 months, if the child does not:

- search for hidden objects
- use gestures to communicate, such as waving
- imitate actions or words

By 18 months, if the child does not:

- vocalize frequently
- point or show things that interest him
- engage in social games, like patty-cake
- play with and explore a variety of toys

By 24 months, if the child does not:

- interact with others during play
- recognize pictures of familiar objects and people by pointing or naming them
- engage in pretend play

By 36 months, if the child does not:

- name pictures
- follow simple directions
- answer questions about recent experiences
- engage in symbolic play

By 60 months, if the child has:

- a lack of curiosity or interest in the surrounding world
- difficulty learning new information despite significant effort and repetition
- difficulty learning new skills despite significant practice
- difficulty solving ordinary, simple problems
- trouble remembering things
- difficulty meeting educational demands

Figure 43. Making Accommodations for Children with Cognitive Impairments

Cognitive impairment, also referred to as "intellectual disability" and once called "mental retardation," describes a condition in which a child has intellectual and adaptive skills significantly below the average for a child his age. It affects 12 in every 1,000 children (Siskin Children's Institute n.d.). It is important to bear in mind that there are many levels of cognitive disabilities, and even the most severely impaired children are able to learn new skills.

Educators can support the development of children with cognitive impairments the same way that they treat all children. Assume that with patience and repetition, all children can learn. Gould and Sullivan (2004) offer these strategies for making your curriculum accessible to children with cognitive impairments:

- Simplify tasks by reducing the number of steps involved.
- Use modelling and cueing.
- Incorporate structure and routine into the daily program. Routines provide opportunities to repeat and practice skills.
- Simplify your language. Short phrases are best. Many children respond well to a rhythmic cadence or having conversation sung to them.
- Arrange furniture to block out distractions.
- Provide ample opportunity for repetition and practice.
- Maintain eye contact with the child while talking.
- Shorten activities to match the child's attention span.
- Use dramatic vocal effects to keep the child's attention.
- Offer only a few choices.
- Provide clear demonstration as needed, accompanied by short, simple sentences. Encourage children to imitate your actions.

Major and Related Theories of Cognition

The theorists you will read about in this section have influenced greatly what we know about early childhood cognitive development and our understanding of best teaching practices for young children. These professionals developed their theories after years of observing children's learning. It is important to be familiar with their theories because they underlie the early childhood field's approach to facilitating children's cognitive development. Theory influences the choices you make in your setting, the materials you provide, your interactions with children, and the experiences you offer them. Your role as an early childhood educator is to translate theory into practice.

Theories of Cognition

Two major theorists of cognition influence modern early childhood practices: Jean Piaget and Lev Vygotsky. Each has had a major impact on the way we support children's development of thinking and reasoning skills.

Jean Piaget

It can be said that no one has influenced educational practice more than the Swiss psychologist Jean Piaget (1896-1980). First published in 1952—and widely disseminated in the U.S. during the 1970s—his theory of how children learn grew out of extensive observations of children in their natural environment rather than a laboratory. At the center of his theory was the assertion that young children's thinking is qualitatively different from adults. Until this time, it was generally accepted that children were miniature adults when it came to thinking. Piaget's revolutionary concept has become the foundation for today's developmentally appropriate educational practices and curricula.

His theory emphasizes that thinking and learning are part of a dynamic, interactive process between children and their environments. In other words, children actively construct their own knowledge through engagement with their surroundings and develop *schemas*, or basic mental concepts, that help people to understand, organize, and think about ideas and objects.

These schemas are continually modified by two complimentary processes that Piaget termed *assimilation* and *accommodation*. Assimilation is the process of incorporating new experiences into old (a child sees a zebra and based on its appearance calls it a horse). We incorporate new experiences into what we already know. Accommodation is what happens when the schema itself changes to accommodate the new knowledge. New information changes what we already know (the child learns that the horse with stripes is a different animal called a zebra). According to Piaget, cognitive development is an ongoing attempt to achieve a balance between assimilation and accommodation, known as *equilibration*. Equilibration is a mental balance whereby we make sense of new experiences and perceptions and achieve a balance in understanding.

Here's how this might work in your setting. Two-year-old Emma has three cats at home, but she has never seen a dog in real life. Your group passes a dog during a community walk. Emma points to the dog and shouts, "Look at that big cat!" (assimilation) You explain to her that the animal she sees is actually a dog—a different animal from a cat. Emma's existing schema that identifies all four-legged, furry animals as cats is now altered (accommodation).

After identifying the dog, you ask the children to tell you what they know about cats and dogs. This is a meaningful way for them to discuss their own learning and understanding about specific animals and for you to support children and their growing knowledge. With this impromptu learning exercise, you have helped to expand Emma's schema about four-legged, furry animals to include dogs. She has also begun learning to categorize. Most importantly, she has changed her behavior based on altered knowledge (equilibrium).

Through his research and observations, Piaget developed four stages of cognitive development spanning infancy to adulthood. Each stage is defined by increasingly sophisticated and abstract levels of thought. These stages occur in sequence and each builds on what was learned in the previous stage. Children proceed through these stages based on maturation and experience (Gordon and Browne 2016):

Sensorimotor birth to 2 years. Knowledge develops through sensory and motor abilities. Children interact with their environment by manipulating objects.

Preoperational 2 to 7 years. Knowledge is represented by language, mental imagery, and symbolic thought. Thinking is dominated by perception, but more capable of symbolic functioning.

Concrete Operational 7 to 12 years. Children can reason logically about concrete objects and events. Logical reasoning begins.

Formal Operational 12 years and above. Children and adults can think deeply about concrete events and can reason abstractly and hypothetically. Children and adults apply logic to abstract thought.

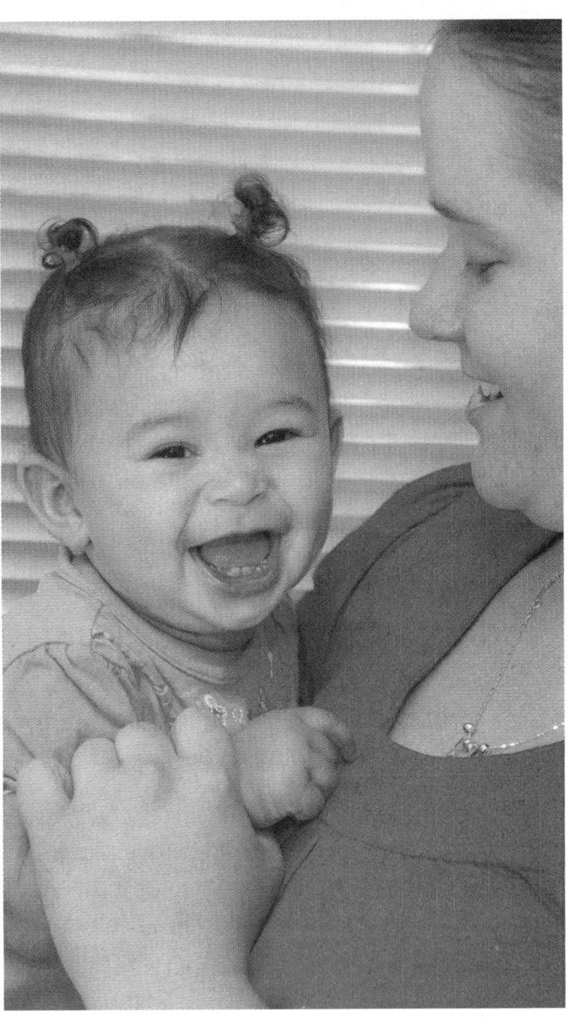

Infants learn best when they feel safe and loved.

The sensorimotor and preoperational stages are most relevant to your work, although some children can master many of the tasks of concrete operations, despite their ages.

During the sensorimotor stage, infants are only aware of what is immediately in front of them, focusing on what they see and do and any physical interactions with their immediate environments. They are unaware of how objects react; therefore, they experiment by shaking, throwing, or mouthing these objects and learn about their worlds through trial-and-error. At about seven to nine months, infants begin to realize that an object exists, even if they can no longer see it. Known as *object permanence*, this important milestone is a sign that their memories are developing. For example, a five-month-old infant who sees you hide an object behind your back will lose interest in the toy. She does not understand that the toy is still there, because she does not understand object permanence.

In the preoperational stage, young children start to think about things symbolically. Their language use matures. They also develop memory and imagination, which allows them to understand the difference between past and future and engage in make-believe. Characteristics of this stage include *egocentrism* (seeing the world from one's own perspective) and difficulty understanding *conservation* (the ability to determine that quantities remain constant despite adjustments in container, shape, or size).

Understanding Conservation

Piaget set up what has become a classic experiment to test when children develop an understanding of conservation—that is the understanding that the quantity of objects or liquids does not change, even though their appearance does. Two identical tall glasses were filled to the same level with milk. When asked how much milk was in each glass, children saw that both glasses of milk were the same. Then, one of these glasses of milk was poured right in front of a watching child into a short, wider glass. Children who had mastered the ability to conserve knew that the quantity of milk in both glasses was still equal. Children who were not able to conserve invariably thought that the taller glass had more milk. Appearance ruled out over logic.

You can see how this works in your own setting. With three-year-old Damien's help, you build two stacks of blocks, each with five blocks in it. Together you count the blocks. You then ask Damien, "Which stack contains more blocks?" He says that the stacks contain the same number of blocks—five.

You now knock down one of the block stacks, and the blocks fall into a pile on the table. You ask Damien, "Are there more blocks in the stack of standing blocks or the stack that fell on the table?" Although Damien saw that there were an equal number of blocks in each stack, he chooses the blocks that have fallen. The fallen blocks appear to take up more space, so Damien reasons that the pile must contain more blocks than the stack.

From this exercise, it's clear that Damien has not yet mastered the concept of conservation and has not yet developed logic-reversible thought which allows him to make judgments by logic rather than by appearance. He does not realize that properties remain constant even when appearances are transformed. Conservation will come about once he is older and has had lots of opportunities to interact with materials. Piaget believed that children in the preoperational stage do not have the cognitive capacity to master this concept. He theorized that conservation occurs at about age seven. In some instances, though, you may find that preschool children are, in fact, learning to conserve.

Children's thought during the preoperational stage is vividly reflected in their speech and actions. Sean sees Patrick playing alone. "Patrick is sad because his Grandpa left," Sean says to you. After asking him some questions, you find that it is Sean who is sad because his own grandfather is no longer living with his family. Sean is in the preoperational stage and assumes everyone feels sad because he does. He also thinks everyone is sad for the same reason he is—their grandfathers are not at home with them anymore. Children like Sean also attribute their feelings to inanimate objects and phenomena, like the weather. Sean may tell you that in addition to Patrick being sad, the falling rain means the sky is sad, too.

Criticism of Piaget's theory of cognition fall into two main categories. The first criticism is that some children may achieve cognitive skills earlier than he describes, as with conservation. Recent research has shown this to be a valid point. We know from research and experience that preoperational children can be taught to take another's perspective, to think logically, and even to develop beginning abstract reasoning skills—developments which Piaget thought impossible at their age.

The second criticism focuses on Piaget's premise that learning goes through distinct stages. Current thinking is that children may not go through stages per se, but there is in fact a sequence to the development of thinking skills. Modern research in neuroscience has shown that brain maturation follows a sequence of development that parallels Piaget's stages of the development of thinking (Gordon and Browne 2016). While Piaget may have overestimated when certain thinking skills develop, his theory provides a strong foundation for educators trying to support cognitive development.

Lev Vygotsky

Another theorist who has had great impact on Western early childhood education philosophy and approach is the Russian psychologist Lev Vygotsky (1896-1934). Vygotsky was a contemporary of Piaget's who died of tuberculosis at a young age, long before Piaget's theory was released. His writings were not introduced to the West until the 1970s. But when they became widely disseminated, Vygotsky had a great impact on early childhood practice. The preschool curriculum *Tools of the Mind*, developed by Dr. Elena Bodrova and Dr. Deborah Leong, is based on Vygotsky's theory.

Although Vygotsky and Piaget were unknown to each other, there are a number of similarities to their theories. Both theorists believed that children are curious, active learners, and that there is an order to the development of cognitive skills. They both supported the need for interaction to promote growth.

Vygotsky's great contribution to the study of cognition was his inclusion of the fundamental role of social interaction in the development of cognition. He theorized that children learn not just by interacting with objects and self-discovery as Piaget described, but also through interactions with adults and more-experienced peers. These adults and peers extend children's learning through conversations that use what the children already know to introduce new information—a concept also known as *scaffolding*. To illustrate, three-year-old Maria has picked up a lacing card for the first time. She keeps running her fingers along the holes bewilderedly. Then she sees that her friend four-year-old Gloria is lacing a piece of yarn through the holes on her own lacing card. "Come here," says Gloria. As Maria sits on the floor next to Gloria, Gloria says, "You need the yarn. I'll show you." Maria sits and watches as Gloria takes the yarn in and out of the holes. "I can do that!" exclaims Maria. She then sits down at the table and starts to lace the card (Gordon and Browne 2016).

A second contribution to practice made by Vygotsky that is absent from Piaget's theory is the influence of culture on learning. Rather than being universal across cultures, Vygotsky theorized the values, beliefs, and tools of individual cultures affect cognitive functions. As noted in the preceding section, the influence of culture on learning is now an accepted tenet of early childhood practice.

Zone of Proximal Development

Central to Vygotsky's theory is the idea discussed above, that we learn from More Knowledgeable Others (MKOs). These are peers (like Gloria) and adults who have better understanding of a concept or a higher level ability than the learner. Vygotsky used the term Zone of Proximal Development (ZPD) to describe the area where children are most sensitive to learning from MKOs. The lower limit of the zone is where children work independently. The upper limit of the zone represents what has been learned and is now known. In between is the area where children can learn under the guidance and encouragement of a more knowledgeable person.

Learning from MKOs in a ZPD is the basis of cooperative learning. Research has borne out that guided learning is often more effective than individual discovery.

Vygotsky's theory also focuses on the role of language in cognitive development. Vygotsky theorized that language plays two crucial roles in cognitive development:

1. It is how adults transmit information to children.
2. It is itself a powerful tool in intellectual development.

The first role is that of social speech, which we are all aware of. The second role involves private speech. Beginning at about age three, children talk themselves through what they are doing in the form of internal monologues. At this point, according to Vygotsky thought and speech merge to produce verbal thinking. In many ways, Vygotsky saw the child coaching himself through inner speech, very much the way a More Knowledgeable Other would.

Vygotsky also theorized that pretend play is the most important vehicle for preschoolers' learning from about age two through age five. He observed that during imaginary play, children assume roles to regulate their behavior. For example, four-year-old Anna understands some of the activities that a mother performs. Pretending to be a mother, Anna defines her actions during play according to her knowledge of a mother's role. This teaches Anna *self-regulation*, or the ability to control her behavior, emotions, and thinking. Self-regulation is linked with children's later success in school (Spiegel 2008).

Along with Piaget, the work of Vygotsky influences our approach to supporting cognitive development in early childhood education today. We encourage young children's acquisition of thinking and reasoning skills by applying their theories to our work with children.

Related Theorists

In addition to Piaget and Vygotsky, there are a number of theorists who did not write about cognitive development per se, but developed theories that have an impact on cognition. In the remainder of this section we examine some of these.

Maria Montessori

The work of famous Italian physician and educator Maria Montessori (1870-1952) overlapped with that of both Piaget and Vygotsky. Her theory of intellectual development is a philosophy that she put into practice. On January 6, 1907 she opened her first school, the Casa dei Bambini (Children's House), in Rome. Following her astounding success in educating children who lived in poverty, she traveled the world espousing her beliefs about how children learn.

What are these beliefs that have made the Montessori approach so popular? First, like Piaget and Vygotsky, she thought that children were not miniature adults, but that they think and develop differently from adults. And like Piaget and Vygotsky, she believed that children learn through self-discovery. All of their theories are considered to be the foundation of the constructivist theory of education, rooted in the belief that children make their own meaning through the interaction of experiences with ideas.

Among the other tenets of Montessori's philosophy are these:

- Children have "absorbent minds" up until about age six. They have an unlimited motivation to obtain competence with their environment and to perfect their skills and knowledge.
- Children's hands are connected to the brain. The sense of touch is as important as vision in learning new concepts.
- The role of the educator is to prepare and adapt the environment to maximize children's learning by making the environment comfortable, stimulating, and encouraging of independence.
- Educators should be observers, not lecturers. They change the environment to meet children's needs.

- The environment is stocked with specially designed materials like letters, blocks, and science experiments that allow for the "work" of the child. These materials are didactic and control for error.
- Educators constantly carry out and record scientific observations of children.
- The area is divided into subject areas and children are free to move about the room.
- Children learn directly from the environment and other children. Educators do not interrupt children when they are concentrating. As Dr. Montessori put it, "Never help a child at a task at which he feels he can succeed "(Daily Montessori 2015).
- All subject area content is interwoven. Children study math, language, geography, art, and music simultaneously.
- Children work for a three-hour period uninterrupted.
- Educators do not award grades or other rewards or punishment. Children are assessed by observation.

From the above description it is readily apparent that many of the principles outlined above would be a part of what any early childhood educator would consider best practices today. Montessori's belief in the power of a child to learn through interaction with a prepared environment is incorporated in all high-quality programming. So is the idea that educators should be facilitators and observers. Some modern critics take exception with the fact that Montessori believed that materials should be used only in one correct way, pointing out that children can use blocks both for building and as a telephone in symbolic play. There is also the current belief that child-initiated learning needs to be balanced with educator-directed instruction at appropriate times, such as when introducing a new piece of technology to the group. Nonetheless, the impact of Montessori's theories and philosophy on early childhood education is undisputed. Twenty thousand schools worldwide use the Montessori model today. They are testament to the lasting power of Maria Montessori's beliefs.

Urie Bronfenbrenner

Russian-American psychologist Urie Bronfenbrenner (1917-2005) developed the ecological systems theory, which examines the impact of children's social environments on their development. He believed that everything in a child and the child's environment affects how a child grows and develops. Bronfenbrenner compared this theory to nesting dolls that fit inside one another. His theory comprises five ecological systems that impact learning and development:

1. **Microsystem.** Refers to the institutions, groups, and individuals that most immediately and directly impact children's development. These include family, school, religious institutions, neighborhood, and friends. For example, children are influenced by the make-up of their families. Do they have any siblings? Does the household include extended family members?

2. **Mesosystem.** Refers to relations between microsystems or connections between contexts, like the relationship between children's families and early educators. If the children's families have trusting and respectful relationships with the early educators, then those relationships will positively impact the children.
3. **Exosystem.** Describes situations in which children do not play active roles, but are impacted nonetheless. For example, a child plays no role in their mother losing her job, but the child and the rest of the family will experience the impact.
4. **Macrosystem.** The largest and most remote set of people and things to do with a child, but it still affects a child's development. It describes the culture, community, and society in which children live. Cultural contexts include developing and industrialized countries, socioeconomic status, poverty, urban versus rural environments, and ethnicity. Members of a cultural group share a common identity, heritage, and values. New generations may change these macrosystems or create new ones over time.
5. **Chronosystem.** Describes the patterning of environmental events and transitions on a child's development over the course of life. This might be the impact of a divorce or the birth of a new sibling (Bronfenbrenner 1994).

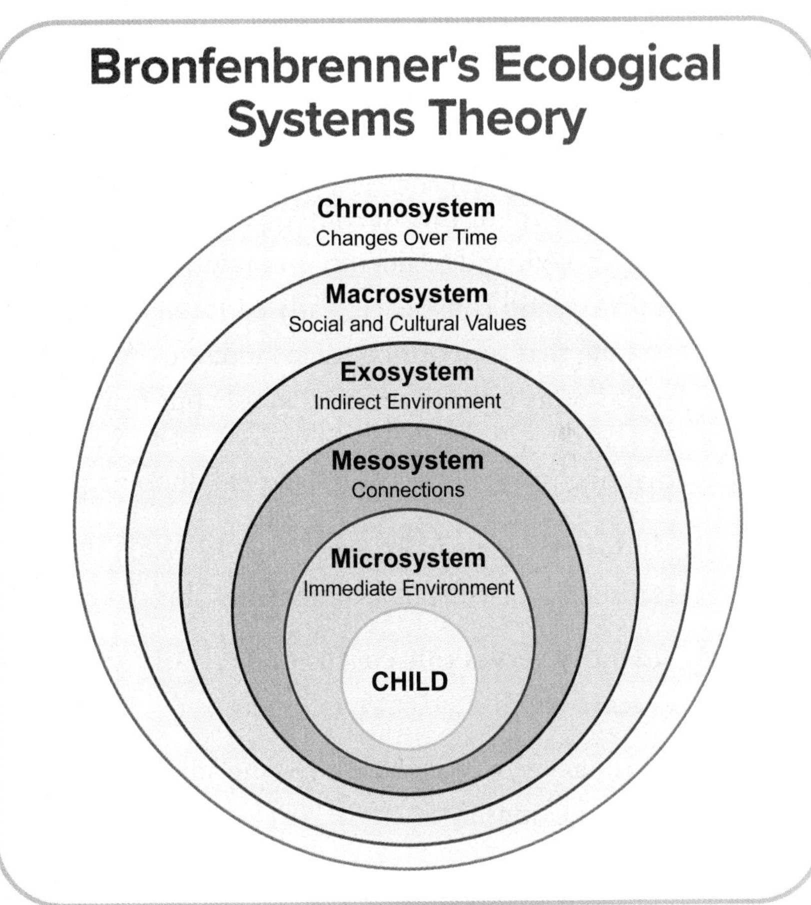

Bronfenbrenner's theory brings psychology, sociology, and anthropology into the realm of education. His multidisciplinary approach to child development was a cornerstone of Head Start. All high-quality early childhood programs today acknowledge the role of the family, the community, and culture in development.

Erik Erikson

Influenced by the work of Sigmund Freud and cultural anthropologists, German-born American psychologist Erik Erikson (1902-1994) devised an eight-stage theory of psychosocial development which underscores the importance of culture and social experience on development. At each stage of development, Erikson theorized, children or adults are confronted with a psychosocial challenge. In order to proceed to the next stage, a balance between the two extremes of this challenge must be met. If this balance is not achieved, Erikson predicted that the child or adult would have ongoing problems related to that issue.

The first three stages are most relevant to your work and are highlighted here:

1. **Trust versus mistrust** (birth to 18 months). During this stage, infants are learning whether they can trust the adults around them and the world in which they live. If infants cry, do early educators pick them up? Do infants' families meet their basic needs? Erikson believed that there is a continuum between trust and mistrust. Infants do not learn to always trust or mistrust someone.

2. **Autonomy versus shame and doubt** (2 to 4 years). During this stage of development, toddlers and young children are learning that they are competent and can perform tasks independently. Adult interactions contribute to children's understanding of their own skills and abilities. If children in this stage are encouraged and supported in their increased independence, they become more confident and secure in their own abilities to survive in the world. If children are criticized, overly controlled, engaged in power struggles with adults, or not given the opportunity to assert themselves, they begin to feel inadequate. These children may become overly dependent upon others, lack self-esteem, and feel a sense of shame or doubt in their own abilities.

3. **Initiative versus guilt** (3 to 5 years). During this stage, children are engaged primarily in play and are further developing their relationships with peers. Children are learning how to get along independently and resolve conflicts while developing empathy, a sense of fairness, and conscience. Early educators support children in this stage by establishing a setting that supports children's interests. A small set of boundaries, limits, or rules exist in this setting and are enforced kindly but firmly (Gordon and Browne 2016).

The remaining five states occur in later childhood and beyond.

4. **Industry versus inferiority** (6 to 12 years). During this stage, children are finding satisfaction in school achievement. This is a child's most enthusiastic time for learning.

5. **Identity versus role confusion** (12 to 18 years). During this stage, children are attaining a sense of self in relation to others.

6. **Intimacy versus isolation** (young adulthood). During this stage, people are building close relationships.

7. **Generativity versus self-absorption** (middle adulthood). During into this stage, adults are finding satisfaction in work and giving back to society.

8. **Integrity versus despair** (late adulthood). During this stage, adults are feeling good about their lives and facing death without regret.

Erikson's theory has had a major impact on early childhood programs. Through an environment and interactions that support the development of trust and initiative, educators support children's development in all areas, including cognitive development.

Abraham Maslow

Abraham Maslow (1908-1970) was a humanist psychologist who developed a hierarchy of needs, in which he theorized people's basic needs must be met before they can reach their full potential. His theory is often presented as a pyramid. The following outlines each set of needs in order from basic needs to the most advanced set of needs:

- Basic or physiological needs: air, food, water, sleep, and shelter.
- Safety and security needs: feeling safe and secure physically and emotionally within the environment.
- Love and belonging needs: social needs, like love, affection, and acceptance.
- Self-esteem: the need for self-respect and esteem from others.
- Self-actualization: state of harmony and understanding that exists while working to achieve full potential and reach goals (Gordon and Browne 2016).

Maslow's theory directly affects children's ability to learn. Be aware of children's needs in your setting. Are they hungry, malnourished, or sleep deprived? Do they feel safe and secure? Does each child have a sense of belonging in your setting? If any of these needs have not been met, children cannot focus on learning. High-quality programs ensure that children's basic needs are met so that true learning can occur in all domains.

Howard Gardner

With his theory of multiple intelligences (MI), American psychologist Howard Gardner (b. 1943) suggests that people's intelligence is multifaceted, not a one-dimensional measure. Rather than focusing on verbal and/or mathematical skills that can be measured by standardized tests, Gardner proposes a broader definition of intelligence. As has been said in regard to his theory, what matters is not how smart you are, but in what ways you are smart. In this theory, first published in 1983 in his ground-breaking book *Frames of Mind: The Theory of Multiple Intelligences* and expanded upon in later writing, Gardner explains that there are at least eight types of intelligences and that each of us possess strengths in multiple areas.

Strength or weakness in one area does not predict strength or weakness in any other intelligence. In Gardner's words (Strauss 2013), "All of us exhibit jagged profiles of intelligences." The intelligences described by Gardner include the traditional areas of math and language, but also domains such as music and kinesthetic movement. They are:

1. **Linguistic.** Using language to express yourself and understand other people. Children who have this intelligence enjoy looking at books, telling stories, and using words to describe their feelings.

2. **Logical/Mathematical.** Manipulating numbers, quantities, and operations. Children with this capability like to count, explore problems, and easily notice patterns.
3. **Musical/Rhythmic.** Thinking in musical terms. Children with this ability hear and recognize patterns.
4. **Bodily/Kinesthetic.** Using your whole body or parts of your body (e.g., hands, fingers, and arms) with great skill. Children with this ability tend to be athletic and can move with ease.
5. **Spatial.** Visualizing the three-dimensional world with ease. Children with this ability enjoy puzzles, drawing, and/or painting. These children may even excel at pointing out directions from one location to another.
6. **Naturalist.** Understanding living things and nature. Children with this ability enjoy hiking, gardening, or learning how to care for the environment.
7. **Intrapersonal.** Understanding yourself, who you are, and what you can/want to do. Children with this intelligence have a realistic grasp of their abilities and challenges.
8. **Interpersonal.** Understanding other people. Children with this intelligence can figure out other people's feelings and abilities.

Gardner also suggests a possible ninth intelligence:

9. **Existential.** Questioning life, death, and spirituality. Children with this intelligence are deep, sensitive thinkers and feelers (Gardner, "Multiple Intelligences").

Gardner's theory has opened up educators to looking at intelligence in a new way. It has gone a long way in helping us appreciate children's differences and unique talents. The MI theory has helped to underscore the importance of individualizing and teaching to children's strengths. At the same time, it has shown educators the need to teach and present concepts that appeal to the multiple ways children learn.

Sara Smilansky

Israeli psychologist Sara Smilansky (1922-2006) researched how children learn through play and the relationship of play to academic success. First published in 1968, her theories state that children go through four stages of play, each building on the previous one. However, these stages do not disappear once a child moves on to a higher stage. Moreover, the various stages may overlap, as when a child moves firemen props into the block area to act out a firehouse scenario:

1. **Functional play.** Sometimes called "practice play," this is how children experiment with things and learn how they work. When a baby shakes a rattle or a toddler bangs cymbals together, she is learning through functional play. Smilansky theorized that children repeat their actions over and over and use the inner thought that Vygotsky described to learn about what is happening. Functional play is the earliest type of play to appear, but it recurs whenever a child explores something new.

2. **Constructive play.** Constructive play goes beyond the exploratory play that characterizes functional play. Children in this stage (which begins in middle to late toddlerhood) create something based on a plan. They organize materials and put things together. Their actions have purpose and are goal-oriented. Constructive play is what you see in toddler and preschool programs as children build with blocks, draw a picture on paper or the computer, or make a kitty out of clay. Constructive play continues throughout childhood.

3. **Symbolic play.** Symbolic play is pretend play. It begins in toddlerhood when children use a tambourine as a crown or a wash cloth as a doll blanket. When children use symbolic pretend play alone, it is called dramatic play; when it involves others, it is termed sociodramatic play. The difference between symbolic play and functional and constructive play is that it is person-oriented rather than object-oriented. And unlike constructive play which is goal-oriented, symbolic play is open-ended.

4. **Games with rules.** In this type of play, children follow prescribed rules and work towards common goals. Games with rules include both table games and movement games, whether children are playing a board game like Chutes and Ladders, or running outside playing Red Light, Green Light.

Educators incorporate Smilansky's work on play every day into center and FCC programming. As we will discuss in a later section, play and learning are intimately linked. Research has linked play to the development of self-regulation (see discussion later in this chapter), creativity, attention, and improved language, literacy, and math skills. Educators can work with children to support their play and their cognitive development.

Brain Research on Cognitive Development

There has been a spate of brain research over the past 25 years that parallels the theories described above. Through MRIs and other imaging technologies, neuroscientists have been able to show how children learn by looking at scans of developing brains. We now have exciting insight on how the brain works and clinical evidence of how children learn to think. Here are some of the major findings that impact you as an early educator (Schiller 2010):

Findings from Brain Research

Research Findings	What These Findings Mean
Cognitive skills are linked to both genetics and the environment. A rich, interactive environment goes a long way in promoting brain development.	The richer the environment and the more intentional and purposeful the interactions and the experiences, the greater the number of brain connections that are made.
The primary task of the brain during early childhood is to make connections.	Experiences wire the brain. Repetition of these experiences hardwires the brain. (When connections are hardwired, they are likely to remain permanent.)
There are sensitive periods when the brain is at its peak for learning. These are known as *windows of opportunity*.	During early childhood, children's brains are developing at a rapid pace, laying the foundation for lifelong learning. Children are developing a range of cognitive skills, including cause and effect and problem-solving.
Children vary their approaches to learning in different situations.	Early educators provide rich learning opportunities for children by using a variety of teaching techniques and appealing to children's multiple intelligences that engage them in the learning experience.
Children use gestures to accompany learning.	Exaggerated movements may indicate a breakthrough in a child's understanding of a certain concept. Be sensitive to children's gestures and regard them as signs that learning is taking place.
Technology can have both a positive impact on the brain (it strengthens neural connections and quickens visual recognition time) and a negative impact on the brain (losing touch with real life relationships and the ability to be intimate with others).	Consider how children are engaging with technology in your room. Spend time speaking with children about what they are working on and learning as they use technology. Encourage children to document their learning with digital cameras or computer art programs. Avoid passive screen time. (See the section on technology in this chapter.)
Children process memories and solve problems during their sleep.	All young children need appropriate amounts of restful sleep to keep their brains functioning optimally.

The findings and ongoing research related to learning and the brain are significant pieces of information that teachers and providers should consider as they plan for and facilitate learning experiences. While individual components are vital to understanding how children learn, it is also critical to remember that the body and brain work together. Separating one aspect or piece from another and only focusing on a singular bit is definitely not conducive to optimizing a child's potential and cognitive development.

By putting several pieces together—as well as examining individual aspects in order to maximize implementation—we can offer experiences and learning options that will benefit all children.

The learning process as it relates to our current understanding of how the brain functions and develops has been briefly covered in the beginning of this chapter. We have looked at theories, developmental milestones and general skills. We will now examine several points more closely in order to make sense of how all of this works together. As stated above, just looking at individual components or pieces without somehow tying it all together can lead to misrepresentation, oversimplification, avoidance or missing out on how cognitive understanding evolves.

All learning starts with relationships: relationships with people, materials, experiences and the broader world. In utero, the developing fetus and the mother are in a relationship that has numerous factors and characteristics unique to the time frame of pregnancy. Once the baby is born, the relationship begins to change by adapting to new and different experiences and environmental factors. Daniel Stern (2002) describes the first relationship as one of mutual regulation. The newborn is thrust into the new environment and we as adults attempt to help regulate the feelings, understanding and interactions that new life is experiencing. In turn, the newborn also regulates us—the parent and teacher. The child lets us know when they are hungry, need a diaper change, want to be noticed and cared for, need space alone or is interested in what is going on in the immediate environment. All of this is the foundation for cognitive learning—and even more specifically what we refer to as executive functions, those higher-order processing skills that represent a depth of knowledge and understanding. Mutual regulation helps to establish the beginnings of a sense of self, as well as knowledge and recognition of others.

Relationships revolve around interactions. Interactions are those experiences between two or more individuals (and possibly include materials, objects, sights or other nonpersonal items) that promote engagement and involve sharing energy and information. When relationships evolve, the potential for learning and development increases.

The teacher or parent provides the opportunities, but it is up to the child to accept or receive and incorporate into the learning experience what the relationship and interaction has initiated. A child cannot be forced to learn anything. A teacher or parent can only provide the experience and interaction. The child's brain and mind determine how the information will be processed and included or rejected.

How can an early educator or parent provide what will positively impact brain development and learning? The interactions and relationships should involve sensory experiences. The often identified five external senses are only a part of the sensory possibilities. The vestibular sense (balance) and proprioceptive sense (the intuition and understanding of how and where body parts are and what they are doing) are additional sensory options. And together, these seven sensory stimuli options provide the basis for the start of the learning process.

In his book, *A Biological Brain in a Cultural Classroom* (2003),), Robert Sylwester, professor emeritus at the University of Oregon, provides an understanding of how to condense the learning process into a simple, four-step pattern, SEAL. The learning process begins with a stimulus (**S**) that is any sensory input—sight, hearing, taste, touch, smell, balance or movement. The stimulus in turn drives an emotional (**E**) response, which tends to be positive or negative, to the sensory input. The emotional response then drives attention (**A**), which ultimately drives learning (**L**).

Every stimulus or sensory piece of information is perceived as positive or negative. Therefore, once the stimulus (sensory information) is provided, the emotional response occurs. If the emotional response to the stimulus is positive—meaning the sensory information is enjoyable, pleasurable, meaningful, playful or important to the child—attention to the sensory input and emotion drives neural connections that promote development of executive functions, those higher-order processing portions of brain development. Learning and the acquisition of knowledge related to the sensory input then occur.

If the sensory input is viewed as negative—it's considered something to be feared, ignored or dismissed as unimportant instead of something enjoyable or exciting—the learning that comes from that kind of attention is limited to survival.

Since all learning begins with the senses, understanding more about how to include the senses in lessons and the learning environment is critical. For a typically developing child, the more senses that can be included in a lesson, the greater is the likelihood that learning will take place. As indicated above, when there is a positive connection to a learning experience, more attention is paid to the experience/sensation and learning takes place. Another way to think of the senses, brain development and learning is to consider that the more senses involved in a learning endeavor, the greater the understanding of a concept and the fewer times the lesson or activity will have to be performed and conducted.

Children respond to positive and affirmative sensory stimuli. The brain assimilates information and forms the neural connections that are part of learning and understanding.

Some simple observations and documentation can serve to find out what stimuli are most beneficial and helpful to individual children. First, find out what type of learning or stimuli a child is attracted to. Ask families what they have noticed about the child's preferences and then observe for behaviors that align. For example, while conducting a simple reading lesson, notice which children tend to slide up closer to the book or storyboard. Listen for the children who are constantly insisting they can't see, want to see more or just be up close. Unless a child has a true visual impairment, the child's actions may be indicative of a preference for **visual learning**—someone who prefers to see and observe.

Another child may ask you to repeat a story, song, rhyme or book numerous time. It's not that the child didn't hear or understand what was read or recited. Instead, the child may just enjoy the sound of the words, music and tone of voice. The child may be indicating that they have a preference for **auditory learning**.

When sitting at a table for a meal or placing objects out for a small group activity, take note of which children seem to have an uncontrollable urge to reach out and touch or grab food or objects. These children may be demonstrating that they actually have a preference for **tactile learning** and are most comfortable when touching materials or tactilely engaging with the environment.

Yet another set of children may be in constant motion. These children find it difficult to "sit still" or just be seated in a nonmoving manner for an extended period of time. Unfortunately, these children often are considered to have behavioral issues or be incapable of focusing. It's not necessarily the case that a child like this is failing to focus or pay attention. Instead, the child may be letting the teacher know that they have a preference for **kinesthetic learning** and requires movement when engaging with the environment.

All of these characteristics and actions may not be actual indicators of a child's preferred learning style, but they are starting points of reference to see what is necessary to create positive learning experiences for the child and therefore promote optimal brain growth and development.

Learning Through Play

Seeing children at play means different things to different people. Most everyone thinks play is fun—including children themselves. When asked in one study what their favorite activity was, 98% of the children answered play (Bredekamp 2011). Because it is so enjoyable, many family members and some educators think that fun equals frivolous. Play, in their view, is a distraction from learning.

Even those that concede that play can be useful may be quick to cut play from programming in favor of more academic pursuits. Free play has had a hard time surviving in an era where testing and accountability are at the forefront of the educational agenda.

Yet, as more and more research shows the benefits of play, it is once again taking a front seat in early childhood education programs. The link between play and academic success has been firmly established. Albert Einstein observed, "Play is the highest form of research." For young children it is the gateway to learning. According to Sandra Waite-Stupiansky (2015), "Play is the most important way that young children learn." To author and movement expert Rae Pica (2015) play "is no different or less important than [children's] need to eat, sleep, and breathe. For young children, play is every bit as essential."

What do children learn through play that makes it so important? Play is children's entry to the physical, social, and affective worlds. Moreover, play builds all of the cognitive skills we have discussed in this chapter.

Cultural differences in the ways that children engage in play are important to consider. For example, in the Farver & Lee-Shin 2000 study, 54% of Korean-American parents thought it was important that adults play with children, compared with 96% of European-American parents. This cultural value difference may show up in your classroom as confusion on the part of a child who is not accustomed to adults joining their play. This is why it is important that the values and perspectives of families be considered when evaluating play.

Supporting Children's Play

The importance of play is clear. As an early educator you need to support children's play both indoors and outdoors, whether you teach in a center-based program or an FCC home. Here are some suggested strategies for supporting the play of children of various ages.

Young infants (birth to 8 months). Infant play begins at the very start of life when they interact with loving and supportive family members and with other important people in their lives, such as you. Young infants use all of their senses to learn about the world. They crinkle their noses in imitation of adults. They hear the sounds of words and the cadence of conversation as you communicate with them. As they grow physically, their bodies lead them to make discoveries. Reaching and grasping allows them to study objects by hand and by mouth. By 4-7 months, they understand what cause-and-effect means: when they drop a rattle out of their reach, they understand that they either have to make noise for you to retrieve it or move on to something else.

Try playing with young infants by using some of these strategies (Zero to Three n.d.; Zero to Three 2012a):

- Move a colorful object slowly, 10-12 inches from a baby's head and let the infant track the object as you move it all around.
- Hold the same toy (such as a rattle) in each hand and shake them one at a time. Changing focus improves attention skills.
- Offer babies two toys to hold and decide which they prefer to explore.

- Introduce stimulation gradually. If a child likes playing with a musical toy or mobile, let the child get used to the toy, then add the music.
- Show children how things work, such as how you turn the pages in a vinyl book.
- Begin playing interactive games like peek-a-boo.
- Sing and dance together.
- Play ball together.

In addition, spend time letting you and the baby imitate one another's facial expressions. Talk with the infant and ask lots of questions and wait for a response, even though the child's answer will be in the form of a coo or babble, rather than words. Conversation not only sets the stage for language development, but focuses children's attention on what is happening and what they are learning. Here are some ideas of things to say:

- "Whose nose is this" (gently grabbing baby's nose)?
- "Let's look at this book together. It's about a baby just like you."
- "Which rattle do you like best?"
- "What does your stuffed bear feel like? It feels soft and furry and kind of squishy to me."
- "What happened when you shook the bells? It made a lot of noise, didn't it?"
- "Who is that smiling girl in the mirror? Why it's you, Kia!"

Spend time letting you and the baby imitate one another's facial expressions

Mobile infants (9 to 17 months). More than anything, mobile infants love repetition. Rattles, busy boxes, blocks and musical instruments allow children to repeat their explorations with both their bodies and their hands. Mobile infants are starting to pretend with objects—they may pick up an empty cup and drink from it. Children at this stage also start to show preferences for active or quiet play. They enjoy reading books with adults and playing with both open-ended toys that they can push and pull and close-ended toys like shape sorters that teach concepts. They also use toys to learn about cause and effect, as they drop balls into a pail, or use a string to maneuver a pull truck. Having grasped the concept of object permanence, games like hide-and-seek capture their fancy.

Zero to Three (n.d.; 2012b) offers these suggestions for educators playing with mobile infants:

- Have duplicates of favorite toys, as children this age like being around other children, but don't want to share.
- Read board books together, letting the child turn the pages.
- Sing and dance together. Children tend to learn words easier when they are sung to them.
- Let children see how things work, from a jack-in-the-box to a ring stack.
- Show children how to combine objects in play to go beyond the exploration stage.
- Offer as much repetition as you have patience for. Children will fill and empty a pail for seemingly all day. This gives them control over their world, while at the same time they are learning about cause-and-effect and other cognitive skills.

Talk to children as they interact with toys and you. Repeat what they are doing to highlight their actions. Ask questions to extend their learning and leave time for them to respond, even if they are pre-verbal:

- "What happened when you pulled the leash on the toy doggie? Yes, he came to you."
- "What's this a picture of? Yes, it is a cow. And what sound do cows make? Moooooo."
- "You put every single clothespin in the bottle. Excellent."
- "Which hole does this round circle piece fit in? See if you can get it in a hole that looks like a circle."
- "Let's sing the Itsy Bitsy Spider song again. I know how much you like it when the rain comes down."
- "You were just pretending to be asleep. You sure fooled me!"

Milestones in Pretend Play

One of the most important types of play in terms of cognitive development is pretend play. Smilansky designated it the third stage of play. Vygotsky thought pretend play was crucial to thought and learning. In the famous theorist's view, play "is the source of development and creates the zone of proximal development" (Bodrova et al. 2013). Furthermore, Vygotsky theorized that new developmental accomplishments become apparent in play far earlier than they do in other activities. Pretend play, in his view, helps young children think before they act, which leads to abstract thinking.

When are children able to participate in pretend play? Symbolic understanding, which is needed in order to pretend, doesn't usually begin until the toddler and preschool years. However, the roots of pretend play start in infancy. Here are the milestones of pretend play (Schickedanz and Collins 2013):

Age of Child	Milestone
Birth to 10 months	No pretending
10 to 12 months	Uses objects meaningfully, but doesn't pretend
12 to 13 months	Simple pretending; e.g., pretends to take a drink from real empty cup
13 to 15 months	Begins to direct play actions; e.g., pretends to feed her doll
20 to 24 months	Begins to use actions seen in real life; e.g., cooks in house center; animates dolls and stuffed animals
26 to 30 months	Uses objects in play that do not resemble real ones; e.g., picks up a block to be a cell phone
30 months	Verbally states she is taking on role of someone else: "I'm the teacher;" able to play two roles, such as self and baby doll
30 to 48 months	Coordinates own role with that of others
48 months	Increased flexibility in use of symbolic objects

Toddlers (18 to 36 months). Children this age like to build and put things together, using cardboard or rubber blocks. They also like to know how things are used together. Toddlers love observing what happens when they fill and dump objects or sand and water into pails and other containers. The hallmark of play during the toddler years, though, is the advent of pretend play. As they learn to move away from physical play to play with symbols, a broom they used in clean up can become a horse, just as a hat can be turned upside down and become a bowl. Toddlers love playing with other children and like to make up their own rules for play scenarios. They are actively working on all four of Smilansky's stages of play, as described earlier.

Try some of these approaches to support toddler play (Zero to Three 2012c):

- Follow the child's lead. Offer toys and observe what toddlers do with them.
- Create a marching band with instruments and scarves or have them paint a group mural.
- Encourage children's pretend play by providing dress-up clothes and accessories and play props. Toddlers are very social.
- Offer quiet play opportunities like looking at books, drawing pictures, or putting a puzzle together. This allows toddlers to do something different instead of always being on the move.
- Play musical games and finger plays like the Hokey Pokey or The Wheels on the Bus. They teach words, sounds, how to follow directions, and have fun.

- Invite a toddler to join in with another child's play. Children learn social skills, such as negotiation skills and beginning sharing skills. They also learn other new skills from their peers.

Toddlers need time, materials, and experiences to meaningfully learn through play. Engage toddlers in conversation to reinforce and extend their learning:

- "What are you going to serve the animals at your tea party?"
- "How would you get your truck into a parking lot?"
- "You used a lot of bright colors in your painting. How do they make you feel?"
- "What shape cookie cutter did you pick? Tell me why you picked the star shape?"
- "Which instrument would you like to play in our marching band?"
- "How do you think the fish in our tank go to sleep?"

Preschoolers (3 to 5 years). At this age children need ample, uninterrupted choice or free play time throughout the day to develop their memory, attention, and self-regulation skills (Spiegel 2008). Also, because brain connections are hardwired through repetition, extended and uninterrupted play time gives children the chance to make cognitive connections repeatedly.

While children are at play, observe and scaffold their learning by stepping in intentionally when appropriate. Model curiosity and encourage children to ask and answer questions that will help them learn. Figure 44a-b describes ways that you can facilitate preschool children's cognitive growth during their play. Many of these techniques can also be effectively used with toddlers and even younger children:

Figure 44a. Supporting Cognitive Development through Play

Learning Center	How the Child Might Play Here	How the Early Educator Supports the Child	Cognitive Skills the Child is Learning
Blocks	Build towers, bridges, and airports out of hardwood blocks.	• Asks questions: "How can you build your construction higher without it falling down?" • Poses problems: "What would happen if you used this small block at the base of the building?" • Allows the child to suggest and try out solutions; guides the child to success	• Predicting • Problem solving • Understanding cause and effect

Figure 44b. Supporting Cognitive Development through Play

Learning Center	How the Child Might Play Here	How the Early Educator Supports the Child	Cognitive Skills the Child is Learning
Math & Manipulatives	Play an animal lotto game with a small group of other children and the early educator.	• Reviews rules: "We can only turn over one card at a time." • Asks questions: "What book did we read that had a mole in it? Did the mole look like this one?" • Introduces new vocabulary and ideas: "You are right. That animal is a kind of cow. It has very big horns and is called an ox."	• Expanding memory, concentration, and attention skills • Matching and categorizing
Science	Balance rocks on a scale.	• Asks questions: "Which rock is heavier?" "How many other rocks do you think you'll need to weigh as much as this big one?" and "Why do you think this rock is so shiny?"	• Weighing • Measuring • Comparing • Classifying • Predicting • Problem solving
Dramatic Play	Shop at the pretend grocery store.	• Joins the children in play: "I need to get some bread. I wonder what kinds they sell here." • Asks questions: "What does a shopper do?" and "How much does milk cost? I wonder if it's more expensive than the market near my house where the milk costs $3.50 a gallon."	• Comparing and contrasting • Pricing • Predicting • Planning • Taking on others' perspectives • Self-regulation
Music & Movement	Dance with scarves.	• Dances along with the child, playing a tambourine to the beat of the music	• Patterning
Cooking	Participate in small group activity of making English muffin pizzas.	• Prepares recipe card • Reviews knife handling and safety rules • Puts muffins in and takes muffins out of broiler • Asks questions: "How can we cut these muffins in half?" "How many muffins would we need to give everyone in our class one muffin?" "What happened to the cheese when it was in the broiler?"	• Observing physical states • Problem solving • Following rules • Understanding one-to-one correspondence • Counting • Understanding picture-based reading
Outdoors	Study animal tracks on the playground after a light snowfall.	• Provides magnifying glasses • Asks questions: "How many different animals do you think were here last night?" "How can you tell there were three animals out here?" "How are the prints alike and how are they different?"	• Comparing • Counting • Patterning • Observing with curiosity

Play and Dual Language Learners

According to dual language learning expert Linda Espinosa (2015), play is an ideal vehicle for children speaking two languages to practice the new language and make friends. In order to join in play scenarios and imaginative playground play, dual language learners work hard to master English. Being able to play with friends is a powerful motivator. Young children have great incentive to develop new vocabulary and converse in English, when the reward is being able to play together with peers. Communicating well in a new language gives dual language learners confidence and lets them experience success.

Executive Function and Play

Executive function is an umbrella term encompassing a number of cognitive skills including self-control, memory, and attention. The Center for the Child at Harvard University (2015) defines executive function as follows: "Executive function skills are the mental processes that enable us to plan, focus attention, remember instructions, and juggle multiple tasks successfully. Just as an air traffic control system at a busy airport safely manages the arrivals and departures of many aircraft on multiple runways, the brain needs this skill set to filter distractions, prioritize tasks, set and achieve goals, and control impulses."

Executive function underlies learning and development. It depends on three cognitive skills that are connected and overlapping: memory, mental flexibility, and self-control. For a child to exhibit executive function, these cognitive skills must work in cooperation. A child must be able to avoid distractions, focus attention, hold relevant information in working memory, and regulate his impulsive behavior.

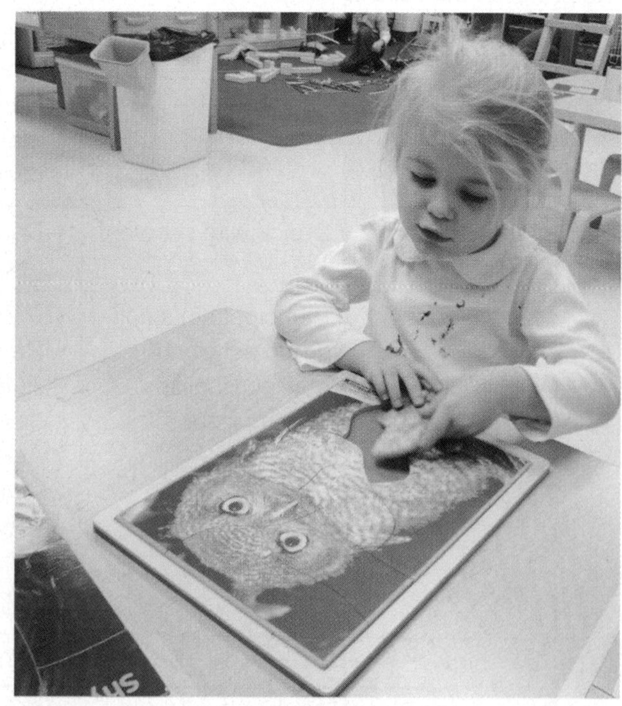

Provide children a wide range of experiences and materials.

Recent strides in neuroscience have found that children who use executive function skills are more engaged in learning (NYU 2015). They can manage their feelings, pay attention, and learn better. Children who possess the skill of executive function are successful learners. Research bears this out: executive function is the single best indicator of school readiness and success—better even than I.Q. (Wardhana 2015).

One of the interesting things about executive function is that, according to brain research, it doesn't develop on its own. There need to be supportive experiences to develop this skill—and one of the best experiences for developing executive function is through play. As you'll remember from the examples of cognitive learnings, children develop through play, memory, attention, and self-control. Pretend play, in particular, leads to development of these skills. The private speech that Vygotsky talks about that occurs during pretend play is fundamental to this joint development. When children take on roles during play scenarios, they have private monologues about what they are going to do and how they will do it. For example, if a child plays a dog going to the vet's office, he knows what the rules of play are: he must bark—not talk—and do what his master and the vet tell him to do. He doesn't have a lot of opportunities to do whatever he feels like. This means he has to control his impulses, delay gratification, exert self-control, and follow social rules. In other words, he has to regulate his behavior.

Self-regulation (or self-control) is a cognitive skill that has been diminishing over the years. In 1940, researchers asked three-, five-, and seven-year-olds to do a number of exercises that measured self-regulation, including standing perfectly still. They found that three-year-olds could not do the task, the five-year-olds lasted three minutes and the seven-year-olds could stand still indefinitely. When the same tests were conducted on children today, researchers found that five-year-olds were acting as three-year-olds did in 1940 and seven-year-olds were not quite at the level five-year-olds were in 1940.

Why the steep decline in self-regulation skills? The answer seems to lie in changes in children's play. In the last half of the 20th century, the way children played changed dramatically. Earlier and throughout history, children played freely using their imaginations. Children made up scripts and rules and regulated their play themselves. They developed executive function.

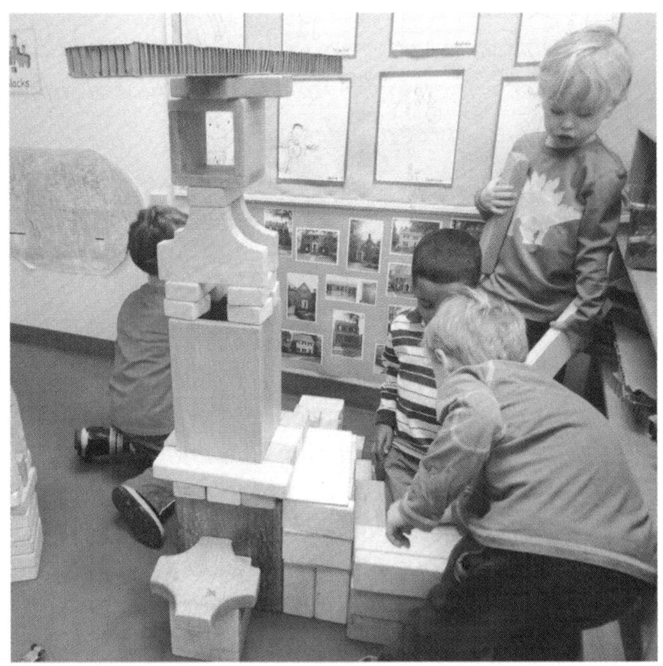

Offer children at least one-hour of uninterrupted time for center play.

Two factors changed things (Spiegel 2008). First, there is an increased concern for safety so children no longer play outdoors without adult supervision. Instead, they participate in structured activities like playing soccer or attending art classes. Second, many popular toys are linked to television and films. Every child has an action figure or doll from the most recent movie. Rather than the focus of play being on activity, it became the toy itself that was important. This new trend in play means that today many children use their imaginations less than children in earlier generations did. And without imaginative, pretend play, executive function skills are waning.

The obvious way to reverse this outcome is to offer many opportunities for pretend play in early childhood settings. Because executive function is a skill that can be taught, the trend can be turned around once again. It is up to early childhood educators to make sure that children have plenty of time for different kinds of play—inside and outside—every day. Encourage families to value spontaneous play at home by asking what kinds of play the children enjoy. Recognize that every family is different, and that trends change over time. Provide opportunities in your program for the kinds of executive-function-building play that may be missing at home.

Learning Throughout the Day

There are a number of ways to incorporate cognitive learning activities in your daily interactions with the children in your setting. Consider these examples:

Choice Time/Free Play. As noted above, pretend play is a prime time for learning. Consider this example.

Leila and Reggie are playing in the dramatic play area, which the children have transformed into a make-believe clothing store. Reggie eyes a dress he would like to purchase for his mother. "It's $93, and it's on sale!" Leila says. Reggie agrees to purchase the dress, and hands Leila a few bills of play money. Leila counts the money and places it in her cash register. She gives Reggie his change, folds the dress, and hands it to him. By taking on roles, the children are developing executive function. Leila and Reggie are also learning about numbers, counting, and social competence.

Their teacher observes Leila and Reggie while they visit different learning centers during choice time. She determines when to lend the children support and when to maintain distance to let the children play and discover independently.

Engaging Children in Their Own Learning

Ms. Thompson observes several children during an indoor gardening activity. Kenya, a five-year-old, impresses Ms. Thompson with her depth of gardening knowledge. Kenya says that she helps her grandfather in his garden on weekends. She knows how to plant vegetables and when, the types of soil to use, and how often to water the plants. Excited by Kenya's gardening savvy, Ms. Thompson invites her to share what she knows about how vegetables grow. She challenges Kenya to predict what will happen if she waters the plants more often or places them in different areas of the room. Kenya realizes she is thinking about plants in new ways.

Days later, Kenya tells Ms. Thompson, "We moved the plant to the window so it could get more sun. Why are the green leaves yellow now?"

Ms. Thompson replies, "Great question, Kenya. I don't know the answer, though. Let's go to the computer and read about plants to see if we can find the answer together." After researching and discussing the information they find, Kenya concludes that too much sun exposure can turn the leaves yellow. Ms. Thompson agrees with Kenya and says, "Let's test this out to be sure." They move the plant to an area away from direct sunlight. She tells Kenya that they will watch the plant over the next few days to see what happens.

Transitions. Help children work on the concept of classification by having them first categorize by one trait. ("If you're wearing red, please get in line.") Then add another trait to challenge the children. ("If you're wearing red and your hair is black, please get your coat.")

Feeding infants. Make these bonding times opportunities to learn. Talk to the baby as you feed her a bottle, describing what you are doing. As you introduce solid foods, engage children in conversation. Wait for a response even though the baby's not yet talking. "Here is a slice of banana. How does it feel when you squish it?"

Snack time. Preschoolers can make their own snacks. Prepare a sign in pictogram form showing how many graham crackers and how much juice children should help themselves to. Children learn about numbers and volume as they prepare their snack and literacy as they "sign" their names to the sheet indicating they've eaten their snack.

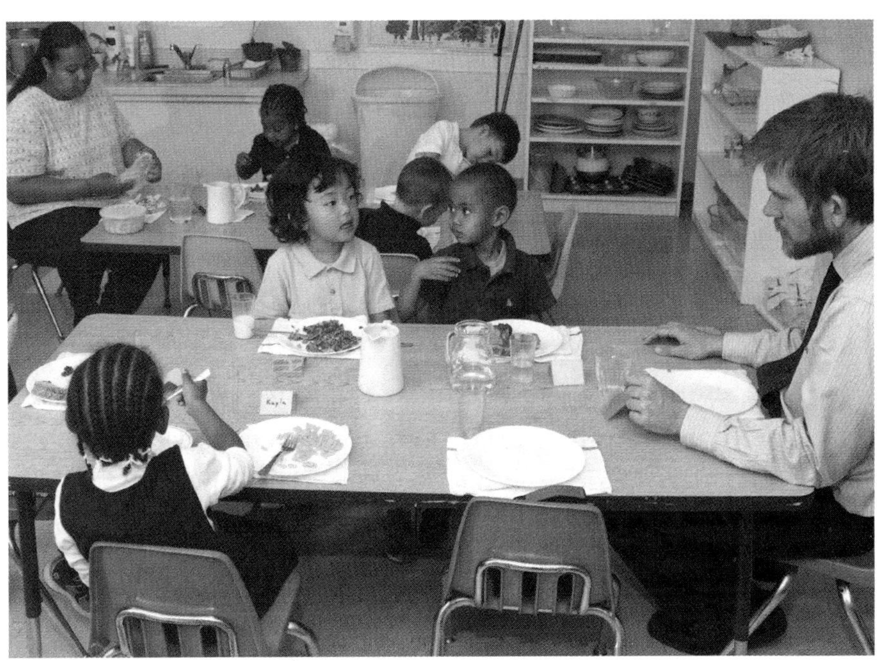

Tackle cause-and-effect scenarios and sharpen children's prediction skills during mealtime discussions.

Family-style lunches with toddlers or preschoolers. Use these mealtimes to introduce the children to new concepts. For example, illustrate cause and effect by noting that the fruit in the gelatin is all at the top or that peeled bananas turn brown. Help children learn to predict outcomes by asking questions, such as: "What would happen to the milk if we didn't have refrigerators?" or "What would we have for lunch if we ate only foods from our garden?" Ask questions that encourage children to make comparisons, like: "How are the raw carrots different from the cooked ones we had yesterday?" Lead children in counting the pieces of food on their plates: "I wonder how many pieces of cucumber you took, Mario? Let's count them together."

Diaper changing and toileting. Respond to children during these routines and take advantage of quality one-on-one time with the child. Initiate conversation, engage the child, and support them in developing a positive attitude about bodily functions and toileting.

Sleep and nap time. Sleep is necessary for children's physical, cognitive, and language development. When infants learn to fall asleep and develop a pattern to comfort themselves, they are learning to regulate their behavior. During sleep and nap time, children also become familiar with the concept of time, discover cause and effect, and learn to identify sleep as a positive experience. For example, when you sing, "Time to go to sleep, time to go to sleep" the toddlers know to move toward their cots. For preschoolers who no longer nap, offer quiet cognitive activities, like working on puzzles while lying on their cots.

Arrival and departure. Help children manage their feelings about separation from and reunions with the people they love. Ask families to bring familiar items from home to keep in your setting, such as photographs and other items. These items will help children settle in at your setting and remain connected to their loved ones. Play games with the children that offer opportunities for people or things to appear or disappear. Read books about separation and reunion.

Ask preschoolers to sign in each morning by placing a symbol or star next to their names. Give children a choice of quiet table activities to work on while the other children arrive—a puzzle, a book, or their journals. Introduce sorting and word sounds by asking children, "If your name begins with the same sound as *tambourine* and *table*, please put your artwork in your cubbies."

Neighborhood walks. Encourage children to be curious and observant. If you see Carrie staring at a ladybug on the ground, join her in a conversation about what she sees. If you see a drain at the edge of the sidewalk, talk with children about what might happen when it rains. Stimulate the children's thinking with follow-up questions, such as: "Where do you think the rainwater goes when it runs down the drains?" Pose a cause-and-effect question: "What happens if water reaches a drain that is clogged with trash?"

Field trips. For example, imagine you are taking a field trip to a busy train terminal. Ask, "Do the people here seem to be in a hurry? Why do you think that's so? Where do you think they're going?" Ask children to count the train cars, guess where the trains are arriving from or departing to, and identify the different types of train cars. Or, on a visit to a shoe store, help children learn about classification as they observe different shoe styles, numbers as they try on different size shoes, and taking on others' perspectives as they pretend to be sales associates and customers. Allow the children to informally interview the real sales associates about their jobs. Follow up with props the children can use to revisit this experience when back in your setting.

Teachable moments. These moments are spontaneous windows of opportunity to extend children's learning and understanding. For example, while playing outdoors, the children rush to the fence to watch high school graduates in caps and gowns walk by. Join the children at the fence and explain the significance of the graduation outfits. Likewise, you and the children see a mound of snow fall from the roof onto the playground. Discuss cause and effect and ask the children to share their theories about why the snow fell to the ground. Weather-related events, like a hailstorm or the sudden appearance of a rainbow, provide opportunities to introduce science concepts.

Identifying and Building Children's Skills and Abilities

As an early educator, what you say and do—including your questions, verbal and nonverbal cues, active listening, descriptions, and suggestions—promote children's learning. Your actions and words help children expand their memories and attention; develop self-regulation and executive function; recognize cause and effect; and sharpen their problem-solving and categorization skills. You also help children understand reading, writing, math, science, art, language, social studies, and technology concepts.

Observe the children in your setting and scaffold their learning. In other words, build on the information the children already know to help them learn new things. Individualize your approach based on each child's skills, abilities, interests, and needs. The following example illustrates how this process works:

> ***Terrell**, age four-and-a-half, says that the insects in the butterfly farm don't look like butterflies.*
>
> ***Mr. Griffin** (Terrell's teacher): "That's a very interesting observation, Terrell. What makes you say that?"*
>
> *(He wants Terrell to articulate his thinking and explain what information he used to reach his conclusion.)*
>
> ***Terrell**: "They don't have wings. They're not flying."*
>
> ***Mr. Griffin**: "You're right about that, Terrell. You made an interesting observation. Butterflies have wings while caterpillars—which is what these insects are—do not. Remember in the books we have been reading we learned that caterpillars will turn into butterflies and then they will have wings."*
>
> *(Mr. Griffin brings over one of the books they've been reading together and asks Terrell to point out both the caterpillars and the butterflies in the drawings.)*
>
> ***Terrell**: "What's that?" (pointing to a picture in the book).*
>
> ***Mr. Griffin**: "That's a chrysalis. The caterpillars form a chrysalis around themselves. Then out of the chrysalis comes a butterfly. Remember how baby chicks hatch from an egg? That's how the butterfly hatches from a chrysalis. Why don't you draw a picture of what you think the caterpillars will look like when they become butterflies?"*

In this brief conversation with Terrell, his teacher learned about and built upon the child's interest and knowledge. He asked questions and brought over a book to remind Terrell of content he had previously been introduced to. Terrell's vocabulary increased when his teacher explained the scientific term "chrysalis." He scaffolded Terrell's learning by helping him relate what he already knew about chickens and eggs to new information about butterflies and chrysalises.

Mr. Griffin helped Terrell expand the following cognitive skills:

- Curiosity about the world around him (how caterpillars and butterflies live).
- Cause-and-effect (what makes caterpillars turn into butterflies).
- Connections between what he already knows and what he is experiencing (how chickens hatch from eggs and butterflies from chrysalises).
- Predicting (imagining the new butterflies).
- Representing his thoughts symbolically (drawing what he thinks the butterfly farm will look like in the future).

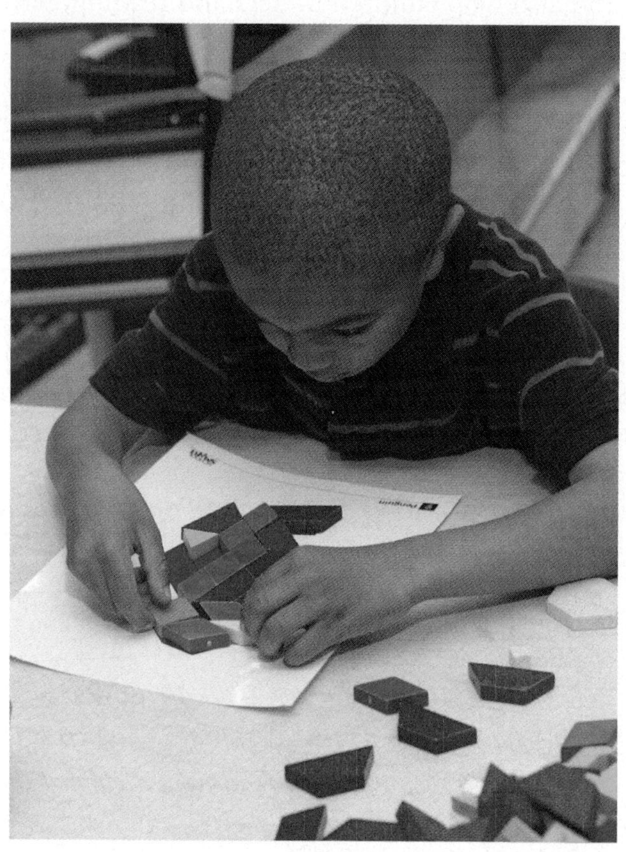

Sometimes children exhibit strong skills or knowledge in a particular area.

Let's take a look at another example.

Ms. White, an FCC educator, notices that three-year-old Linda is having a difficult time completing puzzles. The teacher starts her off with a puzzle with just five or six large pieces and watches to see if Linda still has difficulties. She does, so she offers her a puzzle that has pieces with knobs. She prompts Linda to turn a piece she is having difficulty placing in a different direction. This helps Linda remain focused without feeling overwhelmed. Ms. White then hands Linda one piece at a time to simplify the process. She gives her tips on completing puzzles, like noting colors: "What color is this piece? Yes, it's blue. Do you see another puzzle piece that has this same color blue? Let's see if they might fit together" (Tomlinson and Hyson 2012). Once Linda is confident assembling these puzzles, Ms. White introduces her to more complex ones, perhaps with 10 to 20 pieces with no knobs. She continues to work with Linda, doing just enough to help Linda finish the puzzle on her own.

Consider daily how you can best support the growth and learning of children like Terrell and Linda. Observe all of the children over time and keep individual records for each child. After you have collected sufficient data, analyze it and make conclusions about each child's progress. This information will guide you in customizing learning goals and curricular approaches both for individual children and for groups. In addition, when you speak with children's families about their children's growth and progress, or about obtaining additional assistance for their children, you will have accurate records to provide the family members and other professionals who will work with the children in the future.

Supporting Children's Content Learning

Not only do children refine their cognitive skills during play, they also acquire content knowledge in areas like language and literacy, math, science, art, social studies, and technology. Learning takes place from the moment children arrive at your setting each day to the moment they leave. However, as with all areas of development, children learn through play. For example, children learn a gravity lesson (science) when they build a block tower and knock it down. In the cooking center, you help children read (literacy) the recipe you will use to cook. They may be responsible for measuring (mathematics) the necessary ingredients. When you ask Claire to add 1 teaspoon of *nutmeg* to the mixing bowl, she learns a new word (language) at the same time that she is doing math.

In their play, children act very much like scientists in their approach to learning. Even the youngest infants conduct experiments, analyze data and, begin to, in the words of Alison Gopnik (2010) "form intuitive theories of the physical, biological, and psychological realms." To make sure that children are learning the content that experts think they should know, consult the early learning standards that govern your program. Knowing these standards, you can be intentional in the way you prepare the learning environment, the materials you stock your setting with, and the interactions you have with children. Remember that children bring cultural knowledge and experiences from home as well. Be sure to consult families and examine the funds of knowledge about different content areas that children bring with them. Find ways to incorporate the various background knowledge that children bring to the classroom into your teaching and learning.

In Chapter 6, Communication, you will learn about language and literacy. The arts are covered in Chapter 7, Creativity. The remainder of this chapter, explores how you can support children's development of math, science, social studies, and technology.

Mathematics

Mathematics is a way of describing our world. It is "a way of thinking, knowing, and problem solving that is accessible to all children regardless of their prior knowledge and experiences" (Virginia Early Childhood Development Alignment Project 2008). Children have an intuitive sense of math that begins in infancy. According to Alison Gopnik (2010), baby brains are more flexible than adult ones. They have many more connections between neurons in their brain than do adults plus a chemical that makes a change of connections easy. They are primed for learning.

Observe children during play to understand where they are developmentally.

So how do you introduce math concepts to these eager learners? It's very easy. Math is everywhere and you are probably teaching math without even realizing it (Greenberg 2012). When you use words like "more" or "taller" you are talking measurement. When you ask a child to put a piece of playdough in front of every chair at a table, you are teaching one-to-one correspondence. When you hand a mobile infant a shape sorter to play with, she is learning geometry.

Your job as an early childhood educator is to maximize these unintentional lessons by making them intentional. It is up to you to make all of the math that occurs in daily life both concrete and visible (Greenberg 2012). A good starting point is to familiarize yourself with the components of math, so you know what content children should be learning. They include number and operations; measurement; shapes and spatial relationships (geometry); patterns and relationships; and data collection and analysis.

Number and Number Operations

Infants have an emergent understanding of numeracy, as they attend to more than one object at a time. As you begin counting objects and people in their environment, they start relating the concept of number to your counting. The more you count in relation to their actions, the better their understandings. For instance, you might say to a mobile infant: "You said 'dada' four times this morning. This was the fourth time!"

Keep using this strategy until children can take over the task of counting themselves, which usually happens during the toddler years. Other things you might do with infants and toddlers to set the stage for numeracy are:

- Count children's facial features and body parts. Example: "You have two eyes, two knees, two legs, two arms, two hands, and two feet."
- Sing songs and finger plays that use numbers.
- Read stories that include numbers.
- Count all similar items that infants see.
- Provide number-related toys to play with, such as soft fabric blocks with numbers on them.

If you ask two-year-old Eliza how many bears she has, touch each one saying, "one, two." Eliza is showing that she understands how numbers and counting work; finger counting is an important component of learning about numbers (Bredekamp 2011).

Toddlers and preschoolers will learn to count over time with practice and repetition. Touching the objects makes them concrete. The following tips will help you get toddlers and preschoolers started. By the time they are five, most preschoolers will be counting up to 20, counting five objects in a scattered configuration, recognizing quantities of five or more objects without counting, and writing numbers up to 10. Keep in mind that in numeracy skill development, young children should be working with quantities and naming numbers long before they should be expected to associate a numeral with a quantity. The written numeral 4, for example is a symbol representing the quantity of four objects. Give children plenty of time hearing the number words and manipulating quantities of objects before expecting them to connect that symbol to a quantity

- Count everything, from the number of books in your library to the number of seats at the art table. Touch each object as you count it.
- Sing and act out counting songs and finger plays, such as "There Were 10 in a Bed."
- Read and act out counting books, like *How Do Dinosaurs Count to Ten?* by Jane Yolen, numerous times.
- Set up the dramatic play area for scenarios that lend themselves to numbers and counting, such as a grocery store.
- Use charts to teach number sequence. Ask the children to write their names on a numbered chart as they arrive each day. Children will be able to see who is present and the order in which each child arrived.
- Introduce counting during meals and snacks:
    - o "You can have two graham crackers for morning snack."
    - o "Do we have enough chairs for everyone? Let's count to be sure."
    - o "Look at the chart to see how many slices of bananas are available for your afternoon snack."
    - o "I'm going to eat one of the strawberries in the bowl. How many will be left?"
- Ask questions during play: "How many more blocks will you need to make the towers the same height?"
- Make up problems involving numbers: "I buried three treasures in the sand. Can you find them?"
- Use counting to solve real-life problems: "There are five of you and three tricycles. How many of you can ride right now?"
- Make silly counting mistakes and let the children correct you: "Let's count the children in the circle during group meeting time—1, 2, 3, 10, 4 …"

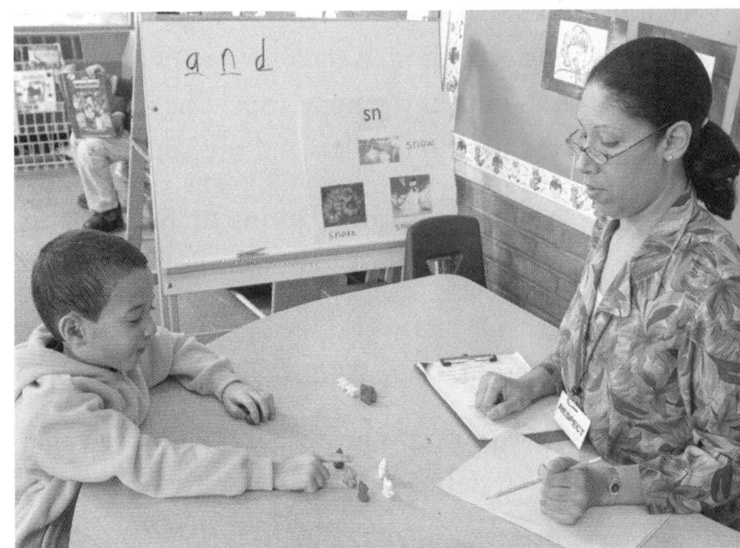

Observe children's progress and record what you see.

Measurement

Measurement allows us to determine quantity-like qualities: size, weight, volume, and time. Understanding begins in infancy and takes off during the toddler and preschool years. Start infants off by using measurement–related words in your conversations with them:

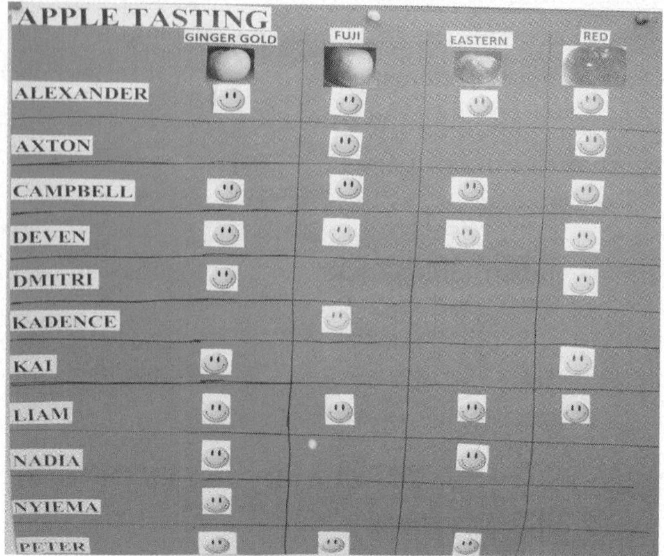

Make a chart of the children's likes and dislikes.

- "I think that toy is a bit too *heavy* to pick up. Try pushing it instead."
- "This rattle is *bigger* than the other one."
- "It feels like you've *gained* another pound since I picked you up yesterday."
- "You drank all of your bottle. The milk is *'all gone'*."
- "There are *fewer* children here today than yesterday."
- "Do you think that this pail is *big* enough to hold the balls?"
- "You completely *filled* the basket with dolls."

As children become verbal, they start asking questions like: Who's taller? Who's bigger? How much does that stone weigh? How high is the climber? And, with your guidance, will start measuring according to their own rules. The rocket ship they constructed using Lego® building bricks is as long as the jump rope. The teddy bear weighs the same as three bean bags. Here are some ways to help toddlers and preschoolers practice measurement:

- Model measuring. During dramatic play, ask the pretend party hosts for a cup of lemon tea with two teaspoons of sugar.
- Provide real-world measurement examples. "Let's make some modeling clay today. I have the recipe here. Who's going to help me measure out the ingredients?"
- Pose problems for the children. "How many cups of water do you think it will take to fill the watering can?"
- Perform measurement activities. "Let's line up from tallest to shortest."
- Ask and answer questions that encourage children's thinking. "If this measuring cup holds half a cup, could we use it to measure two cups of flour? How could we do that?"

For children who are ready to make the transfer from using alternate forms of measurement such as the jump rope in the example above, introduce children to real measuring tools such as rulers and tape measures. "The computer has a 17-inch monitor. Did you know that it's measured diagonally instead of from top to bottom? Let's use the tape measure to measure the screen both ways." Remember that introducing young children to measurement tools, and the language of inches, centimeters, etc., is not the same as expecting them to be able to use these measurement tools accurately. That will come later. For now, experience with these tools and terms will help develop their understanding and interest.

Geometry (Shapes and Spatial Relationships), Patterning, and Organizing/Representing Data

Geometry, patterns, and organizing/representing data are math concepts that young children are exposed to already in their environments. As with other math concepts, build on infants' growing awareness of these processes. Offer them toys like shape sorters that teach geometry concepts and puzzles that will give children practice learning shapes and patterns. Comment on what you see as they play that relate to these mathematical concepts. Over time your words will begin to make sense to the infants.

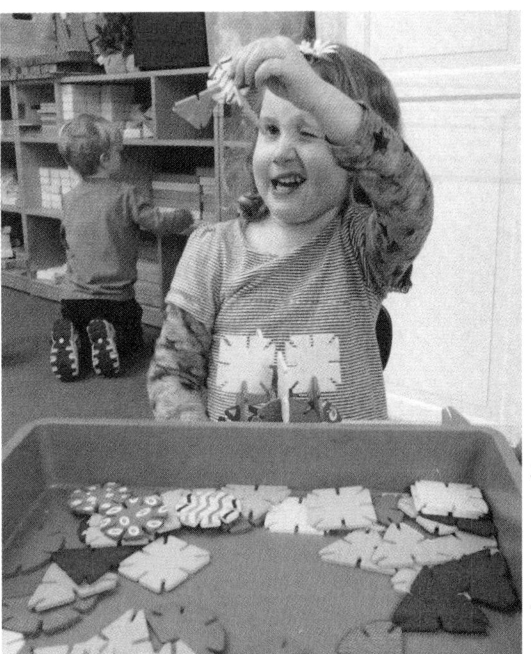

During play, children learn geometry, patterning, and how to represent data.

- "Look at all the different shapes on your mobile. There are stars and squares, and circles, and triangles."
- "Do you want a round cracker or a square-shaped one?"
- "The muffins are round and so are the raisins on them."
- "Bob's shirt has stripes on it. They go red-black-red-black."
- "Look at the keys on this instrument: they go fat key, skinny key, fat key, skinny key."
- "Everyone in our group is putting on a jacket to go outside."
- "All of the balls go in a basket."

As toddlers and preschoolers gain a better grasp of these math concepts, the following activities are opportunities to apply the concepts:

- Ask questions to stretch children's thinking. "How can you create a pattern with these blue and yellow pot holder loops?" (patterning)

- Make graphs. Involve children in creating graphs to show their favorite foods; how much light plants need to grow; or the most popular storybooks the children like to hear you read. (data representation)
- Pose problems. "Which plant container will hold the most soil? The short, fat one or the tall, skinny one?" (geometry)
- Point out patterns in music and lead children in singing them. (patterning)
- Read aloud books about shapes (*When a Line Bends ... A Shape Begins* by Rhonda Gowler Greene) and patterns (*Pattern Fish* by Trudy Harris). (geometry/patterning)
- Ask the children to clean up after block play by matching shapes. Clean up props stored on pegboards by matching objects to adhesive paper shapes. (geometry)
- Challenge children to create different shapes, like a pyramid, when building with hardwood blocks. (geometry)
- Help children string beads in different patterns. (patterning)
- Clap the patterns to songs and chants. (patterning)
- Identify objects in the room by their shapes. Children sit in a *circle* at group meeting time, the window is *square*, or the table is *rectangular*. (geometry)
- Help children find and discuss math in the world around them. "See the interesting shape of the statue's base?" (geometry)
- Provide toys that allow children to create patterns.

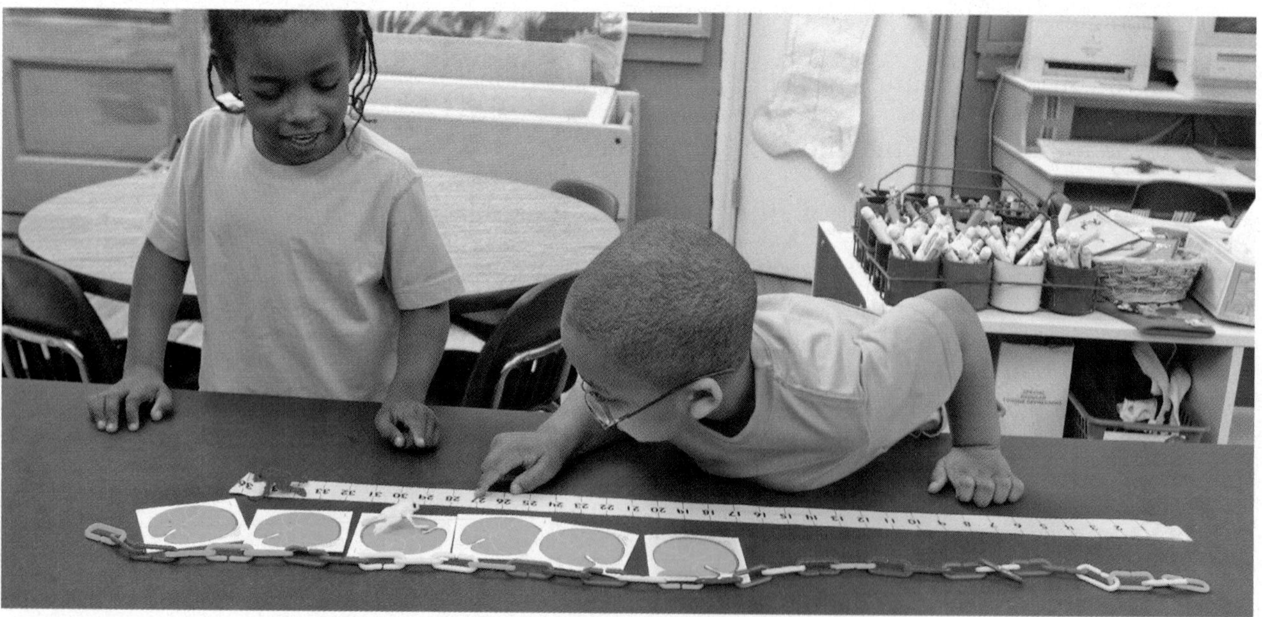

Provide real-world measuring experiences.

Science

Teaching children science encourages them to examine the physical properties of materials and objects, living things (people, plants, and animals), and the earth and environment. Here are some ways you can introduce infants to these concepts:

- Include growing plants in the environment.
- Include living things like an aquarium with fish in the environment.
- Use scientific words such as observe, describe, compare, contrast, and experiment when talking with children.
- Use recycled materials for play and talk to children about why it's good to recycle.
- Offer sensory experiences with natural substances like sand and water.
- Observe scientific phenomena together: "The sun is out and the snow is starting to melt."
- Point out science in everyday life: "That puddle is turning the nearby soil into mud."

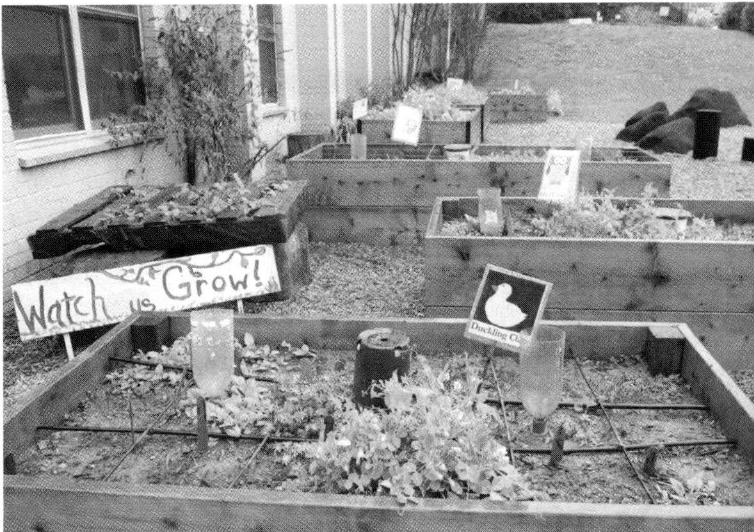

Help the children plant and tend a vegetable garden.

Toddlers and preschoolers can begin to understand and apply the concepts you have introduced. Try some of these strategies to teach science content:

- Provide an environment that invites exploration: stock the science center with tools like magnifying glasses tweezers, scales, binoculars, stethoscope, and microscope and things to explore, like leaves, twigs, bones, seed pods, feathers, pine cones, plants, prisms, an ant farm, etc.
- Add science to other learning centers through books, scales in the cooking area, burying bones in the sand table, gears in the blocks area, and props in dramatic play center such as a stethoscope and thermometer in a doctor's office setting.

- Help children to make charts representing data from their experiments on topics such as the colors of leaves, how tall plants grew, how long it took a block of ice to melt in the water table.
- Work with children to use the computer to document their observations. For example, they can create a PowerPoint presentation of graphs, photos, and drawings.
- Encourage children to make predictions: how long will it take the carrots in our garden to appear?
- Read books together on subjects like worms, bugs, butterflies, tornadoes, and magnets.
- Encourage children to make daily weather reports and record their findings.
- Set up a recycling program for the classroom or FCC home.

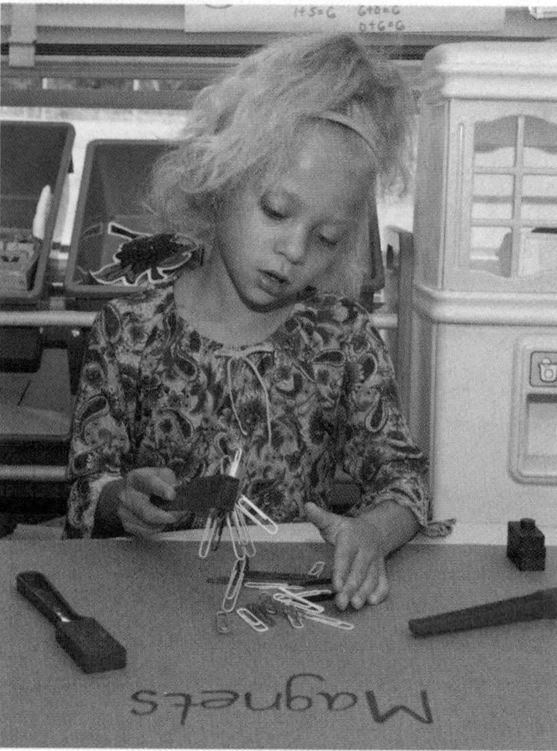

Provide an environment for children that invites exploration.

- Engage children in cooking experiences and observe together the changes in physical properties. “What happens to dough when you add yeast?”
- Take children on nature walks and have them collect leaves, pinecones, and acorns to explore, examine, and experiment with.
- Measure shadows at different times of day.
- Open a “repair shop” to fix broken items in the setting.
- Observe animals outdoors in their natural habitats. Ask the children questions about what they see and document their observations.
- Ask questions that have more than one correct answer, such as, “What do you think might happen if we put something in our compost heap besides leaves and food waste?”
- Plant a vegetable garden. Use the vegetables and herbs in cooking projects and for snacks.
- Encourage children to observe and feed fish in an aquarium.
- Pose challenges, such as “How can you turn the red paint a different color?” or “What will happen to the popcorn when you put it in the microwave?”

- Suggest activities: "Today is sunny, let's go outside and draw our shadows on the ground. We can check again later and see if our shadows grow or change." Or, have children paint the outside walls of your school or FCC home with water and watch it evaporate. Rather than grand demonstration experiments, allow children to explore and inquire about the things they experience on a daily basis.

Teaching children science encourages them to examine the physical properties of materials and objects, living things, and the earth and environment.

- Introduce science into teachable moments: "What do you think made the rainbow suddenly appear?"

Technology

Technology content differs from math, science, and social studies content in that technology refers to both a content area and the tools that are used to learn that content. Everyone is aware that we are now in a digital age, which is changing our world. According to the joint position statement of the National Association for the Education of Young Children (NAEYC) and the Fred Rogers Center for Early Learning and Children's Media at Saint Vincent College (2012):

> The pace of change is so rapid that society is experiencing a disruption almost as significant as when there was a shift from oral language to print literacy, and again when the printing press expanded access to books and the printed word. The shift to new media literacies and the need for digital literacy that encompasses both technology and media literacy will continue to shape the world in which young children are developing and learning.

The definition of technology goes far beyond our definition of a few years back when the technology tools included a desktop computer with a mouse and printer, along with a TV, a VCR, tape recorders, light tables, projectors, and microscopes. The ever-expanding definition now includes tablets, smartphones, interactive whiteboards, electronic toys, cameras, DVD and MP3 music players, and e-book readers. How you use these devices with children determines not only how they learn but what they learn.

Technology differs also from other content areas because it's not something that you want to introduce to children of all ages. The American Academy of Pediatrics (AAP) discourages the use of any screen media other than video-chatting for children under 18 months. Although there are quite a number of software programs and applications developed for and marketed towards infants, do not be tempted to use them. Babies need interactions with real people and objects that they can actively explore with their senses. Being passive viewers in front of a screen goes against everything we know about how babies learn.

For children 18 to 24 months of age, the AAP says that their use of digital media should include only high-quality programs and apps and that technology use should be with an adult. They note that this approach responds to how toddlers learn best. They state that it is best to avoid letting children use media by themselves.

For children older than two years, the AAP recommends limiting media use to no more than 1 hour or less per day of high-quality programming. Again, they remind adults to spend time with children while they engage with media and do other healthy activities together such as reading or playing games.

Preschoolers, however, can benefit greatly from interactions with technology, if used thoughtfully. "Thoughtfully" means when children use a desktop computer or a tablet it is a social rather than a solitary experience. Place two chairs at each screen and let children work in pairs.

Warren Buckleitner (n.d.), a pioneer in using technology with children, suggests that early childhood educators approach technology by:

- Introducing new technology to the group during group meeting times.
- Having children interact with the technology on their own while you are there as a facilitator; there is no need to try to "teach" children how to use technology once you have introduced it.
- Providing opportunities for children to use technology in dramatic play talking on a smartphone or using a tablet in imitation of their family members.
- Making technology interactive through the choice of appropriate software and apps.
- Setting up search functions to show images rather than words. Let children come up with the search words.
- Using a digital camera to document children's work.

In terms of content to focus on, consult the early learning standards that apply to your program. However, not every state and governing body has technology standards in place. If this is the case in your program, remember that there are also standards developed by the International Society for Technology in Education (ISTE 2012). These standards cover four areas: 1. creativity and innovation; 2. communication and collaboration; 3. research and information; and 4. critical thinking, problem solving, and decision making.

It is this fourth area that concerns cognitive content. Included here are the development of these skills:

- To be able to identify and define authentic problems and significant questions for investigation.
- To plan and manage activities to develop a solution or complete a project.
- To collect and analyze data to identify and make informed decisions.
- To use multiple processes and diverse perspectives to explore alternative solutions.

Early childhood educators can help children master this content by picking up on children's natural curiosity and asking guiding questions, such as:

- "Carrie, you were asking why all of the flower stems in our garden are green. Let's look that up on our computer. I think that would make an interesting study."
- "You really enjoyed playing the kora in our marching band, Jack. I like your idea of seeing if there are other instruments that come from Senegal that we might get for our band. Let's try researching this."
- "Why do you think the birds don't like the seed we put in the feeder? What should we look up on the tablet to help us figure this out?"
- "I know that you want to do more drawings for the book that you are making about your dog Chessie. Let's try out this new drawing program and see if you can make a drawing that you'd like to include in your book."
- "It says on the fire department web page that we can contact our fire station by calling them, writing a letter, emailing them, or visiting them in person. How do you think it would be best to contact them to ask them your question about smoke alarms?"
- "We printed out three recipes from our Class Cookbook. What recipe should we make for our family celebration party?"
- "Can you make the same structure on the computer that you made out of Legos® using this program that lets you move Lego blocks around the screen?"
- "How is reading this story on the e-reader the same as and different from when we read it in a regular book?"

Technology is especially helpful when working with dual language learners and children with disabilities. The repetition and reinforcement technology provides is ideal for both groups' needs. Also, computer programs will give you the correct spelling of words in the children's home languages for labeling objects in your setting. Always remember to check with families about the specific words used in their homes as many terms are regionally or dialectically specific. These programs can also teach you the correct pronunciation of words in other languages so you can better communicate with dual language learners and their families. Be careful of using translation software online without having an interpreter double check for accuracy. Language nuance is not something easily duplicated and errors can cause problems and misunderstandings. For children who are blind, have manual dexterity problems, or are deaf, assistive hardware and software can offer accessibility to technology. Work with a special educator to identify and locate these accommodations. To illustrate, *Talk and Draw* software, a federally-funded project, helped children who couldn't use their hands to operate a computer by using their voices to command objects on the computer screen to draw. For some children with severe cerebral palsy, this was the first time they had ever created artwork. Though this software is no longer available, it is the precursor of similar voice recognition software products today that can fulfill this need. Technology can be more than an excellent teacher of cognitive content; sometimes it is a lifesaver. ■

CHAPTER 6:

Communication

CDA® Functional Area 6: Candidate uses a variety of developmentally appropriate learning experiences and teaching strategies to promote children's language and early literacy learning, and help them communicate their thoughts and feelings verbally and nonverbally. Candidate helps dual-language learners make progress in understanding and speaking both English and their home language.

Communication

Introduction

When we communicate, we express thoughts, ideas, information, and experiences through speech, writing, and the use of nonverbal cues, like facial expressions and crossed arms. We develop these skills at an early age. Children learn to speak and build their vocabularies through direct interactions with more competent speakers, including older children and adults.

Language and literacy development are closely related. Gaining language skills—both talking and listening—supports reading and writing and vice versa. In addition, children's language and literacy development allow them to explore and learn content (for example, what kinds of trees grow in the playground or what iguanas eat, now and in the future).

As an early educator, you play a pivotal role in helping the children in your setting develop a strong foundation of language and literacy. They will use these skills to communicate with you and the other children, to get involved in play, to learn to love books and learn from them, and to express their feelings and ideas in spoken and written forms. You achieve this through your learning environment and how you interact with the children within the environment. Responding with a smile when a baby coos at you, introducing toddlers to new vocabulary words, reading aloud to children of all ages, inviting children to share ideas in small and large group meetings, and holding conversations during daily routines, are all ways that you support language and literacy skills.

In this chapter, we will examine the following ways in which you can foster children's language and literacy development:

- **Understanding the Language and Literacy Development of Infants, Toddlers, and Preschoolers**
- **Creating a Language and Literacy Learning Environment**
- **Supporting Children's Oral Language Development**
- **Fostering Children's Reading Development**
- **Fostering Children's Writing Development**
- **Supporting Dual Language Learners**
- **Partnering With Families**

Understanding the Language and Literacy Development of Infants, Toddlers, and Preschoolers

Before infants can understand or say words, they begin to communicate using gestures like facial expressions or by crying. For example, infants may cry to indicate that they want to be held. Over time, children learn to understand and respond to others' speech and express with their own words what they know and feel. For example, infants begin to respond to hearing their own names and to very simple, familiar requests. Mobile infants can shake their heads or ask for an item by looking back and forth from the item to you. Many families and centers will use baby signs with infants to support communication before a child is ready to speak words. Their first words are ones that have a personal meaning, like mama. Between 18 months and 24 months, children learn hundreds of words and combine two words to form a simple sentence, like "Want juice" or "All gone." Toddlers and preschoolers can communicate using words or signs, although there will be times when they need to be reminded to use them.

> Learning to read and write starts long before first grade and has long-lasting effects. Learning to read and write is an ongoing process from infancy. . . . From the earliest years, everything that adults do to support children's language and literacy is critical (Strickland and Riley-Ayers 2006).

As Strickland and Riley-Ayers note, young children's language and literacy development is an ongoing process. Infants turn toward the person who is speaking, begin to make sounds back and forth with a conversation partner, and turn to look at an object a family member or educator is talking about. "Yes, Jaime. We are talking about the squirrel on the windowsill." They like looking at books and listening while a favorite person reads to them. By the time they are toddlers, children join in songs and rhymes, use words and non-verbal gestures to communicate needs, and follow simple directions. "Kion, please get the red ball from under the tree and put it in the basket. Then we can carry the basket indoors." In the preschool years most children have built an impressive vocabulary and can use it to make their needs known, share their ideas and interests, engage in play with one or more children, and explore books and writing. "Veronica, there are a lot of letters in your name. I see you are working hard to learn how to write all of them."

It is important to note that writing involves both composition and letter formation or handwriting. Children compose stories orally from a very young age, and can use tools like magnet letters to compose words (like their name) long before they have the bone development and muscle control in their hands to hold a writing tool correctly and scribe the letters. We can talk about writing stories even when it is the adult who does the scribing.

Communication describes the skills and strategies used to share and exchange ideas and feelings with others. Talking, listening, writing, reading, gesturing, smiling, touching, and crying are among the many forms of human communication. Children and adults communicate for a purpose—our goals might include solving problems, answering questions, requesting help, learning about a topic of interest, sharing and listening to ideas, expressing feelings, thinking and planning, and providing information. To communicate well, we need to build skills in listening, speaking (or use of sign language), writing, and reading. These skills are closely connected to each other and closely tied to cognitive development. Thinking skills help children make sense of the language they hear and they use language skills to talk about a wide variety of topics. Physical development plays a role too, as children need fine motor skills to hold writing implements, turn the pages in books, and use touch screens and keyboards. Language and literacy skills support social development as well. Children with strong language skills are better able to engage in play, make friends, express ideas, and build relationships with adults and peers. The development of communication skills is typically referred to as "emerging literacy."

Effective communication requires presence and engagement. The skills associated with early literacy are and can only be as strong as the interactions and engagements between children and teachers, and other adults in a child's life.

In her book Raising a Talker (2013), Renate Zangl, a psycholinguist, states:

"You can jump-start a child's communication skills by providing a language-rich learning environment from her earliest moments. You are much more than a bystander! You can shape and enhance what and how much she takes in, which affects how much she can learn—now and later on—and how she will communicate with you."

Zangl goes on to discuss how that communication (language and ultimately literacy) revolves around actual physical engagement with a live adult or verbally proficient play partner. Very young children only learn and pick up language (vocabulary, specifically) in a live situation. Computer games, talking books, electronic gadgets, toys that reproduce words, videos, and other non-human voicing objects just are not good at sparking language learning. Young children—babies and young toddlers in particular—need more than just the sound of language. Babies and young toddlers are reading cues and clues that are part of the broader aspect of communication. Baby and toddler brains are quickly associating the sound of words with other visual or sensory data much faster than when words are used on a screen or electronic device, and there is then a delay in the "labelling." As Zangl notes, the timing is off.

Interactions and repeated utterances of words are critical. But communication and opportunities for young children to USE language and communication are what create understanding and comprehension. According to Lev Vygotsky, "language solidifies thought" and demonstrates how communication is effective. It is through the usage of verbal expression—or other communicative devices—that conceptual knowledge becomes a part of the child's experience. Noted linguist Michael Halliday also stresses that "language is the essential condition of knowing, the process by which experience becomes knowledge." In other words, it is in the "doing" of communication that understanding and knowing develop.

As stressed above, communication is so much more than just the use of words, saying something, reading something, working with print or other physical means of expressing ideas. Historically, too, research that emphasized the sheer volume or number of words a child hears was considered the basis for language, literacy and communication programs and efforts. In recent years, our understanding has moved on to examine the quality of interactions and word usage, along with consideration of other environmental factors influencing when and how a child is exposed to vocabulary. Other factors that play a part in language and cognitive development include cultural expectations and means of communicating. Additionally, the child's individual temperament, or how the child communicates, in also a critical factor. Some children are simply more "verbal" while others may not necessarily use as many words in expressing themselves and share their understanding of ideas through other avenues—drawing, dance, constructions, body maneuvers, expressions, and so on. Cultural differences in the ways that families express emotion, give directions, or expect attention from children can influence the communication expression styles of children as well. Recognizing that a cultural style of requesting cooperation ("Can you clean up those legos now?") may be confusing to a child who is accustomed to being given directives ("Put those legos up now, it is time to go."). This confusion often results in discipline issues in the classroom when a child answers a request to clean up in the negative thinking they have been given a choice, and the teacher perceives this as defiance. Understanding the communication styles of the home is essential for avoiding these cultural conflicts in the classroom. This is why Vygotsky's notion that "language solidifies thought" must be understood in the broader context of communication.

Practitioners and advocates who recognize and support the many ways children communicate and express themselves can reference the philosophical and research support that has come from Reggio Emilia, Italy. Over the years, members and participants in the schools and programs found in Reggio Emilia (which has influenced countless other individuals and programs worldwide) have described a core idea of their work as recognizing, encouraging and supporting the "hundred languages of children" (Edwards, Gandini, Forman, 2011). Obviously, they are not literally referencing a hundred (verbal) languages that children might use but the notion that children use a multiplicity of communicative devices to express ideas and understanding.

It is critical that the means and methods of communication that children use be understood as just that—means and methods. Specifically, children will have a dominant or "first" language. However, as indicated above, when given opportunities and options, children will become communicative in a variety of ways. Some children will have the experience of being in a family, community or situation where they can actually learn more than one verbally oriented language. We want to encourage that as much as possible. Being able to express oneself, communicate and share information with persons other than those in a limited circle is a skill to be embraced.

To be understood and to understand are basic human needs. Communication—in whatever form—promotes understanding when any two or more individuals take the time to actually try to make sense of what is said or done.

The selected resources that follow can serve as works that help promote communication, vocabulary acquisition, and the vital interactions that create a basis for assisting children with important and meaningful relationships. Communication starts with the very young and should continue throughout our lives.

Language and literacy skills develop in tandem. Each set of skills depends and builds on the other. Thus, language skills support both reading and writing: reading leads to larger vocabularies, and writing allows children to understand connections between spoken and written words.

Building Language Skills

Language includes receptive language—listening to and making sense of spoken words—and expressive language—using spoken words to share thoughts, ideas, and feelings. Receptive language includes information received by hearing sounds and words or by observing another person's facial expressions. Expressive language includes speech as well as sign language and use of devices such as a communication board or a tablet. Most children gain receptive language skills before they develop expressive language skills. That is, they can understand many spoken words in their environment—whether directed to them or in the background—before they are able to speak. This means children might be able to follow simple directions before they use oral language.

When children are immersed in language—that is, when they have many opportunities to hear older children and adults speak—they are likely to be fluent speakers of their home language by around age three. This language immersion includes many spontaneous, natural interactions with adults, as when a parent lifts a baby from his crib, looks into his eyes, and says softly, "Good morning, Graham. I heard your gurgles telling me that it's time to get up." Having pleasant interactions such as this over and over again, helps infants learn how conversations work—first I say something, then you say something in return—and they learn to enjoy communication with others. Parents and caregivers should be urged to sing, talk, and read to babies as soon as they are born. Even though the baby will not respond in language that adults understand, they are hearing language and absorbing new words daily (receptive vocabulary). Most of all they will gain an understanding of the give and take of conversation and the joy of hearing their caregiver's voice. Language immersion can also be planned as when an educator introduces sophisticated vocabulary to go along with a project or study or leads children in a lunch-time discussion about their morning walk through the neighborhood. As young children's receptive and expressive vocabularies grow, they become skilled communicators who use their language skills to ask questions, get their needs met, provide information, and to enjoy playing and learning with others.

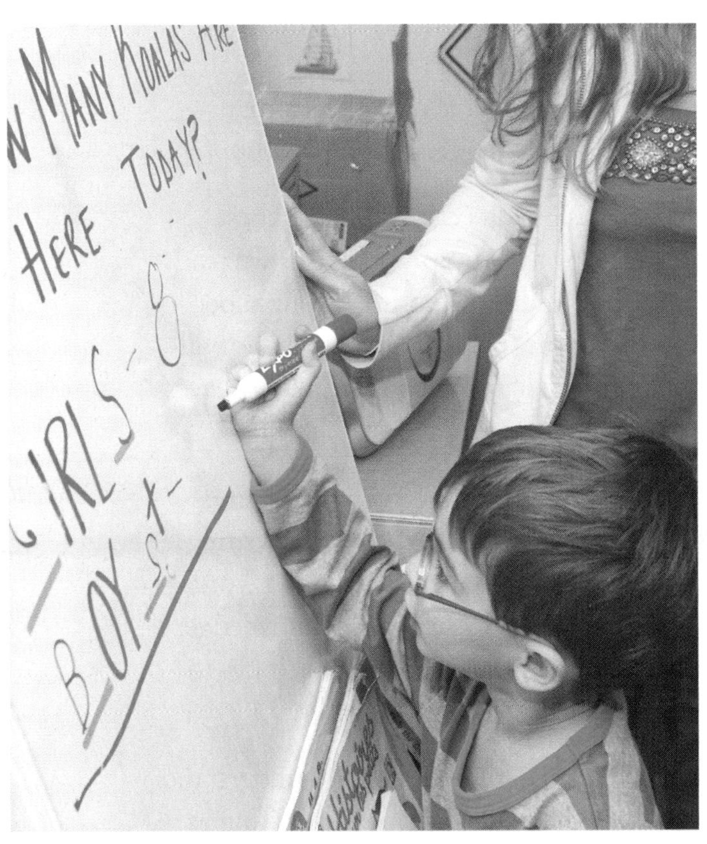

Model writing to demonstrate that print has meaning and motivate children to begin scribbling and writing.

Learning about Writing

Mobile infants and toddlers first explorations of drawing and writing are in the form of random scribbles. They use fine motor skills, visual perception, and hand-eye coordination to hold a chubby crayon or chunky marker and draw on paper. After a while, children come to realize that their actions—moving the crayon on paper, for example—are the cause of the marks they see on the paper. This is one of many ways young children come to understand an important concept: cause and effect.

Young children pass through stages as they learn to write and eventually understand conventional forms of writing—the way older children and adults write. Each stage builds on the ones before. Consider how Reynaldo moves through the stages of writing:

Early scribbling. When given a crayon, Reynaldo, 12 months old, uses his senses to explore it. He holds, smells, and tastes it. When his early childhood educator places a piece of paper on the table where he is sitting, he grasps the crayon in his fist and make marks on the paper. Reynaldo finds it very satisfying to move the crayon back and forth on the paper. He enjoys the process of scribbling, but is not very interested in the product of his work. He is busy practicing what it feels like to hold and use his first writing tool.

Controlled scribbling. Several months later, after having plenty of practice scribbling, Reynaldo, now a toddler, discovers that he can control the crayon and plan what marks to make. His fine motor skills and hand-eye coordination have improved and he can think before acting—he has some control over impulses. Reynaldo's controlled scribbling includes different techniques, colors, and strategies for using crayons, markers, and other writing tools. His scribbles include lines, circles, and zigzags and sometimes he repeats his actions, filling the entire piece of paper with circles.

Basic forms. As a young preschooler, one day Reynaldo looks at his scribbles and says, "I made a square. And here's another one." His small muscle control and hand-eye coordination have improved so much he can repeat what he did and make more squares if he chooses. Sometimes he puts scribbles and squares on the same paper. He does not plan to draw something specific, but when he is done he names his drawings, "It's a cat." The adult can write the label "cat" on his picture so he sees he has composed or written something that others can understand. Some days, Reynaldo makes horizontal, linear scribbles that go across the page. They don't look like letters, but have the connected loops and lines that an adult might use when writing a list or a note.

Pictorial. Reynaldo, now a preschooler, can make marks and shapes and plan ways to use them in his drawings. When he shows his drawings to other people they can begin to recognize what is in the picture: "I see you have drawn two people. Tell me about them." He now knows that pictures—and words— are symbols for real things.

Reynaldo continues to include scribble writing next to his pictures. Adults can transcribe these compositions to support his developing writing. He understands print concepts—such as we read words but not pictures—and sometimes he writes an "R," for Reynaldo. He knows the alphabet too, so he might also write an "R" and a few other letters found in his name. Occasionally he will write other letters he knows too. He is on track to be writing his whole name by the time he leaves preschool and heads off to kindergarten.

Now that Reynaldo has learned to say the alphabet, he may write letters according to the sounds of the letters he knows. For example, a note that reads "I LV U." This is the start of "real" writing, even though it uses invented spelling (writing words according to the way the letters in the words sound). This is a natural stage in children's writing development. Reynaldo's teacher acknowledges and accepts his writing, so he sees himself as a competent and confident learner and continues to refine his writing skills.

Over time, as they practice writing and observe adults writing, young children come to understand that writing is an important skill that serves many purposes. They begin to understand writing as the way that what is said can be captured on paper. They incorporate writing in play scenarios, use a variety of writing tools, and write on paper and other surfaces—such as a white board or a touch tablet. They learn about writing at the same time as they learn about language and reading. Writing helps children understand print concepts and how they are related to speech.

Learning about Reading

As noted earlier, listening, speaking, writing, and reading skills are closely connected. Children who have many opportunities to listen to and express themselves through speech are likely to become skilled readers and writers. Children who can put their ideas in writing become better readers. Children who are read to often learn to love reading, and they become better listeners, speakers, and writers.

Readers use two processes when reading: decoding and comprehending. Decoding is translating the written words into their spoken versions, and comprehending is understanding the meaning of what is read. Typically, children learn these processes in the primary grades. Before they reach this stage, however, they have had many emerging literacy experiences that build a foundation for learning conventional reading.

Oral vocabulary is extremely important to reading comprehension. This is especially true when children have had many interesting first-hand experiences through which they learned vocabulary as part of the activity. Vocabulary knowledge also results from listening to families and educators read aloud from interesting story books and non-fiction texts. Children build their vocabulary over time. Typically, they understand more words than they can say.

Phonological Awareness

Reading also relies on phonological awareness, which is the general ability to notice and manipulate sounds in words. Phonemic awareness, understanding that sounds make up words and that words can be broken into sounds, is one type of phonological awareness. Each of the 6,000 languages in the world uses a different assortment of phonemes—the distinctive sounds used to form words. Babies are born with the ability to distinguish these differences. Their babbles include many more sounds than those used in their home language. At about 6 to 10 months, babies begin to ignore the phonemes not used in their home language. They babble only the sounds made by the people who talk with them most often.

Learning to write requires children to notice and understand that speech is made up of small sounds. This understanding is applied when children write. Thus, when a child writes "TRK," meaning a large vehicle, she is not using conventional spelling, but she is showing that she understands that the word, "truck" has three phonemes, T, R, and K. According to Yopp and Yopp (2009), "A child's ability to reflect on language itself, specifically the sounds of language and especially the phonemes, supports the child's understanding of the logic of the written code. That we use symbols to represent small sounds makes sense because the English language consists of small sounds."

Phonological awareness also includes awareness of the sounds and rhythms of speech, rhymes, and sound similarities. For example, phonological skills include recognition that "hat" rhymes with "cat" and that the "P" at the start of the name Peter is the same sound as the "P" in picture.

Beginning in 2002, the National Early Literacy Panel (NELP 2008, 153) reviewed research on language, literacy, and communication in young children from birth through age five. One of NELP's key findings was the significant relationship between children's knowledge of *phonological awareness* and success in reading and writing. Educators can help young children develop these four phonological skills:

- **Rhyming:** producing words that end with the same sound (e.g., name and flame).
- **Alliteration:** recognizing words beginning with the same sound (e.g., ***br**aid, **br**ain, and **br**eakfast*).
- **Sentence segmenting:** hearing each separate word within a sentence.
- **Syllable segmenting:** being aware of "chunks" in words; understanding that words can have beginning, middle, and ending sounds. (For example, the word "daffodil" is made of three chunks.)

Print Concepts

Print concepts are another set of skills that develop from infancy through the early childhood years when children have many experiences with books and listening to books read aloud. These concepts include knowing the parts of a book, how to hold a book, and that we read from the top to the bottom and from left to right on the page (in English). Children learn concepts such as up/down, front/back, left/right and the associated vocabulary. This helps them understand how words are read and written on a page.

Alphabet Knowledge

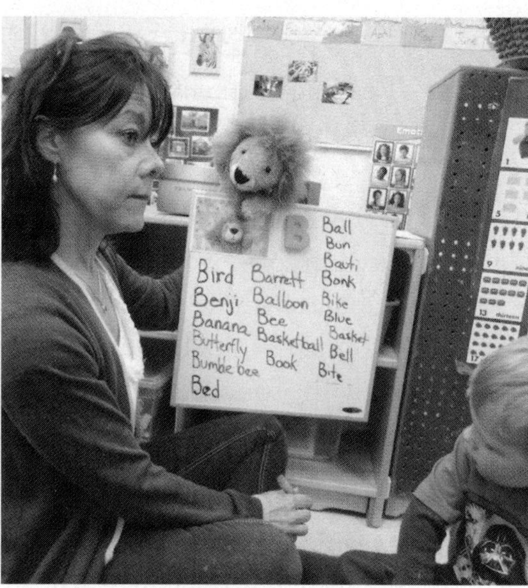

Begin working with young children on literacy skills, like alliteration (words beginning with the same sound).

Alphabet knowledge—being able to name letters and match their sounds to the letters—is another precursor to reading. This involves visual discrimination to recognize and name the letters and auditory discrimination, knowing the sounds that match each letter. These skills are distinct, but they develop together.

Here are some of the other understandings children gain in the early years that support their literacy learning:

- Written names and words are symbols for the actual person or object.
- There is a specific way to write each letter and word; the sequencing of the letters is critical to it making sense.
- Words are made with letters.
- Letters represent specific sounds.
- Symbols and words have consistent meanings. (For example, a pencil in the basket is called a pencil today and will still be called a pencil tomorrow, even if it is in another place.)
- Concepts and vocabulary such as up/down, front/back, left/right.

Language and Emergent Literacy Development

The children in your setting come from various backgrounds and are likely to have had a range of experiences with language and literacy before entering the program. Figure 45a-c includes examples of the typical language and literacy behaviors and skills of young children in different age groups. They are provided as a guide as every child and every group of children is unique and their language and literacy development are influenced by culture, family, exposure to language and books, and other factors. This guide can support you in knowing what kinds of experiences to expect and encourage at what age, but not to determine red flags or concerns. Children who are multilingual may be far more advanced in some areas than you can recognize if you are not fluent in their languages, and other children may be more limited by having exposure to only one language or by having had limited language support at home.

Figure 45a. Language and Literacy Skills for Young Children

Age	Developing Language and Literacy
Young Infants (birth–8 months)	• Can hear all of the phonemes (smallest sounds of language) present in all human languages (this ability decreases as child hears home language more and more). • Smile, coo, and gurgle back and forth with conversation partners. • Learn about the give and take of conversations through playing games such as peek-a-boo. • Switch to babbling (at 6 to 9 months). • Shake their heads to say "No." • Mouth books and explore them with their hands and eyes. • Pay attention to pictures in books.

Figure 45b. Language and Literacy Skills for Young Children

Age	Developing Language and Literacy
Mobile Infants (9–17 months)	• Understand about 50 words by 12 months; understand meaning of a new word every other day. • Say from 3 to 60 words by end of this age period. • Use words and gestures to communicate. • Point at objects for adults to name; remember words when adults name objects. • Distinguish between their home language and other languages. • Follow simple directions. • Recognize the names for many familiar objects. • Follow a few simple phrases and questions. • Scribble on paper using markers and crayons; make circular marks with occasional straight lines. • Bring book to adult and asks to be read to. • Enjoy listening to stories—but have a short attention span. • Point to items in book illustrations or photos; begin to name them.
Toddlers (18–36 months)	• Understand 200 or more words at 18 months; by 24 months 500 to 700 words; by 30 months 800 to 900 words; during this period may learn one or two words per day. • Can say about 500 words by end of period. • Have some difficulty with pronunciation. • Follow one and two step directions. • Use most parts of speech in sentences, such as "I ate an apple" instead of "I ate apple." • Make sounds associated with different animals and vehicles. • Repeat language from picture books while playing: "My bear loves his white shoes." • Hold books and turn the pages. • Have favorite books and want to hear them again and again. • Use one word, varying tone, to express comments versus questions. For example, "Daddy go" and "Daddy go?" • Combine words to form phrases and sentences. For example, "Out now," means "Please get me out of my crib now!" • Pretend to read to dolls and stuffed animals. • Ask "What's that?" when reading with an adult. • Recite and chime in with familiar words and phrases in books, songs, and rhymes. • Enjoy predictable books and simple stories. • Look for favorite pictures in books. • Notice and protest when adult leaves word out or skips page when reading aloud. • Recognize familiar symbols as on traffic signs or food packages. • Scribble zig zags, loops, and possibly the first letter of their name; may arrange scribbles in a line and in rows. • Begin to understand that writing has a purpose. Might ask an adult, "Put my name on this please." • Sing ABC song and recognize and name a few letters.
Young Preschoolers (3–5 years old)	• Understand about 1,000 words at age 3 and 1500 words before turning 4; typically learns 4 to 6 words per day from adults, from being read to, and from new experiences. • Continue to grow expressive vocabulary (it is hard to measure from this age on). • Have greater ability to listen to and understand stories, conversations, fingerplays, and more. • Follow multi-step directions. • Understand explanations when supported by use of concrete objects. "Hold your bread with one hand and spread the cream cheese with the other one."

Figure 45c. Language and Literacy Skills for Young Children

Age	Developing Language and Literacy
Young Preschoolers (3–5 years old) ***continued***	• Improve pronunciation; are easier to understand. • Initiate conversations. "Want to see my new sneakers?" • Still learning the rules of conversation, such as taking turns to speak. • Notice when words rhyme and may point them out to adults; enjoy rhyming games. • Know that words are read and pictures have meaning, but are not read. • Pay attention to stories with familiar characters or about experiences they can relate to • Memorize the text to predictable books. • Retell simple stories they have heard repeatedly. • Ask questions using who, what, where, and why. • Begin to be aware of categories of books—stories versus informational texts, for example. • Notice environmental print and asks what it says. • Make marks that look like writing and ask, "What does it say?" • In second half of year some write letters of their names, not necessarily in a linear fashion. • Ask adults to write for them. "Write, this is Jan's painting." • Name between 5 and 10 letters. • Know that letters are used to form words but do not why certain letters are chosen for a given word; understand that the same letters are used to form many words.
Older Preschoolers 4–5 years old	• Understand about 2500 to 3000 words at age 4; gains about 3000 more during this year; gains 4 to 6 words per day from adults, from being read to, and from new experiences. • Continue to grow expressive vocabulary (is still hard to measure). • Make very few errors in pronunciation. • Follow multi-step instructions with and without demonstration using concrete objects. • Speak in complex and compound sentences. • Tell stories about self. • Start conversations and master conversational skills. • Identify and generate words that rhyme. • Name words that begin with the same sound. • Know how books are organized, for example, the title and author are on the cover and words on pages are read from left to right (in English). • Prefer to listen to a book read aloud from start to finish before discussing it with others. • Have memorized several predictable books and can recite them word for word. • Attempt to read. • Ask and answer questions and make comments and evaluations about the characters and plots of books. • Use information books and other resources to find answers to questions and to learn more about a topic. • Create some recognizable upper case letters; may begin to write lower case letters. • Isolate beginning and ending sounds in words. • Understand that print carries a message. • Write a few words from memory, e.g., their names, love, from, yes, and others that hold special meaning for the child. • Understand that letters represent the sounds in words. • Make books with writing and pictures. • Begin to write words phonetically—using the letters that they hear when the word is spoken (e.g., HRS for horse or KT for cat). • Identify familiar logos, signs, and labels. • Recognize familiar words.

Creating a Language and Literacy Learning Environment

To support all children's language and literacy development you will need to create and maintain a "literacy-rich" learning environment that includes children's home languages as well as English. Ensure that writing, books, and language are displayed everywhere in your setting for children of all ages to use. Consult Figure 46a-c when choosing books.

Providing a Print-Rich Setting

Children learn that print carries meaning when they see how it is displayed and used to share information with others. Over time, they might notice that when you and the children are picking up together, you look at the label on a basket before putting things inside. Or, perhaps they see you make a list of the ingredients needed for tomorrow's bread-baking activity. Children learn that print is a form of communication and begin to associate words with meanings. It is not necessary or appropriate to label every item in the setting. Use labels when they make sense. In addition, for younger children it's best to use either a photo or picture along with the written label. For example, the Duplo® container could feature a photo of a child building with these blocks along with the written label, Duplo®. Whenever posting or adding print to the environment, be sure to include English and home language versions of the written material. Color code each language to help children pay attention to their home language. However, remember to speak the words on the labels because the labels may confuse children who are not yet literate and cannot read the signs. If you are encouraging the use of home languages, the signs may support both you and the child to remember and use the terms.

Figure 46a. Categories of Children's Books

Include a variety of these types of books—both fiction and non-fiction—for the young children in your setting. Unless noted, you can find appropriate books in each category for infants, toddlers, and preschoolers. Be aware of the importance of exposing children to stories with children who are like them and who are like people they may not get to see on a daily basis. Representation is important for building a sense of agency in young children, so be careful that your books don't portray stereotypes or exclusively hero biographies. Stories of children who look, talk, dress, and act like real children do will provide opportunities for discussion and connection. The best way to avoid books with stereotypes is to ensure that stories are written by authors from the communities the characters represent. Stories about animal characters can be wonderful, but they can also carry hidden stereotypes, so check your libraries and keep an eye out for new and important books being released to stretch your library beyond the classics.

Figure 46b. Categories of Children's Books

- **Cloth and vinyl books** tend to be indestructible so a good introduction to the wonders of books and reading for infants. Some have flaps and textures as well as colorful pictures and a few words. They are washable so ideal for an early childhood setting. Examples include *Baby Love* by Sandra Magsamen, *Fuzzy Bee and Friends* by Roger Priddy, and *Find the Bear* by Manhattan Toy.
- **Board books** are small with thick cardboard pages. They are designed so mobile infants and toddlers can hold them and easily turn the pages. Some picture books for preschoolers come in board book versions but may not be appropriate for younger children. Examples of board books that are appropriate for younger age groups include *All Fall Down* by Helen Oxenbury, *Global Babies* by Maya Ajmera, and *Trucks* by Byron Barton.
- **Wordless books** are stories told through pictures and few or no words. For example, *A Ball for Daisy* by Chris Raschka, *Freight Train* by Donald Crews, and *Wave* by Susie Lee.
- **Picture books** include classic and new texts in which words and pictures tell a story about real or imaginary characters and events. For example, *Blackout* by John Rocco, *Make Way for Ducklings* by Robert McCloskey, and *Last Stop on Market Street* by Matt De La Peña.
- **Traditional rhymes and stories** such as nursery rhymes, fairy tales, fables, and folktales from various cultures. For example, *The Wooden Sword: A Jewish Folktale from Afghanistan* by Ann Redisch Stampler, *Pretty Salma, A Little Red Riding Hood Story from Africa* by Niki Daly, and *Joseph Had a Little Overcoat* by Simms Taback.
- **Poetry books** feature one or several illustrated poems. For example, *Honey, I Love and Other Love Poems* by Eloise Greenfield, *Read-Aloud Rhymes for the Very Young* by Jack Prelutsky, and *Here's A Little Poem: A Very First Book of Poetry* by Jane Yolen and Andrew Fusek Peters
- **Books with elegant writing and vocabulary** that have been acclaimed for their prose. For example, *It's Mine!* by Leo Lionni, *Extra Yarn* by Mac Barnett, and *Charlie Parker Played Be Bop* by Christopher Raschka.
- **Books with engaging illustrations**, whether drawings, paintings, collages, or photographs, that spark imaginations. For example, *The Tortoise & the Hare* by Jerry Pinkney, *Sophie's Squash* by Pat Zietlow Miller, and *Rah, Rah Radishes* by April Pulley Sayre.
- **Books on tender topics** that relate to toddlers' and preschoolers' experiences. Topics might include death of a loved one, parental separation, illness, overseas deployment of a family member, or any other experience that is sure to raise strong emotions. It's best to be very intentional in use of these books and educators will need to determine on an individual basis when and how to share them. For example, *Nana Upstairs and Nana Downstairs* by Tomie DePaolo, *My Dad's a Hero by Rebecca Christiansen, and The Family Book* by Todd Parr.
- **Predictable/pattern books** have repeating and rhyming text that let children join in. For example, *Brown Bear, Brown Bear, What Do You See?* by Bill Martin Jr., *Ten Little Fingers and Ten Little Toes* by Mem Fox, and *Goodnight, Goodnight Construction Site* by Sherri Duskey Rinker.

Figure 46c. Categories of Children's Books

- **Concept books** use pictures or photographs to focus on familiar objects or ideas such as colors, shapes, opposites, or sizes. For example, *Color Dance* by Ann Jonas, *What Do Wheels Do All Day* by April Jones Prince, and *Daddies and their Babies* by Guido Van Genechten.
- **Alphabet books** offer fun and colorful illustrations of the letters of the alphabet. For example, *Eric Carle's ABC* by Eric Carle, *Creature ABC* by Andrew Zuckerman, and *Z is for Moose* by Kelly Bingham.
- **Counting books** offer fun and colorful illustrations of numbers. For example, *Curious George Learns to Count from 1 to 100* by H. A. Rey, *Moja Means One, A Swahili Counting Book* by Muriel Feelings, and *One Gorilla, A Counting Book* by Anthony Brown.
- **Informational and non-fiction books** introduce facts about a specific topic and are illustrated with realistic pictures or photographs. For example, *Bugs* by Joan Richards Wright, *Under Ground* by Denise Fleming, and *Actual Size* by Steve Jenkins.
- **Reference books**: resources for learning. For example, *The American Heritage Picture Dictionary, National Geographic Little Kids First Big Book* by Amy Shields, and *Around the World: A Colorful Atlas for Kids* by Anita Ganeri.
- **"Easy readers"/beginning chapter books**: limited vocabulary, rhyme, and repetition for beginning readers. For example, *The Foot Book* by Dr. Seuss, the *Little Bear* series by Else Holmelund and Maurice Sendak, and the *Elephant and Piggie* series by Mo Willems.

(Adapted from Reading Is Fundamental [RIF] n.d.)

Here are some other ways you can provide a print-rich environment for children of different ages. Be sure to include English and home languages that you are using in the classroom.

Young and Mobile Infants

- Display colorful pictures of familiar people and objects at eye level. Label the photos with the names of the people and objects pictured. You could also use the pictures to make books—glue or tape the photos to heavy paper or cardboard, and laminate, or place in zipper plastic bags, and bind it by sewing one side or punching holes and attaching a loose leaf book ring.
- Write information in front of infants so that they can see you doing it. Provide non-toxic chubby markers and crayons and paper so they can write too.
- Offer playdough and other manipulative toys to encourage children's fine motor skills that are needed for turning book pages and holding writing tools.
- Use signs, pictures, labels, and charts to communicate important information. Talk out loud while you refer to the information. "Yum. We are having mac and cheese for lunch today."
- Provide age-appropriate books throughout the setting that you and mobile infants can access.
- Label cubbies with photographs and names.

Toddlers

- Provide materials and toys that encourage communication and pretend play. For example, provide several toy cell phones so children can call their families and chat with each other or with you.
- Create books and sets of picture cards together.
- Include props and activities that support the development of fine motor skills children need for writing.
- Label shelves with pictures and print to identify the materials that belong there.
- Create a few simple interest areas where toddlers can explore toys and materials and spend time playing alongside each other.
- Add books and writing materials throughout the setting.
- Write down children's ideas, stories, and words.
- Label containers with pictures and written descriptions to communicate which items belong inside.
- Create and use signs to convey messages. For example, when you leave the setting, write and place a sign on the door that tells others where you have gone: "Gone for a walk. Be back soon." Tell the children what you are doing and why.

Preschoolers

- Post children's names, along with their photos, on cubbies.
- Display a wide variety of books—including ones children create.
- Provide real-world reading materials—including newspapers, menus, magazines, and store catalogs.
- Store children's journals in a prominent and easy to access location.
- Place photos of children and their families in your setting. Label them with the names of the people pictured and their relationships.
- Create and post items (using words and pictures) that the children can refer to gain or provide information. These include:
    - Daily schedule
    - Attendance chart
    - Daily jobs chart
    - Signs identifying each area of the setting and the learning centers

- o Experience charts created after field trips or nature walks;
- o Signs protecting children's work (e.g., "Please do not touch");
- o Handwashing steps in pictures and words;
- o Recipe cards or charts
- o Alphabet strips
- o K (what I think I know), W (What I want to know) L (What I learned) charts related to studies or themes
- o Charts indicating preferences—e.g., after a taste test of oranges and apples

- Hang samples of children's writing.
- Label children's artwork with sentence strips.
- Label photos and other documentation of children's learning with written descriptions.
- Label children's creations with signatures or sentence strips (e.g., "This sculpture was designed by Keisha.").

Establish a Classroom Library

Although most children do not read independently until they reach kindergarten or first grade, the early years are critical in ensuring that children will be ready to learn to read. Their early experiences will lead them to read so well that they can read to learn. The books in your setting should be appropriate for the ages, cultures, family structures, home languages, interests, and skill levels of the children.

Most experts suggest having at least five to eight books on display per child in the setting. This does not mean that you leave the same books out all year. Instead, replace books the children have lost interest in, add books related to current interests and studies, and add books that you think the children will like, based on your knowledge of individual children and of development in general.

Consider the number of pages in the book, the format, and the amount of text on each page. Think about how old a child would need to be to engage with each book. Children should be able to identify with the topics, photos, illustrations, characters, experiences, and plots of the books you provide. For example, a toddler who is particularly interested in trucks, will probably want to read any of the vehicle books by Byron Barton. They are colorful, short, and have just enough words to match a toddler's attention span. An older child with a similar interest might enjoy *Good Morning Digger* by Anne Rockwell because it tells a story, has detailed illustrations, and offers interesting information about all the steps involved in erecting a building.

Include books that represent the setting's community (urban, rural, or suburban) as well as other places children have heard of or are completely new to them. Also teach children to handle books carefully and when books suffer some wear and tear, show children how to repair the damage. Provide a basket of supplies that are used to fix bindings or tape pages back together. Instill the value of books in children and encourage them to be lifelong readers—people who read because they enjoy books and because they enjoy learning.

Here are some other ideas to ensure that you include age-appropriate books in your learning environment. Review Figure 47 for more guidance.

Young and Mobile Infants

Choose washable cloth and vinyl or wipeable board books because infants will mouth and explore them. At this age infants are learning about books and enjoying time spent reading with someone special. Good books for infants offer:

- Stories about infants, families, animals, and everyday experiences.
- Songs, chants, and rhymes.
- Simple bright pictures and/or photographs with one or two objects per page.
- Experiences infants know, like bathing and shopping with family members.

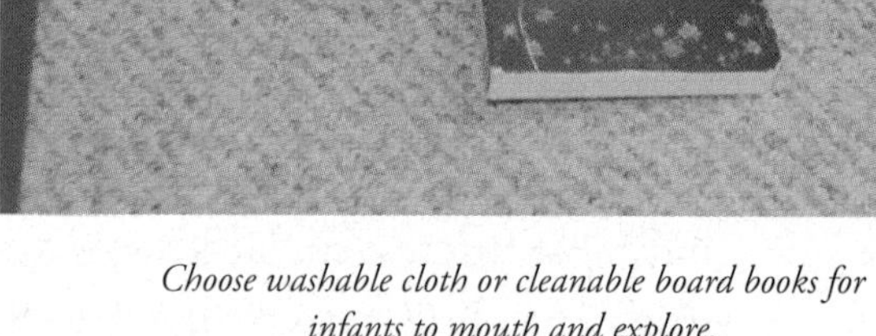

Choose washable cloth or cleanable board books for infants to mouth and explore.

Toddlers

Ideally, by the time infants become toddlers, they are already very familiar with books—board, paperback, and hardback books—and the pleasures of reading. They may show strong preferences for certain books and ask you to read them again and again. Good books for toddlers offer:

- Vocabulary that is more sophisticated than everyday speech, so children can learn new words.
- Stories about families, infants, toddlers, everyday experiences, familiar animals, and feelings.
- Simple concepts like size, shape and color, children's interests, and self-help skills.
- Familiar items in the illustrations to point to and label.
- Repetition, rhymes, and predictable text so toddlers can join in.

Preschoolers

Read interesting books that introduce children to new vocabulary.

Like toddlers, preschoolers may have favorite books they enjoy hearing again and again. You may see a preschooler thumbing through a book and retelling the story to a stuffed animal or doll. They also have favorite characters and authors and come to recognize the unique style of certain illustrators. Good books for preschoolers offer:

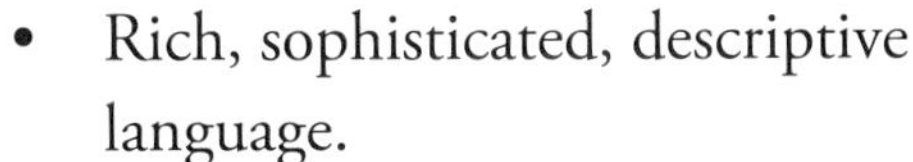

- Rich, sophisticated, descriptive language.
- Easy-to-follow plots about real or imaginary events.
- Compelling, multi-dimensional characters who take action.
- Aesthetically pleasing illustrations.
- Information about science, history, nature, machines, and other topics of interest to individuals and the group
- Stories that reflect children's past or future experiences (for example, moving to a new house or having a new baby in the family).

Figure 47. Evaluating Books for Young Children

The following questions will help you determine whether the books you are considering are right for the children in your setting:

- Is the book free of all bias—including gender, ethnicity, culture, age, family structure, income status, abilities, and sexual orientation?
- Does the book enable children to see their own experiences reflected? (Mirror book)
- Does the book offer a glimpse into the experiences of others? (Window book)
- Does the book contain large, bright, colorful illustrations?
- Are the pages easy to turn?
- Will the story spark conversation?
- Will children want to reread the book?
- Will children be motivated to seek out another book by this author or illustrator on the same topic?
- Is the book worthy of children's time?
- Does the book have an engaging story or provide interesting information?
- Does the book have a purpose other than to promote toys, television shows, movies, or merchandise?

Identifying Excellent Children's Books

The children's librarians at your local library are a great resource for learning about children's literature and non-fiction texts. Many librarians are eager to share their expertise with early childhood educators. In addition, the following resources provide useful information on selecting age-appropriate books that match the cultures, languages, interests, and development of the children in your setting:

- The **Association for Library Service to Children [ALC]** is home to a number of awards for children's books. Lists of current and past winners appear on the website: *www.ala.org/alsc.*
  - **The Caldecott Medal** is given annually for the best illustrated picture book. Awards are also given to honor books, many of which are truly excellent.
  - **Notable Children's Books** are honored for outstanding contributions to young people's literature. They include all of the ALC award winners for the year and other exemplary titles.
  - **The Pura Belpré Award** is presented annually to a Latino/Latina writer and illustrator of children's literature with a focus on Latino culture. Pura Belpré, was the first Latina librarian at the New York Public Library.
  - **The Coretta Scott King Book Awards** are given annually to outstanding African American authors and illustrators of books for children and young adults. The award commemorates the life and work of Dr. Martin Luther King, Jr., and honors the ongoing work of his wife, Mrs. Coretta Scott King.
- **The Children's Book-A-Day Almanac**, is updated daily by Anita Silvey, former editor of the Horn Book and a long-time publisher of children's books. The Almanac includes an archive of books for toddlers to teens, organized by age, genre, and theme: *childrensbookalmanac.com.*
- **The Children's Book Committee at Bank Street College of Education** helps families, and teachers select excellent books for children. The Committee reviews over 6000 titles each year then names the best 600 books, both fiction and nonfiction. The final list is organized by age and category. The Committee also issues several awards: *www.bankstreet.edu/center-childrens-literature/childrens-book-committee*.
- **The Cooperative Children's Book Center** is an examination, study, and research library of the University of Wisconsin-Madison School of Education. The Center's website offers a wealth of information on children's books including topical book lists by age group. The Center issues the annual Charlotte Zolotow Award for the best writing in a picture book published in the United States: *ccbc.education.wisc.edu.*
- **The International Reading Association** publishes Choices Reading List an annual collection of the favorite books of children, teachers, and young adults: *www.reading.org/choices.*
- **National Association for the Education of Young Children** publishes two periodicals that include columns on books for young children. Teaching Young Children offers *Now Read This,* Young Children includes *The Reading Chair* and maintains an online archive: *www.naeyc.org/yc/columns/readingchair.*

Setting Up a Literacy Center

In Chapter 3, you learned tips for configuring the learning centers in your setting for toddlers and for preschoolers. Although they will look different and include different materials, a well-planned and thoughtfully stocked literacy center will support literacy development of both toddlers and preschoolers. Designate the literacy center as an area where children can learn the fundamental skills used when learning to read and write. (They will also be building these skills in other learning centers, but this one is focused specifically on language and literacy learning.) Divide the center to accommodate each activity. Stock the center with materials and equipment that help to create positive language and literacy experiences for each child.

Book Area

In this area, children can peruse books alone, with a friend or two, or in small groups. They can listen to early educators read books aloud. Older children can also recreate or reenact stories and perform puppet shows based on the books you read to them. Whether for toddlers or preschoolers, your literacy center's book area could include the following:

Display books so that their covers are visible. Children recognize books by their cover art.

- Various children's fiction and non-fiction books that children can access and browse. Young children cannot read book spines. They recognize books by their cover art, so display the books so that their covers are visible.
- Comfortable chairs, a rocking chair, a small table and chairs, and nooks (e.g., tents or lofts) where children can look at books alone or take breaks from the group.
- Carpeting or an area rug and big pillows or cushions for reading while sitting on the floor.
- Puppets, a puppet stage, felt characters, and a felt board for dramatizing and retelling stories.
- A book repair basket filled with materials needed to make repairs. (This will be used with an educator's supervision.)

Writing Area

Include the following items in the writing area so that children can explore scribbling and practice writing, draw pictures, learn the alphabet, make signs, write cards, make books, and dictate stories to you.

For toddlers and preschoolers

- Various writing tools (e.g., pencils, pens, markers, chalk, and crayons of sizes appropriate for the age group)
- Various writing surfaces (e.g., paper of different sizes, stationery, chalkboard, and whiteboard)
- Journals or portfolios for preschoolers to document and record their own learning
- Blank labels
- Magic Slates or doodle boards
- Envelopes
- Table and chairs

For preschoolers

- Ruler, stencils, stapler, hole punch, and erasers
- Lap pads and clipboards
- Alphabet strips
- Sandpaper letters
- Letter stamps
- Index cards for making personal dictionaries of words that children use often

Listening Area

Include the following equipment and furnishings so that toddlers and preschoolers can listen to stories, poems, or songs. Some toddlers may need help using the equipment.

- Audio recordings of books, poems, lullabies, and favorite songs. This audio could be commercially produced or recorded by staff or children's family.
- Device for listening to recordings
- Headphones
- Microphone
- Comfortable seating

Include headphones in the listening area of the literacy center so that children can listen to stories, poems, or songs.

Technology Area for Preschoolers

This area may include the following equipment and materials that allow preschoolers to learn the alphabet, tell stories, listen to books read aloud, and practice typing. They can also view websites and use software applications with early educators. This equipment list is desirable, not essential:

- Computer with developmentally appropriate software that can run in several languages
- Printer and paper
- Scanner
- Digital camera
- Shared computer station and two chairs per computer
- Touch tablets like the iPad® and/or smartphones with developmentally appropriate applications

Evaluate computer software and tablet/smartphone applications before making them available to the children in your setting. Determine whether the software and applications are developmentally appropriate and whether they foster children's learning through engagement. When evaluating these technologies, consider the following criteria:

Evaluate computer software and smartphone applications before making them available to the children in your setting.

- Application and software is interactive.
- Content is sound and interesting to children.
- Children can follow instructions and navigate the program.
- Children can use the software/application independently.
- Children can experience success.
- Program is bias-free and violence-free.
- Programs can be individualized and children can use at their own pace.
- Program is flexible and can be adapted for children with disabilities and dual language learners.

The following resources can assist you in locating appropriate software and applications for children 2–5 years old:

- *Children's Technology Review*: a monthly newsletter of reviews and trends in children's interactive media (*www.childrenstech.com*)
- *SuperKids® Educational Software Review*: evaluations of children's software by teachers, parents, and children (*www.superkids.com*)

Publishing Area for Preschoolers

Children can make their own books either using a computer or tablet or by writing on paper. Their illustrations can be drawn, painted, or made using photographs or clip art. Supplies for making covers and binding books are nearby.

- Access to computer/tablet/papers, markers/crayons/paints, hole punch, and ruler
- Cardboard or poster board
- Laminator
- Blank books
- Stapler
- Yarn or laces for binding
- Finished books on display
- Table and chairs for doing work

Be sure that all the supplies for the publishing area are nearby and easily accessible.

Figure 48a. Creating Literacy-Rich Learning Centers

To make language and literacy a natural part of the entire setting, include related materials in every learning center. Label the center and materials in English and children's home languages. Include relevant books that children can easily access, and provide writing materials so children can draw or write about what they are learning and make props to go with their play.

Toddlers

Learning Center	Language and Literacy Materials
Blocks	Paper, index cards, and markers for creating signs, wooden traffic signs, and board books on construction (such as *Roadwork* by Sally Sutton and *Tip, Tip, Dig, Dig* by Emma Garcia).
Art	Playdough and props; chunky crayons, markers, and pencils; large pieces of sturdy paper, books (such as *Mouse Paint* by Ellen Stoll Walsh and *Alphaprints ABCs* by Roger Priddy).
Dramatic Play	Chunky crayons, markers, and pencils; large index cards; pads of paper; magazines and calendars; books related to children's experiences and families.
Gross Motor	Alphabet songs on tape or DVD, books that accompany songs (like *The Wheels on the Bus* and *The Itsy, Bitsy, Spider* by Kate Toms).
Cooking	Snack menu with pictures and words, illustrated hand washing chart, board books such as *My Very First Book of Food* by Eric Carle and *Yummy, Yucky* by Leslie Patricelli).

Preschoolers

Learning Center	Language and Literacy Materials
Blocks	Paper, index cards, and markers for creating signs, wooden traffic signs, blueprints and floor plans, road maps, architectural magazines, and books on construction (such as *Building with Dad* by Carol Nevius and *One Big Building: A Counting Book About Construction* by Michael Dahl).
Art	Recipe cards with step by step instructions for making play dough and cloud dough; alphabet stamps, sponges, stencils and cookie cutters; catalogs and magazines for collages; materials for creating greeting cards; sentence strips under children's art; and books about art and artists (such as *Beautiful Oops!* by Barney Saltzberg and *Vincent's Colors* by The Metropolitan Museum of Art).

Figure 48b. Creating Literacy-Rich Learning Centers

Preschoolers (continued)

Learning Center	Language and Literacy Materials
Dramatic Play	Magazines, newspapers, books, catalogs, telephone books, address books, mail, shopping lists, greeting cards, stationery, cookbooks, calendars, business cards, healthy food containers and cans, "to do" lists, job chart for family members, pens, pencils, markers, notepads, and literacy-related props and materials for pretend scenes (such as a doctor's office, library, bookstore, clothing store, restaurant, diner, or post office).
Music & Movement	Alphabet songs on tape or CD, songbooks, sheet music and charts, books that accompany songs (like *I Know an Old Woman Who Swallowed a Fly* by Nikki Smith), books about music (like *M is for Music* by Kathleen Krull), or books about musicians (like *The Deaf Musicians* by Pete Seeger).
Science	Graphs, pens, pencils, markers, notepads, clipboards, blank books, paper, chart paper and stand, maps and globes, informational text and books, and books with photographs and pictures (such as *I Love Bugs!* by Philemon Sturges and *The Very Busy Spider* by Eric Carle).
Math & Manipulatives	Magnetic letters, alphabet puzzles, alphabet lotto, alphabet bingo, letter-sorting games, alphabet blocks, score sheets and pencils, and picture books that parallel toys and games (such as *My Book of Alphabet Games* by Kumon Publishing and *Stick to It: Toys—A Magnetic Puzzle Book* by Kate Stone and Jeff Cole).
Sand/ Water Play	**Sand:** Alphabet cookie cutters and picture books (such as *Jump Into Science: Sand* by Ellen Prager and *Dirt: The Scoop on Soil* by Natalie Rosinsky). **Water:** Alphabet sponges, chart paper and chart stand, markers, vinyl bathtub books, and picture books (such as *Water Play* by Leon Read and *Will It Float or Sink?* by Melissa Stewart).
Cooking	Recipe cards, cookbooks, snack sign-in sheet, snack menu, handwashing chart, alphabet cookie cutters, letter molds, and picture books for children (such as *My Foodie ABC: A Little Gourmet's Guide* by Puck and *Hola! Jalapeño* by Amy Wilson Sanger).
Outdoors	Sidewalk chalk; paintbrushes and buckets of water; papers, crayons and markers; seed packets; bird identification charts; clipboards and paper; and baskets of picture books (including books about gardening, identifying insects and birds, and taking nature walks).

Support Language and Literacy Learning for Children with Disabilities

Speech and language impairments are the most common type of developmental delay in early childhood, ranging from mild (difficulty articulating certain sounds) to severe (deaf and mute). If you suspect a child's vocabulary is extremely limited for the age group or the child is struggling with speech, continue to observe and keep a written record of your observations. Ask families what they notice at home. Share what you have observed with the child's family, and with their permission, share them with specialists who can assist. By law, children with identified disabilities-including speech and language impairments--can receive support services. Children under age three will have an Individualized Family Service Plan (IFSP) and children ages three to five will have an Individual Education Program (IEP). Both are developed by a team with the family included as a valued and important member whose contributions support the child's development. Here are some suggested strategies and materials that can help children with disabilities build communication skills.

To support language development

- Slow the pace of your own speech and repeat statements and questions as needed.
- Speak simply to children and give them one-step directions. For example, ask a child to "Please clean your lunch plate" (one step) instead of "Please clean your lunch plate when you're done. Then go brush your teeth" (multiple steps).
- Use sign language, picture boards, and gestures to help children communicate.
- Encourage children to express their ideas through the arts—including painting, sculpting, dancing, and playing music.

To support writing skills

- Provide a variety of materials, such as shaving cream, sawdust, and hair gel, so children with dexterity problems can practice tracing letters with their fingers instead of holding a writing tool. Pay close attention to local licensing regulations for what materials are allowed with different age groups.
- Provide letters with texture—made of sandpaper, glitter, or other materials—for children who learn by touch.
- Provide hand-over-hand guidance (place your hand over the child's hand). Reduce this support as children no longer need it.
- Ensure that children can keep their bodies stable. In order to write, children need to have their feet solidly on the floor and the table height should fall between their waist and chest.
- Place sponge rollers on the handles of brushes or pencils so that children can hold them more easily.

Support Language and Literacy Learning for Children with Disabilities (continued)

- For children with severe manual dexterity problems, voice-activated software programs allow children to use their voices—instead of their hands—to write.
- Tape paper to the table or to a large tray to keep the paper stable.
- Let children know consistently that you value any and all of their "attempts" at writing.
- Use technology. Children can use a computer or tablet to listen to stories and type at their own pace and levels of ability. Work with the children's families and specialists to match appropriate technology to children's needs.

To support reading skills

- Begin with simple, wordless or photograph-based books.
- Use large, simple, and bright letters in signs, charts, and labels.
- Encourage children with fine motor challenges to look at books independently to gain practice holding books and turning pages.
- Ensure that all children are seated comfortably for read-aloud sessions. If a child has gross motor delays, ask a specialist for help in finding a comfortable seating position.
- Give children who struggle with concentration a small, soft toy to hold and squeeze during a read aloud session. This helps to release excess energy and minimizes the need to fidget.
- Give children who struggle with attention individual copies of the book you are reading aloud to look at independently. Explain to the other children, "This helps Sophia understand the story better. You can understand by looking at the big book I'm holding."
- Select books that appeal to the senses, such as texture or scratch-and-sniff books.
- Modify existing books by adding texture to illustrations and outlining numbers and letters in glue.
- Select books with cardboard pages that are easy to turn. Or glue ice-pop sticks to the pages as an aid.

(California Department of Education 2000)

Encouraging Vocabulary and Conversation Skills

The topic of supporting oral language development is addressed in the next section, however, there are things you can do to create an environment that encourages children to build their vocabulary and learn to take part in conversations. When thinking about how the room is arranged or what materials are available to children, it may be easy to forget about the people who are also a part of the environment. You and your colleagues, the children, and their families are all critical pieces of the learning environment. In terms of language development, you are a model and a conversation partner. You introduce new words—sometimes called "50 cent" words—with multiple syllables and precise definitions. From you, children learn that blue can be "blue," but it can also be described as "aqua" or "navy" or "cerulean" or "azure."

The presence of other children invites everyone to build language skills so they can talk and play with each other. Children can be models for others, introducing new vocabulary based on their unique experiences, cultures, and interests. "We went to the aquarium this weekend. I saw an anemone and a clownfish."

The way you arrange the environment and plan for routines, transitions, and activities also contribute to vocabulary and conversations skills development. Below are some examples.

- Feeding a baby in a rocking chair or glider gives you time to focus one-on-one. You can talk about what you are doing and what will happen next. And, when the baby looks up from her bottle with a smile, you can smile back—a first step in learning to take part in a conversation. If you work with older children, find ways to include one-on-one time with them too.
- Having small chairs and tables for mobile infants and toddlers allows them to eat together, like a family, with you at the table too. You can model good manners and taking turns during conversations. Of course preschoolers will continue this tradition of family-style dining.
- Establishing places where two or three children can play, read, and talk together allows preschoolers opportunities to get away for a while from the large group. A small couch, a few bean bag chairs, and a blanket spread under a tree communicate to children, "This is a place where you can talk, listen, and respond without interruptions." This arrangement applies to younger children too, who also need places for quiet interactions with peers.
- Building in opportunities for children to share ideas and feelings can be part of your planning from large group time and small group activities. You might include opportunities at the end of choice time for children to talk about their work. "This is our store and these are the things we are going to sell and these are the prices."

Supporting Children's Oral Language Development

Even before children can speak actual words, young children communicate through cries and gestures and interpret others' sounds, body language, and speech. Oral language blends the drive to speak with the desire to be social. Children have an innate ability to learn the rules of the languages used in their environments but communication requires thought, knowledge, and skill.

A strong, consistent, and positive relationship exists between the amount of time a child communicates with an adult and later literacy skills.

The Linguistic Society of America states that young children who are exposed to speech solely through TV and radio will not learn to talk. Children need human interaction to learn to speak (Birner n.d.). By talking with young children and engaging them in conversations throughout the day, you can help children develop strong oral language skills and ensure their future reading and writing success.

There is a strong, consistent, and positive relationship between the amount of time a child communicates with an adult and later literacy skills (Dodici et al. 2003). The Harvard-sponsored longitudinal Home-School Study of Language and Literacy Development also documents a strong connection between early reading success and the number of complex conversations children engage in with adults in both their homes and schools (Dickinson and Tabors 2001).

However, some early childhood experts have found that conversations that go beyond the "here and now" have the most impact on literacy development as opposed to conversations rooted in the immediate environment. For example, when you say to a child, "Put the puzzles back on the shelf" or "Try tasting the carrots," you are conveying a message, but the language you used omits elements related to literacy. Conversations that promote literacy development require language that reflects the past and the future, as well as real and imaginary events. For example, when you talk to children about how much they enjoyed the field trip to a farm earlier in the year, or when you ask them to tell you the questions they want to ask the firefighter when he comes to visit their class next week, the children use language that goes beyond the present. These types of conversations require children to use their developing cognitive skills to represent ideas—a process that is important to the development of reading comprehension.

In addition to using language that surpasses the here and now, Dickinson, Tabors, and their colleagues found that beneficial conversations have the following attributes:

- A balance of adult and child input (taking turns).
- Attentive listening.
- Extended talk that stays on a topic of interest to the child.
- Vocabulary that is introduced in an intentional way.

As with all areas of learning, promoting oral language development requires early childhood educators to think about each child as an individual. Children develop at their own pace and their experiences influence their language and literacy development. Some infants may start babbling and cooing sooner, some are more intent listeners, and others may use lots of nonverbal communication. Talk to families to build your knowledge of each child's skills, interests, abilities, culture, home language, and life experiences so you can decide on the best ways to incorporate that information into your practice to strengthen their language skills.

Use Everyday Experiences to Strengthen Language Skills

As noted earlier, there are direct and positive relationships among the amount of time children communicate with adults, the complexity of these conversations, and literacy development. The following tips will guide you in incorporating language-building conversations into your daily interactions with the children in your setting:

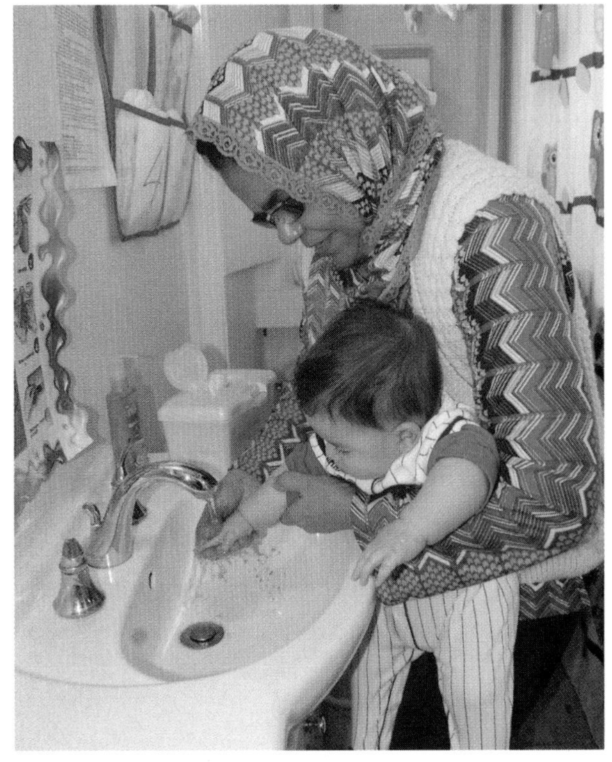

Speak gently to infants throughout the day—including during routines, like handwashing.

Young Infants

- Speak gently to infants throughout the day, including during routines, such as diapering and feeding. These are great opportunities to strengthen your bonds with all children and incorporate additional words into their day. These "conversations" also show infants that you respect them as you describe what you are doing. "I am going to change your diaper. May I please take your pants off? Thanks! Wow, you are wearing diapers size 2 now. You are growing. Thanks for letting me lift your legs. Yes, you are smiling. I am sure you feel good now."
- Describe what you are doing—or provide infants a "play-by-play"—as you care for and

play with them. Infants need to be surrounded by language long before they can actually produce words themselves.

- Provide pleasant sounds and music when children are likely to listen. Notice how infants respond to music and continue to play music they enjoy.
- Sing lullabies to infants as they fall asleep.
- Respond to infants as if they were talking. Coo and smile back at infants, modeling the give-and-take of a conversation. Infants are learning that they can communicate with others. Mirror their expressions and use standard forms of language. Incorporate home languages, particularly words and phrases they are likely to hear at home. "Estoy rodando la pelota para ti. I am rolling the ball to you."

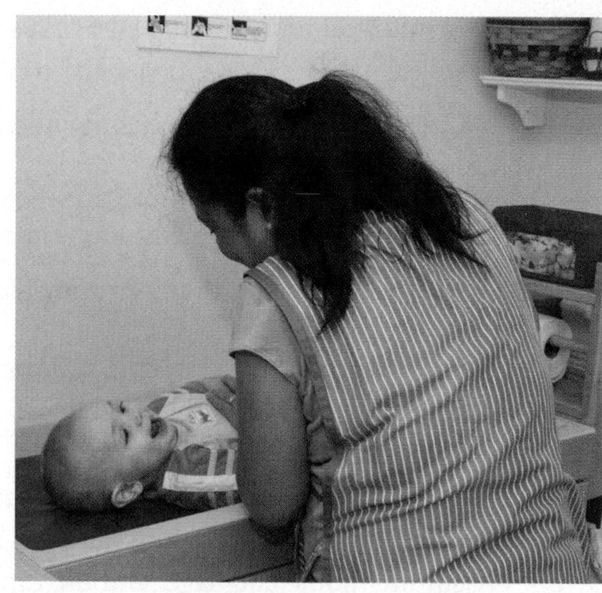

Coo and smile back at infants if they are talking.

Mobile Infants

- Model language that expresses what infants seem to be communicating. ("Ariel, you are waving your arms. I think you want me to pick you up.") Incorporate home language when appropriate.
- Respond to all their attempts to communicate. Talk to all infants who respond and to those who do not. After speaking, wait and provide time for infants to respond. Model the give-and-take of a conversation.
- Use proper language as you describe what you are doing and what they are doing. Speak in the standard dialect.
- Show or point to materials that you are referring to as you talk about the object.
- Talk about their experiences at home.
- Sing lively versions of songs, especially ones with motions. Make up or personalize songs.
- Tell stories.
- Recite poems.
- Sing lullabies as infants go to sleep.
- Play music when infants are likely to listen. Notice how infants respond to music and continue to play music they enjoy.

Toddlers

- Elaborate on toddlers' speech instead of correcting pronunciation or grammatical errors. "I go higher." "I think you want me to hold your hand while you climb the ladder. Here you go. Hold my hand."

- Plan an activity for two to three toddlers. Introduce the activity, give a few simple directions, and encourage the children to talk with each other. "I taped this paper to the table. You can all scribble on it at the same time."
- Expand toddlers speech. When a two-year-old says, "Milk," reply, "Oh, would you like some milk?"
- Introduce new vocabulary and use language that will continue to build toddlers' skills.
- Show or point to materials that you are referring to as you talk about the object.

Be sure to have conversations with toddlers throughout the day, every day.

- Speak and sing in the preferred language of the child's family—including singing or cueing for those who are hearing impaired.
- Have conversations with toddlers throughout the day, every day.
- Describe and explain the child's actions and those of other people.
- Name and describe objects, actions, people, and feelings.
- Read interesting books that introduce new vocabulary.
- Offer a small collection of songs they can learn.
- Introduce music and movement opportunities when toddlers are likely to listen and participate.
- Personalize the songs as much as possible when singing individually or to the group.
- Sing silly songs and songs with repeated words and verses.
- Recite rhymes and make up silly new ones.

Preschoolers

By the time children leave the preschool years, most are using sophisticated vocabulary and grammar and have nearly accurate pronunciation. These language skills are the result of having many opportunities to participate in conversations, ask and answer questions, take part in discussions, and have interesting experiences that support vocabulary learning. When conversations are natural and social, children are more eager to participate. Keep in mind that children are born with different temperaments, and some are more open to conversations while others prefer to watch and listen before engaging. The goal is not to make all children the same, but to offer all children the same opportunities to participate, the same access, and whatever supports each child needs to be successful. Accept their unique responses. The following tips will help you make your conversations more meaningful to them.

- Model conversation skills in your conversations with other adults as well as with children. For example:
    - o To start or join a conversation, say something and wait for a response from the other person.
    - o When the other person replies, look at that person, listen to what is being said, and wait at least five seconds after the person has stopped talking before responding. The idea of not interrupting your conversational partner can be traced back to the writings of Cicero in 44 B.C. (The Economist 2006).
    - o When it is your turn to speak again, add some information related to what was said, ask questions for clarification, stay on topic, avoid unnecessary details, and give the other person a turn.
    - o To keep the conversation going, say something new and interesting about the topic. You might also share your own experiences, ask open-ended questions, explain yourself, and express agreement or concern.
    - o When you are finished with the conversation, let the other person know. Do not end your conversation with an abrupt stop.
- Listen to children attentively during conversations.
- Encourage children to talk during discussions, rather than focusing on correct answers.
- Try to understand what children want to say and help them to express it.
- Offer extra support to children who seem reluctant to talk; encourage children to express themselves. For example, you say to three-year-old Marcus, "Your block tower is very tall." Marcus places another block on his tower but says nothing. "Wow. Now it's even taller," you say. This time Marcus smiles and responds, "It's almost as tall as the ceiling!"
- Expose children to correct grammar. Many of the grammatical errors that young children make in speech, such as "I wented to the store" or "I saw three sheeps," signal that they are applying rules they know, but struggling to learn the rules and exceptions of the English language. Instead of correcting them, respond using correct grammar: "Did you buy anything when you went to the store?" "I saw those three sheep, too."

Scaffold Children's Language Development

A basic element of developmentally appropriate practice is to offer children challenges slightly beyond what they now know or can do. In Chapter 5, you learned the term *scaffolding*, which describes the way adults help children by building on children's current knowledge, providing

Talk with children during play.

challenges, and stepping in to support when necessary. Incorporate this idea into the way you talk with children. Speak to children using language that is more complex than the words the children use now so that they continue to build their vocabularies:

Ask open-ended questions that require children to respond with more than one or two words. Open-ended questions are conversation starters, especially when they are sincere and acknowledge a child's interests. They are also effective ways to extend conversations with children. Use open-ended questions to encourage children to discuss their thinking process rather than to give a "right" answer. For example, you might ask a toddler, "Where are you going to push your wagon this morning?" Then give the child time—approximately five seconds—to reflect and respond. If needed, restate the question or try asking another one. "What are you going to put in the wagon?"

Talk with children during play. If you are sitting with a mobile infant and see that she is taking items out of a basket or you are sitting with a group of toddlers who are playing with cardboard blocks, describe their actions. For example, say "I see that you are taking the blocks off the shelf," and "You have placed three long blocks in a row on the floor." As children get older, ask questions that are both open-ended and go beyond the here and now: "What vegetables could we plant in our garden that we could later serve for snack?" Ask older preschoolers to predict or form hypotheses: "What do you think will happen when you mix those paint colors together?"

Make the most of reading times. The quantity and quality of book reading are associated with literacy gains. Reading books best supports language and literacy development when you talk about and revisit the book you are reading. Invite children to share their ideas about the main character, discuss what they might do in a similar situation, and compare the story to other stories or experiences. Provide props so children can practice language skills as they reenact the stories with peers.

Take advantage of children's dramatic play scenarios. Children stretch their thinking as they imagine themselves in different scenarios. If children are taking a while to plan what they will do, intervene and scaffold their learning. For example, you might join in by sitting at the table and saying, "Boy, am I hungry! What are we having for dinner?"

Retell stories. Children enjoy hearing the same stories repeatedly, which provides you the opportunity to teach them about story elements.

Hold conversations during mealtimes. There are strong positive relationships between mealtime talk during the preschool years and children's scores on literacy measures when the children are 5 years old (Dickinson and Tabors 2001). Sit with the children and help them reflect on what happened during the day and discuss issues and interests. Because young children primarily relate to the world around them from an egocentric perspective, they are inclined to talk about topics that interest them the most. This characteristic also means that you may need to help them stay on the current topic rather than introducing a new one.

Encourage Vocabulary Development

The term *vocabulary* refers to the bank of words we know and use to communicate effectively. This bank is divided into four types:

- Listening vocabulary refers to the words we understand when we hear them.
- Speaking vocabulary consists of the words we use when we speak.
- Reading vocabulary refers to the words we understand when we read them.
- Writing vocabulary consists of the words we use in writing.

Children's listening and speaking vocabularies develop first, just as learning to listen and speak precedes the ability to read and write. As children develop their listening and speaking vocabularies, they gain a foundation for understanding printed words. Printed words expand all four vocabularies over time.

Vocabulary is most closely linked to reading comprehension. The larger and more varied children's listening and speaking vocabularies are, the more likely that they will become readers (Tabors, Beals, and Weizman 2001). Historically, educators regarded vocabulary development as an isolated task. They introduced children to new words and required them to memorize definitions. However, vocabulary development is a natural process. Children need to hear new vocabulary in context to understand meanings.

But most adults do not naturally use large and varied vocabularies when they speak. Oral conversations are typically limited to about 15,000 commonly used words. After analyzing 65 minutes of speech in more than 60 preschool classrooms, the Harvard Home-School Study of Language and Literacy Development discovered that, on average, teachers used only 43 words that researchers classified as relatively sophisticated—the types of words likely to stretch children's vocabularies (Dickinson and Tabors 2001).

A popular and influential study on oral interactions and their impact on children's language was conducted at the University of Kansas by researchers Betty Hart and Todd R. Risley (Hart

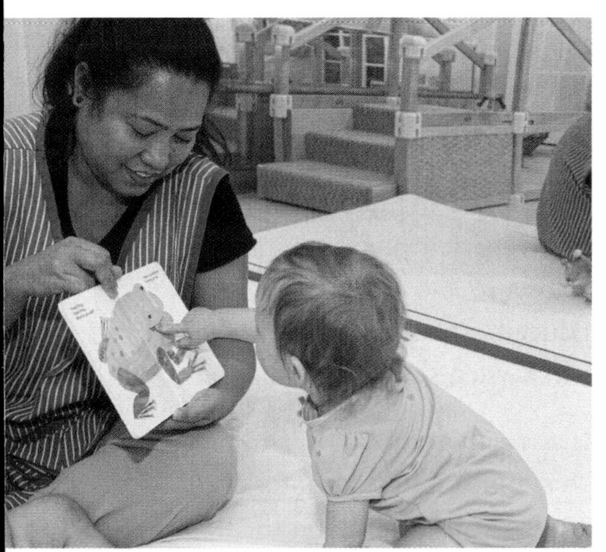

Use the book's illustrations to help children understand the story.

and Risley 2003) Commonly referred to as the "30 Million Word Gap," these researchers found that upper income families used more words with their children than lower income families, resulting in large differences in the children's vocabulary sizes by age four. Although their study has since been criticized as biased, research on language gaps in the early years continues to show that a family's socioeconomic status and parental education levels heavily shape children's learning. Critics emphasize that the research on language gaps in the early years can miss more fundamental takeaways about the deeper racial and economic inequities affecting a child's life living in poverty. And while those need to be addressed through public policy, it nonetheless remains important to help adults understand the power of engaging in early conversations with young children (D. Sperry, L. Sperry and Miller 2019).

As an early educator, it is critical that you be intentional in your use of sophisticated vocabulary. As a life-long learner, continue to add to your own vocabulary. Consider ways to incorporate new and more sophisticated words into your everyday speech throughout the day. Mealtime conversations, reading books with children, dramatic play scenarios, choice time, small group activities, and field trips are a few key situations that are most effective for introducing the rich, sophisticated vocabulary words associated with literacy development. Book reading provides an opportunity to learn vocabulary from two sources—the book and the early educator discussing the book. Dramatic play and field trips lend themselves to fantasy and trips to the unknown—places that are filled with exciting new words. Indoor and outdoor choice time helps you introduce new vocabulary by using new names or descriptions for items with which children are playing or working.

Fostering Children's Reading Development

After reviewing more than 10,000 research studies, the Commission on Reading of the National Academy of Education concluded that there was definitive evidence to support that reading aloud is the overall best predictor of reading success (Anderson 1985). In numerous studies, the number of stories children had been read is the strongest variable that impacts children's school success (Braunger and Lewis 2006).

In this section you will learn strategies to help you begin laying the groundwork for reading success by reading aloud with infants, toddlers, and preschoolers.

Introduce Books to Young Infants

In the first months, babies need an adult to gently hold their head upright so they can see the pictures in a book. They do not see well yet, and tend to prefer images with high contrast, such as books with black and white shapes. They also enjoy looking at faces and many books for this age group include large photos of faces. Make sure there is a wide diversity in the faces that children are seeing. To get infants used to sitting in a lap and listening to a loved one talk, any book will work. Barbara Bowman, a renowned early childhood educator, frequently shares that her daughter enjoyed hearing her father read medical journals to her when she was an infant.

After a few months, infants are better able to hold up their heads and can grasp books and bring them to their mouths. Board books and cloth or vinyl books with simple, colorful photos and pictures are most appealing. Soon they will begin to point, find books in the basket on the floor, and understand a few words.

To support young infants' language and literacy development, early childhood educators can:

- Read books every day, but expect that you will only read a page or two at first.
- Follow infants' interests. If they indicate that they are no longer interested in the book, then allow them to engage in other activities.
- Read and offer board books and washable cloth and vinyl books infants can touch and mouth.
- Use clear speech when reading and read with a variety of expressions.
- Offer a toy to hold and chew while you read.
- Read books with one or two pages with stories about infants, families, animals, and everyday experiences.
- Select books with songs, chants, and rhymes.
- Provide books with simple bright pictures and/or photographs with 1–2 objects per page.
- Provide books on different races, genders, and abilities.

Build on Mobile Infants' Growing Skills

At this stage, infants understand more words. They are movers who can bring books to you. They no longer have to depend on your choices. Their fine motor skills have developed to the point that they can manipulate objects such as flaps in books.

Toward the end of this stage most children will be walking and beginning to talk using single words to name people and things. They may pick up a book and "read" to themselves using babbling that sounds like a person reading, as opposed to talking.

To support mobile infants' language and literacy development, early childhood educators can use any of the above strategies that are still appealing to this age group:

- Provide a variety of books that reflect experiences with which mobile infants are familiar, like bathing and shopping with family members.
- Provide books that show how children from other cultures or communities experience these as well.
- Encourage infants to choose the books they want to read (they may have strong preferences).
- Encourage infants to participate in telling a story. "Mister Brown can moo, can you?" "Moo, moo, moo."
- Allow infants to touch the book while you are reading, and ask questions such as, "Where's the . . . ?"
- Read expressively and make sure children can see the book's pictures.
- Invite infants to "read" to you. Listen to and acknowledge their communication.
- Follow infants lead. When they lose interest, let them engage in other activities.

Read To and With Toddlers

Toddlers have rapidly growing vocabularies, gaining several new words a day. They speak in sentences—short ones at first and later more sophisticated in style. When they are read to often and consistently, they may learn up to one-third of their new words from books read aloud. They can think and pay attention for a longer time so they enjoy longer stories and can talk about the books. Concept and theme books are popular as are predictable books. Toddlers greatly enjoy chiming in with words they know and enjoy reading the same book over and over again. Knowing what comes next gives toddlers a sense of competence. They do look at books on their own now and may talk to themselves about the illustrations or characters.

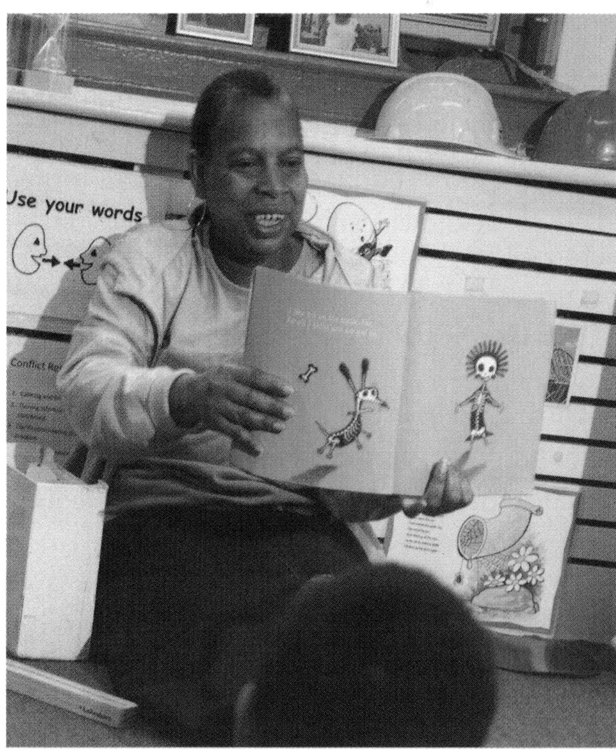

Hold books so that children can see the illustrations while you read.

To support toddlers' language and literacy development, early childhood educators can use any of the above strategies that are still appealing to this age group and:

- Provide board, paperback, and hardback books and both fiction and non-fiction titles.
- Select books about families, young children, everyday experiences, familiar animals, and feelings. Also include books about simple concepts, like size, shape and color, race, and ethnicity, children's interests, and self-help skills.

- Offer concept and theme books related to seasons, community, experiences, and events. For example, if the program is near the ocean, include books about going to the beach. If you are in a city, include books about urban life. Remember not to exclude books about the experiences of others. Include books about farm life, or books about living in apartment buildings no matter where your program is located.
- Read books to children individually and in groups of two to three. Allow children to come or go as they gain or lose interest in the story.
- Choose books that are written with sophisticated vocabulary so that children can learn new words. Use the words yourself at other times to reinforce their learning.
- Provide opportunities for toddlers to interact and discuss the book. Conversations surrounding reading are most helpful in building language.
- Ask open-ended questions that start with why: "Why do you think the ladybug was grouchy?"
- Ask additional questions that will help children expand their thinking and relate the story to their own lives: "Have you ever felt angry like the grouchy ladybug?"
- Become very familiar with the books you read so you can vary your voice by character and bring the story to life.
- Encourage children to participate in making sounds or repeating words and phrases. Ask them to predict what will happen next in the story.
- Allow toddlers to "read" to you (or recite the plot from memory). Listen to and acknowledge their communication.

Help Preschoolers Gain Specific Skills

During their research review described above, NELP found that experts pinpoint four strategies early educators should employ to promote reading among preschoolers (NELP 2008; Espinosa 2010):

- Teach the alphabet.
- Introduce children to rich vocabulary words that stretch their thinking.
- Help children develop phonological awareness.
- Read aloud to children every day.

Strategies for introducing rich vocabulary were discussed in the previous section. The other three strategies are discussed below.

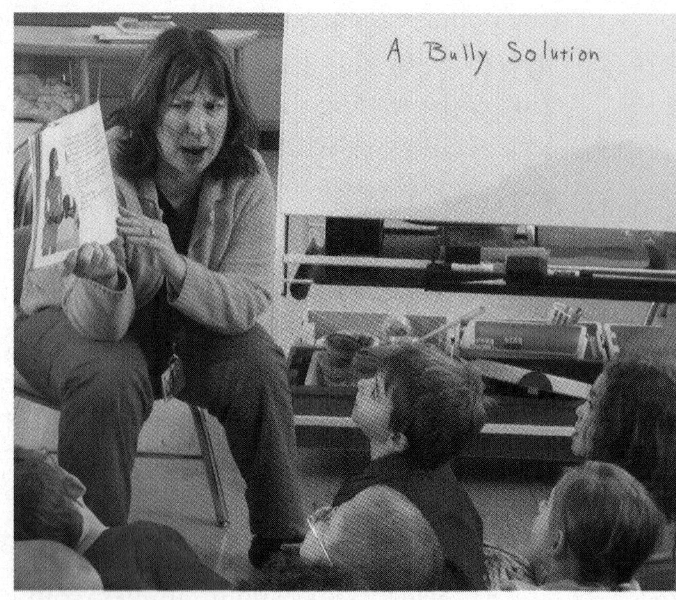

Read with expression and bring the characters and events to life.

Teach the Alphabet

Children's first exposure to the English alphabet is usually through the alphabet (or "ABC") song. Help children relate the letters they sing in the song to the letters on an alphabet strip. Point out the letters on a strip, chart, or white board as they sing. Encourage them to begin the song in the middle or sing it backward. Make up chants or songs that include the letter names and sounds they make.

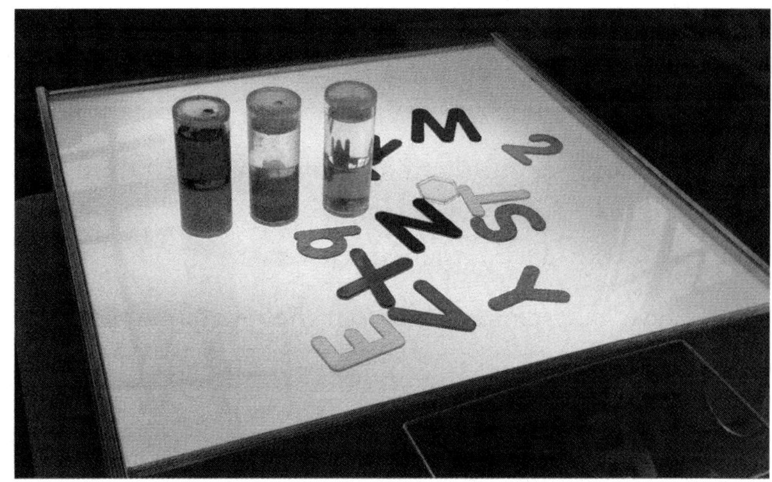

Include items like sandpaper letters in the writing area of your setting's literacy center.

Make learning the alphabet meaningful and fun for children and incorporate their learning into your natural interactions. The following strategies will also help you to begin familiarizing children with the letters of the alphabet:

- Read alphabet books aloud with the children, pointing out the letters as read.
- Sing songs with letter play, such as "B-I-N-G-O."
- Play alphabet matching and concentration games that require children to identify and name letters.
- Display alphabet strips at children's eye level in areas where children are likely to use them, like the writing area of the literacy center.
- Incorporate alphabet props in the learning environment (e.g., alphabet cookie cutters in the cooking center; sandpaper letters and rubber stamp letters in the writing area; alphabet sponges in the sand and water play center; magnetic letters, alphabet blocks, and alphabet puzzles in the math and manipulatives center; and alphabet stencils in the art center).
- Point out letters as you help children write sentence strips, record their words on chart paper, read a book, or see signs on a neighborhood walk.
- Give children lots of opportunities to develop their writing skills, like making signs, publishing their own books, and creating writing samples.
- Teach children to read and write their names. Once they know the letters in their names, other letters may become more familiar to them. For example, Carl sees that *cat* begins with "*c*," like his name does, and that *rabbit* begins with "*r*," like the third letter in his name.

Promote Phonological Awareness

As noted earlier, phonological awareness is a key indicator of success in learning to read. It includes awareness of the sounds and rhythms of speech, rhymes, and sound similarities. To help children build phonological awareness, try the following activities:

- Sing and act out rhyming songs, chants, and finger plays. Set aside time every day for children to sing silly, rhyming songs like "The Name Game." Perform chants and finger plays like "Five Little Ducks."
- Have older children clap out the syllables of words.
- Experiment with rhymes. Two-word sets like *Henny Penny* are appealing to young children because the words sound identical except for the beginning sounds.
- Make up silly songs and substitute your own rhyming words for the actual lyrics.
- Read aloud and encourage children to memorize rhyming poems.
- Read aloud rhyming books and books that play with language, like books by Dr. Seuss.
- Sing and read books that accompany rhyming songs, like "I Know an Old Lady Who Swallowed a Fly."
- Have children act out their favorite rhyming songs and chants.
- Play games in which children find objects or pictures that start with the same sound or that rhyme.
- Focus children's attention on rhymes during daily activities: "If your name rhymes with *plain, rain,* or *cane,* you may get in line now... *Jane!*"

Read Aloud Every Day

As they did when they were toddlers, many preschoolers enjoy hearing the same book read over and over, because they learn through repetition and are most comfortable with what is familiar. Repeated readings help children gain a sense of competence, control, and self-esteem.

To support preschoolers' language and literacy development, early childhood educators can use any of the strategies used with infants and toddlers. (RIF n.d.) In addition, try these read aloud tips.

- Establish a regular time for reading aloud.
- Find a quiet, comfortable place where children can listen to the story free from distractions.
- Invite a child onto your lap. Have at least 10 minutes of reading together one-on-one daily.

- Assemble groups of four to six children for reading aloud to ensure that all children have an opportunity to participate. Children who hear stories in small group settings have higher comprehension skills than children who are read to one-on-one or in large groups (Morrow and Gambrell 2002).
- Select book that you like and that you think the children will like, too. Make sure that it is engaging for your students and written with rich vocabulary. Feature books in all children's home languages about all different people in different kinds of communities. Choose a mix of fiction and non-fiction books, and include books about important topics like race and difference.
- Practice reading aloud. Read to your colleagues and in front of a mirror.
- Let children know why you selected the book. Note the similarities this book shares with other books you have read to them, like author or subject matter. Encourage children to choose which books they want you to read.
- Read the title of the book and the author's and illustrator's names. As you introduce a new book, ask children to predict what the book is about. Draw children's attention to the cover illustration.
- Read with expression and bring the characters and events to life.
- Practice contrasts with your voice, like loud and soft, fast and slow, high and low, to keep readers engaged. Also, employ pauses in your reading. The words on the page will inform your tactical choice (Fox 2008).
- Hold the book to one side so that children can see the illustrations while you read.
- Read slowly enough for children to absorb the words and see the pictures. Use your finger to show children the words they are interested in. Move your finger as you read to them and point out that print in English is read from left to right.
- Use the book's illustrations to help children understand the story. Incorporate children's experiences to help them relate to the plot.
- Read the book again. This time, stop throughout the reading to ask children questions about what might happen next or how they believe a character is feeling. Ask them how they would react in a similar situation.
- Watch the children's body language. They may need a break or even to end a session early. Try to determine whether the children's need to fidget or the book choice is causing the problem.
- Talk about the book afterward and elicit the children's reactions. Ask and answer questions.
- Pose open-ended questions that will spark conversations about the book: "What do you think the bears did to Goldilocks?" Highlight the rich or new vocabulary words. Help children make connections.

- Ask the children to retell the story in their own words.
- Have children act out the story.
- Encourage children to draw, paint images, or write about the story.
- Keep the book available in the literacy center for children to view alone or in small groups.
- Create an audio recording of the book for children to enjoy in the listening area of the literacy

Shared Reading

Shared reading is a variant of reading aloud. "Shared-reading activities are often recommended as the single most important thing adults can do to promote the emergent literacy skills of young children" (NELP 2008, 153). This activity transfers the responsibility for reading from the adult to the children. To spark shared reading, select a big book or other large-text book to share with a group of children. Predictable books, in particular, encourage children to participate in the reading. As you read, point out the words. This action helps children learn the concepts of words and print and that the eye moves from left to right while reading. During subsequent readings of the book, ask new questions and challenge children to predict the plot and chant predictable phrases. Focus on building and extending their understanding of the book. During other readings, focus on decoding (learning and applying knowledge of letter-sound relationships) or the book's language and vocabulary. As children become more familiar with the story, invite them to "read" the text (or recite the plot from memory) out loud to the group.

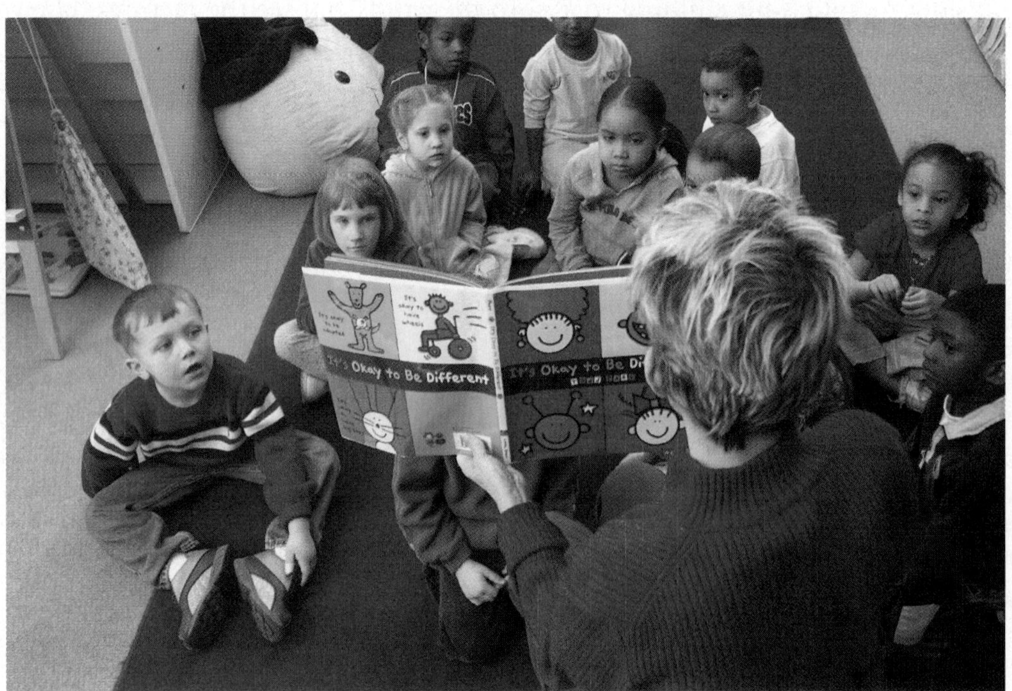

Find a quiet, comfortable place where children can listen to the story free from distractions.

Fostering Children's Writing Development

In this chapter, you have learned that children develop their reading and writing skills simultaneously. For example, alphabet knowledge supports both reading and writing. Furthermore, vocabulary development, phonological awareness, and hearing books read aloud also help to develop their writing skills.

Early childhood educators can model writing to demonstrate that print has meaning and motivate children to begin scribbling and writing. When children observe you writing, they learn that this is a valuable skill. Let them watch you filling out forms, sending in the lunch order, or writing notes to send home to families. Because you do it, writing becomes something they want to do, too.

Encourage Fine Motor Development

Writing relies on children's fine motor development so they need opportunities to practice and use these skills. Encourage children to practice grasping writing tools appropriately in the "tripod grasp." The pads of a child's thumb and index finger should encircle the pencil, which rests on the middle finger near the first knuckle. All fingers should apply equal (but not heavy) pressure.

Many preschoolers have trouble correctly positioning writing tools in their hands. They may hold a pencil with their fists or wrap their thumb around the pencil and tuck it between their first two fingers. This is common due to undeveloped hand muscles. However, inefficient grasps, caused by forcing children to write too soon can prevent the development of appropriate muscles and place stress on children's finger joints. Preschoolers can easily develop writer's cramp, which keeps them from wanting to try to write. Provide lots of opportunity to play with writing and to build fine motor skills before requiring children to hold writing tools before they are ready.

Additional ideas for supporting the fine motor skills used for writing appear in Chapter 4, Physical.

Help children learn to hold a pencil correctly through both modeling and direct instruction. Maintain a relaxed attitude so children are not self-conscious. In addition, handwriting experts provide the following tips (Colker 2010b):

- Place a sticker or rubber band on the part of the pencil where children should grasp.
- Have children practice with small pieces of chalk or miniature-golf pencils to gain control.
- Encourage children to write on vertical surfaces, such as easels or chalkboards, to strengthen muscles and position their wrists appropriately.

Work With Children on Writing Projects

- Create charts and graphs of experiments in the science center.
- Post documentation panels of children's work.
- Publish books and stories with children.
- Ask children to dictate stories to you that you record on chart paper, in journals, or in children's portfolios.
- Send class thank you notes to program visitors.
- Develop, write, and post a set of rules for your setting.

Invite Children to Write their Names

Young children are egocentric (seeing the world from their perspectives), so help them learn to write the most important word in their vocabularies—their names. Children develop this skill in stages:

1. Using scribbles to represent their names.
2. Using actual letters from their names (one letter, the first few letters, or the first and last letters).
3. Writing their names in ways that others can recognize, but not always ordering the letters correctly.
4. Writing the letters, generally, in conventional order, but with some letters reversed or transposed.
5. Writing their first and last names conventionally.

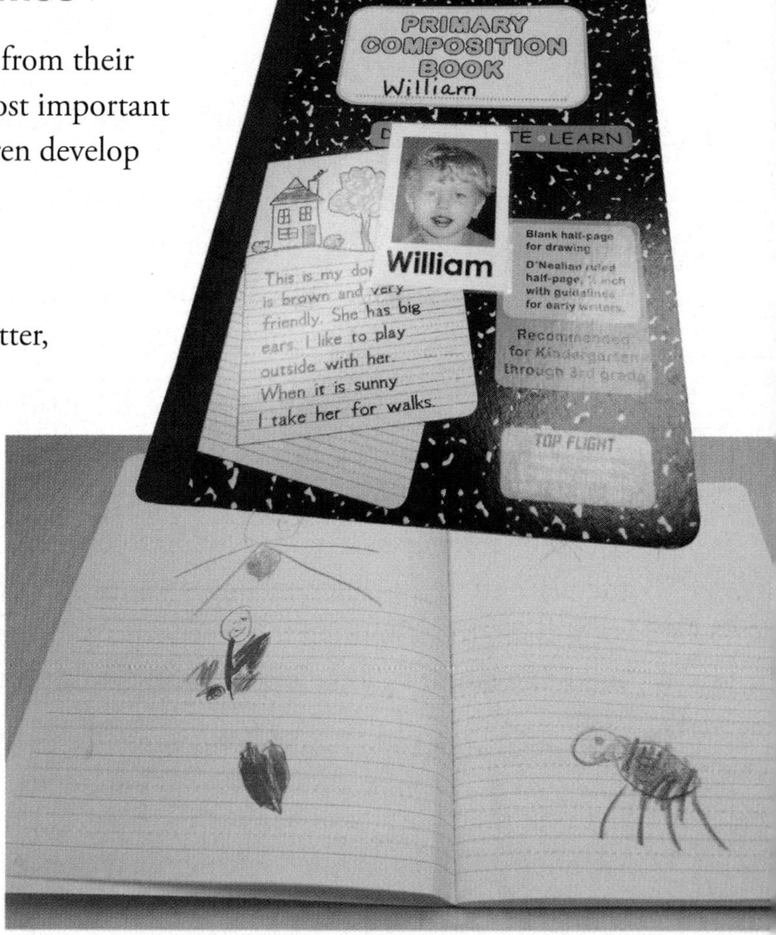

Include journals in the literacy center's writing area so that children can document and record their own learning.

As they learn to write their names, encourage children to sign their artistic masterpieces or create nameplates for their books. Children can practice writing their names on the attendance sheet or by signing up for turns for making snacks, using the computer, or riding a tricycle. These "real-life" reasons to write help children understand that there are purposes for writing, one of which is to share information.

Supporting Dual Language Learners

Language learning is a fundamental part of early development for all children. If a child is raised in a home where English is spoken, the child will learn to speak English. On the other hand, if a child is raised in a home where another language is spoken, the child will learn to speak that language. And if the child is raised in a home where two languages are spoken, the child will become bilingual. Monolingual children may also become **bilingual** if they attend programs, like those in family child care settings, where another language is spoken. These **dual-language learners**, as they are called, have the cognitive ability to maintain two languages instead of just one.

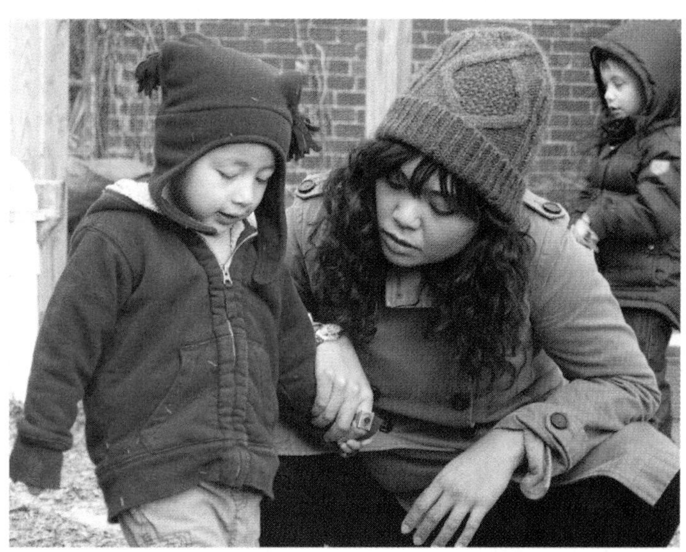

Work with dual language learners one-on-one or in small groups so that you can give children maximum attention.

Eighty-four percent of Head Start programs serve children who speak two or more languages (Severns 2010). These children are dual language learners, or "young children who are learning a second language while still developing basic competency in their first language" (Espinosa 2010). Most infant and toddler dual language learners are able to learn English and their first languages simultaneously. Your goal with all dual language learners in your setting is to foster their ability to speak, read, and write in English while maintaining and supporting the learning of their home language (Tabors 2008).

Historically, educators believed that exposing children to more than one language at a time would confuse them and hinder their mastery of English. Actually, the opposite is true.

Teaching children in their home language promotes their speaking, reading, and writing skills in a second language. This may seem counterintuitive—wouldn't immersing children in as many hours of English instruction every day lead to the most success? Children, in fact, benefit from having solid knowledge of both languages so they can properly sort which vowels…or other parts of language can be transferred from their home language to English and (just as importantly) which ones do not (Goldenberg 2008).

Young dual-language learners may lose fluency in their first or home language when their second language is the dominant one of a nation where they live. This is a source of concern since the children may also lose touch with their culture or family traditions. It may even diminish their chances for academic success. Research shows that the dual-language learners who do best in school are those who have a strong grounding in their home language (Collier, 1987).

Nemeth (2012) cites these reasons why educators should support children's home languages:

The home language is the foundation for cognitive growth. Young dual language learners have acquired most of their knowledge in their home languages. Children transfer literacy skills developed in their home language to new languages. Therefore, early educators should teach these children beginning reading skills in their home languages. Children can readily learn the English alphabet once they have mastered letter and word recognition in their home languages.

Children feel valued when their home language is respected. Children's self-esteem and confidence are bolstered when early educators value them for who they are. When children are free to speak their home languages with their families and within your setting, they receive the message that their home languages and cultures are important.

Families are valued when their home language is respected. Families are more likely to partner with early educators when they see that their cultures are valued in the setting. Even parents who may initially feel that it is better for their children to attend a setting where only English is spoken will be relieved to find out that their home language is not only important, but essential to their child's learning.

It is typical for infants and toddlers who are learning two languages simultaneously to acquire them in similar ways. On the other hand, children who already understand their home languages learn a second languages in a different way. Dual language learning experts have mapped out these steps that children undergo in acquiring a second language (Nemeth 2012):

1. **Home language only.** First, children speak the only way they know how—in their home language—whether or not you and their peers understand them.
2. **Possible silent period.** Children stop talking as they observe and listen. They rely on gestures to communicate.
3. **Actions show understanding.** Children understand what is said to them, even though they do not speak. They can follow instructions and participate in activities as directed.

Use active play activities to introduce vocabulary instead of flash cards.

4. **Formulaic speech.** Children use short phrases and words to communicate. This parallels the speech patterns of two-year-olds learning their first language.
5. **Informal language.** Children speak in sentences and communicate well. This type of language is referred to as *playground language*, because it tends to be informal.
6. **Academic fluency.** Similarly to older children speaking their first language, dual language learners speak in more complex and sophisticated sentences.

Use Conversations to Encourage Dual Language Learners

When communicating with dual language learners in English, make eye contact with them as you speak slowly. Repeat what you say and use clear gestures or visuals so children can understand. Learn at least a few key words and phrases in each child's home language. Ask colleagues, children's family, and community volunteers to suggest ways to enhance your communication with dual language learners.

Use online translation services to learn how to write and say certain words in a child's home language, but check with a fluent speaker or interpreter, from the child's family background, to ensure that what you found online is correct and not confusing.

If you are fluent in the children's home languages, think about how you can use them in conversations. Here are some other ways you can support dual language learners (California Department of Education 2000; Espinosa 2010; Nemeth 2012):

- Be intentional in your use of gestures, facial expressions, and body language.
- Vary your voice inflection for emphasis.
- Work with children one-on-one or in small groups so that you can give them maximum attention.
- Use visual supports like photos, illustrations, props, gestures, and puppets.
- Learn at least a few welcoming words in all children's home languages.
- Post key words and phrases you can pronounce in all children's home languages throughout the room so you can read them to children— including suggested questions to ask children in each learning center.
- Give children time to repeat activities over time and in different contexts.
- Narrate your actions so children can hear models of English spoken correctly: "I'm going to do a head count" and "send in our lunch order now."
- Assemble children who speak different home languages at various mastery levels together in small groups so that they learn from each other.
- Start conversations with simple, closed-ended questions that children can answer with a nod or other gestures.
- Use active play activities to introduce vocabulary.
- Create a word wall displaying vocabulary words the children have recently learned.
- Use books filled with predictable phrases and repetition.
- Give children plenty of examples to help them understand word meanings.

- Select books in which the illustrations closely match the text to help children discern word meanings.
- Help children notice that in the English language words are written with the letters going from left to right, words are written and read from left to right, and from the top of the page to the bottom.
- Display all children's writing samples in whatever language they used.

Create an Environment that Supports Dual Language Learners

Write the words and phrases on charts, labels, signs, and other kinds of print in English and the children's home languages. Thus, the sign for the Blocks would also say "Bloques" and the sign indicating a block structure should be left standing would say, "Please save. Por favor guarder." Offer books in children's home languages and books that have the same text in English and in another language. Do not expect that children will spontaneously read the messages in both languages. Instead, strategically read labels to and with children so they learn both the English and home language word. Here are some additional strategies for ensuring that the learning environment supports dual language learners.

- Include labels and books in each of the children's home languages.
- Color-code the labels used for each language. For example, label the shelves in the art center with a picture of the tool or materials and the English word describing it written in black ink. Include the Spanish words for the items written in green ink. Keep the colors consistent throughout the learning environment; ensure that all signs in Spanish are written in green ink. Mark books, newspapers, and cookbooks written in Spanish with green stickers.
- Represent all children's languages with your labels and signage. Children who have a strong command of their first languages can more easily learn to speak, read, and write English. This tactic also tells children that they are valued and respected in your setting and helps them appreciate each other's home languages.
- Include clear and appropriate pictures or photographs alongside written labels. Also, include the phonetic spelling of some of the words written in the children's home languages to help other adult visitors pronounce these words correctly (Nemeth 2012).

Partnering With Families

Creating a partnership with each family strengthens the quality of education you provide and deepens your understanding of each child's interests, skills, and needs. When you learn about children's favorite stories, books, and songs that are shared at home you can include them in the learning environment. This will help young children transition into the setting and feel a sense of belonging. This information will also assist you in helping children make connections between the stories, books, and songs they enjoy in at home and those they engage in at your setting.

Families with young children are often focused on language and literacy development because they want to be sure their children will enter kindergarten fully prepared to be successful readers and writers. They may ask for concrete evidence that their child is progressing in these areas. Your ongoing observations and documentation can provide examples of the child's work and learning.

Share with families the effective research-based strategies you use to promote language and literacy development. Exchange information about their child's favorite books, stories, poems, and songs at the program and at home. This information can suggest ideas for fun activities at home and ideas for meaningful ways to support their child's language and literacy development at the program.

Weikle and Hadadian (2003) found that successful readers tend to have parents or other family members who did the following:

- Served both as reading and writing models.
- Regularly read aloud to their children.
- Took time to interact with their children.
- Provided reading and writing materials for children to use.
- Believed themselves to play an important role as their child's teacher.

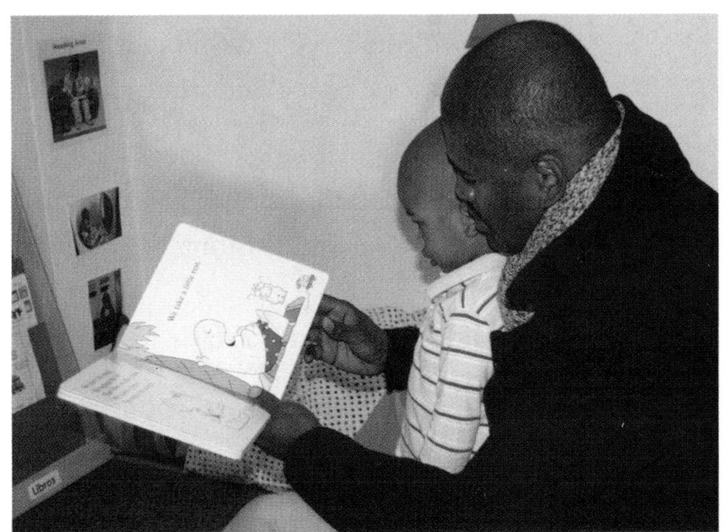

Successful readers tend to have family members who read aloud.

Ask families how they might incorporate the following language and literacy practices at home. These are some of the effective ways they can support their child's learning and enjoyment of language and literacy, through partnerships with educators.

Create a literacy-rich home environment.

To support this strategy, educators can:

- Establish a lending library. Stock it with literacy backpacks that include a children's book, suggested follow-up activities, and materials and props to enhance the learning.
- Make writing backpacks too. Include paper, journals, clipboards, and writing tools.
- Look for used children's books, in good condition, at yard sales and secondhand stores. Give these books to families so children can have their own books at home.

- Engage families in planning a book fair. This can be a way to acquire books as well as being a fund raiser.

Read with children every day.

To support this strategy, educators can:

- Encourage families to read to children in their home language.
- Recognize that in some families the adults are not literate or may work in the evening. You can create a handout that suggests having older siblings read to young ones. Also, note that an adult and child can look at the illustrations and make up a story to go with them.
- Use the information in this chapter to create a handout on reading aloud. Provide a written version in English and the relevant home languages.
- Make a video of you or a colleague reading aloud to post on a video-sharing site so families can see read aloud strategies in action.
- Encourage families to take books with them wherever they go to take advantage of opportunities to read aloud. For example, parents can read aloud while waiting for an appointment or while visiting the neighborhood playground.

Talk with children about their day.

To support this strategy, educators can:

- Provide a list of creative conversation starters that children are likely to respond to—similar to ones you use in your setting. For example, if a child brings home a painting, his dad might say, "Tell me how you made these circles" or "When I look at this painting I see floating clouds. What do you see?"
- Invite families to share their traditions with each other. For example, one family asks the children to share something that happened that was a "rose," and something that was a "thorn." Ask families to suggest times and places where conversations can take place. For example, while preparing, eating, or cleaning up after meals or at bedtime.
- Suggest times and places where conversations can take place. For example, while preparing, eating, or cleaning up after meals or at bedtime.

Take family outings and talk about these shared experiences.

To support this strategy, educators can:

- Suggest that families take photos and use them as prompts to encourage children to recall and discuss their outing.

- Ask families to make a note of any new vocabulary words that came up on the outing. You can reinforce them in the setting while they do the same at home.
- Suggest books and activities that will build on these family outings.
- Explain that to young children, an outing can be as simple as a trip to the hardware store.

Join children in play.

To support this strategy, educators can:

- Make and share a list of the strategies educators you use to join in children's play—providing new props or suggesting new characters that expand the scenario, for example.
- Acknowledge that it can feel strange to join in the play at first, but that the discomfort wanes very quickly.
- Explain that children learn from playing with someone with more advanced skills—such as a parent. Playing can be pretending, rolling a ball back and forth, or trying out a new board game. Recognize that playing with children is not supported in some cultures, and do not pressure or judge families based on other cultural standards.

Sing songs and say rhymes with children.

To support this strategy, educators can:

- Ask families to share with you the songs and rhymes their children enjoy at home so their child and other children can enjoy them at your setting.
- Share the songs and rhymes the child enjoys at the setting. You can even make a recording of the children singing in the classroom that families can sing along with at home.
- Suggest making up songs and rhymes about the child and substituting the child's name in a song or rhyme. "Old MacLucy had a farm . . ."

Write with and in front of children.

To support this strategy, educators can:

- Use the information in this chapter to prepare a handout about the stages of children's writing. Provide a written version in English and the relevant home languages.
- Explain to families what children learn from watching them write. Suggest that they talk while writing so children understand the purpose of writing. "I need to go grocery shopping. Let's look in the refrigerator to see what we need. Looks like the milk carton is almost empty. I'm going to write 'milk' on my list." ■

CHAPTER 7:

Creative

CDA® Functional Area 7: Candidate uses a variety of developmentally appropriate learning experiences and teaching strategies for children to explore music, movement, and the visual arts, and to develop and express their individual creative abilities.

Creative

Introduction

Creativity involves generating novel ideas in alternative, previously unimagined ways. It engages curiosity, risk taking, and imagination. Creative behavior must be original, relevant, fluent (occurs frequently and with ease) and flexible (uses nontraditional approaches) (Isenberg and Jalongo 2010).

In this chapter you will learn the following ways to support children's creativity:

- **Recognizing Creativity**
- **Making A Case for the Arts**
- **Designing Environments That Promote Creativity**
- **Supporting Creativity Through Daily Interactions and Experiences**
- **Promoting Creativity Through the Visual Arts**
- **Fostering Creativity Through Music and Movement**
- **Encouraging Creativity Through the Dramatic Arts**

Recognizing Creativity

Two-year-old Shamar picks up two hardwood blocks, joins two friends who are banging on drums to music, and hits the blocks together to accompany the drumming. Four-year-old Ilona is in the art center. She picks up a packing peanut from the collage box, dips it in paint, and begins to paint a picture, using the packing peanut as a paint brush. The children's early childhood educators watch Shamar and Ilona and think to themselves: "How creative!"

What is it about Shamar and Ilona's actions that made them creative? For one thing they were unexpected. In their settings, blocks are usually used for building constructions and packing peanuts are typically used in collages. Shamar and Ilona weren't limited by the intended use of these materials. They went beyond what was typical to invent new uses.

To be creative is to be able to (Schirrmacher 2011):

- See things in new ways.
- Break boundaries and go beyond the information given.
- Think unconventionally.
- Make something unique.
- Combine unrelated things into something new.

It is important to note that creativity is an attitude rather than a skill. It involves imagination, an ability to go beyond the conventional way of doing things, and to "think outside the box." Consider this example.

Ms. Cicero, a toddler educator, is sitting with two-year-old Aretha at the art table. Aretha is trying to grasp the crayon so that she can draw, but her awkward grip makes drawing frustrating. Ms. Cicero gets up and goes to the first aid kit and comes back with a cotton ball that she places between Aretha's ring and pinky fingers. Voila! Aretha has a firm enough grip to draw. Ms. Cicero found a creative solution to a problem by using a common object in an unexpected way.

In order to be creative children also need to feel that it is okay to make mistakes. Children need an environment that allows and encourages them to take risks and make mistakes without fearing that their efforts will be seen as failures. Mistakes are what allow us to test out hypotheses and make discoveries. If we never know why an answer is wrong, we'll never come up with a novel solution. As Thomas Edison famously said, "I have not failed. I've just found 10,000 ways that won't work." Children need to feel free to invent their own light bulbs.

Creativity is also a process, which may or may not result in a completed product. In the earlier example, Ilona's endeavor to paint with a packing peanut may or may not lead to a painting she wants to display or take home. For her, the experimentation with the painting technique is what is important; the completed painting is just a byproduct of her newly-invented technique.

According to researchers in both education and neuroscience, creativity is composed of seven components that span the cognitive, social, emotional, and physical domains (Hadani 2015):

1. **Imagination and Originality (Cognitive).** Creativity is rooted in being able to imagine and explore novel ideas or to look at existing ideas in new ways. In early childhood education, this begins with pretend play, invented scenarios, and make-believe playmates.

2. **Flexibility (Cognitive).** In order to modify pre-existing concepts, children need to have flexible thinking. They have to be open to new experiences and able to see things from differing perspectives.

3. **Decision Making (Cognitive).** Making thoughtful choices is a necessary component of creative thought. While we tend to see creativity as being exemplified by divergent thinking (exploring many possibilities), convergent thinking (focusing on a limited number of choices) is also needed in order to select the best solution to a problem.

4. **Communication and Self-Expression (Cognitive, social, and emotional).** Creative children are driven to express their thoughts, feelings, and ideas across domains—verbally, through art, dance, drama, and music.

5. **Motivation (Social-emotional).** Motivation is what inspires children to explore and experiment. Research has shown that the more intrinsic and meaningful the rewards—without the promise of external validation—the more creative children are.

6. **Collaboration (Social-emotional).** Working as a team encourages the consideration of differing perspectives and the need for children to explain and possibly revise their viewpoint as they work towards a shared goal.

7. **Action & Movement (Physical).** Exercise and physical activity are correlated with better attention and memory skills. Physical activity acts as a "cognitive enhancer to promote creativity" (Hadani 2015).

For many years, we thought that creativity was rare—a gift that only a lucky few of us possessed. True, we are naturally drawn to notice children who paint realistically, sing with perfect pitch, or dance with grace and flexibility. However, while talent and creativity may overlap, they are not the same. Talent is an innate natural interest or ability that develops with practice while creativity is an ability to invent or imagine an original idea, approach, or solution to a problem. The figures in some creative children's paintings are unrecognizable. Some creative children also sing off-key and move with less grace. Nonetheless, these children are learning to experiment, risk failure, try new things, and think with flexibility and originality. Your role as an early childhood educator is not to be a "talent scout." Rather, your job is to foster every child's creativity—regardless of its perceived degree—in your early childhood setting (Isenberg and Jalongo, 2010). Along with this, it's important to explain this concept to families. They too can encourage their child's creativity at home by noticing and responding positively.

Although your role is not to be a "talent scout," you can foster every child's creativity.

As an early childhood educator, you can nurture the creativity in every child by respecting and valuing the creative process. Children need (Hadani 2015):

- Uninterrupted time to become involved in creative activities
- A place where it is safe to be unconventional
- Encouragement to explore the unknown

In the remainder of this chapter we will explore the specifics of fostering creativity in every child that you teach. Creativity is vital to both children and society. In his 2011 State of the Union Address, President Barack Obama said:

> The first step in winning the future is encouraging American innovation. None of us can predict with certainty what the next big industry will be or where the new jobs will come from. Thirty years ago, we couldn't know that something called the Internet would lead to an economic revolution. What we can do—what America does better than anyone else—is spark the creativity and imagination of our people. We're the nation that put cars in driveways and computers in offices; the nation of Edison and the Wright brothers; of Google and Facebook. In America, innovation doesn't just change our lives. It is how we make our living.

Making a Case for the Arts

With so much agreement on the need for creativity and innovation, it may strike you as odd that for many years now, there has been a backlash in American education against focusing on the arts, which are the backbone of creative expression. The argument was that to be competitive, American children need to be grounded in academic content like reading and math, not art, music, or drama. Consequently, many K-12 curricula have drastically reduced or even entirely dropped arts education. While early childhood education has, for the most part, been spared from having the arts cut out of the curriculum entirely, there has been an accompanying shift in thought that arts-related programming is not as important as language, reading, writing, science, and math. As a result, many early childhood educators have thought of the arts as the "fun" part of their day—not as serious learning.

Thanks to ongoing research, we now know that the visual arts, music, movement, and dramatic play are every bit as important to children's growth and development as are the teaching of academic skills. Indeed, some would claim that the arts are even more important. Take for example, a recent study by social scientists at the University of Arkansas that found that students who are exposed to cultural institutions (e.g., museums, performing arts centers) "not only have higher levels of engagement with the arts, but display greater tolerance, historical empathy, as well as better educational memory and critical thinking skills" (Miller 2013). This study echoes a report by Americans for the Arts that found that children who participate regularly in the arts are "Four times more likely to be recognized for academic achievement . . . than children who do not participate" (Lynch n.d.).

The Reggio Emilia Approach to Art and Creativity

Since the 1940s, the people of Reggio Emilia, a town in northern Italy, have believed that infants, toddlers, and preschoolers are best educated when teachers and families work together closely. In the Reggio classroom, children—not lesson plans—drive the curriculum. Teachers deem any topic the children are interested in worthy of study. They follow these interests closely to conduct long-term studies and investigations that are documented in photographs, pictures, and the children's words and works.

After teachers and parents, the Reggio classroom itself is considered the children's third teacher. Aesthetically pleasing environments are designed purposefully. The classrooms are flooded with natural light and contain beautifully crafted materials. In the bathrooms, there are glass containers of colored water. Mobiles with clear beads, aluminum foil, and coins hang from the ceilings, reflecting light.

Creativity lies at the heart of the Reggio program. Part of the famous philosophy is that there are "100 languages of children," meaning that children need to express their ideas and feelings not just through words, but through all the arts—visual, music, dance, and dramatic play. Observers of a Reggio program note the sophistication of children's artwork. As they express themselves artistically, observe their surroundings, and predict outcomes, these children produce remarkable creations.

What is it about the arts that contributes to young children's growth, development, and academic success? Here are some answers:

Social and emotional development. Art is a window to children's feelings and emotions. Children can express their joy, sadness, fears, and feelings of contentment through painting, music, dance, and drama. Children build self-esteem when they learn skills or how to use a new medium such as clay or move in a novel way. Children learn important social skills when they paint a group mural, march or dance together, or perform a dramatic play scenario.

Language development. The arts carry with them their own vocabulary, which enriches children—words like collage, stabile, assemblage, kazoo, recorder, maracas, glide, gallop, dialogue, monologue, and so much more.

Physical development. Art contributes to the development of both large and small muscle skills in natural ways that children enjoy. Children develop gross motor skills when they paint at an easel or on mural paper on the floor, march with instruments, dance with abandon, wave a scarf through the air or perform in a skit. Fine motor development is a natural byproduct of painting, drawing, pasting, and cutting—and a necessity when learning to write. Playing a triangle, piano keys, or a xylophone demand fine motor coordination. Many types of dramatic play, like making a meal or being a doctor, also develop fine motor skills.

Cognitive development. All of the arts require that children use symbolization. They represent their thoughts as well as their feelings in what they create. Symbolization is, of course, important because it is a foundation skill in learning to read and write. Art also requires children to make decisions when drawing, creating music, and performing interpretive dances. They need to decide what medium they want to use, how they want to arrange a display, how long they want to work on their effort, and what they think of their work.

In addition, children learn many individual cognitive skills through their art, such as problem solving (How to make purple paint. By adding blue paint to red); seriation (Which bell is the loudest?); cause-and-effect (If I keep breathing out, the horn will blow); one-to-one correspondence (giving each person in the class a book to read while playing school in the dramatic play area); science (painting with water outdoors to illustrate the principle of evaporation); social studies (playing music from various cultures); and technology (using a computer app for drawing).

Visual learning. Children learn visual spatial skills when they hang objects on a hanger to make a mobile or jump like rabbits through a field. The visual arts, in particular, lead to graphic symbolism, which is considered a necessary skill in our digital world. As Dr. Kerry Freedman (Lynch, n.d.) has observed: "Children need to know more about the world than just what they can learn through text and numbers. Art education teaches students how to interpret, criticize, and use visual information, and how to make choices based on it."

Inventiveness. The arts encourage children to take risks which gives them a spirit of innovation. As noted earlier, we live in a society that needs creativity and inventiveness. There is no better preparation for this than the arts which force children to express their feelings and thoughts in non-traditional ways.

Appreciation of diversity. Whether it's through music, the visual arts, dance, or drama, the arts introduce children to artists and cultures throughout the world. Since these artists interpret reality through their art, art immerses children in an understanding of culture they may not get in any other way.

There is one final reason to make sure that children receive an arts education. And this is a reason that goes beyond developmental benefits. Art is important in its own right. We need to teach art for art's sake. Though there are major academic reasons to include art in the early childhood curriculum, such justification should not be necessary. Art is what makes civilizations great; it brings beauty to our lives and stimulates our intellect and emotions. Without the arts, we would be lesser beings.

Designing Environments That Promote Creativity

Albert Einstein, the theoretical physicist, is credited with the quote, "Imagination is more important than knowledge." Emily Dickinson, the poet, said, "Imagination lights the slow fuse of possibility." When considering the idea of creativity and how to encourage or promote innovative and provocative ideas, it is truly of value to consider the use of imagination. Thinking about what can be, could be, ought to be, should be, might be or will be is a driving force behind the creative process.

In order to foster the creative process, we must examine the spaces and opportunities we offer for children to be creative. In other words, how do we promote imagination and imaginative thinking that brings about creative ideas and physical expressions of those creative notions? As we have stated above and will explore in more physical terms in the coming text, imagination and subsequent creativity are part of the human development schema related to various processes and developmental areas. However, other—often less tangible but perhaps even more important to supporting the process—aspects of a learning environment either promote or hinder imagination and creativity.

Play. That four-letter word that gets misunderstood and misappropriated in many cases is critical to the creative process. Play is a "concept" as well as an action. Play is a feeling. Play is uniquely suited to each individual. Play is perceived—it is based on perception of what is going on or what is available for use. What one person deems to be playful is not necessarily seen as playful by another person. Even if two children are engaged in the same "playful" scenario, each child—based on their previous experience and engagement with materials and the environment —will view the activity in an individual and unique way. Play is therapeutic. When providing similar objects, time, space and opportunity to any child or group of children, a teacher will notice the individually centered manner in which the child engages. To have expectations, preconceived notions of what can and should be done or to limit personal expression diminishes and negates the benefits of play.

Because play is therapeutic, from a clinical or mental health perspective, we can also examine the role of play and its creative nature. In the book *Play & Creativity in Psychotherapy* edited by Terry Marks-Tarlow, Marion Solomo and Daniel J. Siegel, we find these meaningful words: "Apart from other mammals, children's play is uniquely characterized by imagination—an important aspect of the psychotherapeutic process that has been historically overlooked and theoretically undervalued. When lost in the fun and pleasure of a moment in play, children explore novel forms [creativity] of thought, speech, action and social interaction." So, play and the creative process seem to be supportive of quality mental health and well-being.

Sandra W. Russ, in *Affect & Creativity: The Role of Affect and Play in the Creative Process*, provides a foundation for considering how affect—observed or expressed emotional response—a feeling, or emotion as distinguished from cognition, influences creativity. It is how a child feels or how an adult facilitates or hinders creative thinking in a situation or environment that seems to also impact the creative process. So, setting up a classroom or home with numerous, varied and explicit opportunities and experiences that drive positive emotions becomes extremely important for letting creativity thrive.

Russ (2016) also describes personality traits that are important in the creative process. Those traits include:

- Tolerance of ambiguity
- Openness to experience
- Possessing unconventional values
- Independence of judgement
- Curiosity
- Preference for challenge and complexity
- Self-confidence
- Propensity for risk-taking
- Intrinsic motivation

While some of those traits may not necessarily be observable in very young children, the right environment and opportunities for children will promote the development of some or all of those characteristics.

Unfortunately, many environments and classroom settings do not encourage or provide experiences where imagination and creativity can flourish. Limited resources, abbreviated time schedules, lack of space, staff members' inexperience or lack of understanding, unwillingness to be more tolerant teacher-directed, restrictive experiences/activities, and other influences frequently hinder creativity.

The learning environment you create—the design of your setting and the materials and people within that setting—dictate the types of experiences children will have. Children need uninterrupted time to explore and experiment, get messy, and take pride in their efforts. For the visual arts, having a nearby sink makes clean-up feasible. Take music, movement, and dance outside whenever possible, so children have the space needed for grand moves and can roam without bumping into room dividers or other children at play. Design your learning environment as described in Chapter 3, in a way that supports creativity. Children should know that they are free to be themselves, take risks, and stretch their minds and ideas. These principles apply to both center-based and FCC settings.

Infant and Toddler Settings

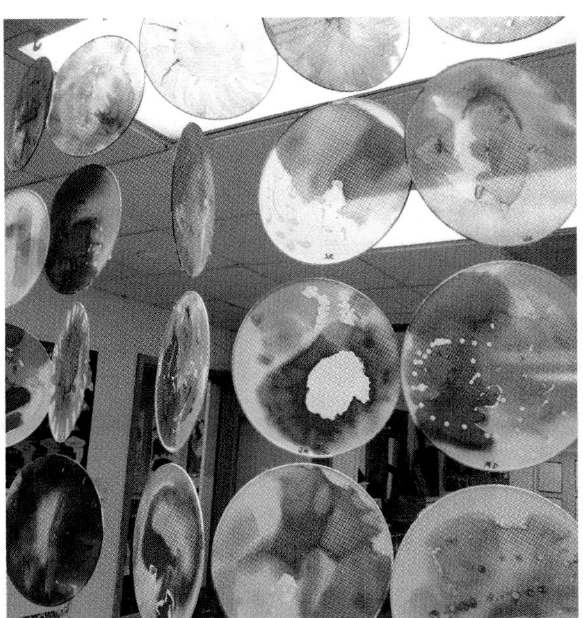

Incorporate a variety of sensory materials.

There is a strong connection between curiosity and creativity. As humans, we have an innate sense of curiosity about the world around us. Infants and toddlers are sensory explorers. As they explore and test new materials and objects, children are making new discoveries in the physical world.

Young Infants. You set the stage for creative thinking and the entire setting can be a creative space for this age range. All of the principles of room arrangement explained in Chapter 3 apply here. You will want to design safe, open spaces and incorporate a variety of sensory materials that promote exploration. Include toys, such as teething rings, balls, rattles, squeaky toys, various containers, stacking toys, and blocks. Also include a variety of safe household items such as empty boxes, plastic containers, or margarine tubs that children can grab, punch, shake, and mouth. For young infants who are not yet mobile but are able to grasp, place these items within their reach. Exploring these items helps infants learn about the toys' physical properties and learn that different toys have different functions. Make sure that babies have uninterrupted time to explore and that you provide toys that are interesting and varied.

In addition, because the arts involve aesthetic appreciation, you want to have an environment that provides a sense of beauty. You want to have walls that are painted in soothing colors, an environment brightened by sunlight, decorations hung where babies can see them, and a space that is neatly organized and welcoming. Fresh flowers and pleasant scents also set a tone for beauty. Music too can be a part of the aesthetic environment. Cultural differences in aesthetic taste are important to recognize too. Take the time to visit families in their homes, or to ask families about the colors and styles in their homes so you can incorporate these into your environments as well.

Mobile Infants. Older babies have beginning language and motor skills that enable them to experiment with materials. They know that they can make things happen—and happen they do. They are busy making finger paintings, pushing and pulling every type of toy vehicle, making music and noise (depending on your viewpoint), playing games, searching out hidden objects (now that they've mastered object permanence), clapping for themselves, and having a great time. They are also starting to solve problems and have beginning understandings of symbolism. Leon gives a stuffed lion a slice of pear from his snack while Aisha flattens a piece of play dough and holds it to her ear as an earring.

Like young infants, mobile infants need safe, open places. They need to move freely and have uninterrupted time to explore the toys and materials housed in their setting. In addition to the usual toys listed in Chapter 3, try giving mobile infants safe household items like pots and wooden spoons they can bang to make music and empty plastic containers they can fill and empty. Materials in the environment should especially support creative endeavors in art, music, movement, and play.

Figure 49 presents some ideas for adding creativity to an infant setting. These apply to programs in both centers and FCC homes.

Figure 49. Promoting Creativity Throughout an Infant Environment

Area	How You Can Promote Creativity
Transition	• Display photos of children and their families. Cover photos with clear adhesive paper and secure them to the floor in front of each child's cubby so crawlers and waddlers can see the photos. • Make a montage of photos of children at play that draws families into your program.
Diapering	• Sing nursery rhymes to babies as you change them. • Narrate what you are doing in song. • Hang a mobile over the changing table for babies to explore with their eyes and feet. • Play peek-a-boo hiding behind the diaper.
Napping	• Play classical music in the background to set a tone for rest. • Sing a lullaby to babies as they settle in for sleep. • Play pre-recorded lullabies from the families, sung in their own voices. • Greet waking babies with a song.
Tummy Time	• Give children lots of open-ended toys to explore like nesting bowls, a pail and shovel, building blocks, wooden animals, and people figures. • Post art work on the wall that appeals to infants—bold colors and clear designs—and art from various cultures. • Hang mobiles that children can move safely and observe shapes and colors.
Individual and Group Play	• Provide children with art and music experiences—finger painting with non-toxic paint, cloud dough (which is edible if swallowed), and instruments to explore. • Play music with varying beats and of varying genres from classical to rock to world music. • Read books that children can hold, touch, and chew like *Fuzzy Bee and Friends* by Roger Priddy. Books like *Baby Beluga* by Raffi and Ashley Wolf allow children to enjoy a story and a song together.
Gross Motor Play	• Offer children soft/light blocks of foam or cardboard to arrange as they please. • Provide balls for children to roll and toss. • Offer children push-and-pull toys that they can move any way they imagine. • Offer children boxes to climb in and out of.
Kitchen	• Invite children to feed themselves, using hands, flatware, scoops, and cups. • Make the area aesthetically pleasing—add a plastic tablecloth, a plant, and boldly illustrated posters. • Change the decor to represent different cultural kitchens.
Outdoors	• Plant a garden that children can explore with all of their senses. • Gather flowers for children to touch, shake, and smell. • Bring an MP3 player outdoors and let children move to music.

Toddlers. Highly creative in the way they explore and manipulate objects, toddlers express themselves using a variety of symbols and media. With encouragement, toddlers enjoy solving problems and are motivated to learn new things. Their constant "why" questions need answers. As children explore and experiment to get their questions answered, they begin to build their self-concepts and self-esteem. They start to feel confident about what they can do and discover, which in turn makes them more motivated to develop creative solutions to problems. They also begin to express their ideas and feelings through imaginary and dramatic play, paint, crayons, clay, blocks, music, and movement.

Provide a range of materials that engage toddlers' five senses. Include crayons, collage, clay, and finger paint in the art center and different sizes, shapes, and types of blocks in the block center. Be sure to include both the familiar with the new and materials that reflect the children's home languages and cultures.

As you observe toddlers at play, continue to note which materials interest them the most and which materials they never use. Either put away the items that are not used or make a point of introducing them to the children, in case they have not noticed them or do not know what to do with them. Reflect on the different ways children can use or manipulate a toy or object. Observe the children's play to make sure that you are providing materials that engage all of their senses. How long do children spend exploring different materials and new objects? Where do they spend the most time engaged? Can you incorporate objects with multiple uses, purposes, or ways that can be manipulated? How can you support children to use materials in different ways? For example, when a toddler marches pegboard pegs across the table, note this as an example of creative thinking.

You'll want to evaluate the learning environment configuration. Does it allow toddlers to roam and explore freely? Can children access materials for different purposes independently? Be sure to keep the environment neat and attractive. Among other things, this will promote creative thought. An aesthetically pleasing space sends children the message that this is a place where they are welcome to play and explore. You want children to be comfortable and feel valued so that they feel encouraged to risk doing inventive things.

In Figure 50 you'll find ideas for spurring toddlers' creativity throughout your setting. These apply to both center-based programs and FCC homes.

Figure 50. Promoting Creativity Throughout a Toddler Environment

Area	How You Can Promote Creativity
Transition	• Decorate the area with photos of the children at play. Help toddlers make creative frames for the pictures out of construction paper, weavings, or wooden frames decorated with acorns, buttons, or sequins. • Make the area aesthetically pleasing with use of colors, painted lines, plants, and so on to "invite" children into the setting.
Diapering	• Post pretty things to look at that you can point out in talking to children. • Make homemade air fresheners using baking soda or herbs like rosemary and lavender or orange peel to "sweeten" the environment. • Post photos of family members by the changing table and point out the faces and clothing to talk about with children.
Literacy	• Do lots of finger plays combined with songs such as *Head, Shoulders, Knees, and Toes* or *Con mi dedito/With my little finger.* • Read books together that feature silly rhymes like *If You Have a Hat* by Gerald Hawksley or *Where Is the Green Sheep?* or *Donde esta la oveja verde?* by Mem Fox.
Dramatic Play	• Encourage children to use body parts and materials from the setting to symbolize dramatic play props. For example, a plate can be a steering wheel or a hand can become a cell phone. • Offer children lots of dress-up clothes, hats from various occupations, and accessories that stimulate dramatic play. Include open-ended materials, like pieces of fabric, so children can create their own clothing and props.
Block	• Provide cardboard and foam blocks that children can use to pile and construct. • Set out cardboard people and animal figures to make children's play more interesting and elaborate.
Gross Motor	• Provide space for children to move like animals—ducks waddling, horses galloping, bunnies hopping. • Encourage children to dance to music from all over the world.
Cooking	• Set up so it appeals to children's senses—brightly colored tablecloth, flowers in a vase, children's art on the wall. • Involve children in presenting food so it is attractive. • Incorporate foods from home cultures and decorate accordingly.
Art	• Introduce children to a variety of art techniques—painting, drawing, collage, sculpting. • Take art outside for children to experience painting and drawing in sunlight and wind.

Preschool Settings

Preschoolers need an environment where they can express their creativity by dabbling in the arts, solve problems, conduct scientific experiments, and approach materials with flexibility and innovation. Set up your program as described in chapter 3, which provides a sample layout. As you design your environment, keep these tips in mind:

Provide lots of open-ended materials that children can use in multiple ways. Materials related to the arts—art supplies, musical instruments, movement and dance props, and dramatic play items—tend to be open-ended by definition.

Provide opportunities for outdoor creativity. Include loose parts, such as stones, branches, buckets, and fabric that children can use in their own ways. Set up a mud kitchen, build a stage for impromptu performances, and offer a basket of cloth strips to weave through the fence. Make drums out of upturned plastic buckets and hang wind chimes from tree branches.

Display materials neatly on open shelving. Use labels (picture and written and in all languages spoken by the children) so that children can use them independently.

Provide places where children can display their creations. A child might want to share his building made of blocks, a mobile, a sculpture, or a homemade instrument after choice time has ended. Help children make signage that will protect the creation from being moved by others.

Decorate the walls with children's artwork and writing samples. Framing the work sends a message that the children's creative works are valued. Display the works at children's eye level so that they can revisit their work and think and talk about the process and materials they used and who they worked with.

Designate spaces indoors and outdoors where children can be messy. Provide smocks and protected flooring so that messes can be easily cleaned and not interfere with children's creative play.

Follow a schedule that includes at least one-hour blocks of time. Children need sufficient time to express themselves creatively, test out hypotheses, and try out their innovative ideas.

Take photographs and document children's creative processes and outcomes. Art work, block creations, and innovative ideas such as Ilona's painting technique can all be documented. Be sure to make observational notes about the children's creativity to keep in their portfolios and share with families.

Figure 51a-b provides specific ideas for promoting creativity in each of the learning centers in your setting. These tips apply to both center-based and FCC settings. The goal is to design your entire indoor and outdoor environments to foster creativity.

Creative

Figure 51a. Promoting Creativity Throughout a Preschool Environment

Learning Center	How You Can Promote Creativity
Block	• Provide a full set of hardwood unit blocks—enough for the size of the group. They are open-ended and can be used for building in multiple ways. • Make sure there is ample, traffic-free space for children to build constructions so they don't have to limit their imaginations. • Encourage children to make signs to keep their creations on display after center time has ended. • Provide prop farm and zoo animals, road signs, vehicles, and people, to use with the blocks. Vary the props to respond to group and individual interests and experiences. • Challenge children to solve problems. For example: "How can these cars get across the river?" or "The tower keeps falling down, what do you think we need to do to ensure that it stays upright?" or "The tiger might eat different foods than the polar bear. How can you create a home for both animals?"
Art	• Provide open-ended materials for painting, drawing, printing, sculpting, and making collages or mobiles. • Comment on the techniques, tools, media, and designs of children's work; remember the processes are typically more important to preschoolers than the final products. • Encourage children to express their thoughts and feelings through their art. • Frame and display children's artwork, with their permission. • Invite older preschoolers to tell you about their work; write their descriptions on paper strips that accompany the work. • Plan small group activities to introduce new tools and media; then leave children to explore ways to use the new items on their own.
Literacy	• Encourage children to create rhymes, poems, and books. • Read and discuss books with individuals, pairs, and small groups daily. • Invite children to act out stories from books and finger plays. • Have children write and act out their own plays. • Include puppets for making up new stories. • Incorporate foods from home cultures and decorate accordingly. • Display books about artists, musicians, dancers, and about creative works from different cultures and countries. • Encourage children to use computers for drawing and creating stories.
Dramatic Play	• Provide gender-specific and gender-neutral dress-up clothing and accessories so that children can assume various roles. • Provide materials and fabrics from around the world that children can use to create their own clothing and accessories. • Provide prop boxes for role-playing scenarios at a grocery store, beach, or hair salon. • Provide props that will stimulate children's imaginations, such as a stethoscope or a cash register. • Enter the children's play on occasion to stimulate the action or pose a problem to solve ("I'm hungry. When will you be serving lunch?").

Figure 51b. Promoting Creativity Throughout a Preschool Environment

Learning Center	How You Can Promote Creativity
Music & Movement	• Encourage children to dance and perform creative movements using various props indoors and outdoors. • Provide materials and step by step instructions so children can create homemade instruments; leave the materials out so children can invent new instruments. • Incorporate children's home languages and cultures by offering a variety of music, songs, and dances. • Sing spontaneously and during transitions; invite children to make up new verses to familiar songs. • Make up songs and dances with the children. • Play different types of music and invite children to draw pictures or move to express how the music make them feel. • Include a variety of musical instruments and support children in playing them.
Math & Manipulatives	• Provide open-ended materials such as Legos, marble runs, magna-tiles, beads with stiff string, parquetry blocks, and geoboards. • Provide standard and non-standard measurement tools and pose challenges, such as: "How many baby shoes long is the book shelf?;" "How many tissue boxes long is the tower you built?;" or "Let's take this yardstick and measure how tall Adam is." • Provide both table and floor space for assembling puzzles so children can work alone or as a group. • Provide cardboard, markers, dice, and other items needed to create puzzles and toys; work with children to make these items. • Suggest that children devise their own rules for games.
Sand/Water Play	• Bury a variety of items of different sizes and textures; have children discover, from touch, what objects are buried in the sand. • Offer numerous items and encourage children to predict what objects will sink or float in water; then have them figure out how to find out if their predictions are correct. • Provide open-ended props children can use in many different ways. Examples include: measuring cups, acrylic tubing, funnels, sifters, pulleys, ladles, and screening. • Ask lots of open-ended questions to stimulate children's divergent (atypical) thinking. For example: "What tools could we use to find out if there is buried treasure in the sand?"
Cooking	• Encourage children to create and record their own recipes. Try these new recipes during your cooking experiences using fresh and healthy ingredients. • Provide garnishes for children to decorate dishes. • Encourage children to put their own "stamp" on recipes. • Ask children to create placemats, centerpieces, and inviting table settings. • Cook recipes from children's home cultures and decorate accordingly.
Outdoors	• Invite children to help with landscaping. • Bring process-oriented activities, such as art and woodworking outdoors. • Provide straws, wires, strawberry baskets, six-pack rings, and plastic hangers for children to use as wands while blowing bubbles. • Invite children to make up outdoor games they can play.

Family Child Care Settings

Family Child Care educators also need to create settings that inspire beauty, allow for flexibility, and set a tone for risk-free discovery and experimentation. Children of all ages need to have the space and time to be creative. Using the guidelines presented in Chapter 3, think about how you can best use the space to offer creative experiences like art, music, movement, dance, and dramatic play. The same materials noted above lend themselves to creative use in an FCC home.

If you have a child-size table and chairs, that is a good place to conduct art activities like painting, drawing, sculpting, and making collages and other artwork. Alternatively, use the kitchen or dining room tables, with high chairs and booster seats as needed. You want to allow children to feel free to create, so either set up the table on an area with washable flooring, or use an old shower curtain, drop cloth, or newspapers to protect the carpeting. The closer this area is to a sink, the easier cleanup will be.

Music, movement, dance, and dramatic play can take place anywhere in your home where there is uncluttered space. Often times, you will want to take these activities outdoors where the space is ample. For all of the activities, offer props and related materials on low shelving so children can take out and use the materials independently.

Because creativity is an attitude and an approach—and not a skill—the most important thing you can do when setting up your environment in any type of setting is to create an atmosphere that lets children know that creativity is not only encouraged, but expected. Set a tone for discovery, invention, and the testing of children's hypotheses. If you expect children to be creative, then they will do everything they can to meet that expectation.

Supporting Creativity Through Daily Interactions and Experiences

In Chapter 5, you learned that young children think differently than adults. Like cognitive development, creativity looks different in children, too (Runco 2012). Children tend to be less inhibited than adults and focus less on finding the "right" answer. Because they are less concerned with what others think about them, creativity comes naturally for most children.

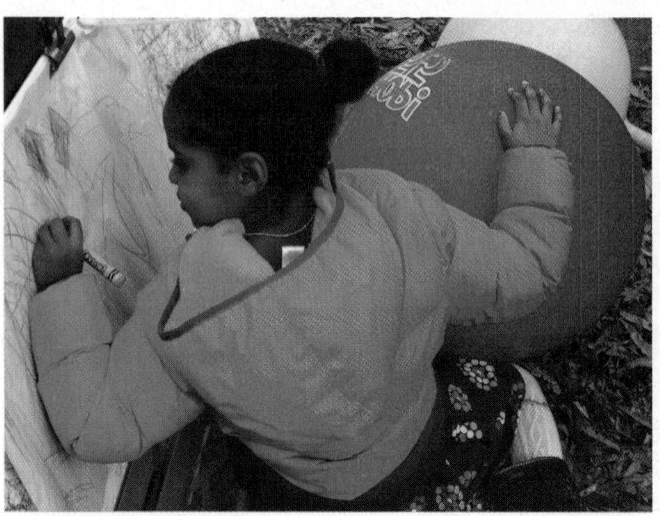

Because they are less concerned with what their painting or drawing looks like, children tend to be naturally creative.

Infants

Creativity is born in infancy. It needs nurturing, though, to develop. While you can't teach creativity, you can promote its growth in all children. You do this by first creating an environment where creativity can flourish and then interacting with children in ways that will encourage its growth. Early childhood educators encourage creativity in infants when they:

- Sing nursery rhymes or silly songs to babies while changing diapers.
- Have hands-on interactions with the child, such as playing games of peek-a-boo or singing Where Is Thumbkin?
- Encourage children's explorations and comment on their concentration, actions, and ways of using things: "I bet you would enjoy playing with this rattle. Last time you held it you shook it, you banged it, you tasted it, and you smelled it. I wonder what you will do with it today."
- Allow children time to explore on their own, such as seeing what happens when they kick a foot-operated toy (e.g., a kick-and-play piano) or wear a wrist bell.
- Add novelty to the familiar. For example, occasionally introduce a new toy or mobile to shake things up.
- Introduce the arts at an appropriate developmental level. To illustrate, put your hands over the baby's and together clap to the beat of the music. Hand a child a musical instrument (like a maraca) to explore. Offer a mobile infant play dough to squeeze.
- Model creativity so that children learn this is something you value. For example, talk to children in rhymes and make up nonsense words.
- Provide opportunities for infants to mimic your creative behaviors, such as making singsong sounds.
- Encourage mobile infants to mimic adult behaviors with dolls and stuffed animals: "Do you want to burp your bunny like I just burped you?"

Toddlers

While toddlers are busy moving everywhere, testing limits, saying "no" and asking "why," educators have many opportunities to promote creativity. Try some of these strategies:

- Acknowledge that toddlers are more interested in the process than the product of creativity: "I saw you pound and flatten the play dough over and over again."

- Follow a flexible schedule so toddlers have time to be creative: "You've really enjoyed playing with the cardboard blocks this morning. Instead of listening to Ms. Montgomery's story, you can stay with the blocks if you like, Freddy."
- Capitalize on children's love of movement: have them wiggle like snakes, leap like frogs.
- Read books aloud with children and change or extend the ending: what happens after the "happily ever after" part?
- Encourage children to find answers to their "why" questions through exploration: "Sandy, you asked why we saw worms in the garden before but don't see them now. Why don't you try raking the ground and we'll find out if there are any worms hiding in the dirt?"
- Build on children's beginning interest in pretend play: "I wonder if this stuffed cow needs to be milked?"
- Challenge children to be creative: "Can you make up a lullaby that the doll might like to hear before you put her to bed?" or "What can you do with the items in this box?"
- Help children see new ways to use toys and materials: "Which body parts other than your fingers could you use to paint with?"
- Provide lots of open-ended experiences with the arts: "I brought in some bells today. Who would like to play with them and see how they work?"
- Pose problems for toddlers to solve: "How can we fit all of the foam blocks on this shelf?" Avoid giving too much instruction. Over-instruction inhibits toddlers' creativity.

Preschoolers

Preschool children have the cognitive, physical, social, and emotional skills and traits needed to be creative. As you observe and interact with children during play, think about the following tips for promoting creativity as preschoolers explore, experiment, and engage in art, music, movement, and dramatic play:

- Point out and comment on children's creativity, letting them know you think these actions are worth noting: "I see that you are using lots of bright colors in your painting. The orange paint makes the paper almost glow."
- Ask lots of open-ended questions: "What do you need to set up a book shop in the dramatic play area?" "Why did you decide to ride trikes today?" "How can you get this statue to stand on its own?"
- Use direct instruction to introduce new materials and equipment, but let children take the lead in deciding how to use them. According to Allison Gopnik (Kuszewski 2011),

"Too much direct instruction—showing a child what to do, rather than letting him figure out the solution himself—can severely affect his ability and/or instinct to independently and creatively solve problems, or to explore multiple potential solutions."

- Pose challenges. Observe and think about how you can scaffold children's learning by focusing on how and what they are learning. "You got the toy car home from the airport by building a highway of blocks. Now how can you get the car across a river where there is no bridge?"
- Use family style dining as an opportunity to spark creative thinking: "How could we eat our mac and cheese if we didn't have forks or spoons?" "What could we serve for lunch if all of the foods had to be red?"
- Think of how to help children use materials in new and exciting ways. "Bobby and Annie are using the box of collage materials right now. Here are some paper clips and tissues that you can use to make a collage while they have the collage box. What other things might you use for a collage?
- Provide children time to fully explore. Do not rush young children from one activity to the next. Allow them to focus on the activities and materials in which they are most interested and curious.
- Value children's art and understand their scribbles, splatters, and blobs are appropriate for their stage of development. Instead of asking what it is, ask children to describe their work and what they did to create it.
- Consider dividing your dramatic play area into two parts. One half would support housekeeping play and the second area can rotate for specific scripts. For example, if you are located near lake or ocean, you might want to set up a beach area where children's scenarios could involve swimming, collecting shells, or picnicking.
- Encourage children to express their feelings through their play: "I know that you're feeling upset that your dad isn't living at home with you, Lucas, but I can't let you hurt Manny. Why don't you take all of that energy and play at the water table outside for a while? You can splash and hit the water as much as you'd like."
- Encourage children to represent their thoughts in multiple dimensions. For example, have them draw a picture of the way music makes them feel or to act out a story you just read them.
- Have children revisit (and rethink) their work. When people are allowed time to return to an idea, they often see things in a new way and experience a breakthrough in their thinking.

Figure 52. Supporting Creative Thinking for Children of All Ages

- Respect all children's responses and ideas.
- Let children know that messes are not only tolerated but, sometimes, invited.
- Give children lots of "practice" time to test their ideas and thoughts and experiment with materials.
- Offer children constructive feedback and encourage them to provide each other the same.
- Limit competition; encourage cooperative learning.
- Offer ongoing encouragement, not empty praise.
- Teach children strategies for creative thinking, and place few restrictions on their ideas.
- Help children see their mistakes as opportunities to learn, not as failures.

(Isenberg & Jalongo, 2010; Chrysikou, 2012)

Promoting Creativity Through the Visual Arts

Drawing, painting, sculpting, and creating collages and mobiles are all expressions of children's creativity. The visual arts allow children to be original and fulfill their need to communicate their ideas and feelings. When given open-ended materials and encouraged to create something of their own design rather than to attempt to reproduce a preconceived model, the visual arts can be the very definition of creativity.

Set the tone for creativity by designing your setting to support art exploration and introducing children to different media and tools: "Today I'm going to introduce you to a new tool for working with clay and dough. It's called an 'extruder.' Raoul, can you please help me? Show the children what happens when you put clay in it and push down. Everyone will have lots of time to explore and experiment with it."

Introduce children to other art-related vocabulary and concepts as you work with them on art experiences (Schirrmacher 2011):

- Color: "You picked dazzling colors to paint with—flamingo pink, lavender purple, and mustard yellow."
- Line: "You filled the whole paper with strong, wavy lines."
- Pattern: "You were able to keep the pattern going in the potholder. You wove of one green and two orange loops."

Creativity and Divergent Thinking

Coined by the psychologist J.P. Guilford in 1967, *divergent thinking* is spontaneous, free-flowing thought which allows us to generate multiple solutions to problems. Divergent thinking is contrasted with *convergent thinking*, where we follow rules and arrive at a single "correct" solution. Creativity, of course, is based on divergent thinking.

Faced with a problem, such as how to make a sculpture stand when it is falling over, a creative child who thinks divergently will brainstorm possible solutions: they could use sand paper to even out the bottom, they could take some play dough or gak and wedge it under the wobbly part, or they could try repositioning the sculpture on its side to achieve better balance. They can then test out these hypotheses one by one and decide which solution works best. When it comes to creativity, there is no one best solution.

- Shape: "I see several shapes in the recycled items you are going to use for your mobile. The hanger is a triangle and the lids are circles. What other shapes will you use?"

Through hands-on, open-ended art explorations, children of every age learn about creative self-expression and about themselves as individuals. It's best for these experiences to be child-initiated, child-directed, and proceed at the child's pace. Avoid worksheets and coloring pages. Instead, let the children's imaginations take charge. If twelve children in your setting are painting today, then the day should conclude with twelve distinct paintings. The styles, colors, and subjects of each painting should reflect the personalities, ideas, and feelings of the artists. Encouraging children to explore with art materials however they see fit is the best way to nurture creativity.

However, it is not enough for educators to just put out art materials and wait and see what happens. Early childhood educators need to engage children in thinking about their art. As children paint or draw, describe their actions or ask respectful questions about their work: "I see that you are placing red paint next to the green paint." "How did you make that blue shape?" "You filled up the whole paper with your drawing." "It looks like you added some texture to the clay." If children indicate that they are drawing pictures of their homes or sculpting blue jays out of play dough, encourage their creative thinking. Ask them to describe their work or tell you how they made their creative decisions. Avoid asking children, "What is it?" or making assumptions about their artwork.

Scribbling, Drawing, and Painting

Young children's artistic explorations begin with scribbling, drawing, and painting. In an attempt to discover what tools like crayons and paintbrushes can do, they explore and experiment with these tools, learning along the way about shape, color, size, and creative self-expression. As an early childhood educator, be aware that children go through distinct stages when learning to draw and paint (Zero to Three n.d.). As you'll notice, these stages overlap with the development of emergent writing, as described in Chapter 6.

1. **Random scribbling** (15 months to 2 ½ years). Children grasp a crayon or marker and find that it will leave a mark on paper, illustrating the concept of cause and effect. Marks grow into squiggles, which children find exciting.

2. **Controlled scribbling** (2 to 3 years). As children gain hand control over a marker or crayon, they perch them between their thumbs and forefingers rather than grasping the writing tools in a fist. Scribbles turn into circles and lines. Instead of touching the paper randomly, children place marks on paper with intentionality.

Children's artistic explorations begin with drawing and painting.

3. **Lines and patterns** (2 ½ to 3 ½ years). Children realize that they can convey meaning through their drawings. They work hard to include in their art the curves and lines that they see in real objects.

4. **Pictures of objects or people** (3 to 5 years). Children are now able to put circles and lines together. Because these early drawings are often unplanned, children frequently do not know what they will be drawing until it happens. Later, as they gain both physical control over drawing tools and the intellectual skill to understand that their thoughts can be represented visually, they plan their art. By the end of this period, children draw with intentionality and have a finished image in mind.

Knowing and understanding these stages will help you support children in exploring and experimenting with drawing and painting tools. Again, your observations of children's interests and skills are critical. Each child is unique and will master different skills at different times.

Early educators can help children move through these steps and help them learn how to hold and use drawing and painting utensils. Crayons and markers are held in the "tripod grasp." The pads of a child's thumb and index finger should encircle the tool, which rests on the middle finger near the first knuckle. All fingers should apply equal (but not heavy) pressure.

Help children learn paintbrush techniques and ensure that you have a variety of brushes available to best meet children's needs. For example, while all children may benefit from using seamless brushes with metal bands, older toddlers and younger preschoolers have more success with flat, one-inch brushes. Older children can use round or flat brushes. After children are familiar with scribbling, drawing, and painting, they will embrace other art forms eagerly.

Most young children enjoy experimenting with art forms such as the following:

- **Collages** (mobile infants, toddlers, and preschoolers). Children tear or cut tissue and magazine photos to paste onto paper or cardboard; embellish the design with feathers, confetti, ribbons, or sequins.
- **Doughs** (mobile infants, toddlers, and preschoolers). Children form dough into sculptures or mounds; roll dough or cut out letters or shapes with cookie cutters.
- **Clay** (toddlers and preschoolers). Children roll, shape, pinch, and sculpt modeling clay; paint hardened baking clay.
- **Three-dimensional constructions** (older toddlers and preschoolers). Children build and create three-dimensional structures that stand (stabiles) or hang (mobiles).
- **Weaving** (preschoolers). Children use potholder loops or freestanding looms to create potholders, fabrics, and designs. Group weaving could take place on a standing loom in the classroom or outdoors on a fence or in the crook of a tree.
- **Woodworking** (preschoolers). Children saw and glue wood pieces together to create constructions and projects (under adult supervision).
- **Puppetry** (preschoolers). Children use stuffed socks, papier-mache covered balloons, or paper bags to form hand puppets; use the fingers of a glove to make finger puppets.

How each child approaches the visual arts depends of course on their stage of development. Think about the children you care for as you read through the following sections. Figure 53 suggests adaptations for children with disabilities.

Young Infants

Infants use all of their senses to discover and learn. As they look at, listen to, smell, touch, and taste objects in their environment, they gain an appreciation for the textures, shapes, colors, and design of the world. With experience, they start to show a preference for particular textures and shapes. This is the foundation for art. Give babies an opportunity to do activities like these:

- Offer pieces of fabric, ribbons, and carpet pieces infants can feel against their cheeks—velvet, corduroy, felt, terry cloth, carpeting, and netting offer a full range of textures; leave them out where they can touch them on their own.
- Hang a prism in a sun-filled window and delight an infant with the dancing colors of the rainbow.
- Offer natural items for infants to touch and smell—sea shells, pine cones, flowers.
- Hang a shape mobile over the changing table, give it a tap so the baby can watch the shapes move.

- Read board books that let babies feel different textures, such as *Touch and Feel Farm* by DK Publishing and the classic *Pat the Bunny* by Dorothy Kunhardt.
- Place the baby on a patchwork quilt for tummy time.
- Lift a baby to touch the leaves on a tree and watch the leaves blow on a windy day.
- Let an infant touch, pick, and eat a cherry tomato from your organic garden.

Mobile Infants and Toddlers

Curious toddlers want to get involved with art. They want to discover what art materials are like—and then they want to do something with them. To introduce art to mobile infants and toddlers. Early childhood educators can let them explore art tools and demonstrate some beginning art techniques and activities. Children this age will start to show a preference for colors and styles of art. The goal is for children to learn how to express themselves emotionally and creatively through art experiences. Here are some specific things early childhood educators can do:

- Give children smocks to wear so that they know they can be as messy as they like.
- Let children explore how a jumbo crayon works. Tape some butcher paper or newsprint to a table or floor and let children move the crayon around, making marks and scribbles as they go. Start with one color, and add different colors as children grow and become more familiar with using crayons.
- Take children outside with a sponge or a painter's brush and pail of water and let them paint trees, steps, walls, and rocks. Indoors, children can paint with water on vinyl floors, or in kitchens and bathrooms of FCC homes.
- Give children tissue paper to tear into designs. Older toddlers can paste the tissue on paper to make a collage-like design.
- Let children experiment with jumbo chalk, either indoors on a chalkboard or with outdoor chalk on cement.

Should Food Be Art?

Using pudding to finger paint or pasta to create collages is not as straightforward an art technique as you might think. Indeed, using food in art is highly controversial. Some find the use of food innovative, inexpensive, and safe should the food be accidentally eaten by exploring infants and toddlers. Others find it wasteful, even offensive, when there are children who go hungry every day.

The use of food as an artistic medium is a complicated issue with no clear-cut, right or wrong answer. Find out your setting's policy regarding the use of food as art. If there is no policy in place, encourage staff and families to discuss this issue and devise a policy together.

- Give children edible play dough (in case they decide to see how the dough tastes) to pound, flatten, and pinch.
- Let mobile infants finger paint with pudding, expecting that this will also be their snack. (See box on previous page.) Toddlers can use homemade finger paints made from sugar, cornstarch, and water.
- Tape paper to a table and invite several children to draw on it. They will enjoy being part of the group and can use broad arm movements to make their marks.

Assemble lots of novel materials.

Preschoolers

Preschoolers are developmentally at a stage where they can independently paint, draw, sculpt, and mold. They build on their knowledge of these basic techniques to do activities like printing, etching, weaving, and puppetry. For younger preschoolers the process is all that counts. However, with increasing skills, the idea of a completed product starts having appeal. Having a drawing or painting to hang in the setting or take home to post on the family refrigerator starts to be a motivator for creating art. Children will choose colors and media that reflect their mood and can tell you how their art and the art of others make them feel. There are many things early childhood educators can do to facilitate children's creativity through art:

Most young children enjoy experimenting with art forms.

- Introduce new painting techniques to inspire children to try them. Some variations are spatter painting (put a screen over an object such as a leaf or flower and use a toothbrush to force the paint through the screen); blow painting (blow paint through a straw onto paper); squirt bottle painting (use empty ketchup or mustard squeeze bottles to squirt out thick paint); folded painting (place paint on unfolded paper, then fold and unfold); ball painting (fill an old deodorant container with a ball top with paint); pom-pom painting (use dishwashing poms); resistance painting (paint over crayon designs); string painting (run a string through paint and over paper); and marble painting (dip a marble in paint and roll it over paper).
- Vary the types of paints, again to spark new creations. For example, water colors and textile dyes add different dimensions.
- Offer children different surfaces to draw and paint on. These might include butcher paper, chart paper, Manila paper, grocery bags, tracing paper, coffee filters, doilies, construction paper, poster board, paper plates, tissue paper, baked clay sculptures, and even sidewalks.
- Establish a variety of places where children can paint: two- or three-sided standing easels (indoors and outdoors), plastic taped to the wall or floor, butcher paper hung on the wall or laid on the floor for murals.
- Try painting with other body parts besides hands: feet can be used for printing and face painting for celebrations.
- Set up a printing area where inks can be rolled on rubber stamps, sponges, corks, golf balls, and cut potatoes (if the program uses food with art).
- Provide a variety of doughs to shape, sculpt and mold. For example, clay, play dough, cloud dough, silly putty, and gak. Let children experiment with oobleck, which is both a liquid and a solid. Pick it up and feel it melt. Throw it in the air and it will flatten. (See recipe that follows.)
- Offer children standard and nonstandard tools from a variety of cultures to use with doughs such as mallets (or a meat tenderizer), rolling pins, cookie cutters, pizza cutters, potato mashers, ricers, mortar and pestle, sushi rolling mats, and melon ballers.
- Collect natural materials with children's help to add to the standard collage materials, such as acorns, seeds, nuts, leaves, flowers. Avoid using foods in art projects, as it may be impossible to know when a family is experiencing food insecurity or difficulty keeping food on the table, and seeing food used for art can be a source of stress or trauma for families.
- Encourage children to use paste, glue, and scissors in ways that will lead to successful experiences. For children who can't yet use scissors, give them opportunities to develop their fine motor skills by tearing papers.

- Assemble lots of novel materials, with the children's help, for making mobiles and stabiles such as driftwood, twigs, dowels, rulers or yardsticks, rubber bands, paper clips, yarn, twine, twist ties, wires, pipe cleaners, ribbon, wire, and tapes. Invite families to make contributions too.
- Provide different weaving experiences beyond potholders on a loom—crepe paper on a link fence; handmade looms formed from chicken wire, Styrofoam balls and boards, egg cartons, empty strawberry containers, or mesh vegetable bags. Weave with aluminum foil, rubber bands ribbons, old stockings, shoelaces, yarn, and twine.
- Plan woodworking experiences and opportunities to hammer golf tees into dry wall and screws into layered cardboard. Let children use hand drills to screw nuts and bolts into wood and then make them into stabiles. Provide safety goggles and supervision.
- Demonstrate how to cover a balloon with papier-mache and invite older preschoolers to make their own puppet heads. Provide pieces of fabric, old socks, buttons, yarn and large needles, and invite children to make puppets of people, animals, and characters of their own imagination.
- Invite children to make homemade art materials with you. Investing them in the process sparks creativity and guarantees that they are using non-toxic art supplies. Make recipe cards that use rebus-like images to illustrate the ingredients and directions. Some favorites are (Colker 2009):
    - Playdough: Combine and knead 2 cups flour, 1 cup salt, 2 tablespoons oil, 1 cup water, and 3 drops food coloring
    - Crafting clay: Add 2 cups baking soda, 1 cup cornstarch, and 1¼ cups water to a saucepan. Cook over medium heat until mixture is consistency of mashed potatoes. Remove from heat and let cool. Knead until smooth, adding food coloring if desired.
    - Oobleck: Place 1 cup cornstarch in bowl. Pour ½ cup water over cornstarch. Mix and let sit until hardened.
    - Face paint: Place 1 teaspoon cornstarch in bowl with ½ teaspoon cold cream (as used on skin). Add ½ teaspoon water and mix. Add food coloring and mix.
    - Finger paint: Place ½ cup cornstarch in bowl. Add 1½ cups cold water and mix. Add 2 envelopes unflavored gelatin to separate bowl. Add ½ cup cold water to gelatin and mix. Let sit for 2 minutes. Pour cornstarch mixture into saucepan. Add gelatin to cornstarch and heat until thick and glossy. Stir in 1 cup powdered laundry detergent. Add food coloring and mix.

Figure 53. Art Adaptations for Children With Disabilities

Every child in your group should have access to art materials every day. If there are children in your program with disabilities, you can readily adapt the curriculum to meet their needs. Here are some examples.

For children with vision impairments/blindness:
• Add textured materials and scents to paint and play dough. • Provide a cafeteria tray or cookie sheet to work on which will define boundaries for the child. • Choose bright, fluorescent paints that contrast with background papers. Border the paper with reflective safety tape. • Pair a sighted child with a visually-impaired one.
For children with auditory impairments:
• Use rebus charts with pictures illustrating art processes. • Communicate with the child using sign language, lip reading, or gestures.
For children with vision impairments/blindness:
• Provide chunky or jumbo markers, chalk, and crayons. • Apply non-skid tape to handles of art tools to provide a better grip. • Provide squeezing scissors or a cutting wheel and cutting mat instead of regular scissors. • Use adhesive paper with the sticky side up so that children can make collages without gluing. • Use Velcro on paintbrushes and mittens so the brush can be attached to the mitten without having to be gripped. • Invite children to use a paint roller on taped paper instead of a brush.

Fostering Creativity Through Music and Movement

Music and movement experiences support children's total development—physical, cognitive (especially math), language and literacy, social, and emotional. Music helps bridge children's thinking from the concrete to the abstract. As it is dependent on symbols, much like language and literacy, higher level critical thinking skills come into play as children explore and experiment with music and appreciate its patterns of loud, soft, fast, and slow. Combining rhythmic movement with speech and song is correlated with inner speech and self-control, components of executive function described in Chapter 5. Both large and fine motor skills are developed through music, movement, and dance. Gross motor skills develop naturally as children leap, crawl, bend, and stretch. Fine motor skills are developed as children play musical instruments.

Consider the following additional benefits:

- Music and movement experiences teach spatial relationships.
- Children develop confidence and self-esteem as they learn and perform songs and dance to the beat of the music with support from adults and peers.
- Children practice counting when they clap their hands four times and then stomp their feet four times, following the beat of the music.
- Music is a form of communication.
- Music has a calming effect on emotions and is an outlet for expressing and coping with feelings.
- Music promotes language skills, by using voice to make musical sounds of tonality and rhythm with words, phrases, and sentences.
- Music is a part of people's souls. Every culture's roots include music and every important personal and social event from birthdays to sporting matches celebrates with song.
- Movement and learning are linked; movement increases children's attention and memory skills.

As with all of development, children master specific skills as they grow. Figure 54a-b presents the developmental progression of music and movement skills.

Figure 54a. Developmental Progression of Music and Movement

Young Infants (0-8 months):
• Turn heads towards music • Respond to sounds by vocalizing • Use body to communicate needs, e.g., reach arms to be picked up
Mobile Infants (9-18 months);
• Show preference for particular types of music • Clap hands and move to music • Enjoy making their own music, e.g., shake a maraca • Attempt to sing to music • Like to be rocked to music while being held • Begin to understand that sounds and music affect behavior • Enjoy hearing their names sung • Imitate vocal characteristics of adults

Figure 54b. Developmental Progression of Music and Movement

Toddlers (19-36 months):	
• Explore musical instruments to see how they work • Respond to changes in musical tempo, beat, sound level • Seek out favorite songs • Participate in finger plays and body plays • Use gestures in music to convey meaning • Memorize short, simple songs • Experiment with sounds	
Preschoolers (3-5 years)	
• Use music and instruments to create moods • Play musical instruments alone and with group • Choose songs and music of own liking • Know words to favorite songs • Make up their own songs • Dramatize songs • Create new lyrics for songs • Enjoy silly songs • Use music to reflect feelings • Follow musical clues to get ready for nap or clean up after choice time	• Use music and instruments to create moods • Understand basic principles of tone, tempo, genre, and pitch • Participate in group games (like the Hokey Pokey) and circle dances • Imitate movements of people and animals on request • Select movements that fit mood • Understand relationship between movement and good health

(Colker n.d.; Pica 2012, 38-39)

Setting Up for Music and Movement

Designate a spacious area for music and movement. In the music and movement center, include the following:

- Instruments representing and used in music of the children's home cultures, like steel drums from the West Indies or rain sticks from Native American tribes.
- Homemade instruments: drums from oatmeal boxes, cymbals from metal pie plates, and maracas from shakers.
- Rhythm instruments: triangles, ankle bells, drums, rattles, shakers, tambourines, and xylophones.
- Software for listening to and composing music and learning about dance.
- A wide range of recorded music—including children's songs, music from children's cultures and home languages, classical, rock, pop, country, hip-hop, jazz, and show tunes.

- Props like streamers, scarves, ribbons, flags, costumes, low stilts, and hula hoops for moving and marching to music. These props exaggerate movements and help children stretch their creativity.
- Quiet areas and headphones for listening to music in private.

Three basic activities take place under the umbrella of music and movement: (1) singing, (2) moving to music, and (3) playing instruments.

Singing

There is a sequence in learning to sing. Children go from listening as babies, to "tagging on" as toddlers, to joining in groups and singing independently as preschoolers. Children are born aware of sounds and rhythms. Their first exposure to music as a newborn is a parent or family member talking, cooing, and singing. They turn towards the human voice and smile. A musical mobile over the changing table and a toy that makes musical sounds captivate their interest. Try placing a baby on her back and move her arms and legs to the beat of the background music.

If you or a colleague plays an instrument, play it to accompany the children's singing.

Infants. You can soothe babies by rocking and swaying them gently in your arms while singing lullabies. When you sing, you expose infants to new vocabulary, sounds and rhythms, facial expressions, and creative expression. Learn a few songs in the baby's home language to help her feel secure in the setting. You'll also find infants a receptive audience for your singing. Even if you sing off key, it is "music" to a baby's ears.

Mobile infants. As children's bodies develop, so too do their reactions to music. Introduce older babies to songs with hand gestures like "Where Is Thumbkin?" and "Cinco ratoncitos" (Five little mice). This helps mobile infants who are learning to coordinate their hands and fingers to explore their bodies through music. They may imitate your movements and will begin to sing and make sounds around 10–12 months old.

Singing the "Itsy Bitsy Spider" gives mobile infants a chance to throw themselves into action. Mobile infants will bounce up and down, clap their hands, and sway and swoon to the sounds of music. They learn to imitate what they hear and start to hum, sing, and chant.

By the age of two, most children are doing what can be termed singing. Much of their singing is spontaneous and in snippets, growing out of motor activity or language play. Between the ages of two and three, children make remarkable progress in being able to sing songs all the way through. They sing and shout words they know and make up their own silly verses to songs. They do not care whether they or you can carry a tune, stay on key, or keep time to the beat. They just want to sing with you or anyone else who wants to join in.

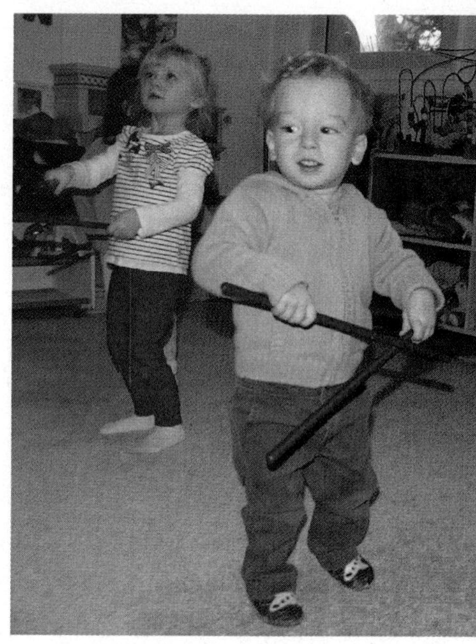

Allow children to move in ways that reflect their moods.

Preschoolers. At this age, children prefer songs with strong rhythms, repetition, and whimsy. They also conform their actions to the mood of the songs they are listening to. Lullabies set a tone for napping while a John Phillip Sousa song will get them up and grabbing an instrument to march. They learn the rhythms and patterns of language as they join in chants and hone cognitive skills when they make up lyrics or change the focus of songs. Instead of singing B-I-N-G-O, Oskar may prefer his song to spell out O-S-K-A-R. Be sure to sing songs children know from their families and cultures—in their home languages. Consult families, colleagues, and the Internet to find many examples (including audio and video) of culturally relevant songs for children.

Figure 55. Pick a Song, But Not Just Any Song

To introduce songs to toddlers and preschoolers, experts recommend the following (Brewer 2006; Schirrmacher 2011; Dodge et al. 2010):

- Select a song that children can readily remember.
- Choose a song with repetition and a predictable pattern; the younger the child, the more important this is.
- Pick a song with a chorus so the children can join in.
- Consider how the song lends itself to movement; opportunities to move have great appeal.
- Avoid songs with high notes or difficult leaps.
- Choose songs with words that the children understand. If phrases are long, consider shortening them.
- Learn the chosen song ahead of time.
- Tell the children a story about the song.
- Sing slowly and clearly when introducing the song for the first time; then repeat it.
- Invite children to sing along with you. Again. And again. And again.
- Use props like puppets and flannel boards to help children remember the song.
- Add motions to the song to aid children in remembering the lyrics.
- Record the children singing alone and in a group. Share the recordings with the children and their families.
- Try putting new lyrics to the song once the children have mastered it.
- Encourage children to compose their own songs.

Music, Movement, and Culture

When you incorporate children's cultural dances and movements, you provide them opportunities to learn more about themselves and each other. You also encourage them to express themselves in an environment in which they feel respected and valued. Ask: What dances do children do at home and in their communities? Do children enjoy practicing these dances and movements? Can these dances be incorporated in meaningful ways? As a culturally responsive early childhood educator, understand that music and movement carry various meanings among specific religious, ethnic, and cultural groups. Some religions may prohibit certain types of music, instruments, and movements. Communication with families is critical to ensure that all children know that they are respected and valued in your program.

Make singing an opportunity for both group fun and individual expression. The following are ways to make singing a regular part of the day:

- Sing songs as a part of routines and transitions (e.g., to alert children of cleanup time or to demonstrate the amount of time children need to wash their hands. [Remember in Chapter 2, you learned that children need to wash their hands for as long as it takes to sing the Happy Birthday song twice.]).
- Sing during group meetings.
- Play games that include singing in English and home languages.
- Read and sing song-based books, such as *There Was an Old Lady Who Swallowed a Fly* by Simms Taback or *De Paseo En El Autobus* by Jane Massey.
- Make up songs with children that narrate what they are doing.
- Record audio versions of songs to play for the group or for children to listen to alone.
- Invite family members to teach the children songs from their culture or in the family's home language.
- Sing from a class songbook of favorite songs; make print and audio copies for families.
- Encourage spontaneous singing.
- If you or a colleague plays an instrument, play it to accompany the children's singing.
- Let children stand up when they sing to help them "feel" the music.

Playing Instruments

Young children are fascinated by musical instruments and the sounds that they produce. Nearly every baby loves to bang on a pot and will delight in the drum-like sounds they produce. They shake their bodies, clap their hands, and stamp their feet, making music of sorts with their bodies. By the time they are toddlers (see Figure 54b), children are ready to explore instruments and see how they work. Gradually they become skilled at ringing a triangle, shaking a tambourine, and playing a xylophone. Preschoolers can bang an instrument to accompany a recording or play their own music in a marching band.

To inspire children to use instruments, provide some that can be used to keep rhythm, some that are melodic, some that represent different cultures, and some that are there just for fun:

- **Rhythm instruments** such as drums, tambourines, maracas, sticks, cymbals, triangles, sandpaper blocks, shakers
- **Melodic instruments** include xylophone, keyboard, tone bells, kazoos
- **Instruments from other cultures** like kalimba, didgeridoo, rainstick, steel drums, cajón, castanets
- **Fun instruments** such as music boxes, musical toys, and sound containers

Help children differentiate music by tone, tempo, genre, and pitch.

Prior to showing children how to use any of the instruments, you want to do these two things:

1. Provide ample time for children to explore and experiment with the instruments to see how they work. They will find out about pitch, timbre, rhythm, and melody on their own.
2. Encourage children to express rhythm through creative movement.

This approach predisposes children to using the instruments creatively, rather than by rote. Once you demonstrate to children the appropriate way to use an instrument, let them take over from there. Encourage your classroom musicians to experiment with sounds and enjoy the experience.

You can motivate children to play with musical instruments by inviting them to join you in making homemade ones:

- Rattles: place gourds in window for several weeks. Turn every few days. Seeds will fall away from inside walls.
- Didgeridoo: decorate the cardboard from a roll of giftwrap paper.
- Maracas: place pebbles in empty dishwashing detergent bottles.
- Banjo: place rubber bands across bottom of a shoebox.
- African drum: fasten circular piece of canvas over end of a terracotta planter with a rubber band.
- Castanets: place plastic milk/juice bottle lids in paper plate. Fold plate in half, with lids inside, and glue closed.
- Cymbals: assemble two like-sized pot lids.
- Water xylophone: fill identical glasses with sequential amounts of water. Clang with a metal spoon.
- Ankle and wrist bells: sew bells onto elastic band.

Encouraging Creativity through the Dramatic Arts

In Chapter 5, you read about the development of pretend play and how children learn through play. Dramatic play involves one child using his imagination to create a make-believe scenario. Sociodramatic play involves two or more children taking on roles as a family having breakfast together, astronauts on a spaceship, or shoppers picking up groceries and checking them out. Higher levels of sociodramatic play involve a group of children acting out a scenario for days and weeks at a time.

Children recreate their own experiences in dramatic play. For example, if they've been well cared for and nurtured, the doll is likely to be fed a bottle, tenderly burped, and rocked to sleep. They also use dramatic play to make sense of experiences, overcome fears, and practice for upcoming events.

As Isenberg and Jalongo explain (2010):

> Children learn about their world not only from their interactions with it, but also from the way the world interacts with them. These concrete, personal experiences provide the basis for their developing abstract thinking. Because drama is always concrete, specific, and personal, it helps children more easily understand how their physical and social worlds work and connect. In other words, dramatic play provides a wonderful vehicle for children to explore and learn about the social and physical world they live in.

Sociodramatic Play

Play fosters imagination, new ways of thinking, and problem-solving skills. Sociodramatic play, in particular, helps children understand and experiment with social roles.

Through these roles, children see things from others' perspectives, and act as adults and feel grown up. It also provides an arena for children to face their fears. For example, a child who is afraid of shots can pretend to be a doctor administering shots to others. Play also helps children develop abstract thinking skills as they use objects to represent or symbolize other things or ideas. For example, "This marker is my pretend hotdog." Play stretches children's imaginations as they pretend to act as people and animals in their world might act.

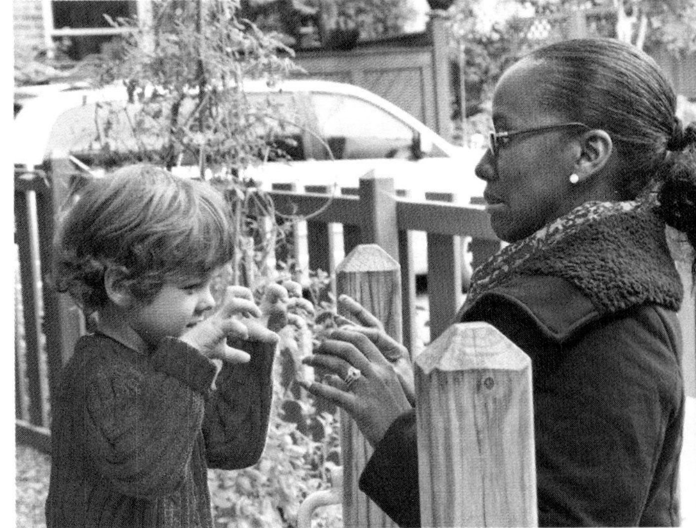

Although children are the stars of dramatic play scenarios, early educators facilitate and sometimes play along.

As infants, children begin to imitate facial expressions, an action that lays the foundation for later dramatic play. The quality of experiences for infants and toddlers will impact their creative thinking and play as they get older. Secure and happy children will begin to develop more extended and imaginative play episodes. Around eighteen months, children begin to engage in symbolic play, where a block can be used to represent a car or other object. As children grow, their pretend play experiences become more intricate. By three years old, play scenarios generally have three components: plots, roles, and props. Children make plans, assume roles, and use objects to express their feelings and ideas.

You are the children's play facilitator, ensuring that dialogue and action do not end abruptly.

Although it is the children who are the "stars" of dramatic play scenarios, early childhood educators serve as facilitators. You are the children's play coach, ensuring that dialogue and action do not end abruptly. As the facilitator, you might enter the action when children's play has lost momentum. For example, three-year-old Derek is pretending to make soup and appears to not know the next step in this scenario. Suggest that he pour some soup into two bowls so that each of you can taste it. Or you might ask open-ended questions that spark his thinking, like: "How did you decide what to make for dinner? "What did you do at work today?" "What books do you have that I might borrow?" "Can you show me how to train the dog so she doesn't bark so much?" "Can you help me plan a birthday party for my grandma?" "Whom should we invite?"

During dramatic and sociodramatic play, there are no right or wrong answers, so questions like these offer children situations in which they can be creative. Encourage children to revisit their play scenarios. This will give them an opportunity to go more in-depth in their plots and to take a fresh look at problems and possible solutions. You can read more about sociodramatic play in Chapter 9.

Figure 56. Adding the Children's Culture to Dramatic Play

Since the dramatic play center is where children recreate their home lives as well as imaginary settings, it is important that it offer materials that represent the children's families, cultures, and languages. You can readily do this by selecting props with the children's families in mind. For example:

- Rubber and plastic foods representing the children's cultures
- Food containers representing the children's cultures and community
- Clothing, hats, scarves, shoes, and accessories representing the children's backgrounds
- Dolls representing diverse ethnicities.
- Eating utensils children might use at home, including chopsticks and Asian soup spoons
- Cooking utensils used in children's homes, including a wok, bamboo skimmer, tortilla press, chapatti press, and the like.

(Schirrmacher 2011)

What if Dramatic Play and Storytelling Turn Violent?

Children's media these days are filled with superheroes who can kill and maim in ever more creative ways. Talk of guns and war fill the air waves. It's no wonder that children's dramatic and sociodramatic play reflects the violence of the real world. Young children feel powerful when they can use their superpowers to conquer enemies.

What should early educators do when faced with children taking on the roles of violent superheroes and gunmen in their play and storytelling? Banning this type of play rarely works. It resurfaces over and over. Experts like Diane Levin (2003) suggest that you turn children's imitative play into creative play: "Take time to observe the play and learn what children are working on and how. Use this information to help children move beyond narrowly scripted play that focuses on violent actions. Help children gain skills to work out the violent content they bring to their play, learn the lessons you aim to teach, and move on to new issues."

One of the most effective ways of doing this is to focus children's attention on the good things superheroes do—like save lives, promote peace, and act with kindness. Making superheroes models of prosocial behaviors (see chapter 9 for more information on prosocial behavior) rather than icons of violence turns the focus away from violence and on to goodness. It also allows children to use their imaginations and thus become more creative in the process. As stated earlier, children use play to work out emotions around experiences. Children who have witnessed violence in their home, neighborhood, in a war-torn country, or through the media may need to act out these scenes to make sense of them. Being there to support this kind of processing is an important role for the early childhood teacher. Patience and empathy will help everyone to be able to move on through their play scenarios.

Storytelling and Story Retelling

Story retelling also facilitates children's creative thinking and problem-solving skills. When children retell a story they have heard, read, or created, their understanding of the story is deepened. For example, children can retell and reenact a favorite story or book or dictate a story idea to you. In these instances, they know the gist of what they want to say, if not the exact wording, and the sequence of events.

The creativity in story retelling rests in the presentation of the story. Children's expressions, timing, enthusiasm, and interpretation reflect their creative thinking. Promote creativity during story retelling by allowing children to choose the books or stories. This builds their personal motivation and support for the story. Help children secure appropriate props and costumes, and give them time and space to plan and practice. Prepare questions in advance to focus children's attention on how their characters feel and act. Revisit the reenactment afterward and link back to the story. Instead of acting out the plot of a favorite story, some children may opt to use puppets to tell the stories. Help children build a stage, announce the story on a chalkboard, and collect tickets to the special performance.

Competency Standard III:

To support social and emotional development and to provide positive guidance

Developmental Contexts

Functional Area 8: Self

Young infants *(birth–8 months)*, during the first few weeks and months of life, young infants begin to build a sense of self-confidence and security in an environment where they can trust that an adult will lovingly care for their needs. Infants are only emerging in their ability to regulate their temperature and recognize signs of discomfort, such as hunger or feeling cold. An adult who cares for a young infant provides immense support for future abilities in self-regulation by being consistently available. The adult feeds the child when hungry, keeps the child warm and comfortable, soothes the child when distressed, and offers learning opportunities by providing interesting things to look at, taste, smell, feel, hear, and touch.

Mobile infants *(9–17 months)*, a loving provider is a resource or "home base" who is readily available and provides warm physical comfort and a safe environment to explore and master. This emotional stability is essential for the development of self-confidence as well as language, physical, cognitive, and social-emotional growth.

Toddlers' *(18–36 months)* sense of self and growing feelings of independence develop at the same time that they realize the importance of their parents and other providers. The healthy toddler's inner world is filled with conflicting feelings and ideas — independence and dependence, confidence and doubt, fear and curiosity, hostility and love, anger and tenderness, aggression and passivity. Understanding the wide range of toddlers' feelings and how they might be expressed can help support the adult's ability to provide a calm and emotionally secure environment.

Preschoolers *(3–5 years old)* experience many conflicting feelings and ideas: independence and dependence, confidence and doubt, fear and power, hostility and love, anger and tenderness, and aggression and passivity. They continue to need a reliable environment and secure relationships with adults as they deal with these feelings and learn more about themselves in an expanding world: peers, school, neighborhood, and society. They are proud of their new skills in caring for themselves, developing friendships, building and making things work, understanding and achieving. Adults can support them by respecting and recognizing the strengths and needs of each child within the cultural contexts of their home and family, and by providing experiences that help them grow as individuals.

Functional Area 9: Social:

Young infants *(birth–8 months)* enter the world with an innate capacity and need for social contact. Yet each baby is unique in styles of interacting and readiness for different kinds of interactions. Infants need both protective and engaging social interactions with a few consistent, caring adults who get to know them as individuals. When adults respond to the cues and signals of young infants, they model social interactions. It is through these early experiences that infants learn to read and respond appropriately to the cues of others.

Competency Standard III (continued)

Mobile infants *(9–17 months)* are curious about others but need assistance and supervision in interacting with other children. They continue to need one or a few consistent adults as their most important social partner(s) and as a bridge to creating additional social partners.

Toddlers *(18–36 months)* social awareness is much more complex than that of younger children. Toddlers can begin to understand that others have feelings too — sometimes similar to and sometimes different from their own. They imitate many of the social behaviors of other children and adults. As toddlers become increasingly interested in other children, adults should guide and support their interactions, recognizing that they continue to rely upon familiar adults for emotional stability.

Preschoolers *(3–5 years old)* welcome social interactions with adults and children. Their social skills develop rapidly, first through parallel play, near other playing preschoolers, and gradually through more cooperative play, with them. Adults can promote understanding and respect among preschool children by providing experiences in sharing materials, responsibilities and social problem solving. Preschoolers can begin to learn about differing individual and group needs in a positive way.

Functional Area 10: Guidance

Young infants *(birth–8 months)* begin to adapt their rhythms of eating and sleeping to the expectations of their social environment through the gentle guidance of sensitive early educators who meet their needs. Infants basic trust in adults and their environment that is established at this time directly affects the child's responsiveness to positive guidance later and promotes the development of self-regulation.

Mobile infants *(9–17 months)* want to do everything but they have little understanding about what is permissible and may not remember rules. Adults can organize the environment in ways that clearly define limits and minimize conflicts. While respecting the child's experiments, they can reinforce positive social interaction (for example, hugging) and discourage negative behaviors (for example, biting) through the use of positive encouragement and redirection.

Toddlers *(18–36 months)* move through recurring phases of extreme dependence and independence as they gain new skills and awareness. They require an understanding provider who remains calm and supportive during their struggle to become independent. Adults must be resourceful in recognizing and encouraging self-regulatory behavior while setting consistent, clear limits.

Preschoolers *(3–5 years old)* can participate in the process of setting group rules and can benefit from learning why those rules are necessary. They require an understanding adult who remains calm and supportive as they continue to become self-regulated. They will continue to "test" limits from time to time as they grow more confident and independent. Adults can support them by acknowledging their feelings and remaining consistent about expectations, routines, and limits.

Remember that these developmental stages may vary in age range based on cultural expectations and norms. Our role is to support children within the contexts of their family culture and not to make them change to fit our expectations.

CHAPTER 8:

Self

CDA® Functional Area 8: Candidate develops a warm, positive, supportive, and responsive relationship with each child, and helps each child learn about and take pride in their individual and cultural identity.

Self

Introduction

In Chapter 5, you learned about Abraham Maslow's hierarchy of needs, which includes basic or physiological needs (air, food, water, sleep, and shelter), safety and security, love and belonging, self-esteem, and self-actualization. Maslow theorized that all these needs must be met before people can reach their full potential. Early childhood educators work to meet children's needs to build a sense of self (the roles, behaviors, and attributes we associate with ourselves), and develop healthy self-esteem (pride in who we are, what we can do, and how we behave and interact with others). They do so by observing and getting to know each child individually and acknowledging, respecting, and appreciating who each child is. When you help children build their sense of self and meet their needs for self-actualization, you help them develop healthy self-esteem and empower them to take on challenges.

Children are motivated to learn when their interests, preferences, families, home language, culture, and race are reflected in their learning environments. Help children appreciate the characteristics that define them uniquely—such as their gender, temperament, strengths, and approaches to learning—and support them in valuing who they are as members of families, cultural groups, communities, and society as a whole.

In this chapter, we will explore the following ways in which you can help children develop a strong sense of self:

- **Understanding the Emotional Development of Infants, Toddlers, and Preschoolers**
- **Promoting Children's Sense of Self**
- **Helping Children Develop Self-Esteem**
- **Guiding Children in Expressing Their Feelings**
- **Helping Each Child Flourish**

Understanding the Emotional Development of Infants, Toddlers, and Preschoolers

Emotional development includes children's ability to identify, express, and manage feelings about themselves, other people, and their experiences at home and in other settings in which they play and learn (Epstein 2009). It includes the emotions a child experiences and how they communicate them, their understanding of emotions and where they come from, recognizing the emotions of other people, and eventually, regulating or managing their own emotions.

Emotional development is a difficult concept to isolate. Like all developmental domains in the early years, children's emotional development grows in conjunction with other kinds of development, most notably social development. Often these two domains are joined and called social-emotional development. Also included in emotional development are gaining a sense of self—"What makes me a unique individual?" and healthy self-esteem—"I am proud of who I am, what I can do, and how I behave and interact with others." In addition, emotional development includes self-regulation skills. These skills are also connected to other domains, including cognitive development. As noted by Ida Rose Florez (2011), "Self-regulation is clearly not an isolated skill. Children must translate what they experience into information they can use to regulate thoughts, emotions, and behaviors."

In this chapter, we focus on how children develop emotional skills and how educators can support this development. Many educators agree that emotional development is a critical part of a child's overall development. Children use these skills now and in the future. With well-developed emotional skills young children can:

- Develop social skills needed to play and learn with others.
- Feel and display empathy towards other children and adults.
- Resolve conflicts using problem solving and language skills rather than through physical aggression.
- Regulate and recognize their own emotions which, in turn, builds a sense of self and healthy self-esteem.
- Focus on learning and achieve success when they move on to kindergarten and school.

Children who lack emotional skills are at risk for peer rejection, unhealthy attachments, mental health issues, and even criminal behaviors. Clearly emotional development should be an important focus in early childhood settings (PAL n.d.).

How children express their emotions is influenced by individual experiences at home and in the program, and in particular, by cultural practices and expectations. For example, in one culture, children may be encouraged to express and share their feelings, ideas, and accomplishments. In another culture, however, children receive the message that it is best to not talk about yourself until an adult asks you to make a contribution to the conversation. Educators can tailor their practice to respect and accommodate each child's cultural norms.

Infants

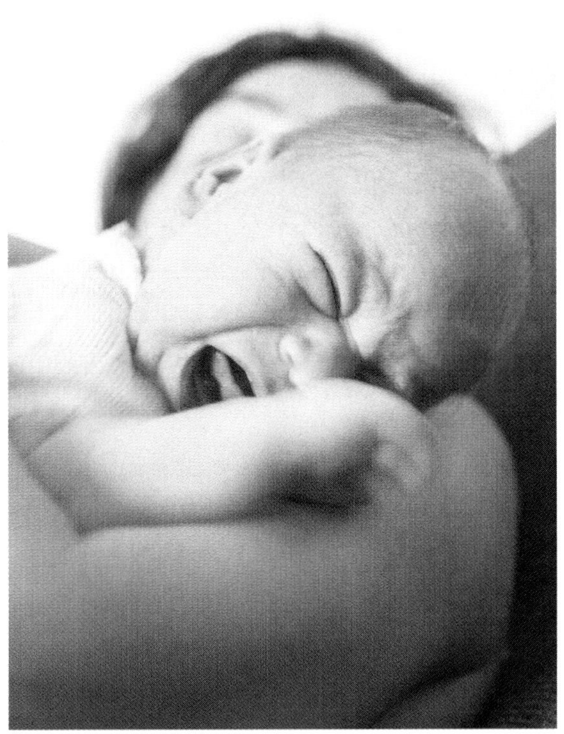

Infants' use of different kinds of crying to communicate different needs.

Often, the first sign that a young infant feels an emotion is a smile. At first, the smile may be reflexive, but by about six months, infants smile and coo to communicate that they feel happy and content. Crying is another tool for expressing emotions. Frequently, infants cry to show their displeasure due to physical discomforts such as hunger. Many parents and early childhood educators come to recognize infants' use of different kinds of crying to communicate different needs—"I need a new diaper, I am lonely, I am very tired." From about three or four months of age, infants start to laugh. What strikes them as amusing can vary greatly among children and may not be something an adult would find funny at all. Nevertheless, when adults and infants interact and play games together, laughter is likely to ensue. Infants also learn to express negative emotions, such as fear and anger. A fearful infant might cry or cling to an adult. An angry infant, perhaps because he does not want to go to sleep or stop playing so he can have his diaper changed, might try to wiggle out of an adult's arms. How infants express their feelings is related to temperament, as discussed later in this chapter. Some babies tend to be easy going while others have strong reactions to experiences.

Young as they are, infants are beginning to build the self-regulation skills that will support them through childhood and beyond. Young infants look to caring adults to help them calm their strong feelings. As they grow into mobile infants, babies begin to adopt their own strategies for coping with emotions. For example, an infant might still look for a caring adult to help reach a toy, but when feeling sleepy, the same infant might get her blankie from her cubby to hold for a while.

Young infants learn about themselves by exploring all the parts of their bodies and then figuring out what they can do with their hands and feet, and how they can move their bodies in place and then from one place to the next. Understanding that they are separate from others is an important milestone in building a sense of self. They learn their names and respond when they hear them used. Mobile infants begin to explore other children—they use their senses—typically touch and taste—to do this, just as they use them to explore other parts of their environment.

Toddlers

In the toddler years, children expand their sense of self. They know and can repeat their names and those of their friends. When asked they can tell you who is in their family, how old they are, what they like to do, and what they are learning. Many toddlers describe themselves using characteristics, such as hair color, gender, race, and size, and compare themselves to others in the group.

Toddlers' emotions are both strong and contradictory. "I want to do it myself." And "I want you to be available when I need you." "No," becomes a frequent and powerful word for toddlers. They feel a sense of control by being able to express themselves with this word, which usually garners lots of attention. It is one of the ways they build a sense of self—"I am an individual who can have his own views." Towards the end of the toddler years, a sense of self also allows for more complex emotions, such as feeling shy or guilty.

Many toddlers can "read" the expressions on adult faces—for example, Ursula sees her mother's frown when she refuses to put her boots on, and Nico notes his educator's raised eyebrows when he pushes Jay out of his way. During this period, children begin to understand that they are separate from other people—an important part of being ready to have empathy for others.

Toddlers are learning the words that name the emotions they feel. More verbal children may say, "I am angry," or "I feel happy." Less verbal children are more likely to continue to use crying or other gestures to express themselves.

Towards the end of the toddler years, many children can express their emotions through words, gestures, and facial expressions, in most situations. They do not do so all of the time. They recognize their own feelings, and those of others, and show a level of concern when others are hurt or upset. Many times toddlers will try to "make things better."

Preschoolers

In the preschool years, children experience a wide range of emotions—both positive and negative—related to their current situations and experiences. As they move through this age period, they will gradually learn to recognize, name, and express their own feelings and those of others, experience empathy more frequently and in more situations, and come to understand who they are and how they are similar to and different from their peers.

Three-year-olds tend to have a rich fantasy life. They act out different roles, assign emotions to dolls and toys, and may stay in the pretend role during routines at home and in the program. They enjoy the sense of control that comes from controlling their fantasies—where their imaginations take them. Some three-year-olds have one or more imaginary friends who are part of their lives for a day or two or for a longer period of time.

Three-year-olds are still learning how to separate thoughts from actions, so self-regulation is a challenge. Polly might think, "I want to ride the blue trike," then grab it from Leon even though he already has his hands on it. Young preschoolers do not hold back. If they feel happy, they express it. If they want something, they take it.

Some three-year-olds lose control—they may have tantrums or laugh uncontrollably. Fears are common, and typically irrational, such as asking to have a light on at night. They can handle minor disappointments and frustrations, but often seek adult help to manage intense emotions. Three-year-olds notice and identify with other children's distress. When a playmate falls and cuts her knee, a child will hurry to get the teacher to help. At this age, children are aware of their own physical and behavioral characteristics. They feel good about their accomplishments, and will talk about them when asked. They identify as a member of a family, racial or ethnic group, and feel connected to others in the community.

By age four, many children are developing a sense of humor. They tell the same jokes again and again, finding each retelling as hilarious as it was the first time. They tend to be less fearful, understanding now that dreams are not real. They become more aware of individual characteristics and compare themselves to others. They now are clear that other people have feelings too and are more often empathetic than in the past. They have begun to pick up the subtle expressions of preference and bias in the books, media, and people around them

Although adults are important sources of comfort, four-year-olds pay attention to and apply the emotion management strategies suggested by adults. They might squeeze a foam ball, take deep breaths, or sit in the corner on one of the bean bag chairs for a while. They now notice and experience more subtle or complex emotions, such as feeling embarrassed or worried.

Four-year-olds are gaining both a sense of self and a healthy self-concept. They can describe themselves in greater detail and include interests and skills in addition to physical characteristics. They have internalized the spoken and unspoken norms of the larger society and their immediate surroundings. They show a sense of belonging to the group, their family, and their communities. During group times or in smaller gatherings they share their ideas and opinions, often telling others about their accomplishments.

By the time they turn five years old and are nearing the end of their time in a preschool setting, children have made great strides in being able to control impulses. The result is that they can feel something without acting on it. Most five-year-olds can use words to express themselves and delay gratification while waiting for a turn or for lunch to arrive. They are unlikely to use aggression to get what they want or express anger or hurt feelings.

Five-year-olds can identify and describe their unique characteristics. Included are interests, talents, and skills along with culture, home language, family, and race. They may say positive things about themselves such as "I am a good friend" or "I worked hard on my picture."

See Figure 57a-b for a summary of young children's emotional development.

Self

Figure 57a. Emotional Skills for Young Children

Age	Developing Emotional Skills
Young Infants (birth–8 months)	• Express feelings through facial expressions, body movements, gestures, gurgling, and cooing. • Attend with interest to others' emotions. • Cry when a child in close proximity cries. • Laugh and make happy sounds. • Quiet themselves/stop crying when rocked/held. • Have specific attachment to primary caregivers.
Mobile Infants (9–17 months)	• Use attachments to family members and educators as secure base to explore. • Show stranger anxiety. • Have separation anxiety. • Use "my" and "me" with pride. • Show beginning signs of self-consciousness. • Check adult's facial expressions for encouragement or to stop behavior. • Respond to others' emotions by expressing a similar emotion. • Experience and express wide range of emotions, including fear and sadness. • Express concern when child in close proximity cries. • Begin to show negative emotions. • Seek comfort from trusted adult when distressed. • Self-calm by sucking thumb. • Act on impulse.
Toddlers (18–36 months)	• Show strong sense of self; resist help. • Have tantrums triggered by frustration. • Are shy with strangers, but less fearful. • With adult help, begin to use strategies to control emotional expression. • Show emotions like guilt, embarrassment, and pride. • Recognize feelings when labeled by adults. • Show empathy towards those who are hurt or sad. • Find regulation of emotions difficult. • Have extreme emotional shifts. • May be possessive and clingy. • Develop fears; afraid of noises.
Young Preschoolers (3–4 years old)	• Recognize feelings and emotions of others. • Express a sense of individuality and personal preferences. • Label feelings based on facial expressions and tone of voice. • Describe feelings of characters in books, with adult support. • Have developing ability to cope with stress. • Comfort others in distress. • Try to help others with simple tasks. • Feel responsible for everything that happens. • Use various strategies to calm selves. • Respond positively to emotional support from others.

Figure 57b. Emotional Skills for Young Children

Age	Developing Emotional Skills
Older Preschoolers (4–5 years old)	• View adults as trusted role models. • Express their sense of self in terms of abilities and preferences. • Notice subtle/complex emotions in self and others. • Are aware that not everyone views the same situation identically. • Gain understanding of the causes of feelings. • Recognize feelings of characters in books/photographs. • Able to use words to describe own feelings and feelings of others. • Are learning coping strategies to manage feelings. • Recreate feelings through dramatic play; use pretend play to gain control of fears. • Exhibit definite personality. • Tend to feel secure.

(Adapted from PBS Parents n.d.; Administration for Children and Families 2015)

Promoting Children's Sense of Self

Experiences and relationships within our families, cultures, communities, schools, and other settings shape our identities over time. During early childhood, children develop a self-concept, or sense of self as they recognize and understand who they are—what makes them similar to and different from other people. They notice the characteristics—attributes, abilities, attitudes, and values that define them as unique individuals.

Sense of self, or identity, includes the roles, behaviors, and attributes we associate with ourselves—including descriptions, such as "I'm strong," "I'm tall," or "I am the oldest child in my family." Development of a sense of self begins in infancy. A child's sense of self is about who he is, not what he can do.

Positive experiences and strong, reciprocal relationships with loved ones help children understand that they are important, valued, and respected. From birth, children develop a sense of belonging when they feel accepted, develop secure attachments, and trust those who care for them. When children feel safe, secure, and supported, they develop the confidence to explore, take risks, and solve problems. The relationships among you, the children, and their families play a key role in building children's identities.

Truly knowing and understanding the children in your setting requires observation, time, and commitment. This knowledge allows you to customize the environment, materials, curriculum, and your interactions with individuals and groups to best serve each child.

The following are ways you can bolster children's developing self-concept and strengthen your relationships with each child:

- Respond to children's needs promptly and consistently. Infants develop a sense of trust when they know that their needs will be met. This trust leads to feeling safe enough to explore and learn in the early years and beyond. Toddlers and preschoolers can wait longer for needs to be met, but they too need consistency and to know that you are there to provide the limits that keep them safe.
- Include families in the setting. Post photos of children and their families in several places so children can "visit" them during the day. Create "All About Me" books that feature photos of children's families, pets, and friends and include documentation of the work and learning that they select. Digitize the books if possible to make it easy to update and expand them over time.
- Incorporate children's home languages and cultures. Include oral and written language, and books, music, recipes, and artifacts representing children's cultures.
- Create a home-like setting. Allow children to bring their favorite items from home—including blankets, stuffed animals, and books. Offer dress-up clothes and props that will be familiar to children from their own homes.
- Post documentation of children's learning. Include artwork and photographs of their experiences and accomplishments within your setting. Talk with children about their experiences so they can revisit what they did and learned.
- Encourage children to practice and master age-appropriate skills. These might include self-help skills, such as grooming, feeding, and dressing, social skills needed to play and cooperate with others, literacy, math, and other pre-academic skills.
- Provide many opportunities to make choices and express preferences. Infants can reach for one rattle or another, toddlers can choose a book to read, preschoolers can determine which pieces of art, writing samples, and photos they would like to take home, display in the setting, or place in their portfolios or "All About Me" books.
- Give each child one-on-one positive attention every day. Hold and talk with infants about what they are doing and what you are doing. Nurture and respond to each child during daily routines, transitions, activities. Observe and join in their play as appropriate.
- Help children develop the ability to express emotions. Encouraging them to clap hands, reach, smile, wave, point, and talk using gurgles, sounds, artwork, writing, and speech.
- Help children distinguish themselves from others. Use saying the infants' names and the names of family members when viewing and pointing to photographs.
- Acknowledge and name visible physical disabilities and racial differences between individuals. Invite and normalize conversation about race and ethnicity so that young children become comfortable asking questions and clarifying their interpretations about social hierarchies.

Which Impacts Children's Development More: Nature or Nurture?

Scholars have debated for centuries the impact of genetics versus environmental influences on human development. Both nature (our genetic or inherited make-up) and nurture (the influence of the physical and social environment) impact our physical and social traits. For example, consider a malnourished child whose growth is stunted due to lack of food or inadequate diet. Then consider a child who is surrounded by supportive and nurturing family members. How are the children's development and sense of self impacted in each situation?

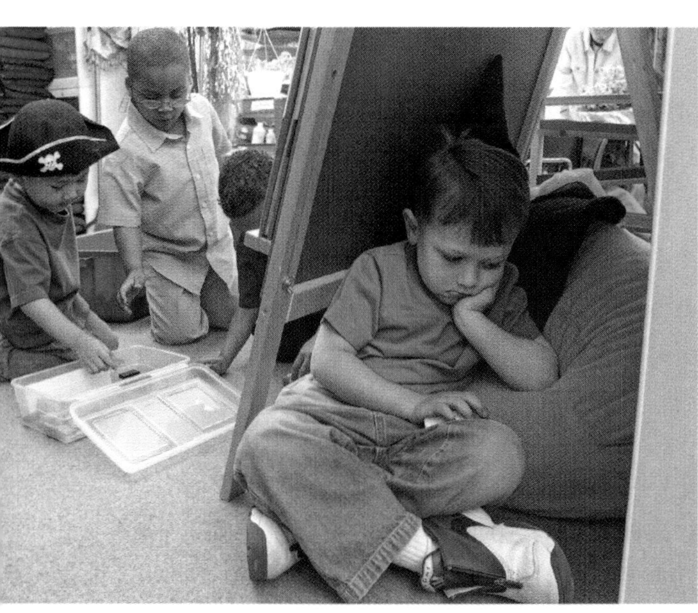

While temperament does not define or predict behavior clearly, it can help you understand how children react and relate to the world around them.

When given opportunities, young children can be active participants and decision makers in your setting. Respect and work with each child's unique skills, qualities, and abilities. Understanding children's developmental milestones, as described in the previous section, will help you select materials, employ teaching strategies, and interact in ways that meet children's needs, reflect their interests, and ensure their progress, growth, and learning. It is also important to understand and see the impact of each child's gender, temperament, approaches to learning, strengths and challenges, and cultural and racial identity. Each of these factors contributes to the development of the whole child. These topics are discussed below.

Gender

At around age two, children begin to form their own ideas concerning gender. By the time they are three years old, most children know whether they are boys or girls and will begin to form opinions about gender roles (Martin and Ruble 2004). Just as they are learning about differences between colors and shapes at this age, children are also beginning to categorize people. Many three- and four-year-olds discuss physical differences between themselves and others, specifically between boys and girls.

Children learn about gender by observing others' behavior, absorbing societal norms, and processing media and environmental messages. When using shared bathrooms (as most toddlers and preschoolers do), children collect data on what makes a girl different from a boy physically. However, for young children, gender is more about behavior than anatomy (Derman-Sparks and Edwards 2010).

If you send children the message that they are free to try out different roles, they will feel comfortable doing so. This includes having a welcoming attitude about girls doing woodworking or playing with blocks and boys tending to dolls or playing a mom or a baby in the housekeeping area. Early childhood educators can help children develop a positive sense of gender by allowing them to experiment with gender roles through play.

Temperament

Temperament describes the way a person approaches and reacts to the world. It influences our behavior and the way we interact with others. It is fixed at birth and driven by both nature (genetic or inherited make-up) and nurture (the influence of the physical and social environment). While temperament does not define or predict behavior clearly, it can help you understand how children react and relate to the world around them.

To define types of temperament, researchers looked at a child's activity level, adaptability to routines, responses to new situations, intensity of reactions, sensitivity to the environment, adaptability to change, and distractibility and persistence when doing an activity. They defined the following three types of temperament—each of which is equally acceptable.

> **Easy or flexible** children tend to be happy, regular in sleeping and eating habits, adaptable, calm, and not easily upset.
>
> **Active or feisty** children may be fussy, have irregular feeding and sleeping patterns, be fearful of new people and situations, get easily upset by noise and stimulation, and have intense reactions.
>
> **Slow-to-warm or cautious** children tend to be less active or fussy, and may withdraw or react negatively to new situations. But, over time, they may become more positive with repeated exposure to a new person, object, or situation (Allard and Hunter 2010).

Early childhood educators and families need to accept a child's temperament, while gently encouraging the child to "step out of his comfort zone." Although temperament is fixed, an individual's behavior need not be controlled by temperament. A child or adult who is cautious, as described below, can learn to be open to meeting new people or trying out new situations.

It's also important for educators and families to view all temperaments as equally worthy and appropriate. The child who is typically calm and easygoing is not "better" than the child who is easily upset by loud noises. Both children were born this way and both children need support to develop emotionally and in other domains.

Being aware of a child's temperament can increase your understanding of her unique characteristics and how she is likely to react to the people and events in her life. It is not helpful, however, to use it as a label or as a way to definitively predict future behavior. Instead, this information can help early childhood educators provide individualized, supportive interactions. For example, if you know that Ricardo is easily distracted by noise and activity, provide a nook or corner where he can read or work alone. Similarly, if Elizabeth is cautious about entering groups, teach her what she can say to make joining others at play easier: "Can I build with you?" or "This is my favorite puzzle. Would you like to do it with me?" Model how to enter a social situation, such as during dramatic play: "Elizabeth and I would like to join you for tea today. What are you serving?"

These suggestions, adapted from the Center on the Social and Emotional Foundations for Early Learning (CSEFEL) (Allard and Hunter 2010), can help you individualize support based on types of temperament.

For a child with an easy or flexible temperament:

- Check in regularly and pose questions focused on the child's feelings. These children are less likely to seek attention or express needs or distress.
- Help the child notice and understand their emotions, feelings, and reactions. You can help by recognizing the child's feelings and letting them know that it's okay to have such feelings.
- Let the child know they should feel free to ask for help and to tell others how they feel. Give the child the words they need to express themselves to others.

For a child with an active or feisty temperament:

- Expect that you will need to be extra flexible and patient when interacting with this child.
- Anticipate that they will have strong emotions and strong responses.
- Offer choices and opportunities for active, gross motor play so the child can expend energy.
- Provide a peaceful setting for these children to calm themselves and prepare for naptime.
- Give individual reminders before transitions by getting down to the child's level. Ask the child to repeat what you said to make sure he understands what will happen next.
- Label a child's strong emotions and describe what the child seems to be feeling. "You are very angry. You wanted to play with the fire truck." Stay calm and reassuring. Once the child is calm, discuss how they can learn to recognize their emotions on their own.

For a child with a slow to warm or cautious temperament:

- Prepare the child for changes in the setting or in the people who spend time there. Talk about this well before the change will take place and repeat the discussion often. If possible, show the child a photograph of the new person.

Self

- Ensure predictability in routines, schedules, environments, and activities, to the extent this is possible in your setting.
- Anticipate the times of the day and situations in which the child will need extra support—and provide it. Scaffold the support provided, so the child can begin to see that they are increasingly independent. "I'm standing right next to the ladder. If you need me to hold your hand you can just ask me. I know you will make it to the top when you are ready."

Approaches to Learning

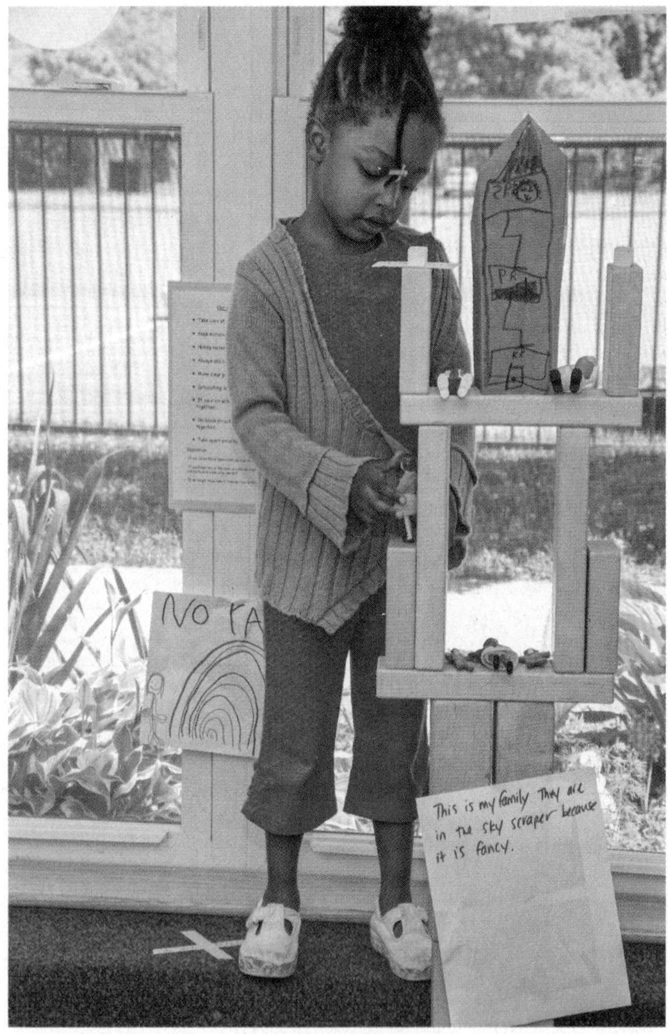

Give children time to become fully engaged in an activity.

Beginning at birth, young infants are able to form relationships with adults, develop trust, and explore the world. With a developmentally appropriate learning environment and nurturing responsive adults, young children can explore and learn. As they gain knowledge and skills across the physical, cognitive, language, and social and emotional domains, children also develop approaches to learning, or specific skills that help direct their learning. There are specific characteristics that determine a child's approaches to learning (Hyson 2008):

- **Intrinsic motivation to learn.** Markus, age four, chooses to research meerkats, not because he has to, but because he wants to learn more about this special interest.
- **Interest and joy in learning.** Toddler Luci squeals with delight when she realizes that she is making marks on paper with her crayon.
- **Engagement.** Six-month-old Gareth, in his FCC educator's arms, stares for long periods of time at the birds at the feeder outside the window.
- **Persistence.** Dina, age three, keeps trying to get her shoes on until she succeeds.
- **Planning.** Preschoolers Justine and Yancey decide to apply their knowledge of the engineering process to design and redesign a house for the pigs that the big bad wolf cannot blow down.

- **Ability to focus and control attention.** Toddler Portia, a slow and determined eater, chooses to remain at the table and finish her macaroni, even though the rest of the children have cleared their dishes and gone off to play.
- **Flexible problem solving.** Two-year-old Graham tries several different ways to get the train up the hill and through the tunnel to the other side of the track.
- **Inventiveness.** A group of preschoolers turn an empty box into a pizza oven and setup a pizza parlor in the dramatic play area.
- **Tolerance for frustration.** Four-year-old Margot stays calm when she has difficulty turning a corner on her tricycle.

Children's approaches to learning are closely linked to school readiness. Children who can plan, focus, and remain persistent, curious, and engaged tend to be more successful in school and are more likely to one day graduate from college. Each child's approaches to learning are different. For example, some children are problem solvers and others are naturally persistent. Evidence that boys and girls differ in their approaches to learning also exists. Early educators can best support children's approaches to learning through effective environments and specific teaching practices. Marilou Hyson suggests the following strategies to arrange an effective setting.

Create an effective environment

- Arrange the setting so it:
  - o Welcomes children and families
  - o Gives clear cues about what to do in each area of the setting
  - o Provide spaces for individual pursuits, lively interactions, and physical activity.
  - o Allows children to choose materials, activities, and playmates, thus supporting self-regulation.
- Establish clear, predictable routines and a flexible schedule that provides enough time for children to get fully engaged in activities
- Organize children in small groups to allow for individualized teaching, interactions, and discussions

Use intentional teaching practices

- Model positive approaches to learning
  - o During group meeting times: "My story hat keeps falling off. I think I will add some ribbons so I can tie it on." (Inventiveness, tolerance for frustration)
  - o In one on one or small group interactions: "I want to learn about meerkats, too. Let's watch this YouTube video together." (Engagement)

- Emphasize learning goals and mastery
    - o Encourage children's curiosity and genuine interest in doing an activity
    - o Provide opportunities to learn specific skills such as using a spoon or cutting with scissors
- Respond to children's ideas and actions
    - o Elaborate and join in with children's play and explorations. "You rolled the ball back to me. Let's roll it to Edward now. He can play too."
    - o Scaffold by providing assistance for a while, then withdrawing the help to allow the child to progress on her own. "It is safer to saw the piece of wood when it is in the vise. I can tell you how to use the vise. Turn this handle to loosen the 'jaws' of the vise. Then put the wood in and turn the handle the other way to tighten it. Now it is secure and you can saw the wood. Next time you can do it and I'll watch."
- Offer meaningful, challenging choices
    - o Plan alternative self-expression opportunities. "How do you feel when you hear this music? Do you want to dance or make a painting or invent a story?"
    - o Encourage children to plan how they will use their time. For example, while transitioning to outdoor play you might say to toddlers, "Think about what you want to do when we get outdoors. Will you ride trikes, pull a wagon, play in the sandbox, or something else? Kim, what are you going to do?"

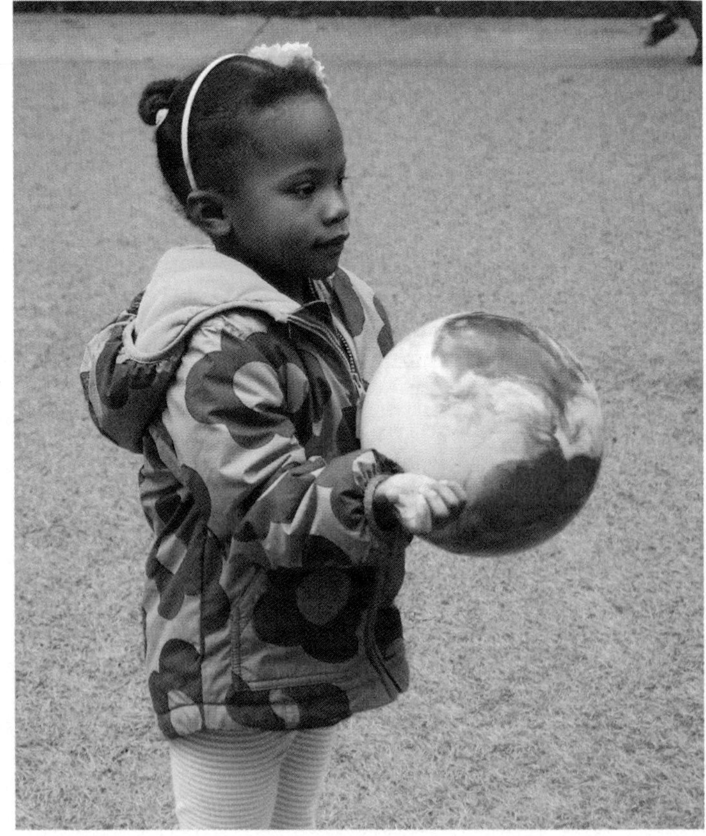

Focus on children's efforts, not their capabilities.

Strengths and Challenges

Every child in your setting will excel at some skills and struggle to master others. For example, Amanda may be able to sing beautifully, but she has great difficulty tossing the beanbags in the laundry basket. Understanding children's strengths and challenges helps you customize activities to work on specific skills, encourage children to learn, and promote their success.

Howard Gardner's theory of multiple intelligences, which you learned about in Chapter 5, details nine ways in which children's abilities are represented by unique talents and personality traits. Children will typically excel sharply in one or two areas that may represent how they learn best. To maintain these children's engagement, challenge them in the areas in which they excel and the areas in which they struggle. The skills, knowledge, and abilities of some children in your setting may be stronger or weaker than what is expected for the age group. In both scenarios, intentionally plan meaningful activities and opportunities that will challenge children and build on their specific strengths.

In some instances, children will benefit from additional screening and support from specialists. Approximately 8% of all children three to five years old receive federal special education services free of charge through the public school system under the Individuals with Disabilities Education Act (IDEA) of 2004 (Office of Special Education Programs [OSEP] 2008). The same law provides early intervention services for infants and toddlers (Part C of IDEA), preschoolers (Section 619 of Part B of IDEA), and school-age children in grades K–12 (Part B of IDEA).

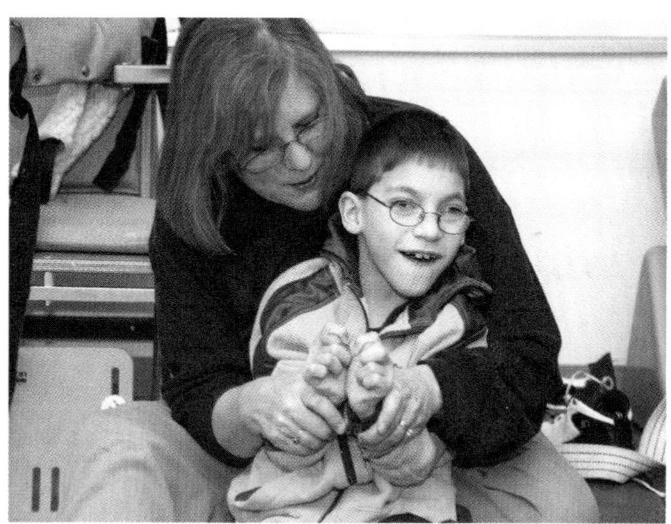

Understanding children's strengths and challenges helps you customize activities.

From birth to age three, children are eligible for free assessment and evaluation and are provided an Individualized Family Service Plan (IFSP) through an early intervention program. This plan is developed with the focus on families as the greatest resource for infants and toddlers.

All preschoolers who are eligible for special education services are provided an Individualized Education Program (IEP). (Many people and even official documents refer to an IEP as an *Individualized Education Plan*. Even though the document is a plan, the official term is *program* [Hayslip, 2012].) The IEP, which is developed by educational staff in concert with parents, specifies the goals for each child and the services that will be provided. These services typically include speech, occupational, and physical therapy. Staff, with the help of special educators and related service professionals, implement the IEP.

When early educators are aware of each child's strengths, it is often possible to harness the strengths to support the challenges.

Beyond more tangible strengths and challenges, early educators can look for attributes and characteristics that seem to support how children fare in any learning environment. As stated above in Howard Gardner's theory of multiple intelligences, children have individual abilities, desires and talents that teachers must consider when planning lessons and setting up a classroom or other learning space. Along with these preferences, seven skills that can be observed or enhanced are precursors or strong indicators that children will be successful, according to Rebecca Parlakian, Senior Director of Programs at ZERO TO THREE. In the publication, *Before the ABCs: Promoting School Readiness in Infants and Toddlers*, Parlakian identifies the following:

- Confidence—a sense of control and mastery of one's body, behavior and world

  When children feel confident about themselves and their environment, they can achieve much and will readily seek out and engage in new endeavors and tasks.

- Curiosity—the sense that finding out about things is positive and leads to pleasure

  The brain (especially the part of the frontal lobe that supports executive functions) responds best to positive stimuli. Curiosity is a natural and initial part of a baby's and young child's developmental trajectory. If curiosity is encouraged and permitted to "mature," the child can embrace newly formed ideas and the means to create more linkages and unique options in the learning environment.

- Intentionality—the determination to act with persistence, an internal drive or emotion expressed outwardly through an action or communication

  Giving children the time, space, opportunity, materials and encouragement to continue and complete a task or endeavor supports becoming persistent. If children feel supported and that their endeavors have meaning, they will continue to develop the intrinsic motivation to complete what they have begun. However, if arbitrary interruptions and limited time or opportunity are a regular feature of a program (whether intentional or not), children will not understand why to continue nor desire to remain focused on what they have started.

- Self-control—ability to modulate and control one's own actions

  As children begin to develop their executive functions, self-control—one of those functions— will begin to be observed as well as practiced. However, it is only through much trial and error, engagement and positive experiences that self-control is recognized and becomes part of the child's person.

- Relatedness—ability to engage with others based on the sense of understanding and being understood by others

In order to maintain and build upon natural inclinations for empathy (understanding the "other"), children must experience ongoing relationship building, interactions, and modeling.

- Capacity to communicate—desire and ability to exchange ideas, feelings, and concepts with others—verbally or otherwise

  Communication is more than just a verbal exchange. Identifying, reading/recognizing, and responding to children's cues and clues promotes greater understanding and leads to a more meaningful experience. Children will increase their learning and more effectively and efficiently respond to their world when they feel in touch with and connect to others.

- Cooperativeness—ability to balance one's own needs with those of others in a group activity

  Accepting the perspective of another person, aiding and assisting someone else, understanding that there is the possibility of more than just one response, and working together to achieve a mutually agreed upon goal require many interactions where needs are met and there is ongoing expansion of ideas. Learning to cooperate is not a singularly achievable act but related to numerous and varied experiences. In turn, children must have opportunities for trial and error—all while being coached to remain vigilant and not give up. The notion of synergy—the whole is greater than the sum of its parts—becomes a foundational principle.

Cultural and Racial Identity

As expressed by authors and anti-bias educators Derman-Sparks, LeeKeenan, and Nimmo, young children's "diverse ethnicities, cultures, religions, languages, and family structures bring both vibrancy and complexities to our communities," Early childhood programs are becoming more and more diverse, with every classroom including children who have many different cultural and ethnic identities. It is an early educator's job to ensure that their setting welcomes all children and families so they will feel comfortable and in the children's case, ready to learn.

Culture

In Chapter 3, you learned that culture refers to the way we eat, sleep, talk, pray, play, and value things and concepts (Derman-Sparks and Edwards 2010). These rules, passed down from generation to generation, describe beliefs, values, and practices.

Culture includes outward symbols, like the way we dress or eat or the languages we speak, and a deep behavioral structure. Cultural rules dictate how we show respect; what constitutes spirituality; our concepts of time and personal space; our values and goals of education; and, in essence, the kinds of people we want our children to become.

Early childhood educators can help children develop positive and accurate identities through showing that their families' home language, cultural beliefs and practices, and racial background are welcomed and a natural part of the setting. Here are some ways early educators can help children "see" themselves in the program.

- Pronounce correctly children's names and the names of their family members. If you are not sure of the pronunciation, ask a colleague to confirm or ask the family member, "Am I pronouncing that correctly?" Most people would rather that you ask them than listen to your mispronunciation over and over again. Keep in mind there are no un-pronounceable names although some take a little more effort to pronounce correctly. Always make the extra effort.
- Represent a wide range of the children's home languages and cultures. Include books, signs and labels, toys, music, foods, decorations, dramatic play dress-ups and props, recipes, and communications that reflect all of the children's languages and cultures, so children are exposed to cultures whether they see them in their classmates or not.

Determine which early childhood practices may conflict with families' cultural beliefs and resolve those differences.

- Learn the "rules, traditions, and expectations" of all the families in the setting. Use this information to develop meaningful relationships and support each culture within the learning environment (Derman-Sparks and Edwards 2010).
- Determine whether there are any developmentally appropriate practices that conflict with families' cultural beliefs. Meet with the family to discuss and resolve those differences. While you cannot compromise on anything that will negatively impact children's health and safety, it is important to show respect and consideration for practices that a given culture might value like the following:

- o Modeling tasks rather than allowing children to do things independently.
- o Valuing interdependence and finding it impolite to acknowledge one child rather than the group.
- o Expecting that children share rather than having them take turns.
- o Deeming eye contact between children and adults while speaking as disrespectful.
- o Viewing boys serving their own meals or girls playing with trucks as disrespectful or inappropriate.
- o Avoiding messy activities so clothing will remain clean.
- o Celebrating or not celebrating certain holidays or birthdays.
- o Speaking simultaneously rather than "turn taking" in typical Western speech patterns.

Should any of these or other culture-based challenges arise, work together with the children's families to devise a plan that will respect individual cultural values and blend them with your setting's best practices. Remain vigilant about questioning where your own priorities and values come from. Ask why it "must" be so before insisting that a child or family conform to your way of doing things. Frequently, if we look beyond the way things have always been done, we find opportunities to be more flexible and accommodating—thereby modeling the empathy, problem solving, and adaptability we want young children to learn.

Race

Though all young children do not understand the concept of ethnicity and racial groups, they notice differences among people. For example, one child may touch another child's hair, because it appears different from their own due to the color or texture. Some children may understand that their skin is a certain color but may not know they belong to a collective racial group. Others may be keenly aware of their racial or ethnic makeup and what it means to others in the world. Even when using formal terms that refer to skin color, children understand the meanings of these words very differently, depending on their own experiences and family culture.

Studies show that toddlers as young as two years old use racial categories to predict people's behaviors. Three- to five-year-olds not only categorize people by race, they express bias based on race (Aboud 2008; Hirschfeld 2008; Katz 2003; Patterson and Bigler 2006).

Although children often attach meaning and positive or negative value to race without adults directly telling them to do so, it is important to note that "the biases children exhibit are not random." In fact, they often "reflect both subtle and not so subtle messages about the relative desirability of belonging to one social group as opposed to another" (Katz and Kofkin 1997). In other words, children notice the ways in which whiteness is normalized and privileged in

American society. This is a prime reason why all children need to see themselves and their ethnicity represented in your learning environment. They also need to see other races and ethnicities, even if those groups are not in your program. All children need to see and learn about race and ethnicity and to be able to identify their own.

It is also important to note that racial identity can include multiple races and cultures. A biracial child might have a Latina mother and an African American father while a multiracial child might have an Afro-Cuban father and a French-Arab mother. Children who are biracial and multiracial need to see all of their races and cultures represented in the images, languages, books, and activities in their learning environment. It is equally important that children who are white and whose family members are predominately white, also see a wide range of races and cultures represented in their learning environments.

Children of color receive conflicting messages from society, which impacts the development of positive racial identities. A lack of exposure to positive images and messages about people of color will lead young children to conclude that it is better to be one kind of person or one race than another. Your goal as an early educator is to help children learn about people of different races, cultures, and ethnicities. If children are not supported in positive identity formation, they can easily incorporate racist or stereotypical messages unconsciously into their view of themselves and others.

Children who learn from the world that they are feared or looked down upon because of racism, xenophobia, and other biases learn to feel shame about who they are. On the other hand, children who learn that they are better, or to be looked up to because they are white, are also receiving inaccurate and disturbing messages. These, often subtle, messages influence the positive or negative values they attach to race. As an early educator, ensure that the learning environment shows evidence of diversity with which young children can easily associate. Ask: Does each child in your class identify with the learning environment? Do the children see themselves and their families represented in valuable ways throughout the setting and throughout the day? Do you have strategies for speaking with children about race in order to normalize discussion? Do you have "ready responses" for children who may make comments that are inappropriate? Create a learning environment that represents all the children fairly and with positive value in your setting.

Equity

As we look at the varied components and pieces related to the sense of self, it is imperative that we also consider how equitable the learning options and opportunities are for children in various settings. Equity incorporates many aspects of good practice along with a focus on the individual within a broader context. Promoting equity requires an understanding of what creates less than equitable environments and then actively working toward overcoming the limitations or barriers.

Many times, the terms equity and equality get interchanged. They are not and do not represent the same idea. **Equality**—or the same for everyone—does not allow for differences, overlooks specific needs, does not take into consideration bias or structural inequities and ignores privilege. **Equity** involves opportunities that are differentiated, takes bias into consideration, examines historical and philosophical perspectives and practices, cultural responsiveness, builds upon and supports relationships, and offers the quality and encouragement necessary for optimal progress and success.

Helping Children Develop Self-Esteem

Self-esteem refers to people's perceptions of their own self-worth. Healthy self-esteem is based on a child's own feelings about herself—it comes from inside and is a realistic assessment of her competence. As noted by Epstein (2009):

> Children develop healthy self-esteem when adults show them respect and support their attempts to try new things. Moreover, children with healthy self-esteem find satisfaction in their own efforts without the constant need for adult approval or praise.

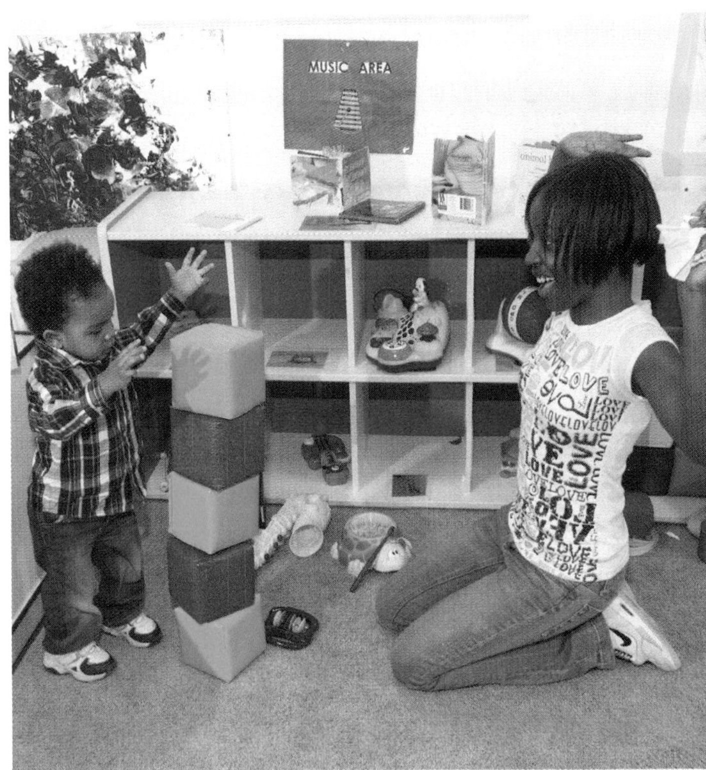

Children's self-esteem may be impacted by their perceptions of being lovable and capable.

Early educators can help children build a healthy self-esteem by first learning the different aspects of self-esteem. For example, self-esteem does not involve boasting or immodesty. Rather, it is about people's feelings concerning who they are and what they can do.

Healthy self-esteem develops and changes over time. It comes from the individual's perceptions of himself and how he believes others perceive him. For instance, as an educator, you give children specific examples of why they are valued members of your learning community. Being specific, explains to children what they did or said that was worthwhile. This helps them see themselves as capable, and leads to healthy self-esteem. With self-esteem comes confidence and increased competence. Children with healthy self-esteem are able to withstand setbacks and accept new challenges and responsibilities.

A sense of agency is closely related to self-esteem. Agency is the idea that you have some power and you can influence the things that happen to you. Children who have a strong sense of self-esteem often find it through noticing how they impact the world around them. Their sense agency leads to stronger self-esteem.

There are a number of ways you can help children develop healthy self-esteem and build their sense of agency:

Build on children's strengths. Plan activities that allow children to apply their skills and achieve success. This will lead to feelings of competence.

Support individual talents and interests. Offer materials, activities, experiences, and interactions that allow children to develop their talents and explore their interests. Celebrate children as they explore and learn new physical and thinking skills. Encourage children, through the language you use, to see the way their actions affect others and the environment.

Encourage children to use their skills to develop new ones. For example, holding and eating with a spoon, rolling a ball to a friend, spreading cream cheese on a cracker at snack time, completing a puzzle, adding a drawing to a get well card, or solving problems when conflicts arise. Then, set challenges for children that are slightly above their skill levels—for example, offer a puzzle with more pieces or provide name cards so children can practice writing their names. As they strive to reach the next challenge, they will build confidence in their growing abilities.

Be a Coach Instead of a Cheerleader

Receiving praise conditions children to work for accolades instead of working toward accomplishing goals. Or, as Galinsky (2012, 2) points out, some children will stop trying to complete tasks altogether for fear that they will not be able to repeat their performances:

> *It is clear that when adults praise children for seemingly in-born characteristics like being smart, it creates the opposite effect. Children become less willing to take on challenges because they don't want to lose their label of smartness. Praising children for their effort and their strategies is much more effective. . . Self-esteem is a by-product of trying hard, making mistakes, failing, and learning to go forward toward a goal.*

Encourage and acknowledge children rather than praising them. Instead of saying, "Good job," keep your feedback specific to children's actions. By describing what they have done, you can help them understand it: "Thank you for putting all of the plates and cups on the table. Now all the children sitting with Ms. Andersen will have their own plate and cup to use."

Have developmentally appropriate expectations for children's behavior and skills. For example, it is typical for toddlers to say "No!" or "Mine!" frequently. They are not trying to annoy you! They do this because they are gaining an awareness of their own self and individual identity and defining what makes them unique and what they have in common with others. Preschoolers are learning about language and literacy; very few are ready for learning to read.

If you expect them to read (or write) before they are ready, you will be setting them up for failure. Failure, especially repeated failures, lead children to see themselves as incompetent and incapable. Help children see that making mistakes is a path to learning and helps them to grow and develop. That way, the occasional failed attempt does not create the feeling of failure that destroys self-esteem.

Speak to children in a supportive, kind, and positive tone of voice. Greet them affectionately every day, and show them you enjoy being with them. Communicate your positive feelings throughout the day. Practice by recording your conversations to make sure your tone is appropriate.

Support a variety of approaches to learning. Offer a wide range of materials and activities so that all children can gain confidence and build independence. For example, some children might be drawn to moving to music while others enjoy yoga. If you provide both options you will be meeting the preferences of several children at the same time.

Spend one-on-one time with each child. Giving young children undivided attention sends the message that they are valuable and others enjoy their contributions. For infants and toddlers, routines are excellent times to build individual relationships. For preschoolers, set a goal of having an individual interaction with each child every day—during activities and choice times, at family-style lunch, when getting ready for nap, or when doing a chore together such as sweeping the trike path on the playground.

Be intentional when interacting with children. Comment on specific behaviors, actions, and results and avoid blanket statements, such as "Good job." Help children notice their own efforts and accomplishments so they can build a realistic and healthy self-esteem and sense of agency. Discourage comparisons to other children's abilities.

Help children understand that plans are not always successful—especially the first time. Talk about times when your plans do not work out and what you will do next. You might say, "The hooks weren't strong enough to hold the gardening tools. I'll have to think of another way to hang up the rakes and shovels." Invite children to talk about their efforts—what did and didn't work and why they think that happened. Focus on efforts rather than accomplishments. "You worked hard trying to get your sock off. One more tug and I think it will work. Can I help you?"

Help children make friends. Making friends is easy for some young children, but most children need an adult to teach friendship skills. You might pair an outgoing child with one who tends to be quiet and reserved. Give them a task to do together and a friendship might blossom. Or, coach a child in how to get involved in play—which is where many friendships begin. Observe together while giving a running commentary on the action. "Diane and Andrew are digging in the sand box. They both have shovels. Looks like they are filling the buckets and making castles, like at the beach. Here comes Tonya. I wonder what she will do. She sits down with Diane and Andrew and asks them what they are doing. Now she is helping them."

Recognizing their own efforts and accomplishments helps children develop a sense of personal competency and self-esteem. Children need to feel worthy if they are to take on new challenges and be eager learners. As an early childhood educator, create an environment where children can express positive feelings and ideas about themselves as they move through childhood into adulthood. Create opportunities for children to take risks, exert effort, and experience success, which will help them develop healthy self-esteem. When children make mistakes or their plans do not work out, they need supportive adults who teach them how to solve problems and encourage them to try again.

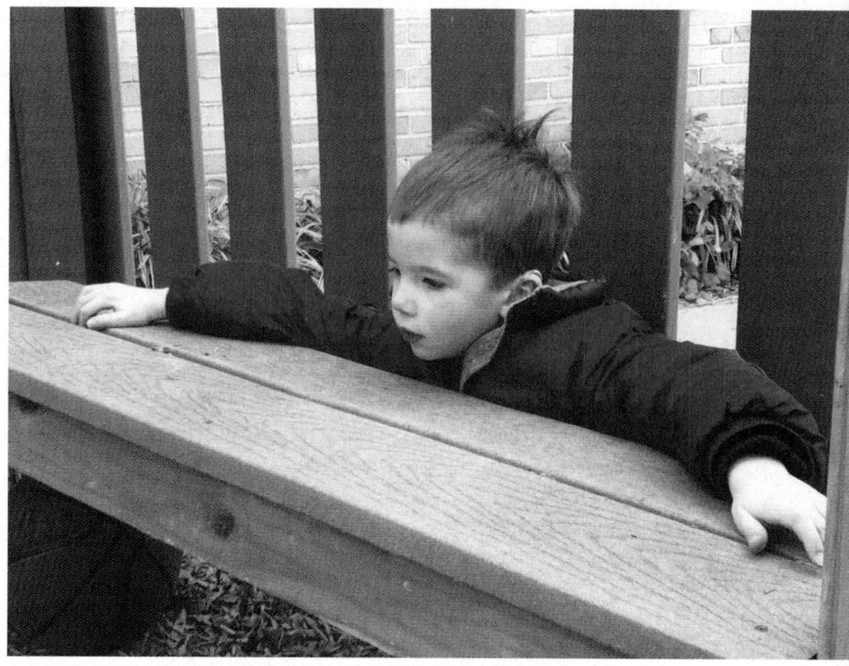

Give children time and space to work through negative emotions.

Guiding Children in Expressing Their Feelings

When you help children communicate their feelings appropriately and effectively, you foster their emotional development, one part of which is building self-regulation. Educators encourage infants' smiles and coos and help a crying baby calm down by meeting her needs or helping her soothe herself. Toddlers need lots of patience and understanding as they gain the language and self-regulations skills needed to express themselves using words. And preschoolers gain a better understanding of their own feelings and those of others and learn to name them as well as express them with words rather than behaviors adults label as disruptive or challenging.

The Center on the Social and Emotional Foundations for Early Learning at Vanderbilt University (n.d.) details a number of strategies you can employ to help children learn to express their emotions appropriately and effectively:

Help children name their feelings. Often, children get frustrated when they cannot articulate the way they feel. Being able to name the feeling can be a big help. When they cannot name the feeling, they act out physically instead. For example, Sarah is angry when she scribbles so hard that her paper tears so she rips it in half. You might say, "Sarah, I think you are angry because your paper tore. You were having a good time scribbling. Do you want to get another piece of paper?"

Give children lots of opportunities to identify feelings in themselves and others. For example, you might say to a child, "Riding the bike is so much fun. I see you smiling. I wonder if you are feeling happy." Or you might point out a situation and ask the child to reflect on what someone else may be feeling: "Joey bumped his head on the slide. I wonder if Joey is feeling hurt, or sad. What do you think? Let's look at his face and see if we can tell what he is feeling. Then we can go ask him."

Help children build a feelings vocabulary. Start identifying basic emotions, such as happy, glad, sad, and angry. Be sure to balance labeling positive emotions as well as those that express negative feelings. Then introduce more descriptive words, such as lonely, excited, frustrated, or grateful. By providing children with more descriptive labels for emotions, they can express their feelings more specifically. For example, Leila is not only *sad* that her grandfather will not be visiting today, she is *disappointed*. Amir is not just *happy* that today is his birthday, he is *excited*.

Use feeling charts and picture books. Help children match facial expressions with feelings. For example, while reading aloud the picture book *David Gets in Trouble* by David Shannon, discuss David's expressions when he is caught doing things he has been told not to do. How does his facial expression change after he apologizes?

Acknowledge when children talk about their feelings. Make your praise specific: "Mike, you remembered to tell me that your feelings were hurt when you didn't get a turn at the computer. It's important to let me know what your feelings are. Now let's see what we can do to can do to help you resolve the situation."

Let children know that feelings are not good or bad, positive or negative, but how you express those feelings can be harmful. Explain to children that there are healthy ways to express big feelings. Whether those feelings are of anger or excitement, jealousy or enthusiasm, when emotions overwhelm us we can sometimes harm others. Dealing with difficult emotions requires adult support and strategies. For instance, they can calm down by sitting on comfortable pillows and reading a book or spending time individually with the pet guinea pig.

Give children space to work through negative emotions. Offer them a book to read, a turn at the sand or water table, or an opportunity to be alone. This is not "time out;" it is space and time to resolve conflict internally.

Model calmness and reason when discussing feelings with children. Wait until children are ready for the discussion. Children will learn from your example that emotions are best discussed calmly and straightforwardly.

Encourage children to resolve peer conflicts independently. Help them put into words how their peers' actions made them feel. Encourage children to devise solutions either individually or in groups, and support them in resolving the conflict.

Practice feeling-related activities. Children can learn from drawing "feeling faces," playing with puppets and dolls, or playing games such as "feeling face bingo" where children cross out feeling faces once they identify the emotion the face demonstrates (Joseph and Strain 2010).

Figure 58. Emotion Words to Teach Young Children*

• Angry	• Proud	• Friendly	• Relieved
• Calm	• Disappointed	• Stubborn	• Interested
• Brave	• Frustrated	• Generous	• Peaceful
• Tense	• Embarrassed	• Shy	• Jealous
• Cheerful	• Silly	• Ignored	• Overwhelmed
• Bored	• Excited	• Satisfied	• Lonely
• Confused	• Uncomfortable	• Impatient	• Loving
• Surprised	• Fantastic	• Safe	• Comfortable
• Curious	• Worried	• Important	• Concerned

*Children generally possess limited vocabularies and need you to introduce them to emotion-related words and their meanings (Joseph and Strain 2010).

(Center on the Social and Emotional Foundations for Early Learning)

Helping Each Child Flourish

If you were to ask families of young children what they want most for their children, a majority would probably say something to the effect that they want their child to be successful—to do well in school and to be a happy, healthy, good person. In other words, they want their children to flourish (Seligman 2011).

In recent years, educators have come to appreciate the role of certain non-cognitive character traits in contributing to children's success in school and life. Chief among these traits are three interrelated and overlapping factors that help children flourish: optimism, resilience, and grit. A major component of all three traits is emotional self-regulation. And what all three traits have in common is that they provide a positive response to adversity. Optimism can be considered part of resiliency and to have grit is to be resilient (Perkins-Gough 2013). In this section, we will identify ways in which you can help children be confident that they will succeed. When they confront problems, one of their first thoughts should be, "I can figure out what to do." When they meet challenges, they should know, "I can do it."

Optimism

Often, children get frustrated when they cannot articulate the way they feel.

The Mayo Clinic defines optimism as "the belief that good things will happen to you and that negative events are temporary setbacks to overcome" (Brody 2012). Suzanne Segerstrom of the University of Kentucky says that optimism involves motivation and persistence. Optimists gladly accept challenges.

Optimists are, by nature, motivated and believe that they are in control of their lives. They have a sense of agency. Pessimists tend to focus on the negative and anticipate the worst outcomes. Optimists tend to do better in school than pessimists and are more motivated to learn. They are also healthier than pessimists and live significantly longer. Pessimists, in contrast, are prone to depression, even as young as preschool age (Seligman 2007). Life would be much easier if we were all born optimists. Unfortunately, not everyone is born to think this way. However, the good news is that unlike temperament which is also inborn but fixed, optimism is something that can be learned. Pessimistic children do not have to become pessimistic adults.

The earlier that children start thinking optimistically, the more they experience educational and health benefits. We must acknowledge that the life circumstances of some children and families may support maintaining an optimistic viewpoint. Children who see others like themselves being successful and having power or control have an advantage when it comes to optimism. Children who see their families and role models being disrespected and put down may struggle to find an optimistic viewpoint. Here are some ideas for helping young children become more optimistic.

Help Children to Identify, Label, and Deal with Their Feelings—Even Negative Ones

Teaching children to think optimistically begins with helping them articulate what their feelings are. How you do this is discussed throughout this chapter. While positive emotions are relatively easy for children and educators to acknowledge and accept, negative emotions like sadness, anger, and loneliness are more difficult for many adults to handle and to handle in children. Experts in learned optimism, like Martin Seligman of the University of Pennsylvania, offer two options (1) turn negative feelings into positive ones and (2) accept the negative feelings, but deal with them in a positive manner.

Teaching children to reframe negative thinking positively is the very heart of learned optimism. You do this by (Pearson and Hall 2006):

1. Acknowledging the child's feelings.
2. Gently challenging the child's expression of feelings by helping them to develop more flexible thinking styles.

The key to changing a thinking style is to discuss what the child is thinking and help him reflect on whether or not he is interpreting events positively or negatively. Some toddlers can begin learning to talk about what goes on in their heads (metacognition). Most preschoolers can become skilled in using metacognition. Help children to analyze how their thinking may be taking them down a harmful path and to see the situation from a more positive light.

One important strategy in helping children change their thinking styles is to point out and show them how to avoid common thinking traps, such as:

- Jumping to conclusions. "Brooklyn's playing with the puzzles again. I bet she won't want me to be in the math and manipulatives center with her."
- Always thinking the worst. "I spilled paint on the carpet. My educator will hate me."
- Being over-emotional. "Anthony won't share with me. I'm never going to talk to him again."

Acting Out How to Deal With Problems

Provide puppets, persona dolls, props, dress-ups, and support so children can put on plays or skits about handling challenges with which they are familiar. This strategy can help children cope with situations, such as:

- Moving away from your friends.
- A military parent or guardian is deployed to a war zone.
- A family member is hospitalized.
- A pet runs away.
- Your sister gets lots of presents and you get none.
- A grandparent goes to live in a nursing home.

You might designate certain puppets or dolls to have particular emotions. The children can use these puppets/dolls to predict what will happen. Then the other puppets/dolls can help them change how they express those feelings. The outcome should be to learn from the adversity and try to see the positive.

Introduce Dramatic Play Scenarios that Children Can Work Through Positively

Some suggestions are:

- All of the food has burned and there's nothing for the chef to serve.
- The "son" doesn't want to clean up his room.
- Your friend's mother won't let her come to your house for dinner.
- Everyone forgot the "daughter's" birthday—and you're the daughter!

Unlike typical dramatic play scenarios where educators are not part of the action, your involvement is needed to ensure that children are resolving things positively. If things aren't going in that direction, ask questions that will guide children to turn things around. At the end of the scenario, spend some time discussing how the positive outcome makes the participants feel.

Read Aloud and Discuss Books that Focus on Optimism

Children's books are one of the most exciting and straightforward ways of teaching positivity. Children identify with the main characters and learn from their experiences. By seeing how the boy in a story succeeds by making optimistic choices, children have a model to follow. Likewise, hearing how the elephant star of a book learns from his mistakes, children are encouraged to do the same.

At group time and with individual children, read aloud a book with a theme related to optimism. Ask questions that draw the children's attention to the problem and adversity, and what the main characters thought would happen. Did the main characters change their way of thinking? What happened in the end? Find ways to relate the main characters' experiences to the children's. Make sure that children understand the book's message and how positive thinking makes life better. Some books to use for this effort are:

- *Dancing with Katya* by Dori Chaconas
- *Grawnma Becky's Bread* by Mark R. Ellsworth
- *The Little Engine That Could* by Watty Piper and George Hauman
- *Sink or Swim* by Valerie Coulman and Rogé Girard
- *When Pigs Fly* by Valerie Coulman and Rogé Girard

Read the book once without stopping so children can get to know the characters and plot. As you read it again, stop to ask pertinent questions and engage children in analyzing a problem. Discuss the choices the main character makes, whether or not the character's reaction is based on facts or fears, and how to resolve the problem positively. Obviously, your choice of questions will vary to fit the plot of the book. These generic questions can guide you in formulating your own:

- What happened to _______________ in this story?
- How do you think this made _______________ feel?
- What do you suppose _______________ was thinking inside his head?
- What would you say to _______________?
- What would you have suggested that _______________ do?
- How did _______________ think things through?
- What do you think will happen next time _______________ has a problem?
- Would you like to have a friend like _______________? Why or why not?
- Would you have ended the story like this? If not, how would you end the book? Why did you pick this ending?

Encourage children to retell and act out the stories in the books you have read them. Use props or puppets to make the experience come alive. Suggest alternative scenarios to act out that might test the main character's optimism.

Use humor and laughter to encourage positive feelings.

Resilience

Resilience is the ability to bounce back from trauma, adversity, violence, and stress. To be resilient doesn't mean that you experience no pain or stress. Life is always going to be filled with stress, change, loss, and pain. Resilience allows you to manage your emotions and lessen the effects of stress by drawing on inner strengths, relationships, and the community. Resilient people identify problems, work through and recover from these problems and challenges, and then move on. Reaching In . . . Reaching Out (RIRO), a Canadian early childhood education resiliency training program. "More than thirty years of research shows that people who are resilient are healthier, live longer, are more successful in school and at work, are happier in relationships, and less prone to depression" (RIRO 2012).

Although some of the components of resilience—like being optimistic—may be inborn, resilience itself develops as children grow and learn self-regulation and coping skills. RIRO reports that children who learn to be resilient possess the 3 Cs (RIRO 2012):

- Control: These children believe that they are in charge of their lives.
- Challenge: They view mistakes as opportunities for learning.
- Commitment: Their active engagement and follow-through provide meaning for their lives.

Resilient children resemble children with a healthy self-concept (Brooks and Goldstein 2003). They feel valued and appreciated, and they understand both their strengths and weaknesses. They are able to set realistic goals, solve problems, and view mistakes and challenges as learning opportunities. Children who are resilient focus on the aspects of their lives that they can control.

The Devereux Center for Resilient Children has developed a strengths-based approach to helping young children develop resiliency, beginning in infancy. They have identified what they call "protective factors" in children (Gartrell and Cairone 2014). Protective factors are (1) environmental factors in the program, the home, and the community, and (2) internal psychological factors that work together to counter the effects of stress or adversity. As you'll note below, they echo the concepts identified by the other resilience projects.

Resilient children feel valued and appreciated.

Figure 59. Resilience Research

In 1955, Emily Werner, a child psychologist, began a 30-year longitudinal study of 505 at-risk children in Kauai, Hawaii. One-third of the children in this group had four or more risk factors that suggested they would struggle with success in life—for example, chronic poverty, dysfunctional, chaotic families, parental divorce, and family drug or alcohol abuse. Yet, one in three of the children in this high-risk group "had developed into a confident, competent adult" by age 18 (p. 2). Even more surprisingly, researchers found that five-sixths of the high-risk children in the study had overcome the adversity of multiple stresses and trauma by their early 30s. From her research, Werner found that those children who grew up to be resilient shared these three characteristics (Werner and Smith 1992):

1. They had been active and sociable infants.
2. They had at least one positive role model who supported their development of trust, autonomy, and initiative.
3. They had at least one skill that gave them a sense of pride and acceptance within their peer group.

Werner concluded that protective factors are more powerful in the lives of children than are the stressful life circumstances that might appear to have foredoomed them. Educators, in particular, were among the most common source of protective factors for children in the study who overcame adversity. And the most powerful protective factor was the caring, supportive relationships that children had with their educators. Helping children build strong protective factors has become the core of resilience-building programs.

We now know that these “high-risk” factors are more common in the population at large than was previously believed. An extensive CDC Kaiser-Permanente study of over 17,000 people conducted between 1995 and 1997 of Adverse Childhood Experiences demonstrated that 70% of the adult population has experienced some of these risk factors and that these people cross every racial, ethnic, gender and economic group. (Felitti, V. J., Anda, R. F., Nordenberg, D., Williamson, D. F., Spitz, A. M., Edwards, V., & Marks, J. S. 1998). Relationship of childhood abuse and household dysfunction to many of the leading causes of death in adults: The Adverse Childhood Experiences (ACE) Study. American journal of preventive medicine, 14(4), 245-258).

Most of us have some adversity in our childhoods that we have overcome, in large part due to the caring supportive relationships we found along the way. Becoming a protective factor for the children we serve is an opportunity for every early childhood teacher in every community.

According to The Devereux Center there are three protective factors that educators can foster or provide to buffer young children from the negative effects of trauma and stress. These are (Devereux Center n.d.):

1. **Attachment and relationships** (for infants, toddlers, and preschoolers). This may be defined as engaging in positive connections with family members and early childhood educators through nurturing interaction.
2. **Initiative** (for infants, toddlers, and preschoolers). This is the ability to assert control and power over the environment by planning activities, accomplishing tasks, and facing challenges.
3. **Self-regulation** (for toddlers and preschoolers). This is the ability to express and manage emotions and behavior in healthy ways and to maintain focus and attention.

Here are some things that educators can do to help children develop these protective factors:

To help infants, toddlers, and preschoolers form attachments and forge relationships:

- Show affection and loving touches to infants; hug toddlers and preschoolers.
- Talk and sing to babies often; especially during routines.
- Mirror a baby's facial expressions, coos, and babbles.
- Help toddlers and preschoolers to make friends by pairing children at a double-sided easel or including a child in pretend play scenarios.
- Make eye contact and scoot down to the child's level when talking to him.
- Use children's names often in conversations.
- Make every child feel special. Children need to have at least one adult who gives them the strength to persevere through difficult times.

To help infants, toddlers, and preschoolers develop initiative:

- Give children lots of encouragement and support in self-help skills like feeding themselves, learning to use the potty, getting dressed and undressed, and brushing their teeth.
- Create a helper job chart so that each child is responsible for a task.
- Let infants decide what toy to play with; older children can choose which learning areas and materials they want to play with.

- Provide children at least an hour of uninterrupted play time so that they can become fully engaged in what they are doing.
- Provide lots of open-ended toys and materials that can be used by different children in different ways.
- Always have on hand some toys that children can do successfully, that they can return to when feeling frustrated.
- Frame children's art work and display it at their eye level.

To help toddlers and preschoolers gain self-regulation skills:

- Play games like *Simon Says* in reverse. This requires children to think and not do something, which helps to build self-regulation.
- Provide activities that require children to follow through. Activities such as cooking using recipe cards or organized sports require children to follow directions.
- Read aloud books that promote self-regulation, such as *The Magic Beads* by Susan Nielsen-Frenlund, *Silver Shoes* by Caroline Binch, and *It's Hard to Be Five: Learning How to Work My Control Panel* by Jamie Lee Curtis are filled with characters who model effective self-regulatory strategies.
- Encourage private speech. By going over in their own heads what they need to do, children prepare themselves to self-regulate.: "I'm scared to go down the slide alone. Look, Julie's doing it now. Everyone knows that Julie's brave. Maybe if I take some deep breaths I won't be so scared. That's what I'm going to do. 1, 2, 3…10. I feel calmer. I think I can go down now."
- Plan stress-reducing activities and exercises. Join in with exercises that will harness children's energy, attention, and focus. Drawing, painting, or using the sand or water table help children relax. Pretend play lets them work through fears of going to a doctor or dealing with a parent or guardian who travels often for work.
- Introduce relaxation techniques like yoga. The calming results of yoga make it a natural partner in teaching self-regulation. Begin with ten to fifteen minute sessions. Each exercise need only last thirty seconds to one minute. You can add more time as children get used to the poses and develop the ability to stay focused.

Remember that the most effective way to help children to develop self-regulation skills is through co-regulation. By soothing and comforting a distressed child and keeping calm in difficult situations, children learn what being regulated looks and feels like.

Cultural Wealth

There are six types of capital that are valued and nurtured by communities of color and collectively form cultural wealth. It is important to view children from a strength-based lens and to acknowledge the cultural capital they bring with them to the early childhood environment (Yosso, 2015). Cultural wealth includes the funds of knowledge and ways of knowing that children possess before entering an early childhood program. The role of the teacher is to use this existing knowledge to enhance the child's growth and development.

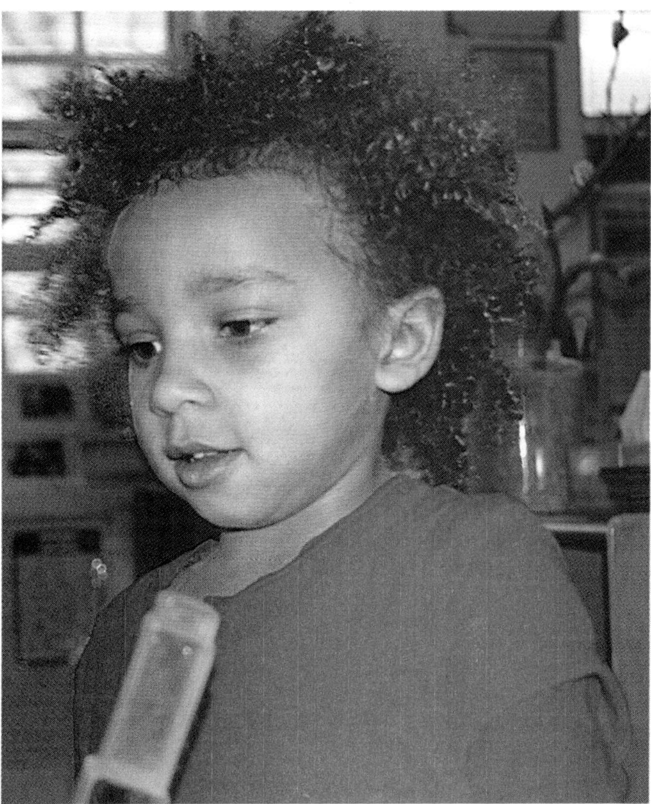

Use existing knowledge of cultural wealth to enhance children's growth and development.

1. **Aspirational capital:** This form of capital is described as persistence and resiliency. It results from experiences that may have been traumatic and from barriers the child and family may have overcome. It includes the child and family's ability to maintain dreams and aspirations in spite of current circumstances. It is the ability to maintain hope against all odds (Longmire-Avital, Buffie, 2019).

2. **Familial capital:** This capital refers to the strength of the family, extended family, and community. It reflects a collective perspective where the child and family are strengthened, supported, and nurtured by the community. It includes commitment to the well-being and an understanding of fictive kinship that extends beyond biological family.

3. **Social Capital:** Social capital is about connections to the community and community networks. It is about the broad base of support that children and families depend on and count on in times of need. This might include the church, the barber, social organizations, and cultural centers where there are shared values, norms, and understanding.

4. **Resistant Capital:** This form of capital is what empowers children and families to oppose and challenge inequities. It is the ability to stand firm in situations of unfairness and to speak up on one's own and others' behalf. When an environment feels hostile or unwelcoming, resistant capital is used to challenge situations where the child, family, or community feels silenced, ignored, or invisible.

5. **Navigational Capital:** Navigational capital is the ability of children and their families to navigate unwelcoming and hostile environments. It empowers children and families to maneuver through unsupportive, biased, and racist spaces and cultivate skills to respond to microaggressions and other forms of adversity.

6. **Linguistic Capital:** This form of capital refers to the various language and communication skills children have. Languages spoken and developed in the home include all languages and dialects, including "Spanglish," African American Vernacular English (AAVE), English, Spanish, Creole, Patwa, and any languages the child, family, and community speaks. It also includes the forms of communication used by the child, family, and community, such as storytelling, memorization, recollection of detail, call and response, and rhythm and rhyme. Linguistic capital also includes the use of facial expressions, body gestures, and other forms of nonverbal communication.

CHAPTER 9: Social

CDA® Functional Area 9: Candidate helps each child function effectively in the group, learn to express feelings, acquire social skills, and make friends, and promotes mutual respect among children and adults.

Social

Introduction

Social development is the process of learning the skills and strategies used to build relationships with, get along with, and enjoy the company of others. Developing and maintaining social skills begins in infancy and for many of us is a lifelong journey. The secret to many happy families and successful careers is having strong social skills. Respect for the views and contributions of others, sharing and taking turns, resolving conflicts amicably, joint problem solving, and building friendships are all skills that children begin to develop in the early years.

As an early childhood educator, you play a major role in the development of children's social skills by arranging your setting to promote small and large group social activities throughout the day, fostering the kinds of play that support social development, and encouraging authentic friendships. You also encourage prosocial behaviors (behaviors intended to benefit another person, such as helping, sharing, or comforting) and partner with families to ensure that children build the social skills needed to enjoy life and do well in school. Strong social skills are the foundation for success in school and work.

We will examine five basic components involved in helping children develop social skills:

- **Understanding the Social Development of Infants, Toddlers, and Preschoolers**
- **Using the Environment to Encourage Positive Social Interactions**
- **Supporting Children's Play**
- **Encouraging Children's Positive Relationships**
- **Fostering Prosocial Behavior**

Understanding the Social Development of Infants, Toddlers, and Preschoolers

As noted by author and educator Ann S. Epstein, social development and emotional development are closely related topics. Emotional development—learning about oneself and being able to recognize, express, and manage feelings—was addressed in the previous chapter. Nevertheless, readers are likely to see that there is significant overlap between social and emotional development. Thus, the term social-emotional development is often used to describe these interconnected areas of learning. According to Epstein (2009):

Social learning comprises the principles and strategies for interacting successfully with others. Dealing with one's emotional state is often a prerequisite for socializing effectively with others.

In this section, we focus on how and when children develop the skills needed to establish and maintain meaningful, reciprocal relationships with adults (at first with parents and other family members and later with early childhood educators) and with other children as they play, learn, and take part in a community together.

Young Infants

Newborn infants look to their mothers, fathers, and other close family members to meet their needs. They rely on these important people to provide food, clean and dry diapers, and comfort. As a baby's needs are met through consistent, caring, loving responses, a strong social relationship is formed. Most infants love to be held and touched gently. They enjoy their caregivers' communications—smiles, coos, laughs, and babbles—and soon begin to respond with smiles, coos, and laughs of their own. Adults—both family members and early childhood educators—provide relationship-based care. They interact with each infant as an individual, getting to know each child's unique interests, likes, and dislikes, and responding with caregiving that is just right for that child.

In early childhood settings, the educators are the first playmates of young infants. They introduce toys—for example, shaking a rattle so a baby can see and hear it, and eventually placing it in the infant's hand so she can shake the rattle on her own. They point out interesting things—"Look there's a red cardinal on the branch"—and introduce new experiences—"I'll put you on the platform at the top and hold your hand while you slide down." FCC educator, Ms. Kianna responds, "Rhonda, I see you smiling and I hear you cooing. I can smile and coo, too. You are so much fun to be with."

Through many responsive interactions in the early months, infants form attachments to their loved ones which in turn lead infants to trust the world. A sense of trust allows infants to feel safe exploring beyond the familiar.

Mobile Infants

Mobile infants begin to show interest in other babies. They play alongside each other and on occasion might interact—cooing or smiling at each other. As an early childhood educator, you continue to be the infants' most regular playmate. You might roll a ball back and forth, play a game of peek-a-boo, or encourage a baby to crawl through a box tunnel. Educators can demonstrate different ways to use the same toy or material. For example, you might show a mobile infant how to use a spoon and bowl for stirring or turn the bowl over and show how the spoon can now be a drum stick.

During this stage mobile infants may experience stranger anxiety—being fearful of new people—and separation anxiety—expressing strong feelings at drop off and pick up times when special adults leave or return. Caring and patient parents and early educators can help children get through these stages by remaining calm and reassuring. Rituals—doing the same thing every day—can be helpful for separation. For example, a mother could give her baby three hugs and count them while she does so or the educator could hold the baby at the window to wave goodbye to her daddy. Following the child's cues with regard to stranger anxiety is important. Let the child stay close until they are comfortable meeting the new person.

Towards the end of the mobile infant stage, the almost toddler is beginning to enjoy the company of others, still playing alongside others rather than with them. They explore different kinds of toys and materials, learning through trial and error and repeating play activities that were fun. Some children begin to use private speech (talking to themselves) and some notice and react when another child is upset.

Toddlers

Toddlers spend a lot of time watching—paying attention to you and to the other children in the group. Most toddlers want to be independent, whether ready or not. They may balk at holding your hand to cross a busy street or collapse in a heap when you say "no" to something they want to do.

Having multiples of popular toys, such as telephones, is a way to encourage beginning forms of dramatic play.

Toddlers are still building a sense of self and feelings of security. As they develop a sense of who they are, they tend to focus on their toys—needing to feel a sense of possession before being willing to share. As you may already know, this is one of the reasons why it's best for early childhood settings to have multiples of the most popular toys such as telephones and firefighter helmets. Having multiples of these items is also a way to encourage beginning forms of dramatic play. With two phones, two older toddlers might call each other or two children might both decide to don the helmets and put out a fire.

Toddlers are learning about lots of feelings, in particular, the feeling of love. They show affection—hugging and kissing others, with and without an invitation. Older toddlers are likely to refer to other children in the group as friends and may prefer playing alongside or with one or two children in particular. With rapidly expanding language skills, toddlers are beginning to work together to carry out a shared goal. "I see you are both pushing the wagon. Nicki is holding one side of the handle and Lester is holding the other. It's a big wagon so it takes two strong children to push it."

Preschoolers

By the time children enter the preschool years, they have already gained a number of social skills. They have strong, reciprocal relationships with caring adults and rely on them for support when needed. Their interest in other children is growing and they have developed preferences for specific playmates. These preferences are based on inferences and interpretations young children make about the world and the people around them. Children will have absorbed the biases of society, their families, and their school settings by this age. For this reason, it is important that we surround young children with positive images of children that look and sound like them, and that look and sound different from themselves. This builds those positive associations that counter the racial, ethnic, and gender biases of American society. When seeing a group of children at play, preschoolers know how to get involved by copying what they are doing or offering a toy to share. Cooperative play is possible, now that children have the cognitive and language skills needed to develop and carry out plans for roles and scenarios. They may spend a long time planning, enjoying the sharing of ideas and working out compromises as much as the actual play. Sociodramatic play may be planned one day and carried out over the next few days. Early childhood educators can help to keep play going by making small suggestions to take it to a deeper level or offering props that will enhance the possibilities of what children can do or say in the play.

Although prosocial behaviors are observed in children as young as infants (as when one baby pats the back of another), in the preschool years they are more pronounced. They include sharing, taking turns, and helping at clean-up time. In addition, they include more sophisticated caring behaviors such as showing empathy when another child is hurt or frustrated or left out of an activity. In short, empathy is being aware of another person's feelings and identifying with those feelings. Preschoolers who are aware of and can label their own feelings, are most likely to be able to experience empathy for others. Other prosocial behaviors likely to emerge in the preschool years include the tendency to be generous, cooperative, and kind to others.

The children in your setting are growing up with diverse cultures, home languages, family structures, economic backgrounds, and experiences. All of these factors will have an effect on their social development. Figure 60a-c includes examples of the typical social behaviors and skills of young children in different age groups. They are provided as a guide as every child and every group of children is unique and their social development is influenced by culture, family structure and relationships, language skills, community, and other factors.

Figure 60a. Social Skills for Young Children

Age	Developing Social Skills
Young Infants (birth–8 months)	• Develop a sense of attachment to important people in their lives. • Build trust and interest in exploration in a safe world. • Like being held and cuddled; enjoy playing with adults. • Recognize familiar voices. • Imitate sounds and gestures. • Coo and make other contented noises. • Show interest in the people around them. • Prefer the faces of people from races they are most exposed to. • Respond to adults' attempts to relieve their discomfort. • Turn head towards familiar voices. • Communicate needs and desires through crying, looking, smiling, and pointing. • Seek attention by manipulating objects (might drop items on purpose). • Aware of self as separate being. • Touch and explore other children's faces. • Smile in response to others (known as the social smile); respond differently to frowns. • Smile at, reach out to, or touch familiar children. • Play peek-a-boo with adults. • Watch other children's play; may try to reach for or take away toy. • Engage in solitary play—explore toys by themselves and play with adults. • Respond to "No."
Mobile Infants (9–17 months)	• Seek support from familiar adults. • Can get upset during separation from family members. • Get close to familiar adult when stranger is present (is fearful of unknown people). • Take hand of familiar adult and lead them to something desired or needed. • Engage in back-and-forth interactions with an adult or another child, e.g., babbling and using a few words (towards the end of the age period). • Imitate each other's behavior. • Seem to prefer spending time with a few other children in particular. • Know some children by name and by individual likes and dislikes. • Prefer children of races they are most exposed to. • Make same sounds as another child or play a game of chase (following each other around the room or through a tunnel). • Engage in "parallel play" (beside other children using the same materials). • May resist adult requests by crying, kicking, or falling to floor. • Respond by looking up and smiling when hearing name.

Figure 60b. Social Skills for Young Children

Age	Developing Social Skills
Toddlers (18–36 months)	• Have friendly, positive interactions with familiar adults in a variety of situations. • Become more comfortable with strangers. • Rely on familiar adults to help when feeling tired, stressed, or frustrated. • Look to familiar adults for reassurance when meeting new people. • Ask for help when faced with difficulties. • Initiate play and conversations with other children. • Respond to other children's invitations to play or talk. • Develop preferences for particular play mates and may form friendships. • Prefer to make friends with children from races they are most exposed to. • May react with aggression when conflicts arise with other children or may ask for adult help. • Have difficulty waiting, taking turns, and sharing. • Engage in parallel play; begins to play with friends (associative play). • Take turns during play, some of the time. • Work with other children to accomplish a shared goal—e.g., digging a hole. • Are aware of and react when another child is in distress; e.g., may cry as well or seek adult help. • Might give another child a spontaneous hug or kiss, or a toy to play with. • Enjoy simple forms of dramatic play; wear dress up clothes; imitate adult behaviors, then invent own scenarios. • Use toys to represent real things (e.g., use a block as a phone).
Young Preschoolers (3–4 years old)	• Show affection for special adults. • Separate easily from family and primary caregivers (most of the time). • Ask adults to help solve problems. • Gain prosocial skills (taking turns, sharing, and so on) over time. • Follow rules, most of the time. • Talk to self. • Cooperate, most of the time. • Move from associative to cooperative play. • Plan and carry out pretend play with others. • Recognize and describes conflicts; suggest solutions with guidance from adults. • Are interested in other children and copy their actions. • Form friendships. • Prefer to make friends with children from dominant culture and class, regardless of their own race, culture, and class. • Assist friends in need (e.g., retrieve a child's hat from her cubby for her). • Accept suggested compromises.

Figure 60c. Social Skills for Young Children

Age	Developing Social Skills
Older Preschoolers (4–5 years old)	• Initiate, respond to, and continue reciprocal conversations with adults. • Respond positively to requests and instructions. • Respond positively to reminders of rules and appropriate behaviors. • Uses prosocial behaviors with adults and other children. • Change moods without much warning. • May have imaginary friends. • Prefer playing with certain children. • Have formed social judgements about children from various races based on societal biases. • Play with others for increasing periods of time. • Engage in cooperative play with other children. • Continue existing and form new friendships. • Make and carry out sophisticated plans for sociodramatic play with other children. • Recognize and describe conflicts; resolve simple conflicts without adult intervention. • Seek adult help when faced with greater challenges. • Help other children solve problems and handle needs. • Exclude other children from play at times. • Use words instead of aggression to express feelings and desires, most of the time.

Using the Environment to Encourage Positive Social Interactions

In early childhood settings as described in Chapter 3, Learning Environment, the environment contains the following elements: the setting itself (indoors, outdoors, and all materials and equipment); the people within the setting (early childhood educators, children, family members, volunteers, administrators, and visitors); and any learning experiences, routines, and schedules established within the setting. In this section, we highlight how each of these elements contributes to setting the stage for positive social interactions.

The way the setting is configured and the materials available for children can support children's play, learning, and development of social skills. A well-designed setting offers open and protected spaces, places to safely get away from group life, and a wide variety of familiar and new materials that offer challenges, without causing frustration. The age-specific charts that follow Figures 61a-c, 62a-c, and 63a-c, offer tips for using your setting (including your interactions with children as an important part of the setting) to support social development. Early educators who work in family child care settings will find most of the suggestions applicable to their situations as well.

Figure 61a. Promoting Social Development Throughout an Infant Environment

Area	Tips for Supporting Social Development
Transition (used by all infants and families)	• Make sure space is large enough to accommodate stress-free drop-off and pick-up times when some infants may experience separation anxiety. • Post recent photos in the communication center of the infants at play so families can talk with their babies about their experiences at the program.
Diapering (used by all infants)	• Store all supplies within easy reach so most of the diapering experience is focused on building a relationship with each infant. • Post interesting things to look at and talk about with individual infants. • Include photos of family members and people of various races and abilities. • Have hand-held toys available to keep infants busy while being diapered. • Invite older infants to hold the clean diaper or show them how to help take off their socks so they can be assistants. • Take your time during diapering so you can get to know, smile, coo, babble, and laugh with each infant. • Arrange the area so you can see what infants are doing in the rest of the room.
Napping (used by all infants)	• Encourage infants who are able, to fall asleep on their own. Self-soothing is an important skill that is the first step in building self-regulation, but only develops when children have been effectively soothed and have experienced co-regulation first. • Help infants who are restless fall asleep by co-regulating—holding, rocking, and gently rubbing their backs or singing softly, before placing them on their backs in the crib. • Sit in a rocker, comfy chair, or glider when feeding bottles to infants. Provide 100% individual attention whenever possible. • Watch and listen for waking infants so they do not have to wait in their cribs.
Tummy Time (used mostly by young infants so they can safely explore out of the way of mobile infants)	• Create a safe place where you and young infants can play, sing, look at books, and talk—you will be teaching them about the give and take of relationships and that it's fun to be with other people. • Place babies near each other so they can begin to notice each other and their activities; remember they might reach out and touch someone's face—which may or may not be welcomed. "Dionne, let me hold your hand while you touch Keon's hair. Together we can be gentle." • Offer encouragement when infants raise their heads or move in other ways; make comments that let infants know you notice them. "Penelope, I think you are almost ready to roll over."

Figure 61b. Promoting Social Development Throughout an Infant Environment

Area	Tips for Supporting Social Development
Individual and Group Play (used mostly by mobile infants—crawlers and walkers)	• Arrange and stock this area with mobile infants in mind; reflect their abilities, interests, home languages, families, and developmental milestones. • Offer blocks, props, and vehicles—to be used by mobile infants playing alongside each other. ("The truck goes 'vroom, vroom.'") • Provide duplicates of popular items so infants do not have to share or wait for a turn. "Emily can play with this ball. Here's one for you." • Attach an unbreakable mirror to the wall so infants can look at themselves and each other. "Who's that? Let's both smile together." • Include dolls of various races and stuffed animals to cuddle and care for. "Baby Stella looks tired. Is she going to sleep?" • Add simple doll care accessories (e.g., bottles) for older mobile infants. "Did Baby Stella wake up? Is she hungry?" • Provide cloth, vinyl, and board books with illustrations or photographs of babies from a variety of races and familiar items from home and from the setting. • Make and display books and posters about infants' families so they can "visit" them during the day. "Your grammy is holding you up so she can look into your eyes." • Offer toys infants can manipulate with their hands that build fine motor skills that can one day be used for self-help activities. "You can hold the "Oball™ and toss it. There are lots of holes in it." • Place bean bag chairs or pillows in a corner so a child can take a break from the group for a while.
Gross Motor (used mostly by mobile infants)	• Arrange and stock this area so mobile infants can safely crawl, cruise, walk, and climb, while building gross motor skills and a sense of competence while playing alone or alongside others. • Provide multiples of push and pull toys; expect infants to have their own ideas about how to use them. • Include balls of many sizes and textures to roll, toss, kick, and pick up. Balls are a wonderful first toy to enjoy with a friend. • Have low padded platforms that invite mobile infants to climb to new heights. • Offer low riding toys to be pushed or pulled. • Setup tunnels or boxes for first chase games, as one mobile infant imitates or chases another child.

Figure 61c. Promoting Social Development Throughout an Infant Environment

Area	Tips for Supporting Social Development
Kitchen (used by all infants)	• Keep this area well-organized and clean so it's easy to retrieve and warm bottles. "I'll be right there with your bottle, Yancey. I know you are hungry." • Have low chairs with trays for infants who can sit and are ready to try eating solid foods, with support from the early childhood educator. You can give the child individual attention and make eating solid foods an engaging experience. • Have a low table with chairs for mobile infants who are ready for self-feeding. Several children can sit at the table and enjoy each other's company at snack and mealtimes. • Invite children to take part in preparing, serving, and cleaning up after snack and meal times. • Be aware of cultural differences in timetables and expectations for the development of feeding skills like toileting, solo sleeping, and other skills. Cultural norms can differ widely and should be supported.
Outdoors (used by all infants)	• Provide equipment that can be used by younger infants who tend to play alone and items that invite mobile infants to interact with others, if they choose. • Spread blankets or mats on the ground for young infants. Offer the same kinds of materials as provided for tummy time. • Provide a large wagon that an educator can use to pull several children around the playground. • Include big pails of water and giant paint brushes so older mobile infants can work together to "paint" the sidewalk. • Bring music and movement outdoors; offer rhythm instruments, a big drum with multiple drum sticks, colorful scarves to wave, and a portable CD or MP3 player to offer music to move and dance to. • Introduce infants to the sights, sounds, and smells of nature. Lift them to see into trees, grasp leaves, and notice colors. Shake a branch to show them how the leaves move.

Figure 62a. Promoting Social Development Throughout a Toddler Environment

Area/Center	Tips for Supporting Social Development
Transition (used by all infants and families)	• Make sure space is large enough to accommodate stress-free drop-off and pick-up times when some toddlers may experience separation anxiety • Post recent photos in the communication center of the toddlers at play, so families can talk with their children about their experiences at the program. • Encourage families and toddlers to sit on the bench to remove boots and put on indoor shoes.
Diapering and Toileting	• Store all supplies within easy reach so most of the diapering experience is focused on building a relationship with each toddler. • Include family photos and pictures of people from a variety of races. • Post interesting things to look at and talk about with individual toddlers. • Have books and toys available to keep toddlers occupied while being diapered. • Invite toddlers to hold the clean diaper or help take off their pants so they can help during the diapering routine. • Use diapering times to have conversations with individual children; while recognizing the signs that they would prefer to finish and get back to their play. • Arrange the area so you can see what toddlers are doing in the rest of the room while engaged in one-on-one diapering and talking with a toddler. • Collaborate with families when toddlers show the signs that they are ready for toilet learning; follow the same approach at home and at the program. • Anticipate that toilet learning will take time; stay calm and positive when toddlers do not make it to the bathroom on time.
Literacy	• Display books about friendship such as *Dog and Bear* from the series by Laura Vaccaro Seeger. Read them with one or two children at a time and talk about what Dog and Bear do for each other as friends. • Include puppets that go with particular books and puppets that invite joint play. • Include books and images that reflect children's families, cultures, and home languages, as well as families and cultures NOT represented by children in your classroom community. • Spend lots of time reading and talking with individual toddlers and with 2 or 3 children in a small group. • Have recordings of books made by the children's family members. Point out that this book is read by "Lark's grandpa," or "Justine's auntie." • Provide duplicates of all items that are particularly popular at any point in time; toddlers will not have to share and will be more likely to enjoy playing alongside each other.

Figure 62b. Promoting Social Development Throughout a Toddler Environment

Area/Center	Tips for Supporting Social Development
Dramatic Play	• Provide male and female dress-up items and gender-neutral accessories, such as back packs and belts as well as pieces of fabric and scarves from around the world that can be made into all kinds of clothing items by children. • Include realistic items (e.g., bottles for dolls) and open-ended items that children can use to represent props needed for their play (a paper towel tube can be a spoon; yogurt containers can be cups; a basket can become a hat). • Set up the area for housekeeping play—the most popular play scenario for toddlers who are likely to copy what they have observed and experienced. • Join children in play—assume a role and pretend alongside them; make comments and offer props that can take the play in a new direction. • Offer dolls and caregiving props that reflect a variety of ethnicities, cultures, home languages, and family structures.
Dramatic Play	• Provide male and female dress-up items and gender-neutral accessories such as back packs and belts as well as pieces of fabric and scarves from around the world that can be made into all kinds of clothing items by children. • Include realistic items (e.g., bottles for dolls) and open-ended items that children can use to represent props needed for their play (a paper towel tube can be a spoon; yogurt containers can be cups; a basket can become a hat). • Set up the area for housekeeping play—the most popular play scenario for toddlers who are likely to copy what they have observed and experienced. • Join children in play—assume a role and pretend alongside them; make comments and offer props that can take the play in a new direction. • Offer dolls and caregiving props that reflect a variety of ethnicities, cultures, home languages, and family structures.
Blocks and Group Meetings (music props are kept here too)	• Include plenty of space for pairs and small groups to build together. • Offer variety—wooden blocks, cardboard blocks, Duplos or similar building bricks. This gives children choices and opportunities for parallel play. • Respect toddlers' short attention spans. Keep group meetings active, small (4 to 5 children, depending on group size), and short (5 to 10 minutes). • Encourage a sense of community by creating group time rituals such as always beginning with the same short song, rhyme, or finger play. • Offer rhythm instruments—two or three of each kind—and colorful scarves to wave during movement activities. Invite toddlers to wave scarves alone or with a partner.

Figure 62c. Promoting Social Development Throughout a Toddler Environment

Area/Center	Tips for Supporting Social Development
Gross Motor	• Arrange and stock this area so toddlers can safely walk, climb, balance, push, pull, and jump while building gross motor skills and a sense of competence alone and with other children. • Provide an indoor structure with stairs and a slide. Offer to help any child who seems to needs support to use the stairs or slide. • Provide balls of many sizes and textures to roll, toss, kick, and pick up. Provide boxes or baskets to toss balls into. • Use tunnels or boxes—longer than those for mobile infants. If they are large enough, you can join in the fun by crawling through yourself. • Set up other boxes as equipment toddlers can climb in and out of. Point out new ways for two or more children to use the boxes.
Cooking	• Provide tools, equipment, and serving pieces from a variety of cultures needed for toddlers to safely explore food preparation in a small group. • Set up low tables and chairs where toddlers and educators can enjoy family-style meals and develop and use social skills, such as taking turns and sharing. • Serve snack in this area too. Set up illustrated cards to show toddlers how many or how much to take as a serving for snack. • Understand and accept that learning to cook, serve and feed oneself, and preparing snacks can be a messy undertaking. Have clean-up materials on hand—ideally in toddlers' reach—so they can help.
Art	• Avoid judging toddlers' work; instead comment on the colors and characteristics of the art or the techniques used. • Model social conversation skills by talking with toddlers about the process—what they are doing with the art materials. • Plan a few art experiences that two or three children can enjoy together such as finger painting on cafeteria trays or on the table; scribbling on a large piece of paper taped to the table; painting with brushes and other items—for example with toothbrushes, straws, and the soles of shoes (old, worn out ones!!).

Figure 63a. Promoting Social Development Throughout a Preschool Environment

Area/Center	Tips for Supporting Social Development
Transition	• Make sure space is large enough to accommodate stress-free drop-off and pick-up times when a few preschoolers might experience separation anxiety. • Post recent photos in the communication center of the preschoolers' activities so families can talk with their children about their experiences at the program. • Set up the area so preschoolers can use self-help skills to remove and hang up coats, stow boots, write on the sign-in chart (as many letters of their name as they know), and so on. • Greet children warmly upon arrival and let them know what activities are available; help them choose whom to play with and what to do.
Science	• Offer materials that invite children to explore and discuss what they find; for example, place a dried sunflower blossom in a shallow box with several magnifying glasses alongside. Remind children to tell each other what they discover. Change items frequently to maintain and spark interest. For example, items from nature may be seasonal or regional (pinecones, gourds, seashells, rocks, wasp nests, cicada husks, dried corn, colorful leaves, nuts, and seeds) and others can emphasize specific science concepts that students can explore independently (prisms, flashlights, clay, soil, seeds, fabrics of different textures, smells, weights, bug boxes, tweezers, goggles, color paddles, batteries wires, and lights, etc.). • Plan small group activities that encourage children to experiment and makes sense of science concepts; for example, making an ocean in a bottle and making kaleidoscopes. • Have one child learn how to use a new piece of equipment—such as a microscope—then teach it to another child, who then teaches it to another, until the whole group are experts.
Art	• Use double-sided easels to encourage conversations between artists. • Visit the art center and encourage the "artists" to observe and comment on each other's techniques and use of color. • Provide opportunities for individuals to create as well as activities for small groups to work together, for example to paint a mural or make a giant thank you card to send to the violinist who visited the group. Remember that the product is not what children at this age are, or should be focused on. Their attention is generally on the process of using the medium or on the process of making something with the medium. Keep conversations focused on process (you are making such big strokes) rather than on the products (what a pretty cat) to best support children in productive commenting on one another's work.

Figure 63b. Promoting Social Development Throughout a Preschool Environment

Area/Center	Tips for Supporting Social Development
Cooking	• Set up snack so children can serve themselves when hungry and eat with their friends if they like. • Plan and lead small group cooking activities that allow children to take turns using the tools and completing the steps in the recipe (for example, children can take turns using the hand beater and punching down the risen bread dough). • Vary the types of tools and cooking you do so that children learn about foods from other cultures. • Serve the results of children's cooking, family-style, to invite discussions about how to make the foods served and other topics of interest to the children.
Sand and Water	• Take advantage of the limited physical and group size of these activities to encourage social interactions. "Julie, you and Sydney are both filling and dumping containers of water. I wonder whose container is smallest?" • Observe to see which props are most popular—this week—and provide extras of those items so children do not get frustrated by having to wait too long for a turn which can lead to disagreements with each other. • Offer multiples of clean-up items so children can work together to mop up spills (several sponges) or sweep sand (two brooms and dustpans).
Math and Manipulatives	• Stock the center with materials for children to use in pairs and groups as well as items likely to be used alone. • Play games with children to help them learn the rules; continue as a play partner as long as they need reminders of how to play the game. • Encourage joint building projects—e.g., with magnetic tiles—by making sure there is space to save the project so the builders can continue the next day. • Create an atmosphere where cooperative learning is valued. "Portia and Andrew, you are both ready for a more challenging puzzle. You could work on it together."
Music and Movement	• Plan and lead partner activities such as sitting back-to-back and trying to stand up. • Lead activities that require cooperation for children to be successful, such as keeping a beach ball or balloon in the air by tapping it when it is within reach. • Teach children partner dances.
Blocks and Group Meetings	• Make sure there are plenty of blocks and props—enough so children can carry out their plans without having to wait for another child to return them to the shelf. • Use group meetings to establish a sense of community; make announcements, introduce new activities or materials, solve problems jointly, and invite children to share their own news, work, and stories. • Provide opportunities for all children to access the group meeting so everyone is included. Help students understand that "attention" may look different for one child or another, but they are still a part of the group. • Provide fidget toys, low chairs, lap blankets, assistance from another adult, or any other support that scaffolds for children with differing physical and developmental needs to access and participate in the group.

Figure 63c. Promoting Social Development Throughout a Preschool Environment

Area/Center	Tips for Supporting Social Development
Dramatic Play	• Provide culturally relevant props, dress-up clothes, and child-size furniture so children can play house. • Create prop boxes based on current interests. • Observe and respond to children's interests by providing props for new scenarios; ask children what kind of pretend setting they would like and involve them in setting it up. • Join the play scenario and model the social skills used during play such as cooperating, compromising, problem solving, taking turns, and so on. "What can I do to help? Is there any cleaning or ironing I can do?" • Notice and provide specific suggestions to children who have difficulty getting involved in group dramatic play. "Celia, it looks like this bodega could use a cash register. Can you get the one from the shelf and use it to ring up the groceries?" Over time, Celia will be able to apply your suggestions and get involved in group play on her own.
Literacy	• Include books about typical issues that preschoolers are likely to encounter. For example, *The Boy Who Wouldn't Share by Mike Reiss and Different Kinds of Goodbyes* by Shelly Rotner and Sheila M. Kelly. • Provide persona dolls and puppets that portray different ethnicities, identities, and abilities—including those of the children in the group. After educators model their use, children can act out stories and solve problems, such as how to ask a friend to play. • Have children write and draw illustrations for joint books. For each page the partner can create a page about the same topic or in response to their friend's page. • Provide cozy chairs and pillows where two or three friends can read.

Supporting Children's Play

As discussed in Chapters 5 and 7, play, particularly pretend play, is a unique and effective learning medium that paves the way for academic and social success. Studies confirm the superiority of play-based models in comparison to academic curriculum models (Trawick-Smith 2009). These study results are especially pronounced for children with language delays, perceptual impairments, and autism. In addition, play has been found to be one of the best predictors of children's later language and learning (Lewis et al. 2000). Dual language learners use more elaborate first and second language during their free play, which leads to increased language learning.

In the late 1920s, sociologist Mildred Parten from the Institute of Child Development in Minnesota, studied young children's play and identified six stages that begin in infancy and continue through the preschool years. These categorizations of play continue to apply today.

1. **Unoccupied play:** Typical of newborns and very young infants whose movements seem random and unplanned. The infant is observing people and things in the environment.
2. **Solitary play:** Infants play by themselves (and with adults who initiate the play). They might shake a rattle, bang two blocks together, or look at a cloth book. The infant is focused on what they are doing, not the play of others.
3. **Onlooker play:** The child watches other children's play but does not join in. The primary activity is watching. Toddlers, while still developing social skills, may engage in onlooker play.
4. **Parallel play:** In this type of play, common among toddlers, children sit side-by-side, playing in the same area or with the same materials, but do not play together. For example, two children sit side-by-side in a sandbox. One digs and the other pours sand through a sieve. Copying another child's play is a characteristic of parallel play so the digger may pick up a sieve and start sifting or the sifter might switch to digging.

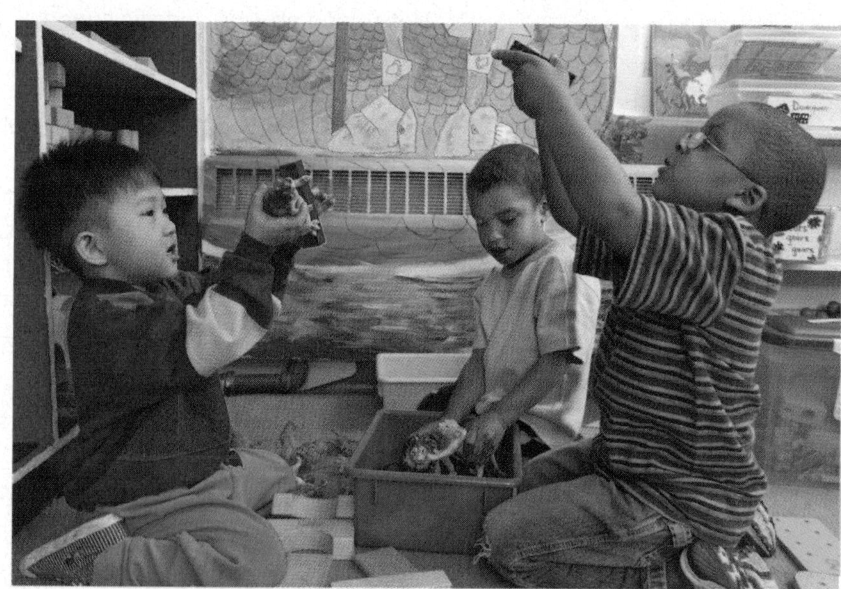

You promote play in your setting with the materials you provide to children and the design of the learning environment.

5. **Associative play:** Typical of older toddlers and young preschoolers, children are interested in each other and moving from playing alone to being a member of a group at play. They engage in separate but related activities, may exchange materials, and discuss what each child is doing.
6. **Cooperative play:** By the time children are preschoolers, most children are able to participate in cooperative play. Two or more children work together to complete a common goal, such as planting a garden or painting a mural. The children discuss their common goal, devise a plan to achieve it, and celebrate the accomplishment together. Cooperative play comes naturally to preschoolers who have developed the social skills needed to get along with others. For example, Irene and Thad are sitting next to each other in the block center. They decide to build something together—a racing boat. While planning how to proceed, they share ideas, negotiate, and compromise—skills that help them reach their goal.

As children get older, they spend more time engaged in the final two types of play, both of which require use of social skills and interactions. They still enjoy the previous stages, but appear to find playing with other children to be the most enjoyable.

Psychologists view pretend play as the "intersection of cognitive development and social experiences" (Seifert 2004). While pretending to engage in social interactions, such as eating a family meal or dressing a doll for bed, children use social cues to fill in the blanks. For example:

- Donald, 22-months-old, takes off his shoe and holds it up to his ear like a telephone and pretends to talk to someone on the other end of the line. His beginning pretend play represents a real-life experience and shows that he understands symbolism—a cognitive leap.
- Violet and Roberto, both three-year-olds, have each selected a doll stroller. Violet buckles a stuffed bunny in her stroller; a stuffed bear sits in Roberto's stroller. The two children take their "babies" for a walk around the room. Their play is social and mimics an experience they have seen at home—both have baby siblings.
- Older preschoolers Gerard and Emma are planning a tea party, like the one Miss Spider had. They envision the bevy of foods and teas on the table and figure out together the best way to serve the treats. They spend a significant amount of time planning their play before carrying out the plans.

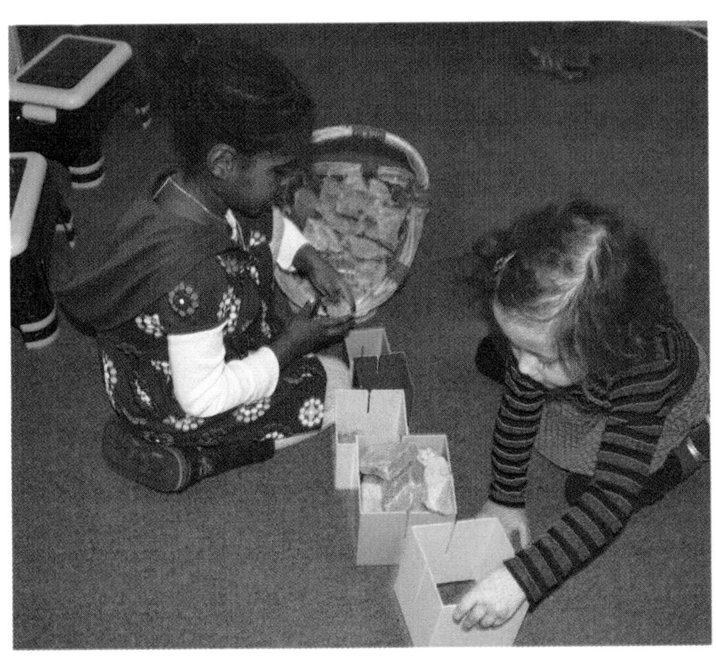

By the time children are preschoolers, they are able to participate in cooperative play.

During play, children use social circumstances to make cognitive gains. By learning to read others' expressions, children determine how they should respond. This is called social referencing. For example, when preschooler Bruce enters a pretend medical office in his family child care home, Emily, his pretend doctor, eyes him and nods toward the chair. Bruce sits down and remains quiet. In this pretend play session, Emily and Bruce understand the roles they are assuming, how they have been integrated into the scenario, and how they should react to each other.

As described in Chapter 7, dramatic play helps children understand and experiment with social roles, consider others' needs, and appreciate different values and perspectives. *Emotional self-regulation* (control of emotions, behavior, and impulses) is linked closely to and develops through dramatic play. When children talk to themselves during play about the tasks they will complete and how to complete them, this is evidence of developing self-regulation skills. Once children can self-regulate, they are open to mastering and employing social skills, like sharing and taking turns.

Each time children enter a dramatic play scenario, they learn more about how others live and work in the world. The home area is the focus of most dramatic play learning centers. Here, children assume family roles, like mom, dad, children, grandchildren, and pets. Using pretend foods and child-size furnishings, pots, cutlery, and dishes, children prepare, serve, and clean up after meals. They engage in family discussions over meals and dress for school and work.

Early childhood educators can work with the children to add other settings that are relevant to children's lives and experiences. Typical settings include a grocery store, a business, a veterinary clinic, the post office, a unisex hair salon, or a medical office. In each new setting, children learn more about how people live, work, and interact with one another. By assuming the roles of cashiers, hair stylists, or entrepreneurs, children can explore these relationships further.

Preschoolers can help select and create a new dramatic play setting by sharing the experiences, interests, and materials that appeal to them. For example, Shantel tells her teacher, Mr. Trent, about an upcoming appointment at the doctor's office and says, "I'm scared she's going to give me a shot. I know it will hurt." Mr. Trent and Shantel work together to design and plan materials for a new doctor's office setting. Because Shantel could make choices about her play, participating in creating this new setting can empower her. Mr. Trent helped Shantel understand and master her fears, even if it is just for pretend. The more details included in the setting, the more realistic and fun the experience will be.

Fantasy scenarios can also foster children's imaginations and creativity. Depending on the group's interests, they might enjoy a giant bird's nest, rocket ship, castle, or log cabin. Involve them in deciding what to create and ask them what materials they need for their play. Engaging children in determining the topics and designs of dramatic play settings will both scaffold children's learning and engage them in the learning process.

Opportunities for child-initiated and child-directed play is a critical feature of developmentally appropriate early childhood settings. Although children's play is authentic and meaningful when self-directed, there are times when you, the early educator, can enter their play to scaffold their learning. For example, Sarah is shy and afraid that the other children will not want to play with her. Sit next to Sarah at the table in the dramatic play learning center and announce to the children, "Sarah and I have had a long day at the office. What can we make for dinner?" Your participation can ensure that the play is the kind of high level play that is linked to school readiness and language development, and supports children's understanding of the world around them.

Assembling Prop Boxes

One way to respond to children's interests is to create theme-based prop boxes. Each box includes a collection of props, materials, and accessories related to the theme. The items are stored in a container—plastic storage bin, cardboard filing box with handles, or a basket. The props for a "Going on a Picnic" prop box could be stored in a wicker picnic basket or a thermal cooler.

Prop boxes are appropriate in any setting, but can be an especially useful way to offer diverse experiences in family child care settings. They do not take up much space and can be easily stored when not in use.

Prop boxes are an excellent tool for supporting or enhancing children's interests, building on their experiences, and offering new content and challenges. Be sure to include enough materials for several children to assume roles and plan and carry out a play scenario. Also, think about the vocabulary words you can introduce and reinforce as part of the play. Here are examples of prop box themes and what you could include in the box:

Optometrist (created because a child recently visited the optometrist)

- Book, such as *The Adventures of Anthony as Seen through His Eyes* by David B. Miller
- Eye chart
- Small paddle to cover one eye when reading the chart
- Small flashlight
- Eyeglass frames
- Calendar
- Magazines
- Pad of paper and pencils
- Mirror on a stand
- White medical jacket (like an optometrist might wear)

Roles: customer, receptionist, optometrist, assistant, and optician (to fit the glasses)

Vocabulary: optometrist, optician, lens, vision, iris, pupil, cornea

Car wash (the weather just started to be warm enough for outdoor water play; access to water is required; set up near the garden so the water is reused)

- Cardboard and markers for makings signs
- Tricycles, wagons, and other vehicles
- Sponges
- Squeegees

Assembling Prop Boxes - Car wash (continued)

- Towels for drying "cars"
- Buckets
- Hose
- Spray bottle
- Chamois cloths
- Cash register
- Play money

Roles: customers, car washers, tire cleaners, car dryers, cashier

Vocabulary: chamois, vehicle, exterior, interior, recycle, process

Encouraging Children's Positive Relationships

Group life, including interactions with early educators and peers help children learn about social skills and roles naturally. As children grow, they watch the world around them, noting people's similarities and differences. This provides a prime opportunity to talk about race and justice with young children. Consider adding books about race and mirrors so children's spontaneous conversations don't shy away from a topic many adults in their lives may be uncomfortable with. Children also learn how social groups operate and determine ways to join and participate in groups successfully. Talk about fairness and the ways that some groups and individuals are treated based on their race identity or ethnicity to help children value equity and grow away from societal biases in their interactions. You can help children engage in successful social interaction by developing attachment-based and respectful relationships with each child and ensuring a friendly, supportive community within your setting.

Foster Attachments and Build Relationships

Attachment—the foundation for trust and understanding the importance and significance of relationships—has a historical foundation in the work of John Bowlby and Mary Ainsworth. Initially, **secure attachment** was seen as only occurring between a mother and child. Over time, however, observation and further research have shown that **secure attachment** is available and sustainable in a relationship with a significant other. Yes, a mother, father, sibling, extended family member or primary early educator can initiate secure attachment. Secure attachment is vital to well-being, outlook on life, engagement with others and additional positive life outcomes.

Unfortunately, **secure attachment** is only one of four generally identified types of attachment. **Insecure attachment**—or the absence of trust and meaningful relationships—breaks down into three subcategories based on the interaction and relationship with the parent or other significant adult in a child's life. Those three subcategories are usually identified as avoidant attachment, anxious attachment and disorganized attachment.

While these categories may seem cut and dried, there is much discussion about the fact that outside of laboratory situations, attachment may fall more on a spectrum and be harder to cleanly assess in real life. There are also differences in the ways that children show attachment that may be cultural (specifically Japanese children express attachment in ways that look different from more Western expectations). As our understandings about early childhood, stress, and trauma evolve, we understand these expressions of attachment may be shaped by factors other than the caregiving relationship. Even so, it is valuable to examine these attachment types to help understand the importance of the caregiving relationship providers must form with each and every child.

How are attachment types identified? As noted above, research over time has provided opportunities to identify the different types of attachment. By using a procedural technique and assessment called the Infant Strange Situation, young children are observed and the reunion between a child and parent after a brief separation is examined (video examples of this research procedure are available on YouTube). What happens during the reunion, and how it occurs, provides the observer with the attachment type that exists between the child and parent.

As demonstrated during the procedure, upon reunion with a parent, securely attached children will be comforted and gleefully reengage in a mutual warm, caring relationship. Observation clearly reveals the child's sense of trust that the parent is meeting their needs and that the relationship is significant.

Avoidant attachment occurs during a parent and child reunion if the child appears reluctant, shows hesitation or simply ignores the parent's return. This is generally indicative that the young child's needs are not being met, the parent is often "not present" and a lack of trust in the relationship exists.

When the young child has a reunion with a parent that does not seem to be consistent with how the child has responded or interacted earlier, an anxious attachment is probably indicated. A mixed emotional response to the interaction and feelings of insecurity or uncertainty are indicative of the **anxious attachment**. The child is showing that their needs are not always met and trust is a concern.

Disorganized attachment is perhaps the most distressing for the observer as well as the child. Disorganized attachment is often related to more disturbing circumstances as represented in the lack of a meaningful, loving, caring or sincere relationship with the parent. At the reunion, the child may demonstrate behaviors and actions that look much like emotional disturbance, irritation, personal angsts and more.

While every person/child experiences different types of attachment to a parent, family member or teacher, the type of attachment that becomes a guiding or significant part of a young child's life has implications for long-term results. It is imperative that all persons in a child's life are aware of how their relationship and interaction with that young child influence who that child develops into as a member of society.

As mentioned above, attachment was historically thought to be what happens between a mother and child. But we now understand that the attachment a child forms with any significant person in their life plays a very important part in governing other aspects of their existence.

The quality of young children's relationships with their early childhood educators is related both to children's future academic success and future social relationships (Hyson and Taylor 2011). Young children who grow up experiencing more secure attachment relationships are more likely to get along with peers, develop empathy, and make friends easily and are less likely to become bullies or the victims of bullies (Riley, San Juan, Klinkner, and Ramminger 2008).

As an early childhood educator, you can form secure attachments with children beginning in infancy as you use feeding and diapering routines as opportunities to talk, nurture, and meet infants' social and emotional needs. Your verbal and nonverbal communications can let the children know that you care about them and that they are special. Use children's names, offer appropriate hugs, and play, talk, and laugh together often. If you do not speak a child's home language, learn a few important words and phrases and ask the family to suggest songs, books, and other materials to help the child feel a sense of belonging in the setting.

Once children are verbal, you can ask about what they like to do at home with their families. Talk with their parents regularly and make home visits when appropriate. Children feel extra secure when they see their families and educators working together to support their learning. As an early childhood educator, you share a significant part of children's lives, and they come to rely on you. They need to believe that you care about what happens to them and their family members.

These attachments help you provide an environment that supports individual and developmental needs and respond to children's culture and language. When you create strong bonds with children, you make them feel safe and secure, help them form relationships with peers and other adults, and give them the confidence to take risks and solve problems. Children are also more likely to imitate respectful relationships because you have been a caring role model.

Three practices fuel the types of relationships that foster attachments and show children you care about, appreciate, and value them unconditionally (Dodge, Colker, and Heroman 2002):

1. Talking and listening to children respectfully.
2. Being sensitive to children's feelings.
3. Validating children's accomplishments and progress.

Also low child-to-educator ratios, small groups, primary caregiving, continuity of care, responsive routines, and engaging learning environments all encourage the formation of your relationships with each child and their relationships with each other.

Create a Learning Community

Your setting is where staff, children, and their families all connect. Though these connections define the dynamics of your learning community, you set the tone for the ways children relate to others and others relate to the children. Focus on helping children develop the skills they need to participate as a member of the learning community. Use your relationships to help older children understand rules and expectations, play with others, and participate fully in the learning community. Providing children with these positive experiences fulfills a core philosophy and ensures that they have the opportunity to be successful and reach their potential.

Although they are rapidly developing and gaining new skills, infants are not aware of being part of a learning community. As they get older, however, they become more aware of other children and what they can and cannot do. They are also keenly aware of their own individual characteristics—including what they know and can do and what they are learning.

Within the learning community in your setting, children take part in different groupings throughout the day. You might begin with group time for everyone, or almost everyone, then go on to choice time and small group activities. Toileting routines might be individual if the bathroom is in the room or in a family child care home, or carried out in pairs or small groups if the bathroom is down the hall. Regardless of the size of the group, however, when children work together to achieve common goals, they learn how to work as a team, support one another, and value and respect each other's thoughts and feelings. Educators can help promote this kind of learning community by planning projects children can complete in groups, like decorating the setting, writing thank you notes to guests, tending a garden, or doing what educator Nancy Jones calls "Big Jobs" (2005). In her program the children work together to sweep the driveway or carry a bag of balls outside.

Nancy Jones also describes the use of group sizes and arrangements as a way to promote friendly social learning. Her suggestions include the following:

- Plan an errand: An educator asks a child to do a task such as retrieving a book from the shelf. The child feels valued, like someone needs his assistance, and perhaps gains enough confidence to invite another child to play.
- Ask a child for help: Plan a one-on-one activity; when one child is done ask her to tell the next participant it's their turn.

- Provide opportunities for children to support one another. A buddy who is able to do a task might support a child who struggles with or has a disability related to that task. This provides access for the child who is learning, and empowers the child who is helping.
- Make all children experts: Encourage children to ask each other a question or for a reminder of how to do something, before coming to an adult.
- Encourage team work: Instead of filling the water table before children arrive, have plenty of buckets on hand so children can work as a team to fill the table.
- Use different spatial arrangements when gathering as a group: Sit on the steps in a triangle formation so everyone can see; form a circle, a friendlier way to gather than forming a line; use a line only when it makes sense, for example when washing hands and both sinks are in use.
- Designate a waiting place: When moving from one place to the next, keep track of the children who go too far ahead by telling them a specific place to wait for the rest of the group. For example, we're going inside now. When you get to the gate, stop and wait for the rest of us.

One way to encourage cooperation is to play non-competitive games that have no winners or losers. Play expert Rae Pica (n.d.) says that when given the choice, most young children prefer to play cooperative games over competitive ones. Competition pits children against one another, raises stress levels, and reduces group trust and motivation. Cooperation, on the other hand, makes children feel good about themselves and each other, increases self-esteem, fosters group trust, and increases motivation. When children cooperate during games, they develop critical listening skills, support and encourage each other, take turns, and find pleasure in others' successes. Consider how a game like "Musical Chairs" results in one winner and everyone else losing. The satisfaction of playing a game where everyone engages and no one is left feeling they were unsuccessful is greater for everyone.

The following are additional ways in which you can provide a positive, supportive learning community throughout the day:

Choice time: (indoors and outdoors). Children can choose to play or work alone or with others in small or larger groups depending on interest. They learn to share, take turns, enter groups of children at play, and observe how other children use materials, objects, and equipment. Outdoors

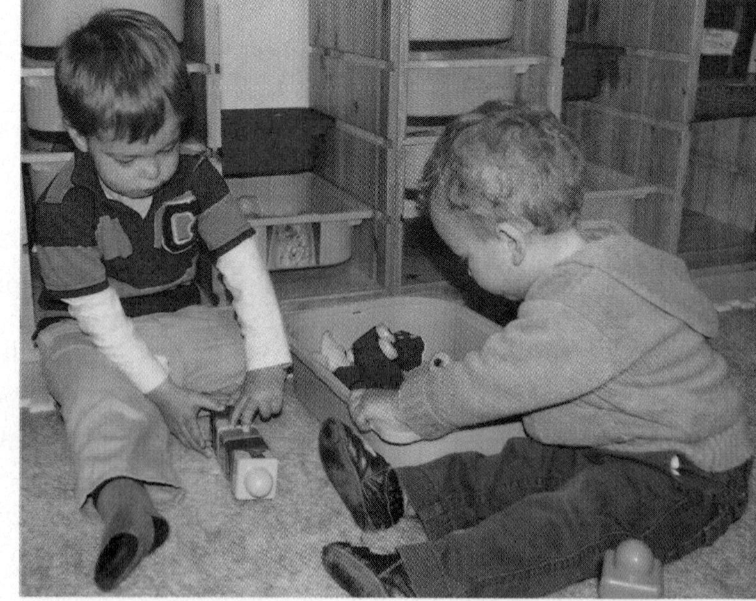

Parallel play involves two children sitting near each other but performing two independent tasks.

children can join small group activities, such as gardening, cooking in the mud kitchen, or woodworking. They can study leaves, read, or use climbing equipment, bikes, and the sandbox independently or with other children.

Group meetings. These gatherings should be engaging and brief. With a new community of learners, start with a short daily meeting that lasts about 10 minutes. Extend the duration over time until meetings last 15–20 minutes. Children can sit on a carpet tile or other defined spot, to minimize crowding (some children particularly need to have space around them). Over time you can help them learn to keep their arms and legs away from others and respond when called upon. Encourage participation during group songs, finger plays, and dances and include opportunities for children to share examples of their work and play. If children do not want to participate in group meetings, excuse them to play or read alone quietly. If children opt out of group meetings, consider the reason for this preference. You might need to make the meetings shorter or more engaging, or observe the child at other times of the day to see if she often has strategies that work for her at other times of the day. If she does, explore further to learn what you can do to help her develop those strategies for use in group meetings. The family can be one source of additional information about ways to engage and accommodate a child who is not interested in group meetings.

Small group activities. These adult-planned experiences are typically led by an educator or a volunteer. Educators form the groups intentionally, perhaps by skill level by language, or by interests, and perhaps to encourage certain children to get to know one another. Depending on the activity, the children might work individually or as a group. For example, while four children make applesauce, each child sits at the table and carries out the steps. They all dice one or two apples, consult the recipe then measure the correct amount of cinnamon, and take turns stirring.

Mealtimes. During family-style dining, children take turns serving themselves and passing items to each other. They converse with and learn about their tablemates (including educators) and discuss weekend activities and their favorite foods. Mealtimes are opportunities to begin to develop friendships.

Help Children Form Friendships

Learning how to start and maintain friendships is a critical life skill that children learn in the early childhood years. The social skills used to have and be a friend begin to develop when young infants see themselves as separate beings, mobile infants begin showing preference for certain children in particular, and toddlers respond to another child's invitation to play or talk. By the preschool years, children have gained the confidence and social skill, such as being able to compromise and solve disagreements amicably, needed to form and maintain friendships and children take great pleasure from the experience of friendship.

Laura Berk, a developmental psychologist who has published widely on the effects of children's development, defines *friendship* as "a mutual relationship involving companionship, sharing, understanding of thoughts and feelings, and caring for and comforting one another in times of need" (2002). The friendships children establish during the preschool years create a sense of belonging and security. Successful friendships in early childhood contribute to children's quality of life and give children what Lilian Katz and Jean Mendoza (2011) call a sense of "having a place." Friendships are essential for mental health and social–emotional well-being.

Children who have developed strong self-regulation skills can play and relate well without adult intervention.

Most children can learn the skills needed to make friends and keep friends. They enjoy social interactions, have a positive sense of self, and are liked by their peers. They can use social skills such as waiting for a turn and compromising. Children with strong social skills are resilient in the face of rejection (Dewar 2009). They are able to explain their rejection ("Perhaps Rachel already had too many friends to play with"), bounce back, and reach out again ("Rachel's playing alone with the dolls. Maybe I can play with her now.").

It is important for each child to develop prosocial skills, form friendships, and treat each other with respect, compassion, and kindness. However, it is not realistic or authentic to teach children that everyone is friends with every single other person they encounter. Though it is beneficial for all children to get along, they should develop friendships on their own. Adults should never force children to become friends with everyone.

Early childhood educators can support friendship in the following ways:

Create opportunities for children to play and work together. Mix the membership of small groups so children can learn from and get to know each other in a variety of contexts. Give children who are shy or reluctant additional support and coaching.

Model what to say to express interest in playing with others: "Jimmy, Andy was wondering if you'd like to work with him on this new alphabet puzzle," or "Jimmy, let's get these cars ready for the race. Miguel, may we join you in racing our cars?" With practice, children can reach out to potential friends. Explicitly teach these friendship skills.

Discuss the subject of friendship during group time. Use puppets to tell a story about friendship. Work with the children to make a list of what it means to be a friend. Remind them that friends can look and sound different, but what they have in common is caring about and enjoying each other

Read and discuss books that include friendship as part of the story. There are many to choose from such as *My Friend Isabelle* by Eliza Woloson, *How Do Dinosaurs Play with Their Friends?* by Jane Yolen, and *Sam and Dave Dig a Hole* by Mac Barnett.

Coach children when they are working together on a task. Describe their shared efforts and encourage them to see how their teamwork contributed to their success. Sometimes friendships are formed just by sharing common experiences.

Model the joys of friendship. Talk to the children about your own friendships and the pleasure they bring.

Plan joint projects and events. For example, several children could take a turn eating a picnic lunch outdoors, a group could make a chalk drawing together on the sidewalk, or several children could turn a refrigerator carton into a cabin. Children tend to feel close to those they work with cooperatively.

Provide targeted assistance when social skills make it hard to make friends. Sometimes children act out when they are upset and others are quiet or reluctant to join in group play. Others have difficulty taking turns, sharing, or being close to other children. And some children have had few experiences in groups and have not had opportunities to learn the social skills needed to play and form friendships.

No matter how children behave, nobody benefits or learns from being rejected and excluded, but everyone benefits from learning to accept "no" gracefully and come back to try again.

The following are ways you can support children who find it hard to make friends:

For children who physically express frustration:

Provide acceptable choices. For example, "McKenzie, I can't let you hurt Star. I know that you want to play house with her, but when you grab the dolls and push Star down, that hurts her and she doesn't want to play together. Last week we talked about what you could do when you feel frustrated or angry. You could try another activity, like playing at the water table. Or you can talk to me about how you feel." Teach all children to identify "big" feelings and strategies for calming down.

Agree on a "safe" phrase or gesture a child can use when losing control. For example, shouting the word rabbit will alert you that Jasmine feels like she is losing control. Jasmine can sit in the "calm down" area and take deep breaths, blow bubbles, use a sensory bottle, hug a soft animal, smell a scented sachet, do chair pushups, color, or listen to calming music until she feels calm and has regained composure. This strategy can support a child with self-regulation and would make him seem like a more appealing play partner to the others in the group.

Talk with a child after a frustrated outburst. Once you and the child feel calm it will be easier to discuss what happened and why and what were the consequences. If the child does not know what triggered the behavior, suggest what you think might be the cause. "I think you want to play superhero too and you felt angry when Ian and Hannah said you couldn't play. It's okay to feel angry, but it's not okay to kick them. What could you have done instead?"

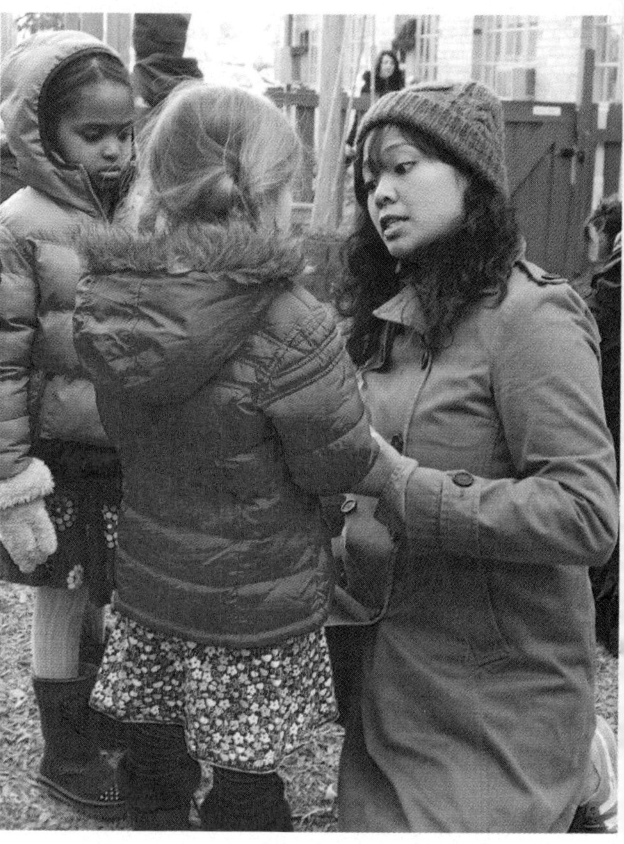

Use the children's own words to repeat each child's side of the situation and to let them know that you heard them.

Spend one-on-one time with the child. Children often need more time with caring adults who will convey to them that they are unconditionally valued and appreciated. Many children simply don't know how to make and be friends yet and need to learn to manage their emotions safely. Building a relationship will help the child feel safe. One on one time could be as simple as reading a book together or laughing at a silly joke. Or, it could be an opportunity to let the child know that you noticed her. "Anita, I was looking out the window this morning when I saw you and your sister getting off the bus. You were very gentle with her, holding her hand and making sure she had her mittens on. She is lucky to have you as a big sister."

For children who seem to be shy or reluctant to join in:

Help children feel safe engaging with others. Some children, including some children with disabilities may not understand another person's social cues. They may need your help to learn what behaviors are likely to support play and friendships. Children with developmental delays, however, are able to reach out to others much like the rest of their peers (Yu, Ostrosky, and Fowler 2011).

Observe and interpret for the child what the others are doing. "Let's sit in the loft and watch the pizza makers. Marco is putting on an apron. Maybe he is the chef. Katie is getting the cash register out. I think she will be the cashier. And Peter has a pad of paper and a pencil. What do you think he is going to be?"

Offer specific suggestions of what a child could say and do to join a group in play. For example, the child could ask questions about the play scenario and roles, offer a new prop, or focus on playing with one child at first, Coach the child to say, "Marco, I will help you make the pizzas. I think we will need a lot of them."

Pair the child with another child who has similar interests. Educators can pair children to run an errand, do an activity, perform a job, or water the garden. During their joint activity the children will get to know each other better and may join each other in play in the future.

For children who are avoided by the others in the group:

Help children ask questions about physical characteristics that may be new to them or misunderstood. While getting to know each other, young children tend to focus on only one aspect of another person at a time. Help children talk openly about what they see and wonder. Invite them to ask questions about how to play with a child in a wheelchair, or why a child is wearing certain clothes, or differences they notice in skin or hair. Read books that feature children with physical disabilities, such as *Rolling Along: The Story of Taylor and His Wheelchair* by Jamee Riggio Heelan and *Some Kids Wear Leg Braces* by Lola M. Schaefer. Books about different physical characteristics, such as *I Love My Hair* by Natasha Tarpley or *Don't Touch My Hair* by Natasha Tarpley, or *Eyes that Kiss at the Corners* by Joanna Ho, or *Shades of People* by Sheila M. Kelly and Shelley Rotner can help children start conversations about differences that might get in the way of friendships otherwise. Providing persona dolls with a visible disability, or other identity differences including one who uses a wheelchair, is another way to help children welcome all of their peers.

Observe to learn more about the child's social behavior. Conduct your observations at different times of the day and in different settings, both indoors and outdoors. Review and analyze your notes, looking for patterns in the child's behavior and the responses of the other children.

If you are leading a small group activity, children can work individually or in groups to follow along with the activity.

With this information you can intentionally plan ways to help this child gain the social skills needed to play and make friends now and in the future. Once a child has been rejected it is critical to break this cycle as soon as possible so it does not continue in the future.

Fostering Prosocial Behavior

Prosocial behaviors are voluntary actions intended to benefit another person. They require empathy and include compassion, cooperation, taking turns, generosity, being fair, feeling and showing affection, being kind, and helping. These behaviors develop over time, beginning in infancy. An infant might cry when she hears another baby crying. When adults use angry voices, babies notice and may reflect their mood by being upset. A mobile infant might try to return a toy to another baby who dropped it. Toddlers are likely to comfort a friend who is upset. Preschoolers learn how to put someone else's needs before their own needs. They might share a banana, offer a toy to a peer, or comfort a friend who is upset.

Children who behave prosocially in early childhood settings continue to behave this way throughout their lives.

To behave prosocially, children must know how to empathize (identify with what another person is feeling) and understand another person's perspective. As defined by Quann and Wien (2006) empathy in young children is "the capacity to observe the feelings of another and to respond with care and concern for that other" Prosocial development of infants and toddlers relies on the respectful, responsive care of adults whose own prosocial behaviors are visible every day. "By being treated with respect by adults, infants learn they are valued and, in turn, how to value and respect others" (McMullen, M. 2013).

Establishing positive interactions among all children and adults creates an atmosphere of mutual respect and support, encourages prosocial behaviors, and develops a supportive community of learners. Moreover, children who behave prosocially in early childhood settings continue to behave this way throughout their lives.

Early childhood development and education expert Marilou Hyson says that adults often forget that prosocial behaviors are voluntary (Hyson and Taylor 2011). For example, if Ricky apologizes to others only when his FCC provider tells him to do so, his actions are not prosocial, because they are involuntary. However, with adult support and facilitation, children can learn prosocial behaviors.

The following are ways in which you can help children gain empathy and other prosocial skills:

- **Provide consistent, individualized care.** This is important at any age and teaches children that they can count on you to keep them safe and that you value them as individuals.
- **Help children understand and identify their own feelings and those of others.** For example, "When you threw the lotto pieces on the floor, you looked very frustrated. It's upsetting when a game seems too difficult." "Omar is feeling sad this morning. He misses his Dad. They are going to Skype tonight but that seems like a long time away."
- **Read books where you can discuss or ask children to describe the characters' feelings.** For example, "Mr. Worm is sad that no one came to Baby Worm's party." Ask children why a character may be feeling a certain way once the emotion is identified. "Yes, Mr. Worm looks sad. Why do you think he feels this way?"
- **Help children to interpret facial expressions.** "Ms. Deanna raised her eyebrows and widened her eyes. I wonder what that means?"
- **Plan activities that involve the whole classroom community.** Teach the children some simple songs to sing to the residents at the nursing home next door, have them make pumpkin bread to serve at the family math fair, and make a video of children sending get well messages to their program director who is recuperating from surgery.
- **Model prosocial behaviors during the day.** For example, warmly greet families and follow up on past conversations, establish times when children can share something (a painting, block building, science discovery, or new skill) with the group, take lots of photographs and revisit them with the children ("Do you remember when the grapes rolled all over the picnic cloth?"), and help your colleagues ("I'll get that door for you, Ms. Kim. I see your hands are full.").
- **Involve children in projects that benefit the community at large.** Ask them for ideas on how to show community members that they care about them. You can organize the group to perform acts of kindness such as donating used toys and books to the pediatric clinic waiting room, weeding the flower beds at the park, or cooking snacks to bring to a homeless shelter.
- **Highlight children's acts of kindness at group time.** Establish a regular routine (daily or weekly, depending on your preference) of highlighting individual children's acts of kindness. Observe and make notes of these acts, then share them with the group. "This morning, Joshua moved his block building so the group working on the zoo structure would have space to build. Thank you, Joshua."

Once children have learned empathy, they can relate to others' feelings, which begets kindness. Children can now be caring and comfort their peers. Model kindness for the children in your setting and be respectful and caring toward others. Children's development of these skills and attributes will be uneven. Continue to support them all in the development of these skills and attitudes.

CHAPTER 10:

Guidance

CDA® Functional Area 10: Candidate provides a supportive environment and uses effective strategies to promote children's self-regulation and support acceptable behaviors, and effectively intervenes for children with persistent challenging behaviors.

Guidance

Introduction

It's choice time in a family child care setting and all of the children seem to be playing peacefully. Suddenly, there is a loud screech. Preschoolers Melissa and Brian are having a tug-of-war over a toy train. Within seconds, Melissa stops and says, "How can we both use the train?" Her FCC educator uses a positive guidance approach so Melissa has learned how to resolve conflicts on her own. In Chapter 9, we discussed creating a caring community of learners and helping children build the social skills needed to play and learn with each other. Several other chapters also described developmentally appropriate practices that support learning and positive behavior. In this chapter, we will focus on supporting and guiding children's behaviors. You will learn six important things you can do to maintain a responsive, caring environment that teaches children how to use positive behavior:

- **Setting the Stage for Positive Behavior**
- **Using Positive Guidance as a Teaching Strategy**
- **Understanding and Addressing Challenging Behaviors**
- **Replacing Time-Out With Time-In**
- **Stopping Bullying Behaviors Among Preschoolers**
- **Partnering With Families**

Setting the Stage for Positive Behavior

As the old adage states, "An ounce of prevention is worth a pound of cure." When applied to early childhood settings, this means that one of the most effective ways to guide children's behavior is to set the stage so children are more likely to share, take turns, use their words, and so on. Some of the ways you do this are by creating an appropriate, home-like environment, by having positive interactions with children, and by teaching children how you want them to behave. Of course, in addition to promoting positive behavior, you will be helping children to see themselves as competent individuals and will be preventing many problems. Several examples of how you can set the stage for positive behavior follow (Koralek 2007).

Follow recommended adult-child ratios and group size. For example, when early childhood educators must care for too many infants or the group size is too large, it will be very difficult to respond to children's needs quickly, consistently, and while building relationships. This is likely to lead to children feeling insecure in the setting and more prone to crying, frustration, and disengagement from adults. On the other hand, if the group size is appropriate and each educator has a small number of infants for whom she provides primary care, attachments will form and infants will learn to trust. Both attachment and trust are precursors to impulse control and other positive behaviors. "I whimpered a little to let you know I am hungry and need to be fed very soon. I trust you to meet this need so I can wait without crying."

Maintain appropriate expectations for each stage of development. For example, toddlers can do many things, but sharing and taking turns are skills that are still developing. If educators expect toddlers to use these prosocial skills, then toddlers are likely to act out because they are not yet able to do so. However, if the setting is stocked with multiples of popular items, toddlers can focus on their play and will not have to meet inappropriate behavioral expectations. It is also important to have appropriate expectations for individual children. Perhaps more than half of the two-year-olds are learning to use the toilet. It's fine for those children who are not ready to take their time preparing for this developmental milestone.

Be prepared to help children cope with feelings. For example, children may arrive at the program tired or hungry or upset about something that happened at home. They too may act out or be reluctant to participate. The simple solution is to offer breakfast upon arrival and set up a cot in the corner so the sleepy child can rest. Give some one-on-one attention to the child who is upset. If the child seems interested in talking, ask a colleague to take over for a bit while you listen and learn about what is causing the upset. The result will be more positive behavior and less use of behaviors that challenge the rest of the children and adults in the learning community.

Often, children get frustrated when they cannot articulate the way they feel.

You can set the stage for positive behavior by applying your knowledge of child development and good practice to create a supportive setting. Such settings foster positive behaviors and minimize behaviors that challenge everyone. The following suggestions are organized by age group—infants, toddlers, and preschoolers.

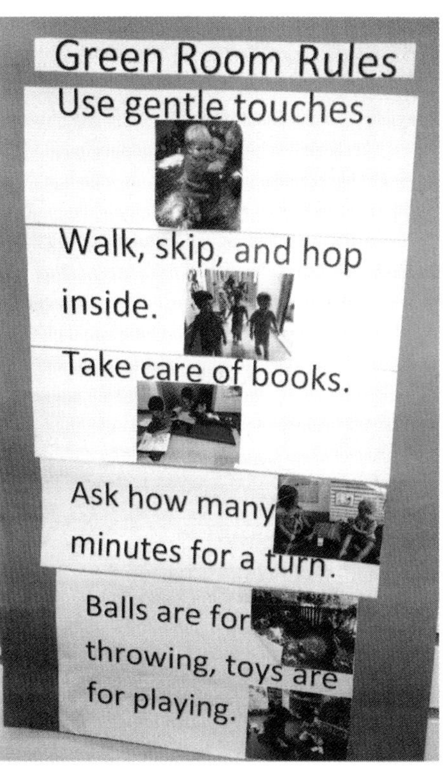

Most children in your setting are still learning to read, so represent rules with pictures.

Arrange the Space to Support Individuals and the Group

Infants

Provide separate play areas for infants and mobile infants. A protected tummy time area is ideal for young infants who tend to play and interact in a small space. Mobile infants can move and explore in other parts of the room. That way the mobile infants won't accidently harm the younger ones and the younger ones won't get in the way of the mobile infants' explorations.

Situate the diapering area so it provides visual access to the whole room. This allows you to give one on one attention to the infant being diapered while also keeping an eye on the other babies. The individual infant will be getting what she needs—a caring relationship—while the other children can continue playing and learning.

Observe and keep track of infants' rapidly growing skills. Young and mobile infants gain new skills seemingly overnight. One day Tyshawn is lying on her back holding and shaking a toy. The next day you find her on her tummy—she rolled over. From now on you will have to be extra vigilant to keep her safe and make sure there are no objects that get in the way of her using this new skill.

Offer mobile infants materials such as playdough and markers in a protected space. Mobile infants are ready to explore these materials using their senses and their fine motor skills, but it's best for them to do so in an area where the young infants can't get in the way or be harmed by these materials.

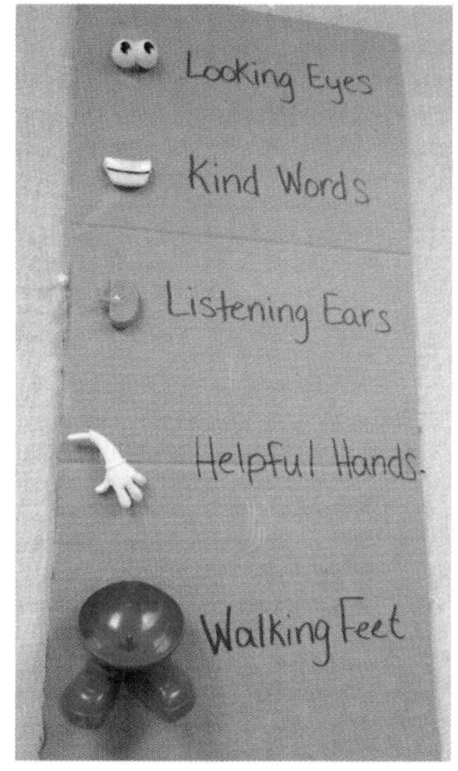

Do not overwhelm the children with rules; start with three to five.

Toddlers and Preschoolers

Set up a be-by-myself center. Include a single chair and a table or desk with a basket of soothing items—squeezable balls, small stuffed animals, table blocks and props, finger puppets, crayons and paper, and books. This can help children decrease stimulation, calm down, and learn to self-regulate their behavior and emotions.

Provide a self-service snack area. Place food and drinks on a table so children can eat and drink when they are ready. There is no need to interrupt children's play and activities to serve snack to everyone at once. Be available to help toddlers and older children as needed.

Include duplicates of popular items. Toddlers are still learning to share and take turns and often want to use the same item in their play. Preschoolers are much more able to share and take turns than they were as toddlers. They can, however, act out when the toys and materials needed to carry out their plans are not available.

Offer relaxing music and headphones. Suggest children listen for a while when they need a break from the group's noise and commotion. Wearing headphones blocks out the noise from the group and ensures the music will not bother anyone else.

Create small cozy places. Two beanbag chairs in a corner, a wading pool filled with pillows, a small tent, or a blanket-covered table are places where one or two children can play or relax alone or together.

Prevent accidents. Disagreements and outbursts can occur when children unintentionally get in each other's way. For example, place the fire trucks on a shelf that can be accessed without walking through the block center. Children who want to play with the trucks can get them without bothering the block builders or accidently toppling other children's creations.

Provide a group meeting space. Group meetings are times when children can take part in activities and discussions that pertain to everyone. Group meeting times give children a voice and a sense of being a community member. They are less likely to act out if they have had an opportunity to share a concern and to take part in problem solving. In settings that do not have room for a dedicated group meeting space, the meeting can take place in the block or music and movement center.

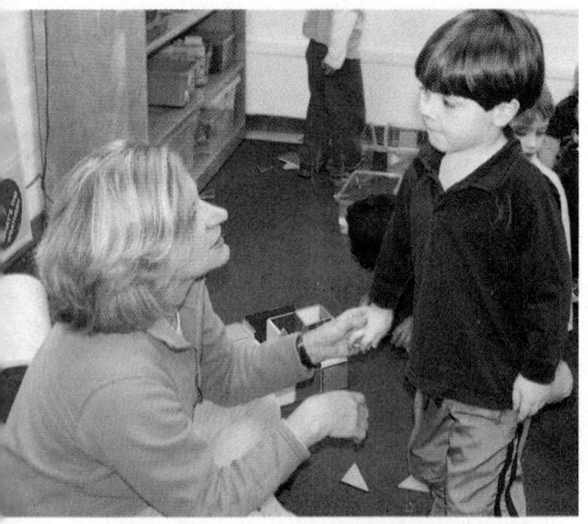

Positive guidance is the best approach for you to support children and help them maintain control of their behavior and emotions.

Maintain Appropriate Expectations Based on Child Development and Individual Needs

Infants

Build a caring, reciprocal relationship with each infant in your care. Your relationship-based care will teach the infant that she is important and valued—because you communicate these feelings to her each time you feed her a bottle or change her diaper or put her down to sleep on demand and not according to a schedule. Soon she will have warm feelings for you too. Caring, reciprocal relationships lead to attachment and trust, which in turn lead to a positive sense of self.

Building trust between early educators and children.

Accept that although some behaviors can be annoying, they are signs of development. For example, when one baby cries, another, and then another may join in. These infants are beginning to develop empathy—an important prosocial skill. A mobile infant might be developing his pincer grasp, so he doesn't have the fine motor skills needed to place his piece of pear back on the tray. Later, he discovers that he can drop things on purpose and wants to practice this skill again and again. The result might be several pear slices on the floor. You can provide some less slippery things to drop so he can continue building his fine motor skills.

Show infants who are ready to get to know their peers how to do so. Infants may not realize that they can hurt another child—when they pull Bunny's floppy ear he doesn't cry. Take the baby's hand and show her how to gently touch another child; play roll the ball with two mobile infants until they get the hang of it; and explain, "Your banana is on the plate in front of you; Omar's banana is on his plate. Omar wants to eat his banana himself."

Use "no" sparingly. By about 10 months, infants are aware that you might not appreciate all of their behaviors. They note that your tone of voice differs when you want them to stop doing something. Save "no," for when infants' safety is in jeopardy. They will learn to take these strong words seriously and stop what they are doing.

Let infants know you value their positive behavior. When infants coo, respond by cooing, too. When 16 month old Lucy moves to sit next to another child you might say. "Lucy you are sitting next to Joe. You're becoming friends. That's wonderful!" The children will begin to understand the joys of relating positively to others.

Toddlers

Acknowledge and support toddlers' interest in being independent. At the same time, be sure to remember toddlers still want and/or need your help sometimes. Involve them in routines and let them do tasks on their own. They can wash and dry their hands, select a book for a read-aloud session, and hold a sign for a game of "red light, green light." When they do seek you out, provide the one-on-one attention they need.

Provide opportunities for toddlers to experience success. This can help toddlers gain self-esteem and come to understand positive behavior. For example, toddlers can do simple tasks such as getting their own mats at nap time. Respond with specific praise that recognizes the child's effort and accomplishment. "Polly, you know how to get ready for nap. First you got your mat and then your blankie and now you are taking off your shoes."

Provide opportunities for toddlers to say, "No." Play games where you say, "Yes," and they say, "No." Sing songs that include the word *no* and read books that ask yes/no questions. Ask silly questions such as, "Do you wear shoes on your ears?" and act surprised when they say, "No." Exploring and experimenting with control helps toddlers learn to monitor their behavior.

Adapt a family-style dining approach to match toddlers' skills. For example, on the day the children have peas for lunch, provide spoons as well as forks. Hungry children will find it easier to scoop up the peas than try to stab them with a fork. Demonstrate how to hold a platter with both hands while passing it to the next person—to your left. Remind toddlers to not let go until their lunch companion has grasped the platter. Introduce good manners by having children wait until everyone has food on their plates before starting to eat. To make the waiting time pass quickly, sing a song together. You can end the song when all have served themselves.

Provide limits that tell toddlers what they can do. Toddlers really do not know what is permissible and what is not. It's up to adults—families and educators—to communicate a few clear limits. Limits tell toddlers what they can explore, where they can go, and what they can do. They give toddlers opportunities to begin developing self-regulation. Reminders are important too and should be stated in positive language. "You can only use the stool at the sink." When Polly carried the stool to the window sill and used it to climb on top, her early educator said, "The stool is to be used at the sink. Do you need my help to see outside?"

Preschoolers

Help preschoolers understand others' point of view. This is an important skill preschoolers are still working on. For example, three-year-olds Tony and Lisa are building with blocks. He places a block on his structure and Lisa responds with tears. "You took my block. I was saving it for my building." Tony looks puzzled. Their FCC educator steps in to explain, "Lisa, Tony did not know that you had set aside that block. Tony, Lisa is upset because she thinks you took her block on purpose." This explanation may or may not resolve the problem. If not, the educator will help the children figure out a solution.

Teach preschoolers the words that name their feelings. Having strong, negative feelings—anger, frustration, sadness—can be scary for preschoolers and can make them feel out of control. Being able to name their feelings returns some control to the situation and allows them to talk about the reasons for their feelings and how they might overcome them. Knowing the names for positive feelings is important too—a happy child probably wants to be able to express their joy as well as feel it.

Provide many opportunities to make choices, every day. Preschoolers are cognitively ready to make many decisions on their own. You can help them practice this skill by letting go of rules and guidelines that are not needed, and offering opportunities to make choices. For example, preschoolers can decide who to play with, which learning centers to visit and what to do there, how many carrots to put on their plate, what book to take to their cot at naptime, and whether their hands are cold enough to warrant wearing gloves. When preschoolers can make choices, they gain a sense of control and are more likely to follow the few simple rules for group life.

Offer toys and activities that are challenging, but not so difficult they cause frustration. When preschoolers get bored because they are not challenged to learn something new, they may express that boredom with challenging behaviors. In addition, preschoolers can be overwhelmed by toys that are too hard to enjoy (for example, a puzzle with too many pieces) or when they are expected to know how to do something they just cannot do yet (for example, writing their name when they do not have the fine motor skills needed to hold a pencil). It's best to offer a variety of toys and materials to meet a wide range of skill levels and to know and respond to each child's abilities (perhaps by planning activities that help a child build fine motor skills).

Anticipate and Plan for Behaviors that Can Cause Problems

The following suggestions are appropriate for infants, toddlers, and preschoolers.

Know and accommodate children's temperaments. Be aware of each child's typical responses to new people and events and plan accordingly. For example, if 12-month-old Ariel is highly active, expect that she will be eager to try the new climber and stay close by in case she needs help. Or, if four-year-old Karl tends to be extremely persistent, understand that he will need time to finish his puzzle before cleaning up and getting ready to go outdoors.

Plan how to include physical activities on cold and rainy days. Children still need to move their bodies and expend energy even when the weather is not ideal. Ask families to provide appropriate clothing for the weather, including waterproof boots and jackets. Have extras on hand for children whose families forgot to send them in weather-proof gear. Depending on the setting, you might be able to use an all-purpose room or hallways for trike riding and playing with balls.

Be aware of the experiences taking place in children's families. For example, Margot's mom is pregnant and due any day now. Expect that this two-year-old will need some extra one-on-one attention before and after the birth of her sibling. Include plenty of dolls and caregiving props so she can mimic the ways her mom and dad care for the new baby and perhaps work out some of her strong feelings about having to share their attention.

Help children prepare for major transitions. In many programs, children move to a new group in September or when they have a birthday. Often this means they must leave behind a familiar setting and other children and early educators. They will have to get used to a lot of new things at one time. Some children find this easy to do, others struggle to get used to their new situation. Help can take the form of having the children visit the new setting before they leave your group for longer and longer periods of time and having the new early educators spend time with them in their current setting. Sometimes, even thoughtfully planned transitions are not enough. For example, when three-year-old Jackson moved from the Butterflies to the Cool Cats he sat in his new cubby for much of the day, despite his new educator's attempts to help him feel at home. After observing for a while, eventually he came out of the cubby and joined in the play.

Prevent and Reduce Stress Throughout the Day

The following suggestions are appropriate for infants, toddlers, and preschoolers.

Offer plenty of opportunities for children to move their bodies—indoors and outdoors. Encourage kicking of legs and waving of arms, bouncing, pushing and pulling, cruising, walking, climbing, running, jumping, dancing, doing yoga poses, riding tricycles, and pulling wagons so children can expend energy and release endorphins, which often leads to happy feelings.

Plan individual and group options for doing an activity. For example, use baby baths or dishwashing tubs for individual water and sand play. Offer the same kinds of props found in the group sand and water tables. Some children are not ready to share props and work alongside others at the group tables.

Limit the time children have to wait. Have an infant's bottle ready before he wakes up—you know how long he typically sleeps so you can do this. Plan for trips to the bathroom or hand washing sink so standing in line doesn't lead to frustrated outbursts. Sing songs, do fingerplays, retell or add to stories, or play games when a short wait is unavoidable.

Reduce the buzz and glare from overhead lights. Turning off a few overhead lights often has a calming effect on children. If it seems too dark, turn on a lamp or two.

Spend one-on-one time with each child. Read a book, talk during routines and transitions, and comment on a child's activities. In short, focus complete attention on a child—even if just for a few minutes—as many times a day as possible.

Establish routines and rituals. Individualize rituals to reflect what children do at home so that they begin to regulate and organize their own behavior. For example, sing the same song (in the same language) at the start of nap time or rub toddlers' backs to lull them to sleep.

Have some fun. Make funny faces and noises, read a humorous book, act it out with puppets, create and wear silly hats, and invite children to laugh. Create an atmosphere where children enjoy being part of a caring, joyful community.

Involve Families So Children Feel Connected to Their Loved Ones

The following suggestions are appropriate for infants, toddlers, and preschoolers.

Communicate with families daily. Parents of young infants tend to be particularly interested in eating, sleeping, and diapering—they want to know details from when their baby was in your care and want to tell you about how they care for their baby at home. For families of older children, exchange news (in person or in a text, note, or e-mail) about what excites, upsets, and interests a child. Include photos if possible. Share what the child does and plays with at home and at the program. Use this information in conversations with children and to adjust the environment, interactions, and activities if needed.

Help families devise a unique ritual for drop-off and pick-up times. This can make these transitions less stressful for all. For example, perhaps Wiley's dad lets her gently push him out the door when she is ready for him to leave. This tip doubles as a strategy for helping Wiley feel a sense of control.

Reflect families and their home languages and cultures in the setting. Post family photos and posters (include all family members on these) on the wall and in scrapbooks; invite family members to critique the environment, interactions, and use of their home language so you can be sure you are offering a culturally appropriate program.

Encourage families to visit during the day, if they are available. Greet the visitors warmly; invite them to eat lunch with their children; ask visiting family members to read with a small group; help a child find her lost shoe; or share a talent or interest with the children.

Make and show brief slide shows or videos of daily life at the program. You can upload them to a computer or tablet and have them playing in a continuous loop at drop-off and pick-up times.

Set a Few Simple Rules that Match Children's Development and Keep Them Safe

Start with a few rules. Very young children are just beginning to develop the capacity to remember. Start with just three to five essential rules that keep everyone physically and emotionally safe, like the following:

1. Walk inside; run outside.
2. Talk in regular voices inside; use loud voices outside.
3. Be kind.
4. Put away the things you play with.
5. Take care of our play materials.

These few rules may be enough to maintain a positive learning community. If you do add additional rules, review them periodically to make sure they are really necessary. The following strategies can help you set and maintain a few rules.

Involve toddlers and preschoolers in establishing rules. Children are most invested in rules that they have suggested and discussed. They will be motivated to remember the rules and to remind others.

Communicate rules and reminders by stating what to do. Young children understand and remember positive wording more readily than being told what not to do. If the rule's intent is for children not to do something, you can still state the rule positively. For example, "Use blocks for building." "Walk inside." "Use your words." Teach and practice rules by reviewing them frequently and having children help repeat them.

Gently remind children of rules when they forget. "Conor, I think you left some toys on the table. Remember our rule "put away the things you play with." Please put them away before getting ready for outdoor time."

Explain why a rule is needed. For example, young children are starting to understand cause and effect. They can predict that if they run indoors, they might knock down and hurt another child or trip and hurt themselves. Therefore, children can understand why they should walk inside.

Display rules accompanied with photos or illustrations. Post the rules and review them as needed. Most children in your setting are still learning to read, so it's helpful to post the rules with pictures. Take photos of children following the rules, and use them to prompt discussions and reminders.

Work with colleagues to apply rules consistently. Young children work hard to remember and follow the rules—as long as there are not too many of them. They find it confusing when one adult applies the rule and another does not. There may be instances, however, when it is appropriate to adapt a rule for a particular child or situation. In these cases, explain the reasons for the change to the other children—they are likely to be understanding.

Should I Change My Practice?

Though you cannot prevent all problem behaviors, observing and reviewing your own practice may identify causes for some of them. If you find that problems tend to arise in one area or during one time of the day, ask yourself the following questions:

- Are any areas or learning centers overcrowded? Should I limit the number of children who can use this area or learning center at one time?

- Do children tend to use only a few of the toys and materials? Have I provided toys and materials that are appropriate for children's ages, developmental levels, interests, culture, and home languages? Do I rotate and offer new toys and materials regularly?
- Do the children seem distracted or bored during activities? Do I plan activities that are engaging and respond to children's interests?
- Do the children seem overstimulated or overwhelmed by the activities? Do I plan activities that are appropriate for children's cultures and skill levels?
- Do the children refuse to clean up? Have I scheduled enough time for play so they can carry out their plans? Are materials displayed on low, open shelves so children can reach them? Are items labeled—with pictures —so children know where things belong?
- Do children have difficulty during transitions? Do I plan for transitions so children do not have to wait with nothing to do?

Review your responses and make changes as needed.

Using Positive Guidance as a Teaching Strategy

Young children have many things to learn in the early years. We do not expect newborn infants to know how to dress and undress, climb stairs, or write their names. Instead, we introduce these skills when it is developmentally appropriate. Through a variety of teaching strategies—from providing an environment in which children can build these skills on their own to offering direct instruction when appropriate—educators foster children's learning. Similarly, young children do not know what behaviors are acceptable and what behaviors are not. They can figure out some of this on their own—"pulling Rachel's hair feels good, but she screams when I do that, so it's not a good idea," but positive guidance from families and educators is most likely to encourage children's positive behavior.

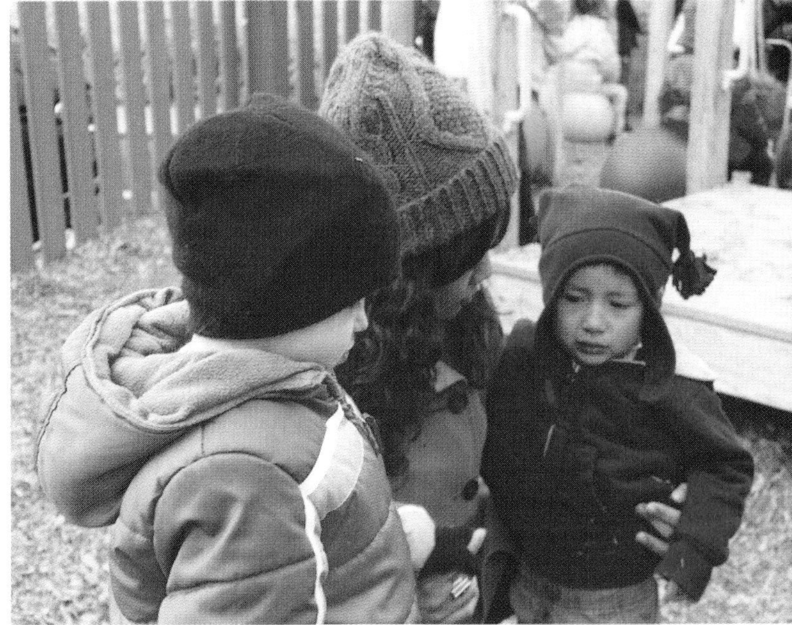

If children are struggling to resolve a conflict, kneel to the children's eye level and help them devise a resolution.

Positive guidance includes all the things educators do to set the stage for positive behavior as described in the previous section. It also includes interactions and direct instruction to help children actually learn about what behaviors are acceptable and how they can control their impulses and manage their strong feelings.

The overall goal of positive guidance is to help children gain self-regulation—being able to manage their own behavior, without adult intervention and reminders. As defined by educators Elena Bodrova and Deb Leong (2008), "Self-regulation is a deep, internal mechanism that enables children as well as adults to engage in mindful, intentional, and thoughtful behaviors." Self-regulation includes emotional and cognitive applications. Children use emotional self-regulation in social interactions and cognitive self-regulation while thinking, as described in Chapter 5, Cognitive and Chapter 8, Self.

Self-regulation involves:

1. controlling impulses and stopping when doing something (e.g., using words to express a need or desire instead of aggression)
2. doing something because it is necessary, even if you do not want to (e.g., sharing, waiting for a turn)

Self-regulated children can delay gratification, suppress impulses, and consider the consequences of their actions. They can think of alternatives that would be more acceptable to the situation. Positive guidance strategies help children gain the self-regulation they need for success in social and cognitive activities.

Figure 64a. Punishment Versus Positive Guidance

Discipline (training that corrects, molds, or perfects) is commonly associated with *punishment* (a penalty for rule violations). However, punishment rarely corrects children's behavior, because it is often hurtful, shameful, arbitrary, and unrelated to the behavior itself. "Punishing children for their wrongdoings will not create change—just a need for more punishment" (Bailey 2001, 8). Both punishment and discipline-based reward systems fail to teach children what to do instead of using the problem behavior. Children are overwhelmed by negative messages about what they *cannot* do, which weakens the emotional bond between early educators and children. Children are unable to feel secure when they are constantly scrutinized for what they do "wrong."

Positive guidance supports and teaches children as they develop the skills to manage their feelings and emotions, share materials and resources, treat others with respect and kindness, and care for their surroundings. For young children, learning appropriate behaviors is a process. They need lots of practice before they can master these skills.

Figure 64b. Punishment Versus Positive Guidance

Punishment and *positive guidance* impact children differently:

POSITIVE GUIDANCE	PUNISHMENT
Builds self-esteem.	Makes child feel worthless and angry.
Gives confidence.	Embarrasses.
Respects children.	Shames children.
Focuses on what children can do.	Focuses on what children cannot do.
Examines causes of behavior.	Focuses on eliminating undesirable behavior.
Empowers children.	Intimidates children.

(Kersey and Masterson 2013; Gartrell 2004; Klein 2008)

Why Rewards Are Not Effective

Guidance approaches that rely on rewards or stickers are also an ineffective way to teach children what behaviors are expected. Some early educators use them, because they believe children will want to change their behaviors to receive the rewards. In the short term, these systems appear to work. Over time, however, children become dependent on these external rewards—controlled by adults--and behave just to obtain them. When children no longer receive the rewards, their behaviors regress. A more effective approach allows children to develop internal self-discipline or emotional regulation.

The following teaching practices underlie a positive guidance approach:

Building trusting relationships. Early educators establish reciprocal, caring relationships with children and let each child know they are valued and belongs. Educators communicate expectations for children's behavior, emphasize children's positive qualities, and believe in children's abilities to make appropriate choices. These strong relationships govern children's behavior and give them the desire to solve conflicts (Bailey 2001).With your support and encouragement, children can learn to self-regulate out of choice—not coercion or manipulation—inside and outside your setting.

Supporting social and emotional development. As discussed in Chapters 9 and 10, strong emotional and social skills allow children to regulate their behavior and enjoy playing and learning with others.

Helping children learn how to solve their own problems. "Guidance teaches children to solve their problems, rather than punishing them for having problems they cannot solve" (Gartrell 2001, 9). Educators scaffold the teaching, gradually withdrawing support until children can apply problem solving skills on their own.

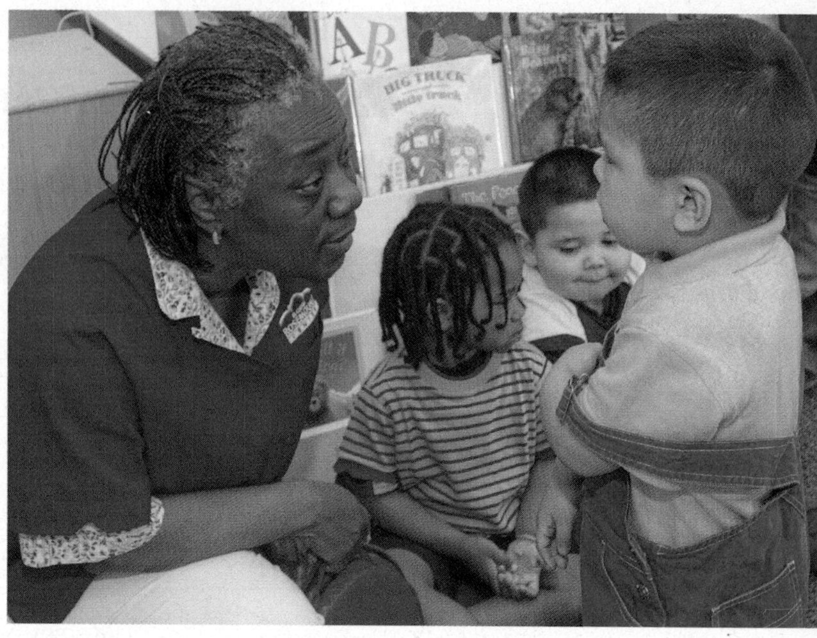

Kneel to a child's eye level and coach them to express how they are feeling.

Building on children's strengths. Every child has abilities that can be harnessed to promote positive behavior. For example, the highly verbal child might have such a strong need to talk that he interrupts the group meeting conversations repeatedly. Plan ahead by asking the child to be ready to share a story with the group. He will be able to use his verbal skills in a successful way. In another example, the child with strong gross motor skills who usually runs ahead of the group, can help you carry the bag of balls outdoors. Or, consider the child whose loud voice typically fills the room with instructions for his playmates. Ask him to use his voice and leadership skills in a different way, as the reminder at clean up time. "Carlos, please visit every learning center and whisper to the children that it's time to clean up."

Consider the Reasons for a Child's Behavior

A positive guidance approach includes finding the root causes and motivation for children's behaviors. Educators must learn behavior as a form of communication and ask, "What is the child trying to say by behaving in this way?"

When the cause of a behavior is not clear, observe and look for patterns in children's behavior. Identify what happens before and after the behavior occurs to identify its cause (Miller 2013). For example, when three-year-old Tyler sits down for lunch, often he starts rocking in his chair, and does not eat. He could be sick, tired, nervous, upset, or reacting to an issue at home. Perhaps his medication affects his appetite. Through a series of observations you learn that Tyler normally plays happily with Marcus before lunchtime. After clean up time and handwashing, he walks to the table, muttering to himself.

Could Tyler be upset that lunchtime interrupts his play time with Marcus? Now that you think you have determined the cause of the problem, ask: What should I do about this? Perhaps you could find more opportunities during the day for Tyler and Marcus to play. Or seat Marcus and Tyler at the same table or next to each other during lunch. Experiment with a few solutions to see what works.

Also, at times children use behaviors that are challenging for us because they are still learning how to express their feelings and emotions. They may lack the verbal skills needed to say what they want or they may lack the social skills needed to get along with others. When the child engages in behavior that is challenging, use the opportunity to coach her. For example, toddler Meesha bumps Daria with the wagon. Daria pushes Meesha. Kneel to Daria's eye level and coach her to express how she is feeling. Coach Meesha too so she can explain to Daria that it was an accident.

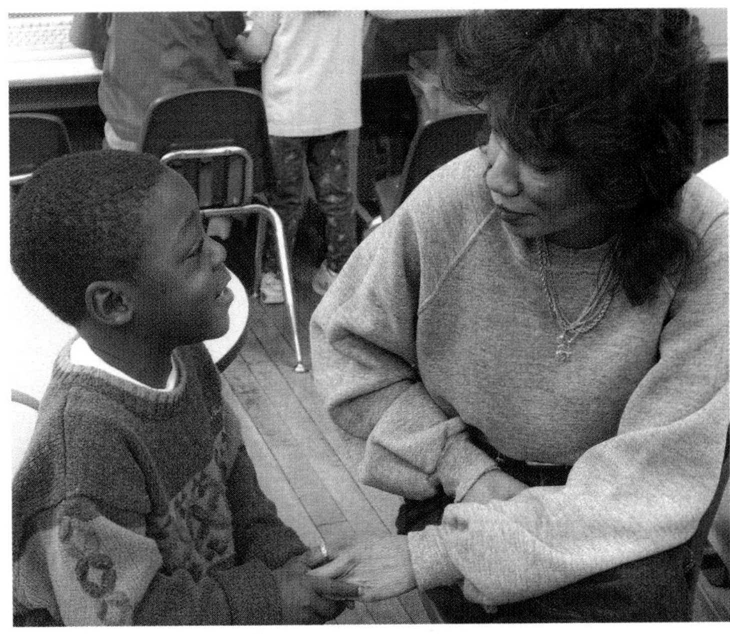

Spending time with children helps you strengthen your relationship with each child.

Understanding and Supporting Children with Autism Spectrum Disorder

Autism from the child's perspective: *(adapted from Ten Things Every Child with Autism Wishes You Knew (3rd Edition), by Ellen Notbohm, 2019)*

- First and foremost, I am a child.
- My senses are out of sync.
- Know the difference between "I won't" and "I can't."
- I think concretely and literally.
- I try to communicate in a variety of ways.
- I am visually oriented.
- Focus on what I can do rather than what I can't do.
- I need help with social skills.
- Learn what triggers my meltdowns.
- Love me unconditionally.

Some facts about Autism Spectrum Disorder (ASD):

- ASD is a medical condition that affects about one and a half million people in the US.
- The term autism spectrum disorder (ASD) describes certain brain development disorders that lead to difficulties in social interactions and communication; some people with ASD perform certain behaviors repetitively.
- ASD is 4 to 5 times more common among boys than girls.
- Around 1 in 68 children in US are identified as having ASD.

Understanding and Supporting Children with Autism Spectrum Disorder (continued)

- ASD affects over 3 million individuals in the US.
- ASD symptoms and signs typically show up between 2 and 3 years of age.
- There is no medical way to detect ASD and there is no cure for autism.
- Early intervention is vital for children diagnosed with ASD.
- Asperger syndrome is at the “high functioning” end of the ASD spectrum. Those with Asperger syndrome do not have serious delays or difficulties in cognitive or language development.
- About 40% of people with autism have average to above average intelligence.
- Many people with autism have exceptional visual, music, and academic skills.
- Many children with ASD attend early childhood programs with their typically developing peers.

Below are "red flags" that a child may be at risk for ASD. If a child exhibits any of these, discuss your observations with the family so the child can be further evaluated.

- No big smiles or other warm, joyful expressions by six months or thereafter.
- No back-and-forth sharing of sounds, smiles, or other facial expressions by nine months.
- No babbling by 12 months.
- No back-and-forth gestures, such as pointing, showing, reaching or waving by 12 months.
- No words by 16 months.
- No meaningful, two-word phrases (not including imitating or repeating) by 24 months.
- Any loss of speech, babbling, or social skills at any age.

A child with ASD might have:

- an obsession with certain objects: for example, a piece of cloth or a collection of forks.
- prolonged interest in common occurrences: for example, watching water swirl down the drain.
- ritualistic behaviors: for example, arranging food in a certain order.
- repetitive (stereotypic) behaviors: for example, hand flapping or repeating the same phrase over and over.

What children with ASD need in an early childhood setting:

- Structure and a predictable routine.
- Environments free of distractions, such as a quiet center.
- Verbal reminders of what happens next.
- Picture schedules.
- Nothing that will overwhelm their senses.
- Social skills support, including how to greet people, behave in social situations, and play with others.

Understanding and Supporting Children with Autism Spectrum Disorder (continued)

To understand what a child with ASD is communicating through behavior, educators ask themselves:

- What was the child doing just before the behavior started? For example, an educator is talking with the child before a small group activity. The rest of the children sit down and she begins the activity. The child with ASD begins to scream. This may be because he wants to regain the teacher's attention.
- What in the environment might have triggered the behavior, outburst, or tantrum? Children with ASD can be upset by loud noises, bright lighting or sunshine, and unfamiliar aromas.
- What is the child trying to say through his behavior? The child might be communicating, "There is too much commotion for me," "I don't want to do this," or I want your attention." A clue can be found in what the child does after the behavior.
- Can I predict when the child will behave in a certain way? In some instances, yes, in others, no. Observing and documenting the child's behavior over time can provide answers, some of the time. For example, if a child repeats a sound repeatedly every day after outdoor time, this may mean that she does not want to go indoors. Her educator can devise a way to give her a warning a few minutes before outdoor time is over so the child has time to end her activity and prepare for the transition.

(Willis 2009)

Individualizing Positive Guidance

Just as an educator might individualize teaching of content areas or physical skills, so too is it important to individualize the use of positive guidance strategies. There is no "one-size-fits-all" set of strategies that will work for every child in every situation. The positive guidance strategies you implement must consider each child's unique interests, temperament, personality, knowledge, experiences, skills, and cultural and family expectations. Even after you tailor the strategy to the individual, it still may not be effective, for that child.

Teaching children problem-solving techniques, giving appropriate encouragement, listening actively, and modeling appropriate behaviors are all effective positive guidance techniques. If you have formed strong relationships with the children, then you have a good idea about the strategies that work best with each of them. For instance, you know that three-year-old Louisa has a hard time staying focused and sitting still during group times because of her age and temperament. You ask her if she would prefer to go to the art center or pick a book to look at quietly. You also know that Mario, who has a developmental delay, throws things when he is upset. Because he is on an IEP (Individualized Education Program), you follow the strategies the special educator suggests for helping him calm down, and then give him choices. The following practices will enhance effectiveness of any strategy you employ (Kaiser and Rasminsky 2012):

Spend time with children. Children need consistent and ongoing guidance. Spending time with children helps you increase your knowledge and understanding of their interests and skills and strengthen your relationship with each child.

Remain calm and in control. You cannot expect children to control their emotions if you cannot control your own. Speak to children in a low, steady voice, maintain distance between you and them, and keep your arms at your sides. Communicate warmth and understanding to children. If their actions overwhelm you or test your patience, ask a colleague to relieve you until you feel calm enough to face the children again.

Support the whole child. If children struggle with problem behaviors, focus on their positive attributes and target the specific issue. Avoid labeling children. For example, never refer to or label them as "troublemakers."

Talk with the child privately. Young children embarrass easily. If they feel humiliated in front of the group, then they will not be receptive to what you say.

Believe in the children. Positive guidance can almost always be successful if you are respectful, firm, clear, and caring toward children. Give children time to develop the self-control and motivation to want to self-regulate. Let children know that you are always there for them and that they can talk to you whenever they are upset.

The following positive guidance strategies can be tailored to address the needs of individual children and situations (Adams and Baronberg 2005; Klein 2008).

Use the word no in extreme situations only. Reserve the word no for very dangerous situations. For example, if Kevin is about to swing a bat, which could accidently hit Thalia, you would say, "Kevin, no!" Or, if a child lets go of the walking rope while you are all crossing the street, you would immediately say, "no," to keep them safe. In both cases you would later revisit the experience to help the child understand why their actions were not safe.

Provide acceptable alternatives. Empower young children to make good choices by offering them appropriate and acceptable alternatives. For example, explain to a toddler, "We have time to read this book or this book. Which one do you want to read?" Or, when there is no room for Zora at the water table. Acknowledge the preschooler's feelings, "I know you want to play at the water table, but right now it's full. Only four children can play here at one time to keep it safe. I see space at the art easel, at the sand table, and in dramatic play. Which one of those do you want to try?"

Use natural consequences when appropriate. *Natural consequences* are the inevitable results of a child's behavior that are not imposed by an adult. They can be effective guidance techniques, especially when children are unhappy with the results of their behavior. For example, if Maureen throws her favorite doll on the floor in anger and the doll breaks, then Maureen must deal with the natural consequences of her behavior—her doll is broken and she can no longer play with it.

Observe all children and continue to learn new things about them each day. Record notes daily and reflect on children's behaviors and actions so that you can learn how to best support each child—including children who are too young or unable to speak for another reason. Review and reflect on your notes to determine possible causes for a child's behavior. Through observation you may, for example, identify a problem with the environment that can be addressed immediately.

Watch for a while before stepping in to resolve a conflict. Often, young children can work things out on their own or what looks like a problem, really isn't one. For example, toddler Hannah might just pick herself up and continue on her way when Peter accidentally bumps into her and she falls down. Or, preschoolers Andi and Nia might come up with a way to take turns playing with the doll they are both grasping. These are instances when children learn more from solving their own problems than from your interventions.

Coach children and support them in resolving conflicts independently. If children are struggling to resolve a conflict, kneel to the children's eye level and help them devise a resolution. The resolutions must be acceptable to each child who is involved. You can coach and support them through this process. See Teaching Children How to Resolve Conflicts, a summary of HighScope's six-step approach to conflict resolution. Also, gently remind the children of previous conflicts they resolved or link this situation to stories you have read together.

Teaching Children How to Resolve Conflicts

Conflict is a normal part of children's lives. Having different needs or wanting to use the same thing when only one is available, can easily lead to disagreements. In the early years, disputes usually involve toys, relationships, ideas, space, and power. Children might argue, use aggression, or back away and avoid each other. These behaviors do not solve the problem.

Early educators can help children learn ways to resolve their conflicts—at first with adult support, and eventually on their own. The goal is to help children see conflict as a shared problem that they can solve by understanding both points of view and finding a solution with which everyone can agree.

Conflict resolution is a process for resolving disputes or disagreements. HighScope (2012) developed a six-step approach for helping children resolve conflicts:

1. **Approach calmly, stopping any hurtful actions.** Make sure that everyone is safe by inserting yourself between the children. Work to manage the children's anger so everyone can calmly assess the situation.
2. **Acknowledge children's feelings.** Let the children know that you understand they are angry, upset, or hurt by the situation.

Teaching Children How to Resolve Conflicts (continued)

3. **Gather information.** Let the children know you are going to help them solve their problem, but first you must know what is wrong.

4. **Restate the problem.** Use the children's own words to repeat each child's side of the situation and to let them know you heard them. "Lindsey, Emilio says that he was riding the tricycle, and you pushed him off and took it. Can you tell me what happened?"

5. **Ask for solution ideas and choose one together.** Each time children offer a solution, repeat their words aloud. "Lindsey, you suggest that Emilio ride the tricycle this morning, and then you ride after lunch. What do you think, Emilio?" Encourage children to reflect on their feelings, plan alternative solutions, predict the consequences, and determine which idea makes the most sense (Epstein 2003). If children cannot devise a suitable solution, or if they suggest a solution that is too punitive or unrelated to the problem, step in and propose your own solution.

6. **Be prepared to provide follow-up support.** Everyone needs to understand the reasons behind the conflict and resolution. If a similar problem occurs in the future, the children can reach a resolution more easily. Evaluate how well the chosen resolution worked and consider whether the children could reach a more effective solution in the future.

Ultimately, the goal is for children to resolve conflicts on their own, acknowledging each other's feelings and devising possible solutions that will satisfy both parties.

Understanding and Addressing Challenging Behaviors

The Technical Assistance Center on Social Emotional Intervention for Young Children, funded by the U.S. Department of Education, Office of Special Education Programs, defines challenging behavior as follows:

> . . . any repeated pattern of behavior, or perception of behavior, that interferes with or is at risk of interfering with optimal learning or engagement in pro-social interactions with peers and adults. . . . Challenging behaviors may be defined as behaviors that interfere with the development and maintenance of reciprocal, positive, and nurturing relationships with the parent or caregiver. . . . (Powell, Dunlap, and Fox 2006).

In this section we discuss the kinds of challenging behaviors that hinder development and learning and harm the child using them or other children. They are pervasive, long-lasting, and not likely to disappear on their own. The adults in a child's life need to work together to determine the cause, what might trigger the behavior, and what the child's behavior means. Together, they will develop a joint plan for addressing the behavior. They also need to agree on how to respond to the behavior now, while the plan is helping the child learn alternative behaviors.

The Importance of Addressing Challenging Behaviors

Supporting children who use challenging behaviors has become a national concern among educators and administrators. In a study of 4,000 preschool settings in 40 states in America, 10.4% of teachers reported that they had expelled a child in the previous year due to behavioral problems (McCabe and Frede 2007). Children's family circumstances impact their behaviors. Some children may exhibit ongoing challenging behaviors when there is stress at home, parents are separating or divorcing, a new baby arrives, or a parent or guardian loses a job or becomes ill. Although most children eventually manage to cope with these experiences, they benefit from extra support and understanding from you and their families. Other children may exhibit repeated challenging behaviors when they get frustrated, do not have the skills to communicate their emotions and feelings, or are struggling to make friends.

If not addressed, children's challenging behaviors could continue, multiply, and lead to lifelong problems. For instance, research has found that children with challenging behaviors are unlikely to have success in school and will be burdened with social and emotional problems later in life—including mental illness. Challenging behavior in preschool is one of the strongest predictors of delinquency, drug abuse, and antisocial behavior in adults (McCabe and Frede 2007).

Ideally, no child would ever be expelled from an early childhood setting and early childhood educators would prevent and handle challenging behaviors using positive child guidance techniques consistently. Educators need to treat children with respect and focus on their positive actions. Though challenging behaviors may test your patience and even anger you at times, never let your anger and frustration show. Be calm, objective, and professional at all times. Your relationships with the children are your greatest aids. When early educators and young children have strong bonds, children have better interactions with their peers and are more eager for positive attention (Powell, Dunlap, and Fox 2006). Gartrell (2008) says that early childhood educators should "reach out to children at risk for stigma and help them turn around their lives by building positive attachments with them, assisting them to find membership in the class, and teaching them democratic life skills".

Responding to Challenging Behaviors

Challenging behaviors may emerge in the toddler and preschool years. The term does not apply to the kinds of behaviors that infants might exhibit. Examples appear below; keep in mind that these are not one-time or even occasional behaviors. They are part of a repeated pattern of behavior.

- Biting
- Kicking, hitting, damaging property, and other forms of physical aggression
- Tantrums
- Using inappropriate words and gestures
- Crying frequently and for long periods of time

Responding to a challenging behavior begins with *defining* what it is the child does. For example, instead of assuming that everyone will know what you mean by saying the child's behavior is "disruptive," take time to record a simple statement that defines the behavior that is challenging: "When transitioning from choice time to clean up, Gareth throws the toys and materials he was using." This allows everyone to have the same clarity about what behavior is challenging.

Next, you need to *gather information from multiple sources* to gain an understanding of when and why the challenging behavior takes place. This step involves several focused observations, consultation with the family to learn whether similar behavior happens at home, reviewing documentation of the child's play and activities, and conversations with colleagues and specialists who also work with the child. Even when you know that a child's challenging behavior is an expression of anger or a need for attention, it is critical to find out the underlying cause of this anger or need. The information you collect will help you plan ways to eliminate the causes of challenging behaviors instead of just treating the symptoms. For example, Owen kicks Seth's cot during nap time. When Seth asks Owen to stop, Owen kicks the cot harder. You intervene by sitting quietly with Owen and asking him to talk with you about what is making him so angry. He tells you that he cannot sleep and that he does not like lying on his cot. You offer him the options of either looking at a book while lying on his cot or assembling a puzzle quietly.

Next, to make sense of the information you collected from multiple sources, *review and analyze* all of your notes and *summarize* what you have learned. This is an important step because it allows you to note patterns in a child's behavior, which can lead to determining the cause. For example, you might learn that the child is more likely to use biting in the morning than later in the day. This might be a clue to the cause. Is the child arriving at the program tired because his new baby brother is keeping him awake or is he hungry because his family thinks he can wait to eat breakfast at the program?

At this point, it is time to hold a meeting among educators, specialists, and the child's family. The goal of the meeting is to review the information collected and develop a specific plan for helping the child replace the challenging behaviors with specific, alternative behaviors. The plan will include:

1. Positive guidance strategies to use at home and at the program.
2. How to monitor, document, and share signs of progress.
3. When to meet again to review and adjust the plan as needed.

As noted by Daniel Gartrell (2011), the meeting is positive, because everyone shares a common purpose—the good of the child.

Replacing Time-Out With Time-In

The term time-out is actually short for the phrase "time out from positive reinforcement from the group," meaning the early educators and community of learners. This tactic, which is a form of discipline, is typically employed when children have been acting out, ignoring rules, or disrupting the group. Often children use these behaviors to communicate that they want attention or connection. Through their behaviors they are asking for *time-in*— time spent with an adult who can help the child express emotions and learn how to cope with strong feelings in appropriate ways.

The term time-out is actually short for the phrase "time out from positive reinforcement from the group."

As designed, during time-out, a child remains in the same room with the group, but is asked to sit outside of the activity area where she caused the problem. This isolates children from the activity and gives them time to calm down and think about their behaviors. During time-out, the early childhood educator remains calm, objective, nonthreatening, and respectful. Time-out lasts one minute per year of a child's age. For example, a four-year-old would remain in time-out for four minutes. Time-out would allow children to calm themselves. These children would then rejoin the group, ready for a hopefully successful experience.

In reality, however, time-out is rarely used as described above. More often than not, it turns into punishment, as when an educator angrily threatens to send a child to time-out. Rather than being an effective guidance technique, time-out can damage children in the following ways (Kaiser and Rasminsky 2012):

- Children receive the message that you can control others if you have power.
- Children feel that their early childhood educators and their peers do not like them.
- Children from cultures that value group participation feel that they are being shunned.
- Time-out interferes with learning.
- Time-out violates children's sense of safety and security.
- Time-out severs the positive relationships educators have with children.

Positive guidance is almost always successful if you are respectful, firm, clear, and caring toward children.

Sending children to time-out can reduce their confidence and self-esteem and can cause them to feel worthless. When children feel hurt or humiliated, it is difficult for them to think about how to alter their behavior to avoid being sent to time-out again. Often children in time-out are labeled as "troublemakers" and are the first to be accused of misconduct. Once children accept this label, it is easier for them to be "troublemakers" than to fight the misnomer.

Because of time-out's misuse, overuse, and possible negative effects, most guidance experts recommend alternate ways to teach children how to build self-regulation skills and learn to behave in acceptable ways. Here are some effective strategies to give children "time in:"

Time-away. Sometimes called "cool-down" or "private time," time away performs the function that time-out should, but with very important differences. Time-away puts the power in the child's hands and is proactive, not reactive. For example, Katie feels angry, and upset, and has the urge to do something she is not allowed to do. She tells you that she wants to move to a quiet area, such as the sand table or literacy center or the be-by-yourself space where she remains until she feels better. Katie determines how long she remains in this area, and returns to the group when she is ready (Kaiser and Rasminsky 2012).

Bringing children in close. Dubbed the "anti-time-out," the "bringing children close" technique involves children coming to you for hugs when they feel out of control or they are disturbing the group. The purpose of the cuddle is not to reward children for bad behavior. Your hugs provide them a safe space to calm down. If children are flailing (and you are certain they are not having a seizure), you might keep a warm hold using your arms and knees. It is tough for an overwrought child to listen, so say nothing during this time except, "I'll hold you until you feel calm" (Porter 2008).

Teaching democratic life skills. According to Gartrell, time-out, like all forms of discipline that shame children, must be abolished. He argues that early educators should replace these practices with positive ones that build on "an encouraging classroom." The goal of positive guidance, in his view, is for children to learn *democratic life skills*, or the social–emotional skills they need to become healthy individuals and contributing members of society. These skills include the following abilities (Gartrell 2001, 14):

- Seeing one's self as a worthy individual and a capable member of the group.
- Expressing strong emotions in non hurting ways.
- Solving problems ethically and intelligently.
- Understanding others' feelings and viewpoints.
- Working cooperatively in groups while accepting the human differences among members.

This strategy lets children know you care about them even if you dislike their behavior. It also unites you and the children and strengthens trusting and respectful relationships. Most importantly, it gives children the support they need to be in control of their emotions. Most early childhood educators report that as children gain self-control, calming takes less time, and the problem behaviors disappear.

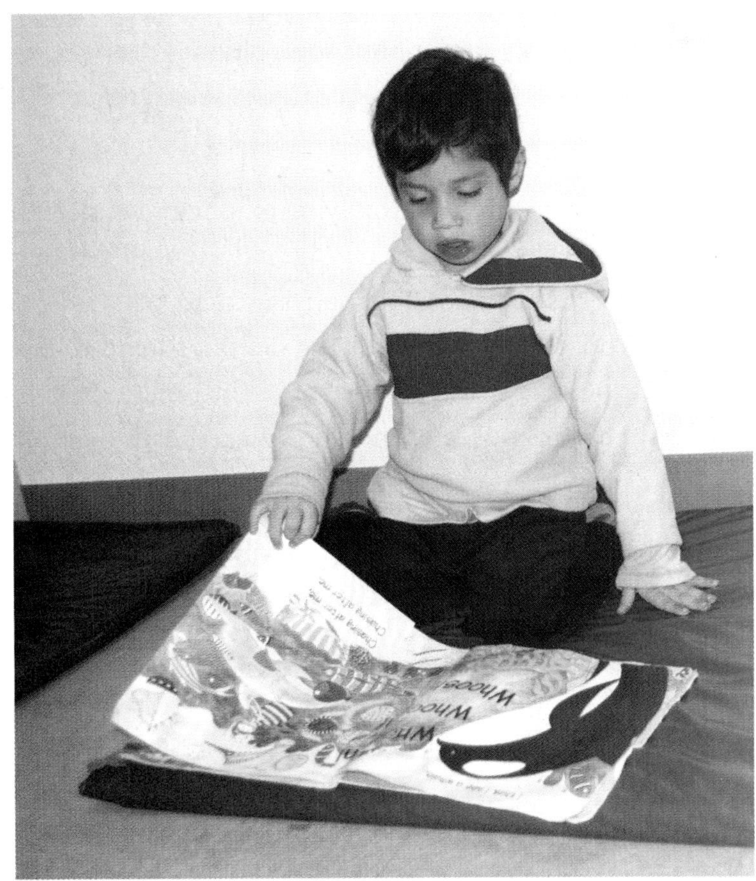

Give children a choice to choose a quieter activity to engage in.

Learning democratic life skills is an ongoing process for children. The challenge, according to Gartrell (2001, 14), is "for teachers—and children—to recognize conflicts as opportunities for teaching and learning." Early childhood educators should teach children these skills through all of the day's events—not just when problem behavior exists.

Stopping Bullying Among Preschoolers

Dan Olweus (1997), who has studied bullying problems among youth for nearly 40 years, defines bullying as the continual and damaging actions of one child against another that are not provoked by the target. Direct bullying is physical or verbal, involving hitting, kicking, name-calling, or teasing. Indirect bullying is less obvious, involving threatening and teasing. Boys who bully tend to be direct and physically aggressive, while girls who bully tend to be indirect and spread rumors, tell secrets, exclude other children, and make threats. In preschool, bullying behaviors occur most frequently in social play, with peers as the targets.

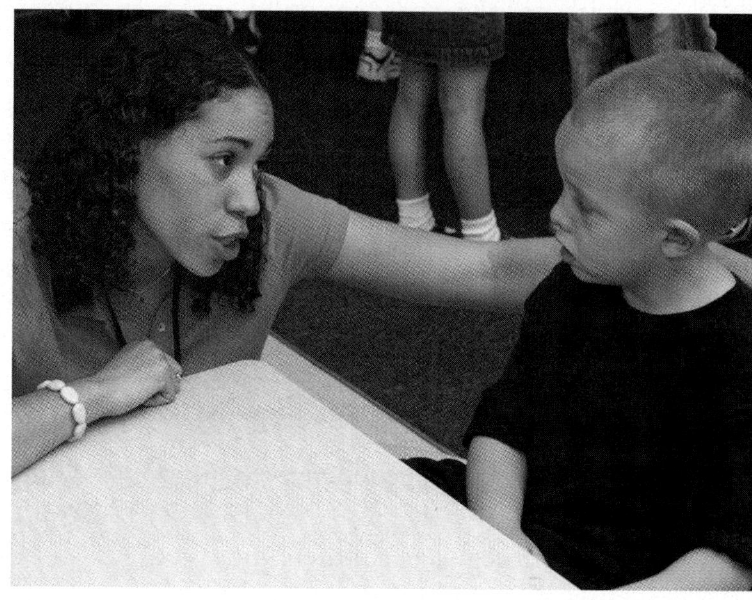

Whatever method you employ to end bullying in your setting, be positive and compassionate.

Researchers agree that bullying among preschoolers results in part because at this age children are still developing social skills and the ability to regulate their emotions. As children's social and emotional skills develop, bullying incidents tend to decline. Researchers have also learned that preschoolers who use bullying behaviors tend to have many friends and are well-respected by their peers (Snow, K. 2014) . On the other hand, children who are the victims of bullies typically have few friends, and thus are vulnerable to being bullied.

There are three kinds of aggressive behaviors used by preschoolers. Over time, when there is an imbalance of power, these aggressive behaviors could become bullying:

Physical aggression includes hitting, pinching, kicking, and pushing. One child might be more physically powerful than the other children. In these instances, there is an imbalance of power that can lead the dominant child to target others (Raisor, J.M. 2012).

Instrumental aggression is used to achieve a goal, such as getting to be first in line or the only one to use a particular toy. It can emerge due to most preschoolers' inability to understand or take on the perspective of others and their lack of language skills to express their feelings and desires.

Relational aggression involves repeated, hurtful exclusions of one child by others. For example, the child who threatens, "You can't come to my party," is using relational aggression. As with the other forms of aggression, over time it can become so severe that it has become bullying.

Positive guidance, again, offers the best approach to ensure that every early childhood setting is free from bullying. Here are some positive suggestions for preventing and reducing bullying in your setting (Kaiser and Rasminsky 2012; EDC 2008):

Teach needed social skills. Many children who use aggression, and perhaps bullying behaviors, lack problem-solving, self-regulation, and calming skills. Children who are the victims of aggression and bullying tend to lack assertiveness. All of these social skills can be taught through direct teaching, modeling, and role playing. See Figure 65 for strategies children who are victims can use to empower and reduce children's feelings of helplessness.

Speak to children positively. Treat both the child who uses aggression and the child who has been victimized with care and respect. Work with children to express their feelings and observe them carefully to get at the heart of what is causing the problem. For the child who is overly aggressive, find positive outlets for leadership abilities. For the target, reassure this child that you will help keep him safe.

Use books and puppets to help children work through their feelings (bibliotherapy). Children can use puppets to help express their thoughts and feelings. You can read aloud and discuss books to help children see how their lives relate to the characters in the story. Here are some recommended books to encourage discussions:

- *Stand Tall, Molly Lou Melon* by Patty Lovell
- *The Grouchy Lady Bug* by Eric Carle
- *When Sophie Gets Angry—Really, Really Angry . . .* by Molly Bean
- *A Bad Case of Stripes* by David Shannon
- *The Recess Queen* by Alexis O'Neill
- *The Juice Box Bully: Empowering Kids to Stand Up for Others* by Bob Sornson and Maria Dismondy

Whatever method you employ to prevent or address bullying in your setting, be positive and compassionate. Get to the root cause of the behaviors and offer bullies choices that will have a positive outcome.

Figure 65. Strategies Children Can Use to Respond and React to Bullying Behaviors

Adapt these strategies for preschoolers. Practice with preschoolers so they feel prepared and can respond to bullying behaviors in the future.

- Ignore the teasing.
- Use I-messages to communicate ("It hurts my feelings when you tease me. Please stop.").
- Agree with the facts (a girl teases a boy about his new glasses, and the boy agrees, "Yes, I do have new glasses.").
- Ask a question about the behavior ("Why are you teasing me about my glasses?").
- Use positive self-talk ("I like my new glasses.").
- Reframe: change a negative statement into a compliment ("Thank you, my glasses are new.").
- Ask for help.

(Freedman, J. 2007)

Partnering With Families

Partnering with families long before guidance concerns are discussed is critical. Families should hear many positive aspects of their child's experience in your environment before behavioral issues are discussed. Begin the guidance conversation with families before any problems arise. Explain that it is part of an early childhood educator's job to teach children all kinds of things, including how to use acceptable behaviors and express their feelings in positive ways. Spell out your guidance philosophy in a guidebook or manual, or as part of your setting's orientation materials. At the start of the year or whenever a new child enrolls in your setting, invite families to meet and discuss the approach you use.

Establish shared goals. You and a child's family are partners, each supporting the child's development and learning. Listen carefully to the family's goals for their child and identify areas of agreement. Explain that positive guidance helps children learn to be self-regulated, solve problems for themselves, and cope with and express strong emotions. "Of course we want the children to follow the few rules they helped to set and to behave appropriately. But we also want

Invite families to meet and discuss your settings guidance policy.

them to learn social and emotional skills that will help them face academic challenges and persevere when something is difficult." Most families will have this goal for their children too. They may not have thought about positive guidance as being connected with academic success.

Cite the research. Have findings on hand that support the positive guidance strategies and techniques you use. This evidence will help you explain how your policy and practice is rooted in best practices. For example, instead of announcing to families that punishment is bad for children, explain that your setting's staff do not employ punishment, because researchers have found that not only is it ineffective, but it can also make a problem worse. Families that use punishment may feel defensive or feel the need to resist what you say. Write a newsletter article about research on the effects of punishment. Then families can read about the subject themselves.

Some families may disagree with your positive guidance approach, because it differs from the way they were raised. For example, a mother might say, "I discipline my child so the world won't," and tell you that you have her full permission to punish her child. Listen carefully and respect her perspective, but do not punish the child. Politely but firmly let the parent or guardian know you cannot comply with this request. Describe the strategies you will be using and share examples (while maintaining confidentiality) that demonstrate their effectiveness. Explain that positive guidance is rooted in child development. You maintain expectations based on children's stage of development and skill levels. Solicit her help in working together to prevent and address problems and, should they arise, challenging behaviors. Perhaps the parent or guardian has suggestions that are aligned with developmentally appropriate practice that you can incorporate into your repertoire of positive guidance strategies.

Maintain ongoing, reciprocal communication with families. Check in with them during drop-off and pick-up times, and communicate through e-mail, texting, newsletters, or regular meetings. If an ongoing problem behavior exists, discuss it with the child's family privately, politely, and nonjudgmentally. Begin the conversation discussing the child's strengths and then plan ways to build on them. Also share information with parents and guardians that you think they will find helpful. For example, send home tip sheets on positive guidance, information on active listening, or pamphlets about how to help children express their feelings. Understanding appropriate expectations will help family members know when children are acting appropriately for their age or when they are having a true behavior problem. Keep families abreast of what is happening in the setting and offer parenting resources, such as books, classes, or workshops when appropriate.

Discuss children' challenging behaviors with families. If children's behaviors are severe and interfering with their participation in the program, meet with family members in person. During these meetings, listen intently and contribute to the conversation. Hearing what happens at home will help you analyze the causes and functions of the behavior and determine what the child is trying to communicate through the behavior.

The best outcome of these meetings is for you and the child's family to brainstorm a common approach for addressing challenging behaviors. When children receive the same support for learning new behaviors in your setting as they do at home, the joint approach is more likely to be successful. ■

Competency Standard IV:

To establish positive and productive relationships with families

Developmental Context

Functional Area 11: Families

Young infants *(birth–8 months)* are establishing patterns of sleeping, waking, eating, playing, and social activity. They can be supported in developing some stability in these routines by the sensitive and consistent responses of adults. Families and providers can anticipate needs and respond more appropriately to the infant's signals when they share details with each other about the baby at drop off and pickup times.

Mobile infants *(9–17 months)* may have difficulty separating from the family members even when the provider is a familiar and trusted person. Providers can support infants and their families by recognizing that it may be upsetting both for the adults and the child and providing strategies to ease the separation. Providers should recognize the potential for competition between themselves and parents and work to avoid it, remembering that infants can have more than one important adult in their lives. Providers and families also need to agree on reasonable and safe limits as children begin to explore and wander.

Toddlers *(18–36 months)* develop their own special routines and rituals in order to feel safe and secure. It is essential that families and providers share their experiences and understanding of the child's patterns and provide consistent, dependable support for the toddler's developing sense of self-competence and confidence.

Preschoolers *(3–5 years old)* move back and forth from their family to the child care program more independently than younger children. They are also more sensitive to the differences between the two environments and observe carefully the interactions between their families and educators/providers. Educators/providers should build a "partnership" with each family to best support the needs of each child. They should keep each other informed of important developments in children's lives and provide mutual support in nurturing each child's physical, social, emotional, and cognitive development.

CHAPTER 11:

Families

CDA® Functional Area 11: Candidate establishes a positive, responsive, and cooperative relationship with each child's family, engages in two-way communication with families, encourages their involvement in the program, and supports the child's relationship with their family.

Families

Introduction

Developing and maintaining reciprocal partnerships with children's families is a recurring theme in this textbook. Early childhood research and advocacy organizations, like the National Association for the Education of Young Children (NAEYC), agree that early care and education should be a collaborative effort between families and early educators. "The experts have been polled and the results are in: a positive parent–educator relationship contributes to school success" (PBS Parents). The two most stable presences in children's lives are their families and the professionals who care for and educate them.

When true partnerships exist among early educators and families, children feel safe and secure and are able to explore and learn in their early childhood setting. These partnerships also ease children's transitions between home and school.

It is important to remember, however, that parents are a child's first and forever teachers. Early childhood educators contribute to learning during an important stage of a young child's life. But families are forever. In most cases they will care for, nurture, and educate their child throughout childhood.

In this chapter, we will discuss the components involved in establishing and maintaining reciprocal partnerships with families:

- **Defining Family**
- **Partnering With Families**
- **Encouraging Family Engagement**
- **Communicating With Families**
- **Holding Formal Meetings With Families**
- **Supporting Child Development at Home**

Defining Family

When asked what it means to be a family, many of us think of the traditional nuclear and extended families whose members are related biologically. In reality, however, the U.S. family model of the 1950s and 1960s—a father who works outside of the home and a mother who stays home to raise the children—now applies to just 15% of all families (Hare and Gray 2008). The U.S. Census Bureau defines the term *family* as "a group of two people or more (one of whom is the householder) related by birth, marriage, or adoption and residing together."

However, in a 2010 survey, 60% of Americans said people can be family simply because they deem themselves to be. Fifty-one percent of those surveyed even thought that pets should be a part of the definition of a family, too (Hare and Gray 2008).

> Families share emotional bonds, common values, goals, and responsibilities and contribute significantly to each other's well-being. When a family includes children, one or more adults (parents and others) may play an involved role in the children's lives. These adults can include biological parents, partners of the child's parent, grandparents, stepparents, aunts and uncles, foster parents, adoptive parents, and any other person who fulfills a significant portion of the parenting and care for the child. These adults may not necessarily be biologically related to the child or even live with the child all of the time.

Types of Family Structures

Today's families exist in structures such as these:

Nuclear families. About two-thirds of families in the US fall into this category—two parents live together with their children. Some nuclear families include a parent who works and one who stays at home—either parent might work in or outside the home in either a full- or part-time capacity. Both parents might be employed or unemployed. Families of young children can include two heterosexual or two homosexual parents. The children in these families are either biologically related to one or both parents or adopted.

Cohabiting families. These families resemble nuclear families, but the parents are not married or legal domestic partners.

Today's families exist in various forms.

Single-parent families. Single parents head one-fourth of all families in the United State. Though either men or women may head these families, women head 88% of single-parent families. It is estimated that in the U.S., 60% of all children will spend some part of their lives in a family with this structure (Hare and Gray 2008).

Blended families. These families are typically the result of divorces and remarriages. Children in these families may be biologically related to one parent or both.

Grandparent-led families. Eight percent of children live with a grandparent for a variety of reasons, from death of a parent to a parent's inability to care for the child.

Interracial, multiracial, and transracial families. In biracial families, each parent is of a different race and the children are biracial. If the parents are biracial, however, the children are multiracial. (For example if a mother is Spanish and French and a father is African-American, any children would be multiracial.) Transracial families consist of parents and their adopted children who are of different races than the parents themselves.

Foster- and group-home families. These temporary families are formed in the best interest of the children, who are often placed with the families by the courts or other government agencies.

Kinship care families. In these families, an arrangement (either legal or informal) exists for relatives (for example, a grandmother), instead of parents, to care for children.

Commuter families. These nuclear or cohabitating families include parents who live and work away from the rest of the immediate family. These situations usually exist because of job responsibilities, educational needs, or military obligations. For example, a woman's husband and children may live in one city, but she lives and works in another during the workweek.

Transnational families. These families live part of each year in different countries. This dynamic can exist in various forms:

- **Children reside with the same set of parents in both countries.** For example, the family's primary residence is in the United States, but they live in China in the summer.
- **Children reside with one parent in both countries.** For example, a mother and children's primary residence is in the United States, but they live in India in the summer.
- **Children reside with one parent in one country and the other parent in another country.** For example, the children's primary residence is in the United States, but their father works in Brazil. The children live with their father in Brazil in the summer and with their mother in the United States the rest of the year.
- **Children reside with parents in one country and grandparents in a different country.** For example, the family's primary residence is in the United States, but the children's maternal grandparents live in Ethiopia. The children live in Ethiopia with their grandparents in the summer and in the United States with their immediate family the rest of the year. All of these family structures are important to know about. Understanding that all family structures are valid and should be represented in your classroom is what matters. The various labels are not what matter.

You will notice that in this chapter and throughout this textbook, the words *families* and *parents* are used interchangeably. Both words refer to the people who are primarily responsible for the children in your care—whether they are parents, stepparents, grandparents, aunts and uncles, cousins, guardians, foster families, or other members of the children's households.

It shows respect, builds trust, and supports children when you represent all families in the setting and within the learning environment. Consider these family structures when choosing the books, materials, photos, and daily activities. When children see themselves and their families represented, they learn that you value them and their cultures. Figure 66a-b is a list of children's books featuring diverse families. These books are just a beginning. As you search for books to add to this collection, be aware of using books written by authors from the cultures represented by the books, and for children depicted in everyday situations. These will be the books children are most likely to relate to.

Figure 66a. Children's Books Depicting Diverse Families

Family Structures

- *And Tango Makes Three*, by Justin Richardson and Peter Parnell, illustrated by Henry Cole, Simon and Schuster, 2005.
- *Daddy, Papa, and Me*, by Lesléa Newman and Carol Thompson, Tricycle Press, 2009.
- *Dear Juno*, by Soyoung Pak, illustrated by Susan Kathleen Hartung, Puffin Books, 2001.
- *Families*, by Ann Morris, HarperCollins, 2000.
- *Heather Has Two Mommies*, by Lesléa Newman, Anniversary Edition, illustrated by Laura Cornell, Candlewick, 2015.
- *The Family Book*, by Todd Parr, Little Brown, 2010.
- *Living with Mom and Living with Dad*, by Melanie Walsh, Candlewick, 2012.
- *Marisol McDonald Doesn't Match: Marisol McDonald no combina*, and others in this series by Monica Brown, Illustrated by Sara Palacios, CBP, 2013.
- *Market Day: A Story Told with Folk Art*, by Lois Ehler, HMH Books for Young Readers, 2002.
- *Mei-Mei's Lucky Birthday Noodles: A Loving Story of Adoption, Chinese Culture and a Special Birthday Treat*, by Shan-Shan Chen and Heidi Goodman, Tuttle, 2014.
- *Our Grandparents: A Global Album*, by Maya Ajmera, Sheila Kinkade, and Cynthia Pon, Global Fund for Children, 2010.
- *Stella Brings the Family*, by Miriam B. Schiffer, illustrated by Holly Clifton-Brown, Chronicle, 2015.
- *Whoever You Are*, by Mem Fox, illustrated by Leslie Staub, HMH Books for Young Readers, 2007.

Diverse Children and Families

African American

- *Baby Dance*, by Ann Taylor, illustrated by Marjorie van Heerden, Harper Festival, 1998.

Figure 66b. Children's Books Depicting Diverse Families

- *Bippity Bop Barbershop*, by Natasha Anastasia Tarpley, illustrated by E. B. Lewis, Little Brown, 2009.
- *A Chair for My Mother*, by Vera B. Williams, Greenwillow, 1982.
- *He's Got the Whole World in His Hands*, by Kadir Nelson, Dial Books, 2005.
- *Lola at the Library*, and others in this series by Anna McQuinn, illustrated by Rosalind Beardshaw, Charlesbridge, 2006.
- *More, More, More, Said the Baby: Three Love Stories*, by Vera B. Williams, Greenwillow, 1990.
- *Mufaro's Beautiful Daughters: An African Tale*, by John Steptoe, Puffin, 2008.
- *Peekaboo Morning*, by Rachel Isadora, G. P. Putnam and Sons, 2008.
- *The Princess and the Pea*, by Rachel Isadora, Puffin, 2009.

Asian

- *Apple Pie 4th of July*, by Janet S. Wong and Margaret Chodos-Irvine, HMH Books for Young Readers, 2006.
- *Dim Sum for Everyone*, by Grace Lin, Dragonfly, 2003.
- *Ganesha's Sweet Tooth*, by Emily Haynes and Sanjay Patel, Chronicle, 2012.
- *Round Is a Mooncake: A Book of Shapes*, by Rosanne Thong, illustrated by Grace Lin, Chronicle, 2000.

Latino/Hispanic

- *Bravo, Chico Canta! Bravo!*, by Pat Mora and Libby Martinez, illustrated by Amelia Lau Carling, Groundwood Books, 2014.
- *Family Pictures, 15th Anniversary Edition / Cuadros de Familia, Edición Quinceañera*, illustrated by Carmen Lomas Garza, CPB, 2005.
- *I Love Saturdays y domingos*, by Alma Flor Ada, illustrated by Elivia Savadier, Atheneum, 2002.
- *In My Family: En mi familia*, by Carmen Garza, CBP, 2013.
- *Niño Wrestles the World*, by Yuyi Morales, A Neal Porter Book / Roaring Brook Press, 2013.

African and Middle Eastern

- *Deep in the Sahara*, by Kelly Cunnane, illustrated by Hoda Hadadi, Schwartz and Wade, 2013.
- *Golden Domes and Silver Lanterns: A Muslim Book of Colors*, by Hena Khan, illustrated by Mehrdokht Amini, Chronicle, 2015.
- *Two Parrots*, by Rashin, NorthSouth, 2014.

How Culture Impacts Family Dynamics

As an early childhood educator, your role in building and maintaining positive partnerships with families can be both highly challenging and extremely rewarding. Strong communication and listening skills, along with the ability to be a flexible and creative thinker, will contribute to your success.

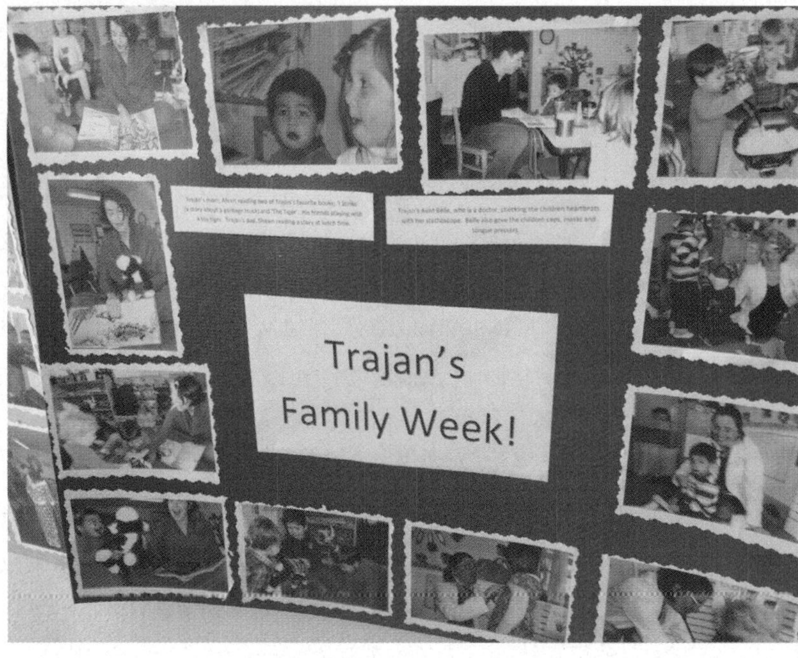

Children will benefit from seeing their families represented in your setting.

Each family has unique relationships, communication styles, expectations for children's learning and behavior, and beliefs about the roles of educators and parents. Parents' and early educators' own family experiences and cultures influence their perceptions of roles and relationships. For example, in some cultures building independence in the early years is not a priority. A family from this culture may believe it is not appropriate to give a young child too much responsibility and may prefer that their child receive greater assistance at meal times or when getting dressed. In another culture, families may believe that their children should learn to obey adults without talking back or questioning a request. You may serve some families where physical punishment is considered appropriate. This may be their preferred form of discipline, but it is not allowed in your setting, either by policy or by law.

Although some families' cultural practices may appear to run counter to the program's policy and practice, early childhood educators must listen to the family's requests and the reasons behind them. With this information, you are more able to build trusting partnerships built on mutual respect. Listen to parents' concerns and respectfully discuss your setting's policies and practices. Be ready to adjust your expectations where it would be reasonable and responsive to do so. For example, when a parent asks you to punish their child, begin by listening to their reasoning. Then take your turn, explaining your policies and sharing information about other techniques, like positive guidance, that are effective in the moment and help a child gain self-regulation, a skill to be used throughout life.

There may be times when it is most appropriate to schedule a meeting with a parent to discuss the topic in detail. Listen intently to a family's culturally-based reasons for why it is inappropriate to teach a child to be independent, and then explain why your setting values this goal. When a family's views do not align with your setting philosophy, or with child development research, it is still critical to respect and listen to the family's concerns and show that you value and respect them. Sometimes it may be important to consider the historical grounding of the policy and to see if adjustments may be called for.

On the other hand, behavioral expectations for the home may differ from those in your setting. Anti-bias educators Louise Derman-Sparks and Julie Olsen Edwards (2010, 40) explain that children in your setting may not be exhibiting "deviating behavior that needs adjustment." Rather, their behavior may be the result of a clash between the cultural practices at home and at the program setting. In these situations, your first reaction should be to carefully examine your values and experiences.

Schedule a formal one-on-one meeting with parents to discuss the issue and/or the child's behavior. Make sure you have planned enough time to carefully listen to and come to understand their viewpoints. It's also important to have time for discussion and for you to have the opportunity to explain the program's position and research-based evidence, if appropriate, to show why you believe the program practice supports children's development and learning. Mutual understanding of the origin of both sets of beliefs helps to strengthen the family-educator relationship, thereby also benefiting the child. Families need to feel that they can retain their fundamental values while working with the program to find an agreeable compromise or acceptable solution.

After the meeting, continue to follow up with the family by sharing the child's experiences each day at your setting. "My colleagues and I will observe and keep track of the positive guidance strategies we use to help your daughter learn what behaviors are accepted. We'll share those notes with you so we can discuss what did and did not work. Hopefully, you can try some of positive guidance suggestions at home and let us know how they are working." There may be times when a family finds the setting's program's beliefs, policies, and practices conflict greatly with their own values, and compromise is not possible. As a result, they may withdraw their child and seek a program that better fits their needs. However, many parents will welcome a chance to learn about the developmentally appropriate practices that underlie your setting's approach. In turn, hearing the families' viewpoints can expand your thoughts and support you in clearly articulating the reasons for your teaching practices.

Partnering With Families

The relationships in our lives—whether they are with family members, friends, or neighbors— transform into partnerships when the people involved all share a common goal and the responsibility for reaching it. Your relationships with families become partnerships because you all want to support their children's development and learning and will work together to achieve this.

Most parents find a setting visit so rewarding that they are eager to return.

All partnerships stem from positive relationships and require all partners to do the following:

- Regard each other as equal partners who contribute to the partnerships in different ways.
- Value and respect each other for what they think, even if there are differences.
- Listen and talk to each other.
- Make an effort to understand and trust each other's points-of-view.
- Confer with each other when making important decisions.
- Actively work on rooting out personal and cultural biases that may get in the way of these partnerships.

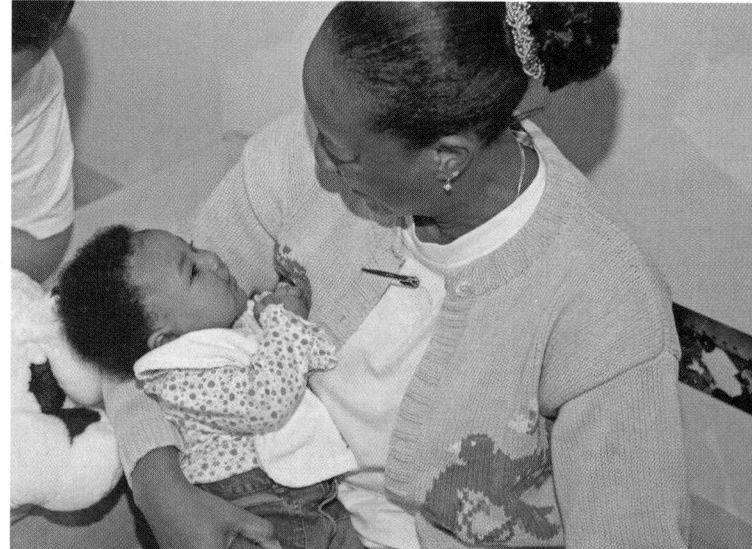

Parents of infants can spend time cuddling, cooing, and playing with their infants.

Many parents, particularly new or first-time parents, may be anxious about leaving their children in the care of adults outside their networks of family and friends. They need to truly believe that their child is in a safe and nurturing place before they will be comfortable with the early childhood setting. Through strong partnerships and clear two-way communication, parents can gain a deeper understanding of what you and the children do each day and how the learning environment, materials, and interactions foster development and learning. They will learn the "why" behind teaching practices and the program's policies. Their confidence in the quality of your setting and you as a skilled early childhood educator may prompt them to encourage other parents to enroll their children.

When you articulate the importance of play and how and what children learn from play, families gain confidence in you as a professional. Your competence will give them ideas for things to do at home to further support their child's development and learning. It can also open the door for parents to share more information about their child and their values to help you understand the child better. Use this information to reflect on how you can tailor your teaching practices to support their child. Regularly sharing with families documentation of their child's learning will encourage parents to share their thoughts and engage in their child's development and learning.

In addition, children will feel most comfortable in the setting if they feel safe and secure. This sense of security, coupled with clear behavioral expectations for older children, gives children the trust they need to explore, try out new materials and activities, and make friends with the other children. Security comes in part from children seeing that their interests, experiences, and materials from home are also part of the early childhood setting. This creates strong links between the children's homes and your setting. A child might think, "This is a place that welcomes me. It feels like home." For example, André went to the beach with his family last week. During the trip, his parents took photos of the sand castles André built. They gave the photos to his teacher to include in André's portfolio. Now André can revisit the photos and describe his vacation. His teacher can link his experience building sand castles at the beach with his experience playing at the sand table or in the sandbox outside. Andre can look at the photos throughout the day or even try to build another castle using blocks or Lego® building bricks.

Strong, reciprocal partnerships with families, offer you a clearer understanding of each child's strengths. Information, like family values, parenting styles, and events in the child's life, can equip you to identify why children react or behave in a certain way. You are more likely to develop stronger bonds with children if they feel that you are connected to their families.

Initiating Partnerships

When families enroll their children in your setting, let them know that you want to partner with them on behalf of their children. Communicate this message through your words and your actions. Take advantage of all opportunities to introduce yourself. Be as open as possible with families. Let them know about you! Where you live, who is in your family, your interests, your culture and identity, your experience as an early childhood educator, and so on. You will be with their child for most of the day for up to five days a week. They want to get to know you.

The following are a few suggestions for how to initiate partnerships with families:

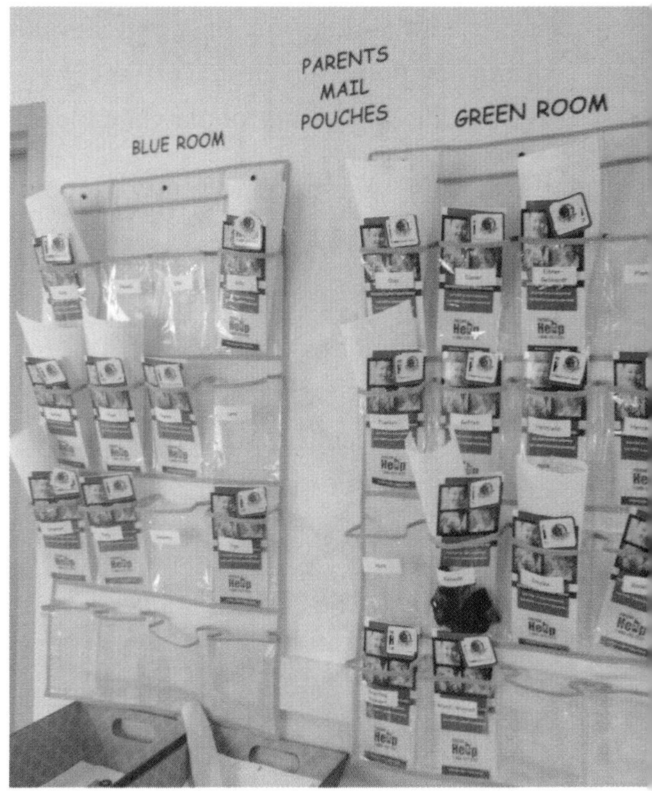

Be sure to show families where they can find their mailboxes.

Develop a family welcome packet. The bulk of this welcome packet should anticipate and answer the kinds of questions families might have about the program. These are likely to vary, depending on the age of their child. Keep in mind that for families of infants, and sometimes toddlers and preschoolers too, this is the first time they are leaving their child in the care of someone other than a family member.

Include information about hours of operation, sick child policies, emergency plans, and field trip rules (including back-up plans in cases of inclement weather). Also include your setting's mission and philosophy, approaches to learning, and a description of the curriculum used. Use the packet to communicate your vision for partnerships with parents, invite parents into your setting, and create opportunities for safe and respectful dialogue.

Consider including a list of frequently asked questions to address common family concerns. Include a form in the front or back and ask parents to sign and return the form to acknowledge that they have received a copy of the packet. If you change policies during the course of the year, notify family members and provide written updates in English and home languages. Review the welcome packet each year to ensure that the content is current and that the text and photos or illustrations welcome families and illustrate the setting's diversity. Get the packet translated into each language spoken by children's families. (Head Start and Early Head Start programs are required to issue parent welcome packets or handbooks in accordance with the Head Start Program Performance Standards [2007].)

Hold an orientation open house. Invite families to tour your setting before their child's first day to establish a friendly and respectful rapport with families. Demonstrate your commitment to professionalism by speaking with them in a serious, yet friendly manner. Review the welcome packet with families and answer their questions. Introduce your curriculum and walk families through a typical day in the setting. Show them how transitions occur between activities, and explain the importance of play in children's learning.

In addition, use this opportunity to show the ways that you welcome families into your program. Let them know that the following features are part of the program:

- The program is accessible to all families whose children are enrolled. Families do not need to make an appointment to visit during the day.
- Every family has an individual mailbox. Both educators and families can use the mailbox to exchange information.
- Signs provide information in English and every family's home language. They include children's names on cubbies and critical signs, such as a reminder to wash children's hands upon arrival, the names of the learning centers, and a job chart for older children.

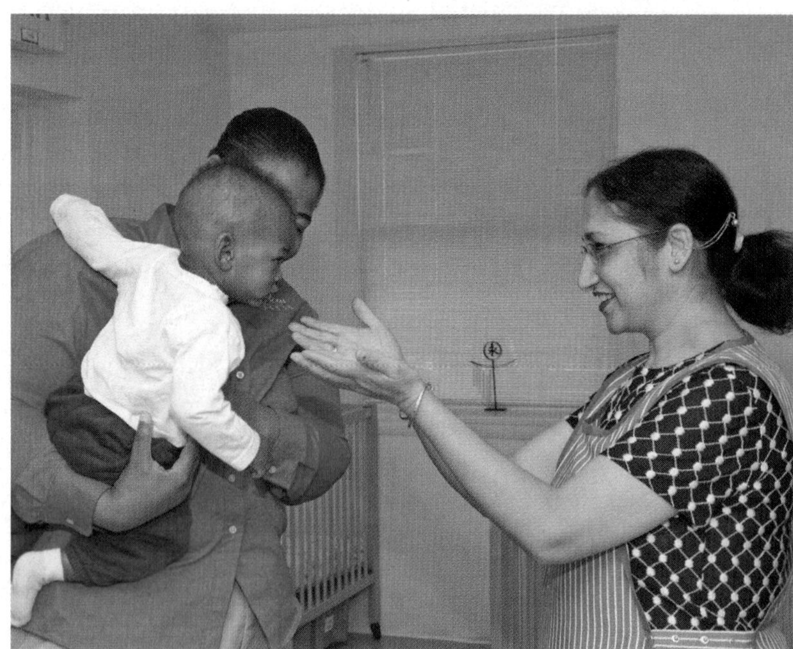

Developing strong partnerships with parents will help them feel secure knowing that their child is in a safe and nurturing setting.

- A family bulletin board displays notices of interest to families.
- Every child and early childhood educator has a family poster, displaying photos of the important people (and pets) in their lives.

- Daily reports detail infants' and toddlers' feeding, diapering, and activities.
- Sign-in and sign-out sheets are used at drop-off and pick-up times.
- Family members can store their coats, purses, and other personal belongings in a locked cabinet while they are visiting the program.
- Parents can sit in adult-size chairs to read a story or join children for a meal.
- Documentation panels with photos and text describe what children are doing and learning.
- Parents can use the program's digital camera to take photos to be included in homemade books and to post in the setting.
- Sample comments and questions, in English and home languages, are posted in the room so family members can use them to engage and interact with children.
- Resources on child development and learning and parenting are available for families to borrow.
- Bags filled with books, toys, or puppets are provided for children to borrow and play with at home.

Conduct an Intake/Enrollment Interview

Make family involvement an important component of your setting's philosophy.

Upon enrollment, all settings conduct a brief initial meeting with families to complete written forms and obtain critical information about the child and family. Conduct this meeting in person and in a comfortable area. Offer snacks and beverages during the meeting. If the family does not speak your home language and you are not fluent in theirs, learn how to pronounce their names and a few words in their home language, such as "welcome" and "thank you" to show respect. In addition, ask a staff member or interpreter who is fluent in both languages to attend the meeting or invite the family to bring a trusted interpreter with them. Pose questions, such as, "Tell me about a typical day at home for Michael. When and where does he nap and what foods does he especially like?"

Below are some important questions to ask families. Explain that you do not mean to pry, you are just trying to get to know them so you can work together to support their child. Allow sufficient time for them to ask you questions, too. This is not a one-sided interview; it is a time to begin building your partnership. The questions are just suggestions and you are likely to change the wording to fit the conversation and circumstances.

The Family

- Do you have any family pets?
- What language do family members speak at home? What languages do family members speak with and around your child?
- Who are the members of your family? Who typically lives in the home with the child? Describe their relationships with your child. Which extended family members live in your home or nearby? Does your child have a special relationship with specific family members or family friends?
- Do you have any traditions you would like you us to include in our program?
- How would you like to be involved in the program in your child's development and learning?
- What more should we know about the family's culture, values, traditions?

The Child

- What activities does your child like best? What are your child's favorite toys? Activities? Books?
- What is your child especially interested in—this month?
- Describe your child's routines for nap time and bed time. How long does your child usually sleep? What are your child's bedtime rituals? Does your child have a special toy or blanket to sleep with? Do they usually wake up in a specific mood (e.g., happy, grumpy, enthusiastic, confused, or something else)?
- How do you comfort your child when they are upset?
- What are your child's greatest strengths?
- What are your child's greatest challenges?
- Does your child have any fears? How do you and the child cope with them?
- Has your child ever been diagnosed with a disability? Does your child have an IFSP (Individualized Family Service Plan) or an IEP (Individualized Education Program)?
- What are your goals for your child's development and learning? What are your wishes and dreams for your child in the future?

- Describe your child's health history. Does she have any food allergies? Is she on medication? Please provide the name and phone number of the child's physician, emergency contacts, and procedures in case your child gets sick or injured.

Feeding and Mealtimes

- For younger, nursing infants: What times does the mother nurse the child? Will she be nursing at the setting and/or providing breast milk or formula? Will the child be transitioning to solid foods at the setting?
- For older infants, toddlers, and preschoolers: Describe mealtimes at your home. Which family members eat together? Do you have any mealtime traditions or rituals we should include in the setting? What are your child's favorite foods? What foods do you like to eat and what foods do you never eat (because you do not like them or for religious or cultural reasons)?

Permissions

You can ask these questions during the meeting, but families must also answer them in writing:

- Who is allowed to pick up your child? What is their relation to your child? What are their names and phone numbers?
- Do we—early educators and staff—have permission to photograph your child for educational use in our setting or in publications or videos publicizing the setting?
- Do you grant permission for your child to take supervised field trips for educational purposes?
- Do you grant permission for your child to ride on buses or in private vehicles for these activities?

You probably will not get all of the information you need during this initial intake interview. Getting to know a child and family takes time and is an ongoing process. The interview may overwhelm some family members. For others, you may be the first early childhood educator they have met, and they may feel intimidated by your position. Others may be reluctant to share what they feel is private information. For example, a family may be reluctant to share that they live at a homeless shelter or are dealing with immigration worries (Derman-Sparks and Edwards 2010). Some families may even think you are judging their parenting styles and abilities.

If parents seem uncomfortable with your questions, focus on priorities like getting the signed permission forms or learning about the child's eating and sleeping preferences. Answers that focus on parental hopes and dreams for their child can wait. Parents are just getting to know you. Perhaps once your reciprocal partnership is further developed, they will want to share additional information.

When Families and Early Childhood Educators Have Conflicts

Collaborating and establishing positive relationships with families helps you gain their trust and respect so you can jointly support their child's development and learning. A primary goal is for parents to feel comfortable sharing their ideas and suggestions and talking to you about issues and concerns related to their child. Perhaps, families will also actively participate in any events or experiences in your setting and become more involved in programming and planning.

However, there may be a family with whom you have difficulty bonding. Perhaps your personality clashes with their interaction style—or vice versa. Or you may sense hostility from this parent—for no apparent reason. Some families may limit their contact with you because they have had unpleasant experiences with educators in their own schooling or because educators are held in high esteem in their culture and they believe it is inappropriate to question your practice. Others may be suspicious of your intentions.

Despite family members' feelings or actions, it's important for early childhood educators to remain open and proactive in forming relationships with them. If you are having difficulty connecting with a child's family, figure out a different, more effective approach. As a professional, you will need to find a strategy that is effective. You will benefit from your heartfelt efforts to learn all you can about families and their beliefs and desires for their children.

Encouraging Family Engagement

Families should know that they are welcome in your setting at all times to observe and participate in meaningful ways. Some settings, like Head Start, have a long history of parent involvement. Other settings, like co-ops or the Sure Start program operated by the Department of Defense Dependents Schools (DoDDS), require parent participation. Engaging families supports children. It should be an important component of your setting's philosophy. (See Figure 67a-b for more information about family engagement.)

Engaging families in meaningful ways takes careful thought. Some families may be reluctant to participate. They may think that they will know what to do. Often parents' work schedules do not allow them to visit the setting during the day. Gently encourage these parents to get involved in the activities they are comfortable doing and have time to do.

Figure 67a. Family Engagement

"Family engagement occurs when there is an ongoing, reciprocal, strengths-based partnership between families and their children's early childhood education programs" (Halgunseth, Peterson, Stark, and Moodie 2009, 3).

The term family engagement describes meaningful partnerships between early childhood educators and the families of young children. Engagement is ongoing, reciprocal, and based on the strengths of all parties. The chart below lists the six factors that are essential parts of family engagement and examples of ways early childhood educators and families contribute to each one.

FAMILY ENGAGEMENT FACTORS	EXAMPLES OF EARLY CHILDHOOD EDUCATOR AND FAMILY CONTRIBUTIONS
1. Early childhood education programs encourage and validate family participation in **decision making** related to their children's education. Families should act as advocates for their children and early childhood education program by actively taking part in decision making opportunities.	At monthly meetings, families contribute to decision-making about classroom activities. "I think the toddlers would love to have a water wall like the one the preschoolers use. We could make one that is less complicated and sized for their height. I'm willing to help." Both families and educators serve on the book selection committee to make sure new books are just right for the children in the setting.
2. Consistent, **two-way communication** is facilitated through multiple forms and is responsive to the linguistic preference of the family. Communication should be both school and family initiated and should be timely and continuous, inviting conversations about both the child's educational experience as well as the larger program.	Educators and families regularly exchange e-mails about individual children's experiences at the program—written in the language families prefer (with help from a translator if needed). Families frequently share photos and stories about their child's home experiences, "Look, here she is crawling up the stairs. Now we will all have to watch her carefully in case she falls."
3. Families and early childhood education programs collaborate and **exchange knowledge**. Family members share their unique knowledge and skills through volunteering and actively engaging in events and activities at schools. Teachers seek out information about their students' lives, families, and communities and integrate this information into their curriculum and instructional practices.	Educators invite family members to share their special talents with the children. "I know you play the saxophone. Would you have time to come to visit to show your instrument to the children—and play a little music?" Family members volunteer to support the program. "I am really good at details. I'd be happy to help organize the book fair this year. It's a great fundraiser."

Figure 67b. Family Engagement

FAMILY ENGAGEMENT FACTORS	EXAMPLES OF EARLY CHILDHOOD EDUCATOR AND FAMILY CONTRIBUTIONS
4. Early childhood education programs and families place an emphasis on creating and sustaining **learning activities at home** and in the community that extend the teachings of the program so as to enhance each child's early learning.	Educators visit community businesses and invite business owners to come to the program. "Miss Louisa, the children loved visiting your bake shop and they have been getting ready for your visit to the classroom all week." Family members help the program network with the community. "My dad's assisted living center is filled with seniors who are eager to read with young children. Let's figure out how to get them together with the preschoolers."
5. Families create a **home environment** that values learning and supports programs. Programs and families collaborate in establishing goals for children both at home and at school.	Educators stock a lending library with children's books and suggestions for follow-up activities to do at home. "You'll find everything you need to do the activity in the bag along with the book." Educators and families jointly set goals for children during biannual family-educator conferences: "So we both agree that it's time to begin toilet learning at home and at the program."
6. Early childhood education programs create an ongoing and comprehensive system for promoting **family engagement** by ensuring that program leadership and teachers are dedicated, trained, and receive the supports they need to fully engage families.	Educators work as a team to plan the many strategies the program as a whole and individual staff will use to engage families. Colleagues regularly support each other's efforts by sharing ideas and successes.

To ensure effective family engagement, these six factors interact and work together. Family engagement requires a culture that supports and honors reciprocal relationships, commitment from program leadership, a vision shared by staff and families, opportunities to develop the skills needed to engage in reciprocal relationships, and practices and policies that support meaningful family engagement (Halgunseth, L.C. and Peterson, A. 2009).

Ask families about their interests and listen carefully to identify their passions—then build on them. A parent who talks about the quilt she is making might be willing to bring it to the program to show the children how quilts are made. Or, a parent who oohs and aahs at your collection of items from nature, might have time to go on a nature walk with the children. Finally, a parent who is active on social media, could help you update the website or share short videos of the children via an e-mail to all of the families in the group.

Visiting the Setting

Families who are able to visit during the day can begin by observing to see and hear the experiences that take place in a typical day. On future visits they can join in play their child and other children. Parents of infants can spend time cuddling, cooing, reading stories, and playing with their infant. Parents of toddlers can explore the setting with their child and other toddlers, play games, narrate what the toddlers are doing, and read stories. Preschoolers' parents can ask open-ended questions and expand children's play and learning.

Help parents notice and make sense of your practice by introducing the specific strategies you use to support children's learning. For example, explain that you talk with infants during diapering, telling them what you are doing and what they are doing in response. In this way you are building a relationship with the child and helping the child gain attachment, which will set the stage for trust and a sense that the world is a safe place to explore. With toddlers, you could discuss and model the importance of having age-appropriate expectations. This is why you have multiples of favorite toys so toddlers do not have to share before they are ready. With preschoolers, a parent could play a simple game of catch with a few children. Your tips could focus on why most preschoolers are neither emotionally nor physically ready for competitive sports.

Once families do get involved, they are usually pleasantly surprised and excited to observe teaching and learning. Seeing how proud their child is to have them there is often all it takes. Most parents find the experience so rewarding, they are eager to return.

The following are a few activities that parents can engage in while visiting the setting:

- Feed a bottle to their infant or another child.
- Roll a ball back and forth with a mobile infant or toddler.
- Help a toddler put her shoes on—again and again, perhaps.
- Make smoothies with a small group of three toddlers.
- Lead a small group activity, such as playing lotto, putting together a puzzle, or blowing bubbles outdoors.
- Read a story aloud to one, a few, or a small group of children.
- Sing with the children or leading a finger play during meeting times.
- Work with the children to turn a cardboard refrigerator box into a house.
- Introducing children to the music of their culture.
- Cooking a family's favorite recipe with the children.
- Talking to the children in the dramatic play center about their occupations.
- Overseeing a woodworking project.
- Accompanying the group on a field trip.

- Reading aloud a book in their home language.
- Teaching children some common words in their home language.

Orienting Families Who Visit the Setting

Remember, parents are used to being with their own child or children, but they may be meeting the other children in your setting for the first time. Playing and interacting with children they do not know may be a new experience. This is one reason why observing on the first visit can be an excellent way to get a feel for the setting and what the adults and children do there.

In toddler and preschool groups, parents might be willing and able to lead a small group activity. Follow these steps to help them prepare.

1. Share the goals for the activity.
2. Provide an opportunity to observe you or a colleague doing the activity.
3. Review the steps and materials to be used. Answer any questions.
4. Observe while the family member conducts the activity.
5. Discuss what the children did and said and learned. Answer any questions.
6. Have the family member lead the activity alone; stay nearby to provide support, if needed.
7. Discuss what the children did and said and learned. Answer any questions.

Create tip sheets for activities that parents can lead, and get them translated into all of the home languages spoken by family members. See Figures 68a-b, 69, 70 and 71a-b.

Figure 68a. Reading Aloud

Share these tips with parents who read aloud in your setting. Explain that some of the tips for one age group are appropriate for other age groups too.

For all children

- Read slowly enough for children to take in the words and look at the pictures.
- Read with expression.
- Have fun bringing the characters and plot to life.
- If children lose interest or decide they want to do something else, allow them to follow their interests.
- Watch the children's body language. Children may need a break or even to end the session.

Figure 68b. Reading Aloud

For infants

- Cuddle up with the infant in your lap.
- Read as much or as little as the infant likes.
- Expect infants to use all of their senses to explore books—they are likely to touch pictures, chew the corners, and reach for the pages.
- Describe and name things, animals, and people in the pictures.
- Ask older infants to point to things, animals, and people in the pictures.

For toddlers

- Ask toddlers to choose a book they like.
- Cuddle up and read with one or a few toddlers at a time.
- Read books with rhymes, songs, and repetition; stop so toddlers can join in.
- Expect to read the same book again and again.
- Spend plenty of time looking at and talking about the pictures.

For preschoolers

- Select a book that you like (and have read before) and that you think the children will like, too.
- Gather a group of 4 to 6 preschoolers in a comfortable area where everyone can sit on the floor. Sit on a chair so all the children can see the book.
- Point out the names of the book's author and illustrator and the cover illustration. See whether the children can predict what the book will be about.
- Talk about the book afterward. Encourage children to retell the story in their own words.
- When you read the book again, stop to invite children to complete a predictable phrase or sentence, to guess what might happen next, or to think about how they might react in a similar situation in real life. Ask older children open-ended questions about how a character might be feeling or why they think the situation occurred.

Other Ways to Be Involved

Many family members can't visit the setting during the day because of their work schedules. However, these parents can still contribute by doing tasks at home. For example, a willing parent could:

- Make a recording while singing some favorite children's songs.
- Sew a tablecloth for the housekeeping area, new dress-up clothes for a particular theme, or floor pillows for the reading nook.
- Translate materials and songs in children's home languages.
- Mount and frame children's artwork.
- Repair toys or make parts for puzzles and games to replace lost pieces.
- Chair the planning committee for a fundraiser such as a book sale.
- Follow instructions (provided by you) to make safe toys out of recycled items. For example, a parent could make a tugging box for infants and toddlers. Poke holes in a shoe box; thread ribbons through two holes and tie knots at both ends; tape the box shut.
- Establish good morning and good night routines and activities with the child.
- Use bath time to talk about the day or for very young children, just explain what is happening as the bath progresses.
- During diapering or toileting, explain your role, procedures, item names, and invite the child to "help" by doing what they are capable of doing based on age and experience.
- During snacks or meals, talk to the child about what they are eating. Prior to the meal invite the child to help set the table (depending on age) and discuss how the food was prepared. If the child accompanied you on the shopping trip to the grocery store, remind the child of how they "helped" with the shopping, and describe textures, colors, flavors and seasonings used with the food.
- If the child takes a nap, explain why the nap is important and what will occur when the nap is over.
- While the child is getting dressed, explain the names, colors and textures of the clothes they are putting on. If the child will be going outside, explain why the particular clothing was chosen and is appropriate for the weather. Discuss the names of the parts of the clothes the child will be wearing.
- When you and the child are playing with toys, be sure to name the toys, talk about the parts, shapes, and colors of the toys, and any sounds associated with them. If the child is old enough, ask the child to talk about different ways they might want to use the toys.

- Use a special time to just talk to the child—perhaps tell a story about growing up, make up a story, do pretend together, or describe events that the child may have already experienced.
- Read books and other materials to the child or just look at a magazine together and talk about the pictures or what is on the pages.
- Enjoy different types of music together with your child.
- Encourage the child to move and dance to the music or use instruments or objects to "accompany" the music and sing songs together.
- Provide the child with art or craft materials to experience different textures, colors, shapes, sounds, and senses. Take a walk with the child to find and gather assorted natural objects you can use to create projects. There's no need to spend a lot of money since the experience and selected items will suffice.
- Get outside together as much as possible. Take a walk, use the senses to explore the neighborhood (find different things to look at, touch, listen to, possibly taste and smell), go to a park or find a large, open space to provide opportunity for lots of movement.

Though it is helpful to have help with these tasks, encourage parents to spend time in the setting with their children if they can possibly arrange their schedule to do so.

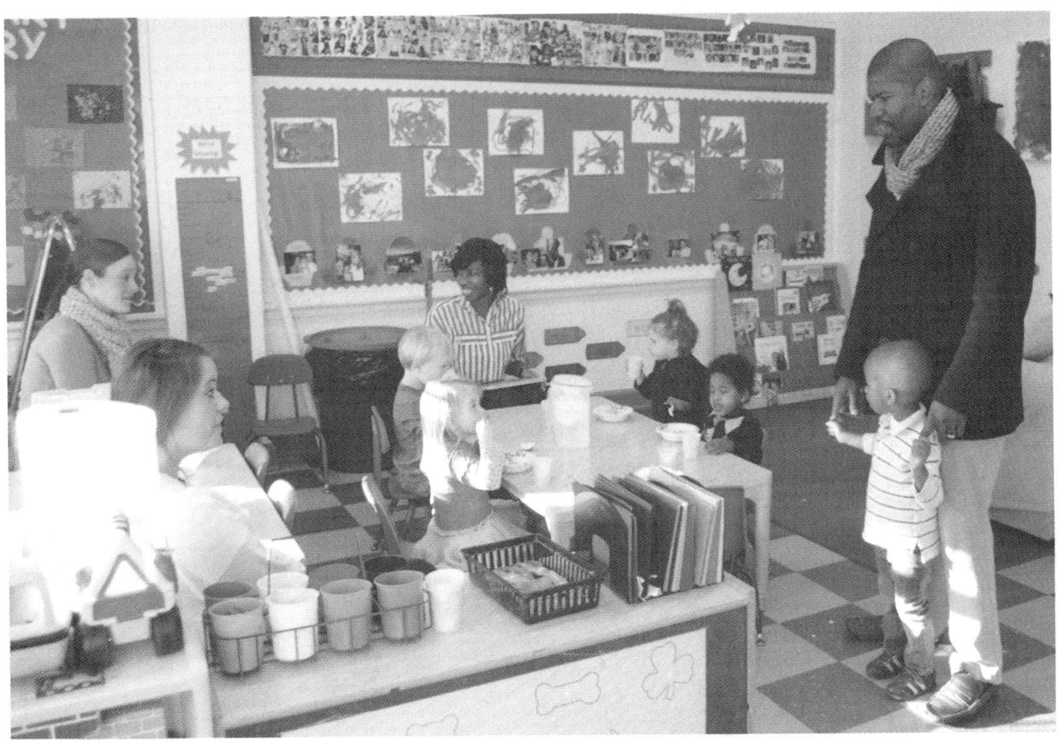

Through strong partnerships and clear communication, parents will have a deeper understanding of your daily schedule and routines.

Figure 69. Ten Tips for Being With Infants

Make and post this list in several places in your setting to guide parents' interactions with infants. Translate them into the families' home languages. Explain that the examples are just a few tips for being with infants and examples of what adults might say. Leave space on the signs so parents can add more tips.

1. Tell the infant what you are going to do before you do it. "I see you are awake. I'm going to lift you up out of the crib."
2. Describe what you are doing and what the infant is doing. "You rolled the ball to me. I'm rolling it back to you now."
3. Show and talk about things in the room and outdoors. "There's a red cardinal on that tree branch. Oh, look, he is flying away."
4. Respond when infants coo and gurgle to you. "Yes, I see you and I hear you. It's fun to be with you."
5. Acknowledge infants' feelings. "You are crying because I put you on the floor. You wanted me to carry you. I think you can crawl to the mat."
6. Remember that infants gain new skills very quickly. "Last week you could get to your knees. Today you can stand up while holding on to the railing."
7. Play with infants so they can learn that it's fun to be with other people. "Peek-a-boo. Where is Yancey? Oh, now I see him."
8. Meet infants' needs quickly and consistently. "I got your bottle ready when I saw you waking up. We can sit in the rocker while you drink your milk."
9. Offer a variety of play materials that infants can use in different ways. "You can bang these two blocks together or you can put one on top of the other."
10. Expect infants to use their sense to explore. "I saw Teresa chewing that toy. Let's put it in the wash basin and get you a clean one."

Figure 70. Sample Questions/Comments for Toddlers

Make and post this list in several places in your setting to guide parents' interactions with infants. Translate them into the families' home languages. Explain that the examples are just a few tips for being with toddlers and examples of what adults might say. Leave space on the signs so parents can add more tips.

ROUTINE/ ACTIVITY	WHAT CHILDREN DO AND LEARN	SAMPLE QUESTIONS/COMMENTS
Diapering and Toileting	The parts of the body; self-help skills; self-regulation; conversation skills.	• "I see that you pumped just enough soap to get your hands clean." • "Tell me what you want to do when we're finished changing your diaper." • "You wiped from front to back. You'll be nice and clean."
Snack and Mealtimes	Conversation skills; fine motor skills; nutrition; self-help skills; counting.	• "You have 2 graham crackers and 3 apple slices. Let's count together?" • "What does the kiwi taste like." • You have a red fork and a blue spoon. Which one will you use?"
Reading Aloud/ Looking at Books	Print has meaning; pictures are related to the text of the book; how to hold books; new vocabulary.	• "Can you bring me a book to read?" • "Where is the rabbit's furry tail? How does it feel to you?" • "I wonder what will happen if the four monkeys jump on the bed."
Pretend Play	To copy adult behavior; make sense of experiences; develop self-regulation; be creative.	• "What's in your bag? Where are you going?" • "You are pushing the stroller very fast." • "Who is calling on the telephone?" • "Peek-a-boo! I see you!"
Blocks and Table Toys	Build fine and large motor skills; explore size and shape; play alongside a friend; talk to themselves about what they are doing.	• "Are the cardboard blocks heavy or light? Can you make a tower with them?" • Where does that puzzle piece go? Do you see a shape that looks like this one? • "You did put the pig in the truck? Is there room for any other animals?"
Drawing, Painting, Using Playdough	Build fine motor skills; learn about cause and effect; express feelings; handle stress; learn vocabulary.	• "Wow. I saw you push down hard with your marker. What happened when you did that?" • "I like how this playdough feels. How does it feel to you?" • "You made straight lines in the fingerpaint. How could you make wavy lines?"

Figure 71a. Sample Questions/Comments for Preschoolers

Post sample questions on the side of a divider shelf where parents can consult them during preschoolers' play. Explain that the examples are just some of the things children learn and some of the ways adults might respond.

CENTER	WHAT CHILDREN DO AND LEARN	SAMPLE QUESTIONS/COMMENTS
Blocks	Geometry (shapes, sizes); balancing; develop fine motor skills; write.	• "Which blocks will you put at the bottom of your tower?" • "How might you keep the building from falling down?" • "How many of these small blocks will it take to make a large block?" • "What should we write on the sign next to your construction?"
Art	Express feelings and ideas; use color and texture; develop eye–hand coordination; develop aesthetic sense.	• "Why did you choose to use dark colors?" • "How does this collage make you feel?" • "If you tell me about your drawing, I'll write down your words on this sentence strip." • "Do you want to post your painting on the wall here, or would you rather take it home?"
Literacy	Letters, words, and print awareness; discover how books work; gain an appreciation of books; write their names.	• "There's a picture of three rabbits eating carrots on the cover of this book. What do you think this book might be about?" • "This word begins with a P sound? Can you think of any other words that begin with a P sound?" • "This book is by Eric Carle. Do you remember any other books you've read by this same author—Eric Carle?" • "Let's act out the story we just read using puppets. Who would like to be the little boy?"
Dramatic Play	Try out roles; work through experiences; develop executive function and self-control.	• "May I join you for dinner? What are you serving?" • "What does your little girl need to do to get ready for school?" • "Would you like to be the doctor who gives children shots? You can make sure that you don't hurt them." • "May I join your tea party? I'd like to bring my friend Maria with me."

Figure 71b. Sample Questions/Comments for Preschoolers

CENTER	WHAT CHILDREN DO AND LEARN	SAMPLE QUESTIONS/COMMENTS
Music & Movement	Patterns and relationships; express themselves; music appreciation; phonological awareness.	• "How would a rhinoceros move?" • "How could we make a drum out of this oatmeal box?" • "Why does this bell make such a high sound?" • "Which songs did you like best?"
Science	Apply scientific method; experiment; graph; observe.	• "How do these leaves look the same? How are they different?" • "What colors do you see when you hold the prism in the light? Are the colors always in the same order?"
Math & Manipulatives	Counting; seriation; matching; more than/less than; fine motor skills.	• "How did you know where to put that last puzzle piece?" • "What other card has a picture that looks like this piece of fruit?" • "Tell me about your LEGO® construction." • "How many pegs are on the pegboard now?"
Sand & Water	Express feelings; experiment; observe; predict; build fine motor skills; volume; patterning.	• "Do you think this rock will sink or float in the water?" • "How did you use the shell to make these patterns in the sand?" • "If we were to turn the water table into an ocean, what should we put in the bottom of the table?" • "What happens to the sand when it gets wet?"
Cooking	Letters, words, and directionality with recipe cards; observe properties change; measurement, volume, and number.	• "How many steps are there in this recipe for pineapple salad?" • "What happened to the popcorn kernels when they were heated?" • "How do we know when the bread is done?"
Outdoors	Develop large muscle skills; explore nature.	• "How did you feel when you got to the top of the climber?" • "Why don't you take the magnifying glass and see whether you can discover what the ants are doing?" • "How will you know when the tomatoes in your garden are ready to be eaten?" • "Let's see how long our shadows are. What should we use to measure them?"

Communicating With Families

Strong two-way communication is imperative to maintaining effective partnerships with families. If children are transported to the program by a family member, it is possible to communicate with families daily. For children who are transported by bus or van, daily face-to-face communications are not possible so you will have to use creative alternatives.

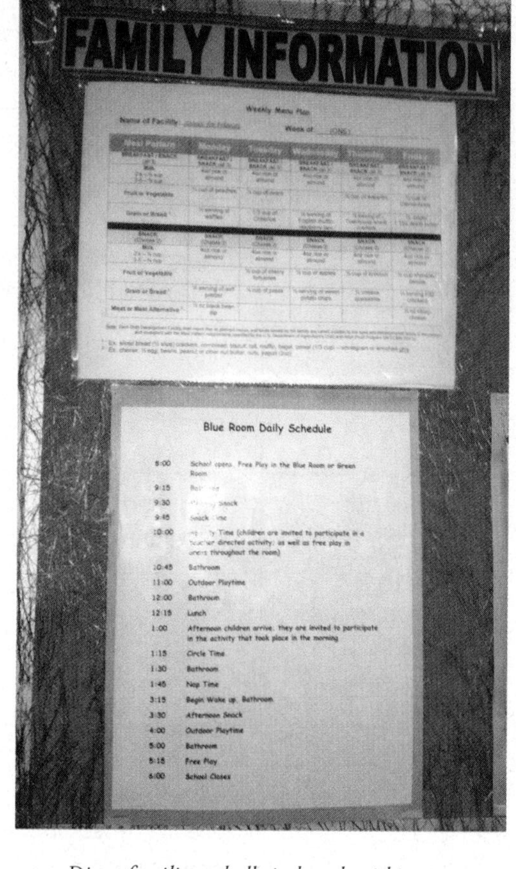

Direct families to bulletin boards within your setting so they can obtain important information.

Whatever the frequency or type of communications you exchange with families, it's important to avoid using technical jargon. Child development and early education terminology may be second nature to you, but it can get in the way of clear communication when families are not equally familiar with the language.

In addition, keep in mind that although educators are knowledgeable about early childhood development, the National Association for the Education of Young Children (NAEYC 2011, 23) agrees you do not need to know all the answers to parents' questions:

> Parents do not feel like partners in the relationship when staff members see themselves as having all the knowledge and insight about children and view parents as lacking such knowledge. In reciprocal relationships between practitioners and families, there is mutual respect, cooperation, shared responsibility, and negotiation of conflicts toward achievement of shared goals. Practitioners work in collaborative partnerships with families, establishing and maintaining regular, frequent, two-way communication with them.

When communicating with families, admitting that you do not know the answer to a question and being willing to seek the information demonstrate keen self-awareness (Gillespie 2006). As parents describe their experiences and perspectives, encourage two-way communication with active listening and empathy.

Here are some suggested mediums and times through which you can communicate effectively with families:

Welcome letter. Before children's first day, send families a one-page letter that lets them know that you and the staff are excited that their children are joining your setting. Describe briefly your setting's philosophy and what your goals are for the children. Explain that you are eager to hear their goals too. Alert families to the setting welcome packet they will receive soon. The packet will describe your responsibilities and the responsibilities you hope parents will agree to assume. Let them know you will be in touch to schedule a home visit and the date and time of the orientation meeting. Reassure them that you will be available to answer all of their questions. Also, send toddlers and preschoolers postcards to welcome them personally to the setting.

Morning drop-off. When parents bring their children to the setting, you can have daily conversations with them. Informal meetings like these help you and the family forge bonds. Greet family members by name (be sure to use correct pronunciation) and ask about their evening or weekend and how their child is doing. Listen attentively as family members share or ask questions. Share anecdotes about their children too and ask questions if you know the answer will be a quick one. Many parents are hurrying off to work so they just can't take too long to chat.

Afternoon/evening pickup. This brief meeting time, like morning drop-off, is another opportunity to connect with families. Parents will want to know how their child's day went, so share something positive. Describe children's actions or what specific activities they did. For example, "Aaron tried hard to crawl today." Respectfully listen to parents as they respond to the information you provide. For example, if a parent is upset to see their son playing in the cooking center, listen to their concerns, consider them carefully, then respond in a way that respects their views and upholds early childhood education practices and the reasons supporting them. While parents of infants and toddlers typically seek detailed information regarding their children's diapering and feeding each day, be sure to also exchange information about the child's explorations and experiences at home and at the program.

Remind toddlers and preschoolers of the things they need to take home and wish them a good evening. Some children may have been asking, "When will daddy be here?" for the past hour, while others watch quietly while other children and parents leave for the day. Some children are so engrossed in an activity that they need a gentle reminder to see their parents have arrived. You can tell them that they will be able to return to the activity the following day.

Children who cling to you at pick-up time may be unhappy that their parents left them that morning or stayed away for so long. They may say that they are angry with or do not like their parents. Help these children reconnect with their family members. "Your daddy looks so happy to see you. He's got your coat in his hand and is ready to help you put it on. I know you are going to have a fun evening." Give all the children a warm goodbye so that everyone will be eager to return the next day.

Phone calls, texts, and e-mails. Depending on families' preferences, set up a regular schedule and method for contacting them. During this check-in, talk about their children's progress, discuss any concerns, and chat about future plans. Include specific examples of children's learning and work or whether you are noticing any changes in children's sleeping and eating patterns. Sending families photos of their children engaging in play is another way you can regularly communicate with families and strengthen the partnership.

Encourage family members to contact you via phone, text, or e-mail if they have concerns or want to discuss something with you. An e-mail or text request affords you time to gather records or other material you might need for your discussion or to discuss their questions with a colleague. If parents have no access to either a computer or phone, arrange to meet them in person.

Newsletters. Weekly or monthly family newsletters provide information of interest to all or at least most families. You can include information, such as a photo-illustrated review of the children's activities last week or month, snack and mealtime menus, requests for donations or volunteer assistance, and reminders of upcoming field trips or family workshops.

You might also write short, informative articles about topics, such as how the children are learning the steps in problem solving so they can discuss and solve conflicts. A "family volunteer of the month" could be a regular feature. Feature stories might inspire some reluctant family members to become more involved in the setting. Desktop publishing and web-based software can help you produce a professional-looking newsletter with photographs. The newsletter does not need to be grand, and can be distributed in print or via e-mail. Co-editing or translating the newsletter would be an ideal volunteer opportunity for a family member—especially one whose schedule does not allow them to visit the program during the day.

As an early educator, when you support the family, you also support the child.

Website: Consider creating a website for the setting, or asking a colleague or volunteer family member for help. A website can keep families informed through stories, photos, and videos and document the explorations, play, and work of children from infancy through preschool age. Since these photos/videos will be posted to the internet, obtain permission from families before posting. Anyone around the world can view your website, so think carefully about the information you post. You'll also want to think about the images you are displaying, since anyone can see them. See Figure 72 for a list of websites that can help you create your own.

Blogs: Depending on your time, interest, and technical skill, you and your colleagues could contribute to a blog about life in your setting. A blog presents an opportunity to tell families about daily happenings in your setting. Limit your blog posts to objective observations only. Do not say anything controversial, embarrassing, or hurtful about the children and families in your care. Focus your blog on factual information while telling stories with humor and personality.

Children's portfolios: Several times a year, send children's portfolios home and so they can share their learning with their families. Families can document learning at home and contribute the documentation for the child's portfolio. Children will be excited to see that they can learn in both home and program settings.

Exchanging information with families is likely to improve your own practice as you use what you learn to individualize the program. Encourage family members to reach out to you with any questions or concerns, and make it easy for them to contact you. Always inform parents of all special occasions— especially when you and the children take field trips. Even if parents provide written consent for their children to go on field trips, make sure that parents know where their child is that day.

Generally, you should share all information with families about their children's time in your setting. An exception to this suggestion is when a child reaches a particularly important milestone. For example, if an infant takes his first steps in your setting, hold off on informing the parents until they excitedly show you a phone video of their son walking from the couch to a table. Other milestones with this kind of significance include when a toddler asks to use the potty or when a preschooler recognizes her name in print.

Figure 72. Resources on Creating Websites and Blogs

Here are a few websites that will guide you through creating and hosting a website for your setting:

Websites

education.weebly.com
www.shutterfly.com/share-photos/classroom-websites.jsp
www.classicwebsites.org
www.educatorpages.com
doodlekit.com/home

Blogs

edublogs.org
education.weebly.com
classblogs.us
classblogmeister.com

Some of these sites will connect you to fellow early childhood bloggers around the world. You can communicate with them about your practice and exchange ideas about effective curriculum and using technology to communicate with families.

Holding Formal Meetings With Families

Formal meetings, such as a home visit or parent-educator conference, are opportunities for family members and educators to discuss a child's activities, interactions, interests, experiences, progress, and goals openly, confidentially, and at length. Family meetings and workshops, on the other hand, are times to discuss and exchange information and ideas as a group.

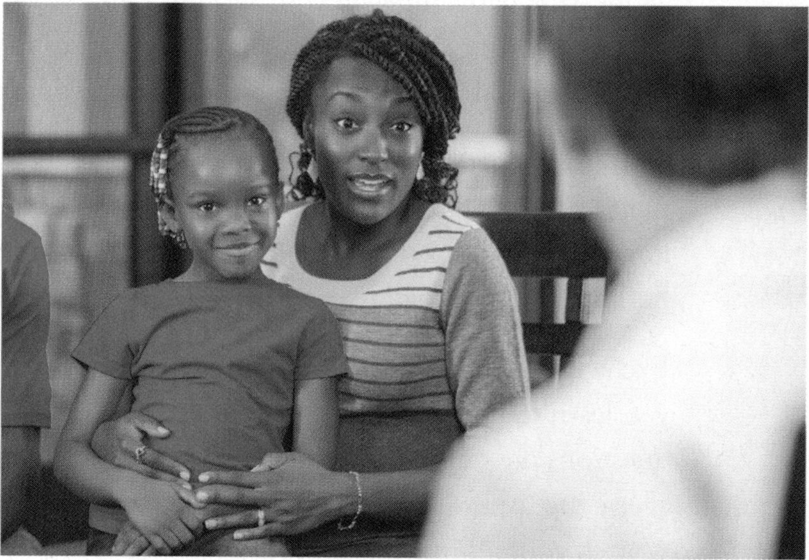

Regular parent–educator conferences allow you to speak in-depth with children's family members about their child's progress.

Home Visits

Home visits help early childhood educators and families get to know each other. They are also opportunities to learn about the children's home environments. Conducting these visits before enrollment reduces anxiety for children and families and eases their transition into the early childhood setting. Home visits also help you deepen your understanding of parents' values, child-rearing practices, and goals for their child's development and learning. For example, if you know how the parents comfort their crying baby, you will be able to use the same practices when caring for the infant. "I see that Justine likes the football hold. She stopped crying almost immediately. I'll be sure to use it when she is in our care."

Arrange the home visit by sending a postcard letting families know of your request, which is to spend time getting to know them and their child before the child's first day in your setting. Be sure to explain that it is of course a time for them to get to know you. Follow up with an e-mail or phone call arranging a date and time that is convenient for the family and when the child is likely to be awake. Reassure family members that there is no need for special arrangements or accommodations. It's a good idea to conduct home visits with a colleague, for safety reasons and to have an extra set of eyes and ears during the conversation. If you do not speak the family's home language, invite a colleague who does to come with you. One of you can engage the child while the other speaks with family members. When you arrive at the home, smile and be friendly, open, respectful, warm, and non-judgmental. This may be a family's first impression of you, so make it a good one. Be able to pronounce their names and their child's name correctly. Pronounce your name, slowly and clearly if necessary.

Consider bringing a welcome gift for the child—something from the setting that the child can engage with at home. This gift could be a book about the child's new early educators with photos of the different areas within the setting's learning environment. This links the child to your setting and makes the idea of being there seem like less of an unknown. Other options are a small box of crayons with a pad of paper or a soft ball.

During the home visit, provide an overview of your early childhood education beliefs and describe a typical day in your setting. Often it is the seemingly small things that families want to know—Who will help their child put on his shoes? Where are each child's diapers stored? What if their child doesn't like the food served? Introduce the welcome packet and invite them to the orientation meeting. "I hope you will be able to attend. It's a wonderful opportunity to meet the parents of your child's classmates."

Review the policies that come up most often—for example, when fees are due and what happens when a child is injured. Be sure to leave time for them to ask questions and raise concerns—and for you to address them. Introduce the concept of partnership—you and the family are working together to ensure their child's success.

Before leaving, go over what happens on the first day—or the first few days if your program uses a gradual transition process so new children have time to adjust to the new setting. Determine which family member will drop off the child in the morning. Discuss how the family member will stay with the child at the setting on the first few days, what the family member might do, and what to expect. Ask the parent to be sure to say "goodbye" to their child and to let the child know when they will return. Reassure the parent that their child will be safe and secure in your setting. You might share some of the goodbye rituals that you have seen other families use and suggest that they make one up for their child. For example, they might sing part of a song with their preschooler, then promise to finish it when they see them again.

Discuss the first day of attendance and strategies for reducing separation anxiety. Bring a camera with you to take pictures of family members that you can print and display in the setting. Explain that their child will feel comforted by having these photos in the setting where he can look at them at any time.

If a family member is absent from the home, think about how you can represent them in your setting. For example, Orlando's father is in the military and has been deployed to another country. Get the details of Orlando's father's deployment. Ask the family for a photo of his father or video of him singing or reading to Orlando. If Orlando's feelings about his father's deployment surface at your setting, you can talk with him while looking at the photo or recording. These items reaffirm the father's place in Orlando's life.

With the parents' permission, ask the child to give you a tour of the home. Many children like to show off the rooms where they sleep and play. As you tour the home, look for signs of the child's favorite playthings, pets, music, and foods. Use this information to help make the child feel a sense of belonging in your setting. "I like being here. There are dinosaurs to play with."

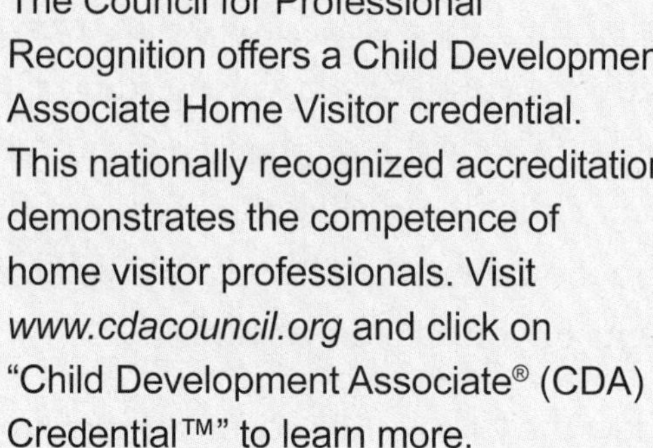

National Child Development Associate® (CDA) Credential™

The Council for Professional Recognition offers a Child Development Associate Home Visitor credential. This nationally recognized accreditation demonstrates the competence of home visitor professionals. Visit *www.cdacouncil.org* and click on "Child Development Associate® (CDA) Credential™" to learn more.

On the other hand, sometimes scheduling a home visit is not possible. Perhaps safety issues prohibit your visit. Or families may not want you to come, feeling that your visit would be an invasion of their privacy. Others may be uncomfortable to have you in their homes. Some families are homeless. Respect families' wishes. If you cannot go to their homes, then invite them to meet at a place in the community, like a local coffee shop, community center, or library room where you can talk.

In addition to the initial home visit, we recommend that you conduct two other visits, one at midyear and another a month before the end of the program year. During the midyear home visit, focus on the child's progress and how well the home and program settings are supporting the child's efforts and accomplishments. Review and plan for the coming year during the end-of-year visit.

Parent–Educator Conferences

Regular parent-educator conferences allow family members and educators to have in-depth conversations about the children's experiences and progress, and plan for the future. Typically early childhood programs hold two or three conferences per year. One or more of these might take place during a home visit. Here are some tips for conducting effective parent-educator conferences:

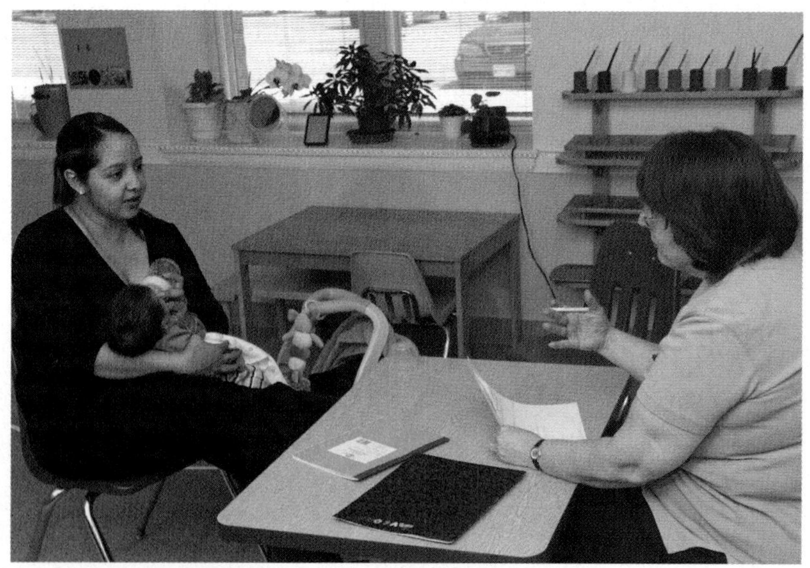

Choose a comfortable, distraction-free area to conduct the conference.

Schedule conferences for dates and times that are convenient for family members. It may be difficult to take time off from work, so prepare for early morning, evening, or weekend meetings. Offer families three date/time options that fit your schedule, and allow them to choose the one that works best for them. Once you agree on a meeting time, follow up with a reminder note. Ask parents to think about the signs of learning they have seen in their child at home, jot down notes about any anecdotes they would like to share, and bring a list of questions or concerns to be discussed. When it seems appropriate, suggest topics that you hope they can think about before the meeting. If lack of transportation or child care gets in the way of a family's attendance, be flexible. Offer assistance if you can. As a last resort, consider holding the meeting via phone this time, or changing the date and time to accommodate the family's needs.

Develop a general, flexible meeting agenda in advance. The focus of the meeting should be the child's progress, so gather all the necessary data—including notes from your observations, formal assessments, and the child's portfolio. Summarize this information into a one-page fact sheet. This sheet will provide you with talking points for the conference and a handout for parents to take home. Organize all materials and information prior to the meeting. This is a meeting of partners so be sure to include plenty of time for the family's active participation.

Choose a comfortable, distraction-free area to conduct the conference. A conference room or staff lounge would work well. Sit on adult-sized chairs and use a table to hold your papers. Avoid sitting behind a desk opposite family members because you do not want parents to think you are in charge and that they are there to listen to you.

Begin the conference with a positive anecdote about the child. Show the parent one of the child's paintings or a photo of the child lifting her head during tummy time. Keep conversation natural and make sure the parent is at ease.

Be aware of cultural considerations. Avoid physical contact if it is not culturally appropriate. Maintain a distance from parents that is typical and comfortable in their culture. If they do not speak English and you do not speak their home language, arrange for a staff person or interpreter who speaks the language to attend the meeting as well. Let the family know before the meeting that you have made this arrangement.

Stay focused on jointly promoting the child's development and learning. Explain that you will be taking notes to create a record of the meeting and topics discussed and offer to share a copy. Stop frequently so they can ask questions and make comments. If they do not do so on their own, ask questions such as, "Have you seen that happen…?" "What would you suggest… ?" and make comments like, "I'd love to hear your views on…" Through your words and actions convey that you are all there to listen, talk, share, and plan.

Ask family members how they think their child is progressing in your setting. Then follow parents' cues to discuss the following topics:

- How the child is adapting to and thriving in the setting.
- The child's interests and engagement.
- Examples of the child's growth and learning.
- The results of your observations and assessments.
- The child's skills in relation to goals that were set.
- Any concerns you or the child's family might have.
- Goals you and the child's family have for the child in the future.
- Next steps.

Reflect on the child's progress in each domain. Share and refer to written and dated observations, photographs, and short videos that you have taken of the child. "Here Graham is holding his fork in one hand and picking up food with the other. In the next photo, a week later, he is using the fork to pick up his macaroni." Ask parents about growth and progress that they have noticed in the child. For older children, point out changes in the child's work— including art and writing samples that indicate the child's learning.

End the parent–educator conference on a positive note.

Indicate any behaviors that have prompted specific concerns about a child. Avoid using judgmental labels, such as *aggressive, destructive, slow,* or *hyperactive.* Concentrate instead on concrete, documented examples of behaviors. Keep your observations objective and factual.

Although some parents may be reluctant to acknowledge their children's challenges, draw out this information gently. Ask them what they have observed at home. If you think it would be helpful to provide them with information about child development, have these resources available during your meeting. Likewise, suggest materials and activities families can do with children at home. Devise a plan of action together.

End on a positive note. Remember, you and family members are partners in supporting the child's growth and development. After the parent-educator conference, give family members a written copy of the plan you jointly developed. Families can use this to monitor progress. The plan can also serve as the starting point for the next conference.

As a closing, share and discuss ideas each of you has for the future for the whole group. This might include activities, field trips, the transition to the next year, or changes to the setting.

Family Meetings and Workshops

At times, early childhood educators invite all of the children's family members to attend parent meetings, which are informational or educational. They also plan family workshops, which engage participants in hands-on activities, like making musical instruments for the setting or discussions about topics related to children's development and learning.

Invite subject matter experts to speak to the attendees about the meeting topic. They lend the content extra credibility and may make the meeting seem more important to some parents. For example, invite a nutritionist to speak about healthy nutrition for young children and weaning infants from the breast or bottle. Or invite a child development specialist to speak about the benefits of play. Allow plenty of time at every meeting and workshop for questions and answers.

Planning for these gatherings is similar to preparing for parent-educator conferences. Publicize events well in advance using flyers, e-mails to families, your website, and word of mouth. Check with family members a few days ahead of time to get an approximate head count so that you can set up the room accordingly and order enough refreshments. Ensure that everyone has directions to the location and knows what time the meeting will begin.

Many workshops involve creating play materials or enhancing the setting in some way. Aim to hold workshops at your setting so that participants can use tools and materials on hand and see how their contributions will be used by the children.

Holding workshops on site also ensures that the location is ideally located and accessible to families. However, if your setting is not large enough to accommodate the group, consider reserving a community room with adult-sized seating in a nearby library or religious center. Arrange for refreshments and child care, if possible. Also plan for a translator to be present.

During workshops, tap into family members' creativity, and make the gathering fun. Offer refreshments and play music while the parents work.

See Figures 73 and 74 for suggested family meeting topics and ideas for workshops.

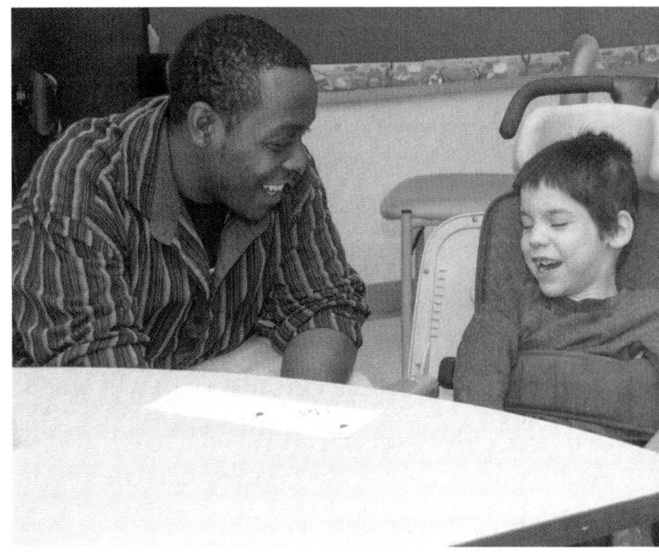

A family with a young child with disabilities will require lots of support from you.

Figure 73. Suggested Family Meeting Topics

- Using positive child guidance
- Following bedtime routines
- Identifying and responding to children's allergies
- Planning healthy and nutritious meals
- Reading to children/choosing books
- Technology and young children/ choosing software and applications
- Video games and young children
- Family life: helping children cope with separation, moving, divorce, and death
- Preventing and coping with stress
- Appreciating diversity
- Raising anti-racist children
- Fire prevention, safety, and sanitation
- Academic learning in the early childhood years
- The value of play
- Ages and stages of early childhood development
- Selecting toys and play materials for young children
- Turning everyday household tasks and routines into learning opportunities; activities to do at home with children
- Infant, toddler, and preschool development—what is and is not typical at each stage
- Supporting dual language learning
- Supporting children with disabilities
- Supporting gifted children
- Community, state, and federal resources for families
- What to expect in kindergarten

Supporting Child Development at Home

During the intake/enrollment interview with each family, you may have learned the family's hopes and dreams for their child. Perhaps they requested information about child development. First-time parents or parents of infants and toddlers may ask you what they should be doing to facilitate their child's growth and development or whether their child's development is typical for their age group. They will want to know when they should be concerned about their child's development and what resources are available to them if they suspect their child has a disability. Parents of preschoolers are often focused on making sure their child will be ready for kindergarten. They want to know how your play-based curriculum supports reading, writing, and arithmetic and what they can do at home to support learning. Here are a few ways to address some of these interests and concerns:

Create a child development resource library. Include reader-friendly books about child development and handouts with milestone charts that explain typical child development. Include information about cultural differences so families have an avenue to discuss their experiences without feeling singled out. Share information from credible websites, borrow books from your local library on behalf of family members, or start small and gradually add to your library as funds allow.

Your state and other applicable early learning standards might also be of interest to families. Post a link to the standards so families can see what some experts believe their children can be learning at a given stage of development.

One excellent way to support parents' interest in learning about child development is for them to participate in child screenings. If your setting performs screenings, encourage families to participate so that they can see what child development information is collected through the screening process. Having family members present also puts children at ease while the screening tool is administered.

Address specific parenting topics. Conduct meetings about parenting issues (for example, self-feeding, toilet learning or making friends) or suggest relevant reading material or websites. The website NAEYC For Families (*families@naeyc.org*) is one source of research-based information for parents of young children. Offer information about local parenting classes and family support groups. Work with your supervisor and colleagues to create a resource file that includes suggested reading or community resources that all families can use.

If an issue arises that involves more than one family, hold a parent meeting focused on this topic. Invite a pediatrician, developmental psychologist, or parent educator to lead the session and answer families' questions.

Figure 74. Ideas for Family Workshops

- Setting up a lending library for toys, books, DVDs, and prop boxes
- Making play materials:
  - cloth or sock dolls
  - puzzles
  - bell bracelets
  - bottle shakers
  - busy boards
  - milk-carton blocks
  - lotto games
  - family books
  - musical instruments
- Planting, tending, and harvesting a garden
- Creating an infant sensory corner
- Landscaping the outdoor play area
- Building and stocking a woodworking center
- Turning family recipes into recipe cards and cookbooks
- Making kits for science projects
- Building a puppet stage and making puppets
- Journaling with preschoolers
- Planning a wellness fair with specialists, such as pediatricians, nutritionists, dietitians, and other health professionals

Supporting Families of Children With Disabilities

A family with a young child who has disabilities will require lots of support from you and others in your program. Most likely they are new to this situation and may feel overwhelmed. They will have numerous questions and few answers and will need assistance to secure the best services for their child. Family members may look to you for help in balancing their lives while caring for their child. Reassure them that you are an advocate for both the child and the family.

If a child has an identified disability, they probably have an IFSP or IEP, developed with your input and in collaboration with the family and specialists. The IFSP or IEP is the blueprint for what you will do in the program and the family will do at home to make sure the child has access to all they need to accomplish the goals set out in the plan. The IFSP or IEP team will conduct a formal review of the plan at scheduled intervals, however it is your role to provide information about the child's efforts and accomplishments on an ongoing basis and to respond to families' feelings and experiences as they arise.

Be sure to tell the family what you and your colleagues are doing to adapt materials, activities, interactions, and the overall environment so their child can participate fully, learn through

YOUNG CHILDREN WITH DISABILITIES REQUIRE:

Their families, early care and education staff, and other service providers to work together as early as possible because...
this creates a solid foundation to support optimal development.

2

Early intervention screening, evaluation, and appropriate services as early as possible because...
strengthening brain and physical development early on can reduce the prevalence of ongoing and future challenges.

Individuals with Disabilities Education Act (IDEA)
is the federal law providing early intervention and special education services to children with disabilities.

Part C of IDEA

Provides early intervention services to children from birth to 3 with disabilities.

Individualized Family Service Plan (IFSP) is a written document outlining:

- The early intervention services a child and family will receive
- The child's needs; the family's strengths and choices; and the Early Intervention team's recommendations

Part B of IDEA (Section 619)

Provides special education services to preschool children with disabilities.

Individualized Education Program (IEP) is a written plan that describes:

- The child's educational goals
- Services and supports in a school setting

3

Early care and education staff can:

- Provide screening and referral for infants, toddlers, and preschoolers
- Individualize services for young children with disabilities
- Listen, support, and strengthen relationships with families, staff, and service providers
- Advocate for and connect families with local community agencies and resources
- Develop and strengthen local community partnerships with Early Intervention, Child Find, and Early Childhood Special Education
- Learn specific intervention skills from community partners
- Visualize the possibilities for all children

4

Inclusion in Head Start means:

- Identifying young children with unique developmental needs
- Ensuring children receive appropriate and timely services
- Helping families navigate eligibility guidelines that are essential for Early Head Start and Head Start programs

The Office of Head Start (OHS) is committed to promoting equity in the systems and services that support young children with disabilities and their families. OHS is dedicated to upholding the principles of equality of access and inclusion that are central to the Individuals with Disabilities Education Act (IDEA).

(HHS, ACF, OHS, and ECLKC 2021)

play, and enjoy the company of other children. Provide specific examples—based on your observation recordings and photos—of how the adaptations allow their child to be engaged in play and learning. Families can also do many of the small things you do—for example, wrapping tape around markers to make them easier to hold—to facilitate their child's learning at home. Explain how and why the adaptations work, how they make it possible for their child to develop and learn. Also, share information about when something was not successful and what you did differently the next time. "I thought it would be easier for Marcus to hold his bottle if I covered it with a sock. Unfortunately the sock was too loose and just fell off. Do you have any suggestions?"

Ask the family about their child's activities at home, too. Always begin these conversations by listening and being open to their insights. Be open and positive and acknowledge the child's hard work and growth. Ask for their suggestions and implement them in the program whenever possible. A strong partnership between you and the family will contribute to their child's progress now and in the future.

Figure 75. Support for Families of Children With Disabilities

These government- and privately-funded organizations provide information on supporting children with disabilities.

General

- National Dissemination Center for Children with Disabilities (*nichcy.org*).
- State-level Parent Centers that are part of the Parent Technical Assistance Center Network [every state has at least one Parent Training and Information Center] (*www.parentcenternetwork.org*).

Specific focus

- The Autism Society (*www.autism-society.org*).
- National Center for Learning Disabilities (*www.ncld.org*).
- Learning Disabilities Association of America (*www.ldanatl.org*).
- LD OnLine (*www.ldonline.org*).
- United Cerebral Palsy (*ucp.org*).
- National Down Syndrome Congress (*ndsccenter.org*).
- National Down Syndrome Society (*www.ndss.org*).
- Alexander Graham Bell Association for the Deaf and Hard of Hearing (*listeningandspokenlanguage.org*).

Maintaining Confidentiality

Many families share personal information with the individual who cares for their child. Early childhood educators must keep this information confidential. The primary concern in a reciprocal partnership between and educator and a family is the child. However, sometimes parents themselves need your assistance. For example, when family members confide in you about financial or health problems, remember that these conditions also impact their children. Being aware of a family's concern can help you understand children's behavior and adjust your expectations and program in response. For example, if you know a mother has lost her job, then you might be more understanding when the child arrives at the program hungrier than usual. You would be sure to have a self-serve snack available so the child does not have to wait until the scheduled time for breakfast. Because you won't always know every situation that every family is experiencing, it is best to plan trauma informed approaches for all children in the program. This includes things like access to food, rest, and comfort on demand. When you support the family, you also support the child.

In addition, store in locked file cabinets all paper copies of family records—including meeting and conference notes, intake summaries, child observation records, and information families share with you. If family members volunteer to help you or other staff manage paperwork, do not allow them access to any children's or family members' records other than their own. Likewise, if parent's reveal information (positive or negative) about other families or children, thank them and let them know that you maintain contact with those children's families. Also inform parents that you will not discuss other children or families with them, just as you would not discuss their child and family with others. Explain that the program staff share personal data only with individuals who have been designated in writing by the family as having a need for this information. For example, a support specialist may need additional information about Deanne's health history or progress in the program and ask to see the child's records and documentation, such as observation notes and work samples. Even if an early childhood educator knows and trusts the specialist, she cannot grant access without Deanne's parents' written consent.

Keeping information confidential is not only ethical, it also builds bonds between you and families and helps to maintain their view of you as a trusted partner. ■

Competency Standard V:

To ensure a well-run, purposeful program that is responsive to participant needs

CHAPTER 12:

Program Management

CDA® Functional Area 12: Candidate is a manager who uses observation, documentation, and planning to support children's development and learning and to ensure effective operation of the program or group. The Candidate is a competent organizer, planner, record keeper, communicator, and a cooperative co-worker.

Program Management

Introduction

Throughout this textbook, we have discussed the various roles you play in fostering children's development. Guiding children's growth and learning is, of course, your chief responsibility as an early childhood educator. Additionally, you fulfill a management role within your setting to ensure that your program runs successfully. Even though center-based educators have supervisors who are managers, there are still management duties that need to be performed related to observation, documentation, and planning. FCC educators, of course, are responsible for all management activities, including matters beyond the scope of this chapter, such as financial operations.

To perform your teaching duties effectively requires you to regularly manage time, space, and resources, and maintain current and accurate records—the same aspects of the workplace that managers handle to ensure efficiency. In this chapter, we will explore the managerial tasks that early childhood educators need to perform to work effectively with young children:

- **Assessing Through Observation**
- **Documenting Children's Learning**
- **Planning and Evaluating**
- **Recordkeeping**
- **Working With Colleagues and the Community**

Defining Terms Used in this Chapter

To ensure a common understanding, here are definitions of key technical terms:

Accountability: Being responsible to funders, taxpayers, politicians, and families for offering high-quality programming that supports children's development and learning.

Assessment: The process of tracking what children know and can do by use of tests that measure how well children have met pre-established benchmarks at specific points in time. Results are used to determine the success of programs/schools and sometimes individual educators.

Authentic Assessment: The process of gathering information about children in real-life situations over time from several sources of evidence and then organizing, interpreting, and using that information to plan an effective program.

Documentation: The process of collecting data, evidence, and artifacts to tell the story and the purpose of an event, experience, or project. Documentation provides information about individual children, the group, and the educators' effectiveness.

Observation: The process of accurately and objectively recording adults' and children's actions, behavior, facial expressions, body language, gestures, babbling, and speech. Observational recordings are used in planning for individuals and the group.

Assessing Through Observation

Keep a clipboard available in the learning environment so that you can record observational notes at any moment.

Assessment is an integral part of the teaching process. You set goals, plan your program, and implement your plans. Then, to see if you have achieved your goals, you have to evaluate the effectiveness of the program. You do this both formally and informally. The kind of assessment you do to evaluate progress towards achieving goals depends on your purpose. There are six purposes of assessment in early childhood programs:

1. To support learning and development
2. To screen children for disabilities
3. To evaluate program effectiveness
4. To monitor trends and needs
5. To assess children's achievement to hold programs (and often educators) accountable
6. To advance knowledge of child development

As an early childhood educator, you will at times be involved in all six types of assessment. However, on a day-to-day basis, it is the first type of assessment that you are most concerned with. You want to regularly assess children to see what they know and can do so you can adjust your teaching to match the children's documented needs. Conventional assessment measures children's progress by using standardized tests at certain points in the year. The results of the testing are norm-referenced, meaning that children are scored and ranked according to how well they compare to the average student their age taking this test. The early childhood field has, however, moved away from the use of conventional tests, deeming them developmentally inappropriate for young children. Samuel Meisels, an early leader in this movement, describes the problem (2006):

> Young children are developmentally unreliable test takers. They have a restricted ability to comprehend such assessment cues as verbal instructions, aural stimuli, situational cues, or written instructions. Further, questions that require complex information-processing skills—giving differential weights to alternative choices, distinguishing recency from primacy, or responding correctly to multistep directions—may cause a child to give the wrong answer. In addition, young children may not be able to control their behavior to meet the demand characteristic of the assessment situation—whether this is because they are affected by fatigue, boredom, hunger, illness, or anxiety, or simply because they are unable to sit still and attend for the length of time required.

Because of these many problems, the field as a whole has turned to alternative testing methods, using what is known as *authentic assessment*. Authentic assessment, as defined at the start of this chapter, does not rely on norm-referenced tests. Rather it depends on various forms of evidence that early childhood educators collect over time.

To be considered authentic assessment, the information must be collected (NYC Department of Education):

- Systematically (There is a specific purpose for collecting the information and the methodology used to collect that information is both unbiased and reliable; if several people observed the same thing at the same time, results would all be the same).
- In natural settings (The information on the child is collected in the classroom or FCC home; the child is not brought to an office or lab for testing).
- During daily routines and activities (Information is collected while the child goes about his daily schedule—during play, while eating, during transitions, and so on).

Early childhood educators use the information gained through authentic assessment to guide curriculum planning and customize the curriculum to meet each child's strengths, needs, and interests. It is designed to "provide strength-based, inclusive, and individualized care; support child-initiated learning; and promote appreciative understanding" (Muskie School of Public Service 2010).

The most common and most important form of authentic assessment is *systematic observation*, which is done often and regularly. Observations document both typical and atypical behavior. Educators record and save their observations, so they can reflect on and use them to guide future teaching practices. Observations can include both informal and formal approaches. You do informal observations when you see six month old Manuel sitting up for the first time and make a note to record this accomplishment or when you see three-year-old Betsy willingly sharing her favorite doll and record a brief note on an index card to help you remember that this happened. These are noteworthy events that you want to document and be able to share with the children's families, so you jot down what you see, being sure to date the notation.

Formal observations of individual children are conducted as part of your program's evaluation, to determine the degree to which curricular goals and program learning standards are being met. In order to determine if a child is meeting a developmental standard, educators have to collect multiple observations on many indicators. You might be observing two-year-old Amad at lunch time to see if he can follow two-step directions. You ask him to clear his plate after eating and then he should go in the bathroom with Ms. Jones to wash his hands. In this case, you use a checklist and note what happens in the comments section.

Observing With a Purpose

Observation (both informal and formal) is a critical part of the early childhood teaching approach. Though we talk a lot about observation, it's not always clear how a particular observation can answer your questions. For example, today you observed that several of the children in your setting seem unusually restless, and no one has played in the dramatic play center. But did you also consider that it is well after 2:00 p.m. and the children did not have outdoor time because of the heavy rain? Or, could the children be bored with the items in the dramatic play center, because the inventory has not changed in 6 months?

It is imperative to observe with purpose and from more than one vantage point. In their book *The Power of Observation*, authors Jablon, Dombro, and Dichtelmiller (2007) define observation as "watching to learn." Determine what it is you want to learn and then conduct your observations at appropriate times and in relevant settings to gather the necessary information. For example, if you want to learn more about how children say goodbye and later reconnect with their families, your observations will take place at drop-off and pick-up times in the transition area of the setting.

The key to planning and implementing a successful curriculum is taking time to see what is really happening in your setting. What are the children doing and learning? When you observe children engaged in the learning environment, you obtain clear and detailed information about what works well and what needs to be changed to further foster development and learning.

A series of observational recordings can answer these questions:

How do I make use of the environment to support children during routines and activities? Are quiet areas separated from noisy ones? Can children play undisturbed? Are young infants separated from mobile infants during active play times? Are there any areas that invite children to run or create "traffic" problems?

How do I encourage active exploration and play: Does the arrangement allow children to move at their own pace? Do children stay engaged? Are there areas of the room that children use regularly? If so, what might be drawing them to the areas?

How appropriate is my inventory of toys and materials? Are there an appropriate number and variety of items available to infants? Are there an appropriate number and variety of items available to toddlers and preschoolers in each learning center? Are there picture and written labels telling toddlers and preschoolers where materials go? Are materials accessible to children? Do children return materials to their designated places on shelves when they are through playing with them?

Are there places where different groupings of children can gather? Where do children come together as a group, work in pairs and small groups, and play and be by themselves when they so desire? Are these areas well used?

Do children follow the daily schedule? How frequently and in what circumstances do older children consult the picture schedule? Do children regularly stay engaged in play at centers for at least an hour of uninterrupted time (as provided in the schedule)? Do children go outside in the morning and the afternoon?

Does the program welcome families? Is there a transition area for families to receive information and ask staff questions? Are there sufficient adult-sized chairs so adults can feel comfortable while playing with children?

Does the outdoor environment promote development of the whole child? How does the outdoor environment allow children to work on social, emotional, and cognitive skills as well as physical ones? Are there spaces where children can play in small groups as well as by themselves?

Does the program promote inclusivity? What accommodations have been made to ensure full participation of children with disabilities? What adjustments have been made to make dual language learners comfortable in my setting? Where can sick children wait for a family member to arrive?

How effective are transitions? Is there a lot of down time while children move from one activity to another? What do children do and learn during transitions? Are there any transitions that could be eliminated?

Do eating times work successfully? Are infants fed on demand? How does family style dining work for toddlers and preschoolers? Are tables within the learning centers used for lunch, or are tables grouped together? Does an adult sit with each group of children? Do children seem to enjoy the food? Are the children learning to try new foods? What kinds of conversations take place at the table groups? What self-help skills can the children develop? How do the children clean up after themselves?

How are nap times working? How are infants put down for naps? Where do toddlers and preschoolers nap? Do most children fall asleep? How do the children who are awake stay occupied? Does the layout promote children's sleeping and comply with health regulations?

How are different family structures represented in the classroom? What photos are available in the classroom? Are all of the children able to see themselves represented in the materials? In the books? In the artwork? What opportunities are there for children to see people of other races? Abilities? Ethnicities? Religions? Identities? Are there provocations (like mirrors) present to spark conversations among the children about differences and similarities?

It is also critical to observe each child individually so you can plan a program that addresses specific characteristics, including home language, abilities, needs, and interests and supports family and cultural practices. Focus your observations so that you can answer questions like these:

- What is this child like? How does the child's temperament affect her play and learning? What personality traits are evident and how do they affect the child's participation in the program?

- How does the child like to be comforted? How and when does the child like to be helped?
- How does the child approach learning? How long does the child attend to a task? Does the child persevere? Does the child seek help from adults or from another child?
- What does the child do throughout the day? Does the child tend to stay engaged with one experience/center or does the child move on after a few minutes?
- How does the child express creativity? Does the child use her imagination? Does the child engage in sociodramatic play?
- How does the child solve problems? Does he make hypotheses and test them out? How does he react when something does not go as planned?
- How does the child communicate? What language skills does the child have in the home language and in English?
- What interests the child? What materials does he like to play with? What are the child's favorite toys?
- What cognitive, language/literacy, social/emotional, and physical skills does the child possess?
- Is the child a dual language learner?
- What specific skills is the child developing and working on? Has the child demonstrated growth in specific areas over time?
- Is the child in good health? Is he developing physically according to developmental milestones?
- Does the child have skills and knowledge beyond that of his age group? Does the child have developmental delays or special requirements?
- What triggers a child's challenging behavior? What positive guidance strategies are most effective in helping the child learn to use safe behaviors?
- How does this child interact with peers? Which other children are likely to be her playmates?
- How does this child interact with educators? Does the child tend to gravitate to certain educators rather than others?
- How does the child interact with his family? How is his family's culture reflected in the program?
- How does the child interact with adults in the program who are not educators, such as classroom visitors and family volunteers?

Observing Systematically

Use a tablet or smartphone app to help you write, track, and sort your observations by child, activity, or center.

Regularly observing the program in operation and the children engaged in activities enables you to plan and implement a curriculum to support both individual children and the group. Your daily teaching practices are so deeply rooted in observation that you cannot perform your job effectively without it.

The purpose of your observations drives when, where, and how you conduct them. As noted earlier, observations occur in natural settings and are integrated into children's daily activities. In other words, observe children's behaviors during typical daily events, like during personal care routines, interactions, and play. For example, if you want to examine how Brandon gets along with his peers, observe him during indoor and outdoor choice times and document his conversations and interactions with others. Likewise, if you want to observe Jessica's progress in developing specific fine motor skills, observe her doing art projects, working on puzzles, and eating lunch.

The more frequent your observations, the greater the likelihood that they will provide accurate information about the child's growth and development. For example, you may observe that Skylar has difficulty stacking blocks to form a tower. Record this information, even though you have seen her stack blocks without difficulty before. A more accurate picture of Skylar's abilities will develop as you observe her over time. Perhaps she is not yet proficient in stacking blocks and is working to refine this skill. Therefore, your observations of her both successfully stacking blocks and having difficulty make sense, since this is a skill she is working on and hasn't fully mastered.

The idea of regularly observing every child in your program can understandably seem overwhelming and you may wonder how you will find the time to do this well. If your program has you observing to complete instruments to determine if local, state, or Head Start learning standards are being met, you will have a great number of indicators of progress in all domains of learning that you have to collect observations for.

Julianne Wurm (2009) and other experts on observation offer these tips to make the observation process a part of your everyday routine, and something you enjoy because it makes your teaching more effective:

Start with small chunks of time and gradually add more. Begin with 5-10 minute periods during which you observe children and take notes. As you feel more comfortable, add another 30 seconds or a minute to this set-aside time. Eventually, the time will add up.

Determine when and where to observe children. Set aside a morning and afternoon time and location for your observations. For example, you might choose 10:00 to 10:15 a.m. each morning for observing indoors and 2:30-2:45 p.m. each afternoon for observing outdoors.

Select a child to observe ahead of time. If you work in a center-based program, you can divide the children up so that you and your colleagues are each responsible for 4-5 children daily. In an FCC home, you will need to observe all of the children daily. Take notes on the children you are assigned to during each observational period.

Plan a focus for the observation. As noted earlier, it is best to have a purpose for every observation. Each week, have one or two prime foci, such as fine motor development and sharing. Over time, you can rotate the foci so that you have an opportunity to directly observe for each indicator addressed in your assessment tool.

Set up the environment to facilitate observations. For example, if you are observing sharing behaviors, take away some of the duplicate toys to see how children will share when there are not enough favorite toys to go around. Likewise, if you are observing to see children's fine motor skills, make sure that each learning area or center has tools available that will promote the development of fine motor skills, e.g., scissors and paste in the art center, puzzles and Legos in the math and manipulatives area, and bells and rhythm sticks in the music and movement center.

Collaborate with colleagues (in a center). Perhaps a colleague can work with the children while you observe and record children's behavior and then you can switch roles. Educators in both centers and FCC homes may have family volunteers who can be with the children while you observe.

Develop a system that works for you. Some educators take notes on address labels that they can then peel off and move to a child's folder or directly onto an observational form. Others take notes on index cards that they keep in an apron pocket. Some educators keep a pen handy in their pocket, while others wear a pen around their neck like a lanyard. Other popular techniques are to keep a poster of observable indicators in each learning center and to have clipboards with paper for recording housed at each interest area/ learning center.

Develop a system of observation that works for you.

Use abbreviations and symbols to record quickly. Children move and talk too fast for most people to record every detail and word. Abbreviations and symbols will help. For example, use the child's first initial to stand for his name. You can use common abbreviations for the centers in your program: SW=sand and water; MM=music and movement; DP=dramatic play. Other abbreviations you might adopt are TT=tummy time, GM=group meeting, or SG=small group. If you are looking at a skill, such as cutting with a scissors or walking unassisted, you might use a check mark to indicate that the skill was observed. Consider underlining or starring thoughts for emphasis. The only rule about abbreviations and symbols is that you must be able to readily interpret them.

Observing Dual Language Learners

If they are children in your program whose home language you do not speak, look to colleagues or neighboring programs for bilingual staff who might be able to assist you, especially when you are observing children's language skills and interactions. If you are unable to get a colleague to come into your program, use a tablet or smartphone to make a digital recording of the child. Next, ask for help in translating what the children said. You can use audio and video observations as you would written observations to make notations of the child's interests, strengths, and challenges.

Keep observational notes simple. You want to capture the essence of what you observe, not write eloquent notes. A short description followed by a quote from the child is often sufficient, along with the child's name, the name of the observer, the date and time of the observation, and the setting.

Take notes that will meet several indicators. Even if you are observing for a specific indicator, such as problem-solving skills, you may be observing an example of team-building and social skills. Because children's behavior is so interrelated, you'll rarely see a skill being worked on without overlapping on other skills in other domains. You will save a great deal of time in observing children if you use the same observational note to illustrate several indicators.

Use technology. A tablet or smartphone can help you write, track, and sort your observations by child, skill area, domain, or learning center. Record observations using a digital or video camera or audio tape then transcribe them later for your records.

With time and practice, you will become more skilled and efficient at performing daily observations. You will be able to observe more children each day, and the time it takes you to record your observations will decrease.

Early childhood educators perform various types of observations, depending on the purpose and the amount of time allotted for the observation. Figure 76a-b lists the most frequently used forms of observation in early childhood education programs. You will note that all of these forms of observation provide specific types of information that will aid you in making decisions about your program.

Figure 76a. Common Forms of Observation

Type of Observation	Description and Use	Written Documentation*
Brief Notes (Educator created)	These quick entries provide data on a child's interests or progress.	Jot down a short note on an index card, an address label, a sticky note, or a log sheet. Date the entry. For easy access, keep these tools on a clipboard to which a pen is tied.
Anecdotal Records (Educator created)	These are short descriptions of incidents involving one or more child. They provide data on a child's interests, interactions, and progress.	Record comments on index cards and include the date, the names of the children observed, and how long the observation lasted.
Running Records (Educator created)	This is the most common type of formal observation. Running records are descriptions of children's behavior recorded objectively, accurately, and chronologically over a specific length of time, typically 10 to 15 minutes. Record children's verbalizations as they occur. Use running records to provide data on a child's interests, interactions, language development, and progress.	Record what you see and hear on an index card or prepared piece of paper. For each observation include the names of the children, the location, and the time it began and ended.
Diary/Journal Observations (Educator created)	These are descriptions of a child's behavior sequentially over time. They are performed with a specific purpose in mind, such as discovering what triggers a child's aggressive behavior or why a child is suddenly withdrawn.	Make entries on index cards or in a notebook. Note the date, time, and setting next to each entry.
Matrices (Educator created)	These grids are specific to a skill or skills. List the names of all the children you are observing. Take brief notes next to children's names regarding their skill levels. Use this format to study group progress in specific areas of development.	Record observations on the grid described.
Event Sampling (Educator created or pre-made form)	This observation documents the number of times a child engages in a particular behavior (such as reading books, building block structures, or cleaning up after choice time) in a specified time period.	Make tally marks on forms designed for this purpose.

* Although early educators have used written forms of documentation with great success, in some programs educators now use tablets and smartphones to record their observations. Most devices have this capacity built in and there are applications with more sophisticated capabilities.

Figure 76b. Common Forms of Observation

Type of Observation	Description and Use	Written Documentation*
Time Sampling (Educator created or pre-made form)	Time sampling records the number of times something happens (whether or not a child socializes with others or how many times a child uses the computer or plays with blocks) during a specified time period (typically 30 minutes).	Make tally marks on forms designed for this purpose.
Checklists (Pre-made form)	Checklists allow you to observe and document information about children's skills, behaviors, or attitudes.	Place check marks on a prepared form whenever you observe the noted skill, behavior, or attitude.
Rating Scales (Pre-made form)	A way of evaluating a child's observed skill, behavior, or attitude from high to low proficiency or frequency. This type of instrument can also be used to observe the environment. Often rating scales include rubrics that specifically describe each point of a rating scale.	A number is selected that corresponds to the proficiency or frequency of the observations on each item in a prepared form.

Observing With Objectivity

Useful observations require *objectivity* (expressing or dealing with facts or conditions). To be objective in your observation, stay focused on the facts. Do not make assumptions or assign causes to what you observe. Avoid words like the ones in Figure 77 that indicate that you have made a judgment about what you have seen.

Figure 77. Words to Avoid While Recording Observations

- Happy
- Sad
- Angry
- Funny
- Lonely
- Bossy
- Mean
- Selfish
- Generous
- Sloppy
- Neat
- Beautiful
- Ugly
- Antsy
- Frustrated
- Anxious
- Petty
- Furious
- Sickly
- Amazing
- Awesome
- Restless
- Creative
- Bored
- Helpful
- Lazy
- Talented
- Nice
- Kind
- Aggressive
- Smart
  Shy
- Scared
- Artistic
- Needy
- Curious
- Intelligent
- Excited
- Pretty

The words in Figure 77 describe conditions that are not observable. They denote abstract emotions occurring inside of a child or reflect your opinion or interpretation of the behaviors you are observing. None of the words denote actual skills or behaviors.

Objective writing is straightforward and can be challenging to write. Examine the following sample narratives:

Warren is contentedly playing at the sand table. Eduardo comes over to join him. Eduardo looks around to see whether anyone's watching (he doesn't realize that I am) and deliberately throws sand in Warren's face. Poor Warren starts crying, so I drop everything to go comfort him.

This narrative includes opinions and judgment words, like *contentedly*, *deliberately*, and *poor*. Also, the observer has interpreted what they believe are Eduardo's motivations. However, the observer has no way of knowing why Eduardo went to the sand table and is unable to know if Eduardo was looking around "to see whether anyone is watching." Now, take a look at this observational note:

Warren is at the sand table. He is making circular shell patterns in the sand. After three minutes, Eduardo takes a vacant place at the table. He picks up a shovel and then puts it down. He looks around the table and digs his hand in, pulling out a stone and putting it down. He again looks around the table. Warren picks up the stone and adds it to his pile of shells. Eduardo looks at Warren and says, "That's my stone" and throws sand at Warren's face. Warren begins to cry.

This objective narrative provides insight into Warren's interests and skills as well as the possible roots of a conflict. It is not biased towards either child, since it reports the facts in the order they happened.

Record all your observations this way. You want them to be factually accurate and recorded in the exact sequence they occur. Ensure that you capture language and dialogue verbatim. These objective observations can help you root out unintended or implicit biases you may be unaware that you hold. Biases about a particular child, or about a group of children can turn up when you notice you are having a hard time remaining objective in your notes. Watch for your tendency to assign blame or value and monitor your self-awareness of hidden biases you may carry.

An Observational Technique that Doesn't Require Objectivity

There is one popular observational technique that doesn't demand that you be objective: learning stories. Based on the work of Margaret Carr and her colleagues (Carr & Lee, 2012) in New Zealand, learning stories are an assessment technique that requires early childhood educators to observe children and then write narrative stories to interpret what children are learning in the particular situation observed. Instead of writing "just the facts" as most observations require, learning stories use storytelling that is subjective and based on personal feelings. And unlike observations, which are intended for the educator, learning stories are directed to the children being observed.

Recorded from the perspective of the storyteller or observer, learning stories describe what is happening with the children, document what learning is taking place throughout the experience, and end with examining next steps. Storytellers share their observations with family members and ask them to contribute to the story. Children also discuss their own experiences, feelings, and learning. A sample learning story is presented in Figure 78.

Figure 78. Learning Story: Building Together With Anthony and Rosie

March 2nd

Today, during choice time, I watched you two work together in the block center to build a tunnel for trains to go through. I could hear you developing a plan for which blocks you were going to use and where you were going to place each block to create your tunnel. You also built a very large train station that had a waiting room for passengers. It took you quite some time, but you both kept working on it until you were happy with what you created. You showed me your train station when you finished, because you were so proud of your work. You couldn't wait to tell me all about the train station and how it functioned. I then left the block center, and you continued to build the station and add more detail. Again you were so proud of your success and brought me over to see the additions that you made.

What Does This Tell Me?

As you were working together to build the tunnel and the train station, I learned that you enjoy working together. You were using your oral language skills while talking to each other, asking questions, and discussing what to do. You also used clear language to share your thoughts and ideas with each other. This ensured that you both understood each other. It took you a long time to build both the tunnel and the train station, and this demonstrated persistence and motivation. You used your knowledge of mathematics, science, and technology to build your tunnel and train station and demonstrated creativity and innovation through your novel design.

Where to Next?

I hope that you continue to work with each other. There will be lots of different activities during which you can work alongside each other. You both have an enthusiasm for building with blocks, and it will be interesting to see whether you continue to use your creativity and innovation to make different things.

Child's Voice

[Anthony] Me and Rosie were making buildings for the trains. It was hard, because sometimes the blocks fell over, but then we got them to stand up. We made a tunnel and a train station so that the people did not get wet when they were waiting to ride the train, because it's raining.

Parent's Voice

[Early childhood educator asks Anthony's family members whether Anthony likes to build at home.]

Anthony loves to build with Legos® at home. He will spend hours with his big brother creating spaceships and rocket ships that they are going to send to the moon. He loves to show his dad his creations and is hoping that we can get new blocks for him to work with.

The learning story is not the same as a case study or a long running record (which is written objectively). They are strength-based narratives that tell a story about learning. Interpretation occurs at the time of the observation, not upon later reflection. It should be noted that because of their narrative nature, learning stories are best used to show the development of children's dispositions—things like curiosity, perseverance, and what is known as *approaches to learning*. Learning stories do not provide valid evidence of the development of knowledge, skills, and understanding (Blaiklock 2008).

Summarizing Observational Information

After completing your observations and recording your findings, reflect on the information you have collected and determine what the next steps should be. You have already completed this work if you used your observations to complete rating scales or rubrics. Further interpretations are not necessary.

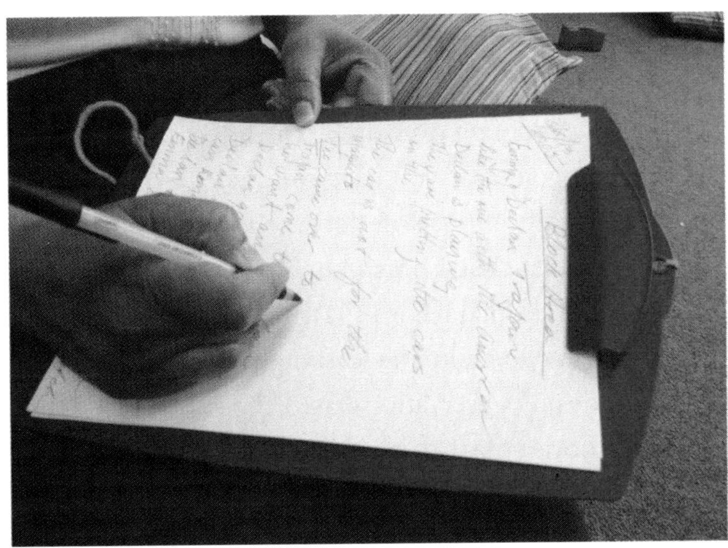

Objective writing is straightforward and can be challenging.

For your other objective observations, it's now time to put on a subjective lens. Review the purpose of your observations, and ask yourself the following questions:

- Looking at the observations as a whole, what have I learned about this child?
- Do any patterns appear?
- What might cause or explain the child's behavior?
- Does this explanation cover everything that was observed? If not, what else might be at work?

Once you have made your best educated guess about why a situation or behavior is occurring, devise an action plan.

How frequently you summarize your observations depends on how you will use the information. At the end of each day, you may want to review the data you collected and modify your future daily plans to incorporate what you observed. Or you may choose to review and summarize your observations weekly to distance yourself from the information, which may help you view the information more objectively (Jablon, Dombro, and Dichtelmiller 2007).

Documenting Children's Learning

Part of being an effective early childhood educator is being able to document the progress of both individual children and the group using multiple sources of information, including observations. Documentation also enables you to share information with families and colleagues.

Portfolios

A portfolio is a collection of children's work samples that together provide a portrait of what a child knows, what the child understands, how the child behaves, and what the child is interested in. It is a celebration of a child's experiences in your program over time. The informal and formal observations that you have conducted, recorded, and stored are a significant part of documenting children's learning and belong in a child's portfolio. Organize and store observational notes, anecdotal records, learning stories, and running records that relate to children's learning in their portfolios. Also include any observation-based checklists, tallies, rating scales, and rubrics that offer insight into the child's growth and development.

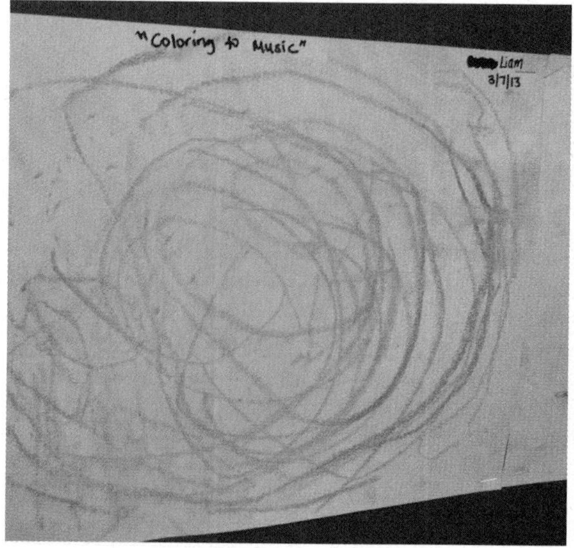

Include children's drawings and paintings in their portfolios.

In addition to your observations, children's portfolios consists of actual samples of children's work that represent development over time. These samples may be real or photographed, depending on their size and fragility. Include dated items such as the following in each portfolio:

- Children's artwork—including drawings, paintings, and collages.
- Writing samples that show the child's scribbling, letters, and words.
- Number samples that show the child's mastery of counting over time.
- Books/stories the child dictated and illustrated.
- Printouts of art, writing, book publishing, and other creative experiences done on the computer.
- Lists of books read.
- Graphs of science-related experiments.

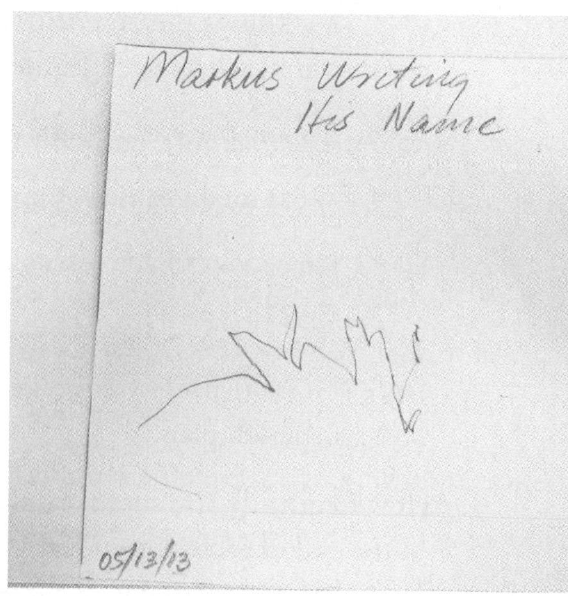

Children's portfolios should include dated writing samples that show the child's scribbling, letters, and words.

Also include photos of the following:

- Artwork—including sculptures, murals, and mobiles.
- Dishes children created during individual and group cooking activities.
- Dramatic play scenarios and puppet show skits.
- Science experiments.
- Physical accomplishments.
- Block creations.
- Routines—including brushing teeth, washing hands, having a meal, napping, and putting on/taking off a jacket.
- Examples of the child at play--working and interacting with others.
- The child on field trips.
- The child at the start and finish of the year.

Date these samples and write notes on them (e.g., "Chandler is sorting leaves by color, which she was not able to do a month ago."). In addition, incorporate children's voices. For example, you might want to also include the following in children's portfolios:

- Notes and comments from children about their work—including audio descriptions of artwork recorded by staff.
- Recorded discussions with children about favorite things to do at home and at the setting.
- Transcripts of recorded conversations among children, their peers, and adults.
- The child's personal reactions to learning experiences.
- Children's evaluations of their work and experiences.

Finally, a child's portfolio can contain information about the child that family members or specialists have contributed. This information should be relevant to the child's growth, learning, or development. For example, a family member might contribute a drawing or writing sample that illustrates one year old Dorine's ability to cover the paper with crayon lines or four-and-a-half-year-old Tara's ability to write "mom."

Portfolios—like all forms of learning documentation—should tell a complete story (Seitz 2008). In this case, the story is about an individual child's learning and development over the course of a period of time. Having this information will help you plan for the children and share information with families. It will also help children revisit their learning. When children revisit their learning they can see how many new skills they have developed and take pride in their accomplishments.

Figure 79. What Does a Portfolio Look Like Physically?

A portfolio can take on a variety of physical forms depending on the program and the educator. Here are some common choices for housing portfolio contents:

- Bankers boxes
- Accordion files
- Folders
- Hanging/expanding files in a file cabinet drawer
- Flash drives
- X-ray folders
- Unused (donated) pizza boxes
- Three-ring binders
- Photo albums
- Plastic containers with lids
- Scrapbooks

Some educators use a dual system: one for three dimensional work samples and another for forms and observations.

Documenting the Group's Learning

In traditional forms of assessment, group learning is determined through testing. Authentic assessment looks to the process of documentation to illustrate the learning and development of a group of children. For example, this documentation could summarize a project investigating children's interest in rain, describe a memorable field trip to a farm, or highlight how children have mastered a specific concept, like measurement.

Use bulletin boards, presentation boards, or documentation panels to prepare this documentation to display at children's eye level. You can also use web diagrams, maps, photographs, slide shows, video clips, or artifacts to tell the story. For example, if you wanted to show children learning to measure, display photos of them measuring plants they have grown, marking their own height against a wall, and using a ruler to measure each other's feet in a shoe store dramatic play scenario. You could also include videos and photos of children using other objects to measure, such as twine to measure a sand-table toy or their own feet to determine the dimensions of a cage for a pet guinea pig. Children can narrate these photos, explaining what object they used to measure and how their methods worked. The idea is to track children's thought processes as they use and refine this skill. The more media you use, the richer your story will be.

This form of storytelling "shows children that their work is valued, makes parents aware of class learning experiences, and allows teachers to assess both their teaching and the children's learning. In addition, dialogue is fostered with other educators. Documentation becomes a tool for teacher research, reflection, collaboration, and decision making" (Institute for Early Childhood Education and Research [IECER] 2012).

Planning and Evaluating

Early childhood educators need to plan for both individual children and the group. They also need to observe and evaluate the plans as they are being implemented to know if they are serving the children optimally. Planning and evaluation should be part of an ongoing cycle of curriculum planning, with each part feeding into the next:

Figure 80. The Cycle of Curriculum Planning

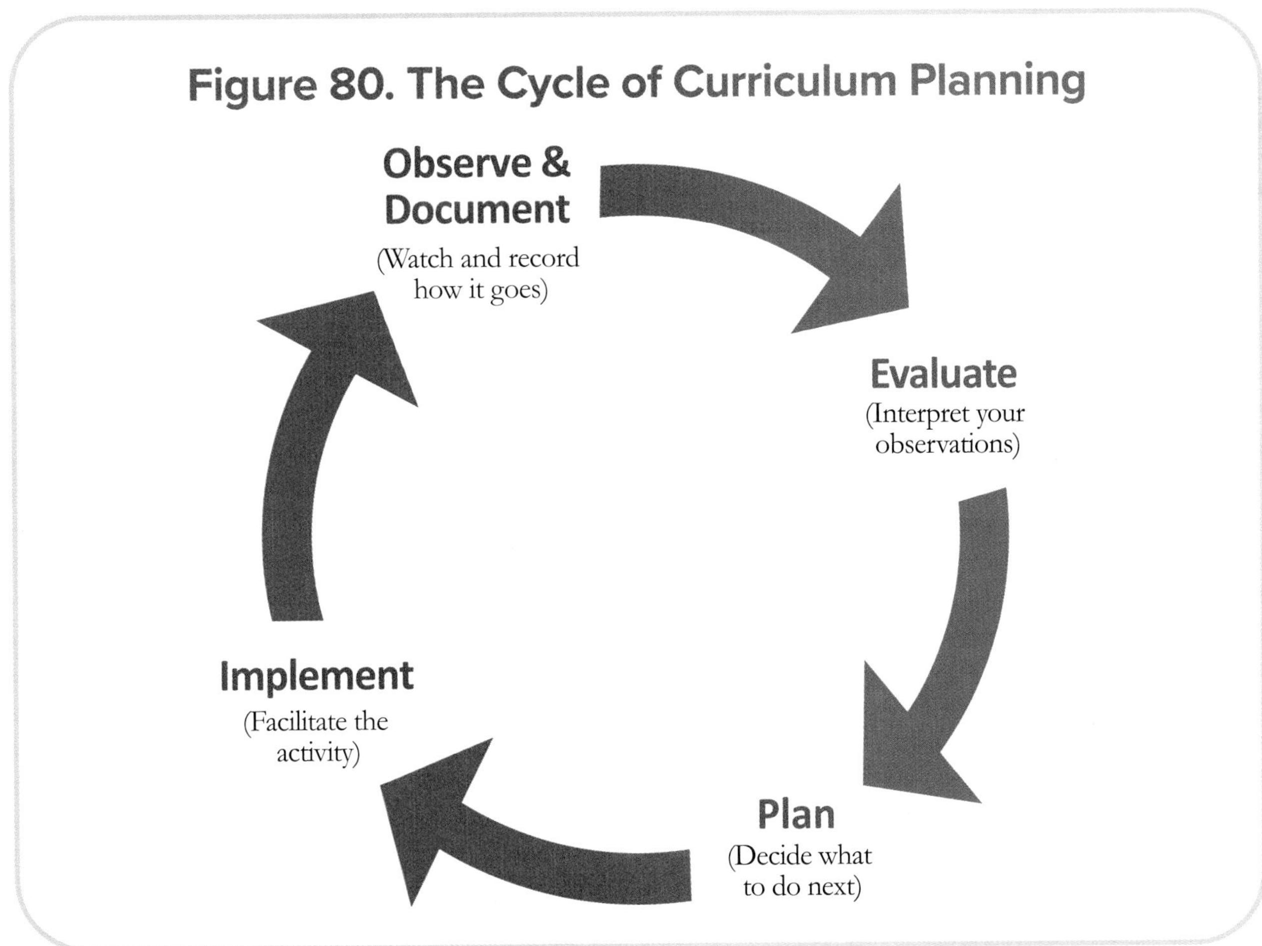

Planning for Individual Children

All the observations, assessment data, family input, and work samples you have collected provide a wealth of information about each child, including the following:

Specific skills, behaviors, and attitudes across the domains of development and learning. Document whether children are meeting specific early learning standards—state, Head Start, or your own setting's standards. At least one of the rating scales, rubrics, or observational scales you have administered will provide you data on each child's physical, social, emotional, cognitive, and language and literacy skills in relation to the standards applicable to your setting. Samples of a child's work, transcripts of conversations with the child, and input from families provide examples of these skills in action that enrich your observations.

For example, you know that four-year-old Miranda has strong fine motor and prosocial skills and that she understands print concepts and speaks in both English and Spanish. This information will help you plan and implement a curriculum that will build on her many abilities, challenge her, and honor her home language while increasing her English literacy. Similarly, you also know that 18-month-old Mohammed has good gross motor skills but is not yet talking. You can create meaningful opportunities for him to hear lots of language. In addition to reading and singing to him daily, make sure that you engage him in conversation during routines like diapering and eating. Even though he's not yet talking, pause in your conversation, waiting for a response. He may start babbling more and even using words.

The child's interests. Your observational records will reveal in which areas of the setting children spend most of their time; the materials they like to use; their favorite books, stories, and games; and any other likes and dislikes. This information tells you how to effectively motivate children's learning, set up the learning environment, engage them in conversation, plan meaningful experiences, and make them feel valued and validated.

The child's temperament and approach to learning. Your observational records will reveal the contexts in which each child learns best, letting you know the best approaches for teaching individual children. As a responsive early childhood educator, create opportunities for one-on-one interactions with the children throughout the day and respond to children's verbal and nonverbal cues. Adapt the learning environment so all children can move freely according to their own abilities and interests.

The child's friendships. Observational notes and family members' input will reveal details about a child's relationships with peers and adults. Use this information when planning for small group activities, conducting group meetings, and supporting children during meal and snack times.

Special requirements. Screening and family input forms, parental conversations, and observations will help you provide a child with needed support during situations, like divorce, or if a child has an identified disability that is being addressed in an IFSP or IEP or if a child is a dual language learner. You can also accommodate family requests concerning their children, such as dietary restrictions.

Organize this information with a planning form, like the one in Figure 81a-b that summarizes the observational and supporting data you have collected on a child. Moreover, defining the learning objectives for each child guides your teaching practices. You can focus on what is important for children to learn and help them master these objectives in a developmentally and culturally appropriate way.

Your program should designate how often you will set learning goals for children and complete individual planning forms. At a minimum, perform these tasks three times a year—a month after the child's first day in your setting, midyear, and at the end of the year. If you conduct assessments on children's learning more often, complete a planning form each time you gather new data. Understanding children's interests, knowledge, skills, and abilities allows you to set appropriate goals and customize your teaching practices accordingly.

Figure 81a. Individual Planning Form

Child's name: ______________________ Date of birth: ______________

Child's home language: ______________________ Class/group: ______________

Early educator's name: ______________________ Date: ______________

Developmental Summaries *(include sources of information for each)*

Gross motor skills: ______________________

____

____

Fine motor skills: ______________________

____

____

Social-emotional skills: ______________________

____

____

Language and literacy skills: ______________________

____

____

Math skills: ______________________

____

____

Science skills: ______________________

____

____

Social studies skills: ______________________

____

____

Skills in the arts: ______________________

____

____

Figure 81b. Individual Planning Form

Technology skills: ______________________________

____

____

Child socializes with: ______________________________

____

____

The child's interests are: ______________________________

____

____

Major strengths: ______________________________

____

____

Areas for growth: ______________________________

____

____

Disabilities/supports (if applicable): ______________________________

____

____

Early earning standards to work on with this child:

1. ______________________________
2. ______________________________
3. ______________________________

Goals for this planning period:

1. ______________________________
2. ______________________________
3. ______________________________

Planning for Children on an IFSP or IEP

Through your screenings and other observations of children, you may have collected information that leads you to suspect that a child could have developmental delays or other disabilities. Discuss your observations with your supervisor (if in a center-based program) and then with the children's families. With parental permission, specialists can then evaluate the child to determine whether they have disabilities in accordance with the Individuals with Disabilities Education Act (IDEA). If disabilities are present, specialists, along with you, the children's families or guardians, special educators, and any relevant colleagues in your setting, will write an Individualized Family Service Plan (IFSP) or Individualized Education Program (IEP) for the children.

Some children may enroll in your program with an IFSP or IEP already in place which states their strengths, specifies learning goals, and designates what services your setting must provide. In accordance with children's IFSPs/IEPs, make accommodations that will enable them to fully participate in the setting's curriculum. This may mean rearranging the setting or providing adapted toys, eating utensils, and computer software and hardware. Or you may need to present information visually or repeatedly. You may need to work with a special educator to learn how to interact with the children in ways that are most effective in supporting development and learning. It is every child's legal and ethical right to be able to access the curriculum. You can read more about the inclusion of children with disabilities in your program in Chapter 13 and throughout this textbook.

Figure 82. Resources for Learning More About Disabilities

Consult the following resources to learn more about children's specific disabilities:

- Alliance for Technology Access (ATA) (*www.ataccess.org*)
- American Speech-Language-Hearing Association (ASHA) (*www.asha.org/public*)
- The Arc (*www.thearc.org*)
- Autism Society (*autism-society.org*)
- Council for Exceptional Children (CEC) (*www.cec.sped.org*)
- Division for Early Childhood (DEC) through the Council for Exceptional Children (*www.dec-sped.org*)
- LD OnLine (*www.ldonline.org*)
- The National Center for Learning Disabilities (*www.NCLD.org*)
- National Disability Rights Network (*www.ndrn.org/index.php*)
- National Dissemination Center for Children with Disabilities (NICHCY) (*nichcy.org/families-community*)
- United Cerebral Palsy (UCP) (*www.ucp.org*)

Planning for Groups of Children

In Chapter 3, you learned that small group times allow you to engage more deeply with a few children at a time, working on specific skills or knowledge. For example, you may notice that a few children find it difficult to hold and write with a marker or crayon. They need opportunities to build their fine motor skills. Other children may be interested in cars. This information will help you choose new materials, like books, songs, rhymes, and stories, to include during large group time and small group activities with children. Reflect on your observations and documentation of children's learning to support and evaluate your planning and implementation. Post your weekly planning on the wall to inform family members of the learning that children are engaging in each day. Refer to Chapter 3 for additional information on planning for infants, toddlers, and preschoolers.

One use of observational data not covered in Chapter 3 is in planning for long-term studies for groups of toddlers and preschoolers. Studies, sometimes referred to as project work, are a technique pioneered by the schools of Reggio Emilia and popularized in the U.S. by educators Lilian Katz, Sylvia Chard, and others. Though they remind many educators of themes, studies are quite different in origin and application. Themes, as you will recall, are topics of study thought to be of general interest to the age group using them—transportation, change of seasons, dinosaurs, or holidays. Many educators do the same themes in the same order year after year.

As you might guess, it is hit or miss if these themes have any appeal to the participating children. Take a theme like change of seasons. For children in New England who can watch the leaves change color and fall in October, following this theme is something they can relate to. But how about children in southern California? They look out their window in October and see palm trees swaying in the warm breeze. They are not likely to relate to the theme through personal experience.

Long-term studies, in contrast, come from the educator's observations of what interests children in their immediate surroundings. As a result of observing children at play and recording their conversations, you know what captivates their interest and what questions they would like answered. Because studies come from what you know about the children, you can tap into ready motivation. Children come to studies eager to learn.

There is one other major difference between studies and themes. Themes last for a pre-set amount of time, typically a week or two. Studies, on the other hand last as long as they hold the children's interests. Because they come from your observations of children, you can be confident that children will have longer-term interest than they would in a theme. Most studies last a minimum of a month. However, if the children's interest wanes, it's time to conclude the project work and move on.

Study Topics/Projects

Phase One—Getting Started

Prepare for the topic/project

- Possible topic emerges
- Initiated by the teacher ***OR*** emerging from the children's interests
- Complete webs on possible questions, curriculum opportunities, resources, and field sites
- Provide focusing activities and common experiences for the group or class
- Decide if topic is appropriate and practical

Phase Two—Developing the Study Topic/Project Work

Implementation and development work

- Reexamine planning webs to identify skills and concepts
- Prepare for field work and expert visitors
- Investigate
- Represent what was learned through writing, drawing, construction, dancing, and dramatic play
- Revisit web to indicate what was learned, identify new questions, repeat investigation and representation

Phase Three—Concluding the Study Topic/Project

Debrief—Review—Share

- Plan culminating event (celebration) for students to share/tell the story of the topic/project
- Complete the culminating event or activities
- Review project and assess achievement of goals

(Chard 1998)

Questions and Provocations to Stimulate Dialogue, Language Usage, and Cognitive Development in Young Children

- Tell me about what you're doing . . .
- How did you do that?
- What do you think will happen if . . .?
- I was wondering if there's another way we can . . .
- How many of you did it take to do that?
- How many (name the objects or items) did it take you to do that?
- Is there anything you would like to change?
- What other pieces do you think we could include?
- Where do you think we can put this so other people can enjoy it, too?
- Let's make a sign so others know about your ____. What would you like to write on the sign?
- Where should you post this sign so everyone can read it?
- Tell me about what you are you making.
- Let me know if you need anything else to . . .
- What do you think will happen if you change this?
- I see you used ____, ____ and ____. Tell me the reason you chose those.
- How many more do you think you could make?
- Who else could we ask to help us with this?
- I see you're dressed like a(n) ____. Tell me about your job.
- Since we can't take this out of the classroom, what can we do to let other people know what this looked like?
- Who worked on this project? What did they do?
- If you work here again tomorrow, will you do the same thing (use the same materials) or something different?
- Let's make a list of all the pieces you used.

Here's how a long-term study might work. Ms. Airs, an FCC educator, observed that the children in her program are very concerned about the bees in their flower garden. They want to know why the bees are just on the flowers and not the vegetables and how the bees can make honey if they spend all of their time with the flowers.

Based on her observations, Ms. Airs considers a study on bees. She wants to be sure that it will meet the criteria below (Dodge et al. 2000; 2002):

- Age-appropriate and relevant.
- Able to be explored in depth through hands-on investigations.
- Allows children to acquire knowledge and apply skills in meaningful ways.
- Explores real world problems.
- Engages and challenges the full group of children.
- Promotes cooperative learning and teamwork.
- Involves families in the children's learning.
- Enables children to develop social/emotional, cognitive, language and literacy, and physical skills.
- Respectful of cultural differences.
- Worth studying.

Finding that the study will meet these criteria, Ms. Airs prepares for introducing the study. She does this by first making a planning web of the big ideas she thinks she will be introducing, such as where bees live, what bee society looks like, what bees eat, how bees make honey, why bees sting, and how bees help our world. Then she brainstorms ways to incorporate language and literacy, math, science, social studies, the arts, and technology while having children investigate these topics. Here's a summary of what she came up with:

Content Area	What We Could Study About Bees
Language and Literacy	Read books (*The Very Greedy Bee*), do finger plays (Here is the beehive), sing songs (Happy Yellow Bumblebee), learn bee-related vocabulary (pollen, hive, drone, beeswax).
Math	Compare sizes of bees, count legs, observe pattern of stripes, observe and count bees in the garden.
Science	Investigate what bees eat and how they make honey, observe honeycomb, study lifecycle of a bee; determine how bees lay eggs and what happens when stung by a bee.

Content Area	What We Could Study About Bees
Social Studies	How to care for bee colonies, and why the world needs bees to survive (book: *What If There Were No Bees?*).
The Arts	Make hives, wear beekeeper costumes in dramatic play; fly/ move to Rimsky-Korsakov's *Flight of the Bumblebee.*
Technology	Use tools (magnifying glass, microscope) to study bees; email an expert with bee questions; Skype with other FCC homes studying bees; document study in slide show.

Confident of her approach, Ms. Airs brings the children together and reads aloud *Are You a Bee?* by Judy Allen. She discusses the book with the children and writes down their questions about bees. She will use their questions to guide the study:

- What do bees do during the day?
- Do bees sleep?
- Why do bees eat flowers? Why don't they eat vegetables?
- Why is the queen bee so big?
- How do bees talk to each other?
- Will bees sting you if you don't touch them?
- Why do bees make noise?
- What do bees do with honey?
- Do baby bees fly?
- Do all bees dance?
- Where can a bee hide?
- Is a bumblebee the same as a honeybee?
- Can bee stings kill you?

Ms. Airs also let the children's families know about the study and urges them to discuss the bee study with the children at home.

Each week for the next six weeks (which is the duration that the bee project lasted), Ms. Airs prepared a weekly planning form and posted it for the children's families to see. Figure 78, presents Week #3 of the bee study:

Figure 83. Weekly Planning Grid for Bee Study

	Monday	Tuesday	Wednesday	Thursday	Friday
Group meeting	Question to talk about: Why don't bees see red?	Discuss tomorrow's visit to bee farm; list questions to ask and what to look for	Prepare for field trip; Discuss how many bees are in a colony	Review field trip; go over questions and answers. Discuss bee communication	Write group thank you letters; Discuss: why only girl bees sting
Learning centers (including book to read in Literacy Center)	Read: *Bumble Bee* by Margaret Wise Brown; Add microscope to Science Center	Read: *The Bee (Life Cycles)* by Sabrina Crewe; Add patterning materials to Math Center	Read: *Honey (What's for Lunch?)* by Pam Robson; Make recipes with honey in Cooking Center	Read: *Busy As a Bee* by Melvin Berger; Add materials to art center for making hives	Read: *The Bee Tree* by Patricia Polacco; Add materials to Art Center for bee-related art
Small group	Use cotton balls to remove pollen from lilies	Have a honey taste test	Explore honeycomb	Make beehives using egg cartons, bubble wrap and other art supplies	Make bee costumes and headbands using pipe cleaners, googly eyes, netting
Outdoor time	Set up beekeeper area for dramatic play	Stretch like bees releasing beeswax	Set up a bee and pollinator garden	Take a nature bee walk; use bee I.D. chart to identify types of bees	Take honeycomb outside and observe bees interact with it
Transitions	Anyone wearing bee colors of yellow and black lines up first	Anyone with striped pattern like bees lines up first	Flap wings like bees to place in line	Do waggle dance in line	Line up as type of bee children studying (carpenter, honey, killer, etc.)

Throughout the study, Ms. Airs stocked the learning centers with materials the children needed to investigate their questions. She encouraged the children to work together and to use the computer to find resources on bees. The children made bee sculptures and mobiles, painted a mural, and wrote their own book about bees. They made costumes and did the bee waggle dance. They studied honeycombs, watched honey harvested at a bee farm, taste-tested various types of honey and made recipes featuring honey. They did investigations and made a poster of bee facts learned (see chart). All the while, Ms. Airs took observation notes that she put in the children's portfolios along with photos of the hive they built, their investigations, art work, and stories.

At the end of the study Ms. Airs invited the children's families to come celebrate the study. They looked at a slide show she made showing the children's work and ate foods made with honey—chicken wings, honey oatmeal bread, and baklava. Everyone thought the study of bees was a bee-utiful choice.

Bee Facts

- Only female (girl) bees sting.
- Smoke calms bees down.
- Bees cannot see the color red.
- The queen bee is twice the size of a worker bee.
- A bee colony has about 50,000 worker bees.
- Bees share food. That's how they talk to each other, too.
- Bees have to visit 2 million flowers to make a pound of honey.
- Bees do a waggle dance to tell other bees where to find nectar.
- There are 10 types of honeybees.
- Our food supply depends on bees.
- Bees have been around longer than people, but are disappearing rapidly.
- We have to save the bees!

Recordkeeping

Throughout this book you have been advised to complete certain forms and records. Chapters 1 and 2, offered guidance on which forms relate to children's safety, health, and well-being. In this chapter, you were coached on how to do observations and assemble portfolios for the children. The forms you need to track include:

- Family intake form
- Current medical information for each child
- Child health record
- Family emergency numbers and information

- Permission slips for field trips
- Individual planning forms for each child
- IFSP/IEPs for children with disabilities
- Incident reports, accident reports, or special problems
- Observation checklists, rating scales, and time and event samples
- Running records, anecdotal notes, and learning stories
- Developmental assessments of children
- Parent-educator conference reports

Part of your role as an early childhood educator is to know how to maintain these records. You want to make sure that these forms will be available when needed. There are five steps that you should follow to maintain records properly:

1. Decide who is responsible for each record. For example, most early childhood educators in centers and all FCC educators would be responsible for making sure that the forms listed above are completed and in their possession.
2. Develop a cover form/checklist—or use software. Use it to indicate you have completed forms. Date and initial each form.
3. Determine which forms are confidential. Typically that is anything that has to do with personal data about a child or family, such as health records, IFSP/IEPs, and developmental assessments.
4. Place the form in the designated storage system, typically a file cabinet or bankers box with hanging folders. All confidential forms must be stored in filing cabinets that can be locked.
5. Review the system periodically and remove unnecessary forms. Consult your program's policies as to how long individual children's forms should be maintained.

Your biggest priority is Step 3, honoring the confidentiality of personal data. You have a responsibility to each child and family in your program to keep personal data private. Only those with a specified "need to know" (for example, a special education teacher working with a child on an IFSP), who have written parental permission, are entitled to access these files. Family members can, of course, have access to their own child's file. They cannot, however, have access to any other child's forms. Likewise, you cannot discuss what is in any child's confidential files with colleagues outside of your program or with anyone who is not a family member of the child. Your confidentiality is every child and family's guaranteed right.

Working With Colleagues and the Community

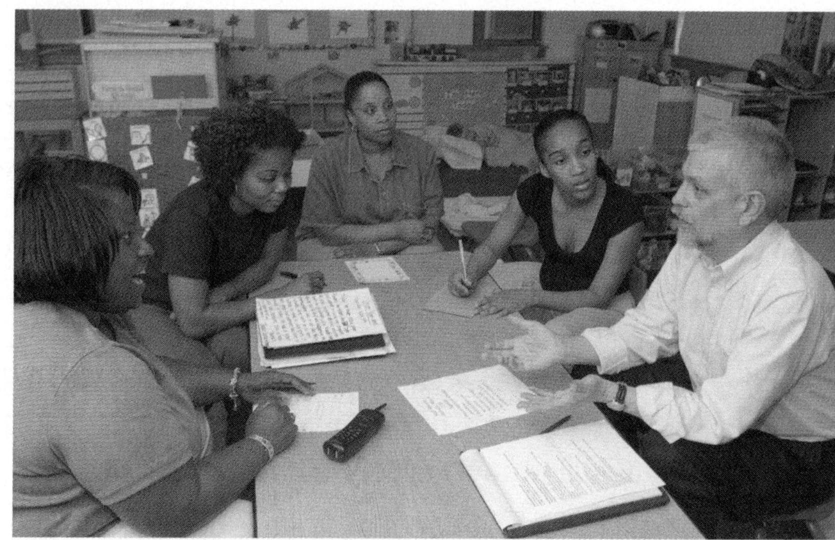

How frequently you summarize your observations depends on how you will use the information.

Early childhood educators who work in centers are surrounded by a pool of concerned adults—family members, colleagues and other staff, program volunteers, community service personnel, licensing staff, special educators, social workers, substitute early educators, supervisors and other administrators, trainers, medical and dental personnel, and consultants. When you think about all your responsibilities, remember that you are not alone. All these adults play a role in your setting, are influenced by the way you manage it, and are personally invested in the children's and the setting's success. FCC educators typically do not have all of these resource people at hand and will have to search out a support team—perhaps by joining an association or identifying other FCC educators in their area. In either type of setting, though, effective educators manage cooperative and respectful relationships with professional colleagues. Their support is vital to your program's success.

Professionalism in a Center

Professional relationships are integral to program management. Present yourself in a professional manner and be open to others' opinions, beliefs, and ideas. You work with colleagues, a supervisor, and the program director every day, and you have established relationships with each of them. Work to maintain strong relationships and partnerships with these colleagues. Collaborate to ensure that the children are supervised appropriately. This helps maintain order in the learning environment and keep everyone safe and healthy.

If you observe an early childhood educator doing something that conflicts with early childhood best practices, express your concern to this person in private. Discuss the situation to see whether there might be an explanation. If there's not an explanation, monitor the situation before discussing it with a supervisor—unless what you observed is harmful to another person. If you have an issue with what a colleague has said, even if it is in a group setting, speak to this person in private and discuss the matter calmly. Tell your colleague in a non-accusatory way what upset you. State the facts, avoid blame, and manage your emotions to help you reach a resolution.

For example, you might tell your colleague, "When you interrupted my story to tell the children what we are having for lunch, I felt disrespected." This gives your colleague an opportunity to both apologize and give you an explanation: "I'm sorry, I certainly didn't mean to disrespect you. The reason I interrupted you is because the cafeteria people came early and I didn't want the food to get cold. I should have gotten your attention rather than interrupting."

If your supervisor gives you negative criticism or feedback, avoid blame and again manage your emotions. You may think that your supervisor has misunderstood something or drawn a conclusion based on incorrect or incomplete information. Try to supply your supervisor with correct or additional information. However, you are responsible for managing the setting, and your supervisor is responsible for managing you. Consider the situation from this person's perspective. Your supervisor is offering you this feedback constructively to help you become a better early childhood educator, so try not to be offended. Accept this person's feedback for what it is: a different perspective on which you can reflect.

In Chapter 13, you will find a section on ethical decision making which provides further guidance on how to deal with colleagues and supervisors whose behavior leads you to feel uncomfortable and what to do if you feel that they are behaving in inappropriate ways.

Substitute Early Childhood Educators

Substitute early childhood educators are often introduced into the setting without having spent any time with you or the children. Prepare to make their time in the setting effective. Create a binder for them that includes the following:

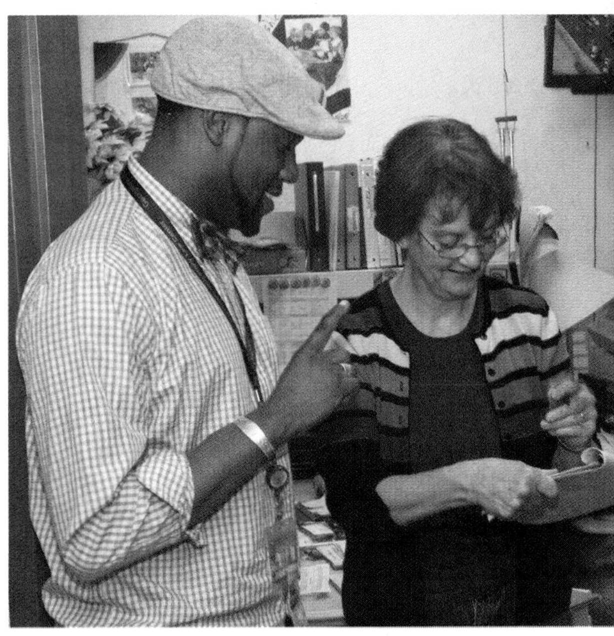

Create a binder for substitute early educators to help make their time in the setting effective.

- A class list, with the names of every child and family member (preferably with photographs).
- All appropriate paperwork, including necessary forms (e.g., incident report forms).
- The list of who is authorized to pick up each child at the end of the day.
- A copy of your setting's rules, daily schedule, and lesson plans that cover the time period the substitute educator will work at your setting.
- A list of any of the children's disabilities (e.g., who has an IFSP/IEP, who has food allergies, or who might need to leave the setting early that day).

External Community

Special educators, social workers, trainers, community service representatives, and consultants are all there to offer you, families, and children support and supplemental services. In essence, they are there to enhance the services you provide. Meet the specific community members who support your setting and the families you serve. Among the organizations that you may want to contact are those that handle the following:

- Domestic violence, including child abuse and neglect and spousal abuse (e.g., organizations like Parents Anonymous, Child Protective Services, and local shelters)
- Homelessness (e.g., local shelters)
- Nutrition (e.g., the local extension office)
- Screening children for disabilities (e.g., Child Find)
- Translation/interpretation
- Library services
- Immigration/refugee support
- Cultural Connections (e.g., community centers)

Figure 84 lists some of the typical resource agencies that serve families. Add to this list by searching the Internet or collaborating with your supervisor if you are in a center-based program. If you are in an FCC home, confer with your licensing representative if you need additional help locating the services your local community offers.

Figure 84. Community Resources

- Parenting programs
- American Red Cross
- Easter Seals
- Safety groups
- Mental health clinics
- Medical clinics
- Dental clinics
- Supplemental Nutrition Assistance Program (SNAP)
- WIC— Special Supplemental Nutrition Program for Women, Infants, and Children
- Financial planning
- Child care resource and referral
- Cultural resource groups
- Resale shops
- Educational supply stores
- Food cooperatives and farms
- Children's bookstores
- Early and periodic screening programs
- Local children's museums and the zoo
- Libraries
- Nature centers
- Service organizations that might contribute resources or funds to your program
- Churches, temples, mosques, spiritual centers

Competency Standard VI:

To maintain a commitment to professionalism

CHAPTER 13:

Professionalism

CDA® Functional Area 13: Candidate makes decisions based on knowledge of research-based early childhood practices, promotes high-quality in child care services, and takes advantage of opportunities to improve knowledge and competence, both for personal and professional growth and for the benefit of children and families.

Professionalism

Introduction

Everything that you do as an early childhood educator—including keeping children safe and healthy, fostering their learning and development, engaging their families in their care and education, and managing a successful setting—commands a commitment to professionalism. Your conduct should always reflect early childhood education best practices and illustrate your dedication to your career, to the children in your care, and to their families. As an early childhood educator, you are a lifelong learner—meaning that you are engaged in an ongoing process of remaining abreast of the latest early childhood education research and best practices, refining your own practices, and growing as a professional.

In this chapter, we will focus on the following skills and traits that contribute to your professionalism:

- **Educating With Intentionality and Reflection**
- **Making Ethical Decisions**
- **Articulating Values, Vision, and Passion**
- **Continuing Your Professional Development**
- **Advocating for Children and Families**

Educating with Intentionality and Reflection

Early childhood educators must have rich and current knowledge of childhood development, and be able to support and scaffold each child's learning. These characteristics help you educate with intentionality and reflect on the effectiveness of your teaching practices.

Intentional Early Educators

Ann Epstein, author of *The Intentional Teacher: Choosing the Best Strategies for Young Children's Learning*, Revised Edition (2014), explains, "Intentional teaching does not happen by chance. It is planful, thoughtful, and purposeful." Intentional early educators observe the children in their care, determine their needs, employ best teaching practices based on these needs, and reflect on the effectiveness of the experience as a whole. They apply a wide range of strategies, thoughtfully applied to facilitate each child's development and learning."

Early Learning Standards

Every state and many organizations have developed early learning standards for children in the early years. Usually organized by domain as well as age range, the standards describe what young children should learn and be able to do at a given point in their education. The U.S. Department of Education defines them as:

A set of expectations, guidelines, or developmental milestones that describe what all children from birth until kindergarten entry should know and be able to do and their disposition toward learning. These standards must be appropriate for each age group of infants, toddlers, and preschoolers and English learners, and for children with developmental delays and disabilities. In addition, the standards must cover all the Essential Domains of School Readiness, and must be developmentally, linguistically, and culturally appropriate.

Intentional early educators continue to question and think about how and why a teaching practice is appropriate for the child and the situation. They are problem-solvers and independent thinkers. These educators ask themselves questions like the following:

- What does each child in my setting need? (Trina, seven months) seems like she is interested in transitioning to use of a sippy cup.)
- What information do I need to determine this need? How will I obtain this information? (I'll ask her parents what they think.)
- What are developmentally appropriate goals for each child? (We can keep giving her bottles as she makes the gradual change to using a cup.)
- What experiences, materials, and interactions will help each child reach these goals? (I'll give her some water in a sippy cup so she can get used to how it feels.)
- What additional information do I need to meet these goals? (If they agree with this plan, I'll ask her family to exchange information about Trina's experiences with her cup at home and at the program.)
- In what areas do I need to develop professionally to support my teaching practices? (I will review information on infant development to see what other self-help skills are typical of babies in Trina's age group.)

Educators Deb Curtis and Margie Carter (2009) say that intentionality is a disposition:

> Intentional teachers. . .have certain qualities that distinguish them from teachers who depend on curriculum activity books, follow the same theme plans year after year, or struggle daily to get the children involved in anything productive. The knowledge and skills of master teachers are not necessarily different from those of other teachers. Rather, these professionals have become improvisational artists. They have developed a set of attitudes and habits of mind that enable them to respond readily to the classroom dynamics and multiple needs of children.

The National Association for the Education of Young Children says that successful early educators are always intentional (Copple and Bredekamp 2009):

> Whenever you see a great program, one in which children are learning and thriving, you can be sure that teachers (and the administrators who support them) are highly intentional. In everything good teachers do—creating the environment, considering the curriculum, and tailoring it to the children as individuals—they are purposeful and thoughtful. As they make myriad decisions, big and small, they keep in mind the outcomes they seek. Even in responding to unexpected opportunities—"teachable moments"— intentional teachers are guided by the outcomes the program is trying to help children reach and by their knowledge of child development and learning.
>
> Having their objectives and plans in mind, intentional teachers are well prepared to tell others—parents, administrators, colleagues—about what they are doing. Not only do they know what to do, they also know why they are doing it and can describe their purposes.

Epstein (2014) adds, "Intentional teachers use their knowledge, judgement, and expertise to organize learning experiences for children." She notes that such teachers can also recognize and take advantage of unplanned situations that support goals for children.

To become this type of intentional teacher, early educator, Schiller (2007) recommends the following three-step approach:

1. **Familiarize yourself with child development and research knowledge to understand which outcomes are best suited to the children in your care.** Be knowledgeable and observant. Understand how children of different ages, dispositions, and interests learn best and the accommodations you need to make to foster their learning.
2. **Select targeted, desired outcomes for children while planning.** Intentional early educators must be exceptional planners who configure the environment, choose materials, and question children in ways that promote learning.
3. **Learn from the children you teach. Understand that teaching involves following and leading.** This may mean that you let the children decide what they will engage in and learn. For example, some children might enjoy sorting leaves, so allow them to do so. At times, you also facilitate adult-guided learning while exploring materials or technology, like a new microscope that will allow children to discover new attributes about leaves. To follow up, intentional early educators might then lead small groups in playing a lotto matching game of leaves or allowing children to create their own matching games.

Figure 85. Characteristics of Intentional Teaching

- **High expectations.** Teachers and providers believe that all children can learn and make progress. They expect children to challenge themselves and persevere. This expectation leads children to want to be capable and competent.
- **Planning and management.** Teachers and providers set appropriate learning objectives for each child, based on early learning standards, but are flexible enough to alter plans to include the children's new interests and unexpected needs.
- **Learning-oriented.** Teachers and providers create a community of learning in which children are dedicated to and value their own interests, skills, and progress.
- **Engaging activities.** Early educators plan meaningful experiences that are related to children's lives and designed to challenge children without frustrating them.
- **Thoughtful questioning.** Teachers and providers customize questions for children to learn what they are thinking and to help stimulate their ideas.
- **Feedback.** Teachers and providers offer specific information that helps children review and evaluate their efforts and accomplishments. Such feedback can encourage children to identify problems in thinking, make predictions, and challenging use their imaginations and creativity.

Reflection

Intentionality and reflection coincide. Using reflection to review and analyze the effectiveness of your teaching, can lead to improvements in your approach and allow you to be even more intentional.

Reflection requires educators to take the time to consciously observe and evaluate their actions and determine whether their strategies are effective in supporting children's learning. Through reflection educators can use what they learn about themselves and the children to make changes in their setting, alter their teaching practices, and make decisions in the future. Consider the following example of a teacher of young toddlers reflecting on a morning activity.

> *While the children are napping, Ms. Singh sits down with her laptop to spend a few minutes reflecting on the morning's events. She had introduced an outdoor activity—blowing bubbles—because it was the first sunny day in a long time. While reviewing the photos she had quickly downloaded to her laptop, she sees the joy in the children's faces and thinks about the interactions she had with these delighted toddlers. She makes a few notes—"Leo seems to particularly enjoy chasing the bubbles; Carrie likes the way the bubbles melt in her hands; and Omar seemed happy to watch for a while before joining in." She remembers introducing some new words to the children and wrote*

those down too—transparent, floating, and drippy. To reinforce children's learning, she and her colleagues can find ways to use these words. She makes a point to find the word for bubbles in each of the children's home languages so she can use it correctly. Ms. Singh plans to review the early learning standards for this age group and see which ones were addressed in the bubble- blowing experience.

Reflection not only provides insight about your learning community and your practices, but it also helps you learn more about you and what makes you "tick." As an intentional early educator, you understand who you are as a human being and as a professional. This self-awareness helps you become more objective and thoughtful about your relationships with children and the way you approach teaching. Reflection helps you to better understand the following characteristics about yourself:

- Your values and beliefs. (I believe that all children can learn.)
- Your strengths and weaknesses. (I am very well-organized and develop detailed plans. I could use help in recognizing when to deviate from the plan.)
- Your teaching philosophy. (Children learn through play and through intentionally planned experiences that are implemented by teachers.)
- Your teaching and learning styles. (I learn best through doing. Reading is not enough, I need to apply new information for it to make sense to me.)
- How past experiences have influenced you. (I have always loved reading so I am always seeking books that will fit the interests of the children in the group.)
- Your understanding and appreciation of diversity. (I came to the United States as a refugee from another country. Therefore, I am particularly sensitive to children and families who are adjusting to life in this country.)

Reflective early educators are better able to see patterns in children's behaviors and uncover issues that impact learning.

- Your understanding and appreciation of dual language learners. (I respect dual language learners by encouraging them to use both English and their home languages. Having skills in both languages is a lifelong benefit for these children.)
- Your understanding of individual children and their learning and behaviors. (Tarik likes to watch and listen before joining in a group at play. He seems to be figuring out what's going on and what role he can assume in the play scenario.)

- Your role in the teaching process. (I am a facilitator. I observe and reflect before deciding what the children might need to expand their play and learning.)
- Your "authentic" self. (I am a work-in-progress.)

Teachers and providers who regularly practice reflection find that it also helps them uncover hidden biases and dispositions. Anti-bias educators Louise Derman-Sparks and Julie Olsen Edwards (2010) challenge teachers and providers to reflect on how their personal biases might affect their practices. For example, they explain, through reflection, a teacher came to realize that four-year-old Jack always "got on her nerves," because his facial expressions were similar to those of her father, with whom she had a difficult relationship. Once she made this connection, she was able to bond with Jack in a way she had not been able to before. Another teacher was annoyed by families who brought their children to school late. Reflection helped her realize that tardiness bothered her because she had been raised to believe it was disrespectful. She had been discounting the explanation of parents when they tried to explain that the bus was often late arriving at the bus stop. She also realized that she had not considered that the children's families could not afford cars and that public transportation, though unreliable, was their only means of transportation. Once she was able to view the situation from their perspective, she was able to change her own views about the children's tardiness and become more supportive of their families' needs.

Reflective early educators are better able to do the following:

- Slow down and take a better look at how they teach.
- Discover patterns in children's behaviors.
- See how they translate theory into practice.
- Determine whether they act with professionalism.
- Recognize and change behaviors that are not consistent with their standards of effective teaching.
- Determine whether their teaching addresses the learning standards.
- Uncover issues that impact children's learning.
- Use multiple sources of information to inform their practice.

Reflection can improve your planning and teaching practices. Ask yourself *what* and *why* questions to increase your own awareness about your teaching practices and the impact they have on children. Questions, like What am I doing? and Why am I doing it? will lead you to ask more questions: How effective is my teaching? What are the children learning? What can I do better? Apply your reflections on what did and did not support children's development and learning when developing weekly plans. For example, you might note that Trey's rapidly developing body and nerves may be causing his fussiness, so the weekly plan could include a way to provide constant soothing primary care and to share this strategy with his family.

Realizing the Truth During Reflection

Today, in the dramatic play center, Mr. Kastle joined the children's "dinner" and talked with them about what they were eating. He and the children laughed and they vied for his attention. He introduced new words, like spatula and seafood.

Later that afternoon, as he reflects on the activity, Mr. Kastle remembers it as being a success. He recalls thinking to himself that the children's families would be pleased to hear them using these new vocabulary words. However, his intent for entering the children's play was to observe firsthand how they were assuming roles and learning skills, such as following rules and regulating their emotions. He had planned to use his interactions with the children to talk about foods and introduce new words. When he analyzes the experience, though, he realize that he lost track of these goals and was caught up in having fun with the children. He sees that he was flattered that the children were vying for his attention and began performing for them. At the time, he considered the experience a success, but now sees that the experience did not focus on goals for the children. They received less out of the experience than he did. Mr. Kastle's reflections lead him to remember to stay focused on his intent in future interactions with the children.

Reflective early educators take a step back and decide whether they are executing plans as effectively as possible. They also tend to be more flexible and open to change than early educators who are not reflective (Stewart 2010). The following tips can help you become a reflective teacher or provider (Beal n.d.; Carter, Cividanes, Curtis, and Lebo, 2010; Pappas 2010; Neas 2012):

- Make time in the schedule for reflection. Just as you make time to observe children every day, commit to reflection time as well. Once you build reflection consistently into your regular schedule in an organized, systematic way, the process will become automatic.
- Focus your reflections. Begin by concentrating on a specific concept, like how you teach individual children, rather than a broad, abstract concept, like how you teach in general.
- Work with a mentor or coach who can guide and critique your work and help you problem-solve and plan strategies.
- Focus your reflections on several children each day, much like you do during observations.
- Maintain a written and/or photo journal or diary. Daily or weekly entries will help you capture experiences more accurately and completely. Describe your immediate reaction and the children's reactions to experiences. Pose questions for yourself that you can reflect on in future entries.

Finding a Mentor

Consider asking a skilled early childhood professional whom you trust and respect to serve as your mentor. Many professionals choose mentors to guide and support them as they face challenges, celebrate successes, and grow professionally. The National Association for the Education of Young Children and Child Care Aware® of America (2011, 10) define "mentoring" as a "relationship-based process between colleagues in similar professional roles, with a more- experienced individual with adult learning knowledge and skills, the mentor, providing guidance and example to the less-experienced protégé or mentee. Mentoring is intended to increase an individual's personal or professional capacity, resulting in greater professional effectiveness." This relationship should be mutually beneficial. You and your mentor need to be clear about the nature of the relationship and the expectations you have of each other so that you can learn and grow together.

- Try collaborative journal writing. Ask colleagues to join you in keeping diaries that you can share and critique while writing feedback for each other.
- Hold regular discussion groups with colleagues about their observations.
- Ask a mentor, coach, or colleague to videotape you with the children. Watch the recording several times, then consider what went well and what you might want to do or say differently in the future.
- Ask a colleague to observe your teaching and give you feedback. Offer to do the same for them.
- Ask the children for feedback about their day. Listen carefully—they know success when they experience it.
- Use learning stories, which you read about in Chapter 12. Write these stories as first-person narratives and focus on a specific child or group of children in your setting with whom you have been working. Write about your experiences interacting with the child or group and discuss your thinking along with your interpretations of the child's actions and thoughts. Think about your actions and goals, offer interpretations, and describe your feelings. Once you have written your story, invite the children and their family members to incorporate their voices into the story.

Figure 86. Reflective Questions

Creating a list of questions to guide your reflection is a useful starting point. There are no *right* or *wrong* questions. Just choose those that will support you. Marge Carter and Deb Curtis suggest the following areas and questions to consider.

1. Know yourself.
   - What captures my attention as the children engage, explore, and talk with each other and with me?
   - What delights me as I watch and listen?
   - How might my background and values influence how I respond to the children?
2. Find the details that touch your heart and mind.
   - What are the children learning from this experience?
   - What do I notice in the children's faces and actions?
   - Where do I see examples of the children's face and actions?
3. Seek the child's perspective.
   - What is the child drawn to and excited about?
   - What might the child be trying to accomplish?
   - Why might the child be talking to and playing with others this way?
   - What ideas might the child be exploring?
4. Examine the physical and socio-emotional environment.
   - How do schedules, routines, the physical space, and materials support or limit the children's play?
   - What changes or additions to the space of materials would help to strengthen children's relationships?
   - How do schedules and routines influence this experience?
5. Explore multiple points of view.
   - How might the child's culture and family background be influencing the situation?
   - What questions could I ask the child's family?
   - What other perspective should I consider?
   - What child development or early learning theories apply to this experience?
   - How does this child's play (or other activity) demonstrate desired early learning outcomes or standards?
6. Consider opportunities and possibilities for next steps.
   - What values, philosophy, and desired outcomes do I want to influence my response?
   - What new or existing relationships could be strengthened?
   - Which learning goals could be addressed?
   - What other materials and activities could be offered to build on this experience?
   - What new vocabulary can teachers introduce?

(Adapted from Carter, M. and Curtis, D. 2009)

Making Ethical Decisions

Throughout the day, you make decisions about everything that happens within the setting—including the following:

- What materials should I make available?
- Is it too cold to go outside today?
- Which children should help set the tables for lunch?
- Should I extend outdoor play, since the children are having so much fun discovering worms?
- Should I let Charles keep napping or wake him for snack, since he ate so little for lunch today?

While all of these decisions require thought and consideration, once you make them, you will probably give them little additional thought. However, other situations, like the ones described below, require you to reflect on what you believe and what you know is best for children before making a decision:

- Lately, Denise has been shoving and pushing other children. You want to discuss her behavior with her parents so that you can jointly devise a plan of action. However, based on previous conversations, you believe Denise's father will punish her severely if he hears how his daughter has been behaving.
- Two-year-old Austin's dad tells you that he does not want his son wearing any of those "sissy" dress-up clothes anymore. "If Austin grows up to be a homosexual, it will be your fault," his father says.

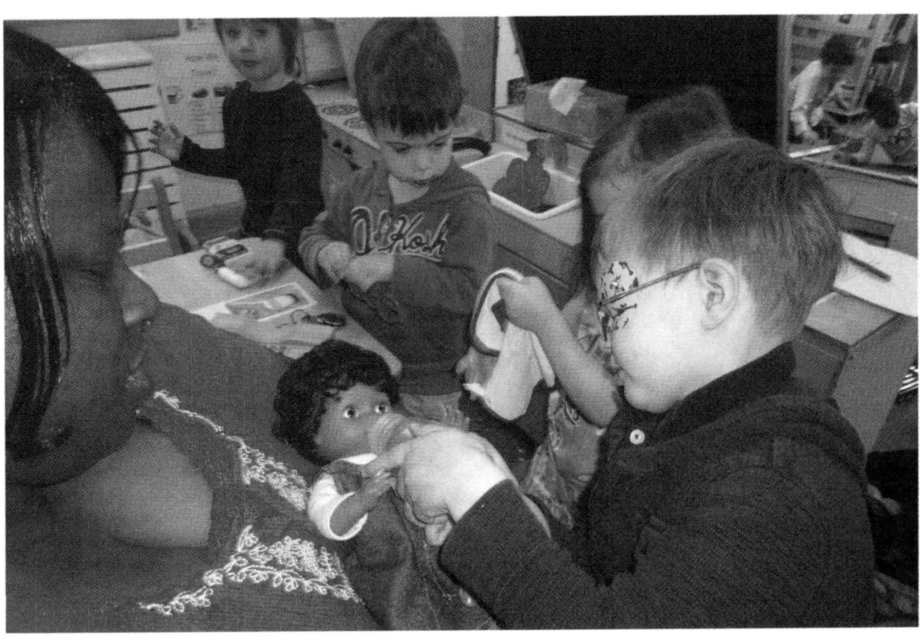

As an early educator, you treat girls and boys equally according to Section 1, Principle P-1.3 of the NAEYC Code of Ethical Conduct. Children of all genders have access to all materials within the setting.

- Aaliyah's mother has volunteered to help you with filing. You accept her offer and give her the keys to the filing cabinets. When you check to see whether she needs your help, you find her looking at other children's portfolios.
- At a staff meeting, your supervisor Tony tells a joke about a particular ethnic group. A few people laugh. Most, like you, look uncomfortable.
- Eddie, a four-year-old on an IEP for emotional disturbance, exhibits screaming outbursts. By constantly working with him in ways his specialists suggest, his screaming has lessened somewhat, and he is participating more in the program. You are very pleased by his progress. However, by devoting so much time to Eddie, you have spent less time with the other children.
- At a parent conference, Penny's mother tells you that her boyfriend is rough with Penny when she talks back to him. After confiding in you, she begs you not to tell anyone.
- Maddy's father arrives at your setting wanting to spend time with his daughter. The program has on file a copy of the court order that restricts his access to Maddy.

What would you do in these situations? To some teachers and providers, the solutions may be readily apparent but difficult to implement. Others may be unsure about what to do and need guidance to make an appropriate and ethical decision.

For those instances in which the answer is not obvious, The National Association for the Education of Young Children (NAEYC, 2005) has developed a *Code of Ethical Conduct* (*www.naeyc.org*) that outlines early educators' professional responsibilities. As Feeney (2010), one of the document's authors, writes, "Professional ethics helps us as early childhood educators to think about our responsibilities to children, families, communities and society and to address some of the difficult situations we face every day."

Because the document applies to all members of the profession, it represents the values and moral responsibility of the field, not of any one individual. It thus relieves early educators from concerns that they are acting alone. When you apply the *Code of Ethical Conduct*, you represent the early childhood field to society.

Using the *Code of Ethical Conduct* as a moral compass in decision-making is straightforward. It is divided into four areas of ethical responsibility:

Children. "Our paramount responsibility is to provide care and education in settings that are safe, healthy, nurturing, and responsive for each child."

Families. "Because the family and the early childhood practitioner have a common interest in the child's well-being, we acknowledge a primary responsibility to bring about communication, cooperation, and collaboration between the home and early childhood program in ways that enhance the child's development."

Colleagues. "In a caring, cooperative workplace, human dignity is respected, professional satisfaction is promoted, and positive relationships are developed and sustained."

Community and society. "Our responsibilities to the community are to provide programs that meet the diverse needs of families, to cooperate with agencies and professions that share the responsibility for children, to assist families in gaining access to those agencies and allied professionals, and to assist in the development of community programs that are needed but not currently available."

Each area provides early educators with ideals and principles they can use in decision-making. One principle, P-1.1 (in "Ethical Responsibility to Children," Section 1), presides over all others:

> Above all, we shall not harm children. We shall not participate in practices that are emotionally damaging, physically harmful, disrespectful, degrading, dangerous, exploitative, or intimidating to children.

Much like a physician's Hippocratic oath, this principle is the early childhood field's credo. It guides your teaching practices and how you support children in learning, growing, and thriving.

Teachers and providers can consult the Code for help in making decisions in difficult situations, like one of the ones presented earlier:

> *Two-year-old Austin's dad tells you that he does not want his son wearing any of those "sissy" dress-up clothes anymore. "If Austin grows up to be a homosexual, it will be your fault," his father says.*

While your immediate reaction may be to address the father's veiled threat or to explain your personal views to Austin's parents, neither response is appropriate. Section 1, Principle P-1.3 of the Code states the following:

> We shall not participate in practices that discriminate against children by denying benefits, giving special advantages, or excluding them from programs or activities on the basis of their sex, race, national origin, immigration status, preferred home language, religious beliefs, medical condition, disability, or the marital status/family structure, sexual orientation, or religious beliefs or other affiliations of their families.

According to this principle, it is ethical to treat girls and boys equally. Children of all genders have access to all materials within the setting. Therefore, children can try on whatever clothes they want as they explore male and female roles. Trying on clothing of another gender is very typical behavior for children under five years old and an opportunity for them to learn social skills, rules, and roles.

Section 2, Ideal I-2.6 states, "to acknowledge families' childrearing values and their right to make decisions for their children." Acknowledge Austin's dad's right to hold different values about what his child should be exposed to in your setting.

Principle P-2.2 provides further guidance, "We shall inform families of program philosophy, policies, curriculum, assessment system, cultural practices, and personnel qualifications, and explain why we teach as we do—which should be in accordance with our ethical responsibilities to children."

According to the Code, you might decide that the best course of action is to find a quiet place in the setting to meet informally with Austin's parents and respectfully discuss the setting's philosophy toward pretend dress-up play. Acknowledging their concern, explain why you do what you do and gently reassure Austin's father that there is no relationship between dress-up play and later sexual identity. To reinforce your position, give him copies of research papers to take home and read. Many parents will accept what you have to say when they see there is research and sound reasoning behind the practice.

Another one of the previous situations presents a real dilemma:

> *At a staff meeting your supervisor Tony tells a joke about a particular ethnic group. A few people laugh. Most, like you, look uncomfortable.*

You are offended that Tony is telling a joke that stereotypes an ethnic group. This joke, in your opinion, is racist. However, Tony is the offender. On the one hand, you want to confront him at that moment before the entire group. On the other hand, you fear that a confrontation would get you fired.

One of the core values in the *Code of Ethical Conduct* "Preamble" is "respect diversity in children, families, and colleagues." Your supervisor's joke was disrespectful to that particular ethnic group and to all people who value diversity.

Section 3, Principle P-3A.2 provides sound advice:

> "When we have concerns about the profession- al behavior of a co-worker, we shall first let that person know of our concern in a way that shows respect for personal dignity and for the diversity to be found among staff members, and then attempt to resolve the matter collegially and in a confidential manner."

Perhaps you could make an appointment to speak to Tony privately. During this meeting, tell him in a factual, nonaccusatory way that you were offended by the joke he told at the staff meeting and that it made you uncomfortable. Let him know that you wanted to bring it to his attention, because he may not have been aware of how the joke was received. Communicate your own reaction to the joke, not the reactions of others. Tell your supervisor that you felt that it was important to discuss the situation with him because of the principles outlined in the *Code of Ethical Conduct.*

The *Code of Ethical Conduct* will help alleviate some of the stress involved in making decisions in difficult situations. This does not mean that the situations will be less difficult or that the decisions will be less painful to implement. What it does mean, though, is that your decisions will be ethical and professional. Additional discussions of ethical dilemmas as published in the *Young Children* column Focus on Ethics, appear online at *www.naeyc.org/resources/topics/focus-ethics.*

Articulating Values, Vision, and Passion

The ability to confidently and clearly explain how children learn, what children learn, and your developmentally appropriate teaching practices that support learning will strengthen your family engagement efforts and your outreach and relationships within the community.

Become familiar with the early learning standards that govern your setting. Search the Internet to find the early learning standards for your state. These standards represent the learning outcomes that all children in your setting are expected to achieve. Be prepared to explain how your setting addresses these standards.

Be prepared to articulate additional state and federal laws, like the Individuals with Disabilities Education Act (IDEA) that emphasizes the strengths and abilities of children and their families. Knowing what IDEA requires will help you work with families and explain how you will continue to support them and their child.

Advocating for Change

Advocacy and activism are two important activities for all practicing professionals. Connecting to an issue of importance to you in your work and joining with others through involvement outside the workplace may be the best way to be an advocate or activist. You can't change the world alone, but working with others you can make a difference.

Including Children With Disabilities

The Individuals with Disabilities Education Act (IDEA) is a Federal law that ensures that infants, toddlers, children and youth with disabilities receive the services they need to succeed in school. IDEA governs how states and public agencies provide early intervention, special education, and related services.

IDEA Part C governs the provision of intervention services to Infants and toddlers (ages birth to 2) who have developmental delays or diagnosed physical or mental conditions that are likely to result in delays. Services are also provided to families of the eligible infants and toddlers. The goal of the services is to help children get the assistance they need to be ready for preschool and kindergarten. Every child who receives services under Part C must have an individualized family service plan (an IFSP) developed with by a team with active participation from the child's family.

Older children and youth (ages 3-21) who have a qualifying disability that adversely affects educational progress receive special education and related services under IDEA Part B. The categories of disabilities are; autism, deaf/blind, deafness, hearing impaired, mental retardation, multiple disabilities, orthopedic impairment, serious emotional disturbance, specific learning disabilities, speech or language impairment, traumatic brain injury, visual impairment including blindness, and other health impairment.

Including Children With Disabilities (continued)

Special education services are provided in what is termed, the least restrictive environment—children with disabilities are included in settings along with children who do not have disabilities. Such environments for 3- to 5-year-olds include early childhood centers and family child care homes. Every child who receives services under Part B must have an Individualized Education Program (IEP). Like an IFSP, it is developed by a team with the family included as a valued and important member of the team.

Teachers and providers, in conjunction with specialists and the child's family, implement IFSPs and IEPs. They might use assistive technology, adapt materials and equipment to allow for the child's participation, provide materials for a wide range of abilities, and work one on one with a child on a specific skill or task.

To learn more about IDEA and inclusion, visit the websites of the US Department of Education, *idea.ed.gov*, the Pacer Center *www.pacer.org*, and the Division for Early Childhood, *www.dec-sped.org*.

Explain the following when discussing your setting's best teaching practices with families or others in the community. Be sure to specify the age groups of the children you work with to help others visualize the program in action.

Best Practice	Explanation
The configuration and materials in the learning environment support learning for all children, including children with disabilities.	We display materials on low open shelves so children can choose what they want to use and return items when finished. Loose items, such as Legos®, are stored in clear containers for the same reason. Self-help items—like Kleenex—are also placed within children's reach so they can be independent.
Educators use of scaffolding and other individualized teaching strategies that build on children's current skills while fostering new ones.	Many times we use scaffolding to meet children at their level and offer just enough support to allow them to take themselves to the next level. We often update materials in response to a child's new skills or interests. Modeling is another strategy that helps children learn knowledge and skills.
Children have many opportunities to learn through play.	Play is an effective way to support young children's learning. It enhances their problem-solving abilities, builds social and emotional skills, and fosters creativity. Play includes make believe, building with blocks, playing games, and riding trikes outdoors.
The daily schedule explains what happens each day and in what order.	Word and picture versions of the schedule are posted so children can "master" the events of the day. They feel more secure when they know what comes next and which activities will take place before it is time for their parents to return.

Best Practice	Explanation
Educators encourage dual language learners to retain their home language skills while learning English.	Dual language learners are both gaining language skills in English and their home languages and using both languages to learn other content. Retaining home language skills allows children to communicate with family members in their preferred language.
Community partnerships can support children and families.	Many young children are growing in the context of a home, a child development program, and a community. They can learn and thrive in all three settings.
Positive guidance teaches children how to behave safely and encourages them to regulate their own behavior.	Young children are still learning about which behaviors are safe in society and which ones are not. Over time, with guidance from caring adults, they will learn to share and take turns, express feelings through words, and cope with frustration and disappointments.
Children's activities and accomplishments are assessed on an ongoing basis and at specific points in time.	Teachers and providers observe and take notes, take photographs and make short videos, and save samples of children's work. These items document children's participation and progress. Valid and reliable standardized assessments are used to summarize a child or group's progress over time.
Educators use a variety of methods blogs, websites, e-mails, newsletters, and so on—to exchange information with families about the program's activities and about their own child.	Every family is unique and has a preferred way to receive and exchange information about their child. Teachers and provides use different methods to make sure they reach and engage every family.

Your ability to explain these practices will strengthen you as a spokesperson for the setting and as a valued communicator for families and community programs. This ability places you in a position of responsibility, and designates you as the voice of your setting—and of early childhood education—to your community.

Continuing Your Professional Development

The early childhood education field, like many other professions, does not remain static. New research informs our practice. As the knowledge base grows, the field's thinking around how children learn shifts. For example, there was a time when some early childhood programs depended on scripted lessons and adult-directed activities. Through research, educators learned that child-initiated activities driven by children's interests and discoveries are more likely to support and motivate children's learning. Today, the intentional early educator opts for a balanced approach. Epstein describes it as follows:

> At some times or for some content, children seem to learn best from *child-guided experience*—that is, they acquire knowledge and skills mainly through their own exploration and experience, including interactions with peers. At other times and for other content, children learn best from adult-guided experience—that is, in planned situations in which their teachers introduce information, model skills, and the like. (p.2)

Education trends emerge because research supports them. These trends reflect the research of the time period. While we are confident that our practices today are best, research may lead us in another direction in the future, and the field will need to make accommodations. If you are not aware of new research, you will not be able to shift your teaching practices and provide what children need at that time. The Federally-funded National Institute for Early Education Research (NIEER) provides a robust and current website with research briefs and reports on a number of topics of relevance to early childhood teachers and providers. Visit *www.nieer.org* for more information and to sign up for the NIEER weekly newsletter.

Professional development opportunities help you stay current in the field, continually improve your teaching practices, and work toward being a better early educator. Lilian Katz believes that early educators' needs for professional development will vary as they mature in their jobs and gain confidence working with children. While beginning early educators are in survival mode, they need on-site support and mentoring. After a year or two at the job, though, most early educators are confident and are improving their teaching practices. They benefit from attending conferences, reading journals, taking webinars, listening to podcasts, and meeting with colleagues. In contrast to beginning early educators, seasoned early educators—with at least three years of on-the-job experience—are able to take a step back and look at their job performance in perspective. They crave depth and insight. For them, all of the methods listed above, in addition to journals, conferences, seminars, and continuing education offer the kind of information they need to excel in their careers.

Resource & Referral Agencies

Ninety-nine percent of zip codes in the United States have a local, government-funded Child Care Resource and Referral agency (CCR&R) that serves two primary purposes:

1. To assist parents in finding child care programs in their area that match their needs.
2. To raise the quality of child care by providing professional development opportunities and various resources to local early educators and early childhood professionals.

Search the Internet to find the name of your local CCR&R and learn about all the ways that it can support you and your work.

Early childhood professional development opportunities come in various forms:

- Reading journals, magazines, books, newsletters, blogs, and websites.
- Participating in on-site training and receiving technical assistance.
- Taking self-directed training courses (e.g., webinars).
- Attending meetings, trainings, and conferences offered by local, state, regional, and national or international professional organizations and associations.
- Visiting other settings to observe and talk with other teachers and providers.
- Attending seminars and institutes.
- Enrolling in community college, university, and graduate degree courses/programs.

Some professional development options are designed to address a particular domain, age group, or setting. Being able to connect and talk with other early childhood professionals can be invigorating. Check with your supervisor to see whether your setting recommends specific professional development opportunities and whether financial support for these opportunities is available. If your setting is unable to support you financially, there may be additional funding available from the state or your community.

Connecting With Professional Groups

Each day, most early educators are only in contact with the colleagues at their settings and FCC providers typically work alone. However, there is great value in connecting with the professional groups in your community and networking with others in the early childhood education field. Some professional groups may be local chapters of national organizations. Others are state groups or groups of locally active early educators.

Find out what early childhood education professional groups are active in your area. Contact several of these groups to learn more about their activities and membership. Visit their websites and peruse their newsletters, journals, or other literature. Select one or two organizations, attend a few of their meetings, and join the group if you think that it and the members are a good fit for you. The more active you are in the group—attending meetings and volunteering for committee or board positions—the more you will get out of your membership and the more you can contribute to the field.

See Figure 87a-b for a list of the major groups dedicated to serving early childhood professionals:

Figure 87a. Early Childhood Education Professional Groups

Organization	What It Does/It's Mission
Association for Childhood Education International™ (ACEI) *www.acei.org* 1101 16th St. NW, Ste. 300 Washington, DC 20036 (202) 372-9986 • (800) 423-3563	ACEI's mission to promote child well-being continues to strengthen and evolve with the changing world environment. The organization commits to bridging the gap between global initiatives and local needs.
Child Care Aware® of America (formerly the National Association of Child Care Re-source and Referral Agencies [NACCRRA]) *www.childcareaware.org* 1515 N. Courthouse Rd., 11th Floor Arlington, VA 22201 (800) 424-2246	Child Care Aware® of America works with more than 600 state and local Child Care Resource and Referral agencies nationwide. These agencies help ensure that families in 99% of all populated ZIP codes in the United States have access to high-quality, affordable child care. To achieve its mission, Child Care Aware® leads projects that increase the quality and availability of child care, undertake research, and advocate child care policies that positively impact the lives of children and families.
The Division for Early Childhood (DEC) *www.dec-sped.org* 27 Fort Missoula Rd., Ste. 2 Missoula, MT 59804 (406) 543-0872 3415 S. Sepulveda Blvd. Suite 1100, Unit 1127 Los Angeles, CA 90034 (406) 543-0872 • (310) 428-7209	The Division for Early Childhood promotes policies and advances evidence-based practices that support families and enhance the optimal development of young children who have or are at risk for developmental delays and disabilities.
Military Child Education Coalition (MCEC) *www.militarychild.org* 909 Mountain Lion Circle Harker Heights, TX 76548 (254) 953-1923	The MCEC's work is focused on ensuring quality educational opportunities for all military children affected by mobility, family separation, and transition. The organization performs research, develops resources, conducts professional institutes and conferences, and develops and publishes resources for all constituencies.
National Association for Bilingual Education (NABE) *www.nabe.org* 8701 Georgia Ave., Ste. 700 Silver Spring, MD 20910 (240) 450-3700	NABE's mission is to advocate for the nation's bilingual and English language learners and families and to cultivate a multilingual, multicultural society by supporting and promoting policy, programs, pedagogy, research, and professional development that yield academic success, value native language, lead to English proficiency, and respect cultural and linguistic diversity.
National Association for the Education of Young Children (NAEYC) *www.naeyc.org* 1401 H Street NW, Suite 600 Washington, DC 20005 (202) 232-8777 • (800) 424-2460	NAEYC is the world's largest organization working on behalf of young children. The organization's mission is to serve and act on behalf of the needs, rights, and well-being of all young children with a primary focus on the provision of educational and developmental services and resources.

Figure 87b. Early Childhood Education Professional Groups

Organization	What It Does/It's Mission
National Black Child Development Institute (NBCDI) *nbcdi.org* 8455 Colesville Road, Suite 910 Silver Spring, MD 20910 (202) 833-2220 • (800) 556-2234	Since 1970, the National Black Child Development Institute has remained steadfast in its mission "to improve and advance the quality of life for Black children and their families through education and advocacy." As a membership organization with volunteer-based affiliate networks in over 20 communities across the country, NBCDI serves as a national resource agency providing strengths-based programs, publications, policy, and trainings focused on the following areas: health and wellness, early childhood development and education, elementary and secondary education, literacy, child welfare, and family engagement.
National Head Start Association (NHSA) *www.nhsa.org* 1651 Prince St. Alexandria, VA 22314 (703) 739-0875 • (866) 677-8724	The National Head Start Association is a nonpartisan, not-for-profit organization committed to the belief that every child, regardless of circumstances at birth, has the ability to succeed in life. The organization's mission is to coalesce, inspire, and support the Head Start field as a leader in early childhood development and education. The opportunities offered by Head Start lead to healthier, empowered children and families and stronger, more vibrant communities. NHSA is the voice for more than 1 million children, 200,000 staff, and 1,600 Head Start grantees in the United States.
Southern Early Childhood Association (SECA) *www.southernearlychildhood.org* 1123 S. University Ave., Ste. 255 Little Rock, AR 72204 (501) 221-1648 • (800) 305-7322	Since 1948, the Southern Early Childhood Association has brought together preschool, kindergarten, and primary teachers and administrators; caregivers; program directors; and individuals working with and for families, to promote quality care and education for young children. Over 20,000 individuals working in every aspect of child care and early childhood belong to SECA.
World Organization for Early Childhood Education (OMEP-USA) *www.omep-usnc.org* Southern Illinois University Carbondale, IL 62901 (618) 453-4246	OMEP-USA is one of more than 70 national committees (chapters) in World OMEP, a nonprofit child advocacy organization associated with the United Nations, UNICEF, UNESCO, the World Health Organization, and others working for healthy, peaceful, equitable, sustainable, and just environments for the world's children today and in the future.
ZERO TO THREE: National Center for Infants, Toddlers and Families *www.zerotothree.org* 1255 23rd St. NW, Ste. 350 Washington, DC 20037 (202) 638-1144	ZERO TO THREE is a national, nonprofit membership organization that provides parents, professionals, and policymakers the knowledge needed to nurture early development. The organization's mission is to ensure that all babies and toddlers have a strong start in life.

Approach your professional development with intentionality and reflection. Periodically, analyze your professional development activities and ask: How are these activities useful to me and the job that I perform? In what ways is my teaching improving? Am I achieving my professional development goals? What other areas do I want to explore? What do I find challenging in my professional practice?

Depending on your answers to these questions, consider making some changes to your professional development plan. Reconsider the groups you have joined and your level of involvement, and ask your colleagues, supervisor, and mentor for advice.

Get Involved at the Local Level

NAEYC is a national organization with local affiliates across the country. Members receive services and resources from both the national office and from the affiliate. One way to get to know other early childhood teachers and providers in your area is to get involved at the affiliate level. You do this by attending meetings, taking part in discussions, volunteering to help plan upcoming events, and perhaps agreeing to run for office. Some affiliates publish newsletters and journals; others have large conferences; and all would want to have you as an active member.

Remember that part of your role as an early childhood professional is to also assume roles that reflect leadership and active membership in a collegial community. Continual learning, professional development, and engagement will prove to be quite valuable over time.

While you may not choose to move into a full leadership role, you still are "leading" and guiding a group of children, families, colleagues and others. Your title may not reflect everything you do, but your active role in the program will benefit everyone.

The following ideas—referred to as "Essential Conditions"—are aspects of leadership and a part of your responsibilities that create a more productive and meaningful workplace.

Essential Conditions

- **Quality of life (meeting the needs of ALL individuals and creating a supportive environment)**

  Make sure you are aware of and get to know each individual child, immediate family member and staff member with whom you work closely. Knowing and interacting with others promotes a more cohesive understanding of expectations, needs and goals. Getting to know others helps you appreciate who they are, so you can intervene in appropriate and respectful ways.

- **Compelling mission**

  Know what, where, how, when and more about your program's ideals and goals. What is it that you are trying to accomplish in the community and with the children? How is your personal involvement important in making things happen?

- **A balance between task and maintenance activities**

  All of us feel overextended between work and life outside our job. Get to know your colleagues, their work style, and what they enjoy doing, their gifts, talents, and likes. Figure out ways of coordinating who does what and what can get done so that no person feels overwhelmed or underappreciated and can be successful. Sharing tasks and obligations that are easier or less troublesome for each person will create a more enjoyable and successful workplace.

- **Open, honest, reciprocal communication**

  Communication is critical in relationships and workplace environments. Having a great working relationship allows for honesty and openness that will benefit workers, children and the learning community.

- **Culture that is cooperative and conducive to collaboration**

  Working together seems to be a natural part of any workplace. But a successful workplace culture will not exist unless coworkers make an effort to understand each other, cooperate, collaborate and foster a meaningful understanding of what is necessary to reach mutual goals.

- **Interdependence (we are all in this together!)**

  Understand that no one person has all the answers, all the expertise, all the skills, or all the ideas. Each individual has something valuable to contribute.

- **Accountability that requires all staff members to work on achieving the mission**

  Accountability, like cooperation and collaboration, plays a significant role in the success of any program. Each and every member of the staff should know how vital, important and needed they are to making a program successful. Maintaining a level of professionalism that reflects the combined efforts of everyone will promote recognition and success.

- **Mutual respect, trust, and trustworthy school environment**

  Recognizing that each individual in the workplace has a role to play in the program's success involves being respectful of differences, trusting that all persons will be professional and strive to do their best, and knowing that the mission and goals are achievable and ideal.

- **Time, resources, and structures that support and facilitate collaboration**

  Being a change agent is sometimes difficult and not always seen as necessary. However, being actively involved in a program, and offering ideas on how to make things better for everyone, is never a bad idea. Are there more time-efficient ways of accomplishing a task? Where can resources be accessed that do not significantly elevate costs? Are there enough resources? Who can be a resource? What are the roadblocks to adequately meeting or exceedingly goals and objectives? How might roadblocks be approached in order to truly meet mission and vision goals? Does everyone involved with or part of a learning community feel wanted, needed, appreciated, understood, and welcome to participate?

Advocating for Children and Families

The early childhood education field needs professionals like you to join the ranks of advocates who rally societal support for young children, their families, and their early educators. Much work is needed to help society understand the benefits and value of early childhood education—and those who teach young children.

Being an early childhood education advocate means that you continually educate the public about the early childhood field—much in the same way that you educate them about your setting—and work with groups to influence legislation in support of the field. These groups often have the staff, resources, and experience to help you advance the cause more effectively. Organizations like NAEYC and the Ounce of Prevention Fund (*www.ounceofprevention.org*), a Chicago-based group that funds and advocates for nationwide access to high-quality early childhood programs, offer toolkits that help you frame your message, target elected officials, and work with the media. These organizations supply you with fact sheets and data to help you present your position to your intended audience. You can subscribe to NAEYC's Children's Champions, to receive regular updates and action alerts on important issues being addressed by Congress and the Administration (*www.naeyc.org/policy/federal/updates*).

Many of the organizations listed in Figure 87a-b include advocacy as one of their services. Figure 88a-b lists some of the other leading organizations that advocate for children and families.

Figure 88a. Advocacy Organizations

Organization	What It Does/It's Mission
Alliance for Justice (AFJ) *www.afj.org* 11 Dupont Circle NW, 2nd Floor Washington, DC 20036 (202) 822-6070	Alliance for Justice is a national association of over 100 organizations, representing a broad array of groups committed to progressive values and the creation of an equitable, just, and free society. AFJ works to ensure that the federal judiciary advances core constitutional values, preserves human rights and unfettered access to the courts, and adheres to the even-handed administration of justice for all Americans.
Alliance for Early Success (formerly the Birth to Five Policy Alliance) *www.earlysuccess.org* PO Box 6756 Leawood, KS 66206 (913) 642-3490	The Alliance for Early Success (formerly the Birth to Five Policy Alliance) is a catalyst for putting vulnerable young children on a path to success. As an alliance of state, national, and funding partners, the organization's goal is to advance state policies that lead to improved health, learning, and economic outcomes for young children, starting at birth and continuing through age 8.
Center on the Developing Child at Harvard University *developingchild.harvard.edu* 50 Church St., 4th Floor Cambridge, MA 02138 (617) 496-0578	The Harvard Center stimulates demand for science-based innovation by communicating-the-science, translating and communicating complex ideas in simple, usable ways and in a variety of forms; develops current and future leaders in the classroom and in the field, supporting them to think, work, and lead differently; cultivates institutional partners for collective ownership by building and sustaining mutually beneficial relationships with fellow travelers who are committed to achieving breakthrough outcomes for children.
Children's Defense Fund (CDF) *www.childrensdefense.org* CDF National Office 840 First Street NE, Suite 300 Washington, DC 20002 (202) 628-8787 (800) 233-1200	The Children's Defense Fund is a nonprofit child advocacy organization that has worked for 40 years to ensure a level playing field for all children. The organization champions policies and programs that lift children out of poverty; protect them from abuse and neglect; and ensure their access to health care, quality education, and a moral and spiritual foundation.
Council for Exceptional Children (CEC) *www.cec.sped.org* 2900 Crystal Dr., Ste. 1000 Arlington, VA 22202 (888) 232-7733	The Council for Exceptional Children is the largest international professional organization dedicated to improving the educational success of individuals with disabilities and/or gifts and talents. CEC advocates for appropriate governmental policies, sets professional standards, provides professional development, advocates for individuals with exceptionalities, and helps professionals obtain conditions and resources necessary for effective professional practice.

Figure 88b. Advocacy Organizations

Organization	What It Does/It's Mission
First Five Years Fund *www.ffyf.org* 33 W. Monroe St., Ste. 2400 Chicago, IL 60603 (312) 453-1835	The First Five Years Fund helps America achieve better results in education, health, and economic productivity through investments in quality early childhood education for disadvantaged children from birth to age 5. The organization provides knowledge, data, and advocacy, helping federal policymakers make investments in the first 5 years of a child's life that create greater returns for all.
National Center for Children in Poverty (NCCP) *www.nccp.org* 215 W. 125th St., 3rd floor New York, NY 10027 (646) 284-9600	Founded in 1989 as a division of the Mailman School of Public Health at Columbia University, NCCP is a nonpartisan, public interest research organization. The organization is one of the nation's leading public policy centers dedicated to promoting the economic security, health, and well-being of America's low-income families and children. NCCP uses research to inform policy and practice with the goal of ensuring positive outcomes for the next generation.
National Council of La Raza (NCLR) *www.nclr.org* Raul Yzaguirre Building 1126 16th St. NW, Ste. 600 Washington, DC 20036 (202) 785-1670	The National Council of La Raza—the largest national Hispanic civil rights and advocacy organization in the United States—works to improve opportunities for Hispanic Americans. Through its network of nearly 300 affiliated community-based organizations, NCLR reaches millions of His-panics each year in 41 states, Puerto Rico, and the District of Columbia. To achieve its mission, NCLR conducts applied research, policy analysis, and advocacy, providing a Latino perspective in five key areas: as-sets/investments, civil rights/immigration, education, employment and economic status, and health.
National Women's Law Center *www.nwlc.org* 11 Dupont Circle NW, #800 Washington, DC 20036 (202) 588-5180	Since 1972, the National Women's Law Center has expanded the possibilities for women and girls in the United States. The organization has succeeded in getting new laws on the books and enforced, litigating groundbreaking cases all the way to the Supreme Court, and educating the public about ways to make laws and public policies work for women and their families. Today, an experienced staff of nearly 60 continues to advance the issues that cut to the core of women's lives in education, employment, family and economic security, and health and reproductive rights—with special attention given to the needs of low-income women and their families.
Voices for America's Children *www.voices.org* 1000 Vermont Ave. NW, Ste. 700 Washington, DC 20005 (202) 289-0777	Voices for America's Children is the nation's largest network of multi-issue child advocacy organizations. The organization's nonprofit, non-partisan network spans almost every state, the District of Columbia, and the U.S. Virgin Islands. It leads advocacy efforts at the community, state, and federal levels to improve the lives of all children, especially those most vulnerable, and their families.

Figure 89. Ways to Advocate for Children

- Be the spokesperson for your setting. As an early childhood education professional, you should be able to communicate your program's story—its philosophy and research-based practices. Because you already represent your setting to families and community organizations, you are well-equipped to explain the importance of high-quality early childhood education to funders and policymakers.
- Team up with your colleagues to form your own advocacy group.
- Join forces with school boards and other local organizations.
- Promote and help plan local events for NAEYC's Week of the Young Child™ (*www.naeyc.org/woyc*). This annual event is designed to focus public attention on the needs of young children and their families and to recognize the early childhood programs and services that meet those needs.
- Vote in local, state, and national elections for candidates who support children and families.
- Attend town meetings and ensure that early childhood issues get on the agendas.
- Introduce the families you serve to advocacy opportunities.
- Start or join letter writing campaigns to urge all elected officials to support stronger and better child care legislation.
- Express your point of view by writing letters to the editor or op-eds (feature articles usually opposite the editorial page) for publication in magazines, journals, and newspapers.
- Start a blog about your work in the field. Include photos of children playing and learning. Remember to get prior written permission from parents to use their children's photos in this way.
- Invite policymakers to visit your program. Plan ahead to maximize the benefits of the visit.
- Hold an open house where visitors can visit your setting and witness developmentally appropriate practices in action.
- Identify a specific children's issue for which to advocate (e.g., obtaining more services for children with disabilities or children whose families are homeless, saving a well-used park, or increasing salaries for child care staff).

Identify the many opportunities around you to become a champion for early childhood education. You could lead efforts, like those listed in Figure 89 or work behind-the-scenes writing brochures or grant proposals, gathering data for policy papers or surveys, or developing advocacy videos. See where your talents and passions lead you, and find a way to show your support for children and families. Young children need **you**. Families need **you**. The profession needs **you**.

You are the ideal advocate because you have completed this textbook and are putting the concepts you learned into practice.

References

Chapter 1 Safe

A Joint Collaborative Project of the American Academy of Pediatrics, American Public Health Association, National Resource Center for Health and Safety in Child Care and Early Education, with support provided by the Maternal and Child Health Bureau. (2011).*Caring for Our Children: National Health and Safety Performance Standards Guidelines for Early Care and Education Programs*. Third Edition.

Administration for Children and Families. U.S. Department of Health and Human Services. (June 25, 2015). *Caring for Our Children Basics: Health and Safety Foundations for Early Care and Education.* http://www.acf.hhs.gov/sites/default/files/ecd/caring_for_our_children_basics.pdf.

American Academy of Child and Adolescent Psychiatry. (2012). Lead exposure in children affects brains and behavior. Retrieved from http://www.aacap.org/App_Themes/AACAP/docs/facts_for_families/45_lead_exposure_in_children_affects_brain_and_behavior.pdf

American Academy of Pediatrics. Healthychildren.org. (April 2012). *A Child Care Provider's Guide to Safe Sleep*. https://www.healthychildren.org/English/family-life/work-play/Pages/A-Child-Care-Provider's-Guide-to-Safe-Sleep.aspx

American Academy of Pediatrics, American Public Health Association, National Resource Center for Health and Safety in Child Care and Early Education. *Caring for Our Children: National Health and Safety Performance Standards; Guidelines for Early Care and Education Programs*. 4th ed. Itasca, IL: American Academy of Pediatrics; 2019.

Centers for Disease Control and prevention (CDC). (September 14, 2015). *Child Passenger Safety: Get the Facts*. http://www.cdc.gov/motorvehiclesafety/child_passenger_safety/cps-factsheet.html

Centers for Disease Control and Prevention (CDC). (June 20, 2014). *Preventing Carbon Monoxide Poisoning after an Emergency.* https://www.cdc.gov/disasters/cofacts.html

Centers for Disease Control and Prevention (CDC). (April 12, 2012). *Protect the Ones You Love: Child Injuries are Preventable.* http://www.cdc.gov/safechild/poisoning/index.html?s_cid

Centers for Disease Control and Prevention (CDC). (July 2, 2013). *Protect the Ones You Love: Child Injuries are Preventable.* http://www.cdc.gov/safechild/NAP/overviews/suffocation.html

Federal Emergency Management Agency (FEMA). (November 2011). *Sample Childcare Evacuation Plan*. https://emilms.fema.gov/is36/assets/EAP_Sample.pdf

Greer, D. (September 2, 2011). *What Does It Mean To Be Safe? A Teacher's View*. http://www.littlepicklepress.com/what-does-it-mean-to-be-safe-a-teachers-view/

Johns Hopkins Children's Center. (March 22, 2010). *A Dangerously Tasty Treat: The Hot Dog is a Choking Hazard*. http://www.hopkinschildrens.org/A-Dangerously-Tasty-Treat-The-Hot-Dog-is-a-Choking-Hazard.aspx

Koralek, D. Dodge, D. & Pizzolongo, P. (2004). *Caring for Preschool Children*. Third Edition. Washington, DC; Teaching Strategies, Inc.

National Highway Traffic Safety Administration (NHTSA). (May 2006). *Seat Belts on School Busses*. http://www.nhtsa.gov/Vehicle+Safety/Seat+Belts/Seat+Belts+on+School+Buses+--+May+2006

National Safe Kids Campaign. (2004). Drowning fact sheet. Retrieved from http://www.preventinjury.org/PDFs/DROWNING.pdf

Savage, M. A., Kawanabe, I. T., Mejeur, J., Goehring, J. B., & Reed, J. B. (2002). *Protecting children: A guide to child traffic safety laws*. Retrieved from National Highway Traffic Safety Administration website: http://www.nhtsa.gov/staticfiles/nti/enforcement/pdf/ProtectingChildren.pdf

South Carolina Child Care Services. (April 2013). *Emergency Plan Guidelines for Child Care Providers*.

State of New York Department of Health. (July 2009). What child care providers need to know about lead. Retrieved from http://www.health.ny.gov/publications/2517.pdf

University of Nebraska Cooperative Extension. (n.d.). Toxicity of common houseplants. Retrieved from http://lancaster.unl.edu/factsheets/031.htm

U.S. Department of Agriculture (USDA). *Basics for Handling Food Safely.* March 24, 2015, http://www.fsis.usda.gov/wps/portal/fsis/topics/food-safety-education/get-answers/food-safety-fact-sheets/safe-food-handling/basics-for-handling-food-safely/ct_index

U.S. Fire Administration. (2003). A fact sheet on fire safety for babies and toddlers. Retrieved from http://www.usfa.fema.gov/campaigns/usfaparents/downloads/508/USFA_FireFacts_508.pdf

Chapter 2 Healthy

American Academy of Pediatrics. (2009). *Caring for your baby and young child: Birth to age 5.* (5th ed.). New York, NY: Bantam Books.

American Academy of Pediatrics, American Public Health Association, & National Resource Center for Health and Safety in Child Care and Early Education. (2011). *Caring for our children: National health and safety performance standards—Guidelines for early care and education programs* (3rd ed.). Elk Grove Village, IL: American Academy of Pediatrics.

Aronson, S. S. (2012). *Healthy Young Children: A Manual for Programs*, 5th ed. Washington, DC: National Association for the Education of Young Children. P. 122.

Centers for Disease Control and Prevention (CDC). (2010). *Proper handling and storage of human milk.* Retrieved from http://www.cdc.gov/breastfeeding/recommendations/handling_breastmilk.htm

Centers for Disease Control and Prevention (CDC). (August 28, 2015). *Vaccines Do Not Cause Autism.* http://www.cdc.gov/vaccinesafety/concerns/autism.html

Colker, L. J. (2005). *The Cooking Book: Fostering Young Children's Learning and Delight.* Washington, DC: National Association for the Education of Young Children.

Colker, L. J. (2009). *Sure start program guide.* Arlington, VA: Department of Defense Education Activity.

Dixon, S., & Rosas, A. (n.d.). *Just a spoonful of sugar: Tips for giving medicine to kids.* Retrieved from http://www.pampers.com/just-a-spoonful-of-sugar-tips-for-giving-medicine-to-kids

Head Start. *Essential Principles for Care.* (February 23, 2015). http://eclkc.ohs.acf.hhs.gov/hslc/tta-system/health/physical-health/education-activities/health_lea_00224_070605.html

Hviid, A., Hansen, J.V., Frisch, M., & Melbye, M. (April 2019). "Measles, mumps, rubella vaccination and autism: A nationwide cohort study." *Annals of Internal Medicine* 170 (8): 513-520.

Karageorge, K., & Kendall, R. (2008). *The role of professional child care providers in preventing and responding to child abuse and neglect.* Washington, DC: Office on Child Abuse and Neglect, Children's Bureau.

National Association for the Education of Young Children. (2011). *Code of ethical conduct and statement of commitment.* Washington, DC: Author

National Resource Center for Health and Safety in Child Care and Early Education. (2013). *Important Information About New Bleach Concentration.* http://cfoc.nrckids.org/bleach/bleach.cfm

The Nemours Foundation. (2012). *Breast or bottle?.* Retrieved from http://kidshealth.org/parent/pregnancy_newborn/formulafeed/breast_bottle_feeding.html#

Santos, A. (2010). New Massachusetts regulation requires tooth brushing in child care settings. Retrieved from http://www.examiner.com/working-moms-in-boston/new-massachusetts-regulation-requires-tooth-brushing-child-care-settings

Thelan, P. & E. A. Cameron. (2012). *Food Allergy Concerns in Primary Classrooms: Keeping Children Safe.* Young Children 67 (4): 106-112.

University of Michigan Health System. (2012). Children with chronic conditions. Retrieved from http://www.med.umich.edu/yourchild/topics/chronic.htm

U.S. Department of Agriculture, & U.S. Department of Health and Human Services. (2010). *Dietary guidelines for Americans, 2010* (7th ed.). Washington, DC: U.S. Government Printing Office. Retrieved from http://health.gov/dietaryguidelines/dga2010/DietaryGuidelines2010.pdf

Zero to Three. (2010). *Potty Training: Learning to the Use the Toilet.* https://www.zerotothree.org/resources/266-potty-training-learning-to-the-use-the-toilet

Chapter 3 Learning Environment

Colker, L. J. (2009). *Sure Start program guide.* Arlington, VA: Department of Defense Education Activity.

Copple, C., & Bredekamp, S. (Eds.). (2009). *Developmentally appropriate practice in early childhood programs serving children from birth through age 8* (3rd ed.). Washington, DC: The National Association for the Education of Young Children.

Early Head Start National Resource Center (Technical Assistance Paper 14). Supporting Outdoor Play and Exploration for Infants and Toddlers. Washington, DC: 2013.

Derman-Sparks, L., & Edwards, J. O. (2010). *Anti-bias education for young children and ourselves.* Washington, DC: The National Association for the Education of Young Children.

Dodge, D. T., Colker, L. J., & Heroman, C. (2002). *The creative curriculum for preschool* (4th ed.). Washington, DC: Teaching Strategies.

Early Head Start National Resource Center. (2010). *Create an environment of YES!* Retrieved from http://eclkc.ohs.acf.hhs.gov/hslc/tta-system/ehsnrc/Early%20Head%20Start/early-learning/curriculum/environment_nycu.htm#CreateanEnvironmentofYES

National Infant & Toddler Child Care Initiative. (2010). *Infant/toddler curriculum and individualization.* Retrieved from ZERO TO THREE: National Center for Infants, Toddlers and Families website: http://www.zerotothree.org/public-policy/state-community-policy/nitcci/multidisciplinary-consultant-module-3.pdf

Nemeth, K.N. & Erdosi, V. (September 2012). *Enhancing practice with infants and toddlers from diverse language and cultural backgrounds.* Young Children, 49-57.

Nemeth, K. N. (2012). *Basics of supporting dual language learners: An introduction for educators of children from birth through age 8.* Washington, DC: National Association for the Education of Young Children.

Owocki, G. (1999). *Literacy through play.* Portsmouth, NH: Heinemann.

Torelli, L. & Durrett, C. (n.d.). *Landscape for learning: The impact of classroom design on infants and toddlers.* http://www.spacesforchildren.com/articles/landc2.pdf

Chapter 4 Physical

American Academy of Pediatrics. (2013). Ages & stages: Baby 0–12 mos. Retrieved from http://www.healthychildren.org/english/ages-stages/baby/Pages/default.aspx

Benelli, C., & Yongue, B. (2004). *Supporting young children's motor skill development.* Farmington Hills, MI: The Gale Group.

Bredekamp, S. (2013). *Effective practices in early childhood education: Building a foundation* (2nd ed.). Boston, MA: Pearson.

Carollo, R.(January 3, 2012). Physical Activity May Help Kids' Grades, Too. http://abcnews.go.com/Health/physical-activity-linked-academic-performance/story?id=15273908

Connell, G. & McCarthy, C. (2014). *A moving child is a learning child: How the body teaches the brain to think.* Minneapolis, MN: Free Spirit Publishing Inc.

Gallahue, D. L., Ozmun, J. C., & Goodway, J. D. (2011). *Understanding motor development: Infants, children, adolescents, adults.* (7th ed.). Dubuque, IA: McGraw-Hill.

Gavin, M. (August 2015). Kids and Exercise. http://kidshealth.org/parent/nutrition_center/staying_fit/exercise.html

Gould, P., & Sullivan, J. (2004). *The inclusive early childhood classroom: Easy ways to adapt learning centers for all children.* Beltsville, MD: Gryphon House.

Herr, J. (2012). Working with Young Children, 7th Edition. Tinley Park, IL: Goodheart-Willcox.

Huffman, M., & Fortenberry, C. (2011). Helping preschoolers prepare for writing: Developing fine motor skills. *Young Children, 66* (5), 100–103.

Jaslow, R. (2013). CDC: 80 Percent of American Adults Don't Get Recommended Exercise. CBS News. http://www.cbsnews.com/news/cdc-80-percent-of-american-adults-dont-get-recommended-exercise/

National Association for Sport and Physical Education. (2004). *Active start: A statement of physical activity guidelines for children from birth to age 5* (2nd ed.). Reston, VA: Author.

Port, D. R. (2015). *Do Babies Need to Crawl? Parenting. Meredith Corporation*. Retrieved from http://www.parenting.com/article/do-babies-need-to-crawl

Shelov, S., Editor-in-Chief. (2014). *Caring for your Baby and Young Child. Birth to Age 5.* 6th Edition. New York: American Academy of Pediatrics.

Siegel, D. J. (2015). *The developing mind: How relationships and the brain interact to shape who we are.* New York: Guilford Press.

Teacher Support Force. (2011). *Brain exercises and physical coordination are benefits of physical education.* Robbinsville, NC: Author. Retrieved from http://www.teacher-support-force.com/brainexercises.html

U.S. Department of Health & Human Services, Administration for Children & Families, Office of Head Start, and Early Head Start National Resource Center. *Children with Special Needs* (Infographic). (2015). English. https://eclkc.ohs.acf.hhs.gov/hslc/tta-system/ehsnrc/comp/children-with-disabilities/infographic.html

Chapter 5 Cognitive

Administration for Children & Families. Office of Head Start. (2015). *Head Start Early Learning Outcomes Framework.* Birth to Five. Washington, DC. https://eclkc.ohs.acf.hhs.gov/hslc/hs/sr/approach/pdf/ohs-framework.pdf

Berk, L.E. (2012). *Child Development.* 9th Edition. Upper Saddle River, NJ: Pearson.

Bodrova, E., Germeroth, C., & Leong. D.J. (Fall 2013). *Play and Self-Regulation: Lessons from Vygotsky.* American Journal of Play, Vol.6, No.1, pp.111-123.

Bredekamp, S. (2011). *Effective practices in early childhood education: Building a foundation.* Boston, MA: Pearson.

Bronfenbrenner, U. (1994). Ecological models of human development. *International Encyclopedia of Education, 3* (2), 1643-1647.

Buckleitner, W. (n.d.). *What Should a Preschooler Know About Technology?* Scholastic. Early Childhood Today. http://www.scholastic.com/teachers/article/what-should-preschooler-know-about-technology

Center for the Child. Harvard University. (2015). *Key Concepts: Executive Function & Self-Control.* http://developingchild.harvard.edu/science/key-concepts/executive-function/

Daily Montessori. (2015). *Montessori Theory.* http://www.dailymontessori.com/montessori-theory/

Gardner, H. (October 16, 2013). *Multiple Intelligences' Are Not Learning Styles.* The Washington Post.

Gopnik, A. (August 15, 2009). *Your Baby Is Smarter than You Think.* New York Times. Op-Ed.

Gopnik, A. (July 2010). *How Babies Think. Scientific American.* www.ScientificAmerican.com.

Gordon, A.M. & Browne, K.W. (2016). *Beginnings & Beyond: Foundations in Early Childhood Education.* 10th Edition. Belmont, CA: Wadsworth Publishers.

Gordon, A. M., & Williams-Browne, K. (2013). *Beginnings & Beyond: Foundations in Early Childhood Education.* 9th Edition. Independence, KY: Cengage Advantage Books.

Gould, P., & Sullivan, J. (2004). *The inclusive early childhood classroom: Easy ways to adapt learning centers for all children.* Beltsville, MD: Gryphon House.

Greenberg, J. (May 2012). Rocking & Rolling. More. All Gone. Empty, Full. Math Talk Every Day in Every Way. Young Children. Washington, DC: NAEYC.

International Society for Technology in Education. (2012). http://www.iste.org/standards

Learning Disabilities Association of America. (1999). *Early Identification—Cognitive Milestones*. http://www.ldonline.org/article/6042/

NYU. (2015). *Focusing on Executive Functions in Kindergarten Leads to Lasting Academic Improvements, Finds Research by Clancy Blair and C. Cybele Raver*. http://steinhardt.nyu.edu/site/ataglance/2014/12/tools-of-the-mind-blair-raver.html

Pappas, S. (October 21, 2013). *Math Ability Starts in Infancy, Study Suggests*. LiveScience. http://www.livescience.com/40576-infant-math-ability.html

Pica, R. (2015). *Memo to the Early Childhood Education Community*. In Bohart, H. Charner, K. & Koralek, D. (Eds.) Spotlight on Young Children. Exploring Play. Washington, DC: NAEYC.

Royal Children's Education Institute. (2011). *How Your Child Learns: The Baby to Preschool Years*. Raisingchildren.net.au. http://raisingchildren.net.au/articles/learning_birth_to_preschool.html

Schickedanz, J.A. & Collins, M.F. (2013). *So much More than ABCs*. Washington, DC: NAEYC.

Schiller, P. (2010). *Early Brain Development Research Review and Update*. Exchange, 26–30.

Shonkoff, J. (October 2005). Speech at OSEP Conference. Washington, DC.

Shonkoff, J. P., & Phillips, D. A. (Eds.). (2000). *From neurons to neighborhoods: The science of early childhood development*. Washington, DC: The National Academies Press.

Siskin Children's Institute. (n.d.). *The Facts about Cognitive Impairment*. http://www.siskin.org/downloads/FactsonCognitiveImpairment.pdf

Spiegel, A. (February 21, 2008). *Old-Fashioned Play Builds Serious Skills*. NPR. http://www.npr.org/templates/story/story.php?storyId=19212514

Stern, D. N. (2002). *The first relationship: Infant and mother*. Cambridge, MA: Harvard University Press.

Strauss, V. (October 16, 2013). Howard Gardner: *'Multiple intelligences' are not 'learning styles'*. The Washington Post. https://www.washingtonpost.com/news/answer-sheet/wp/2013/10/16/howard-gardner-multiple-intelligences-are-not-learning-styles/?utm_term=.95d0b63b3b0f

Sylwester, R. (2003). *A biological brain in a cultural classroom: Enhancing cognitive and social development through collaborative classroom management*. (2nd ed.). Thousand Oaks, CA: Corwin Press.

Tomlinson, H. B., & Hyson, M. (2012). Cognitive development in the preschool years. In C. Copple (Ed.), *Growing minds: Building strong cognitive foundations in early childhood* (pp. 13–23). Washington, DC: National Association for the Education of Young Children.

Waite-Stupiansky, S. (2015). *Memo to Funders of Early Childhood Programs*. In Bohart, H. Charner, K. & Koralek, D. (Eds.) Spotlight on Young Children. Exploring Play. Washington, DC: NAEYC.

Wardhana, G. (September 29, 2015). *Executive Function—The Foundation for School Success*. Scientific Learning.

Wiseman, L. (February 2006). *The Culture-Cognition Connection*. Monitor. American Psychological Association, Vol. 37, No. 2, page 64.

Virginia Early Childhood Development Alignment Project. (2008). *Milestones of Child Development. A Guide to Young Children's Learning and Development from Birth to Kindergarten*. https://www.dss.virginia.gov/files/division/cc/provider_training_development/intro_page/publications/milestones/milestones_one_document/Milestones_Revised.pdf

Zero to Three. (2012a). *Birth to 6 Months. Babies Use their Bodies and Senses to Play*. http://main.zerotothree.org/site/DocServer/stages_of_play_-_birth_to_six_months_-_6-15.pdf?docID=13865

Zero to Three. (2012b). *Stages of Play: 6-12 Months. Babies Discover Connections*. http://main.zerotothree.org/site/DocServer/stages_of_play_-_6_to_12_months_-_6-15.pdf?docID=13862

Zero to Three (2012c). *Stages of Play: 12-24 Months. Young Toddlers Solve Problems.* http://main.zerotothree.org/site/DocServer/stages_of_play_-_12_to_24_months-6-15.pdf?docID=13863

Chapter 6 Communication

Anderson, R. C. (1985). *Becoming a nation of readers: The report of the national commission.* Champaign-Urbana, IL: University of Illinois.

Birner, B. (n.d.). Language acquisition. Retrieved from http://lsadc.org/info/ling-faqs-lang_acq.cfm

Braunger, J., & Lewis, J. P. (2006). *Building a knowledge base in reading* (2nd ed.). Newark, DE: International Reading Association.

California Department of Education. (2000). *Prekindergarten leaning development guidelines.* Sacramento, CA: Author.

Colker, L. J. (2010a). America's early childhood literacy crisis. *Teaching Young Children, 3* (4), 27–29.

Colker, L. J. (2010b). Getting a grip on things: Building fine motor skills. *Teaching Young Children, 3* (5), 26–28.

Collier, V. (1987). "Age and Rate of Acquisition of Second Language for Academic Purposes." *TESOL Quarterly* 21 (4): 617-641.

Dickinson, D. K., & Tabors, P. O. (Eds.). (2001). *Beginning literacy with language: Young children learning at home and school.* Baltimore, MD: Brookes.

Dodici, B. J., Draper, D. C., & Peterson, C. A. (2003). Early parent–child interactions and early literacy development. *Topics in Early Childhood Special Education, 23* (3), 124–136.

Edwards, C., Gandini, L., & Forman, G. (eds.). (2011). *The hundred languages of children: The Reggio Emilia experience in transformation.* (3rd ed.). Santa Barbara, CA: Praeger.

Espinosa, L. M. (2010). *Getting it right for young children from diverse backgrounds: Applying research for improved practice.* Upper Saddle River, NJ: Pearson.

Fox, M. (2008). *Reading magic: Why reading aloud to our children will change their lives forever.* New York, NY: Mariner Books.

Gilkerson, G., & J. A. Richards. (2009). *The Power of Talk: Impact of Adult Talk, Conversational Turns, and TV During the Critical 0-4 Years of Child Development.* Boulder: The LENA Foundation. http://www.lenafoundation.org/wp-content/uploads/2014/10/LTR-01-2_PowerOfTalk.pdf

Goldenberg, C. (2008). Teaching English language learners: What the research does—and does not—say. *American Educator, 32* (2), 8–23, 42–44.

Hart, B., & Risley, T. R. (2003). The early catastrophe: The 30 million word gap by age 3. *American Educator, 27* (1), 4-9.

Heroman, C., Dodge, D., Berke, K., Bickart, T. and Colker, L. (2010). *The Creative Curriculum for Preschool: Objectives for Developing and Learning.* Bethesda, MD: Teaching Strategies.

The Economist. (2006, December 19). The art of conversation: Chattering classes: The rules for verbal exchanges are surprisingly enduring. *The Economist.* Retrieved from http://www.economist.com/node/8345491

Morrow, L. M., & Gambrell, L. B. (2002). Literature-based instruction in the early years. In S. B. Neuman &. D. K. Dickinson (Eds.), *Handbook of early literacy research* (pp. 348–360). New York, NY: The Guilford Press.

National Early Literacy Panel (NELP). (2008). *Developing EARLY LITERACY: Report of the National Early Literacy Panel. A scientific synthesis of early literacy development and implications for intervention.* Washington, DC: Author.

Nemeth, K. N. (2012). *Basics of supporting dual language learners: An introduction for educators of children from birth through age 8.* Washington, DC: National Association for the Education of Young Children.

Reading Is Fundamental (RIF). (n.d.). *Choosing good books for young children.* Retrieved from http://rif.org/us/literacy-resources/articles/choosing-books-for-young-children.htm

Severns, M. (2010). Dual language learners: What early educators need to know [Blog post]. Retrieved from: http://earlyed.newamerica.net/blogposts/2010/dual_language_learners_what_early_educators_need_to_know-28196

Strickland, D., & Riley-Ayers, S. (2006). *Early literacy: Policy and practice in the preschool years.* New Brunswick, NJ: National Institute for Early Education Research at Rutgers University.

Tabors, P. O. (2008). *One child, two languages: A guide for early childhood educators of children learning English as a second language* (2nd ed.). Baltimore, MD: Brookes.

Tabors, P. O., Beals, D. E., & Weizman, Z. O. (2001). You know what oxygen is? Learning new words at home. In D.K. Dickinson & P.O. Tabors (Eds.), *Beginning literacy with language: Young children learning at home and school.* Baltimore, MD: Brookes.

Weikle, B., & Hadadian, A. (2003). Emergent literacy practices among parents of preschool children with and without disabilities. *International Journal of Special Education, 18* (1), 80–99.

Yopp, H. K., & Yopp, R. H. (2009). *Phonological Awareness is Child's Play!* Young Children 64 (1): 12-21.

Zangl, R. (2013). *Raising a talker.* Lewisville, NC: Gryphon House, Inc.

Chapter 7 Creative

Colker, L.J. (2009). *The Cooking Book. Fostering Young Children's Learning and Delight.* Washington, DC: NAEYC.

Colker, L.J. (n.d.) *Child Development Tracker.* Creative Arts. http://www.pbs.org/parents/childdevelopmenttracker/one/creativearts.html

Hadani, H. (2015). *Inspiring a Generation to Create: Critical Components of Creativity in Children.* Sausalito, CA: Center for Childhood Creativity.

Isenberg, J. P., & Jalongo, M. R.. (2010). *Creative thinking and arts-based learning: Preschool through fourth grade* (5th ed.) Upper Saddle River, NJ: Merrill.

Kuszewski, A. (July 7, 2011). *The Educational Value of Creative Disobedience.* Scientific American. Blog. http://blogs.scientificamerican.com/guest-blog/the-educational-value-of-creative-disobedience/

Levin, D. E. (May 2003). Beyond Banning War and Superhero Play. Meeting Children's Needs in Violent Times. Young Children. Washington, DC: NAEYC.

Lynch, G.H. (n.d.). *The Importance of Art in Child Development.* PBS Parents. http://www.pbs.org/parents/education/music-arts/the-importance-of-art-in-child-development/

Marks-Tarlow, T., Solomon, M., & Siegel, D. J. (eds.). (2018). *Play & creativity in psychotherapy.* New York: W. W. Norton & Company.

Russ, S. W. (2016). *Affect & creativity: The role of affect and play in the creative process.* London: Routledge.

Miller, J. (December 9, 2013). *Science Says Art Will Make Your Kids Better Thinkers (And Nicer People).* Fast Company. http://www.fastcocreate.com/3023094/science-says-art-will-make-your-kids-better-thinkers-and-nicer-people

Pica, R. (2012). *Experiences in Movement and Music.* Independence, KY: Cengage Learning

Runco, M. A. (Ed.). (2012). *The creativity research handbook: Volume 2.* New York, NY: Hampton Press.

Schirrmacher, R. (2011). *Art and Creative Development for Young Children.* 7th Edition. Independence, KY: Wadsworth.

State of the Union Address. (2011). https://www.whitehouse.gov/the-press-office/2011/01/25/remarks-president-state-union-address

ZERO TO THREE. (n.d.). *Learning to write and draw.* Retrieved from http://www.zerotothree.org/early-care-education/early-language-literacy/writing-and-art-skills.html

Chapter 8 Self

Aboud, F. E. (2008). A social-cognitive developmental theory of prejudice. In S. M. Quintana & C. McKown (Eds.), *Handbook of race, racism, and the developing child* (pp. 55–71). Hoboken, NJ: John Wiley & Sons.

Administration for Children and Families. (2015). *Head Start Early learning Outcomes Framework: Ages Birth to Five.* https://eclkc.ohs.acf.hhs.gov/hslc/hs/sr/approach/pdf/ohs-framework.pdf

Allard, L. T. & A. Hunter. (2010). *Understanding Temperament in Infants and Toddlers.* http://csefel.vanderbilt.edu/resources/wwb/wwb23.html

Brody, J. E. (2012). A richer life by seeing the glass half full [Blog post]. *The New York Times.* Retrieved from http://well.blogs.nytimes.com

Brooks, R., & Goldstein, S. (2003). 10 ways to make your children more resilient. Retrieved from http://www.familytlc.net/resilient_children_preteen.html

Center on the Social and Emotional Foundations for Early Learning. (n.d.). *Teaching your child to: Identify and express emotions.* Retrieved from http://csefel.vanderbilt.edu/familytools/teaching_emotions.pdf

Davies, L. (2008). *Instilling Perseverance in Children.* Education World. http://www.educationworld.com/a_curr/columnists/davies/davies006.shtml

Derman-Sparks, L., & Edwards, J. O. (2010). *Anti-bias education for young children and ourselves.* Washington, DC: National Association for the Education of Young Children.

Derman-Sparks, L. & D. LeeKeenan & J. Nimmo. (2015). *Leading Anti-Bias Early Childhood Programs: A Guide for Change.* New York and Washington, DC. Teachers College Press and NAEYC. p. 9.

Devereux Center for Resilient Children. Website: http://www.centerforresilientchildren.org/.

Epstein, A. S. (2009). *Me, You, Us: Social-Emotional Learning in Preschool.* Ypsilanti and Washington, DC: High Scope Press and NAEYC. P. 6.

Florez, I. R. (2011). Adapted from *Developing Young Children's Self-Regulation through Everyday Experiences.* Young Children. 68 (4) p. 47.

Galinsky, E. (2012). *Success in parenting—Avoiding the happiness and self-esteem traps.* Retrieved from http://www.huffingtonpost.com/ellen- galinsky/parenting-advice_b_1651941.html

Gartrell, D. & Cairone, K.B. (July 2014). *Fostering Resilience: Teaching Social-Emotional Skills.* Young Children. Washington, DC: NAEYC.

Goodwin, B. & Miller, K. (September 2013.). *Research Says Grit Plus Talent Equals Student Success.* Educational Leadership. Vol. 71, No. 1, pp. 74-76.

Hyson, M. (2008). *Enthusiastic and Engaged Learners: Approaches to Learning in the Early Childhood Classroom.* pp. 86-94.

Joseph, G. E., & Strain, P. S. (2010). *Enhancing emotional vocabulary in young children.* Nashville, TN: Center on the Social and Emotional Foundations for Early Learning.

Katz, P. A., & Kofkin, J. A. (1997). Race, gender, and young children. In S.S. Luthar, J.A. Burack, D. Cicchetti, J.R. Weisz (Eds.), *Developmental psychopathology: Perspectives on adjustment, risk, and disorder* (pp. 51–74). New York, NY: Cambridge University Press.

LeBuffe, P. (February 2014). *Helping our Children Develop Grit.* MK memo. http://www.metrokids.com/Blogs/February-2014/Helping-Our-Children-Develop-Grit/

Longmire-Avital, Buffie. 2019, March 4. *What's Their Capital? Applying a Community Cultural Wealth Model to UR.* [Blog Post]. Retrieved from https://www.centerforengagedlearning.org/whats-their-capital-applying-a-community-cultural-wealth-model-to-ur/

Martin, C. L., & Ruble, D. N. (2004). Children's search for gender cues: Cognitive perspectives on gender development. *Current Directions in Psychological Science, 13,* 67—70.

Office of Special Education Programs. (2008). *Thirtieth Annual Report to Congress on the Implementation of the Individuals with Disabilities Education Act, Parts B and C.* Washington, DC: Author.

Parenting Assistance Line. (n.d.). Adapted from http://www.pal.ua.edu/children-mental-health/nurturing_inf_tod.php

PBS Parents. (n.d.) Child Development Tracker. http://www.pbs.org/parents/child-development/

Pearson, J. & Hall. D.K. (April 2006). *Reaching IN…Reaching OUT.* Resiliency Guidebook. Toronto: Child & family Partnership.

Pearson, J., & Hall, D. K. (2012). Guide 1: Resilience—a brief overview. In D. Smith (Ed.), *Reaching IN. . .reaching OUT resiliency guidebook: "Bounce back" thinking skills for children and adults* (pp. 1–3). Ontario, Canada: Child & Family Partnership.

Perkins-Gough, D. (September 2013). *The Significance of Grit: A Conversation with Angela Lee Duckworth.* Educational Leadership. Vol. 71, No. 2, pp.14-20.

Seligman, M. E. P. (2011). *Flourish: A visionary new understanding of happiness and well-being.* New York, NY: Free Press.

Shechtman, N. DeBarger, A.H., Dornsife, C., Rosier, S. & Yarnall, L. (2013). *Promoting Grit, Tenacity, and Perseverance: Critical Factors in the 21st Century.* Washington: DC: U.S. Department of Education.

Scher, H. (June 2012).The Trying Game: Teaching Perseverance to Kids. *Parents Magazine.*

University of Pennsylvania. School of Arts and Sciences. The Duckworth Lab. https://sites.sas.upenn.edu/duckworth

Werner, E. & Smith, R. (1992). *Overcoming the Odds: High-Risk Children from Birth to Adulthood.* New York: Cornell University Press.

Yosso, T.J. (2005). *Whose culture has capital? A critical race theory discussion of community cultural wealth.* Race Ethnicity and Education, 8 (1), 69 – 91.

Zhivotovskaya, E. (September 21, 2009). *Got Frit? Start with Mindset.* Positive Psychology News Daily. http://positivepsychologynews.com/news/emiliya-zhivotovskaya/200902211582

Chapter 9 Social

Berk, L. E. (2002). *Infants, children, and adolescents* (4th ed.). Boston, MA: Allyn & Bacon.

Dewar, G. (2009). *Preschool social skills: A guide for the science-minded parent.* Retrieved from http://www.parentingscience.com/preschool-social-skills.html

Dodge, D. T., Colker, L. J., & Heroman, C. (2002). *The creative curriculum for preschool* (4th ed.). Washington, DC: Teaching Strategies.

Epstein, A.S. (2009). *Me, You, Us: Social-Emotional Learning in Preschool.* Ypsilanti, MI: High Scope® Educational Research Foundation. p. 4

Hyson, M., & Taylor, J. L. (2011). Caring about caring: What adults can do to promote young children's prosocial skills. *Young Children, 66* (4), 74–83.

Jones, N. P. (2005). *Big Jobs. Planning for Competence.* https://www.naeyc.org/files/tyc/file/BigJobs.pdf

Katz, L. G., & Mendoza, J. A. (2011). Introduction to the special section on social-emotional issues in the lives of young children. *Early Childhood Research & Practice, 13* (1). Retrieved from http://ecrp.uiuc.edu/v13n1/

Lewis, V., Boucher, J., Lupton, L., & Watson, S. (2000). Relationships between symbolic play, functional play, verbal and non-verbal ability in young children. *International Journal of Language & Communication Disorders, 35* (1), 117–127.

McMullen, M. B. *Chapter 3, Understanding Development of Infants and Toddlers*, in Copple, C., S. Bredekamp, D. Koralek, & K. Charner., eds. (2013). *Developmentally Appropriate Practice: Focus on Infants and Toddlers.* Washington, DC: National Association for the Education of Young Children.

Paley, V. G. (1993). *You can't say you can't play.* Cambridge, MA: Harvard University Press.

Pica, R. (n.d.). *When kids cooperate.* Retrieved from http://www.maternitycorner.com/mcmag/articles/child0004.htm

Quann, V. & C. A. Wien. (2006). *The Visible Empathy of Infants and Toddlers.* Young Children 61 (4): 22-29.

Riley, D., San Juan, R. R., Klinkner, J., & Ramminger, A. (2008). *Social & emotional development: Connecting science and practice in early childhood settings.* St. Paul, MN: Redleaf Press.

Seifert, K. L. (2006). Cognitive development and the education of young children. In B. Spodek & O. N. Saracho (Eds.), *Handbook of research on the education of young children* (3rd ed., pp. 9–22). Mahwah, NJ: Erlbaum.

Trawick-Smith, J. (2009). *Science in support of play: The case for play-based programs* (White Paper). Willimantic, CT: Eastern Connecticut State University.

Yu, S. Y., Ostrosky, M. M., & Fowler, S. A. (2011). Children's friendship development: A comparative study. *Early Childhood Research & Practice, 13* (1). Retrieved from http://ecrp.uiuc.edu/v13n1/

Chapter 10 Guidance

Adams, S. K., & Baronberg, J. (2005). *Promoting positive behavior: Guidance strategies for early childhood settings.* Upper Saddle River, NJ: Pearson.

Bailey, B. (2001). *Conscious discipline: 7 basic skills for brain smart classroom management.* Orlando, FL: Loving Guidance.

Bodrova, E. & Leong, D. J. (March 2008). Developing Self-Regulation in Kindergarten Can We Keep All the Crickets in the Basket? Of Primary Interest column. *Young Children.*

Education Development Center. (2008). *What you can do: Recommendations and strategies for adults.* Retrieved from http://www.eyesonbullying.org/cando.html

Epstein, A. (September 2003). *How Planning and Reflection Develop Young Children's Thinking Skills.* Beyond the Journal. Young Children on the web. https://www.naeyc.org/files/yc/file/200309/Planning&Reflection.pdf

Freedman, J. (2007). *Easing the Teasing: How Parents Can Help Their Children.* www.education.com/reference/article/Ref.Easing_Teasing_How as cited by Raisor, J. M. & S. D. Thompson. May 2012. Guidance Strategies to Prevent and Address Preschool Bullying. Young Children. p. 74.

Gartrell, D. (2001). Replacing time-out: Part one—Using guidance to build an encouraging classroom. *Young Children, 56* (6), 8–16.

Gartrell, D. (2004). *The power of guidance: Teaching social-emotional skills in early childhood classrooms.* Clifton Park, NY: Delmar.

Gartrell, D. (2008, January). Guidance matters: Comprehensive guidance. *Beyond the Journal: Young Children on the Web.* Retrieved from http://www.naeyc.org/files/yc/file/200801/BTJGuidanceGartrell.pdf

Gartrell, D. (2011, February/March). Good guidance. The goals of guidance: Democratic life skills. Handout 1: The individual guidance plan. *NEXT for TYC, 4* (3). Retrieved from http://www.naeyc.org/files/yc/file/201107/IndividualGuidancePlan.pdf

Highscope. (Spring 2012). *Putting Training Into Practice.* Highscope ReSource. http://www.highscope.org/file/NewsandInformation/ReSourceReprints/Spring2012/ReSourceSpring2012rev_72.pdf

Kaiser, B., & Rasminsky, J. S. (2012). *Challenging behavior in young children. Understanding, preventing, and responding effectively* (3rd ed.). Boston, MA: Pearson.

Kersey, K., & Masterson, M. (2013). *101 principles for positive guidance with young children: Creating responsive teachers.* Upper Saddle River, NJ: Pearson.

Klein, A. S. (2008). *Guiding young children: 21 strategies.* Retrieved from http://www.earlychildhoodnews.com/earlychildhood/article_view.aspx?ArticleID=578

Koralek, D. (2007). *Creating a Comfortable Environment for Preschoolers.* Teaching Young Children, 1 (1), 6-7.

McCabe, L. A., & Frede, E. C. (2007, December). *Challenging behaviors and the role of preschool education* (Preschool Policy Brief, Issue 16). Retrieved from National Institute for Early Education Research website: http://nieer.org/resources/policybriefs/16.pdf

Miller, D. F. (2013). *Positive child guidance* (7th ed.). Stamford, C.T.: Cengage Learning.

Notbohm, E. (2019). *Ten things every child with autism wishes you knew.* (3rd ed.). Arlington, TX: Future Horizons Inc.

Olweus, D. (1997). Bully/victim problems in school: Facts and intervention. *European Journal of Psychology of Education, 12,* 495–510.

Porter, L. (2008). *Guiding children's behaviour* [DVD]. Adelaide, Australia: Small Poppies SA.

Powell, D., Dunlap, G., & Fox, L. (2006). Prevention and intervention for the challenging behaviors of toddlers and preschoolers. *Infants & Young Children, 19* (1), 25–35.

Raiser, J. M. & Thompson, S. D. (May 2012). Guidance Strategies to Prevent and Address Preschool Bullying. *Young Children.* pp. 70-74.

Snow, K. (October 27, 2014). *Bullying in Early Childhood.* http://www.naeyc.org/blogs/bullying-early-childhood

Willis, C. (January 2009). *Young Children with Autism Spectrum Disorder: Strategies that Work.* Autism Speaks www.autismspeaks.org

Chapter 11 Families

Derman-Sparks, L., & Edwards, J. O. (2010). *Anti-bias education for young children and ourselves.* Washington, DC: National Association for the Education of Young Children.

Gillespie, L. G. (2006, September). Cultivating good relationships with families can make hard times easier! *Beyond the Journal: Young Children on the Web.* Retrieved from http://www.naeyc.org/files/yc/file/200609/RockNRollBTJ.pdf

Halgunseth, L. C., Peterson, A., Stark, D. R., & Moodie, S. (2009). *Family engagement, diverse families, and early childhood education programs: An integrated review of the literature.* Retrieved from National Association for the Education of Young Children website: http://www.naeyc.org/files/naeyc/file/research/FamEngage.pdf

Hare, J., & Gray, L. A. (2008). All kinds of families: A guide for parents. Retrieved from http://www1.cyfernet.org/prog/fam/nontradfam.html

National Association for the Education of Young Children. (2011). *Code of ethical conduct: Supplement for early childhood program administrators.* Retrieved from http://www.naeyc.org/files/naeyc/file/positions/Supplement%20PS2011.pdf

Office of Head Start. (2007). Head Start Program Performance Standards. http://eclkc.ohs.acf.hhs.gov/policy

PBS Parents. (n.d.). The parent–teacher partnership. Retrieved from http://www.pbs.org/parents/goingtoschool/parent_teacher.html

U.S. Census Bureau. (n.d.). Frequently asked questions. Retrieved from http://www.census.gov/hhes/www/income/about/faqs.html

Chapter 12 Program Management

Blaiklock, K.E. (2008). *A Critique of the Use of Learning Stories to Assess the Learning Dispositions of Young Children.* NZ Research in ECE Journal, Vol. 11.

Carr, M., & Lee, W. (2012). *Learning stories: Constructing learner identities in early education.* Thousand Oaks, CA: SAGE Publications.

Chard, S. C. (1998). *The project approach: Making curriculum come alive.* New York: Scholastic Teaching Resources.

Chard, S. C. (1998). *The project approach: Managing successful projects.* New York: Scholastic Teaching Resources.

Dodge, D.T., Colker, L.J., & Heroman. (2000). *Connecting Content, Teaching, and Learning.* Washington, DC: Teaching Strategies.

Dodge, D.T., Colker, L.J., & Heroman. (2002). *The Creative Curriculum for Preschool.* 4th Edition. Washington, DC: Teaching Strategies.

Institute for Early Childhood Education and Research. (n.d.). *Research into practice: Reggio Emilia.* Retrieved from http://earlychildhood.educ.ubc.ca/community/research-practice-reggio-emilia

Jablon, J. R., Dombro A. L., & Dichtelmiller, M. L. (2007). *The power of observation* (2nd ed.). Belmont, CA: Wadsworth Publishing.

Meisels, S. (2006). *Accountability in Early Childhood: No Easy Answers.* An Occasional Paper. Chicago: Erikson Institute.

Muskie School of Public Service. Cutler Institute for Health and Social Policy. (June 2010). *Authentic Assessment in Infant & Toddler Care Settings: Review of Recent Research.* http://muskie.usm.maine.edu/Publications/CYF/Authentic-Assessment-Child-Care.pdf

NYC Department of Education. Division of Early Childhood Education. *A Parent Guide to Understanding Authentic Assessment for Young Children.* http://schools.nyc.gov/NR/rdonlyres/3AC4B691-F21C-43FF-AD89-5EFA1C54F5CB/0/ParentGuidetoAssessmentsfinal13114.pdf

Seitz, H. (2008, March). The power of documentation in the early childhood classroom. *Young Children, 63* (2). Retrieved from http://www.naeyc.org/files/tyc/file/Seitz.pdf

Wurm, J. P. (April/May 2009). *Making Observation an Everyday Practice.* TYC. Washington, DC: NAEYC, pp.6-7.

Chapter 13 Professionalism

Beal, J. (n.d.). *How to become a reflective teacher.* Retrieved from http://www.ehow.com/how_5011663_become-reflective-teacher.html

Carter, M., & Curtis, D. (2009). *The visionary director: A handbook for dreaming, organizing, and improving your center.* St. Paul, MN: Redleaf Press. Retrieved from National Association for the Education of Young Children. Teaching Young Children. Teaching Young Children. Vol. 3, No. 4. http://www.naeyc.org/files/tyc/file/TYC_V3N4_Reflectiveteacherexpanded.pdf

Carter, M., Cividanes, W., Curtis, D., & Lebo, D. (2010). *Becoming a reflective teacher.* Teaching Young Children, 3(4), 1–4.

Copple, C., & Bredekamp, S. (Eds.). (2009). *Developmentally appropriate practice in early childhood programs serving children birth through age 8* (3rd ed.). Washington, DC.: National Association for the Education of Young Children.

Derman-Sparks, L., & Edwards, J. O. (2010). *Anti-bias education for young children and ourselves.* Washington, DC: National Association for the Education of Young Children.

Epstein, A. S. (2014). *The intentional teacher: Choosing the best strategies for young children's learning.* Washington, DC: National Association for the Education of Young Children.

Feeney, S. (2010). Celebrating the 20th anniversary of NAEYC's Code of Ethical Conduct—Ethics today in early care and education: Review, reflection, and the future. *Young Children, 65* (2). Retrieved from http:// http://www.naeyc.org/yc/pastissues

National Association for the Education of Young Children. (2005). *Code of ethical conduct and statement of commitment.* Washington, DC: Author.

National Association for the Education of Young Children, & Child Care Aware of America. (2011). Early childhood education professional development: Training and technical assistance glossary. Retrieved from http://www.naeyc.org/GlossaryTraining_TA.pdf

Neas, L. M. R. (2012). *Ideas to begin reflective teaching strategies in your classroom.* Retrieved from http://www.brighthubeducation.com/teaching-methods-tips/92097-reflective-teaching-strategies/

Pappas, P. (2010). The reflective teacher: A taxonomy of reflection (part 3). Retrieved from http://www.peterpappas.com/2010/01/reflective-teacher-taxonomy-reflection.html

Schiller, P. (2007, November/December). *More purposeful and intentional infant and toddler care.* Exchange, 10–13.

Stewart, K. E. (2010). *The role of reflection: Preschool teachers' use of reflective thinking to translate higher education learning into teaching practice.* Minneapolis, MN: Capella University.

U.S. Department of Education. (n.d.). *Definitions.* http://www.ed.gov/early-learning/elc-draft-summary/definitions

Vojtek, R. O. & Vojtek, R. J. (2009). *Motivate! Inspire! Lead!: 10 strategies for building collegial learning communities.* Thousand Oaks, CA: Corwin Press.

Index

D

F

L

M

N

O

P

Q

R

S